Preserved in the Peat

An extraordinary Bronze Age burial on Whitehorse Hill, Dartmoor, and its wider context

Andy M. Jones

OXBOW | books
Oxford & Philadelphia

First published in the United Kingdom in 2016. Reprinted in 2017 by
OXBOW BOOKS
The Old Music Hall, 106-108 Cowley Road, Oxford, OX4 1JE

and in the United States by
OXBOW BOOKS
1950 Lawrence Road, Havertown, PA 19083

Hardcover Edition: ISBN 978-1-78570-260-0
Digital Edition: ISBN 978-1-78570-261-7

A CIP record for this book is available from the British Library

Library of Congress Cataloging-in-Publication Data

Names: Jones, Andy M., author.
Title: Preserved in the peat : an extraordinary Bronze Age burial on
   Whitehorse Hill, Dartmoor, and its wider context / Andy M. Jones.
Description: Oxford ; Philadelphia : Oxbow Books, 2016. | Includes
   bibliographical references and index.
Identifiers: LCCN 2016019904 (print) | LCCN 2016021504 (ebook) | ISBN
   9781785702600 (hardcover) | ISBN 9781785702617 (digital) | ISBN
   9781785702617 (epub) | ISBN 9781785702624 (mobi) | ISBN 9781785702631 (pdf)
Subjects: LCSH: Bronze age--England--Dartmoor. | Prehistoric
   peoples--England--Dartmoor. | Burial--England--Dartmoor--History--To 1500.
   .| Grave goods--England--Dartmoor--History--To 1500. | Material
   culture--England--Dartmoor--History--To 1500. | Excavations
   (Archaeology)--England--Dartmoor. | Peat--England--Dartmoor. | Dartmoor
   (England)--Antiquities.
Classification: LCC GN778.22.G7 J66 2016 (print) | LCC GN778.22.G7 (ebook) |
   DDC 936.2--dc23
LC record available at https://lccn.loc.gov/2016019904

Printed in Malta by Melita Press Ltd
Typeset in the UK by Frabjous Books

For a complete list of Oxbow titles, please contact:

UNITED KINGDOM
Oxbow Books
Telephone (01865) 241249, Fax (01865) 794449
Email: oxbow@oxbowbooks.com
www.oxbowbooks.com

UNITED STATES OF AMERICA
Oxbow Books
Telephone (800) 791-9354, Fax (610) 853-9146
Email: queries@casemateacademic.com
www.casemateacademic.com/oxbow

Oxbow Books is part of the Casemate Group

Front cover: *The cist in the peat mound (figure 2.10 of this volume)*
Back Cover: *Top left – Photograph: Alan Endacott. Top right – Photograph: Gary Young*

Contents

Section 1: Background

Section 2: Deconstructing and reconstructing the cist

Section 3: Assembling the burial

Section 4: Items with the young adult

Section 5: The cist and the moor: the environmental setting of the site and its wider landscape context

Section 6: The radiocarbon dating

Section 7: Discussion, interpretation and conclusions

Acknowledgements

Acknowledgements are given at the end of each chapter. I would, however, like to give particular thanks here to a smaller number of people who have ensured that the project has reached a successful conclusion.

In particular, I would like to thank Jane Marchand, Senior Archaeologist, Dartmoor National Park Authority and Vanessa Straker, Historic England Regional Science Advisor for helping to steer the project since 2011. I would also like to thank Historic England, for largely funding the post excavation project and the Dartmoor National Park Authority for their support. Thanks are also owed to Duchy of Cornwall on whose land the cist was located and the other individuals and bodies who have helped fund this project including: Devon County Council, Dartmoor Preservation Association, Devon Archaeological Society, Dartmoor Trust, Dr Jeremy Butler, Plymouth City Council and Helpful Holidays. I am also grateful to the Army for providing accommodation during the fieldwork.

The author is grateful to Graeme Kirkham for reading and editing the draft report and to Henrietta Quinnell for reading the concluding chapter and for comment on Dartmoor archaeology. I am also grateful to Alison Sheridan for the huge amount of additional work on the jewellery chapters and to Ralph Fyfe for becoming an additional team member onsite and for subsequent comment. Thanks are also extended to Francis Shepherd for finalising drawings and photographs. I would also like to thank the anonymous referees for their constructive comments. Lastly, but certainly not least, I would like to thank Helen Williams for all the information she supplied during the conservation process and for the fantastic work on the finds.

The Ordnance Survey mapping included within this publication is provided by Cornwall Council under licence from the Ordnance Survey in order to fulfil its public function to disseminate information to a wider audience. Persons viewing this statement should contact Ordnance Survey if they wish to licence Ordnance Survey mapping for their own use.

List of Contributors

JEFFREY J. BLACKFORD
Department of Geography, University of Hull

FIONA BROCK
School of Archaeology, University of Oxford

CHRISTOPHER BRONK RAMSEY
School of Archaeology, University of Oxford

RICHARD BRUNNING
Somerset Historic Environment Service, South West
Heritage Trust

ESTHER CAMERON
Institute of Archaeology, Oxford

GILL CAMPBELL
Historic England

MATT CANTI
Historic England

CAROLINE CARTWRIGHT
British Museum

MAGGIE COOPER
Independent researcher, basket maker and conservator

MARY DAVIS
National Museum of Wales

SHERRY DOYAL
Independent researcher, basket maker and conservator

JOANNA DUNSTER
Cranfield University

DINAH EASTOP
The National Archives, Kew

RALPH FYFE
School of Geography, Earth and Environmental Sciences,
Plymouth University

MARK HARDIMAN
Department of Geography, Royal Holloway University
of London

SUSANNA HARRIS
Institute of Archaeology, University College London

ZOË HAZELL
Historic England

LINDA HURCOMBE
Department of Archaeology, University of Exeter

JAMIE INGLIS
Independent jewellery maker

ANDY M JONES
Cornwall Archaeological Unit

JULIE JONES
Independent charred plant macro-fossil specialist

STUART KING
Independent wood turner

ANNA LAWSON-JONES
Cornwall Archaeological Unit

LINDA LEMIEUX
Independent researcher, basket maker and conservator

SARAH LITTLEWOOD
Department of Geography, Durham University

ALISON MACLEOD
Department of Geography, Royal Holloway University of London

PETER MARSHALL
Historic England

SIMON MAYS
Historic England

QUITA MOULD
Barbican Research Associates

MARTA PEREZ
School of Geography, Earth and Environmental Sciences, Plymouth University

HENRIETTA QUINNELL
Independent finds specialist

HAL REDVERS-JONES
Whitby Jet Heritage Centre

PAULA REIMER
School of Geography, Archaeology and Palaeoecology, Queens University Belfast

NICOLA RUSSELL
SUERC, University of Glasgow

ALISON SHERIDAN
National Museums of Scotland

CAROLINE SOLAZZO
Museum Conservation Institute, Smithsonian Institution

VANESSA STRAKER
Historic England

RUTH STUNGO
Royal Botanic Gardens, Kew

ROGER TAYLOR
Independent geologist

LORE TROALEN
National Museums of Scotland

KATE VERKOOIJEN
Independent researcher and experimental archaeologist

HELEN WILLIAMS
Wiltshire Conservation Centre

Summary

In August 2011, Cornwall Archaeological Unit was commissioned by the Dartmoor National Park Authority to undertake the archaeological excavation of a cist which was located on the western edge of a peat mound which was drying out and shrinking.

At around 600m OD, the Whitehorse Hill cist is the highest to be recorded on Dartmoor and is situated at the southern end of an exposed long north–south ridge. Around 700m to the north is the Hangingstone Hill cairn, which is inter-visible with Whitehorse Hill and occupies a similar position, and it may be significant that both ends of the hill were marked with Early Bronze Age monuments.

When first recorded in the 1990s, the cist was eroding out of the western side of a peat mound measuring approximately 12m in diameter by 1.5m high. The extent of the mound was, however, determined by peat cutting which had left it standing proud of the adjacent landscape. It is therefore uncertain as to how prominent the cist was in the Bronze Age, although it is possible that it was set into a slight swelling in the peat. Analysis of the peat soil above the capstone suggests that the soil had grown over it. This means that the site of the cist would have been visible, at least locally, when first built.

Initial recording had suggested that it was aligned east–west and that the western end stone had fallen off. It was therefore thought that much of the cist had already been lost and the site was expected to be rich in environmental archaeology, but in keeping with many other Dartmoor cists, was anticipated to be an 'empty box'.

However, excavation revealed that the cist was aligned north-west–south-east and that, despite the collapse of a side stone, there was an intact burial. The location of the deposit within blanket mire led to a remarkable degree of preservation and the recovery of an unparalleled assemblage of organic Early Bronze Age artefacts.

The excavation of the mound revealed that it was formed through natural peat growth and that the cist had been set into a cut into the mound, which was lined with stones.

Micro-excavation of the contents of the cist revealed the order in which items inside it had been placed. At the bottom was a layer of purple moor grass, which had probably been collected in the summer or early autumn. This time of year was also suggested by pollen from meadowsweet flowers, which was also found inside the cist. Upon this was a unique composite textile-and-animal skin object, consisting of a panel of finely-woven nettle fibre textile, and edged by piping and triangular appliqués of calfskin. This object may well have been a garment or a sash.

Above this was the pelt from a bear. It suggests that bears survived in southern Britain into the Bronze Age, although it may have been obtained through exchange and may not be local. The pelt was folded around a cremation but it could originally have been an item of clothing. Within the folds of the pelt was a badly-corroded copper alloy pin, which may have been used to secure the pelt. The cremated remains were incomplete and poorly preserved; perhaps they had been carried around in the bundle for a while before burial. It could, however, be established that they were of a young person, aged 15–25. The gender has not been determined but the associated artefactual assemblage suggests that the deceased was a female.

Beside the cremation was a basketry container. This consisted of three sections made from coiled lime bast that had been stitched together with cattle hair to form a lidded cylindrical container.

Within and spilling out of this container were a flint flake and what appears to be a jewellery set, comprising a braided armband or bracelet, a necklace, and two pairs of studs. The band is unique and had been made by braiding long double strands of cattle hair to make a narrow, intricate band, and slotting in small tin studs at regular intervals during the braiding process.

A further object of tin was found inside the container. This was a cylindrical bead that had probably formed the centrepiece of a composite necklace comprising seven amber beads, 92 disc beads of Kimmeridge shale and around 110 chunky disc beads of clay. While the clay was probably local to Dartmoor and the tin had almost certainly come from the south west region, the Kimmeridge shale had travelled around 130km from the east as the crow flies, and the amber could have originated in the Baltic region, although the beads had probably been obtained through links with Wessex. The necklace is the largest and most complete to be found in southwest England.

The two pairs of wooden studs were made from spindle wood. They provide the earliest evidence for wood turning in Britain, setting back its appearance by at least 500 years. The larger pair were probably worn in the ears, but the smaller pair may have been labrets, and worn through the lips.

Lastly, covering the cist contents was a second layer of matted plant material, but it was not sufficiently well-preserved for the plants to be identified.

Radiocarbon dating of the cremation and organic material from inside the cist places its construction and use in the Early Bronze Age, from *circa* 1730 to 1600 cal BC.

Opportunity was also taken to record environmental information from the peat mound beside the cist. Analysis of environmental material included tephra, testate amoebae, pollen, non-pollen palynomorphs, charcoal and soil micromorphology. These analyses reveal that the local environment was changing from a peat bog covered with heather and cotton grasses to one where grasses and other taxa associated with grazing were becoming established, with a hazel and oak woodland growing on the slopes below the summit of the hill. By the time that the cist was constructed, communities may have taken advantage of this change, as the first widespread evidence for burning and fungal spores from grazing animals indicate that it was used for pasture. It may be significant that the hill was marked by a burial at the time when grazing was increasing. This could be argued to suggest a desire to define tenure of the land, or perhaps shows an attachment to a place people frequented with their animals.

The excavation was highly significant: the information recorded from the cist and the surrounding peat mound has provided the first secure dating information from a Dartmoor cist as well as detailed data on the environmental background and pastoral activity. However, it is the unparalleled assemblage of organic objects which are of most importance, as these have yielded insights into a range of materials which have not survived from the earlier Bronze Age elsewhere in southern Britain.

In addition to the remarkable finds and wealth of environmental data, the excavations were also of great importance because they demonstrate the potential for nationally significant archaeological sites to survive in remote areas of Dartmoor where sites were not thought to exist. This challenges the perception of blanket peatlands as entirely natural, non-cultural spaces.

Résumé

Conservée dans la tourbe: Extraordinaire inhumation de l'âge du bronze sur la colline de Whitehorse, Dartmoor, et son contexte plus étendu

En août 2011, l'autorité du Parc National de Dartmoor a commissionné l'Unité Archéologique de Cornouailles pour entreprendre les fouilles archéologiques d'une tombe située en bordure ouest d'un tertre tourbeux qui se désséchait et se contractait.

A environ 600m NGF la tombe de la colline de Whitehorse est la plus haute jamais enregistrée sur Dartmoor et est située à l'extrémité sud d'une longue crête exposée orientée nord-sud. A environ 700m au nord se trouve le cairn de Hangingstone Hill qui est inter-visible avec la colline de Whitehorse et occupe une position similaire, et il est peut être significatif que les deux extrémités de la colline étaient marquées par des monuments de l'âge du bronze ancien.

Quand elle fut enregistrée pour la première fois dans les années 1990, la tombe s'érodait du côté ouest d'un tertre de tourbe mesurant environ 12m de diamètre sur 1,5m de hauteur. L'étendue du tertre était, toutefois, déterminée par la récolte de la tourbe qui l'avait laissé saillant sur le paysage adjacent. Il est donc impossible de dire de combien dépassait la tombe à l'âge du bronze, bien qu'il se peut qu'elle ait été insérée dans une légère enflure dans la tourbe. L'analyse du sol tourbeux au-dessus de la pierre de couverture indique que le sol avait poussé par dessus. Ce qui veut dire que le site de la tombe aura été visible, au moins localement, au moment de sa construction.

Les premiers relevés avaient donné à penser qu'elle était alignée est-ouest et que la pierre de l'extrémité ouest était tombée. On pensa donc qu'une grande partie de la tombe avait déjà disparu et on s'attendait à ce que le site soit riche en archéologie environnementale, mais comme pour de nombreuses autres tombes de Dartmoor, on pensait trouver une boîte vide.

Néanmoins, les fouilles révélèrent que la tombe était alignée nord-ouest/sud-est et que, malgré la chute d'une pierre latérale, elle contenait une inhumation intacte. Le lieu de déposition dans une étendue boueuse a garanti un remarquable degré de préservation et la récupération d'un assemblage sans égal d'objets façonnés organiques de l 'âge du bronze ancien.

Les fouilles du tertre révélèrent qu'il résultait de la croissance naturelle de la tourbe et que la tombe avait été insérée dans une entaille du tertre qui était tapissée de pierres.

Une micro-fouille du contenu de la tombe révéla l'ordre dans lequel les objets avaient été placés à l'intérieur. Au fond, il y avait une couche de molinie bleue, qui avait probablement été ramassée en été ou au début de l'automne. Cette période de l'année était également représentée par le pollen de fleurs de reine- des-prés présent aussi dans la tombe. Là-dessus se trouvait un unique objet composite en textile et peau d'animal consistant en un panneau de textile en fibre d'ortie délicatement tissé et bordé de ganse et d'appliques triangulaires en peau de veau. L'objet pourrait avoir été un vêtement ou une ceinture.

Pardessus il y avait une peau d'ours. Ce qui donne à penser que des ours vivaient encore dans le sud de la Grande-Bretagne à l'âge du bronze, bien qu'elle ait pu-faire l'objet d'un échange et ne pas-être de la région. La peau était pliée autour d'une incinération mais elle avait pu être un vêtement à l'origine. Dans les plis de la peau se trouvait une épingle extrèmement rouillée en alliage de cuivre qui aurait pu être utilisée pour maintenir la peau. Les restes incinérés étaient incomplets et mal conservés ; ils avaient peut-être été portés çà et là dans un ballot avant l'inhumation. On a pu toutefois établir qu'il s'agissait d'une personne jeune, âgée entre 15 et 25 ans. Le genre n'a pu être déterminé mais l'assemblage d'objets façonnés associés conduit à penser que c'est une femme.

A côté de l'incinération, se trouvait une corbeille en vannerie. Elle consistait en trois sections composées d'écorce de tilleul enroulée qui avait été assemblée au moyen d'une couture en crin animal pour former un contenant cylindrique à couvercle.

A l'intérieur de cette corbeille, mais en débordant à

l'extérieur, se trouvaient un éclat de silex et ce qui semble être une parure de bijoux comprenant un bracelet, un collier et deux paires de clous d'oreille. Le bracelet est unique et avait été fabriqué en nattant de longs brins d'une double épaisseur de crin de cheval ou de bovidé pour former une bande étroite et compliquée, et en insérant de petites boules d'étain à intervalles réguliers au cours du procédé de tressage.

Un autre objet en étain fut trouvé à l'intérieur de la corbeille. C'était une perle cylindrique qui avait probablement constitué l'élément central d'un collier composite qui comprenait 7 boules d'ambre, 92 perles en forme de disque en schiste de Kimmeridge et environ 110 grosses perles en forme de disque en argile. Si l'argile venait probablement de la région de Dartmoor et l'étain presque certainement de la région du sud-ouest, le schiste de Kimmeridge avait parcouru environ 130km à vol d'oiseau depuis l'est, et l'ambre pourrait avoir son origine dans la région balte, bien qu'on s'était probablement procuré les perles grâce à des relations avec le Wessex. Le collier est le plus grand et le plus complet jamais trouvé dans le sud-ouest de l'Angleterre.

Les deux paires de clous en bois étaient fabriquées en bois de fuseau. Elles constituent le premier témoignage de tournage du bois en Grande-Bretagne, faisant reculer la date de son apparition d'au moins 500 ans. La plus grande paire était probablement portée aux oreilles, mais il se peut que la plus petite ait été des labrets et portée a travers la lèvre.

Finalement, couvrant le contenu de la tombe, se trouvait une seconde couche de matière végétale tressée, mais elle n'était pas assez bien conservée pour nous permettre d'identifier les plantes.

La datation au C14 de l'incinération et du matériel organique de l'intérieur de la tombe place sa construction et son utilisation à l'âge du bronze ancien, à partir d'environ 1730 à 1600 av.J.-C.cal.

Nous avons aussi saisi cette occasion pour enregistrer les renseignements environnementaux provenant du tertre de tourbe à côté de la tombe. L'analyse du matériel environnemental comprenait téphras, amibes testacées, pollen, palynomorphes non polliniques, charbon de bois et micromorphologie du sol. Ces analyses révélèrent que l'environnement local allait d'une tourbière couverte de bruyère et de linaigrette à une où les herbes et autres taxonomies associées au pâturage commençaient à s'établir, un bois de noisetier et de chêne poussait sur les pentes en bas du sommet de la colline. Venu le moment de la construction de la tombe, les communautés avaient peut-être profité de ce changement, car les premiers témoignages de brûlage largement répandu et de spores de champignons d'animaux au pré indiquent une utilisation comme pâture. Il est peut-être significatif que la colline fut marquée d'une inhumation au moment où le pâturage augmentait. On pourrait argumenter pour proposer un désir de définir la tenure de la terre ou peut-être montrer un attachement à un endroit fréquenté par les hommes et leurs animaux.

Les.fouilles eurent d'importantes conséquences, les renseignements obtenus de la tombe et du tertre de tourbe qui l'entourait ont fourni les premiers éléments de datation certaine d'une tombe de Dartmoor ainsi que des données détaillées sur l'arrière-fond environnemental et l'activité pastorale. C'est cependant l'assemblage sans pareil d'objets organiques qui est le plus important car ceux-ci ont offert un aperçu sur une gamme de matériaux du début de l'âge du bronze qui n'avaient survécu nulle part ailleurs dans le sud de la Grande-Bretagne.

En plus des trouvailles remarquables et de la richesse des données environnementales, les fouilles furent également extrèmement importantes car elles démontrèrent que des sites archéologiques d'intérêt national pouvaient survivre dans des zones isolées de Dartmoor, là où on ne pensait pas que des sites pouvaient exister. Ceci défie la perception de la couverture de tourbières comme des lieux totalement naturels, et non culturels.

Zusammenfassung

Im Torf erhalten: Eine außergewöhnliche bronzezeitliche Bestattung am Whitehorse Hill, Dartmoor, und ihr weiteres Umfeld

Im August 2011 wurde Cornwall Archaeological Unit von der Verwaltung des Dartmoor Nationalpark mit der archäologischen Ausgrabung eines Steinkistengrabs beauftragt, das sich am westlichen Rand eines austrocknenden und schrumpfenden Torfhügels befand.

Mit einer Höhe NN von ungefähr 600m ist die Steinkiste von Whithorse Hill, die am südlichen Ende eines exponierten, langen, nordsüdverlaufenden Höhenrückens liegt, die am höchsten gelegene der im Dartmoor aufgenommenen Gräber dieses Typs. Etwa 700m nördlich liegt das Hangingstone Hill Steinhügelgrab, das von Whitehorse Hill aus sichtbar ist und eine ähnliche Lage einnimmt; es mag von Bedeutung sein, dass beide Enden des Höhenrückens mit frühbronzezeitlichen Denkmalen markiert wurden.

Bei ihrer ersten Aufnahme in den 1990er-Jahren erodierte die Steinkiste aus der westlichen Seite eines Torfhügels mit einem Durchmesser von ungefähr 12m und einer Höhe von 1,5m. Das Ausmaß des Hügels war jedoch durch den Torfabbau bedingt, der dazu geführt hatte, dass der Hügel über die umliegende Landschaft herausragte. Daher ist unsicher, wie markant der Hügel in der Bronzezeit war, obgleich möglich ist, dass er auf einer leichten Erhöhung im Torf errichtet wurde. Analysen des Torfbodens oberhalb des Decksteins legen nahe, dass der Boden über ihn gewachsen ist. Dies bedeutet, dass der Ort der Steinkiste zum Zeitpunkt der Errichtung, zu mindestens lokal, sichtbar war.

Die ursprüngliche Aufnahme deutete darauf hin, dass die Steinkiste Ost–West ausgerichtet und der westliche Abschlussstein umgefallen war. Deshalb wurde davon ausgegangen, dass ein großer Teil der Kiste bereits verloren und der Fundplatz reich an paläobotanischen Resten sei, aber in Übereinstimmung mit vielen anderen Steinkisten im Dartmoor war die Erwartung, dass es sich um eine „leere Kiste" handeln würde.

Die Untersuchung ergab jedoch, dass die Steinkiste von Nordwest nach Südost ausgerichtet war und dass sie, trotz eines umgefallenen Seitensteins, eine intakte Bestattung enthielt. Die Lage der Reste im Decktorf (blanket mire) begünstigte einen erstaunlichen Erhaltungsgrad und erlaubte die Bergung eines unvergleichlichen Ensembles frühbronzezeitlicher organischer Fundgegenstände.

Die Ausgrabung des Hügels zeigte, dass dieser sich durch natürliches Torfwachstum gebildet hatte und dass die Steinkiste in einer mit Steinen ausgekleideten Eintiefung in den Hügel errichtet worden war.

Die Niederlegungsabfolge der in der Kiste deponierten Fundgegenstände konnte im Zuge der Mikro-Ausgrabung ihres Inhalts ermittelt werden. Zuunterst fand sich eine Lage Blaues Pfeifengras, das wahrscheinlich im Sommer oder Frühherbst gesammelt worden war. Blütenpollen von Echtem Mädesüß, die ebenfalls in der Steinkiste gefunden wurden, weisen gleichfalls in diese Jahreszeit. Darüber lag ein einzigartiger Gegenstand aus einem Verbundwerkstoff aus Textil und Tierhaut, der aus einem Feld aus feingewobenem Nesselfaser-Textil mit Paspelierung und dreieckigen Applikationen aus Kalbsleder bestand. Bei diesem Objekt könnte es sich um ein Kleidungstück oder eine Schärpe handeln.

Darüber lag ein Bärenfell. Das legt nahe, dass Bären bis in die Bronzezeit hinein im südlichen Britannien überlebt haben, obwohl es auch durch Tausch erworben und nicht lokaler Herkunft sein könnte. Das Fell war um eine Brandbestattung herum gefaltet, aber es könnte ursprünglich als Kleidungstück benutzt worden sein. In den Falten des Fells fand sich eine stark korrodierte Nadel aus Kupferlegierung, die zum Verschließen des Fells gedient haben mag. Die Reste der Brandbestattung waren unvollständig und schlecht erhalten; vielleicht wurden sie vor der Bestattung in dem Bündel transportiert. Es ließ sich jedoch feststellen, dass sie von einem jungen, 15–25 Jahre alten Individuum stammten. Das Geschlecht konnte nicht bestimmt werden, aber die Beifunde deuten auf eine weibliche Bestattung.

Neben der Brandbestattung lag ein Korbgefäß. Dies

bestand aus drei Teilen, die aus verdrilltem Lindenbast gefertigt und mit Rinderhaar zu einem zylindrischen Behälter mit Deckel zusammengenäht worden waren.

In dem Behälter, und aus ihm herausfallend, fanden sich ein Feuersteinabschlag und möglicherweise ein Schmuckensemble, das aus einem geflochtenen Armband, einer Halskette und zwei Paaren von Doppelknöpfen bestand. Das bislang einzigartige Band wurde aus langen Rinderhaar-Doppelsträhnen zu einem schmalen, komplexen Band geflochten, in das während des Flechtens in regelmäßigen Abständen kleine Zinnniete eingesetzt worden waren.

Ein weiterer Zinngegenstand wurde in dem Behälter gefunden. Dabei handelte es sich um eine zylindrische Perle, die wahrscheinlich das Mittelstück einer vielteiligen Halskette mit sieben Bernsteinperlen, 92 scheibenförmigen Perlen aus Kimmeridge shale (schiefriger Tonstein) und ca. 110 klobigen Scheibenperlen aus Ton bildete. Während der Ton wohl von lokaler Herkunft aus dem Dartmoor war und das Zinn ziemlich sicher aus dem Südwesten kam, stammte der Kimmeridge shale aus einer Entfernung von etwa 130 km Luftlinie in östlicher Richtung und der Bernstein wohl aus dem Baltikum; die Perlen wurden jedoch wahrscheinlich über Verbindungen nach Wessex bezogen. Die Halskette ist die größte und vollständigste, die bislang in Südwest-England gefunden wurde.

Die beiden Holzknopfpaare wurden aus Spindelstrauchholz gefertigt. Sie liefern den frühsten Beleg für die Drechslerei in Britannien, womit der Beginn dieses Handwerks nun mindestens 500 Jahre früher angesetzt werden kann. Das größere Paar wurde wahrscheinlich in den Ohren getragen, während es sich bei dem kleineren Paar möglicherweise um Lippenpflöcke handelt.

Der Inhalt der Steinkiste war von einer zweiten Lage verfilzten Pflanzenmaterials bedeckt, das aber für eine Bestimmung der darin enthaltenen Pflanzen nicht gut genug erhalten war.

Radiokarbondatierungen der Brandbestattung und des organischen Materials aus dem Inneren der Steinkiste datieren ihre Errichtung und Nutzung in die frühe Bronzezeit, von ca. 1730 bis 1600 cal BC.

Es wurde auch die Gelegenheit genutzt, paläoökologische Daten des Torfhügels neben der Kiste zu dokumentieren. Das paläoökologisch analysierte Material umfasst Tephra, Thecamoeben (Schalenamöben), Pollen, Nicht-Pollen-Palynomorphe, Holzkohle und Bodenmikromorphologie. Diese Analysen zeigen, dass das lokale Milieu sich von einem Hochmoor mit Heide und Wollgrass zu einem Moor entwickelte, in dem sich Gräser und andere mit Beweidung assoziierte Taxa fanden und an den Hängen unterhalb des Hügelgipfels ein Hasel-Eichenwald wuchs. Spätestens zum Zeitpunkt der Errichtung der Steinkiste hatten menschliche Gemeinschaften diese Änderung zu ihren Gunsten genutzt, denn es fanden sich die ersten großflächigen Hinweise auf Brandrodung, und Pilzsporen von Weidetieren deuten an, dass das Moor als Weideland genutzt wurde. Es könnte von Bedeutung sein, dass der Hügel gerade zu dem Zeitpunkt mit einer Bestattung markiert wurde, als die Beweidung zunahm. Dies ließe sich dahingehend interpretieren, dass damit einem Bestreben nach Festlegung der Landbesitzverhältnisse Ausdruck gegeben werden sollte, oder vielleicht zeigte sich damit die Verbundenheit zu einem Ort, den die Menschen mit ihren Tieren aufsuchten.

Die Ausgrabung erzielte äußerst wichtige Ergebnisse: die von der Steinkiste und dem sie umgebenden Torfhügel dokumentierten Informationen lieferten die erste sichere Datierung einer Steinkiste im Dartmoor sowie detaillierte Daten zu ökologischem Umfeld und Weidewirtschaft. Am bedeutendsten sind jedoch die organischen Gegenstände, für die bislang keine Vergleiche bekannt sind, denn sie gewährten Einblicke auf eine Reihe von Materialien, die nirgendwo sonst aus der Bronzezeit des südlichen Britanniens erhalten sind.

Abgesehen von den bemerkenswerten Funden und dem Reichtum an paläoökologischen Daten waren die Ausgrabungen auch deshalb von großer Bedeutung, weil sie gezeigt haben, dass selbst entlegene Bereiche des Dartmoor, in denen gar nicht mit der Existenz von Fundstellen gerechnet wurde, das Potenzial zur Erhaltung von archäologischen Fundstellen nationaler Bedeutung haben. Damit wird die landläufige Auffassung der ausgedehnten Moorlandschaften als ausschließlich natürliche, nicht-kulturelle Orte hinterfragt.

Übersetzung: Jörn Schuster
(ARCHÆOLOGICALsmallFINDS)

Section 1:
Background

1. Introduction

Andy M. Jones

The background to the project

In July 2011 the Historic Environment Projects team (now Cornwall Archaeological Unit), Cornwall Council, was commissioned by Jane Marchand, Senior Archaeologist at Dartmoor National Park Authority, to undertake the excavation and recording of a cist on Whitehorse Hill in the parish of Lydford, Dartmoor. The site is located in the National Park and is situated within the boundaries of the military's Okehampton firing range (Fig. 1.1).

The cist was discovered in 1999 and became a Scheduled Monument (National Heritage List Entry 1020871) in 2003. It lay within an area surrounded by peat cuttings and was located on the western edge of a peat mound measuring approximately 12m in diameter and up to 1.5m high which was visibly drying out and shrinking. Continuing efforts were made over a period of eight years to stabilise the monument, and repair works had been grant aided by English Heritage (now Historic England) South West region. As a last ditch attempt to preserve the cist *in situ* a stone revetment wall was built in front of it to prevent further erosion. However, continuing extreme weather conditions coupled with the exposed hilltop setting of the site resulted in the repairs failing and the peat continuing to dry out. It was therefore feared that the cist was in considerable danger of collapsing over the winter of 2011–12 without an adequate record being made of the site.

The objectives of the project

In light of this imminent threat to the cist, a MoRPHE compliant project design (Historic England 2016) was produced for archaeological excavation and recording. It identified a number of objectives which were specific to the project, including the following:

- To record and excavate the cist so that a record was made of it before it collapsed.
- To recover and date suitable sampled material recovered from inside and around the cist, so that its chronology and context in relation to other excavated sites and the surrounding landscape could be better understood.
- To assess and analyse environmental materials from within and especially adjacent to the cist in order to help establish the environment when the cist was constructed.
- To investigate the peat mound to establish whether the peat had formed naturally or if the mound was a partly-constructed landscape feature.

The project design was submitted to English Heritage in the summer of 2011 who agreed to part-fund excavation of the cist together with the Dartmoor National Park Authority and a number of local funders.

Archaeological investigations of the cist and the mound into which it was set took place during the first week of August 2011, during the summer closure of the army firing range. Given the paucity of artefacts from almost all of Dartmoor's investigated cists (Worth 1967, 192–97; Butler 1997, 275–277), it was anticipated that very little in the way of artefactual material would be recovered from inside the cist itself. However, contrary to these low expectations, the results from the excavations led to the discovery of a nationally important collection of organic objects and other items associated with an Early Bronze Age cremation. Excavation of the cist revealed that despite the collapse of one of the side stones, there was an intact burial comprised of cremated bone which was associated with organic artefacts.

The contents of the cist were excavated by Helen

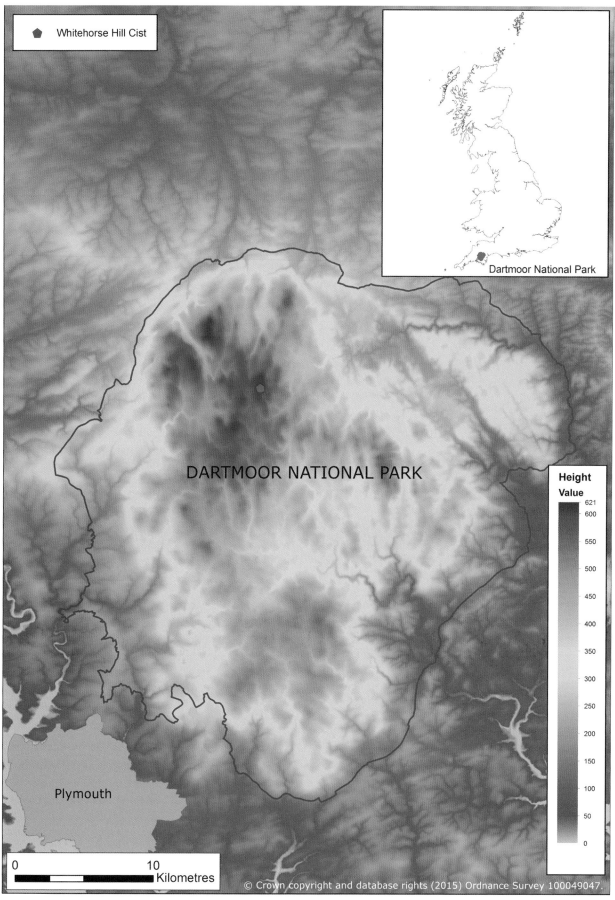

Whitehorse Hill Cist

DARTMOOR NATIONAL PARK

Dartmoor National Park

Height Value

Plymouth

© Crown copyright and database rights (2015) Ordnance Survey 100049047.

Figure 1.1: Location map showing the Whitehorse Hill cist and the boundary of Dartmoor National Park.

Williams at the Wiltshire Conservation Service laboratory in Chippenham (Chapter 3), where it was found that sandwiched between two layers of matted plant material were a cremation that had been wrapped within an animal pelt, a basketry container, a braided textile band with tin studs (an armband or bracelet), and a textile and animal-skin object. The basketry container held shale, clay and amber beads from a necklace, together with a tin bead, and two pairs of turned wooden ear studs or labrets and a copper-alloy pin were found later in the conservation process. In addition to the finds within the cist, two wooden stakes were recovered from the peat adjacent to the cist which may have been used for marking out the site (Chapter 4).

Environmental samples were taken from the cist and the mound and these too were found to have preserved a range of organic materials which required further analysis, including pollen, testate amoebae, non pollen palynomorphs, plant macrofossils and charcoal, as well as several deposits of tephra produced by episodes of volcanic activity. Consequently these materials had the potential to answer important questions about environmental conditions at the time the cist was constructed, as well as providing the first evidence for Early Bronze Age economic practices on the moor.

The spectacular – if rather unexpected – results from the project led to the production of a revised project design with newly identified areas and tasks for analyses which were not included within the original scope of the project. The revised project design also had new research goals which were commensurate with the findings from the excavation. The following research objectives were identified:

- To determine the dates for the construction of the cist and the contents found within it.
- To establish how the various organic objects (the braided band, textile and animal-skin object and basketry container) and other objects found in the cist were made.
- To ascertain the 'biography' of the objects found inside the cist, to establish whether they were new or old at the time of burial.
- To analyse the pelt, so that the type of animal from which it was made could be identified.
- To ascertain how the cist relates to practices associated with wider funerary and ceremonial monument activity at local, regional and national levels.
- To investigate the development of the peat mound, so that its past prominence in the landscape could be established.
- To ascertain what environmental conditions were around the cist during the Early Bronze Age.
- To identify how animals formed part of the economy of the area and which animals were grazing around the cist.
- To help guide future management of Dartmoor's historic environment, by considering the potential for further unidentified sites to exist on the moor.

In addition to these identified aims, the analysis process has inevitably thrown up new questions, as for example when the two pairs of wooden ear studs / labrets were discovered and a copper-alloy pin was uncovered within the fur of the pelt. By contrast, the less precise identification of the tephra layers within the peat mound meant that the environmental sequence could not be as tightly dated as had been hoped at the outset of the analysis stage.

Nevertheless, the wealth of material collected from the excavation has enabled a great deal of information to be gained and the key objectives were not only met but in several cases surpassed what was anticipated at the outset. Overall, the results from many of the analyses undertaken as part of this project represent firsts for the study of the British Early Bronze Age and its material culture.

Report structure

In addition to the revision of the project's aims, in light of the extraordinary information gathered by the project, it was decided to expand the original envisioned excavation report within a journal into a stand-alone publication which would include all the analyses undertaken on the materials from the cist.

This, the resulting monograph, is divided into seven parts with an eighth section of specialist reports at the end. Given the broad spectrum of the finds and environmental material recovered and the potentially diverse audience, it was decided that each chapter would be self-contained with separate bibliographies and acknowledgements so that they can be read as separate papers. They have, however, been arranged by theme, so that they can be read sequentially, and an interpretative overview is given at the end.

This section, the first, outlines the background to the project and its aims. It also describes the setting of the cist and the history of previous recording.

The second section is entitled 'Deconstructing and reconstructing the cist'. It describes the methods and results from the 2011 excavations, especially with regard to the stratigraphy of the peat mound and the cist, as well as the soil micromorphology. It also includes a chapter on the micro excavation of the contents of the cist in the laboratory at Chippenham, Wiltshire, and lastly a report on the wooden stakes which were recovered from the mound.

The third and fourth sections present analyses of the contents of the cist. The third, 'Assembling the burial', contains a range of detailed specialist reports on the cremation itself, the charcoal and textiles found with it and on the matted plant material and pollen from within the cist. The fourth section, 'personal items with the young adult', covers the artefacts from the cist, including the copper-alloy pin, the flint, the jewellery and the organic artefacts.

The fifth section, 'The cist and the moor: the environmental setting of the site and its wider landscape context', provides an overview of the range of analyses which were used to help with providing a wider context for the setting of the cist.

The sixth section is concerned with the radiocarbon

Figure 1.2: The Whitehorse Hill peat mound from the south showing the peat cutting around it. Note the protective wall in front of the cist, just visible on the left hand side of the mound, and the Hangingstone barrow in the distance to the north (beside the military observation post).

dating and modelling of the results. The seventh and final section of discussion, interpretation and conclusions provides a synthesis which draws together the results from the analyses and data from other excavated sites to consider the Whitehorse Hill cist in its wider context and discuss the creation of the burial assemblage.

At the end of the report are a series of specialist contributions which relate to detailed analyses which are referred to in the preceding chapters. These include reports on the X-Ray Fluorescence (XRF) analysis of the tin beads, Scanning Electron Microscope (SEM) analysis of plant materials and proteomic analysis of the animal hairs.

Report conventions

Detailed records of all archaeological features were made during the excavation, with each context being allocated a unique number. All archaeological layers referred to throughout the report are shown within ( ) brackets. The structure number for the cist is presented as an unbracketed number with letters allocated (A, C, E, F, G, I, J, K, L and M) for the stones comprising the cist.

Calibrated date ranges provided in this volume have been calculated using the maximum intercept method (Stuiver and Reimer 1986), OxCal v4.2 (Bronk Ramsey 1995; 1998; 2001; 2009) and the dataset for terrestrial samples from the Northern hemisphere (Reimer *et al.* 2013). Calibrated date ranges are quoted in the form recommended by Mook (1986) with the end points rounded outwards to 10 years (or five years when error terms are less than ±25 BP). Ranges in the volume are quoted at 2σ.

In order to assist with identification of the sites on Dartmoor under discussion, Leslie Grinsell's (1978) numeration system is used where possible (see Table 21.1) and published site names (including the Whitehorse Hill cist itself) are given for those without 'Grinsell numbers'.

Location and setting of the Whitehorse Hill cist

The Whitehorse Hill cist was situated within a small natural peat mound or 'peat hag', which was left standing higher than the surrounding moorland by past peat cutting. It stands at SX 6172 8547 near to the summit of a broad flat-topped hill on the northern part of Dartmoor, located at the southern end of a north–south ridge at a height of approximately 604m OD (Fig. 1.1). The underlying bedrock geology is granite, which is covered by a thin layer of granitic subsoil. For the most part this is in turn buried by thick deposits of peat, except in those areas where peat cutting has taken place or where tracks have eroded deeply though the peat and the underlying granitic subsoil has been exposed. The peat mound in which the cist was set is located not far to the south of a very deeply cut late nineteenth or early twentieth century track and is surrounded by extensive evidence for peat extraction, which historically was cut on an industrial scale as a source of fuel (Newman 2011, 223). These cuttings have obscured the original outline of the mound and left it standing as an island, often literally so during wet periods when the cuttings become filled with water (Fig. 1.2). In consequence, the mound has been artificially enhanced and

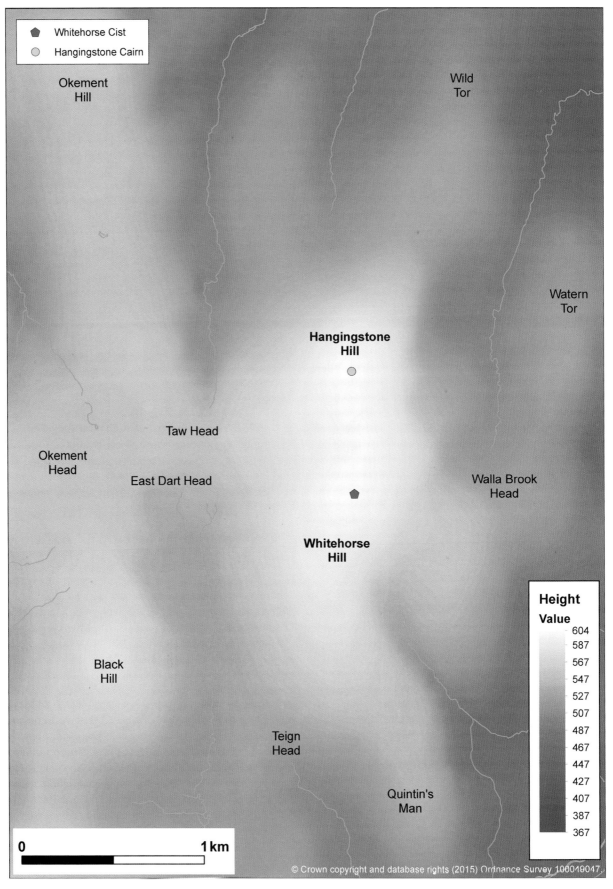

Whitehorse Cist

Hangingstone Cairn

Okement
Hill

Wild
Tor

Watern
Tor

**Hangingstone
Hill**

Taw Head

Okement
Head

East Dart Head

Walla Brook
Head

**Whitehorse
Hill**

Black
Hill

Teign
Head

Quintin's
Man

**Height
Value**

604
587
567
547
527
507
487
467
447
427
407
387
367

0   1 km

Figure 1.3: Location map showing the topography of Whitehorse Hill and the Hangingstone Hill cairn. Note the large number of stream heads and intervening interfluves which surround the hill.

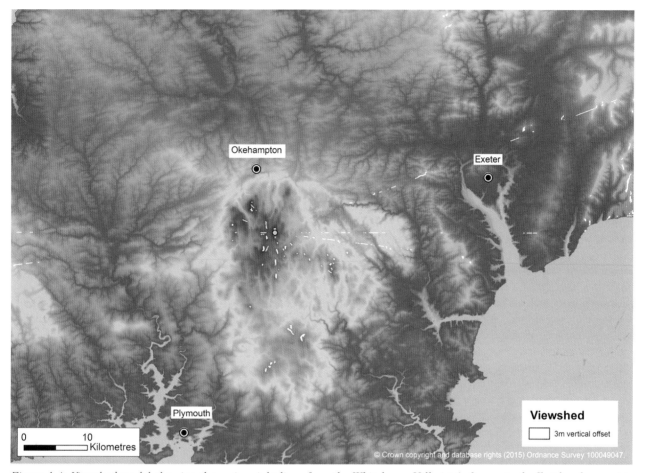

Figure 1.4: Viewshed model showing the major sight lines from the Whitehorse Hill cist (a 3m vertical offset has been set to allow for the height of the mound and a person). The dominant views are those towards the east into lowland areas of Devon.

stands proud of the surrounding land surface. This makes it harder to ascertain the site's original prominence in the wider Bronze Age landscape. In addition to altering the local topography, the peat cuttings have also contributed to the drying out and shrinkage of the peat mound, and it was this process that had resulted in the eventual exposure of the cist in its western side.

The Whitehorse Hill cist is one of the highest to be found on Dartmoor and it occupies a commanding, if isolated position, above several stream valley heads (Fig. 1.3). It has expansive views to the west into Cornwall and particularly to the east, where sightlines extend (in good weather) into Dorset. However, views of the adjacent moorland are rather more restricted, with viewsheds largely confined to other hilltops, rather than into the surrounding valleys. This means that relatively few other monuments are visible from the cist (Fig. 1.4).

The northern end of the ridge, which lies approximately 700m to the north, is occupied by another ceremonial monument, which is visible from the cist. This is a prominent turf and stone barrow known as the Hangingstone cairn (Fig. 1.5). Both sites have comparable landscape settings and are likely to be of broadly similar Early Bronze Age date (Fig. 1.6). Aside from these two sites, no other

prehistoric monuments are recorded on the ridge, although it is quite possible that the deep peat may hide further cists or other features. A prehistoric stone row has recently been found on the high moors at Cut Hill (see, for example, Fyfe and Greeves 2010) and a second Bronze Age cairn has been identified on the lower slopes of Hangingstone Hill (Jane Marchand, pers comm.). Further away, on the southern side of Dartmoor, a pit-circle was found beneath the peat at Headon Down (Dyer and Quinnell 2013). Indeed, it is more than likely that many more examples of the smaller-scale monument forms which are known across the moors in the south-west, such as diminutive stone rows and stone settings, and timber post-rings (for example, Riley and Wilson-North 2001, 27; Jones and Quinnell 2011), await discovery beneath the blanket of the peat. It may therefore be a mistake to see the Whitehorse Hill cist as an entirely isolated monument.

Previous archaeological recording of the Whitehorse Hill cist

The first indication of the archaeological potential of Whitehorse Hill was a cist first noted in 1892 by the

Figure 1.5: The Hangingstone Hill cairn from the east, with a military observation post beside it. (Photograph Andy Jones).

Figure 1.6: The Whitehorse Hill peat mound from the Hangingstone Hill cairn approximately 700m to the north. Although the peat mound appears to look like a sky-lined barrow, its prominence in the early Bronze Age landscape is uncertain because of the changes brought about by later peat cutting. (Photograph Andy Jones).

antiquarian John Chudleigh (1892, 14), who marked its position on the map of Dartmoor antiquities which accompanied his book. It is uncertain, however, whether this represents the site excavated in 2011 or another site which has been lost.

It is certainly the case that the Ordnance Survey did not mark the site, although its position was noted in the 1990s (Fig. 1.7). However, it was not until 2000 that its location was published by Joe Turner (Fig. 1.8), who drew the exposed cist section and produced a short note on

Figure 1.7: The Whitehorse cist photographed in 1999 (scale is 1m). Note that the level of the peat in front of the cist was then much higher than in 2011. (Photograph: copyright Tom Greeves.)

Figure 1.8: First recorded section of the cist, by Joe Turner, published in the Proceedings of the Devon Archaeological Society for 2000. (Reproduced by permission of Devon Archaeological Society and Pat Turner.)

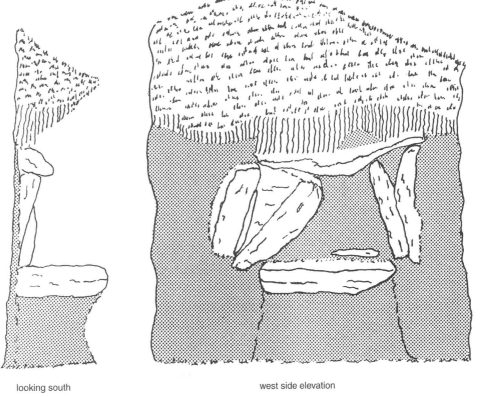

looking south

west side elevation

0   40cm

Figure 1.9: Environmental recording of the peat mound section immediately adjacent to the cist by English Heritage in 2005. (Photograph: Zoë Hazell.)

the site for the *Proceedings of the Devon Archaeological Society* (Turner 2000). Prior to the 2011 excavations, the exposed section of the cist measured up to 0.7m wide by 0.25m deep and 0.35m high. Turner recorded that a stone was missing from the western side of the cist and that this was likely to be the end stone. The previous recording of the condition of the cist also noted that hair moss was growing out of the exposed section (Turner 2000). Visual inspection of the interior by torchlight in 2011 ahead of excavation appeared to indicate that it was a largely empty void except for a peaty fill in the bottom of the cist. It was therefore assumed that the cist was aligned east–west and, based on visual inspection, anticipated that any fill inside it was likely to be either recent or badly disturbed.

Following the identification of the site, environmental sampling of the peat mound adjacent to the cist was carried out by English Heritage in 2005 (Straker 2006) (Fig. 1.9). Analyses of the samples from the monolith tin included assessment of the pollen, the charred macrofossils and testate amoebae. It was decided to take the reporting on the testate amoebae to full analysis and the results from that work are included in this monograph (Chapter 19,

below). In addition, two radiocarbon determinations were obtained from the monolith tin. These suggested that the peat at the level of the base of the cist was of an Early to Middle Neolithic date, 4625±50 BP, 3620–3130 cal BC (SUERC-10199), whereas that from peat level with the top of the cist was of Early Bronze Age date, 3650±50 BP, 2200–1880 cal BC (SUERC-10198). The meaning of these dates was therefore open to question, as the position of the cist within the mound allowed for the possibility that it could be of either earlier to Middle Neolithic or Early Bronze Age date. One possible scenario was that a trench to hold the cist had been cut into the peat, down to the Neolithic level of peat accumulation, and that the stones were inserted into it. The alternative was that the cist was constructed upon the Neolithic ground surface and that the peat had grown up around it during the Bronze Age. The second scenario implied that the cist was a free-standing monument which stood proud of the surrounding contemporary land surface.

Although available evidence suggested that cists were a long-lived site type, analogy with other dated examples across the south-west strongly suggested that where dating was possible, cists post-dated the Neolithic period (for example, Pollard and Russell 1969; Jones 2009–10), and it was therefore unlikely that the site would prove to be of fourth millennium cal BC date. However, as discussed in Chapter 21 below, examples such as Lydford 24 at Fernworthy (Baring Gould 1898) were associated with Beaker pottery, which is likely to predate 2000 cal BC, whereas others, such as Moretonhampstead 6 (Grinsell 1978), were associated with Early Bronze Age artefacts which post-dated 2000 cal BC. Unfortunately, the majority of investigated cists on Dartmoor were excavated a century or more ago, and most produced little or nothing in the way of artefactual material (Butler 1997, 279–280; Table 21.1; Chapter 21, below). Indeed, prior to the investigation of the Whitehorse Hill cist there were no radiocarbon determinations from any of the Dartmoor cists and, in fact, scientific dates from cists in the south-west, as opposed to cairns and barrows, are generally few and far between. Those which have been obtained reflect the same broad chronology as the artefactual assemblages; for example, a recently obtained radiocarbon determination (Wk-20900; 3561±34 BP) from Farway 31 calibrates to 2020–1770 cal BC (Jones and Quinnell 2008), whereas a sample of bulk oak charcoal (BM-402; 3336±53 BP) from Upton Pyne 248b, also in east Devon, provides a *terminus post quem* of 1750–1500 cal BC (Pollard and Russell 1976). As a result, prior to the 2011 excavation, it was possible that the Whitehorse Hill cist could prove to be of later third or early–middle second millennium cal BC date.

Given the uncertainties relating to the possible date of the cist, the considered assumption that there would be an absence of datable artefacts and the uncertain method of construction, the peat mound around the cist was also investigated in 2011 to recover dating and palaeoenvironmental material, which it was thought were unlikely to survive within the interior of the cist itself. It was also hoped that the analysis would be able to establish whether it was an entirely natural mound, or one which had been made more prominent through human activity.

As will be described in the succeeding chapters, the expectations from the project were radically revised in light of the excavation and the outstanding set of results which emerged from it.

Finally, it is also worth noting that the project has generated a considerable amount of public interest and media coverage. The latter included a television documentary called *Mystery of the Moor*, which was shown on BBC TV in February 2014. Between September and December 2014 a very successful exhibition devoted to the Whitehorse Hill cist was held at Plymouth Museum. Replicas of the artefacts from the cist were made for both the television programme and the exhibition, and images of these items feature throughout this volume.

Acknowledgements

I would like to thank the Devon Archaeological Society and Mrs Pat Turner for giving permission to reproduce the section drawing of the Whitehorse Hill cist and Tom Greeves for permission to use his photograph of the cist. I would also like to thank my colleagues Sean Taylor and Francis Shepherd for producing the location and viewshed maps.

References

Baring-Gould, S. 1898. Seventeenth report of the barrow committee. *Transactions of the Devonshire Association* 30, 77–79.

Bronk Ramsey, C. 1995. Radiocarbon calibration and analysis of stratigraphy. *Radiocarbon* 36, 425–430.

Bronk Ramsey, C. 1998. Probability and dating. *Radiocarbon* 40, 461–474.

Bronk Ramsey, C. 2001. Development of the radiocarbon calibration program. *Radiocarbon* 43, 355–363.

Bronk Ramsey, C. 2009. Bayesian analysis of radiocarbon dates, *Radiocarbon* 51, 337–360.

Butler, J. 1997. *Dartmoor Atlas of Antiquities. Volume 5: the second millennium B.C.*. Tiverton: Devon Books.

Chudleigh, J. 1892. *Devonshire Antiquities*. London: H.R. Allenson.

Dyer, M. & Quinnell, H. 2013. Excavation of a group of Early Bronze Age monuments on Headon Down, Sparkwell. *Proceedings of the Devon Archaeological Society* 71, 55–80.

Fyfe, R. & Greeves, T. 2010. The date and context of a stone row: Cut Hill, Dartmoor, south-west England. *Antiquity* 84, 55–70.

Grinsell, L. V. 1978. Dartmoor barrows. *Proceedings of the Devon Archaeological Society* 36, 85–180.

Herring, P. 2008. Stepping onto the commons: south-western stone rows. In P. Rainbird (ed.) *Monuments in the Landscape: papers in honour of Andrew Fleming*. Stroud: Tempus, 79–88

Historic England 2016. Management of Research Projects in the Historic Environment: The MoRPHE Project Managers Guide, Swindon: Historic England.

Jones, A. M. 2009–10. The excavation of a barrow on Constantine Island, St Merryn, Cornwall. *Cornish Archaeology* 48–9, 67–98.

Jones, A. M. & Quinnell, H. 2008. The Farway barrow complex in East Devon reassessed. *Proceedings of the Devon Archaeological Society* 66, 27–58.

Jones, A. M. & Quinnell, H. 2011. The Neolithic and Bronze Age periods in Cornwall, *c* 4000 cal BC to *c* 1000 cal BC: an overview of recent developments, *Cornish Archaeology* 50, 197–230.

Mook, W. G. 1986. Business meeting: recommendations/resolutions adopted by the Twelfth International Radiocarbon Conference. *Radiocarbon* 28, 799.

Newman, P. 2011. *The Field Archaeology of Dartmoor*. London: English Heritage.

Pollard, S. & Russell, P. 1976. Radiocarbon dating: excavation of round barrow 248b, Upton Pyne, Exeter. *Proceedings of the Devon Archaeological Society* 27, 95.

Riley, H. & Wilson-North, R. 2001. *The Field Archaeology of Exmoor*. London: English Heritage, London.

Stuiver, M. & Reimer, P. J. 1986. A computer program for radiocarbon age calculation. *Radiocarbon* 28, 1022–1030.

Straker, V. 2006. Dartmoor 2005: palaeoenvironmental sampling from Cut Hill and Whitehorse Hill. Unpublished report.

Turner, J. 2000. A cist on Whitehorse Hill. *Proceedings of the Devon Archaeology Society* 58, 249–250.

Worth, R. 1967. *Worth's Dartmoor*. Newton Abbot: David and Charles.

Section 2:

Deconstructing and reconstructing the cist

2. Results from the 2011 fieldwork

Andy M. Jones

The archaeological fieldwork was in two stages: first, a topographical survey of the cist and the peat mound into which it was set was undertaken, followed by excavation of the cist and recording of the upstanding section of the peat mound.

Pre-excavation survey

A survey of the site was undertaken by Phil Newman in July 2011 (Fig. 2.1), in the form of a dual frequency GPS RTK survey. A base station was established on Hangingstone Hill for which final grid coordinates were computed using RINEX data from four OS active stations. This enabled the survey to be geo-referenced without the need for fixed identifiable features on OS maps. It also meant that the information could be downloaded into GIS mapping without any correction. In addition, a 12m grid was established over the site. The four corner pegs were subsequently used as reference points during the excavations.

Excavation methods

A protective stone wall recently constructed by the Dartmoor National Park Authority in front of the cist (which was named Cist 10) was removed by hand and the exposed west-facing section of the peat mound was hand-cleaned. A 10m north–south section was established on the axis of the cist and cut back (Figs. 2.2 and 2.3). This ensured that the relationship between the cist and the mound could be established and recorded in profile, as well as revealing the sequence of the site's construction. The remaining portion of the mound was left unexcavated.

The standing section was hand-drawn at a scale of 1:10 (Figs. 2.4 and 2.5). The top of the mound above the cist was then cut back to expose the top of the cist and its *in situ* capstone (Fig. 2.6). A plan was made of the unexcavated cist at a scale of 1:20. After completing the plan, the capstone was lifted and a second 1:20 plan was made (Fig. 2.7).

Excavation of the cist's contents then commenced in spits, which were 100% sampled for plant macrofossils. However, very early in the excavation of the cist a shale bead was identified and cremated bone could be seen beneath a layer of what appeared to be matted 'fur-like' material. At this point the decision was made to block lift the contents of the cist with the base stone of the cist and transport it for detailed laboratory excavation at the Wiltshire Conservation Service laboratory in Chippenham (Chapter 3, below). The stone was wrapped in cling-film and transported some 1.5 km by wheelbarrow to the site vehicle. The following day, a final post-excavation plan was made of the site showing the position of two hazel stakes (Small Finds 1 and 2; Chapter 4, below) which were identified when the remainder of the cist was dismantled.

A black and white archive photographic record was made of the excavations and additional colour digital images were taken. A Total Station was used to survey the stones which comprised the cist. Environmental samples (including plant macrofossil, pollen and testate amoebae) were taken from within the cist and from the surrounding peat mound.

On completion of the archaeological recording the stones from the cist were all labelled with identifying letters, so that the cist could be reconstructed within the peat mound. The cist was rebuilt within the peat mound in 2012; however, peat shrinkage has continued to be a problem.

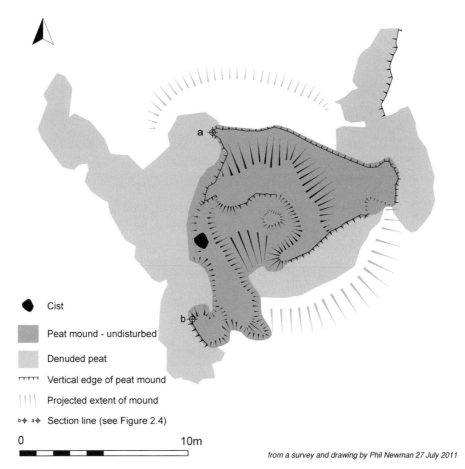

Cist

Peat mound - undisturbed

Denuded peat

Vertical edge of peat mound

Projected extent of mound

Section line (see Figure 2.4)

0   10m

from a survey and drawing by Phil Newman 27 July 2011

Figure 2.1: Plan of the peat mound prior to excavation. The cist was in the western side of the mound. (After a survey by Phil Newman.)

Figure 2.2: The Whitehorse Hill peat mound after the section had been cleaned. (Photograph: Alan Endacott.)

Figure 2.3: A close-up of the cist after the west-facing section had been cleaned back.

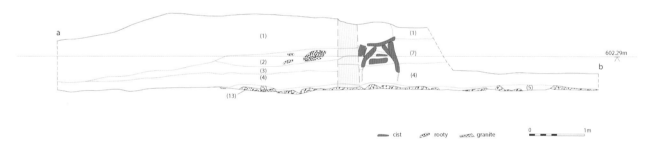

Figure 2.4: The west-facing section of the entire mound.

A full description of the contexts within the mound, of the deposit within Cist 10 and of the stones was given in the archive level project report (Jones 2011).

The site stratigraphy is described below from the bottom to the top of the recorded section.

Results from the excavation

The peat mound into which the cist was set measures approximately 12m in diameter and has a height of approximately 1.5m. The current extent and form of the mound is, however, largely artificial, its edges being defined by the limit of adjacent peat cuttings (Fig. 2.1).

At the base of the section the natural granitic soil or 'growan' (5) and the granite bedrock (13) were exposed. Overlying these deposits was the peat mound, which reached a height in the section of up to 1.3m. When freshly cleaned it appeared to comprise distinct organic layers, (1), (2), (3), (4), (5), (6) and (7), which ranged

from black to mid greyish-brown in colour. However, there was no evidence that the mound was in any way artificial. Although changes in colour of the peat were given conventional archaeological context numbers, in reality these changes reflected little more than the wetness of the peat, and the assigned context numbers cannot be taken to represent meaningful stratigraphical units. This was demonstrated by the fact that when layer (7) on the south side of Cist 10 was cut back (thereby revealing damper peat), it became identical to the wetter layers (2) and (3), which were located on the north side of the cist. In other words, the 'stratigraphy' of the mound relates more to the condition of the mound at the time of recording than to the conventional layer formation or episodes of activity which are normally associated with context numbering.

Two hazel stakes (Small Finds 1 and 2) were found in layer (2) beside Cist 10 (Figs. 2.7–2.9). Small Find 1 was located on the eastern side of the cist and was lying prone at the level of the base of the cist. Small Find 2 was

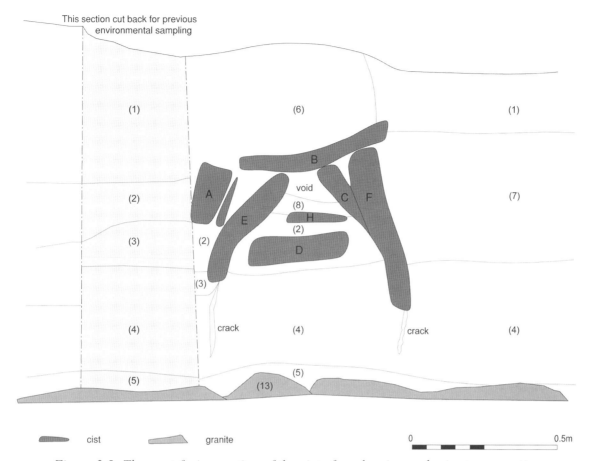

This section cut back for previous environmental sampling

(1) (6) (1)

B

A void C F (7)

(2) (8)

E H

(3) (2) (2)

(3) D

(3)

(4) crack (4) crack (4)

(5)

(5) (13) (5)

cist   granite   0   0.5m

Figure 2.5: The west-facing section of the cist after cleaning and prior to excavation.

situated against the northern side of the cist and was in a vertical position. Three radiocarbon determinations were obtained on the stakes: SF1; SUERC-40124; 3500±30 BP) and two on SF2 (OxA-26377; 3437±28 and OxA-27447; 3457±27) that are statistically consistent (T'= 0.3; T'(5%)= 3.8; v= 1; WH11 – SF2; 3447±20 BP). These three measurements are statistically consistent (T'= 2.4; T'(5%)= 6.0; v= 2) and both stakes could therefore be of the same actual age. Chronological modelling (Chapter 20) provides estimates for the dates of the stakes of *1890–1735 cal BC (90% probability; SUERC-40124; Fig. 20.3)* or *1715–1695 cal BC (5% probability)* and *1870–1845 cal BC (4% probability; WH11 – SF2; Fig. 20.3)* or *1815–1685 cal BC (91% probability)*, probably *1765–1735 cal BC (33% probability)* or *1720–1690 cal BC (35% probability)*. It is suggested below that these stakes may have been associated with the marking out of the mound for the cist (Chapter 20, below), and they therefore provide a *terminus post quem* date for the construction of the cist.

Cist 10 was set within layer (2) (Fig. 2.4) on the west side of the mound. No cut into the mound was found, although it is very unlikely that one would have been identifiable given the plastic quality of the peat. However, micromorphological analysis of the peat adjacent to the cist suggested that it had been disturbed (Chapter 5, below), which would be

Figure 2.6: The Whitehorse Hill cist from the east, showing the exposed capstone (upper left) and side stone G. (50cm scales.)

Andy M. Jones

*Figure 2.7: Plans
of the cist: prior to
excavation (top),
with capstone
removed and hazel
stakes exposed
(bottom).*

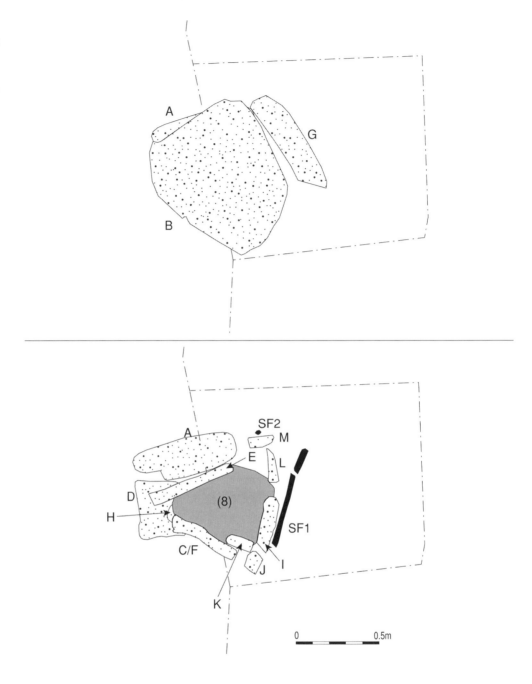

*Figure 2.8: Stake,
Small Find 1 lying
prone on the eastern
side of the cist within
the peat mound.*

Figure 2.9: Stake, Small Find 2 parallel to one of the side stones on the northern side of the cist and within the peat mound.

congruent with a cut having been made into the peat mound to hold the cist. It is also uncertain as to how deep the cut was and how much of the cist stood proud of the mound, although as discussed below it seems likely that the capstone was originally above the top of the peat mound.

Externally, the cist measured 0.78m long by 0.68m wide and 0.3m high. The cist comprised a flat granite base slab (H), measuring 0.7m by 0.48m, around which several wedge-shaped granite stones (A, C, E, F, G, I, J, K, L and M) were set upright within the peat. These stones ranged in length from 0.24m to 0.6m. Most were arranged so that the tapering end of the stone pointed downwards into the peat. One stone, (J), was much smaller and square, measuring 0.1m × 0.1m, and had been used in the south-east corner of the cist to square it off. A large capstone B

was placed on top of the cist. This stone was larger than the others and measured 0.79m × 0.66m. This stone gave the cist the appearance of a large 'stone mushroom' or a miniature megalithic 'quoit' (chambered tomb) (Fig. 2.10).

As noted in the introduction, it appeared initially that the cist was aligned east–west and that the stone at its northern end was missing (Fig. 2.3). However, excavation demonstrated that this appearance had been created by the exposed end stones E, F and C, sinking into the peat layers (2), (3) and (4) and leaning inward, so that they gave the impression of forming the narrow end of the cist (Figs. 2.4, 2.5). Likewise, stone D, originally thought to be the base of the cist, was instead found to be a side stone which had collapsed outwards. A stone (G) opposite it on the eastern side of the cist was also found to have become displaced.

Figure 2.10: The cist in the peat mound. Note the collapsed nature of the side stones and the distinctive large capstone.

This means that the slightly longer axis of the cist would have been north west – south east.

The original shape of the cist is not entirely certain. It may have been rectangular, although it could have been almost square in plan. Alternatively, and unlike most Dartmoor cists, it could have been far more irregular. This might explain the apparent instability of the side stones. It would also mean that the cist is unlikely to have been free-standing as the side stones would not have been able to support the weight of the capstone.

The cist was partially filled by layer (8). This was a peat deposit between 0.05m and 0.15m thick. In the exposed section the deposit was quite rooty and it was initially thought likely that it had formed naturally, rather than being a placed deposit. However, during the excavation of the layer in spits, it was found that it contained a burial

deposit as well as a number of unique organic artefacts (see Chapter 3, below). It seems likely that layer (8) was deposited into or entered the cist after the burial deposits had been placed within it.

The contents of the cist were excavated off-site in the Wiltshire Conservation Service laboratory at Chippenham, where it was established that there was a coherent ordering to the filling of the cist. The detailed account of the micro excavation is given in Chapter 3 but the sequence is summarized here. At the base of the cist there was a layer of matted plant material, largely of purple moor grass; pollen from meadowsweet may indicate that a floral tribute had also been placed into the cist (Chapters 9 and 19, below). Three radiocarbon determinations were obtained on material from the matted plant material 3433+29 BP, 1880–1660 cal BC (SUERC-52450); 3357+30 BP, 1740–

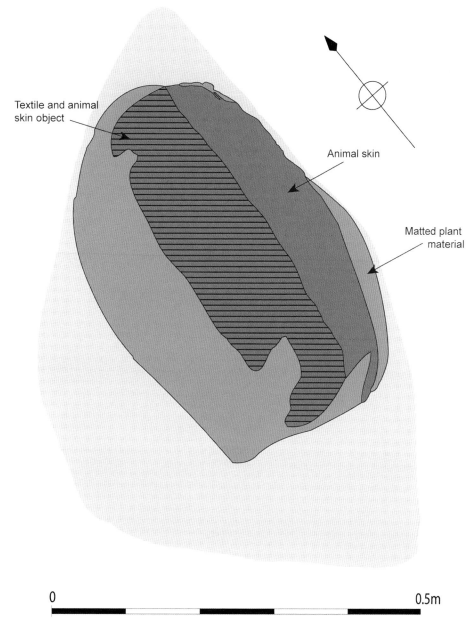

Textile and animal skin object

Animal skin

Matted plant material

0   0.5m

Figure 2.11: Plan of the initial finds placed within the cist (textile and animal-skin object and matted plant material). (After a plan by Helen Williams, Wiltshire Conservation Laboratory, Chippenham.)

1560 cal BC (OxA-30025); and 3378+37 BP, 1760–1560 cal BC (UBA-25301). These measurements are statistically consistent (T'= 3.5; T'(5%)= 6.0; v= 2) and could be of the same actual age. Chronological modelling (Chapter 20) provides an estimate for the construction of the cist into which the matted plant material was placed of *1730–1600 cal BC (95%* probability*; cist_finished;* Fig. 20.3), probably *1690–1620 cal BC (68% probability)*.

Upon the matted plant material was a thin composite textile and animal-skin object made up of two layers of textile made from nettles and edged with calfskin beading fringed with triangles (Chapter 18) (Fig. 2.11). This item may have been a band or sash. Above it, cremated human

bone had been placed within an animal pelt. A small amount of burnt textile was recovered which is likely to have been part of a garment or wrapping around the body when it was cremated (Chapter 8). Charcoal, predominantly of oak but with some hazel and likely to derive from the funeral pyre, was intermixed with the cremation deposit (Chapter 7). A delicate basketry container was placed at one end of the pelt (Fig. 2.12). In the immediate vicinity of this container, pieces of jewellery were found, including a composite braided bracelet or armband, beads forming a composite necklace and wooden studs. The bracelet consisted of braided strands of cattle hair into which had been inserted a large number of small studs, identified as being of tin by XRF analysis

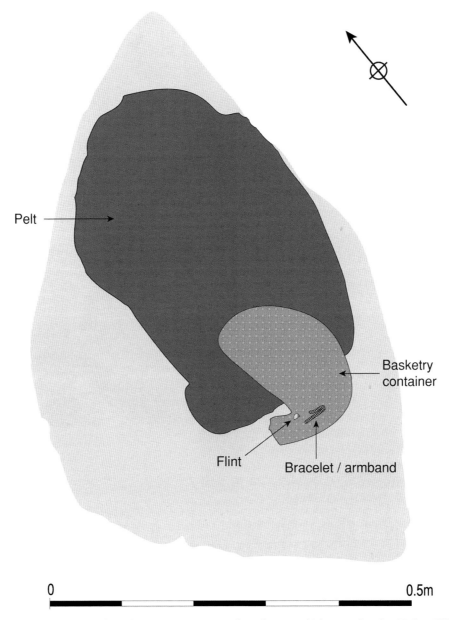

Figure 2.12: Plan of the pelt and basketry container within the cist (After a plan by Helen Williams, Wiltshire Conservation Laboratory, Chippenham.)

(Appendix A and Chapter 14). The composite necklace was made up of over 200 beads, including disc beads of shale, clay and amber and a large bead of tin (Chapter 15). A second tin bead is also likely to have been in the basketry container but only fragments from this survived. Four turned wooden studs made from spindle wood were also found within the basketry container, and a single flint flake tool was also recovered. A copper-alloy pin was found within the folds of the pelt during the conservation process. It is tempting to see this as being used to fasten the pelt or seal the deposit within it (Chapter, 12, below). A further layer of matted plant material covered these objects.

The beads and the copper-alloy pin are diagnostic finds of Early Bronze Age type and therefore gave an immediate indication of an early second millennium date for the burial (Chapters 12 and 15). This was subsequently confirmed by radiocarbon determinations obtained on several artefacts from the cist, including the basketry container, 3405±33 BP, 1870–1620 cal BC (OxA-27543), the pelt 3358±33 BP, 1740–1530 cal BC (OxA-27446), and one of the wooden studs, 3709±33 BP, 2200–1980 cal BC (OxA-27915). Dates were also obtained from the cremation, 3511±29 BP, 1930–1750 cal BC (OxA-26376), the cremation charcoal 3528±29 BP, 1950–1750 cal BC (SUERC-52451), and a charred culm node 3423±34 BP, 1880–1630 cal BC (UBA-25300) (Chapter 20). Chronological modelling (Chapter 20) provides estimates for the dates of material incorporated into the cist spanning a period of *60–280 years* (*95% probability*; Fig. 20.4), probably *125–240 years* (*68% probability*), from *1845–1685* (*95% probability*; *start_cist_contents*; Fig. 20.3) probably *1780–1719 cal BC* (*68% probability*) to *1730–1600 cal BC* (*95% probability*; *cist_finished*; Fig. 20.3), probably *1690–1620 cal BC* (*68% probability*) (Chapter 20).

Cist 10 was covered by layer (6), a friable peat deposit up to 0.37m thick. When the section was cut back two further layers were identified between layer (6) and the top of the capstone. Layer (11) was a thin, 0.02m thick, gritty peat which was directly above capstone B. Analysis of the soil micromorphology suggests that this layer could have developed *in situ* (Chapter 5), which implies that the capstone was left exposed long enough for a soil to form over it. However, it was covered by a second thin peat layer (12), which was darker and grit-free, which did not seem to have developed *in situ* and, in common with the peat sampled in 2005 adjacent to the cist, appeared to be very disturbed.

It therefore seems likely that layers (6) and (12) represent material which had been backfilled onto the top of the cist. Layer (11), however, may have been a soil horizon which had started to establish above the exposed capstone. How long after the cist was constructed any soil development on the capstone occurred is uncertain. Likewise, the date of any subsequent disturbance to the peat above the cist is also unknown. It does, however, seem unlikely that peat layer (6) was dumped straight on top of the cist after its construction, as this would not have allowed time for a peat soil to have formed on top of the capstone. It is therefore more likely that the peat was not deposited over the site of the cist immediately after the burial had been placed inside it. It is also possible that the location of the cist continued to be known in prehistory and the question of 'revisiting' will be discussed later (Chapter 21).

To north and south of the cist, the upper part of the mound section, which post-dated the cist, comprised layer (1), a thick dark peat deposit. It is quite likely that layer (1) was just a wetter version of layer (6) and that in fact they represent the same sequence of peat growth.

Summary of the stratigraphy

The archaeological investigations at Whitehorse Hill in 2011 led to exciting new information about the character of Early Bronze Age burial on Dartmoor. It provides one of the most significant records of funerary practices of this period in Britain and has provided an unparalleled set of artefacts. The site is the first cisted burial on Dartmoor to have been recorded using modern techniques which take into account the stratigraphy of the cist and the surrounding environment.

From the stratigraphy the following information about the construction of the site has been obtained.

The cist was set into a mound of natural peat and to date the site is the only example to have been recorded within a peat mound. Nonetheless, the cist falls within the broad pattern of excavated cists that have been recorded across south-west England.

It seems possible that prior to the construction of the cist, two hazel stakes were pushed into the peat to mark the site. A similar process of marking a site for funerary activity has been suggested for other Early Bronze Age burials, and this will be discussed in Chapter 21.

As noted above, no cut for the stones which formed the cist was visible in the recorded section of the peat mound, although it is unlikely that one would have been identifiable in the peat. It is, however, considered highly improbable that the cist could ever have existed as a free-standing structure. The side and end stones are unlikely to have provided any kind of long-term support for the capstone and the side stones are likely to have collapsed long before a peat layer developed around it. This is also supported by the soil micromorphology analysis which suggests that the peat immediately adjacent to the cist had been disturbed. It is also very probable that the continuing growth of the mound over time would have destabilised a free-standing structure and caused it to collapse. It is therefore very likely that the stones were set around the inside edge of a cutting which had been made into the top of the peat accumulation. The difficulty in cutting a neat shape into the peat might also explain why the cist was somewhat less regular than those that are typically found in the mounds of barrows and cairns, and why the base of the cist had been lined with a large stone. By placing the side stones around the edge of the cut, with their tapering ends pointing down into the mound material, the peat would have provided the stability needed to hold the cist together as a structure. However, the weight of the stones, including that of the large capstone, together with the periodic expansion of the mound would have led to some distortion over time, with some stones sinking deeper into the mound, others moving inwards or outwards. Evidence for this process is reflected in the final slightly contorted appearance of the cist and by the cracks in the peat beneath the large end stones (Figs. 2.5 and 2.10).

The broadly north-west–south-east alignment of the slightly longer axis of the cist conforms to the overwhelming majority of recorded cists on Dartmoor (Chapter 21). Likewise, the overall dimensions of the site are within the range of documented cists. However, the irregular shape and use of small stones to form the sides of Cist 10 mean that it is rather different from most other recorded Dartmoor cists. Typically, these are neatly built rectangular boxes or stone chests comprising a capstone supported by two long side stones and two shorter end stones. A few sites have been found to be constructed from smaller stones, as, for example, at White Hill 4, and a handful of non-rectangular cists are also known (Butler 1997, 172). The base stone is also unusual, as only a very small number of sites have a floor stone or paving (Baring Gould 1898; Grinsell 1978). As will be discussed in the concluding chapter, the final shape of the cist might in part have arisen through its location within a peat mound.

After the cist was constructed, a layer of matted plant material was placed on the base stone and the cremation and the accompanying artefacts were placed upon this. The character of these artefacts will be described in detail in the individual specialist chapters and in the concluding chapter. However, it is worth noting at this point that there is some evidence for complexity in the formation of the deposit. The implications of this will be discussed fully in Chapter 21.

The preservation of the artefacts within the cist is likely to have resulted from it being situated within the peat mound and through the placing or formation of a deposit of peat within it after the cremation and the artefacts had been placed inside. On present knowledge it seems likely that the interior of the cist was intentionally infilled with peat, although the exact point in time at which it entered is unknown. Where archaeological recording has been sufficiently detailed, this pattern of deliberate infilling has been found at other Dartmoor sites, as, for example, at Chagford 4, Peter Tavy 39 and Walkhampton 17, where the interior of the cists had been filled with layers of redeposited subsoil; at Chagford 3 a cist had been filled with a 'black soil' (Baring Gould 1898; Burnard 1897; 1899; Quinnell 2003). Indeed, it was suggested by Worth that, where cists have been found undisturbed, 'every example agrees on this particular' (Worth 1967, 171).

Despite uncertainty as to how high the mound may have stood above the surrounding landscape in the Bronze Age, it does seem likely that the majority of the peat above the capstone had been dumped over it, although a thin layer of soil directly above the stone seems to have been a naturally formed deposit. This has been taken to imply that the capstone was left uncovered for long enough to allow soil formation to commence, and it is therefore likely that the stone would have been a visible marker in the landscape for a period of time after the cist had been constructed. The implications of this are discussed later (Chapter 21).

Acknowledgements

I would like to thank Helen Williams for providing the original drawings of the find locations within the cist and Alan Endacott for supplying the aerial photograph of the mound. I would also like to thank my colleagues Sean Taylor and Francis Shepherd for producing the section drawings and plans. The survey of the mound was carried out by Phil Newman and his data were used to produce the plan. I would also like to thank the excavation team of Sean Taylor and Ralph Fyfe. Onsite environmental sampling was undertaken by Vanessa Straker, Zoë Hazell and Julie Jones.

References

Baring-Gould, S. 1898. Seventeenth barrow report. *Transactions of the Devonshire Association* 30, 77–79.

Burnard, R. 1897. Sixteenth barrow report. *Transactions of the Devonshire Association* 29, 66–71.

Burnard, R. 1899. Eighteenth barrow report. *Transactions of the Devonshire Association* 31, 94–100.

Butler, J. 1997. *Dartmoor Atlas of Antiquities*, volume 5. Tiverton: Devon Books.

Grinsell, L. V. 1978. Dartmoor barrows. *Proceedings of the Devon Archaeological Society* 36, 85–180.

Jones, A. M. 2011. Whitehorse Hill cist, Dartmoor, Devon: Archaeological excavation, 2011 (unpublished archive report). Truro: Historic Environment Projects, Cornwall Council.

Quinnell, H. 2003. Devon Beakers: new finds, new thoughts. *Proceedings of the Devon Archaeological Society* 61, 1–20.

Turner, J. 2000. A cist on Whitehorse Hill. *Proceedings of the Devon Archaeology Society* 58, 249–250.

Worth, R. 1967. *Worth's Dartmoor*. Newton Abbot: David and Charles.

3. The micro-excavation and conservation of the artefacts

Helen Williams

Following the excavation, the contents of the cist (on the base stone) were received at the laboratory in August 2011 for assessment and micro-excavation, having been block lifted on site (Chapter 2). The block consisted of a large granite base slab with layers of peat resting on top. A small section of what appeared to be red coloured fur or hide was visible towards the bottom of the block together with small fragments which were initially identified as bone. The block measured approximately 600mm in width × 400mm in depth × 350mm in height (Fig. 3.1).

Methodology

The block was excavated in 2cm spits to ensure that any further contents were recovered. Adjustments were allowed depending on the extent of finds uncovered. Each spit was plotted onto a sheet of Melinex with the position of any finds recorded and photographed. The finds were also photographed *in situ* and post-excavation.

Finds were separated into material types and bagged accordingly as excavated; no cleaning of any material took place at this stage. Finds were kept in stable cold storage until analysis had been completed and the most

Figure 3.1: Block containing cist contents before excavation. (Photograph: Helen Williams, Wiltshire Conservation Centre.)

appropriate conservation treatments were determined. No consolidants were used.

Details of micro-excavation

Burial block

The block from the cist environment consisted of a clay-like peat, roots, peat and small stone inclusions, most probably granite pieces derived from the surrounding cist slabs. Fur or hide material was visible from a depth of 5cm from the surface of the excavated block, leather fragments were discovered at a depth of 7cm and 10cm (Figs. 3.2 and 3.3). Further potential cremated bone fragments were visible through a hole in the fur/hide material at a depth of 9cm. These fragments were subsequently confirmed as being human by Simon Mays (Chapter 6). A matted layer of plant material had been placed at an angle, to all intents and purposes deliberately, partially covering the burial beneath. This was first recorded at a depth of 7cm to 8cm from the surface (Fig. 3.4).

Central feature

At this stage, with peat layer (8) and loose burial debris removed from around the central 'feature' and bagged, the decision was taken to remove and record the remaining burial items as a separate micro-excavation. Samples of peat and burial material were taken from between each layer for environmental analysis and to determine whether pollen in particular might be present, which might indicate, for example the placement of floral tributes (see Chapter 21).

The objects recovered from the block were, from top to bottom, as follows:

- Upper matted layer of plant material, 0–1cm depth, partially overlying whole burial.
- Basketry container, 1–2cm depth, partially overlying the pelt.
- Shale and amber beads, braided band with tin studs, 2–3cm depth, believed to be part of the original contents from the basketry container, and small detached animal skin triangles from the textile and animal-skin object.
- The pelt, containing a cremation, 3–4cm depth.
- Textile and animal-skin object, 4–5cm depth, placed directly below the pelt with no peat layer between.
- Layer of matted plant material, 5–6cm depth, placed directly onto the granite base slab and similar in appearance to the matted layer recovered from the top of the burial.

Cremation

The cremation within the pelt was divided into four 'quadrants' (Fig. 3.5) and excavated accordingly to determine whether there was any significance to the

Figure 3.2: Leather fragments at 7cm depth. (Photograph: Helen Williams, Wiltshire Conservation Centre.)

Figure 3.3: Leather fragments at 10cm depth. (Photograph: Helen Williams, Wiltshire Conservation Centre.)

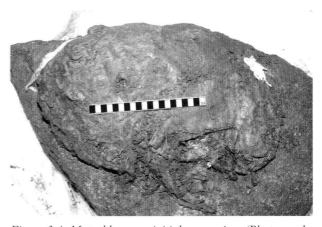

Figure 3.4: Matted layer on initial excavation. (Photograph: Helen Williams, Wiltshire Conservation Centre.)

placement of the material. The condition of the material was variable (Table 3.1). The bone was air dried and any peat removed with a stiff brush to aid identification. Individual fragments were photographed; charcoal and

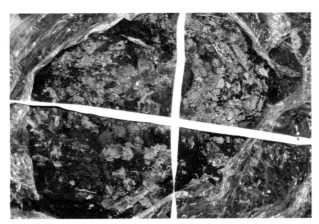

Figure 3.5: Cremation quadrants. Quadrant 1 top left, Quadrant 2 top right, Quadrant 3 bottom left, Quadrant 4 bottom right (Photograph: Helen Williams, Wiltshire Conservation Centre.)

Figure 3.6: Matted layer after excavation. (Photograph: Helen Williams, Wiltshire Conservation Centre.)

Table 3.1: Brief description of the cremated remains, by quadrant.

Quadrant	Description of material recovered
1	Preservation of much of the material is poor, almost sand-like in consistency, large proportion of ash. Some larger fragments retrieved
2	Preservation is better with more recognisable bone fragments visible
3	Preservation is poor as with quadrant 1, some larger fragments retrieved including a tooth root (no enamel).
4	Smaller quantity of material overall, small quantity of loose material and some larger fragments retrieved.

Figure 3.7: Matted layer after conservation treatment. (Photograph: Helen Williams, Wiltshire Conservation Centre.)

other burnt matter were separated out. By agreement with environmental specialists, the charcoal was air dried and vegetable matter kept damp where possible.

Conservation of individual finds

Matted layer of plant material

The surface of the lifted block was partially obscured by peat deposits and debris from the burial environment and was wet and therefore fragile. It consisted of strips of plant material. The upper material was not well-preserved and could not be identified but a similar layer at the base was identified as purple moor grass that had been placed in a linear fashion (Chapter 9). There does not appear to have been any means of holding the material together, such as weaving, for example (Fig. 3.6).

Due to the fragility of the material, minimal peat deposits were removed prior to treatment from the top-facing surface only. The material was treated with a two-stage PEG process (10% PEG 400 and 10% PEG 4000), followed by freeze drying.

Following treatment, the remaining peat deposits were mechanically removed as far as possible without causing further damage. The layer remains fragile but stable (Fig. 3.7).

Basketry container

The basketry container was made from plant material, identified as lime bast (Chapter 13, and Appendix B, below). It consists of strips of the bast fibre which appear to have been stitched to form two circular sections joined by a tube of similar material. The sections are held together with a thick, coarse thread, which has been identified as cattle hair (Appendix C). The contents included beads of shale, clay and amber and one of tin; a flint flake tool and fragments of tin from a second possible bead were also found. There were also two pairs of wooden studs and an armband or bracelet made from braided animal hair

Figure 3.8: Basketry container in situ. (Photograph: Helen Williams, Wiltshire Conservation Centre.)

Figure 3.9: Basketry container on initial excavation. (Photograph: Helen Williams, Wiltshire Conservation Centre.)

Figure 3.10: Basketry container after conservation treatment. (Photograph: Helen Williams, Wiltshire Conservation Centre.)

Figure 3.11: Basketry container, detail. (Photograph: Helen Williams, Wiltshire Conservation Centre.)

decorated with tin studs. The latter was found next to the basketry container but is thought to have fallen out as a result of the distortion of the container during burial (Fig. 3.8) (Chapter 21).

The surface of the object was partially obscured by peat and debris from the burial environment. The material was wet and therefore fragile. The object had slumped sideways in the burial environment causing it to become flattened and distorted. Some of the contents therefore spilled out. A section of the basketry container was inadvertently removed during the discovery of the cist burial on Dartmoor (Fig. 3.9). The section was retrieved from peat samples and treated with the view of attempting a reconstruction if possible. The section was fragmentary at the edges and more deteriorated than the rest of the container, due to not being kept in the same controlled conditions. This section was also found at the front edge of the burial which was more exposed to weather conditions and may have suffered from increased deterioration as a result. The area of the

object that it corresponds to is in a similar fragmentary condition, with one small section completely detached.

Peat deposits were removed as far as possible with a soft brush and distilled water from the interior and exterior of the container and the separate fragment prior to treatment. Both were treated with a two-stage PEG process (10% PEG 400 and 10% PEG 4000), followed by freeze drying.

Following treatment the object is stable with a light buff-coloured appearance. The coarse black stitching was still friable and was therefore consolidated with 5% Butvar (polyethylene butyral) in industrial methylated spirit (Figs. 3.10 and 3.11).

Beads

The beads were part of a composite necklace. This consisted of a tin bead (a second tin bead was indicated by fragments

Figure 3.12: Beads in situ. (Photograph: Helen Williams, Wiltshire Conservation Centre.)

Figure 3.14: Clay bead example. (Photograph: Helen Williams, Wiltshire Conservation Centre.)

Figure 3.13: Shale bead example. (Photograph: Helen Williams, Wiltshire Conservation Centre.)

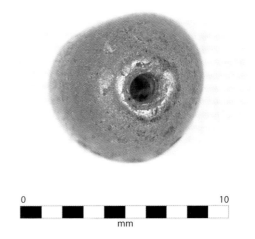

Figure 3.15: Amber bead example. (Photograph: Helen Williams, Wiltshire Conservation Centre.)

in the basketry container), shale disc beads, including one large example, amber beads, clay beads and small clay fragments (Chapter 15). In addition, a small number of beads were found next to the container, presumably having fallen out of it when it collapsed (Figs. 3.12 to 3.15).

All beads were recovered in a damp condition, covered with peat and debris from the burial environment. The tin bead has a thick encrusted layer of corrosion products visible. One section of shale and amber beads may have the remains of threads present (Group F). The amber beads are in excellent condition and appear to have retained their translucency; minor chips are missing from the ends near to the perforations (Fig. 3.15). The very small clay beads are extremely brittle and fragile and are prone to breakage.

Peat and debris were removed from the surface of the beads with a small brush. More stubborn areas were treated with barely damp swabs of distilled water under magnification. The tin bead was mechanically cleaned under magnification.

Following treatment, all are generally in good condition and stable. The amber beads have retained their translucency. The small clay beads remain brittle and fragile.

Flint

This is in excellent condition and has been identified as a flake tool (Chapter 17). Peat and debris were removed from the surface with barely damp swabs of distilled water under magnification.

Wooden studs

The studs consist of two pairs, one large and one small (Chapter 16). One of the large studs has several fragments detached from around the edges (Fig. 3.16). These were retained for treatment with the intention of re-attaching them if possible. The remaining three studs were intact. The second large stud had a small patch of tin corrosion visible on one surface, indicating contact with tin in the burial environment (Fig. 3.17).

Peat and debris were removed as far as possible with damp swabs of distilled water under magnification. The studs and small fragments were treated with a two-stage PEG treatment (10% PEG 400 and 15% PEG 4000) followed by freeze drying.

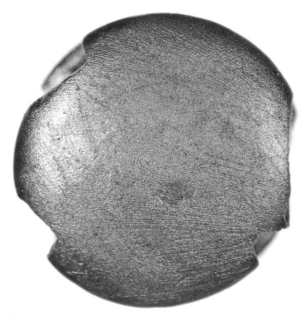

Figure 3.16: Large wooden stud with fragments missing. (Photograph: Helen Williams, Wiltshire Conservation Centre.)

Figure 3.17: Large wooden stud with tin staining. (Photograph: Helen Williams, Wiltshire Conservation Centre.)

Following treatment the studs are in good condition but are prone to damage from environmental fluctuations. Studs 2 and 4 developed cracks that opened up to the extent that small sections became detached. These were repaired using Paraloid B72 acrylic adhesive. The small fragments were reattached to Stud 3 also with Paraloid B72; these also remain fragile.

Braided band with tin studs

The armband or bracelet is made from braided cattle hair with tin studs (Chapter 14). The band was damp and fragile but in generally good condition. One terminal was missing but would potentially have consisted of a loop with which

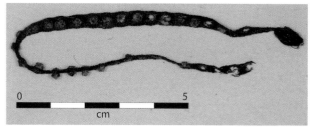

Figure 3.18: Braided band with studs after conservation treatment. (Photograph: Helen Williams, Wiltshire Conservation Centre.)

Figure 3.19: Animal pelt on initial excavation. (Photograph: Helen Williams, Wiltshire Conservation Centre.)

to secure the band closed over the rounded terminal. This section of the band was particularly fragmentary. The rivets were corroded and may have areas of weakness, particularly at the point where the two domed sections join.

X-ray analysis has revealed a good metal content inside the studs and XRF analysis indicated that the metal rivets are made from tin (Appendix A).

The peat and corrosion products were removed as far as possible by first consolidating the band and rivets with 4% Butvar (polyvinyl butyral) in industrial methylated spirit, followed by gentle mechanical cleaning under magnification. Where areas of weakness caused studs to become detached, these were replaced with Paraloid B72 acrylic adhesive. Following treatment the band is fragile but stable (Fig. 3.18).

Animal pelt

The pelt was red–brown in colour when wet, with long dense hairs visible, approximately 39mm in length and coarse in appearance. The hairs appear to be aligned in the same direction with a central fold visible along one edge (Fig. 3.19). There is no stitching present to indicate that more than one animal may have been used (Chapter 11). Samples from the pelt revealed that it belonged to the bear family (Appendix C). Specialist analysis has revealed that the pelt was folded with the skin side innermost

Figure 3.22: Textile and animal-skin object on initial excavation. (Photograph: Helen Williams, Wiltshire Conservation Centre.)

Figure 3.20: Animal pelt after conservation treatment. (Photograph: Helen Williams, Wiltshire Conservation Centre.)

Figure 3.21: Copper-alloy pin. (Photograph: Helen Williams, Wiltshire Conservation Centre.)

(Chapter 11). This has completely deteriorated in the burial environment leaving the pelt extremely fragile and fragmentary. Peat from the burial environment and debris from the cremation were visible adhering to the hair, causing it to clump together in places.

The pelt was frozen in a tub of water before being freeze dried. No surface treatments or consolidants were used. Following treatment the hair appears a light brown/orange colour with the shorter underhairs having a 'fluffy' appearance. Further peat and debris were removed mechanically (Fig. 3.20).

Copper-alloy pin

A small copper-alloy pin was discovered amongst the hairs at one edge of the pelt during cleaning post treatment (Fig. 3.21). This was broken into four sections and has a brittle outer casing. The surface has been cleaned mechanically under magnification and sections reattached where possible.

Textile and animal-skin object

This consists of a woven textile panel with a thin animal-skin seam (Chapter 18). The seam has small perforations visible along its length (Fig. 3.22). There is also a border of small animal-skin triangles running horizontally along each long edge of the panel. The underside of the object may have consisted of a thin panel of animal skin. However, this had completely deteriorated in the burial environment.

The surface of the object was partially obscured by

Figure 3.23: Textile and animal-skin object after conservation treatment. (Photograph: Helen Williams, Wiltshire Conservation Centre.)

peat deposits and debris from the burial environment. The leather appeared to be in a reasonably good condition. The woven panel is very fine and therefore fragile.

The peat deposits were removed as far as possible to aid specialist examination under magnification. The object was treated with a 15% glycerol solution before freeze drying.

Following treatment the woven panel was fragile and required further cleaning and consolidation with 5% Paraloid B72 in industrial methylated spirits (Fig. 3.23).

Figure 3.24: Wooden stake (Small Find 1) after conservation treatment. (Photograph: Helen Williams, Wiltshire Conservation Centre.)

Figure 3.25: Wooden stake (Small Find 2) after conservation treatment. (Photograph: Helen Williams, Wiltshire Conservation Centre.)

Wooden stakes

A wooden stake (Small Find 1), received as two fragments and subsequently identified as hazel (*corylus* sp) (Chapter 4), was found lying horizontally outside the cist (Fig. 3.24). It was in two pieces but with a good join. The larger fragment is in a fair condition, with degradation more emphasized towards the break edge. The smaller fragment is in poor condition. The break is probably a recent one although the fracture probably occurred at an existing weak point. The rod is very straight with only two very small knots. It retains its bark over most of its length and the bark that is missing could be a recent loss which had come adrift during excavation or storage. The unworked end is broken and poorly preserved.

The second stake (Small Find 2) was found vertically outside the cist (Fig. 3.25). The rod is quite straight with no significant side branches but is slightly curved near its complete end. It retains its bark over most of its length and the bark that is missing could be a recent loss during excavation or storage. It was in two pieces that do not join very well.

The peat deposits were removed before treatment with a two-stage PEG process (10% PEG 400 and 15% PEG 4000), followed by freeze drying.

Following treatment the small fragment from small find 1 is extremely fragmentary. The core of the other fragments are intact, the ends are slightly friable. The outer bark has split and warped in several places, smaller fragments have become detached.

Acknowledgements

I would like to thank my fellow specialists: at Historic England, Gill Campbell, Matt Canti, David Dungworth and Joanna Dunster, Karla Graham, Zoë Hazell, Angela Middleton, Simon Mays, Peter Marshall; also Esther Cameron, Caroline Cartwright, Mary Davies, Susanna Harris, Jan Bruun Jensen, Julie Jones, Quita Mould, Alison Sheridan and Henrietta Quinnell. Thanks also to Andy Jones, Jane Marchand and Vanessa Straker for coordinating the project.

Guidelines followed during the conservation work

ADS 2000. *Digital Archives from Excavation and Field Work: guide to good practices*. (http//ads.ahds.ac.uk/project/goodguides/excavation).

Barnard, J. Goodman, L. & Shippen, N. 2010. Excavation and stabilisation of a 17th century wicker basket: new application of a known method. In K. Straetkvern & E. Williams (eds.), *Proceedings of the 11th ICOM-CC Group Wet Organic Archaeological Materials Conference: Greenville 2010*. Np: ICOM-CC working group for Wet Organic Archaeological Materials, 647–656.

Carrlee, E. & Senge, D.K. 2010. Polyethylene glycol treatments for basketry on the Northwest coast of North America. In K. Straetkvern & E. Williams (eds.), *Proceedings of the 11th ICOM-CC Group Wet Organic Archaeological Materials Conference: Greenville 2010*. Np: ICOM-CC working group for Wet Organic Archaeological Materials, 553–570.

English Heritage. 2006. *Management of Research Projects in the Historic Environment*. London: English Heritage.

English Heritage. 2012. *Waterlogged Artefacts: guidelines on their recovery, analysis and conservation*. London: English Heritage.

Karsten, A., Graham, K., Goodman, L., Ganiaris, H. & Domoney, K. 2010. A comparative study of various impregnation and drying methods for waterlogged archaeological leather. In K. Straetkvern & E. Williams (eds.), *Proceedings of the 11th ICOM-CC Group Wet Organic Archaeological Materials Conference: Greenville 2010*. Np: ICOM-CC working group for Wet Organic Archaeological Materials, 595–610.

Kaye, B., Cole-Hamilton, D. J. & Morphet, K. 2000. Supercritical drying: A new method for conserving waterlogged archaeological materials. *IIC Studies in Conservation* 45, 233–252.

Omar, S., McCord, M. & Daniels, V. 1989. The conservation of bog bodies by freeze drying. *IIC Studies in Conservation* 34, 101–109.

Plymouth City Museum & Art Gallery. 2012. *Archaeological Archives Deposition, Version 1*. Plymouth: Plymouth City Museum & Art Gallery.

Raftery, J. 1970. Prehistoric coiled basketry bags. *Journal of the Royal Society of Antiquaries of Ireland* 100, 167–168.

Thickett, D., Cruickshank, P. & Ward, C. 1995. The conservation of amber. *IIC Studies in Conservation* 40, 217–226.

Ward, C. Giles, D., Sully, D. & Lee, D. J. 1996. The conservation of a group of waterlogged Neolithic bark bowls. *IIC Studies in Conservation* 41, 241–249.

Watkinson, D. & Neal, V. 2001. *First Aid for Finds* (4th edition). London: Rescue/UKIC Archaeology Section.

4. The wooden stakes from the Whitehorse Hill cist

Richard Brunning

The stakes

Background

Two wooden sticks or stakes were recovered during the excavation of the Whitehorse Hill cist. Both were found outside the cist and were embedded within peat. Three radiocarbon determinations were obtained on the stakes (Table 20.1). Chronological modelling (Chapter 20) provides estimates for the dates of the stakes of *1890–1735 cal BC* (*90% probability*; *SUERC-40124*; Fig. 20.3) or *1715–1695 cal BC* (*5% probability*) and *1870–1845 cal BC* (*4% probability*; *WH11 – SF2*; Fig. 20.3) or *1815–1685 cal BC* (*91% probability*), probably *1765–1735 cal BC* (*33% probability*) or *1720–1690* cal BC (*35% probability*).

Species

The sticks were identified under a microscope, using Schweingruber (1990) as a reference. Both proved to be hazel (*Corylus* sp). The choice of hazel may be because it is a common species and produces long straight stems. The species selection may have been more significant,

however, as small hazel roundwood has been found in several of the well preserved Bronze Age barrows from Denmark. Six split hazel sticks (*c.* 6–10cm long) with cut ends were found among the well-preserved contents of the Bronze Age Guldhøj barrow and a hazel stick bound with leather strips was found inside the bag of the rich burial at Gardehøj, near Copenhagen (Glob 1973, 93–94, 114). From the same country the Borum Eshøj barrow produced a hazel stick (*circa* 78cm long) beside the log coffin. This stick had notches along one side at regular intervals and was thought to have been a measuring rod used in the construction of the coffin and possibly in the laying out and erection of the mound (Glob 1973, 38–39). Hazel features in both Celtic and Norse mythology but it would be unwise to transfer these associations to a different time and place.

Small Find 1

This stick was found lying horizontally outside the cist, along its eastern side, within the peat mound (Chapter 2). It is in two pieces but there was a very good join between

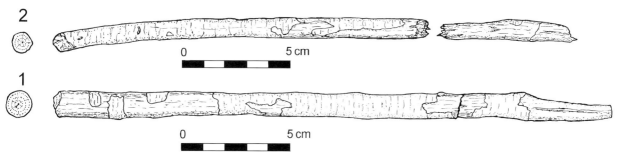

Figure 4.1: The hazel sticks from the cist: Small Find 2 (top); Small Find 1 (bottom). (Drawing: Richard Brunning.)

the two parts. The break is probably a recent one although the fracture probably occurred at an existing weak point. The stick is 520mm long and 26mm in diameter. The rod is very straight with only two very small knots (Fig. 4.1). It retains its bark over most of its length and the bark that is missing could be a recent loss as it is insecurely attached. The unworked end is broken and poorly preserved. The other end has been cut to a point on three faces over 80mm, with the very tip of the point broken off. It had been cut at shallow angles of 2–3°, leaving three facets, flat in cross section with slightly raised ridges between them. This tool-mark evidence is too slight to confidently assign an axe type to its formation.

The cuts at the end were not intended to merely sever the stem but rather to create a point, presumably to aid insertion into the ground. Therefore, although it was found horizontally, there appears to have been an intention to use it vertically at some point. There is no obvious differential decay along the piece that would suggest that it had been partly below ground and partly above for a prolonged length of time. It is possible that it had been inserted to its full surviving length, which would explain the poorer preservation at the uncut end. In such a situation breakage is most likely to occur at the ground surface as this is the point where decay is fastest.

Small Find 2

This piece was found outside the cist, standing vertically alongside one of the side stones of the cist (Chapter 2). It is 464mm long and 18mm in diameter (Fig. 4.1). The rod is quite straight with no significant side branches but is slightly curved near its complete end. It retains its bark over most of its length and the bark that is missing could be a recent loss during excavation or storage. The rod is in two pieces that do not join very well. The shorter piece is from the lower end and was lifted in a block of peat because it was hoped that it would contain a well-preserved worked end. In fact there were no tool-marks on the lower section and it was in a very advanced state of decay, significantly worse than the remainder of the stem. The bottom end was torn on one side over 30mm. The longer section was quite decayed at its lower end, which explains why it was not possible to lift it in one piece. The upper end looked as though it had been deliberately cut across and therefore represents the original end of the object, with some wear slightly obscuring the tool-marks.

The observed decay on this piece is the opposite of what might be expected. Normally the lower ends of stakes are in much better preservation than the tops, unless there is something unusual in the burial environment that causes more rapid decay at depth. There is no evidence of such a cause in the site description. Another possibility is that the piece represents the top of a longer rod that had been set vertically and then decayed significantly at ground level where it broke off, possibly during an attempt to extract it. The broken top part was then inserted vertically again. This

would explain the poor preservation at the bottom section and the tear at the bottom end. As the two stems (Small Finds 1 and 2) are both young hazel it is not impossible that they were once part of the same stem, although the significant difference in diameter suggest that this is not the case unless a joining section is missing.

Comparisons for the worked wood from the cist

The discovery of prehistoric worked wood in an upland peat context is extremely rare in the United Kingdom. A recent review of 739 sites which have produced worked prehistoric wood in England and Wales recorded fewer than half a dozen find spots in upland peat (Brunning 2007, 18–23). The uncertainty of the exact location and local environment for some finds makes a more precise figure hard to assign.

A large proportion of the worked wooden remains discovered in the eighteenth and nineteenth centuries were from Neolithic and Bronze Age barrows on uplands (Brunning 2007, 21–22). The review listed 28 examples of wooden mortuary structures, 17 examples of single planks immediately above or below an inhumation or cremation, 44 examples of tree-trunk coffins and six cases of wooden boxes containing cremations (Brunning 2007, 298).

The records of finds of stakes or poles are quite rare. At Caerloggas Down, Treverbyn, Cornwall, two branches were found on an old land surface under a barrow (Miles 1975, 48–49). A wooden pole was one of the objects found in an Early Bronze Age mortuary enclosure at Wrangworthy Cross 1, East Putford, Devon (Radford and Rogers 1947, 156–163). At Amesbury 164 (G15) barrow, near Normanton Gorse in Wiltshire, Richard Colt Hoare (1812, 205–206) recorded a primary inhumation with two bronze daggers in a wooden box, and a beaker and antlers on an elm plank from which extended three poles to the top of the barrow.

Despite a large number of investigations and increasingly well excavated sites, the twentieth and early twenty-first centuries have produced proportionally far fewer examples of wooden artefacts surviving in barrows (for example, Forde 1939; Elgee and Elgee 1949) than previous centuries. This is due to a combination of factors, including the damage done by antiquarian investigations, the shift away from barrows in archaeological fieldwork and an increasing trend to undisturbed preservation. It may also be a symptom of the general decline in wetland preservation conditions in the United Kingdom that has been highlighted by numerous studies (for example, Darvill and Fulton 1998; Van de Noort *et al.* 2001).

References

Brunning, R. 2007. Structural wood in prehistoric England and Wales. Unpublished PhD thesis: University of Exeter.

Darvill, T. & Fulton, A. K. 1998. *MARS. The Monuments at Risk Survey of England, 1995: main report*. London: Bournemouth University and English Heritage.

Elgee, H. W. & Elgee, F. 1949. An Early Bronze Age burial in a boat-shaped wooden coffin from north-east Yorkshire. *Proceedings of the Prehistoric Society* 15, 87–106.

Forde, D. 1939. Dysgwylfa Fawr Barrow, Cardiganshire: a Food-Vessel and dug-out trunk cremation burial. *Antiquaries Journal* 19, 90–92.

Glob, P. V, 1973. *The Mound People*, London: Paladin.

Hoare, R. C. 1812. *The Ancient History of south Wiltshire*. London: William Miller.

Miles, H. 1975. Barrows on the St Austell granite. *Cornish Archaeology* 14, 5–82.

Radford, C. A. R. & Rogers, E. H. 1947. The excavations of two barrows at East Pudford. *Proceedings of the Devon Archaeological Society* 3, 156–163.

Schweingruber, F. 1990. *Microscopic Wood Anatomy: structural variability of stems and twigs in recent and subfossil woods from central Europe*. Birmensdorf: Swiss Federal Institute of Forestry Research.

Van de Noort, R., Fletcher, W., Thomas, G., Carstairs, I. & Patrick, D. 2001. *Monuments at Risk in England's Wetlands*. Draft V.2. Exeter: University of Exeter.

5. The samples of peat and possible soil from the cist at Whitehorse Hill

Matt Canti

There were three component aims to the micromorphological analysis at Whitehorse Hill:

1. To determine the formation process of the ~ 1cm grey layer immediately above the capstone.
2. To determine whether or not the peat above the cist accumulated *in situ* or was the result of backfilling.
3. To determine the formation process of the dark, possible soil layer beneath the plant material (probably part of the matted feature) on the basal stone of the cist.

Sampling

The sampling had two components, those taken during the excavations and a sample taken during the micro excavation in the laboratory.

In the field

Three Kubiena tins (samples 5–7) were taken, among other palaeoenvironmental samples, from above the capstone and in the adjacent peat (Fig. 5.1). The peat overlying the capstone occupies the upper part of sample 6, and the control peat for comparison is represented by sample 7. The grey layer immediately above the capstone (Fig. 5.2) was best preserved in the base of the vertical Kubiena (sample 6), and is just visible in Figure 5.1.

Figure 5.1: Kubiena tins taken in the field. Samples 5 and 6 are horizontally and vertically oriented tins from immediately above the capstone; Sample 7 (left) is a vertical tin from the peat outside the cist, taken as a control.

Figure 5.2: The point of the trowel picks out the very fine layer approximately 1cm thick resting on the top of the capstone.

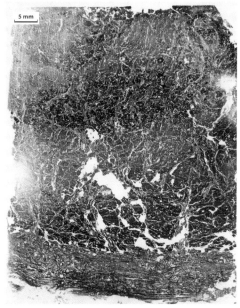

Figure 5.3: The dark possible soil layer beneath the plant material on the base stone.

Figure 5.4: The whole slide produced from sample 6. Note the junction between the unstratified upper peat and lower, highly stratified peat (the fine grey layer) at the base.

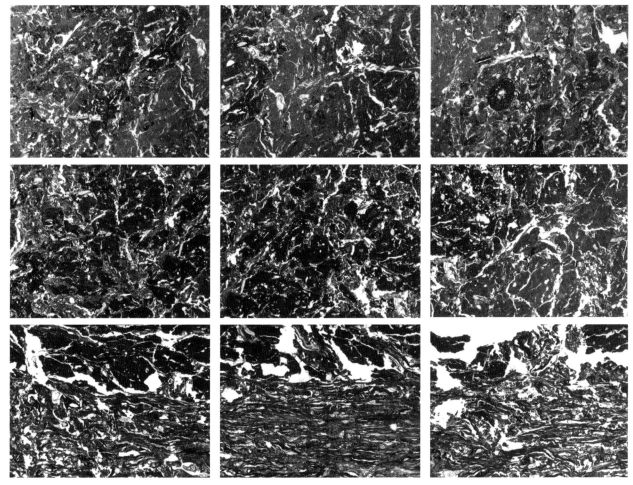

Figure 5.5: Sample 6, the fine grey layer and peat above the cist capstone. Nine ~1cm wide sample microscope views, laid out approximately as they occur on the slide.

Figure 5.6: Sample 6, detail of the unstratified peat above fine grey layer.

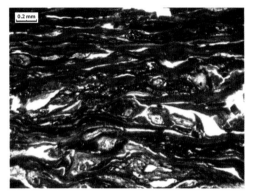

Figure 5.7: Sample 6, detail of the strongly stratified grey layer immediately above the cist capstone.

In the laboratory

A small (approximately 20mm × 20mm) piece of the dark, possible soil layer beneath the plant material was sampled at Chippenham in September 2011 (Fig. 5.3).

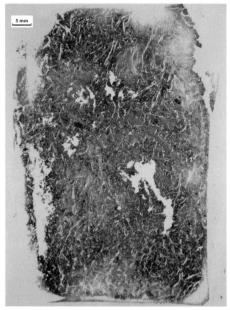

Figure 5.8: The whole slide produced from Sample 7, the peat outside the cist.

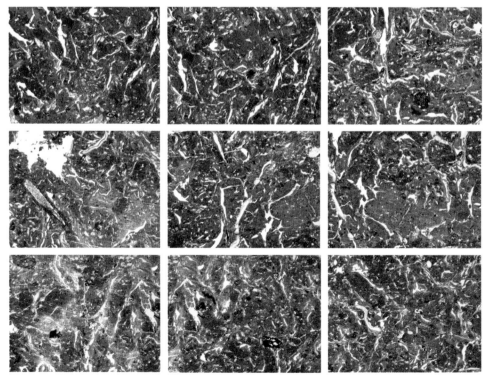

Figure 5.9: Sample 7, the control peat sample from outside the cist. Nine ~1cm wide sample microscope views, laid out in approximately their natural positions on the slide.

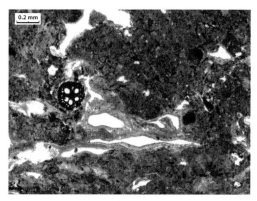

Figure 5.10: Sample 7, detail of the peat from outside the cist.

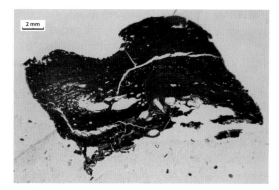

Figure 5.11: The whole sample of the possible soil layer beneath the plant material on the base stone.

Methods

The samples were acetone-replaced in order to try and retain the morphological properties of the organic matter while making them suitable for thin section manufacture. Acetone replacement entails soaking the wet material in acetone, repeatedly pouring off the water/acetone mixture thus produced, and replacing it with pure acetone, so the whole sample gradually becomes wetted only by acetone. The samples were then impregnated with Crystic resin under vacuum and thin sectioned to 30μm for analysis (Murphy 1986). They were examined in plane and cross-polarised transmitted light.

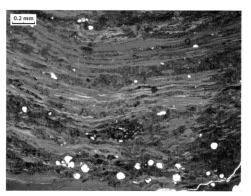

Figure 5.12: Detail of the dark possible soil layer beneath the plant material on the base stone.

Results

Samples 6 and 7

Figure 5.4 shows the whole of sample 6 and highlights the coarse difference between the disorganized upper part of the slide, and the finely stratified grey layer at the base. A more detailed view is presented in Figure 5.5, with nine photographic segments of the slide. The contrast between the two parts of the slide is very clear in the lower three segments.

The upper four-fifths of sample 6 consists of unstratified peat (Fig. 5.6) containing a few roots and occasional dark charcoal fragments, possibly of *Erica* (Gill Campbell, pers comm). This contrasts strongly with the lower one-fifth of the slide, which is the fine grey layer. Although it also consists of rooted peat, it is very strongly stratified and lacks any charcoal fragments (Fig. 5.7). The junction between the two is sharp.

Figure 5.8 shows the whole slide of sample 7, which is the peat from outside the cist. This is very similar to the main body of peat above the capstone, that is to say, the upper part of sample 6 (Figs. 5.4–5.6). Progressively increasing magnifications of sample 7 are shown in Figures 5.9 and 5.10. The whole sample consists of mixed, unstratified, rooted peat with vertical and diagonal voids, as well as discrete areas of different woodiness arranged chaotically.

It also contains the remains of charcoal fragments, again possibly of *Erica* (Gill Campbell, pers. comm.).

The similarity between the peat over the capstone and the control peat outside suggests a similar process formed them. In both cases, the lack of stratification, the disoriented voids and the jumbled, sometimes diagonal or vertical differences in peat quality all combine to give a strong impression that the peat has been built up by dumping rather than by growth.

In stark contrast to this, the fine grey layer directly over the capstone consists of strongly stratified peat which must either have grown *in situ,* or was deposited very slowly so that the fibres could arrange themselves parallel to the capstone surface.

The possibility that the disorganised peat was the result of trampling has been considered, but the sharp junction in sample 6 precludes this. If trampling had been the process that disorganized the upper parts of sample 6, then it would be expected to grade down into the fine grey layer rather than have a sharp boundary.

Dark possible soil layer

The whole of the sample is shown in Figure 5.11 and the detailed view in Figure 5.12. The sample is entirely composed of compressed organic matter, either a remnant of some laid material or of peat that used to be growing on the stone. There is almost no mineral material despite the visible grains on Figure 5.3, which must have been a small patch rather than something which extended consistently into the sample.

Reference

Murphy, C. P. 1986. *Thin Section Preparation of Soils and Sediments*. Berkhamsted: AB Academic.

Section 3:
Assembling
the burial

6. The human remains

Simon Mays

The material

The quantities of human bone recovered from the four quadrants are shown in Table 6.1. In addition, there were some tiny fragments of bone adhering to remains of charcoal (Chapter 7) or other burnt organic material which could therefore not be weighed.

The majority of the bone is highly fragmented, as is customary in early cremations, with a great many fragments less than 1cm long (Fig. 6.1). Fragments are

Table 6.1: Human remains from the Whitehorse Hill cist by quadrant

	Weight (g)	*%*
Quadrant 1	267.2	38
Quadrant 2	152.3	22
Quadrant 3	236.7	33
Quadrant 4	51.6	7
Total	707.8	100

Figure 6.1. The cremation from the Whitehorse Hill cist within the pelt. (Photograph: Helen Williams, Wiltshire Conservation Centre.)

predominantly white or light grey in colour with a few reddish–brown and black fragments.

Identifiable elements were present from most areas of the body (below) but cranial vault and long-bone shaft fragments were few. There is no indication of the presence of more than one individual. There is no evidence for any non-human remains. All epiphyses that could be seen were fused, save the medial clavicle. There was no evidence for any open tooth roots. These observations suggest an age at death of about 15–25 years, based on modern schedules of skeletal development (Webb and Suchey 1985; Cardoso and Rios 2011); these may, however, be a somewhat under-estimate of age in archaeological groups. The mandible has a well-developed mental eminence. The overall impression from the remains is of a small, gracile skeleton, but the extent to which this reflects bone shrinkage during cremation is unclear. It is not possible to determine the sex of the cremated individual.

Discussion

Mean skeletal ash weight measured from people who died in the first half of the twentieth century has been reported as 1550g for females and 2288g for males, giving a mid-sex mean of 1919g (Trotter and Hixon 1974). This would appear to suggest that the Whitehorse Hill remains comprise between about one-third and half of the full amount expected from an adult cremation. Fragments of cranial vault and large long-bones were fewer than customarily seen in ancient cremations. These are strong elements that survive well in the burial environment, so perhaps the 'missing' bone primarily reflects partial deposition of remains in antiquity rather than their destruction by natural processes in the soil.

Bone colour can be used as an approximate guide to firing temperature. The predominant white or light grey colour of the fragments appears to indicate a temperature somewhere in excess of about 650°C (Mays 2010, 322). The temperatures reached in the cremation process may actually have been much higher than this. Simple camp fires can attain 900–1000°C (Stiner *et al.* 1995) and when body fats ignite during the cremation process they burn very fiercely, so that temperatures in excess of 1000°C may be reached (Murad 1998; Schultz *et al.* 2008). The brown and black colours are indicative of lower temperatures – perhaps 200–400°C – for a few fragments (Mays 2010, 322).

In summary, the cremated remains recovered from the Whitehorse Hill cist comprise the partial remains, thoroughly cremated, of an individual of uncertain sex aged about 15–25 years old at death.

Bone fragments identified to skeletal element

Identified elements include fragments of: lumbar, thoracic and cervical vertebrae, metatarsals, right clavicle, left scapula (coracoid), left capitate, ribs, sternum, left proximal thumb phalanx, right ulna, cranial vault, mandible (including second and third molar sockets, and mental eminence), first maxillary premolar roots, mandibular molar, maxillary incisor, right maxilla, right sphenoid, medial end of left clavicle (epiphysis unfused), seven roots from single-rooted teeth, mandibular molar dentine crown (unworn), terminal hand phalanges, molar and premolar roots, left maxilla with sockets for incisors, canine, premolars and first molar, right occipital condyle, sphenoid, zygomatic, sacrum, patella, left pisiform, two proximal hand phalanges, proximal foot phalanx.

References

Cardoso, H. F. V. & Rios, L. 2011. Age estimation from stages of epiphyseal union in the presacral vertebrae. *American Journal of Physical Anthropology* 144, 238–247.

Mays, S. 2010. *The Archaeology of Human Bones* (2nd edition). London: Routledge.

Murad, T. A. 1998. The growing popularity of cremation versus inhumation: some forensic implications. In K. J. Reichs (ed.), *Advances in the Identification of Human Remains* (2nd edition). Springfield: Charles C Thomas, 86–105.

Schultz, J. J., Warren, M. W. & Krigbaum, J.S. 2008. Analysis of human cremains: gross and chemical methods. In C. W. Schmidt and S. A. Symes (eds.), *The Analysis of Burned Human Remains.* London: Academic Press, London, 75–94.

Stiner, M.C., Kuhn, S.L., Weiner, S. and Bar-Yosuf, O. 1995. Differential burning, recrystallisation and fragmentation of archaeological bone. *Journal of Archaeological Science* 22, 223–237.

Trotter, M. & Hixon, B. B. 1974. Sequential changes in weight, density, and percentage ash weight of human skeletons from an early fetal period through to old age. *Anatomical Record* 179, 1–18.

Webb, P. A. O. & Suchey, J.M. 1985. Epiphyseal union of the anterior iliac crest and medial clavicle in a modern, multiracial sample of males and females. *American Journal of Physical Anthropology* 68, 457–466.

7. The wood charcoal

Zoë Hazell

The excavation of the cist buried within peat on Whitehorse Hill uncovered a cremation deposit wrapped in a pelt (Chapter 2). Among the cremated bone of a young person (Chapter 6) were fragments of charcoal.

Sample information

The charcoal (and bone) samples of the cremation deposit were 3–4cm from the surface. The cremation had been sub-sampled by dividing it into four quadrants (Table 7.1) and had been air dried prior to analysis (Chapter 3).

Methods

This analysis follows on from the assessment of the wood charcoal remains (Hazell 2012), for which the charcoal fragments had been separated (through sieving and hand-picking) into three groups: fragments >4mm, fragments 2–4mm and fragments with any one plane <2mm.

For the analysis, all the charcoal fragments recovered from the three groups were examined; 78 in total (of which 48 were >2mm). Where large enough, each fragment was split along the three main planes for identification (transverse (TS), tangential longitudinal (TLS) and radial (RS) sections). The planes were then examined under an Olympus BH high power light reflective microscope (×50 to ×500 magnification), and compared with wood identification texts by Schweingruber (1982) and Gale and Cutler (2000).

Where identification to genus level could not be resolved with certainty – that is, either where fragments were too small to break to see all three planes and/or not enough diagnostic features were visible – the term 'cf' was used. In the case of the fragments with a plane <2mm that appeared to be *Quercus* sp. (oak), but anatomically could

Table 7.1: Samples of burnt material (including wood charcoal and cremated bone) from the cremation feature

Sample ID	Quadrant number	Alignment within feature excavation
Q1	1	Top left
Q2	2	Top right
Q3	3	Bottom left
Q4	4	Bottom right

Table 7.2: Wood charcoal fragment counts from the cremation deposits at Whitehorse Hill, categorized by taxa, quadrant and sieved fraction

Sample ID/ quadrant	Size (mm)	*Quercus* sp.	cf *Quercus* sp.	*Corylus* sp.	Indet.	Total
Q1	>4	7	3	–	1	11
	2–4	5	1	–	1	7
	Plane <2	–	16	–	7	23
Q2	>4	15	1	1	2	19
	2–4	–	–	–	–	0
	Plane <2	–	2	–	3	5
Q3	>4	2	–	–	2	4
	2–4	–	–	1	–	1
	Plane <2	–	1	–	1	2
Q4	>4	4	1	–	–	5
	2–4	1	–	–	–	1
	Plane <2	–	–	–	–	0
Totals	>4	28	5	1	5	39
	2–4	6	1	1	1	9
	All >2	34	6	2	6	48
	Plane <2	–	19	–	11	30
	All frags	34	25	2	17	78

not be distinguished from *Castanea* sp. (sweet chestnut) (on the absence of multiseriate rays); they were assigned to cf *Quercus* sp. based on the abundance of securely-identified larger fragments of oak within the sample. Some fragments could not be identified (for example, root or knot wood, highly vitrified) and were recorded as 'Indeterminate'.

Fragment counts were used in the sample's interpretation, rather than their weights, due to the very small size of the majority of the fragments and the resulting large errors associated with weighing.

Where possible, other features and characteristics of the wood charcoal (Marguerie and Hunot 2007) were noted during the analysis:

- Size of the fragments (radial measurement).
- Information on the growth rings: number (count), curvature (none, weak, moderate, strong, indeterminate).
- Presence/absence of: pith, bark, tyloses, fungal hyphae/mycelium, degradation (insect/rootlet holes), radial fractures and vitrification (I (low), II (strong) and III (total fusion).

Results

Identifications

Only two taxa were identified, *Quercus* sp. (oak) and *Corylus*

sp. (hazel), both of which are hardwoods (angiosperms). Some fragments were unidentifiable (indeterminate).

Quercus sp. was identified based on the combination of: a) ring porous vessel patterning, b) distinctive flame-like patterning of vessels in the latewood, c) both uniseriate and multiseriate rays, and d) the presence of tyloses (indicating heartwood). Due to the presence of the flame-like latewood vessel patterning, it was possible to say that the *Quercus* sp. (Fagaceae family) was a deciduous taxon; within the British Isles this includes only *Q. robur* (pedunculate oak) and *Q. petraea* (sessile oak) (Gale and Cutler 2000, 204).

Corylus sp. was identifiable on the basis of: a) aggregate rays, b) scalariform perforation plates with widely-spaced bars (5–10), c) rays 1 cell wide (2–3 near aggregate rays), and d) large vessel wall pits. *C. avellana* (hazel) is the only native *Corylus* sp. (Betulaceae family) in the British Isles.

Abundances

In total, 78 wood charcoal fragments were recovered from the cremation remains and subsequently examined. Summary results are shown in Table 7.2 and Figure 7.1.

Overall, the total number of wood charcoal fragments recovered was small (78) and the assemblage was dominated by 59 fragments of *Quercus* and cf *Quercus*. Only two fragments of *Corylus* were recovered and the remaining 17 fragments were indeterminate.

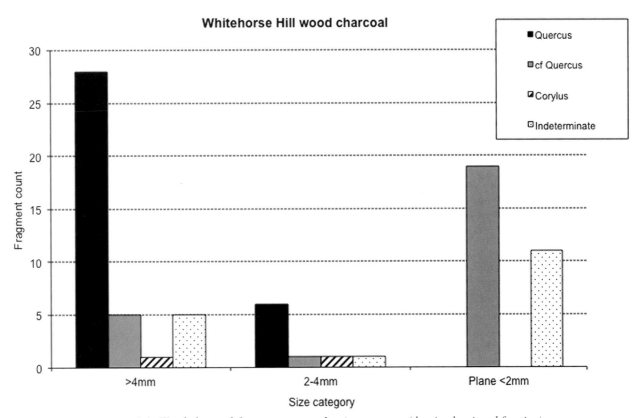

Figure 7.1: Wood charcoal fragment counts, by size category (that is, the sieved fraction).

Size categories

Based on fragment counts, *Quercus* was overwhelmingly dominant within both the >4mm and 2–4mm categories. It was absent from the category of fragments with a plane <2mm, because no firm identifications could be made on these small pieces, which instead were referred to as cf *Quercus*. Similarly, indeterminate fragments were dominant in that same category, because i) the smaller they were the harder it was to identify them, and ii) due to a high level of vitrification (that could have resulted in a more brittle charcoal that fragmented more).

As shown in Table 7.3, the >2mm (combined) size fraction of the sample was dominated by *Quercus* sp. (71%) and cf *Quercus* sp. (13%), which together accounted for 84%. The next abundant group was the indeterminate category at 13%, with *Corylus* sp. the least abundant taxon at 4%.

When the percentage abundances were calculated separately for each of the size categories (Table 7.4), the

results of the >4mm fraction were similar to those values as shown in Table 7.3: *Quercus* sp. 72%, cf *Quercus* sp. 13%, Indeterminate 13% and *Corylus* sp. 3%. This showed that including the 2–4mm fraction counts did not alter the overall percentages much (probably due to the fact that only nine 2–4mm fragments were recovered), and therefore suggested that identifying and counting only the >4mm fragments would have sufficed (in this sample).

Other characteristics

The additional features recorded are summarized in Table 7.5.

Fragment sizes

As well as the small number of total fragments, the sizes of the individual fragments themselves were small, with the radial length of the largest fragment measured at 28.6mm. Thirty fragments (38% of the total) had a plane <2mm.

Growth rings

The maximum number of growth rings on a fragment was approximately 35, on *Quercus* sp. However, this fragment, and some others of *Quercus* sp., had growth rings so close to each other that it was not always possible to differentiate – and therefore count – them, reliably.

Where possible, an average growth ring width per fragment was calculated. cf *Quercus* sp remains had a minimum value of 0.45mm and a maximum value of 2.95mm, which was a larger range than for *Corylus* sp., for which the minimum and maximum values were 0.48mm and 0.83mm respectively (although the total number of *Corylus* sp. fragments was very small; only two).

No strong growth ring curvatures were recorded; and the majority were indeterminate, none or weak, suggesting that larger sections of trees (branches, trunk) were being used.

Other observations

Generally, vitrification commonly occurred in the sample. Level II (strong) vitrification was the most widespread,

Table 7.3: Percentage abundances (using fragment counts) of each taxa calculated from the total number of fragments >2mm

Size (mm)	Quercus	cf Quercus	Corylus	Indeterminate
>4	58.33	10.42	2.08	10.42
2–4	12.50	2.08	2.08	2.08
Total	70.83	12.50	4.16	12.50

(Fragments <2mm were omitted due to the insecure identifications of such small wood charcoal fragments)

Table 7.4: Percentage abundances (using fragment counts) of each taxa calculated separately for each size category

Size (mm)	Quercus	cf Quercus	Corylus	Indet.	Total
>4	71.79	12.82	2.56	12.82	100
2–4	66.67	11.11	11.11	11.11	100
Plane <2	0.00	63.33	0.00	36.67	100

Table 7.5: Summary table showing the main characteristics, by taxa, of charcoal fragments >2mm

Taxa (>2mm fragments)	Radial measurement of fragment (mm) (2dp)		Growth ring curvature	No. growth rings counted		Tyloses	Fungal hyphae	Radial cracks	Vitrification
	Min.	Max.		Min.	Max.				
Corylus sp	1.93	3.30	**I**, M	4	4	**N**	**N**	**N**	**I, II**
Quercus sp	2.09	28.56	**I**, N, W, M	2	*c.* 35	**Y**, Y&N, N	**Y**, N	**Y**, N	I, **II**, III
cf *Quercus* sp	3.80	10.55	**I**	2	*c.* 5	**Y**, Y&N, N	**N**	**Y**, N	**II**, III

Bold indicates the most frequently-occurring categories. For ring curvature: I = indeterminate, N = none, W = weak and M = moderate. For tyloses, fungal hyphae and radial cracks, presence or absence is indicated by: Y = yes and N = no. For vitrification: I = low, II = strong and III = total fusion.

although fragments often contained patches of level III (total fusion). Two fragments >2mm were too highly vitrified for the wood taxa to be identified.

Heartwood and sapwood of *Quercus* sp. was identifiable based on the presence and absence of tyloses within the vessels; of the cf *Quercus* sp. fragments >2mm, all but two had tyloses present in the vessels, indicating that heartwood (that is to say, mature oak wood) dominated the sample. Eight fragments appeared to include the heartwood-sapwood transition.

No fragments with bark or pith attached were observed, and no complete roundwood cross-sections were present. Only one fragment (*Corylus* sp.) appeared to be the outer edge of a round wood, which together with moderate ring curvature could suggest that it was part of a branch.

None of the *Corylus* sp. fragments had radial cracks, but nearly all the cf *Quercus* sp. fragments did. Some research suggests that the density of radial cracks in charcoal could indicate the burning of (unseasoned) greenwood (Théry-Parisot and Henry 2012). It is interesting to note here that radial cracks were present on fragments that seemed to represent degraded wood prior to burning (although no counts were made nor density values calculated).

Thirteen fragments (one of *Corylus* sp. and 12 of cf *Quercus*) were noted as possibly degraded, inferred from the poorly preserved and distorted wood structure. Furthermore, two of those fragments (one each of *Quercus* sp. and *Corylus* sp.) had holes in the wood that could have derived from rootlets and/or insects, and two additional fragments (of *Quercus* sp. and indeterminate) were noted as having fungal hyphae within the vessels. Possible implications for this in terms of wood degradation are discussed below.

Possible evidence of worked wood

On initial inspection one fragment (of *Quercus* sp.) appeared to be a fragment of roundwood, that is to say, with a curved outer edge aligned parallel to the growth rings. But under a microscope it became clear that this was not the case; rather, the regular curved edge was oblique to the growth rings (Fig. 7.2). It is more likely that this characteristic is artificial rather than naturally-occurring, thereby indicating the presence of worked wood.

Discussion

Characteristics of the cremation wood

Fuel types and characteristics

There is very a low diversity of taxa (n=2), typical of deposits resulting from a one-off usage (Asouti and Austin 2005). The two taxa were *Quercus* sp. and *Corylus* sp., suggesting that these were the preferred wood choices for fuelling this cremation. By far the majority of the wood charcoal remains were of *Quercus* sp., with only a couple of fragments of *Corylus* sp. *Quercus* sp. charcoal is commonly recovered from British archaeological sites, so it is not surprising to find it here. Although it is one of the more difficult woods to ignite, once lit it has favourable burning characteristics, releasing high levels of heat, something that would be desirable for burning a human body. Given the difficulty of lighting oak, the *Corylus* sp. fragments could derive from wood used as kindling, as it is easier to set alight but burns more rapidly.

Some of the charcoal showed possible evidence of the wood's degradation and decay, indicated by the observation

Figure 7.2: The Quercus sp. *fragment showing a possibly worked curved edge. Note the multiseriate ray running horizontally across the middle of the fragment (indicated by the arrow). The fragment measures 7.9mm on its longest axis. Image © Historic England.*

of a) poorly preserved and distorted wood structure, b) holes in the wood that could have resulted from rootlet penetration or insect burrowing, and c) the presence of fungal hyphae within vessels. This could suggest that some of the wood was not freshly cut when it was burnt; indeed that it could have been dead long enough prior to burning for decay processes to take place. Although it is not possible to determine whether this wood was collected as dead wood or felled and then stored prior to burning (during which time decay would have occurred), it suggests that it was not cut contemporaneously with or specifically for the cremation.

Worked wood

The presence of an oak charcoal fragment that appears to show signs of having been worked could indicate that worked wood was burnt as part of the cremation, either as part of a cremation structure (such as a worked wood stake) or as an artefact as some kind of offering with the body. If this latter interpretation is correct, with the exception of some textile fragments (Chapter 8), it would represent the only artefact known to have been burnt on the cremation pyre with the body (Chapter 21).

Burning conditions

If the amount of charcoal present is indicative of the burning processes and conditions (rather than any post-cremation processes), the small numbers of fragments recovered indicate that a significant degree of wood combustion occurred during the cremation.

Vitrified charcoal was common in the sample. Currently the conditions and processes that cause vitrification of charcoal are not well understood; although vitrified charcoal is no longer thought to result from the re-burning of wood (that is to say, using charcoal as a fuel) or to be associated with high temperature burning (McParland *et al.* 2010).

Characteristics of the local environment

Quercus sp. and *Corylus* sp. remains are commonly recorded in British archaeological and palaeoenvironmental records. Their presence in these cremation remains suggests that these two taxa were growing in the wider locality (Chapter 19) where the cremation took place – although this location is not known – and need not have been in the vicinity of the stone cist where the cremation remains were ultimately deposited. The presence of wood charcoal of these taxa supports pollen studies from Whitehorse Hill that indicated the presence of these two taxa in the region (Fyfe 2006; Williams 2007, Chapter 19).

Summary

Full analysis of the identifiable components of the wood charcoal remains recovered from the cremation burial at Whitehorse Hill demonstrated that the sample consisted predominantly of oak with very little hazel. This did not vary from the preliminary results of the initial sample assessment; both are commonly-recorded taxa in archaeological samples from the British Isles.

The oak charcoal frequently included heartwood remains, often with minimal ring curvature, suggesting that larger tree sections of oak were preferentially used as fuel. There were also indications that some of this wood was degraded prior to burning. One of the two hazel fragments recovered seemed to be from a smaller (twig) section of tree. Together with the different burning characteristics of oak and hazel, it seems probable that the hazel could have been used to start the fire, and that the oak was used to fuel it once it had taken hold.

During the full analysis, an example of possibly worked wood (also oak) was encountered, suggesting either that wooden artefacts could have been burnt within the pyre, or that the structure of the pyre itself contained worked wood.

References

Asouti, E. & Austin, P. 2005. Reconstructing woodland vegetation and its exploitation by past societies, based on the analysis and interpretation of archaeological wood charcoal macro-remains. *Environmental Archaeology* 10, 1–18.

Fyfe, R. 2006. White Horse Hill, Dartmoor; Phase 1 Pollen analysis. Plymouth: University of Plymouth. Unpublished report for Dartmoor National Park Authority.

Gale, R. & Cutler, D. 2000. *Plants in Archaeology: identification manual of vegetative plant materials used in Europe and the south Mediterranean to c. 1500*, Kew: Westbury Publishing and Royal Botanic Gardens.

Hazell, Z. 2012. Whitehorse Hill, Dartmoor; cremation samples (WHC11): Wood charcoal assessment. Unpublished assessment report: English Heritage.

McParland, L., Collinson, M., Scott, A., Campbell, G. & Veal, R. 2010. Is vitrification in charcoal a result of high temperature burning of wood? *Journal of Archaeological Science* 37, 2679–2687.

Marguerie, D. & Hunot, J.-Y. 2007. Charcoal analysis and dendrology: data from archaeological sites in north-western France. *Journal of Archaeological Science* 34, 1417–1433.

Schweingruber, F. 1982. *Microscopic Wood Anatomy: structural variability of stems and twigs in recent and subfossil woods from central Europe*. Birmensdorf: Swiss Federal Institute of Forestry Research.

Théry-Parisot, I. & Henry, A. 2012. Seasoned or green? Radial cracks analysis as a method for identifying the use of green wood as a fuel in archaeological charcoal. *Journal of Archaeological Science* 39 381–388.

Williams, S. 2007. Environmental change and landscape modification since the Early Neolithic, Whitehorse Hill, Dartmoor. Durham: Durham University. Unpublished undergraduate dissertation, Geography.

8. The charred textiles from the cremation deposit

Susanna Harris

A number of small textile fragments were recovered during micro-excavation of the cremation deposit in a spit 3–4cm from the surface (Chapter 3). These were described as burnt textile by the conservation team and here will be referred to as charred following the usual convention for textiles preserved in this manner.

Method

As the textiles were mostly smaller than 1cm, when determining the thread count per cm measurements were taken over 5mm and doubled. As there is no way to identify which is the warp and which is the weft, the measurements of thread systems are nominated system 1 and system 2. The size, degradation and heavy encrustation on the charred textiles meant that in some cases these technological details could not be identified. Nevertheless, the textiles are significant due to their role in the cremation process as will be elaborated on below. Due to the low likelihood of obtaining a reliable fibre analysis from these poorly preserved samples, no fibre identification was attempted but suggestions of the fibre type are made below.

A catalogue of the textile fragments and the textile components of the textile and animal-skin object is given at the end of this report.

Description of the textiles found in the cremation deposit

Twenty two small textile fragments were recovered from the cremation deposit during the micro-excavation. The size of the small textile fragments ranges from 21 × 16mm to 4 × 3mm. They are all grey or black and appear charred; they are also degraded and dirt encrusted. Some are adhering to fragments of bone. One textile from quadrant 1

of the cremated bone deposit has a shiny, solidified liquid on the surface which is the same grey and black colour as the textiles. This is presumably the remains of a substance which became liquid during burning and solidified shortly afterwards. One of the textiles from quadrant 1 has been pulled and stretched in one direction, possibly where it was wrapped, fastened or tied before it became charred. Five textile fragments from quadrant 2 have two or more layers. Three of the textile fragments are sufficiently well preserved to identify that they are plain weave (Emery 1966, 76). Measured over 5mm, the thread counts of the preserved fragments are: 16/18, 17/17 and 12/10 threads per cm. In a textile from quadrant 1 it is possible to identify that the threads in system 1 are 2 ply and measure 0.3–0.4mm in diameter. Technically these are referred to as balanced plain weave (tabby) because the warp and weft are equally or very similarly spaced and of similar dimensions (balanced) and woven in plain weave; that is, one over and one under, alternating in subsequent rows (Emery 1966, 76).

Small fragments survived the fire and their charred state would have aided their subsequent preservation. On the basis of their small size, charred state, the presence of solidified liquid and presence with the burnt bone fragments, the textiles presumably accompanied the body into the cremation fire. They could have been worn as clothing, added as a wrap or shroud, or used to bind the body.

Interpretation and context

As wool typically burns and does not char with a naked flame, it is most likely that the textiles were made of plant fibres. In addition, they are made of 2-ply threads, believed to be typical of plant fibre yarns in Britain in the Bronze Age (Bender Jørgensen 1992, 19). As outlined in the report on the textile and animal-skin object (Chapter 18), balanced plain weave is typical of textile technology in Bronze Age Britain (Bender Jørgensen 1992, 18–19). The thread counts of British "plain weave" textiles of this period range between 6 and 18 threads per cm, although most are around 10 threads per cm (Bender Jørgensen 1992, 18–19; Henshall 1950, 133, 158–162). With a thread count of up to 18 threads per cm and one recorded thread diameter of 0.3–0.4mm, the textiles from the cremation deposit of Whitehorse Hill cist are at the finer end of the scale when compared to other balanced plain weaves (Bender Jørgensen 1992).

Cellulose fibres are highly flammable (Harris 2010, 106; Hencken Elsasser 2010, 58) and as part of the cremation pyre they would have added to the blaze. It is likely the charred textile fragments come from some kind of binding, wrapping or clothing of the body and can be compared to other Bronze Age textile finds in Britain. At Huntshaw barrow 1, Devon, the remains of a cloth possibly used to wrap charred human bones were found in a cist (Grinsell 1970, 122). Beneath Cairn III at Carvinack barrow, Cornwall, there were impressions of cloth in the clay; this has been interpreted as a bag used to hold the cremation (Dudley 1964, 430). A similar use may account for the preserved fibres found in a cremation at Harlyn Bay, Cornwall, although this is uncertain (Ratcliffe 2011, 93). Layered textiles recovered from an Early to Middle Bronze Age cremation excavated from Over Barrow, Cambridgeshire, were found in a charred, fragmentary state and preserved in multiple, thick layers which suggests they were probably not clothing but some other form of wrapping, padding or binding (Harris 2012). There are hints that cloth was used in various ways in inhumation burials elsewhere in southern Britain. At Bincombe, Dorset, the slightly contracted position of the body and a bronze awl placed at the neck suggest that the body was wrapped in a garment or shroud (Grinsell 1982, 60). At Hemp Knoll, Wiltshire, the inhumation of a Beaker burial was found in a highly flexed position, which suggests it was tightly bound prior to burial (Robertson-Mackay 1980, 141–142, fig. 9). Although these do not provide clear comparisons for the charred textiles of the Whitehorse Hill cist, they act as a reminder of the different ways bodies can be prepared in death and it is possible the textile fragments in the Whitehorse Hill cist cremation deposit were used in one of these ways.

References

Bender Jørgensen, L. 1992. *North European Textiles until AD 1000.* Aarhus: Aarhus University Press.

Dudley, D. 1964. The excavation of the Carvinack barrow, Tregavethan, near Truro, Cornwall. *Journal of the Royal Institution of Cornwall* 4, 414–451.

Emery, I. 1966. *The Primary Structures of Fabrics: an illustrated classification.* Washington DC: Textile Museum.

Grinsell, L. V. 1970. The barrows of north Devon. *Proceedings of the Devon Archaeological Society*, 6, 340–355.

Grinsell, L. V. 1982. *Dorset Barrows Supplement.* Dorchester, Dorset Natural History & Archaeological Society.

Harris, S. 2010. Smooth and cool, or warm and soft: investigating the properties of cloth in prehistory. In E. Andersson Strand, M. Gleba, U. Mannering, C. Munkholt, M. Ringgaard (eds.), *North European Symposium for Archaeological Textiles* X, Oxford: Oxbow Books, 104–112.

Harris, S. 2012. Report on the textiles from Over Barrow, Cambridgeshire, with fibre analysis by Margarita Gleba. Unpblished report submitted to Cambridge Archaeological Unit.

Harris, S. 2015. Folded, layered textiles from a Bronze Age pit pyre excavated from Over Barrow 2, Cambridgeshire, England. In K. Grömer & F. Pritchard (eds.), *Aspects of the Design, Production and Use of Textiles and Clothing from the Bronze Age to the Early Modern Era. NESAT XII.* Budapest: Archaeolingua Main Series 33, 73–82.

Hencken Elsasser, V. 2010. *Textiles: concepts and principles* (3rd edition). New York: Fairchild Books.

Henshall, A. 1950. Textiles and weaving appliances in prehistoric Britain. *Proceedings of the Prehistoric Society* 26, 130–162.

Ratcliffe, L. 2011. The pendant, 91–93. In A.M. Jones, J. Marley, H. Quinnell, & S. Hartgroves 2011. On the beach: new discoveries at Harlyn Bay, Cornwall. *Proceedings of the Prehistoric Society* 77, 89–109.

Robertson-Mackay, M.E. 1980. A 'head and hooves' burial beneath a round barrow, with other Neolithic and Bronze Age sites, on Hemp Knoll, near Avebury, Wiltshire. *Proceedings of the Prehistoric Society* 46, 123–176.

Catalogue of textiles from the Whitehorse Hill cist

Textile adhering to bone from quadrant 1

CIST (10), LAYER (8)

Carbonised textile fragment adhering to bone measuring 12 × 5mm. The textile is difficult to see but has enough diagnostic features to identify that it is woven in plain weave with 16 threads per cm in system 1 and 18 threads per cm in system 2.

Three textiles from quadrant 1 (cremation)

SPIT 3–4CM FROM SURFACE

Three fragments of charred textile measuring 21 × 16mm, 12 × 11mm and 6 × 6mm. They are heavily encrusted. The weave structure of one fragment can be identified and is plain weave. Another of the textile fragments has a shiny, solidified liquid on the surface which is of the same grey and black colour as the textiles. One textile fragment has been pulled and stretched in one direction, possibly where it was wrapped or tied before it was charred.

Textile from quadrant 1 (cremation)

SPIT 3–4CM FROM SURFACE

This is a charred textile measuring 3 × 4mm and originating from the cremated bone sample. It is woven in plain weave. The threads of system 1 are spun in 2-ply and measure 0.3–0.4mm in diameter, the thread of system 2 is 0.3mm in diameter and cannot be further identified. No thread count was taken as the piece is too small.

Four pieces of textile from quadrant 2 >4mm

SPIT 3–4CM FROM SURFACE

The four textile fragments measuring 12 × 8mm, 6 × 3mm, 10 × 6mm and 7 × 8mm. Three of these fragments have 2 layers of textiles. One layer of the largest piece can be identified as balanced plain weave with 17 threads per cm in both system 1 and system 2; the other layer is unclear.

Four textiles from quadrant 2 >4mm

SPIT 3–4CM FROM SURFACE

The fragments measure 6 × 8mm, 3 × 7mm, 4 × 7mm and 4 × 6mm. The weave structure is unclear. The best preserved fragment is probably plain weave, with 12 threads per cm in system 1 and 10 threads per cm in system 2. As the fragment is less than 1cm square, the thread count was taken over 5mm. In one case three layers of textile can be identified.

Two textiles from quadrant 2 >4mm

SPIT 3–4CM FROM SURFACE

Two charred textiles measuring 4 × 3mm and 10 × 8mm. Both consist of several layers of textiles, although it is unclear how many exactly. The weave structure cannot be identified.

Six textile fragments adhering to bone from quadrant 3

CIST (10), LAYER (8)

These six textile fragments are all adhering to small pieces of bone, the largest bone fragment measures 13 × 8mm. The textiles are charred and appear grey and black and the features are indistinct. Although recognisable as textiles there are insufficient weave intersections to identify the weave structure. The thread count for the largest piece is taken in one direction only and is 14 threads per cm, averaged over a thread count taken over 4mm.

Grid impression on bone from quadrant 4

CIST (10), LAYER (8)

The bone fragment measures 16 × 11mm and is grey-black due to charring. There is a grid pattern impressed on the surface but it is unclear whether or not this is a textile impression. It is not classified as a textile.

Textile adhering to bone from quadrant 4 (cremation)

SPIT 3–4CM FROM SURFACE >4MM

This is a much encrusted textile fragment measuring 5 × 6mm with few visible weave intersections. It is possibly plain weave.

Textile component of the textile and animal-skin object

SPIT 4–5CM FROM SURFACE

Fragile, wet preserved textile measuring 350 × 65mm with stitched leather beading and triangle fringe; total width including leather component 105mm. There are two layers of textile, both a uniform brown colour. The upper textile layer is encrusted with a substance the same colour as the textile. The upper textile layer is woven in repp, plain weave. System 1 is composed of z2S threads, medium to loose spun, thread diameter 0.5–0.8mm, 20–24 threads per cm. System 2 is composed of z2S threads, loose spun (65°), thread diameter 1–1.2mm and 5–6 threads per cm. Only one set of threads of the lower textile layer remain. They are composed of 2S threads, diameter 0.8mm (see Chapter 18).

Braided armband or bracelet with tin studs

SPIT 2–3CM FROM SURFACE

See Chapter 14 for description.

9. The matted plant material from the base of the cist

Julie Jones

A matted layer of plant material approximately 325 × 250mm in extent, with the fibres running roughly in the same direction, appeared to have been deliberately placed on the granite base slab prior to deposition of the cremation and of the various artefacts found in the cist. A second layer of apparently similar plant material had been laid over these items after they were deposited. Samples from both these layers were collected as part of the micro-excavation of the cist contents (Chapter 3).

The plant fibres appeared to be in varying degrees of preservation and the samples were taken with the aim of determining whether these had been deliberately placed, whether there were any signs of folding, plaiting or weaving, or if stems had simply been laid around the other cist contents perhaps as cushioning or protection. The aim was also to obtain a species identification and to ascertain the origin of this material, and to determine whether the taxa present were the same as those in the basketry container (Chapter 13).

The matted plant material

The following spits were examined (depth of spits measured from the upper surface of the micro-excavated cist deposit):

BELOW ORGANIC ARTEFACTS (ON BASE STONE)
1. Spit F 5–6cm
2. Spit J (taken from directly above base stone before micro-excavation (equivalent to Spit F)

ABOVE ORGANIC ARTEFACTS (BELOW CAPSTONE)
1. Spit B 1–2cm
2. Spit C 2–3cm

The samples were all examined using a low-powered binocular microscope at magnifications of between ×6 and ×60. They were continually flushed with distilled water from a washer bottle to remove the peat, with each stem removed individually to determine whether there was any sign of weaving or pattern to them. It soon became clear that the plant material from all four spits appeared to be the same, with what were initially labelled as 'yellow stems' and 'brown stems.' These will continue to be referred to as 'yellow' and 'brown stems' during this initial discussion. There was some finer root growth over the top of this material which would appear to be post-depositional.

Spit F 5–6cm (from directly above the stone slab)

This was the best preserved sample. The 'yellow stems' which were more substantial (or better preserved) than the 'brown stems' were all unidirectional. Some of the yellow stems have culm nodes, several of which form a clustered line as shown in Figure 9.1. The presence of culm nodes indicates that these are grass stems, nodes being one of the diagnostic features of grasses. The impression is of a clump of grass gathered, or pulled up, and deliberately placed.

There was also a single basal stem section with several roots preserved (Fig. 9.2) and a stem with two small basal leaves originating from the basal culm node (Fig. 9.3).

The second group of 'brown stems' are more highly degraded, although some show signs of ribbing. Many are broken down into individual fibres and they appear to be laid in a more random pattern.

There were also occasional bracken (*Pteridium aquilinum*) pinnules noted here which occurred on the face of the sample; this also contained occasional fragments of decayed granite, suggesting that this was likely to have been the face which was in direct contact with the granite slab, although there was no indication on the sample bags of orientation.

Figure 9.1: Grass culm nodes clustered together.

Figure 9.2: Basal culm node with roots.

Figure 9.3: Small leaf coming from culm node.

Spit J (samples 2 and 4)

Most of this sample consisted of degraded stems although most were again unidirectional. However, at one end of the sample there was a small cluster of better preserved yellow stems with most of the culm areas roughly aligned at one end.

Spit B 1–2cm

This spit was mostly degraded stems and fibres, although the positioning appears more random here with some clumps at right-angles, some diagonal. No yellow stems were observed.

Spit C 2–3cm

This spit consisted largely of the more degraded brown stems with only occasional examples of the better preserved yellow stems. Most were again unidirectional (all the yellow ones were) but there were other fibres which were at right angles or more randomly positioned.

Following the microscopic dissection of the stems, measurements were made of all the better preserved yellow stems, recording whether these were from node to node, node to broken end or broken end to broken end. The results are as follows:

Spit F 5–6cm

22 stems measured
13 node to node: length: 1.3–4.8cm; average length: 2.7cm; average node width: 1.7cm.

Spit J sample 2

21 stems measured
3 node to node: length: 1.2–2.8cm; average length: 2.1cm; average node width: 1.35cm.

Spit J sample 4

19 stems measured
9 node to node: length: 2.5–5.0cm; average length: 3.46cm; average node width: 1.76cm.

Spit C 2–3cm

10 stems measured
2 node to node: length: 3.0–3.7cm; average length: 3.35cm; average node width: 2.2cm

The results of the initial microscopic examination indicate that the better-preserved yellow fragments are grass stems of similar length, with the alignment of some of the culm areas suggesting that clumps of grass or grasses were collected and laid down on the granite slab. The presence

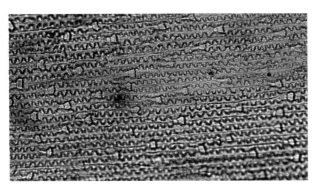
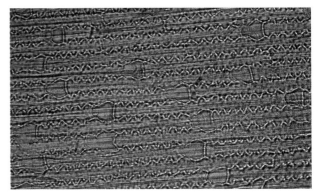

Figure 9.4: Spit J: ×200 and ×400, yellow stem.

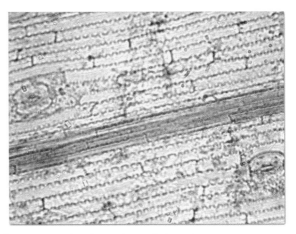

Figure 9.5: Spit F 5–6cm: ×200 and ×400, brown stem showing veins and stomata.

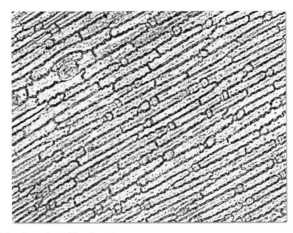

Figure 9.6: Spit F 5–6cm: ×200, small leaf, and ×400, showing stomata.

of a basal culm node, with some root retained, may also suggest that some clumps were uprooted.

High-powered microscopic examination was necessary to confirm species identification. Fragments of both categories of material extracted from the matted feature from spits F, J and C were mounted in Aquamount on glass microscope slides and then examined under ×100, ×200 and ×400 magnification with a photographic record made of distinguishing characteristics (Figs. 9.4–9.6). It soon became apparent that many of the characteristics observed were common to both the 'yellow' and 'brown stem' fragments.

The 'yellow stems' show a distinctive 4-sided cell pattern with very sinuous cell walls. Measurements showed that individual cell width was constantly 10μm, with the length 8–10 times longer than wide. Each of these longer cells was abutted by less sinuous short pairs of cells.

The same cell pattern and dimensions were recorded for the brown stem fragments, although here darker ribbing was noted, representing the veins of a leaf. The sinuous cell walls seem to continue through these ribs, which are seen as a darker colouration. Several stomata were also present in the intercostal zones (between the veins), with stomata width of about 25μm and length 30–35μm, with narrow guard cells. The distance between the ribs varied between 105–120μm. One of the small leaves from Spit F

Table 9.1 List of commonly occurring moorland grasses.

Agrostis setacea		Bristle-leaved Bent
Agrostis tenuis		Common Bent-grass
Agrostis canina	*	Velvet Bent
Anthoxanthemum odoratum	*	Sweet Vernal-grass
Deschampsia flexuosa	*	Wavy Hair-grass
Festuca ovina	*	Sheep's Fescue
Festuca rubra		Red Fescue
Molinia caerulea	*	Purple Moor-grass
Sieglingia decumbens	*	Heath-grass

* Indicates reference slides were made from the grasses. The grass nomenclature follows that of Hubbard (1992).

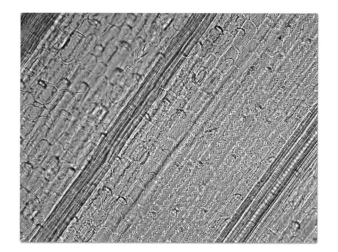
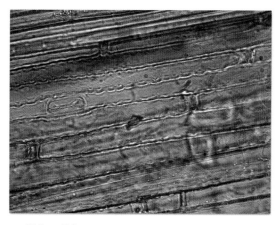

Figure 9.7: Agrostis canina ×200, ×400.

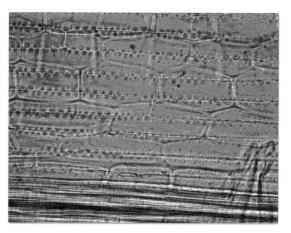

Figure 9.8: Antho anthemum odoratum ×200, ×400.

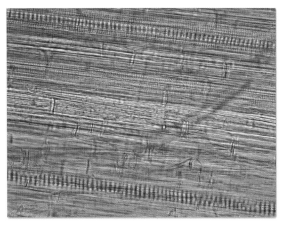
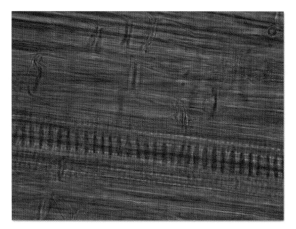

Figure 9.9: Deschampsia fle uosa ×200, ×400.

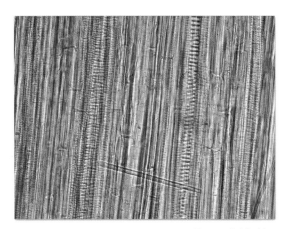

Figure 9.10: Festuca ovina ×200, ×400.

(5–6cm) was also mounted and examined microscopically, with the same cell pattern and stomata observed (Fig. 9.6).

It would therefore appear that the fragments from all spits originate from the same grass species. The culm nodes are only present on the better preserved yellow fragments, suggesting that these are grass stems, with the ribbing and stomata on the less well-preserved brown fragments suggesting that these are the leaf sheaths, which being less substantial have preserved less well.

Identification of moorland grasses

The next stage was to obtain a species identification (following Dickson 1970, 234). Ward *et al.* (1972) distinguish seven vegetation groups which are characteristic today of Dartmoor. These include blanket bog, *Calluna-Molinia* moorland, *Vaccinium* moorland, heath, valley bog and grassland types. Within these habitat groups are a number of consistently recurring grasses, as shown in Table 9.1.

Reference slides were made from the grasses shown with an asterisk (*). Stems and leaves were boiled in distilled water for one hour and then heated at 80°C in potassium hydroxide for an hour. They were allowed to cool before rinsing clean with distilled water and mounting in aquamount on glass microscope slides for examination at ×100, ×200 and ×400 magnification.

Agrostis canina

A fine-leaved grass of damp or wet places, velvet bent is a tufted perennial, 15–75cm tall, with slender creeping stolons, rooting at the nodes and producing fine leafy shoots. The culms often ascend from a bent or prostrate base and it has narrow, often in-rolled leaves.

The cell walls of this species are slightly sinuous, approximately 125μm wide and of variable length, up to 450μm. Stomata have parallel-sided subsidiary cells; dimensions are same as cell width (125μm) and 325μm long (Fig. 9.7). Shorter cells present over the veins.

Anthoxanthemum odoratum

Sweet vernal-grass is a tufted perennial of grassland,

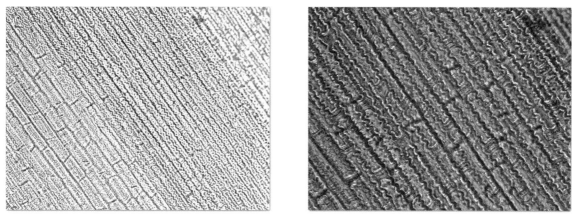

Figure 9.11: Molinia caerulea ×200, ×400.

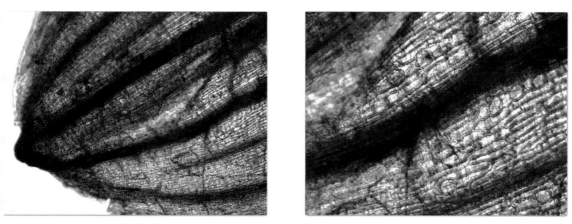

Figure 9.12: Molinia caerulea (leaf tip) ×100, ×200.

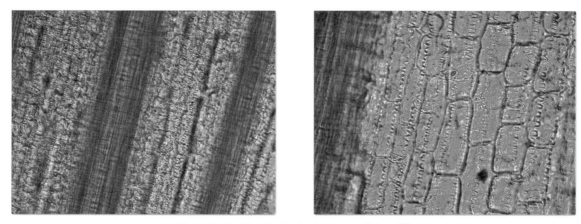

Figure 9.13: Sieglingia decumbens ×200, ×400.

moor and open woods. It is 10–100cm tall, with erect or spreading culms and pointed leaf blades, 1.5–5mm wide.

The leaves have big 5–6 sided smooth-edged short and dumpy cells, but also wavy edged cells, approximately 2μm wide; cells abut each other lengthwise – no smaller inter cell. Cell length varies greatly. Inter-rib width 225μm (Fig. 9.8).

Figure 9.14: Molinia caerulea, basal nodes from spits and modern reference node, ×6.3 (left to right): spit F 5–6cm; spit J; modern Molinia.

Deschampsia flexuosa

Wavy hair-grass is a loosely to densely tufted perennial, 20–100cm tall, with broad, flat leaves with prominent acute triangular ribs, from marshy grassland, moors and damp woodland.

During slide preparation this flimsy grass disintegrated, suggesting fossil preservation may be poor. Bigger smooth-edged cells with stepped ribbing between were noted, with no stomata observed (Fig. 9.9).

Festuca ovina

A densely tufted perennial, 5–60cm high, with very slender erect or spreading culms (Fig. 9.10). From poor soils and in open situations on moors and heaths. This grass was also delicate and had a similar cell pattern to *Deschampsia*, with big smooth edged cells with stepped ribbing between.

Molinia caerulea

A compact tufted, tough-rooted perennial, 15–120cm high that often forms large tussocks on moorland, heaths and commons (Figs. 9.11 and 9.12).

The cell structure on both the stem and a small leaf tip showed narrow cells with very sinuous walls, with cell length eight to ten times longer than wide, with small double cells abutting each cell. The leaf tip fragment showed thick ribs from the leaf veins with stomata present in the intercostal zones.

Sieglingia decumbens

Heath-grass is a densely tufted grass, 10–60cm high, with erect, spreading or almost prostrate slender stems on sandy or peaty soils, frequent on moorland and heath (Fig. 9.13).

Very sinuous cells approximately 50μm wide and of variable length, with single cells at each end of the long cell. Also bigger, more rectangular smooth edged cells 30–35μm wide and approximately 100μm long. Inter rib distance 140–150μm wide. Stomata mostly with triangular subsidiary cells.

Discussion

The examination of a selection of common moorland grasses confirmed that the matted plant material from the cist is purple moor grass, *Molinia caerulea*.

As Hubbard (1992) illustrates, *Molinia* is an erect, compact, tufted perennial grass, 15–130cm high when flowering, which often forms large tussocks or extensive swards (Taylor *et al.* 2001). The leaf sheaths tightly enclose the stem towards the base, then long, thin blades (3–12mm wide) taper to a fine point. The erect culms (stems) are slender to stout with one node towards the base, disarticulating at this node. The basal internode, up to 5cm long, usually becomes swollen and club-shaped in late summer-autumn and filled with food reserves. The growth cycle starts in April–May, with the stem becoming elongated in May–June, with growth showing an average of 5cm between nodes at this time. This corresponds well with node-to-node measurements made on well-preserved culms from spits C, F and J, with all from 1.2–5cm in length. Figure 9.14 illustrates the similarity between fossil and modern culms and how these easily disarticulate at the nodes.

From late June to early July the upper series of leaves open and flowering occurs in July–August. By September the first series of leaves are dead and by November all leaves are dead and most have dropped off (Taylor *et al.* 2001, 139). This annual cycle would suggest that the optimal time for collecting *Molinia* would be late summer–autumn, when the basal internodes are swollen but before the leaves die back. Collection of reference material of *Molinia* in early October 2012 showed how easily the culms and leaves could be gathered from the base of individual clumps, with little root disturbance.

Historically, purple moor grass was used in Orkney and Shetland to make ropes (Gale and Cutler 2000). By harvesting while still green and drying thoroughly before use the natural toughness of the grass was retained. In the Scottish Highlands it has also been used for brooms and thatching (Edlin 1951). *Molinia* grows today in four of the habitats on Dartmoor described by Ward *et al.* (1972), on blanket bog, *Calluna-Molinia* moorland, *Vaccinium* moorland and heath. On blanket bog, where conditions are at least seasonally wet, it is usually abundant and frequently dominates large areas, often to the exclusion of other flowering plants, forming dense circular tussocks from 8–20cm in diameter at the base. On damp or wet heath it occurs in association with *Erica tetralix* (cross-leaved heath), *Calluna vulgaris* (heather) and *Trichophorum cespitosum* (deergrass). However, there is no evidence for the presence of *Molinia* from the analysis carried out in 2008 by Hazell on the peat forming around the cist on Whitehorse Hill. This analysis showed the dominance of ericaceous plant remains but with the addition of *Eriophorum vaginatum* (hare's-tail cotton-grass) and *Sphagnum* (bog moss) in periods of wetter conditions. Generally there was a poor state of preservation of the macrofossil remains within the highly humified peat.

It would therefore appear that clumps of purple moor grass were collected for use as matting around the cremated burial deposit with its associated artefacts. Its abundance today on blanket bog on Dartmoor suggests that it would have been available close to the cist and could easily have been pulled up without the use of any tools, perhaps in late summer or early autumn when the basal culms were swollen, but before leaf fall. A point in late summer is also indicated by the meadowsweet (*Filipendula*) pollen which was found in the cist (Chapter 10).

Acknowledgements

Thanks to Gill Campbell who assisted with the collection of reference material and preparation of slides, and for her support during visits to the Historic England laboratories at Fort Cumberland

References

Dickson, C. A. 1970. The study of plant macrofossils in British Quarternary deposits. In D. Walker & R. G. West (eds.), *Studies in the vegetational history of the British Isles*. Cambridge: Cambridge University Press.

Edlin, H. L. 1951. *British Plants and Their Uses*. London: Batsford.

Gale, R. & Cutler, D. 2000. *Plants in Archaeology: identification manual of vegetative plant materials used in Europe and the southern Mediterranean to c. 1500*. Otley: Westbury and Royal Botanic Gardens, Kew.

Hubbard, C. E. 1992. *Grasses. A Guide to their Structure, Identification, Uses and Distribution in the British Isles*. London: Penguin.

Taylor, K., Rowland, A. P. & Jones, H. E. 2001. *Molinia caerulea* (L.) Moench biological flora of the British Isles. *Journal of Ecology* 89, 126–144.

Ward, S. D., Jones, A. D. & Manton, M. 1972. The vegetation of Dartmoor. *Field Studies* 4, 505–533.

10. The pollen and non-pollen palynomorphs from the cist samples

Ralph Fyfe and Marta Perez

Samples from within the cist at Whitehorse Hill were analysed for their pollen and non-pollen palynomorph (NPP) content, to address the following questions:

1. Was material deposited in the cist (in particular the matted plant material) sourced locally, or could it have been brought to the site from a different part of the wider landscape?
2. Are there any seasonal indications that might be useful for inferring the time of year at which deposition occurred?
3. Are there indications of particular depositional practices within the pollen spectra?

Sample descriptions and methods

Seven samples were prepared for pollen and fungal spore analysis (Table 10.1). Four of these were from artefactual material: material cleaned from the textile and animal-skin object, two samples from inside the basketry container and a sample of the pelt. The remaining three were associated with the matted plant material.

Samples from inside the cist were prepared and analysed for their pollen and fungal content using standard methods (Moore *et al.* 1991; Blackford *et al.* forthcoming). Statistical analyses on the pollen and non-pollen palynomorph (NPP) datasets was undertaken using R (R Core Team 2013) using the package Vegan (Oksanen *et al.* 2013). Diagrams were plotted using the software package C2. Where possible, statistically-significant counts (300 land pollen types) were made, and pollen concentrations were calculated using exotic marker tablets. The data were summarized and plotted and also compared with the pollen samples from the high-resolution stratigraphic section (Chapter 19). This was undertaken by creating a Bray-Curtis dissimilarity matrix for all samples, and then performing an unconstrained cluster analysis.

Table 10.1: details of samples from within the cist used for pollen and NPP analysis

Sample	Description
1	Soil and debris cleaned from the textile and animal-skin object
2	Soil from directly on top of the pelt
3	Soil beneath matted plant material fragment.
4	Matted plant fragments directly on base stone.
5	Fragmentary samples of matted plant material.
6	Soil from inside basketry container.
7	Soil from inside basketry container.

This approach results in groupings of samples which are the most similar in taxon composition and proportions. A glossary of common anmes of pollen taxa is provided in Chapter 19 (Table 19.4).

Results and interpretation

Results from the pollen and NPP analysis are summarised in Figures 10.1 and 10.2.

Pollen analysis

The pollen concentrations from the cist samples are low, and concentrations from the pelt sample were too low for any reliable results to be calculated. The sample taken from the textile and animal-skin object had very low concentration values and only a limited pollen sum (162 TLP) was possible. The pollen samples are all broadly similar. Arboreal types are the most common, including *Corylus* (hazel the most abundant taxa), *Alnus* (alder) and *Quercus* (oak). Poaceae (grasses) and *Calluna* (heather)

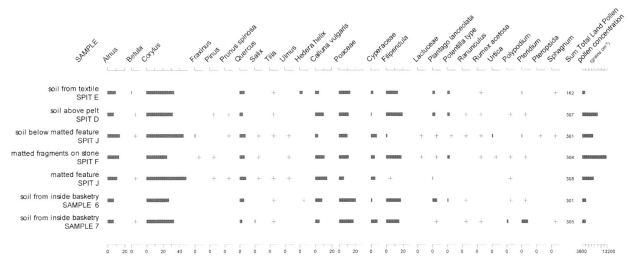

Figure 10.1: Pollen analytical results, samples from within the cist at Whitehorse Hill. No pollen was recovered from the pelt. (Samples 6 and 7 were taken from inside the basketry container.)

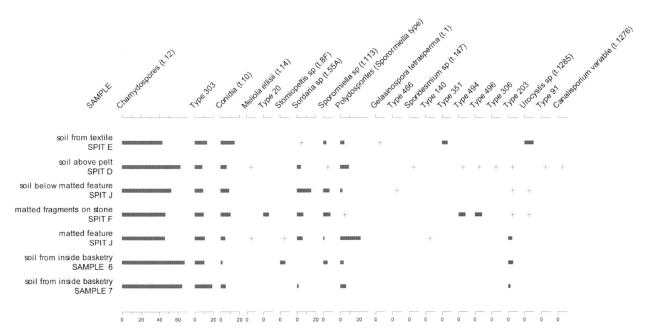

Figure 10.2: NPP analytical results, samples from within the cist at Whitehorse Hill. '(Samples 6 and 7 were taken from inside the basketry container.)

are the most common non-arboreal types and, along with Cyperaceae, suggest an assemblage typical of blanket mire.

Five of the seven samples included *Filipendula* (meadowsweet) at around 15–20% TLP. This taxon only appears sporadically and at very low levels in the continuous peat section (Chapter 19). Particular concentrations of *Filipendula* pollen have been noted from cist burial contexts in Scotland and the Scottish borders; for example, Dalgety Bay, Fife (Whittington 1993; Tipping 1994), and Leetside Farm, Berwickshire (Clarke and Hamilton 1999; Clarke 1999). Ongoing post-excavation analysis from Dagger Cist, Forteviot, Fife, has recovered

Filipendula flower heads within the cist, confirming the use of the flower within Bronze Age burials in Scotland (Glasgow University 2014). Deposition of floral tributes in Bronze Age burials is also inferred from pollen analysis in southern Scandinavia; for example, wood anemone (Lageras 2000). It seems likely, therefore, given the absence in the wider environment of *Filipendula* at levels anywhere near those found from within the cist, that meadowsweet was deposited with the burial.

Filipendula usually flowers between May and August, which suggests deposition during the summer months. This is congruent with the analysis of the matting within the cist which comprised *Molinia* (purple moor grass) stems, most likely pulled or collected during the late summer (Chapter 9).

The cluster analysis (which combined the samples from within the cist and from the section) excluded *Filipendula* as this has been interpreted as an introduced pollen type. The results of the analysis confirm that the pollen samples from within the cist are all very similar (they are placed within the same broad cluster) and are most similar to the pollen samples from 31–33cm depth in the peat section. There are also broad similarities to the samples from 25–26.5cm depth. This strongly supports the notion that the matted plant material used within the cist is local in origin. It does not preclude that it has been brought to site from elsewhere but, if it has, it has come from a very similar landscape context.

Non-pollen palynomorphs (NPPs)

The NPPs are dominated by Type 12 (around 45–60%) and Type 303 (10–20%). Both of these taxa are associated with drier phases in blanket peats. They are not associated with any particular host species but in dry conditions can be locally abundant as they are associated with decomposition of plant tissue. Type 10 is associated with *Calluna* in intermediate phases (between wet and dry blanket bog). The other taxa that appear at significant levels within the samples include *Sordaria* and *Sporormiella*. *Sodaria* is strongly associated with grazing: while it is not an obligate dung fungi (it can also live on decaying and rotting wood and other plant material), it is most commonly associated with other dung fungi. This is supported at Whitehorse Hill as *Sporormiella* is an obligate dung fungi.

The overall assemblage is most similar to the samples from the high-resolution peat sequence between 33cm and 35cm depth; that is, before the explosion of NPP taxa associated with dung (in particular *Sordaria*). The samples from within the cist therefore suggest that while it was being constructed the local landscape included grazing animals.

Conclusion

Considering both the pollen and the NPP data together, several key points can be made:

1. The material deposited within the cist most probably included a floral tribute (*Filipendula*) and the deposition of material probably occurred between May and August.
2. The matted plant material from within the cist,

identified as *Molinia* (Chapter 9), is local in origin, with strong associations with particular phases within the pollen and NPP high-resolution phases. The results suggest drier blanket bog conditions.

3. There is a difference in the results of comparison between the pollen and NPP data from the cist and from the peat section. The pollen suggests 31–33cm depth as the best correlative, the NPP data 33–35cm depth. The difference may reflect the highly localised character of the NPPs (source areas are thought to be in the order of 10m) against the wider pollen rain. Alternatively, it might be used to infer a much more precise date of the cist, at 33cm. Caution is urged over the latter interpretation, though, owing to the source area uncertainty, and a lack of more independent dating of the peat section.

References

Blackford, J. J., Innes, J. B. & Clarke, C. forthcoming. *Guide to Quaternary Fungi*. London: Quaternary Research Association Technical Guide.

Clarke, C. M. 1999. Palynological investigations of a Bronze Age cist burial from Whitsome, Scottish Borders, Scotland. *Journal of Archaeological Science* 26, 553–560.

Clarke, C. M. & Hamilton J. E. 1999. Excavation of a cist burial on Doons Law, Leetside Farm, Whitsome, Berwickshire. *Proceedings of the Society of Antiquaries of Scotland* 129, 189–201.

Glasgow University. 2014. Strathearn environs and Royal Forteviot project http://www.gla.ac.uk/schools/humanities/research/archaeologyresearch/projects/serf/ [last accessed 24 June 2014].

Lageras, P. 2000. Burial rituals inferred from palynological evidence: results from a late Neolithic stone cist in southern Sweden. *Vegetation History and Archaeobotany* 9, 169–173.

Moore, P. D., Webb, J. A. & Collinson, M. E. 1991. *Pollen Analysis*. Oxford: Blackwell.

Oksanen, J., Blanchet, F. G., Kindt, R., Legendre, P., Minchin, P. R., O'Hara, R. B., Simpson, G. L., Solymos, P., Stevens, M. H. H. & Wagner, H. 2013. Vegan: Community Ecology Package. R package version 2.0–10. http://CRAN.R-project.org/package=vegan.

R Core Team. 2013. R: A language and environment for statistical computing. R Foundation for Statistical Computing, Vienna, Austria. ISBN 3-900051-07-0, URL http://www.R-project.org/.

Tipping, R. 1994. 'Ritual' floral tributes in the Scottish Bronze Age – palynological evidence. *Journal of Archaeological Science* 21, 133–139.

Whittington, G. 1993. Palynological investigations at two burial sites in Fife. *Proceedings of the Society of Antiquaries of Scotland* 123, 211–213.

Section 4:
Items with
the young adult

11. The animal pelt

Esther Cameron and Quita Mould

Description

The flattened mass of hair retrieved from the cist represented part of an animal pelt (a skin with the hair, fur or wool present) (Figs. 11.1 and 11.2). Only the hair remained, complete with flecks of blackened tissue around the hair roots, which were taken as evidence that the pelt skin had originally been present in the burial and had subsequently decomposed. A folded edge was evident along one side but as no other regular edges were observed the original dimensions of the pelt are unknown. This folded mass of hair measured 390 × 280mm from which it was estimated that the outline of the surviving pelt when unfolded was a rough rectangle measuring *circa* 560 × 390mm.

The hair was dense, and in the dried state it was an orange–brown colour, darkening to dark brown–black when wet. The two types of hair fibres present, the under-hairs and guard-hairs, were approximately 29mm and 40mm in length respectively. Both were finer and lighter in colour toward the root and darker and thicker toward the tip. The hairs were aligned in one direction along the same axis as the fold (Fig. 11.3). There also appeared to be a slight gradation in density from one edge of the pelt at 'N' to the opposite edge at 'S', decreasing in the direction of the hair tips, although the pelt's damp and bedraggled condition made it difficult to be certain of this.

One animal pelt or many?

As the skin survived only as minute flecks of tissue there was no remaining evidence of whether it had been seamed or stitched. Neither were there any marked changes in hair direction that might suggest that small pieces had been joined. While a single seam joining two similarly aligned pelts would be difficult to detect, if several whole pelts from small animals had been joined, aligned side by

Figure. 11.1: Photograph of the pelt, upper view. Sample spot N is located at the top right-hand corner. (Photograph: M. Wachnik.)

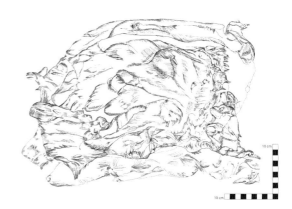

Figure 11.2: Illustration of the pelt, upper view. (Drawing: M. Wachnik.)

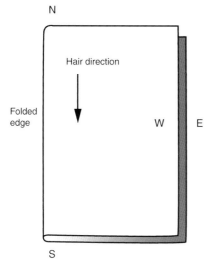

Diagram showing the
sample spots on the pelt

Figure 11.3: Schematic plan of the pelt showing hair direction and sample spots N, S, E, W (Drawing: E. Cameron and M. Wachnik.)

Table 11.1: The weight of hair in mg per 10mm²

N	S	E	W
0.065	0.034	0.045	0.049

Without its skin, the density of hair growth on the pelt was measured by weight of fibres per 10mm² rather than by individual hair count (Table 11.1). A sample approximately 15mm² was removed from each edge N, S, E and W and trimmed to 10mm² using a razor on a grid-marked cutting board. Each sample was gently cleansed with water, dried at ambient room temperature and weighed on a Sartorius balance (Model ME235S) at Begbroke Nano, Oxford University.

It was apparent that N, E and W contained many guard hairs and that S contained very few, as would be expected of hair growth on the butt and near to the region of the belly respectively (Ryder and Stephenson 1968, 357–8). The results showed that hair density on the pelt at N was almost double that at S and that density at E and W was approximately equal and fell between the values for N and S. This, as well as the relative lack of guard hairs in sample S, supports the suggestion that S marks the transition to the belly region, and allows the animal a minimum girth of 780mm (twice the distance from N to S).

The quantity and mixture of hair fibres, which included a high proportion of guard hairs, suggested that at least part of it came from the butt area. In addition, the outline of the pelt implied that the extremities had been removed; its uniform hair direction made it likely that one side of an animal had been utilized, as a complete butt has two hair directions divided by the line of the backbone. A measurable difference in hair volume from top to bottom of the pelt appeared to reflect the transition from backbone to belly. For these reasons the pelt is assumed in the following discussion to be from a single animal but the possibility remains that it may have comprised several smaller pelts sewn together.

side, this might have been more evident as the different hair directions would produce a 'herringbone' effect. The tousled effect of the fur hat from the Ötztaler Alps, achieved by randomly joining small pieces of fur, was not evident in the pelt from the Whitehorse Hill cist. Although there were some areas of the pelt where hair alignments differed slightly, no underlying changes of fibre direction were apparent, although such changes might have been masked by the pelt's clumped and matted condition. The length of the hairs, recorded by Dr Andrew Wilson as up to 50mm (Wilson 2013), did not suggest the short, dense coats of stoats and weasels which have maximum hair lengths of 14mm and 8mm respectively. The observed characteristics of the hair suggested that the pelt was possibly that of a single, larger animal, and subsequent analysis by Caroline Solazzio (Appendix C) has confirmed that it belonged to the bear (*Ursidae*) family.

Orientation of the pelt and estimation of girth

The hair was examined in order to orientate the pelt and establish what part of animal had been used. The strongest and hairiest part of an animal skin is the 'butt', located between the shoulders and the tail, which tends to produce a dense growth of both types of hair (Fig. 11.4). On the belly and axilla regions, where the skin is weaker, hair is less dense and typically grows in several directions (Haines 1981, 17) (Fig. 11.5). The rate at which hair density changes across an animal's flank from backbone to belly tends to vary according to the size of the animal, so any apparent variation in hair density on the pelt may suggest the relative proportions of the animal.

Had the pelt been worked?

There is no evidence for how, or even if, the skin had been treated. It is possible that the animal had been flayed and the fresh pelt placed directly in the burial or that it had been temporarily preserved, possibly with salt, until it was required. The fold in the pelt suggests that the skin was in a soft and pliable condition when it was placed in the cist, which suggests either that it was fresh or that it had been prepared in some way, as unworked skin or rawhide quickly becomes stiff and inflexible. Pelts preserved with salt can be softened when required by the simple technique of repeated flexing and working by hand, although skins which have been treated in this way decay quickly in temperate zones (Rahme and Hartman 2001, 1). Various methods may have been employed to soften or further treat the skin. The available evidence for the preparation of skins points to the use of animal fats in prehistory (Groenman-van Waateringe *et al* 1999; Püntener

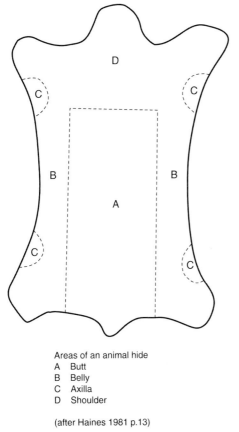

Areas of an animal hide
A   Butt
B   Belly
C   Axilla
D   Shoulder

(after Haines 1981 p.13)

Figure 11.4: Diagram showing the areas of an animal hide (after Haines 1981, 13). (Drawing: M. Wachnik.)

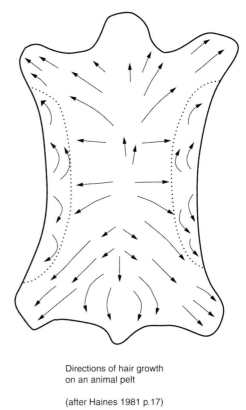

Directions of hair growth
on an animal pelt

(after Haines 1981 p.17)

Figure 11.5: Diagram showing directions of hair growth on an animal pelt (after Haines 1981, 17) (Drawing: M. Wachnik.)

and Moss 2010; Harris 2011). Traditional methods still used today to work a variety of animal hides and skins, including beaver, marten and other smaller mammals, are summarised by Rahme and Hartman (2001) and Rahme (2011). The skin of the pelt from the Whitehorse Hill cist may have been stretched, scraped and repeatedly worked by hand, and animal fats may have been applied, before it was slowly dried. This would render the pelt resistant to microbiological degradation but it would eventually rot if subject to damp or wet conditions for a long period (Thomson 2011, 4), as may have been the case here.

Native American Indians traditionally practiced a method of curing skins that involved the application of animal fat, usually the animal's brain, and smoking over a fire for several days (Harris 2011, 61). For some years it has been supposed that the fur clothing of the glacier corpse from the Ötztaler Alps had been smoke-tanned, as some of the pollen grains found embedded in the hairs were shrunken and bleached as if they had been exposed to smoke (Groenman-van Waateringe 1995). Currently it is thought that Early Bronze Age living quarters were probably such smoke-filled environments that these alone could have caused the pollen grains to shrink. More recent analysis of the Ötztaler clothing samples by IR spectroscopy suggests that the skins were treated with animal fats (Püntener and Moss 2010).

Bronze Age pelts: the wider context

Although the animal has been identified as belonging to the bear genus (Appendix C), some uncertainty exists as to whether a single skin or several skins sewn together were employed, so that comparison with other Bronze Age burial finds remains problematical. This said, the fact remains that the recovery of an animal pelt of any kind in Britain is uncommon. Hair, thought to be probably animal, was present in a log coffin burial at Weaver's Down, Hampshire (Grinsell 1938), and a proteinaceous layer interpreted as the remains of a cloak or hide covered a Beaker inhumation burial at West Overton barrow 6b (Smith and Simpson 1966). The hooves and the head of an ox placed beside the coffin at Hemp Knoll Barrow, Bishops Canning, Wiltshire, may represent a flayed hide, as the absence of any other bones indicates that the entire animal had not been interred (Robertson-Mackay 1980). At Dysgwylfa Fawr, Cardiganshire, a piece of animal pelt, reported to be from a stoat or fox, was found covering a cremation accompanied by a Food Vessel and flint inside a log coffin (Forde 1939; Savory 1980, 80). At Shuttleston, Derbyshire, remains of a hairy skin of dark red colour were found in a barrow containing an inhumation with a copper-alloy dagger and axe (Bateman 1861, 34). Indirect evidence of pelts comes from Gristhorpe, Yorkshire, where the presence of foot bones of fox and pine-martin suggests that the pelts of these animals had been placed in the log coffin burial (Melton *et al.* 2010; 2013).

Scottish Early Bronze Age burials in cists containing fur or ox-hides are tabled by McAdam (1982, 127). In the majority of these ten cists the hairs were identified as bovine, the burial rite as inhumation, and the practice was either to cover the body with a hide or to place it under the head or body. In a cist with a decorated capstone and part-pebbled floor at Cuninghar, Tillicoultry, Clackmannan, the head of the inhumation rested upon a layer of hair fibres identified as possibly stoat (Robertson 1894; Coles 1899; Henshall 1963, 176). More recent finds of Early Bronze Age inhumations in cists include that at Langwell Farm, Strath Oykel, Sutherland, where the body was wrapped in a brown cattle-hide (Lelong 2012), and at Spinningdale, Sutherland, where a 'small tangle of wool' associated with brown sinew-like material, possibly the remains of a sheepskin, lay beneath the body. In this case however, as both ends of the individual fibres examined were broken, the identification of the presence of a sheepskin in the burial can only be tentatively suggested (Walton Rogers 2013).

In the wider European context, the inclusion of a cow skin was commonly part of the burial ritual for both men and women in Danish Bronze Age oak coffin inhumation burials. A cow skin was spread out at the bottom of the oak coffin, hair-side upward, and the body placed on top covered by a textile cloak, the hide was then carefully folded around the body, as, for example, at the man's grave at Trindhøj (Broholm and Hald 1940, 43). Similarly, in the Whitehorse Hill cist, the pelt, although in this case hair-side facing outward, was carefully folded around the cremated bones; it is perhaps in this context of wrapping and display that the Whitehorse Hill pelt should be viewed (Chapter 21).

Summary

Examination and measurement of the hair direction, quality and density suggests that the hair recovered represents half an animal pelt, divided along the backbone, with shoulder, belly and axilla removed. This would imply that the pelt had been prepared carefully and used economically. While it is possible that the pelt comprised several smaller animals joined together, no direct evidence of that was observed and no stitching medium was present. No evidence of whether the pelt had been worked could be provided by the surviving hair.

The bear pelt enclosing the cremated remains within the Whitehorse Hill cist is an important and unusual find as, to date, only one other burial, at Dysgwylfa Fawr, Cardigans-hire, is known to have cremated remains associated with a pelt (Forde 1939). Although the occurrence of pelts within inhumation burials are more numerous they still remain uncommon finds. While the apparent rarity of the identification of pelts within Bronze Age burials may in some part be the result of the bias against the preservation of organic remains in the burial environment and the

inability to detect and recover such ephemeral evidence in the past, it may reflect the value and prestige of such items. In reviewing the Scottish evidence McAdam noted the occurrence of fur and hide in exceptional cists: 'Construction details and grave-goods indicate that fur and hides are found in the graves of individuals of special status whose burials required unusual care and special effort' (McAdam 1982, 126). The Whitehorse Hill cist animal pelt had been placed in the cist with the hair side downward, the cremation placed on its skin surface and one half of the pelt folded over it so that the two resulting layers were 'skin to skin' and hair outward with the cremated remains within. The wrapping or enfolding of the cremated remains within the pelt with the fur / hair clearly displayed would appear to have been a significant part of the burial ritual. It may be that the pelt was a statement of the prestige of the deceased and those who presided at the burial.

Acknowledgements

Andy M. Jones is thanked for references; Roy Thomson for discussions and expert advice, and Magdalena Wachnik for Figures 11.1–11.5.

References

Bateman, T. 1861. *Ten years' diggings in Celtic and Anglo Saxon Grave Hills, in the Counties of Derby, Stafford and York.* London: J. R. Smith.

Broholm, H. C. & Hald, M. 1940. *Costumes of the Bronze Age in Denmark: contributions to the archaeology and textile history of the Bronze Age.* Copenhagen: NYT Nordisk. Arnold Busck.

Coles, F. R. 1899. Notices of the discovery of a cist and urns at Juniper Green, and of a cist at the Cunninghar, Tillicoultry, and of some undescribed cup-marked stones. *Proceedings of the Society of Antiquaries of Scotland* 33, 354–372.

Forde, D. 1939. Dysgwylfa Fawr barrow, Cardiganshire: a food-vessel and dug-out trunk cremation burial. *Antiquaries' Journal* 19, 90–92.

Grinsell, L. V. 1938. Hampshire barrows. *Proceedings of the Hampshire Field Club and Archaeological Society* 14, 9–40.

Groenman-van Waateringe, W. 1995. Pollenanalyse als Indikator für das Gerbeverfahren bei den Tierfellen des Mannes vom Tisenjoch. In K. Spindler, E. Rastbichler-Zissernig, H. Wilfing, D. zur Nedden, H. Nothdurfter (eds.), *Der Mann im Eis: Neue Funde und Ergebnisse*, v. 2, 67–70. Vienna and New York: Springer.

Groenman-van Wateringe, W., Kilian, M. & van Londen, H. 1999. The curing of hides and skins in European prehistory. *Antiquity* 73, 884–890.

Haines, B. 1981 *The Fibre Structure of Leather.* Northampton: Leather Conservation Centre.

Harris, S. 2011. Preparing skins in prehistory: a review of evidence and approaches. In R. Thomson & Q. Mould (eds.), *Leather Tanneries: the archaeological evidence.* London: Archetype, 57–67.

Henshall, A. 1963. *The Chambered Tombs of Scotland, Volume I.* Edinburgh: Edinburgh University Press.

Lelong, O. 2012. Langwell Farm, Strath Oykel, *PAST* 72, 12–14.

McAdam, E. 1982. Comparative background: the cemetery. In

T. Watkins, The excavation of an Early Bronze Age cemetery at Barns Farm, Dalgety, Fife, 120–129. *Proceedings of the Society of Antiquaries of Scotland* 112, 48–141.

Melton, N., Montgomery, J., Knüsel, C. J., Batt, C., Needham, S. P., Parker Pearson, M., Sheridan, J. A., Heron, C., Horsley, T., Schmidt, A., Evans, A., Carter, E., Edwards, H., Hargreaves, M., Janaway, R., Lynnerup, N., Northover, P., O'Connor, S., Ogden, A., Taylor, T., Wastling, V. & Wilson, A. 2010. Gristhorpe Man: an Early Bronze Age log-coffin burial scientifically dated. *Antiquity* 84, 796–815.

Melton, N., Montgomery, J. & Knüsel, C. J. (eds.) 2013. *Gristhorpe Man: a life and death in the Bronze Age.* Oxford: Oxbow Books.

Püntener, A. & Moss, S. 2010. Ötzi the Iceman and his leather clothes. *CHIMIA International Journal for Chemistry* 64(5), 315–320.

Rahme, L. 2011. Tanning with traditional tools and techniques: Inuit, American Indian and Sami people. In R. Thomson & Q. Mould (eds.), *Leather Tanneries: the archaeological evidence.* London: Archetype, 39–48.

Rahme, L. & Hartman, D. 2001. *Leather Preparation and Tanning by Traditional Methods* (revised edition). Portland, OR: Caber Press.

Robertson, R. 1894. Notice of the discovery of a stone cist and urns at the Cuninghar, Tillicoultry. *Proceedings of the Society of Antiquaries of Scotland* 29, 190–197.

Robertson-Mackay, M. E., 1980. A 'head and hooves' burial beneath a round barrow, with other Neolithic and Bronze Age sites, on Hemp Knoll, near Avebury, Wiltshire, *Proceedings of the Prehistoric Society* 46, 123–176.

Ryder, M. and Stephenson, S. 1968. *Wool Growth.* London: Academic Press.

Savory, H. N. 1980. *Guide Catalogue of the Bronze Age Collections.* Cardiff: National Museum of Wales.

Smith, I. F. & Simpson D. 1966. Excavation of a round barrow on Overton Hill, north Wiltshire. *Proceedings of the Prehistoric Society* 32, 122–155.

Thomson, R. 2011. Skins, leather and tanning: some definitions. In R. Thomson & Q. Mould (eds.), *Leather Tanneries: the archaeological evidence.* London: Archetype, 3–7.

Walton Rogers, P. 2013. Organic residue. In I. Arabaolaza, *Spinning the Yarn: a cist at Keas Cottage, Spinningdale.* Glasgow: Guard Archaeology, Archaeology Reports Online ARO5, 13 [online at http://www.archaeologyreportsonline.com/PDF/ARO5_Keas_Cottage.pdf]

Wilson, A. 2013. Report on analysis of Whitehorse Hill cist pelt. Bradford: University of Bradford.

12. The copper-alloy pin

Alison Sheridan, Esther Cameron and Henrietta Quinnell

The incomplete and wholly mineralised remains of a metal pin, presumed to be of copper alloy (Fig. 12.1) were discovered during a late stage in the conservation process of the bear pelt that had been wrapped around the cremated remains. Surviving as four fragments and a flake, it was found inside the edge of the pelt and could have been used to pin the ends of the pelt together. In order to check for the possible presence of any organic components (since the question was raised as to whether this may have been an awl, which could have had an organic handle), the pieces were examined microscopically by Esther Cameron at the Wiltshire conservation laboratory in Chippenham, using a Wild Heerbrugg M8 binocular microscope magnifying up to ×50, under raking fibre-optic light.

The longest fragment, incorporating the pointed terminal of the object, measures 21mm long and 1.25mm in thickness and is an olive green-grey colour; much of the surface had corroded away. Its pointed end is sharp and above the shank is square-sectioned. This fragment does not appear to conjoin with the others. The remaining pieces are blackish and the two largest of these, measuring 9.5mm and 7mm in length respectively and both 1.25mm thick, conjoin. The cross-section here is circular. The larger of these two pieces has an excrescence on its side and a twisted appearance that cannot be explained in terms of the corrosion of the metal (Theodore Skinner, pers. comm.). Instead, it appears that this part of the shank – which probably constituted the middle part of the object – had been deliberately twisted. The 'excrescence' part of the twisted section suggests a degree of complexity in the manufacture process. The fourth fragment measures 5mm x 1mm and the flake (not shown in the photograph, Fig. 12.1), 3 x 1.25mm. Excluding the flake, the overall length of the four fragments totals 42.5mm; when complete, the object would have been longer. No traces of attached organic material were found.

Discussion

That this object had been a garment pin, rather than an awl, is indicated by the twisted shape of the probable mid-shank fragment, and by the fact that the section is circular at this point, but square further down the shank, nearer the tip. With awls, where there is variability in the cross-section shape, the square part is the broadest part of the shaft (often in the middle), while the pointed section/s of the shank has or have a circular cross section; that is, a configuration opposite to the one seen at Whitehorse Hill. (For examples of various awl cross-sectional shapes, including tanged awls with rectangular-sectioned tangs, see Annable and Simpson 1964, 113; Thomas 2005, fig. 55).

Both awls and pins of copper alloy are exceedingly rare in the south west. Just five awls have been found previously, all in Cornwall and Scilly (at Gwithian, Harlyn Bay, Treligga and Highgate, and at Gugh on the Isles of Scilly: Pearce 1983, 373, 376, nos 62a, 100, 150; Christie 1985; Nowakowski and Johns 2015). There is just a single find of a copper-alloy pin, which came from a richly-equipped grave at Upton Pyne, in the Exe Valley, Devon (Kirwan 1872, 643 and pl. 1, fig. 3; Jones and Quinnell 2013). That pin, like the one from Whitehorse Hill, had probably been used to secure the ends of an organic wrapper or container for cremated human remains (originally suggested to be of a woman or youth: Powers 1969), found in what had probably been a wooden cist-like structure. Also present in the Upton Pyne funerary deposit were a knife-dagger, pyre debris and a composite necklace; the necklace is described and discussed in Chapter 15.

The Upton Pyne pin measures approximately 65mm but all that survives is the shaft, with a fragment of a vertebra attached to one end, and it is heavily corroded like the Whitehorse Hill example. Unlike the latter, however, it has an expanded terminal that appears to have been circular

10 mm

Figure 12.1: Photograph of the pin. (Photograph: Helen Williams, Wiltshire Conservation Centre.)

in plan and to have had a concave edge. Kirwan (1872) describes the cross-section of the shank as being squared at its thicker end and, to judge from his engraving, the shank appears to be slightly thicker than that of the Whitehorse Hill pin. It has been claimed (for example, by Edwina Proudfoot (1963, 425) and Sabine Gerloff (1975, 250)) that the shank of the Upton Pyne pin is twisted, even though that feature is not obvious in Kirwan's illustration. If it is indeed twisted, then that provides a point of comparison with the Whitehorse Hill example.

Three other so-called 'screw-shank' Early Bronze Age pins of copper alloy are known in Britain, all from Wiltshire. Of these, the examples from Milston barrow G3

or G7 and from Kennet Hill (lost) are crutch-headed pins (Gerloff 1975, 250 and pl. 57A; Annable and Simpson 1964, 56 and 110, 361; Proudfoot 1963, 425), while the example from Scratchbury (Norton Bavant) barrow G1 survives just as a shaft fragment (Gerloff 1975, 112, 250, pl. 57E). Gerloff and Proudfoot also cite two skeuomorphs in bone, with carved spiral grooves. The example from Dewlish G7, Dorset, is a crutch-headed pin with two sets of three diagonal grooves that do not form a continuous spiral but which do give an impression of spiralling (Proudfoot 1963, 425; Gerloff 1975, 111, 251, pl. 48B; Ann Woodward, pers. comm.). The example from Edmondsham G2, Dorset, survives only as a shank but does have true spiral decoration (Proudfoot 1963; Gerloff 1975, 111, 251). These metal and bone examples vary in their size and thickness, with the Milston example being relatively robust, measuring 159mm long, 19mm across and with a shank diameter of 8mm (www.wiltshireheritagecollections.org.uk/, accessed January 2015), while the Edmondsham example is more delicate, with a shank diameter of approximately 5mm. This variation in robustness appears not to follow gender lines, since the cremated remains associated with the Edmondsham pin were found to be those of an adult male (Lisowski 1963). That pin, like the aforementioned bone pin from Dewlish, was associated with a Camerton-Snowshill-type dagger, a dagger type for which the *floruit* dates to *circa* 1700–1500 cal BC (Woodward *et al.* 2015).

The metal 'screw-shank' pins are part of a range of 'fancy' copper-alloy pins, worn by both male and female members of the elite, that appear to have come into use in Britain around 1700 cal BC and were particularly popular in and around inland and coastal Wessex (Gerloff 1975, pl. 62A). It has been argued (for example, Gerloff 1975, 112) that they indicate a switch in the way that clothes were fastened, from the use of buttons to the use of pins as the preferred mode, although that is not to deny the occasional earlier, Chalcolithic, use of metal pins in Britain (as at Roundway, Wiltshire: Gerloff 1975, 28 and pl. 41A).

The fact that clear Continental parallels can be found for the Early Bronze Age pins, particularly in central and northern Europe in Tumulus Culture contexts, has encouraged the view that here is a Continental style of dress accessory that was adopted in Britain (Gerloff 1975, 118–123; cf Piggott 1938, 85–87; Woodward *et al.* 2015). For example, screw-shank (or 'twisted shaft') pins with variously shaped heads are known from southern Germany, Switzerland, northern Europe and the Netherlands (Gerloff 1975, 122; Piggott 1938, 85). Indeed, Edwina Proudfoot has argued that the metal pins are actual imports from the Continent, while the bone skeuomorphs constitute local attempts to emulate these prestigious dress accessories (Proudfoot 1963, 414), and there may be merit in such a suggestion. Within south-west Britain, the fragmentary bone ring-headed pin found in a Trevisker vessel with a small amount of calcined human bone at Stannon, on Bodmin Moor (Harris *et al.* 1984, fig. 7), may be a skeuomorph of a Continental metal ring-headed pin, as represented at Amesbury barrow G24, Wiltshire (Gerloff 1975, 110).

The inclusion of a metal pin – a rare and precious object – in the Whitehorse Hill funerary assemblage underlines once more the special status of the deceased, and is in line with the nature of the other grave goods, as discussed elsewhere in this volume. Whether that pin had been made on the Continent and imported into Britain is a question that cannot be addressed without undertaking metal analysis, but it remains an intriguing possibility. Given the concentration of fancy metal pins in Wiltshire and adjacent counties, it seems most likely that the Whitehorse Hill pin had been acquired through contacts with the elite in Wessex rather than as the result of any direct links with the Continent. In this respect the pin shows the same concern with participating in the 'vocabulary of esteem' that was current in Wessex as do the composite necklace (Chapter 15) and the studs (Chapter 16).

Acknowledgements

The authors wish to thank Helen Williams for providing photographs and information about the pin.

References

Annable, F. K. & Simpson, D. D. A. 1964. *Guide Catalogue of the Neolithic and Bronze Age Collections in Devizes Museum.* Devizes: Wiltshire Archaeological and Natural History Society.

Christie, P. 1985. Barrows on the north Cornish coast: wartime excavations by C. K. Croft Andrew 1939–1944. *Cornish Archaeology* 24, 23–122.

Gerloff, S. 1975. *The Early Bronze Age Daggers in Great Britain, and a Reconsideration of the Wessex Culture.* Munich: Prähistorische Bronzefunde VI(2).

Harris, D., Hooper, S. & Trudgian, P. 1984. The excavation of three cairns at Stannon, Bodmin Moor. *Cornish Archaeology* 23, 141–155.

Jones, A. M. & Quinnell, H. 2013. Daggers in the West: Early Bronze Age daggers and knives in the south-west peninsula. *Proceedings of the Prehistoric Society* 79, 165–191.

Kirwan, R. 1872. Notes on the pre-historic archaeology of east Devon. *Archaeological Journal* 29, 151–165.

Lisowski, F. P. 1963. Appendix I: The Edmondsham cremation. In E. Proudfoot, Report on the excavation of a bell barrow in the parish of Edmondsham, Dorset, England, 1959. *Proceedings of the Prehistoric Society* 29, 417–418.

Nowakowski, J. A. & Johns, C. 2015. *Bypassing Indian Queens. Archaeological excavations 1992–1994. Investigating prehistoric and Romano-British settlement and landscapes in Cornwall.* Truro: Cornwall Archaeological Unit, Cornwall Council & The Highways Agency.

Pearce, S. 1983. *The Bronze Age Metalwork of South Western Britain.* Oxford: British Archaeological Report 120.

Piggott, S. 1938. The Early Bronze Age in Wessex. *Proceedings of the Prehistoric Society* 4, 52–106.

Powers, R. 1969. Report on the cremated bones from a barrow at Stevenstone Farm, Upton Pyne, Devon (No. 7, fig. 1), excavated in 1869, 76. In S. H. M. Pollard & P. M. G. Russell, Excavation of round barrow 248b, Upton Pyne, Exeter. *Proceedings of the Devon Archaeological Exploration Society* 27, 49–76.

Proudfoot, E. 1963. Report on the excavation of a bell barrow in the parish of Edmondsham, Dorset, England, 1959. *Proceedings of the Prehistoric Society* 29, 395–425.

Thomas, N. 2005. *Snail Down, Wiltshire. The Bronze Age barrow cemetery and related earthworks, in the parishes of Collingbourne Ducis and Collingbourne Kingston. Excavations 1953, 1955 and 1957.* Devizes: Wiltshire Archaeological and Natural History Society Monograph 3.

Woodward, A., Hunter, J., Needham, S. P. & Bray, P. 2015. Daggers and knives. In A. Woodward & J. Hunter, *Ritual in Early Bronze Age Grave Goods. An Examination of Ritual and Dress Equipment from Chalcolithic and Early Bronze Age Graves in Britain.* Oxford: Oxbow Books, 175–181.

13. The basketry container

Caroline Cartwright, Maggie Cooper, Sherry Doyal, Dinah Eastop, Linda Lemieux and Ruth Stungo

The basketry container from the Whitehorse Hill cist is a unique item in a British Bronze Age context. It consists of two stitched or coiled circular discs joined by a longer coiled basketry 'tube', with coarse hair stitching around the edges. As the basket had been flattened and distorted in the cist burial, its exact shape and full dimensions were not clear (Fig. 13.1). The object in its current state measures approximately 197 × 235 × 275mm and has a weight of 28g (Chapter 3).

The basket fibres were examined under a scanning electron microscope (Appendix B) and a piece of the hair stitching was also analysed. The following sections of this chapter include summaries of the results from the microscope and proteomics analysis (below) and present macro study of the bag by a group of expert basket makers, which was undertaken ahead of the production of a reconstruction basket. The chapter also includes unpublished research undertaken by Sherry Doyal.

Dimensions and shape

The basket had become crushed and a fragment had become detached from it (Fig. 13.2). It was too fragile to be eased out to shape and the form is therefore a matter of conjecture (Fig. 13.3). However, there is a general consensus that the basket sat on a circular bottom about 160mm in diameter. The body of the basket rises from this to a mouth that was either circular or oval and it is agreed that this was smaller than the base, which may be evidence a tapering bodied basket.

The body of the basket ends in a tapering of the coil to produce an even lip at the mouth of the basket. Because the basket is crushed the dimension of the rise is an estimate. The estimated measurements are 120–200mm at the base, 90–100mm at mid-point and 140mm at the mouth stretched out of shape. The lid was estimated at 75–80 × 110mm.

Multiple interpretations of the evidence are possible and the initial suggestions considered were:

Figure 13.1: The main section of the basket after lifting from the block. (Photograph: M. Wachnik.)

Figure 13.2: Photograph of the detached fragment of the basket. (Photograph: M. Wachnik.)

- A straight-sided 'duffel'; unlikely, as measurement of the basket varies and the lid was certainly smaller than the base.
- A self-supporting round bottom rising to an oval mouth.
- A softer 'dilly bag'-like pouch which, if slung, would result in a D-shaped opening.
- A 'drum' slung on the basket body side. This would allow a cord to pass through the holes on lid and base. The lid would be captive with an opening at the top. The suggestion of a tapered body makes this less likely.

The basket has a flat (or flattened?) lid or cover. It was suggested that the lid might have an overlap but it is thought that it was not big enough to support this. The lid is evidently carefully shaped with tapering coils and can be described as oval or D-shaped. There is a central hole. It is uncertain if this is a circular start or a hole left by loss of a knob, for example. The lid stitches are slightly finer and have more detail than those of the body of the basket and it is possible that a second, equally accomplished hand was involved. The base may be coarser because it needed to be stronger to give more support. The lid is, in part, sewn to the body of the basket.

Materials

Analysis of the plant fibres revealed that the basketry end panels and the coiled 'tube' which connected them are made up of lime / linden (*Tilia* sp.) bast fibres. Lime bast fibres were also used for the ties or stitching which hold the coils together (Appendix B, below). Lime would have been present in the wide, lower river valleys around Dartmoor but not on the higher parts of the moor itself (Chapter 21).

In a collaborative study of Swiss lake dwelling textiles (Higgitt *et al.* 2011), Harris described some experimental work she has undertaken which may be relevant to the Whitehorse Hill cist, in which both outer and inner bark was removed from the lime tree by cutting across the bark and pulling it away from the sapwood (Appendix B, Fig. B.9). Further processing by water retting for a period of six weeks was then required in order to separate the inner bark (bast fibres) from the outer bark (Harris 2007).

The hair used for the stitching (Fig. 13.4) which secures together the lime bast coiled panels which make up the basket (identified by Sherry Doyal) has been identified by proteomic analysis as being derived from cattle (Appendix C).

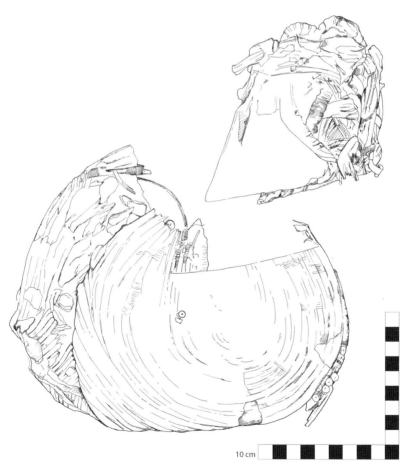

10 cm

Figure 13.3: Schematic illustration of the basket, upper view. (Drawing: M. Wachnik.)

Figure 13.4: Photograph of the stitching holding the sections together. (Photograph: M. Wachnik.)

Technique

The maker of the basketry container was very accomplished: the shaping is careful and the work very regular. The basket is bundle coiled. This is a sewn and not a woven technique, as had initially been thought. In bundle coiling a passive core of material is spiralled and held in place one lift upon another with an active sewn element.

The stitches are plain (overcast) and cover the core. A bundle core is about 6mm per lift. There are 4–6 stitches per 5mm. The sewing elements are finely graded and used flat. Stitches are carefully placed between the stitches of the preceding coil and split the core in places. At the base there were 10 stitches per centimetre.

There are two rows of decorative use of the cattle hair as the active element at the lip of the basket. The dark cattle hair and lime bast alternate as the active element and part of the passive core so that a checker pattern was obtained.

The bundle is a flat band rather than a tube of material, which was carefully graded and tight, and had not been plied. There was the possibility of a slight twist on the core (as if away from the body, coiling clockwise by a right-handed maker; however, some right-handed basket makers do coil anti-clockwise). It is also worth noting

that lime is usually spun with counter-clockwise z-twist (Reichert 2007).

Tools

Tools would have been used to make the basket because of the fine quality of the stitching, which would have required either a needle or an awl. Bone and antler tools are possibilities but these do not survive well in the archaeological record (Gill Campbell, pers comm.).

A bird-bone awl could have been used; as this punctures but also provides a channel to thread through, not unlike a sail-maker's fid; they have been used in lip work such as bee skeps. There may also have been use of a bone or horn ring to size the coil.

A copper-alloy awl could have been used and a pin was found within the folds of the pelt (Chapter 12). However, this could not be directly linked with the making of the basket.

Conclusion

The basket from the Whitehorse Hill cist is a finely made object which was the work of a highly skilled craftsperson.

It represents an unparalleled find in the context of the British Bronze Age. Indeed, lime bast objects are rare and comparanda for them in the British archaeological record are discussed below (Chapter 21). Myking *et al.* (2005) have documented the use until relatively recently of lime bast fibres in Norway for bags and fishing nets (among other purposes), as they are resistant to decay and display minimal water absorption.

Note

Much of the information in this chapter is based on unpublished research on basketry undertaken by Sherry Doyle for Plymouth Museum.

References

Harris, S. 2007. Cloth in prehistoric societies: the social context of cloth in prehistory, with case studies from northern Italy and the Alpine region from the Neolithic to Bronze Age. Unpublished PhD thesis: Institute of Archaeology, University College London.

Higgitt, C., Harris, S., Cartwright, C. R. & Cruickshank, P. 2011. Assessing the potential of historic archaeological collections: a pilot study of the British Museum's Swiss lake dwelling textiles. *British Museum Technical Research Bulletin* 5, 81–94.

Myking, T., Hertzberg, A. & Skrøppa, T. 2005. History, manufacture and properties of lime bast cordage in northern Europe. *Forestry* 78, 65–71.

Reichert, A. 2007. *Bast, Rushes, Stinging Nettles. Textile Materials from the Stone Age. Archaeological Reconstructions by Anne Reichert.* Dithmarschen: Museum für Archäologie und Ökologie Dithmarschen.

14. The composite braided hair armband or bracelet

Alison Sheridan (JAS), Esther Cameron (EC), Caroline Cartwright (CC), Mary Davis (MD), Joanna Dunster (JD), Susanna Harris (SH), Linda Hurcombe (LH), Jamie Inglis (JI), Quita Mould (QM), Caroline Solazzo (CS) and Helen Williams (HW)

The incomplete (but probably nearly complete) remains of a braided band made of hair adorned with metal studs were initially spotted by HW during preliminary inspection of the cist's contents. A fragment around 185mm long, curved back on itself and forming an uneven and truncated oval shape around 80mm long – echoing the band's original shape – was found lying in the exposed interior of the basketry container (Chapter 13), close to its base and on the side facing towards the bottom of the cist (Fig. 14.1.). The contents of the container had been thus exposed due to its having split open after deposition due to crushing pressure from above. Specks of detached corroded metal from the studs were distributed in the vicinity, where the container and other items had been in direct contact with the band. Further details of the structure of the band were revealed, prior to its excavation and conservation, through X-raying. This was initially undertaken at Salisbury District Hospital, but more detailed images (including some in colour) were achieved through the subsequent use of the high-resolution imaging system linked to the X-ray equipment at National Museum Cardiff; that imaging was undertaken by MD (Figs. 14.2. and 14.3.). This revealed that the close-set metal studs are of dumb-bell form, with rounded-conical, roughly flat-based heads joined by a narrow waist (Fig. 14.3. top). It also revealed details of the oval, bobble-like terminal that survived at one end of the band, and suggested that at the heart of this terminal there had been an oval organic item rather like a sunflower seed or a small seed pod of the honesty (*lunaria*) plant (Fig. 14.3, bottom). This will be returned to below.

The second end of the band was not present and may have decomposed completely; at any rate, the frayed end that survives shows no obvious signs of having been cut, and so the deliberate truncation of the object can arguably be ruled out. It may be that the band was never much longer than about 185mm (as measured from the colour X-ray, Fig. 14.2. bottom); it is assumed that it would have had a looped end, which would have articulated with the oval terminal at the other end. Indeed, since the band appears to narrow at its truncated end (Fig. 14.2. bottom) – forming a natural point of weakness – it seems likely that this marks the point at which the terminal loop would have begun. A loop just 20mm long would have sufficed to articulate with the bobble-terminal, making the overall estimated length of the band approximately 205mm. It may well be that the band broke when the lidded container split open, and its narrow and delicate looped end then decomposed, or else frayed and disintegrated into short fragments of fibres.

The band now survives as one long section of paired, braided strands (identified as hairs – see below), around 153mm long, plus a shorter stretch around 12mm long that became detached at a weak point during the conservation process, along with a stud that came away at that break point, and some loose hair and stud fragments (Fig. 14.4). Eleven paired strands had been used, either comprising eleven individual hairs that had been doubled back on themselves (as seems to be suggested by the detailed photograph of the 'bobble' terminal: Fig. 14.4, 4) or else comprising 22 individual hairs that had been knotted together at one or both ends. Either way, long individual

Figure 14.1: Photographs of the braided band in situ, showing its position with respect to the split-open lime-bast container; the detail in the bottom view, showing a line of oxidized tin from the studs, demonstrates its proximity to the binding linking the base to the body of the container. (Photographs: Helen Williams, Wiltshire Conservation Centre.)

hairs had been used: these were either *circa* 205+mm long or, if doubled over, about 410+mm long (assuming that the length had not been topped up by splicing in additional hairs). Each hair is just over 0.3mm thick. At its narrowest the band is only 3mm wide, but it broadens to 4.5mm where it encloses the studs, and to 5.3mm at the oval 'bobble' terminal; that terminal is 8.8mm long (Fig. 14.4, 4).

The remains of 35 studs can be seen as red and yellow-fringed green areas in the colour X-ray (Fig. 14.2, bottom), although in three cases only the holes for the studs survive and in several more cases only a small part of the stud is present. Many of the studs are heavily corroded and have lost much of their surface. The best-preserved examples reveal that they had been around 4.1mm long, around 3mm at their broadest point, and around 2.2mm at the narrowest point of their waist. Due to corrosion it is hard to be certain

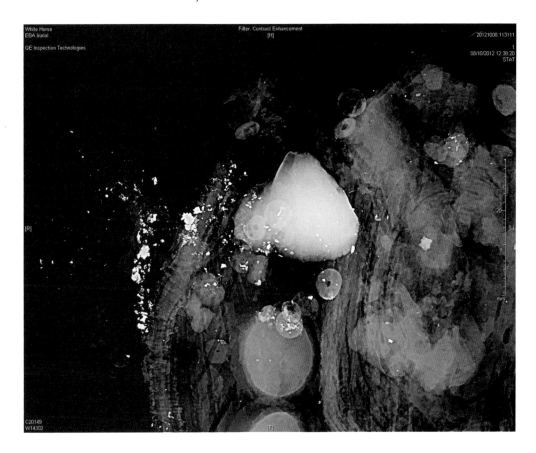

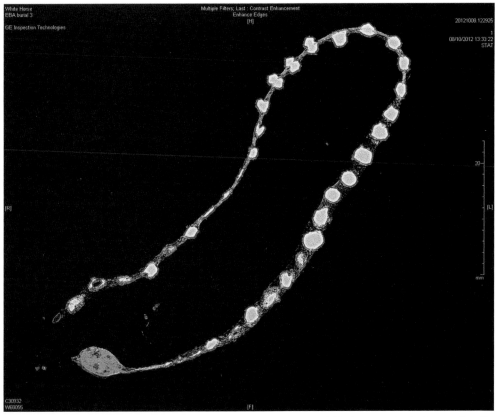

Figure 14.2: X-ray images taken by Mary Davis at National Museum Cardiff, showing (top) the armband's position with respect to the container and to some of its other contents (note that the armband appears as a linear spread and scatter of white matter); and (bottom) the complete armlet, with the tin studs showing as red-fringed yellow areas. The structure of the 'bobble' terminal is also visible.

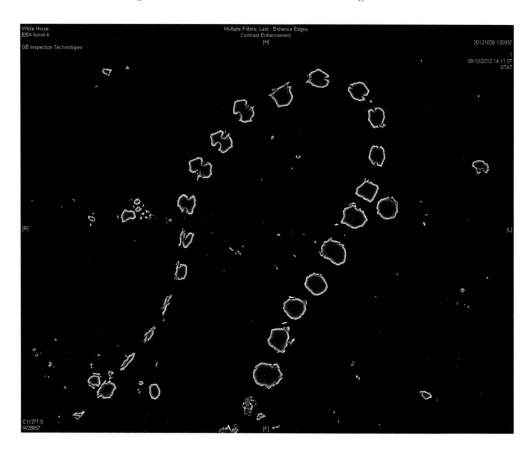

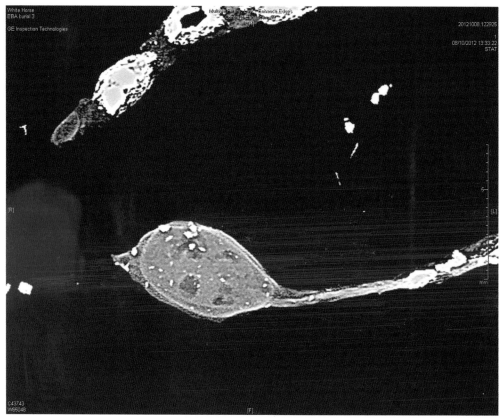

Figure 14.3: X-ray images taken by Mary Davis at National Museum Cardiff, showing (top) the pointed dumb-bell shape of the tin studs, as revealed by the relatively well-preserved studs lying on their side, top left; and (bottom) an apparent inner structure within the 'bobble' terminal, reminiscent of a lunaria (honesty) seed pod. Note its oval outline and four dark spots within the oval area.

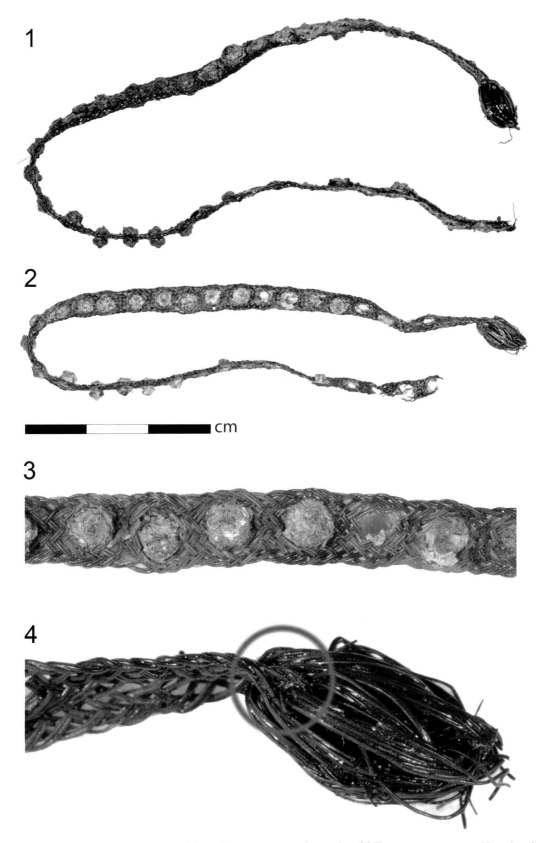

Figure 14.4: 1. The armband as initially lifted from the container. 2. The armband following conservation. Note that the detached fragment is not in its original position. 3. Detail showing the close spacing of the tin studs. 4. Detail of the 'bobble' terminal. The circled area appears to show the articulation between the main body of the band and the terminal, with hairs in the terminal threaded through a looped end of a strand from the band. (Photographs: Helen Williams, Wiltshire Conservation Centre.)

whether both ends of each stud were of rounded-conical shape or whether the end closest to the skin had been a rounder, domed shape; the detailed X-ray (Fig. 14.3, top) would allow either interpretation. The studs had been set evenly and closely along the band, starting approximately 9mm from the 'bobble' terminal, with distances between the centre of adjacent studs ranging between 4mm and 5.5mm (Fig. 14.4, 4).

Raw material identification

Compositional analysis of the metal studs by JD, using portable X-ray fluorescence spectrometry (pXRF), confirmed that they are indeed, as initially suspected, of metallic tin, partly oxidised to tin oxide (Appendix A). When new, the studs would have been a silvery colour; this has oxidised to a whitish and grey colour. They would also doubtless have been burnished to a high sheen, no trace of which now survives due to the corrosion. It was decided not to attempt sourcing of the tin through isotopic analysis (*cf* Haustein *et al.* 2010), not least because the currently available reference material for south-west England does not yet contain enough samples across Cornwall and Devon to characterize the overall variability, although there may be scope for undertaking such analysis in the future.

Identification of the strands was initially undertaken macro- and microscopically by QM, SH and EC. They were able to confirm that they are unspun and suggested further analysis. Two tiny samples were then removed for identification by CC, using a scanning electron microscope (SEM) (Fig. 14.5), and a fibre attached to the aforementioned loose tin stud was examined microscopically by EC (Appendix B). The fibre was identified as animal hair, and the possibility that the hairs could be guard hairs (that is to say, from the outer part of a pelt or hide) was suggested. Even at high magnification (×400), however, the surface of the hair appeared very smooth, with no obvious cuticular scales visible, and thus lacked sufficient features to allow positive identification of the species of animal.

Subsequent analysis of the protein within the hair, undertaken by CS using Zooms proteomics analysis, was able to identify the genus as *Bos*, as this is the only genus that shares the unique peptide peaks that were present in the specimen. (Appendix C.) Hair of the same genus had also been used to join the base of the basketry container to its body, and to adorn the top of the container. Within that genus, yak can safely be discounted as a candidate; but since there is no known keratin sequence for aurochs, the use of auroch (*Bos primigenius*) hair, rather than domestic cattle (*Bos taurus*) hair, cannot be ruled out. As regards the part of the body from which the hair had come, given the hair lengths cited above (either around 205+mm or approximately 410+mm), the tail would appear to be the only plausible candidate. An alternative may be use of hair from the hide of a Highland cow or bull, since this can exceed 330mm in length and would more than suffice

for the shorter of those two lengths. The springiness and pliability of the ancient hair may provide further clues as to species and breed: in undertaking the experimental replication, LH found that the tail hair of a modern Belted Galloway was springier and harder to keep under control than the ancient hair would have been; for that reason, one of the replicas was made using horse hair, which was easier to work. Further experimentation, using hair from the more archaic Chillingham breed of cattle, from Highland cattle and from aurochs, might shed more light on which species or breed is the most likely candidate, in terms of these working properties.

As regards the colour of the hair, while the present mid- to dark-brown colour has no doubt been affected by lengthy contact with peaty water and with the other contents of the cist, and might also have been affected by the process of cleaning and conservation, there is no obvious evidence for the deliberate or dramatic transformation of its original colour through the use of a dye. Cattle tail hair colour can vary from whitish (in the case of albino cattle) to grey, auburn, mid-brown, dark brown and black. While we cannot determine the exact original shade, it is likely that the selection process would not only have focused on obtaining hairs of the desired length, but also on choosing hairs of a particular colour, in order to complement or contrast with the silver of the tin studs, and even perhaps to echo the colour of other elements of the deceased's jewellery. The possibility that the cattle hair and its colour had a symbolic significance, or had been attributed a specific amuletic property, cannot be ruled out. (See Hurcombe (2014) for a discussion of reasons for organic raw material choices in prehistory.)

As for the 'bobble' terminal, while the X-ray suggested that hairs had been wrapped around an oval organic item, and while the initial description of this item by QM, SH and EC as a 'concretion' suggested that it had been a solid object, nevertheless no trace of a seed, nut or other object was found upon microscopic examination or during cleaning and conservation by HW. Furthermore, the application of pXRF analysis (by JD) confirmed that the centre of the terminal had not been metallic. The terminal was not, however, examined using SEM and the possibility must remain that the initial detailed X-ray (Fig. 14.3, bottom) had indeed revealed the presence of ephemeral traces of an oval seed or similar thin, delicate organic item, which subsequently disintegrated. On this hypothetical item the X-ray image appears to show traces of up to four small circular attachments – hence the comparison above with a *lunaria* seed pod. The function and construction of the 'bobble' terminal are discussed further below.

Manufacture

The experimental replication of the band by JI (who made the studs) and LH (who braided the band and inserted the studs) revealed invaluable information about the process of

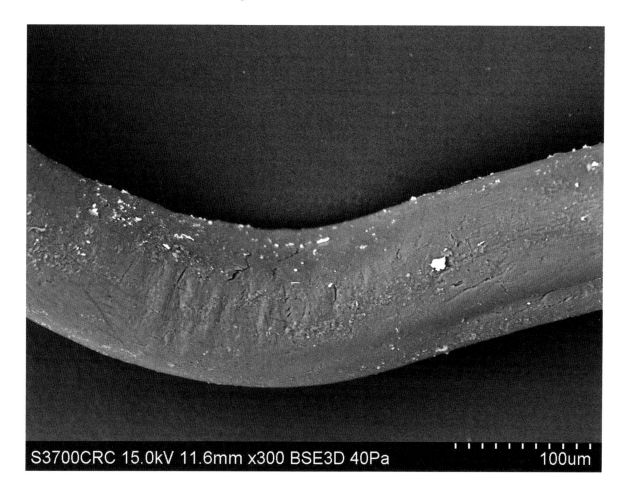

S3700CRC 15.0kV 11.6mm x300 BSE3D 40Pa   100um

S3700CRC 12.0kV 11.2mm x800 BSE3D 40Pa   50.0um

Figure 14.5: High-magnification VP-SEM images of individual hairs from the armband. (Images: Caroline Cartwright, British Museum.)

Figure 14.6: Replica tin studs made by Jamie Inglis. (Photograph: Jamie Inglis.)

Figure 14.7: Detailed view of the armband showing the structure of the braiding. (Photograph: M. Wachnik.)

manufacture and the considerable skill of the person – or probably rather people – who made it.

The tin studs will have been made by first hammering a piece of metallic tin into a swage block to create a rod, circular in cross-section, around 3mm in diameter. Thereafter, various methods could have been used to shape the conical ends and narrow waist; the softness of tin will have made it relatively easy to file, chisel and/or hammer the metal into the desired shape. JI experimented with two techniques, namely riveting and filing. With the first, 4mm long lengths of the tin rod were cut, chiselling the mid-point of each (using a bronze chisel) to start creating the constricted waist. The rod was then fitted into a riveting support made from hinged metal strips, and placed one end into a dome-shaped hollow and the other into a doming punch. Hitting the doming punch then created both domed ends, and a release mechanism built onto the riveting support allowed the stud to be freed. Minimal filing with a bronze file and burnishing to a high sheen then finished the process. The other method involved filing one end of a rod into a cone shape, cutting a waist, then cutting the stud free from the rod and setting the conical end into a pin vice made from a stick with its end hollowed, before filing the other end into a conical shape. (The use of beeswax in the hollow would have provided greater stability.) To finish, the stud was polished and burnished to a high sheen, using a bronze burnishing tool (which was the smooth side of the aforementioned file) and burnishing leather coated with jewellers' rouge (iron oxide mixed with fat). JI concluded that while the 'riveting' method was the quickest

and most reliable of the two methods, it appeared unduly complex, due to the support and release mechanism, and so the simpler 'filing' technique was used to create the studs used in the reconstructions (Fig. 14.6). Making 35 studs in this way took around 10 hours, starting with a ready-made tin ingot.

As for the braiding of the band (Fig. 14.7), initial examination by SH concluded that this had been carried out using an oblique 2/2 twill interlacing technique, to use the fabric structure terminology defined by Emery (1966, 63–64). In this technique, holding one end under tension, one paired strand from one side is interlaced diagonally across the other strands in a two-over, two-under formation (Seiler-Baldinger 1994, 38–39). This method would produce neat edges that appear slightly different on either side, due to the configuration produced by the braiding method.

In undertaking the experimental replication of the band, LH had to consider the following key questions:

- At which end of the band would the process of braiding have begun? (This relates to the need to anchor the strands so as to maintain an even tension throughout the process.)
- Had the pairing of the hairs in each of the 11 strands been effected by doubling over 11 long hairs, or by using 22 hairs? And if the latter, how were they secured together into pairs? Had any additional hairs been braided in if any individual hair had been found to be too short?

- How had the 'bobble' terminal been created, and how does it articulate with the rest of the object? Was it made as an integral part of the braiding, or was it added to the band? How was the springy hair in the band effectively secured into the 'bobble' terminal so that the whole braid could not come apart during use?
- Similarly, how were the ends of the springy hairs prevented from coming loose at the presumed looped end?
- How were the studs inserted into the band?

After careful consideration of these questions, and through a process of experimentation, LH decided that if the 'bobble' terminal had been integral to the rest of the band (for example, by looping the hairs around an oval former to create the 'bobble' and then starting the braiding), the band could not have been started at this end, as it would not have provided the requisite tension. Instead, the braiding was started at the hypothetical loop end, which did permit the requisite anchoring; a macramé board was used to maintain the tension and to manipulate the strands (Fig. 14.8). Having experimented with using long individual hairs that were doubled back on themselves to form the strand-pairs, and finding that this was both fiddly and ran the risk of requiring additional hair insertion to achieve the desired length of band, LH proceeded with paired individual hairs, knotted at the loop end. This, too, was fiddly, and indeed the process of securing both ends of the band proved to be the hardest part of the process. As noted above, it may be that the original maker had indeed used very long hairs doubled back on themselves. Regarding the question of whether any additional hairs had been spliced in to the original band, there had been no indication that this had been the case (except, perhaps, for a single stray hair end seen projecting from the band where it curved around: Fig. 14.4, 1).

As for the 'bobble' terminal, LH proceeded on the assumption that it had been created using the loose ends of the braided band, and worked these ends – with considerable difficulty – into a bobble shape through much fiddly looping, feeding in and knotting. However, another possibility is that the 'bobble' was made by taking additional strands of hair and looping these through the looped ends of doubled-over band hairs (as the detailed photograph, Fig. 14.4, 4, suggests might have been the case), and then working the loose ends of those new strands in on themselves, perhaps with some internal knotting and with considerable deftness. If this had been the case, then it would have been possible to start the band at this end, with the 'bobble' strands serving to anchor the looped ends of the braids at tension. Whichever had been the technique used, LH concluded that it would have helped the original maker to have had some kind of 'core' substance within the 'bobble', to facilitate the anchoring of the ends, to help bulk out the 'bobble' and – if the terminal had been made using the loose ends of the band – to prevent the band from unravelling. As for preventing unravelling at the loop end, as noted above this was achieved through knotting the band around itself.

Inserting the studs proved to be a further challenge. After trying to braid around studs that had been placed at the mid-width of the band – an experiment that met with only partial success – it was discovered that the most effective method was to braid around a cocktail stick, to make a small hole, and having created three such holes, to 'pop' the studs in. There was sufficient 'give' in the braiding to allow the holes to be teased open far enough for the studs to be inserted; and the dumb-bell shape of the studs ensured that, once they had been inserted and the braid re-tightened, they would not then slip out. While it would have helped to have two pairs of hands to carry out this process, LH concluded that a sufficiently experienced braider – as had evidently been the case with the maker of the Whitehorse Hill band – could have achieved this on her or his own.

The final result (Fig. 14.9), which bore more than a passing resemblance to the original, was a very fine, lightweight, semi-rigid band with shiny studs that catch the light. When worn by a young female model, the object fitted her upper arm snugly (Fig. 14.10, top). The band could, however, have been worn more loosely, around the wrist, as a bracelet (Fig. 14.10, bottom).

Discussion

Clearly, this piece of jewellery had been made with considerable expertise and using a material (tin) that would have been precious and much sought-after at the time. As such, it fits the broader picture portrayed by the other artefacts in the cist, as being a special object for a special person. While the extreme rarity of preserved organic objects in Bronze Age Britain makes it impossible to determine whether braided hair jewellery was commonly used at the time, and while tin objects are doubtless under-represented in the archaeological record due to the propensity for tin to oxidise, nevertheless this sophisticated object gives the impression of having been a rare, high-status possession that would have marked out its wearer as belonging to a privileged minority in Early Bronze Age society. The significance of the use of tin is discussed briefly below and in more detail in Chapter 15.

This object is unique, for while the use of jewellery for the wrist is not unknown in Early Bronze Age contexts in Britain, the choice of raw materials certainly is. Furthermore, there is no proof that any of the known Early Bronze Age bracelets or bangles had been worn as armbands on the upper arm, as the Whitehorse Hill band may have been. There is a much later tradition of wearing upper arm jewellery, known from Iron Age Britain and Ireland. In addition to the massive copper-alloy armlets of northern Britain (Hunter 2006), two organic armbands are known, found around the upper arms of adult males of presumed high status whose remains have been discovered as bog

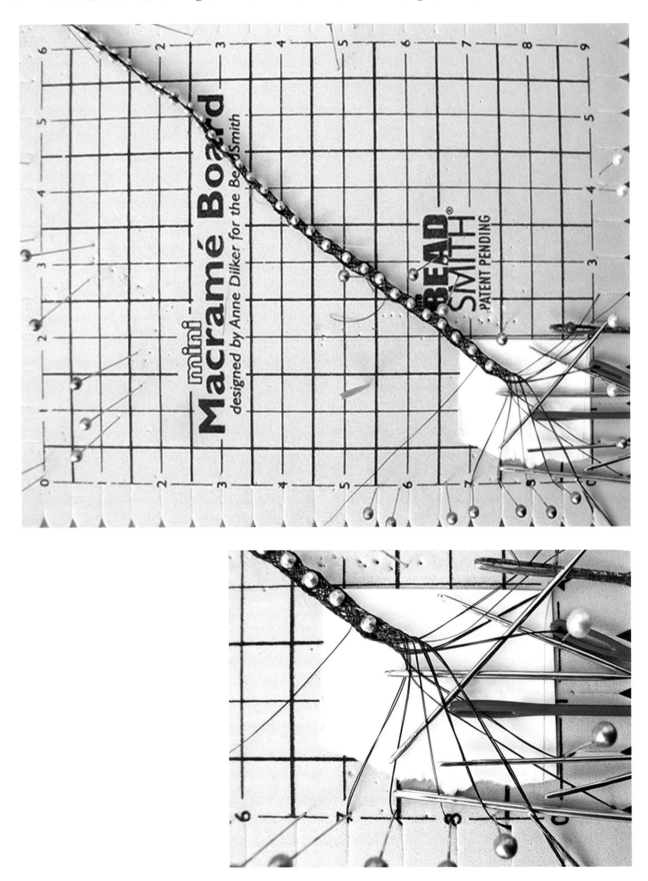

Figure 14.8: Experimental replication of the armband by Linda Hurcombe, using a macramé board to hold the band in tension. Detail shows the individual paired-hair strands during the process of braiding. (Photographs: Linda Hurcombe; detail of Andrew Brown/De Facto Films.)

Figure 14.9: The replica armband, showing how shiny the studs were when new (Photograph: Linda Hurcombe.)

bodies. One, from Old Croghan, County Offaly, Ireland, had been made by interlacing two slit strips of treated animal hide, and ornamenting it with sheet tinned bronze clasp-mounts bearing repoussé circles; the associated body has been dated to the Iron Age (O'Toole 2013, no. 16). The other appears to be a simple band of fox fur, found on 'Lindow Man', Cheshire; this body has been radiocarbon-dated to 60 cal BC–cal AD 130 (Stead *et al.* 1986; weighted mean 1965+46 BP; T'= 6.5; T'(5%)= 6.0; v= 2; calculated from OxA-531; 1920+75 BP; OxA-604; 1850+75 BP and OxA-605; 2125+80 BP). Neither of these offers a close parallel to the Whitehorse Hill cist band, however.

The jewellery for the wrist known from the Early Bronze Age includes bangles of copper alloy and of gold, the former occurring both in sheet metal and as solid bar-bangles, the latter as sheet metal bangles (Needham 2000; Needham *et al.* 2006; Needham and Sheridan 2014). There are also bead bracelets of jet and shale, ranging in form from spacer plate bracelets (Sheridan 1998) to one composed entirely of fusiform beads from Southery Fen, Norfolk (Roberts 1998, 191 and fig. 3) and another made from minuscule disc beads found at Roundway, Wiltshire (Sheridan 2015). However, all or virtually all of these bangles and bracelets will have pre-dated the Whitehorse Hill band and, as noted above, none offers a point of comparison either in its raw material or its technique of manufacture. The only elements of the Whitehorse Hill band that can be paralleled among British jewellery dating to the first half of the second millennium are the shape of the studs and the use of tin.

The gently conical dumb-bell shape of the studs recalls the shape of some ear studs, as discussed in Chapter 16, and also the lower end shape of some 'miniature macehead' pendants, including an example in shale from Stannon Down, Cornwall (Jones 2005). Indeed, the conical or sub-conical form is a recurrent feature of early second millennium ornaments, occurring, for example, on the sheet gold 'button cover' from Hengistbury Head, Dorset (formerly Hampshire), the gold-covered conical ornament from Upton Lovell G2e, Wiltshire, the sheet gold stud covers from the jet macehead from Clandon, Dorset, and the embossed sheet gold cape from Mold, Clwyd (Needham 2012; Needham and Sheridan 2014; Needham and Woodward 2008). In other words, this shape would have been part of the Early Bronze Age 'vocabulary of esteem' and its use would have identified its owner as being an active participant in the elite culture that used that vocabulary. Moreover, when rendered in metal, the conical or domed shape would have served to maximise the visual impact of the ornament, as a convex surface would have reflected incident light more effectively than a flat surface. Therefore, the shape of the studs in the armband was not simply a response to the need to create ornaments that would not slip out of the band: it was a way of maximising the visual and social impact of this piece of jewellery.

As for the use of tin, the few Early Bronze Age *comparanda* are presented in the discussion of the tin bead from the necklace, in Chapter 15. Suffice it to reiterate

Figure 14.10: Replica armband being worn (top) on the upper arm as an armband and (bottom) as a bracelet. (Photographs: (top) Linda Hurcombe; (bottom) Dartmoor National Park Authority.)

here that tin would have been a precious material at the time, and much sought after, principally because it was an essential component of bronze. By the time the occupant of the Whitehorse Hill cist was living, there would have been a well-organized movement of tin – presumably in ingot form – from its production areas in Cornwall (and possibly Devon), not just around Britain and Ireland but further afield, into Continental Europe, almost certainly via Wessex. Control over this flow of tin would have offered a way of enhancing power, wealth and social differentiation, and the use of tin for personal adornment would therefore constitute conspicuous consumption of a valuable resource. Dartmoor may well have been on the route from the production areas to Wessex, and the occupant of the cist – and / or their wider social group – could have played a role in the easterly flow of tin towards Wessex.

There might have been an additional significance to the use of tin in the band. As discussed elsewhere (for example, Haveman and Sheridan 2006), since the production of metallic tin involved a spectacular and mysterious transformation from the raw cassiterite, it may be that the resulting product was attributed special, magical properties. When employed in personal ornaments, it may have been used as an amulet, to protect its wearer, and when used as a grave good, it could have been an element of 'supernatural power dressing', analogous to the use of other special substances such as amber, jet and faience (Sheridan and Shortland 2003). Therefore, its use would not only have signalled the wealth and special status of the deceased, it could also have been intended to protect that individual in the Afterlife. Whether the use of cattle hair in both this object and the container that formerly held the band also had symbolic or amuletic significance is currently an unanswerable question.

References

Emery, I. 1966. *The Primary Structures of Fabrics: an illustrated classification.* Washington DC: Textile Museum.

Haustein, T. L., Gillis, C. & Pernicka, E. 2010. Tin isotopy – a new method for solving old questions. *Archaeometry* 52, 816–832.

Haveman, E. & Sheridan, J. A, 2006. The necklace from Exloo: new light on an old find. *Palaeohistoria* 47/48, 100–139.

Hunter, F. J. 2006. New light on Iron Age massive armlets. *Proceedings of the Society of Antiquaries of Scotland* 136, 135–160.

Hurcombe, L. 2014. *Perishable Material Culture in Prehistory: investigating the missing majority.* London: Routledge.

Jones, A. M., 2005. Settlement and ceremony: archaeological investigations at Stannon Down, St Breward, Cornwall. *Cornish Archaeology* 43–44, 1–141.

Needham, S. P. 2000. The gold and copper metalwork. In G. Hughes, *The Lockington Gold Hoard: an Early Bronze Age barrow cemetery at Lockington, Leicestershire.* Oxford: Oxbow Books, 23–46.

Needham, S. P. 2012. Putting capes into context: Mold at the heart of a domain. In W. Britnell & R. J. Silvester (eds.), *Reflections on the Past: Essays in honour of Frances Lynch.* Welshpool: Cambrian Archaeological Association, 210–236.

Needham, S. P. and Sheridan, J. A. 2014. Chalcolithic and Early Bronze Age goldwork from Britain: new finds and new perspectives. In H. Meller, E. Pernicka and R. Risch (eds.), *Metals of Power: early gold and silver. Proceedings of the 6th Archaeological Congress of Central Germany.* Halle: Landesmuseum für Vorgeschichte Halle, Tagungen des Landesmuseums Band 11, 903–941.

Needham, S. P. & Woodward, A. 2008. The Clandon Barrow finery: a synopsis of success in an Early Bronze Age world. *Proceedings of the Prehistoric Society* 74, 1–52.

Needham, S. P., Parfitt, K. & Varndell, G. (eds.) 2006. *The Ringlemere Cup. Precious Cups and the Beginning of the Channel Bronze Age.* London: British Museum Research Publication 163.

O'Toole, F. 2013. Armlet, Old-Croghan man. In F. O'Toole, *A History of Ireland in 100 Objects.* Dublin: Royal Irish Academy 16.

Roberts, J. 1998. A contextual approach to the interpretation of the Early Bronze Age skeletons of the East Anglian Fens. *Antiquity* 72(275), 188–197.

Seiler-Baldinger, A., 1994. *Textiles: a classification of techniques.* Washington DC: Smithsonian Institute Press.

Sheridan. J. A. 1998. Jet spacer plate necklace and bracelet [from East Kinwhirrie], 34–37. In D. B. Taylor, J. S. Rideout, C. J. Russell-White and T. G. Cowie, Prehistoric burials from Angus: some finds old and new, *Tayside and Fife Archaeological Journal* 4, 31–66.

Sheridan, J. A. 2015. Discussion of disc bead and spacer plate necklaces of jet and jet-like materials. In A. Woodward & J. Hunter, *Ritual in Early Bronze Age Grave Goods. An Examination of Ritual and Dress Equipment from Chalcolithic and Early Bronze Age Graves in Britain.* Oxford: Oxbow Books, 341–362.

Sheridan, J. A. & Shortland, A. 2003. Supernatural power dressing. *British Archaeology* 70, 18–23.

Stead, I. M., Bourke, J. & Brothwell, D. 1986. *Lindow Man: the body in the bog.* Ithaca: Cornell University Press.

15. The composite necklace

Alison Sheridan (JAS)
with contributions by Mary Davis (MD), Joanna Dunster (JD),
Jamie Inglis (JI), Henrietta Quinnell (HQ), Hal Redvers-Jones (HR-J),
Roger Taylor (RT), Lore Troalen (LT), Kate Verkooijen (KV)
and Helen Williams (HW)

The discovery of a small shale disc bead among the peaty contents of the cist in August 2011 was the first indication of the presence of a composite necklace. It was eventually found to comprise one fusiform bead of tin, the crushed and fragmented remains of a second tin bead, seven amber beads, 92 disc beads of Kimmeridge shale and at least 109 disc beads of fired clay, possibly a few more (as discussed below). Following the block-lifting of the cist's contents, and prior to their full micro-excavation by HW in the Wiltshire Conservation Laboratory, an initial indication of the nature and distribution of some of these beads was provided by the high-resolution X-raying undertaken by MD at National Museum Cardiff (Fig. 15.1). This revealed clusters of the shale disc beads, along with some of the clay disc beads and the ghostly outline of an amber bead (Fig. 15.1, 1). It also showed the scattered traces of the disintegrating, oxidised tin bead within one of these clusters, located at the end of the lime-bast basketry container furthest from its base (Fig. 15.1, 2); and it revealed, with particular clarity, the fusiform shape of the better-preserved tin bead, found in the area of the container's base (Fig. 15.1, 3). The X-rays, together with HW's subsequent micro-excavation and detailed mapping of the beads in the laboratory, revealed that the beads were mostly clustered in two areas of the underside of the container (Figs. 15.2, 15.3 and 15.5, 2 and Table 15.1). One of these clusters (HW's 'Groups A–D' on Fig. 15.3, together with 'Group F', shown in Fig. 15.4 and found after the removal of 'Groups A–D') was located around what would have been the bottom of the container before it collapsed and split; this cluster of beads was close to

the braided armband or bracelet (Chapter 14), the wooden studs (Chapter 16) and the flint object (Chapter 17; and see Fig. 15.3). The other cluster, including the crushed tin bead (HW's 'Group E': Fig. 15.3), was at the other end of the flattened container. (Other beads, whose precise location with respect to Groups A–D and F could not be determined although they had been found in the same general area, were given an arbitrary label as 'Group G'.) The beads' distribution indicated that the necklace had originally been inside the container, at its bottom. The separation of the two bead clusters will have taken place when the container became crushed and split; indeed, the direction in which the beads had been moved, and the distance between the clusters, may be an indication that the container had toppled over before being virtually flattened.

The presence of several 'runs' of abutting beads (Fig. 15.5) makes it clear that the beads had indeed been strung as a necklace when they were deposited. Their spatial patterning offered some clues to the necklace's overall shape and bead arrangement, despite the disruption caused by the crushing of the container and the probability that the necklace had lain in a heap within the container rather than as a rigid hoop. The fact that one amber bead (F11) was found abutting the fusiform tin bead (F26: Fig. 15.2, 2), with two other amber beads (F18 and F33) found nearby (Fig. 15.4, 2), suggested that these contrasting-colour beads may have been neighbours and, despite the fact that not all of the tin and amber beads were found grouped together, there is a strong likelihood that they had lain at the front of the necklace to maximize the visual impact of these especially precious beads (which would

Table 15.1: The beads in the composite necklace, by spatial groupings and material. Dimensions (in mm, to nearest 0.1mm) are maxima. Not all beads were measured but the unmeasured examples fall within the size range of the measured beads. See Figures 15.3 and 15.4 for the location of Groups A–F; 'Group' G comprises beads found in the same general area as those of Groups A–D and F, the precise location of which could not be mapped.

Group & no	Tin	Amber	Shale	Clay	Diameter or length (mm)	Thickness (mm)	Hole diameter (mm)
Group A							
1				•	5.7	2.8	1.1
2				•	5.5	2.5	1.3
3				•	5.8	2.8	1.2
4				•	5.7	2.9	1.6
5				•[1]			
Group B							
1			•		7.0	1.3	2.3
2			•		7.0	1.4	2.0
3			•		6.9	1.8	2.2
4			•		6.8	1.4	2.2
5			•		7.2	2.0	2.6
6			•		7.1	2.7	2.3
7				•	5.6	2.6	1.3
8			•		6.7	1.8	2.0
9			•		6.6	1.5	2.3
10			•		6.5	1.4	2.4
11			•		6.7	2.4	1.8
Group C							
1				•	5.6	2.5	1.2
2				•	5.5	2.5	1.2
3				•	6.1	2.6	1.1
4				•	5.3	2.6	1.1
5				•	5.5	2.7	1.1
6				•	5.5	2.7	1.2
7				•	5.9	2.9	1.4
8			•		5.4	1.3	2.0
Group D							
1		•			7.3	6.9	1.4
2			•		6.1	0.9	1.3
3				•	5.7	3.2	1.7
4			•		6.2	1.1	1.3
5			•		6.5	1.3	1.4
6				•	6.0	2.4	1.5
7				•	6.2	2.6	2.0
8			•		5.8	2.5	1.2
9				•	5.5	2.5	1.1
10			•				
11			•				
12			•				
13				•	5.5	2.4	1.5
14			•				
Group E							
1				•			
2				•			
3		•			9.2	4.3	2.3
4			•		6.5	[2]	2.4
5			•		6.7	1.6	1.8
6			•		6.9		
7				•	3.8	c 1.4	
8				•	6.2	c 3.1	1.6
9				•			
10				•			
11				•	4.1	1.5	1.2
12				•	c. 3.8		
13				•	c. 4.0		
14				•	c. 3.7		
15			•				
16			•		6.3	1.7	1.5
17			•		6.3	0.9	1.8
18			•		5.4	1.2	1.1
19			•		5.6	1.2	1.3
20				•			
21				•			
22			•				
23			•				
24			•				
25				•[3]	3.9		
26				•			
27			•				
28			•				
29			•				
30			•				
31			•				
32			•		6.6	2.3	2.0
33				•			
34			•				
35				•			
36			•		6.6	2.4	2.1
37			•		6.9		2.0
38			•		7.7	2.5	2.1
39			•		6.6	1.8	2.2
40			•		5.6	2.5	1.7
41			•				
42				•			
43				•			
44				•			
45				•	5.2	2.5	
46			•				
47			•				
48			•				
49				•			
50				•			
51				•			
52				•			
53			•				
54			•				
55		•			4.0	2.3	1.5
56			•				
57			•				
58				•			
59				•			
60				•			
61				•			
62				•			
63				•			
64				•[4]	4.0		
65				•			
66				•	c. 3.4		
67				•			
68				•			
69				•			
70				•			
71				•			
72			•				
73				•[5]			
74							
75				•[6]	3.3		
76	•						
Group F							
1				•			
2				•			
3				•			
4				•			
5		•					
6				•			
7				•			
8				•			

No.					
9		•			
10		•			
11	•		9.7	5.5	2.2
12	•				
13		•			
14		•			
15		•			
16	•				
17		•			
18	•		8.2	c. 6.0	2.2
19		•			
20		•			
21		•	7.1	1.8	1.5
22		•	9.5	0.9	1.2
23		•			
24		•			
25		•	3.9	c. 0.7	
26	•				
27		•			
28		•			
29		•			
30		•	7.1	1.8	1.9
31		•	6.5	2.1	1.6
32		•			
33	•		9.6	6.0	2.2
34		•			
35		•			
36		•			
37		•			
38		•			
39		•			
40		•			
41		•			
42		•			
43		•	5.6		
44		•			
45		•			
46		•			
47		•			
48		•			
49		•			
50		•			
51		•			
52		•	6.9	1.3	1.8
53		•	6.9	1.6	2.3
54		•	6.4	1.7	2.3
55		•			
56		•			
57		•	7.2	2.0	1.8
58		•	6.7	1.9	1.7
59		•	6.5	1.5	2.0
60		•	6.4	1.8	2.3

No.					
61		•			
62		•			
63	•				
64	•				
65		•			
66	•				
67		•			
68		•			
69		•			
70	•		5.1	2.1	2.3
71		•			
72		•			
73		•			
74	•				
75	•				
76	•				
77		•			
78		•			
79	•				
80		•			
81		•[7]			
'Group' G					
1	•		5.9	2.6	1.7
2		•	7.2	1.5	2.3
3		•	6.6	1.5	2.2
4		•	5.7	1.3	2.1
5		•	5.6	2.6	1.4
6		•	5.9	2.8	1.0
7		•	5.3	2.2	1.8
8		•	5.3	2.4	1/2
9		•	6.7	1.5	2.2
10		•	7.0	1.5	2.1
11		•	6.8	1.4	1.2
12		•			
13		•	5.5	2.7	0.9
14		•	5.7	c. 2.5	1.0
Found during excavation					
–		•	6.8	1.7	1.6

[1]Consists of 6 small fragments, probably all from one bead; [2]Where individual measurements are missing, this is because there was not enough time to complete the measuring process during the laboratory visits; [3]Broken into three fragments; [4]There is a further fragment, E64A, that may be from the same bead as E64; [5]E73 and E74 = from set of tiny fragments from at least two beads; [6]Comprises 12 tiny fragments from at least one bead; [7]There is a further fragment, F81A, that may well be from the same bead as F81.

also have been particularly eye-catching due to their colour and sheen). As for the disc beads of shale and fired clay, which make up 96 per cent of the approximately 210 beads in the necklace, their grading in diameter suggests that the smallest examples – tiny clay beads, between 3.3mm and 4mm across – had probably lain at the back of the necklace, with the larger beads towards the front. The smallest beads were almost all found in Group E. One particular shale disc bead is significantly larger than all the other disc beads (Fig. 15.6, 1, left end and Figs. 15.4 and 15.10, no. 22 in Group F) and this suggests that it could have functioned as a fastener for the necklace, even though it was not found close to the smallest disc beads.

As for the original spatial relationship between the blackish shale and the brown clay beads, it is clear from the 'run' of small beads shown in Fig. 15.5 that the two materials were not segregated, with all the clay beads at the back and the shale beads towards the front; instead, it appears that they were interspersed, probably as runs of beads of one material and then of the other. Indeed, the spatial distribution of the beads as found (for example, Fig. 15.4, 2, for Group F) supports this view, although there are also instances where one or two shale beads were found among several clay beads and *vice versa*. Since the diameter ranges of the clay and shale beads overlap, there is scope for the necklace to have had a fairly smooth gradation of

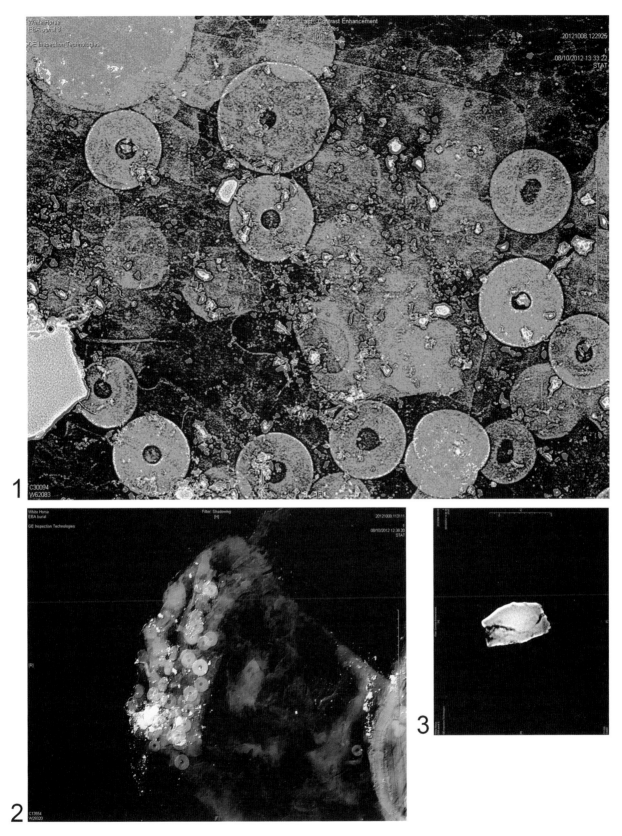

Figure 15.1: X-ray images of beads from the composite necklace: 1. Some of the 'Group F' beads. The shale disc beads (including the relatively large 'fastener' bead, towards the top of the image) appear most clearly. Some fired clay disc beads are also visible as slightly fainter images. The edge of the tin bead F26 is also visible in the bottom left corner and one of the wooden studs appears top left. 2. General view of the 'Group E' beads, showing fragments of the disintegrated tin bead E76 (as the white 'cloud' at the bottom end of the bead cluster, plus scattered white specks). The base of the basketry container is at the bottom right. 3. The tin fusiform bead F26, showing its curving seam. (Images by Mary Davis, National Museum Cardiff.)

Alison Sheridan

Figure 15.2: Close-up view of some of the 'Group F' bead cluster, showing the fusiform tin bead F26 (yellowish, just below centre) adjacent to one of the amber beads (F11: reddish, slightly shiny) and surrounded by disc beads of clay and shale. The large round object on the right side is one of the wooden studs. (Photograph: Dartmoor National Park Authority.)

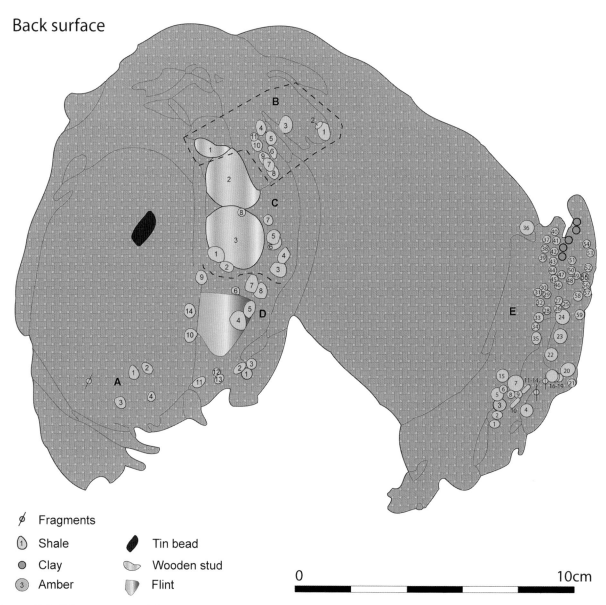

Figure 15.3: Schematic view of the position of some of the necklace beads (Groups A – E) and other finds associated with the basketry container. This view shows the first items that were found when the flattened container was turned over. The position of the fusiform tin bead F26 is shown in black. (Diagram based on information by Helen Williams.

Figure 15.4: 1. Schematic view showing some of the 'Group F' beads, which were found after the Group A–D beads had been excavated. These beads would originally have lain on the base of the container. The grey bead in the centre is the fusiform tin bead F26. (After plan by Helen Williams, Wiltshire Conservation Laboratory, Chippenham.) 2. The 'Group F' beads, as laid out for examination in an 'exploded' version approximating to their respective discovery positions; see Table 15.1 for key to materials. Note: i) amber bead F11 had been adjacent to tin bead F26 when found; ii) the orientation is roughly at 90° to that shown in 15.4, 1; iii) the apparent truncation of some beads (e.g., 49, 52) is due to the fact that they were photographed lying in hollows carved in a foam support. (Photograph: Alison Sheridan.)

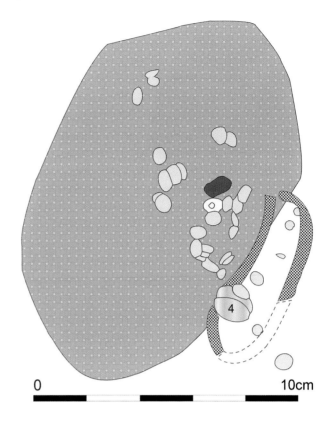

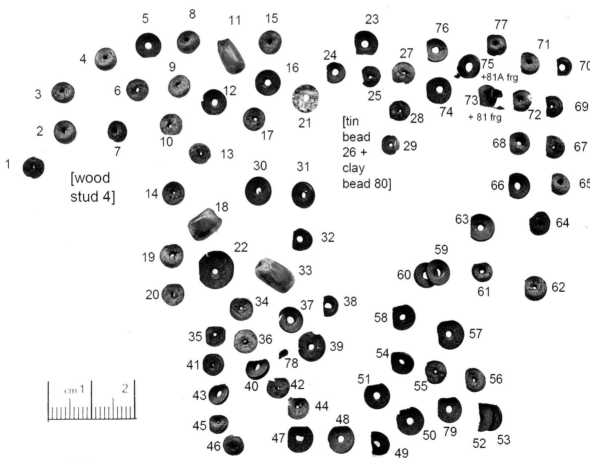

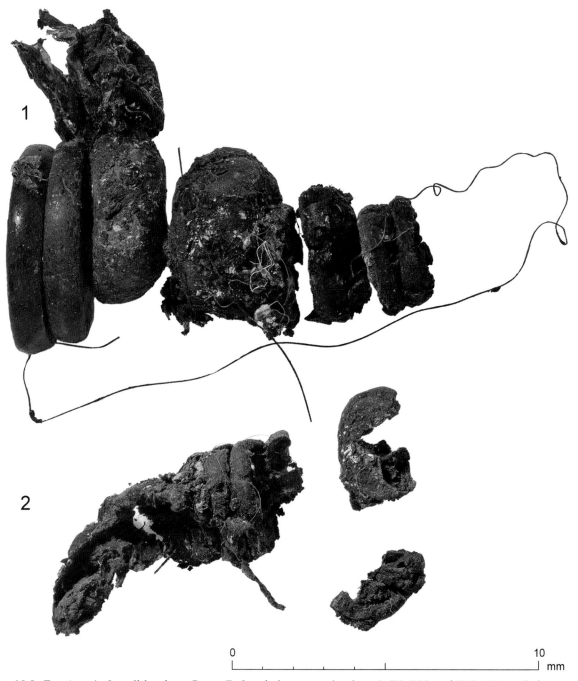

Figure 15.5: Two 'runs' of small beads in Group E, found close to each other: 1. E5–E10 and E60–E63, with fragments of peat still adhering to some beads. Note: i) gradation in diameter; ii) juxtaposition of groups of shale disc beads (i.e., the two on the left, E5–6) and of fired clay disc beads (on the right); iii) long, thin hair-like fibre which could be cattle hair from the container rather than necklace thread. 2. Clay beads E11–E14 and (detached) E64 and E64A; the 'tail' at the left end is peat. Note the hollowness of the beads. (Photographs: Gary Young.)

bead diameter from the front to the back. Whether any disc beads had been used to separate the tin and amber beads cannot be determined, although the juxtaposition of the tin and amber beads shown in Figure 15.2 suggests that this was not the case.

A tentative, hypothetical reconstruction of the arrangement of some of the beads is shown in Figure 15.6, 1, and

Figures 15.6, 2 and 15.6, 3 show one of the two replica necklaces that were made. Neither the reconstruction nor the replicas includes the second tin bead because it is hard to be certain of its shape (as discussed below). Moreover, the replica necklaces do not faithfully replicate the original arrangement of the clay and shale beads, since they show all the shale beads grouped together towards the front

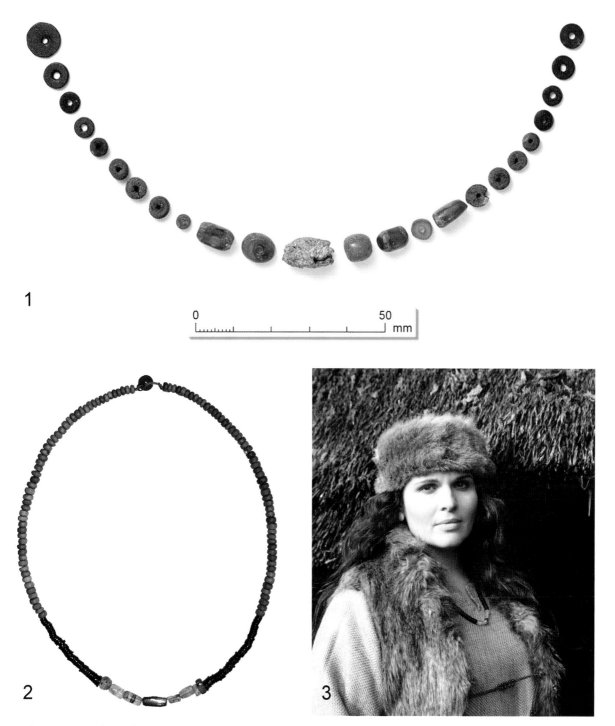

Figure 15.6: 1. Hypothetical reconstruction of arrangement of some of the beads in the composite necklace; note that most of the clay and shale beads have been left out. The large disc bead at the left end (F22) could have been used as a fastener. 2. The replica necklace that was displayed in Plymouth Museum in 2014. (Note: the clay beads are not graded in size as they had been in the real necklace.) 3. Replica necklace, made for the television programme, as worn by model. (Photographs: 1. Gary Young; 2. Plymouth Museum; 3. Dartmoor National Park Authority.)

(except for the fastener), and all the clay beads (actually Fimo modeller's 'clay', in the version shown in Fig. 15.6, 2) grouped towards the back. However, since some uncertainty remains as to the actual overall arrangement of the shale and clay beads, this departure from what we can propose as the actual arrangement can arguably be forgiven.

The replication of the necklace proved to be a valuable exercise in demonstrating the striking colour contrasts between the different materials – which would certainly have been a prominent characteristic of the original necklace – and in showing how it would lie when worn. The calculated overall length of the original necklace, based on an average thickness of 1.64mm for the shale beads and an average thickness of 2.63mm for the clay beads, and estimating a length of about 15mm for the crushed tin bead, is around 520mm (nearly 20.5in). Assuming that there was not a significant length of bead-free thread at the back of the necklace when worn, this corresponds roughly to 'matinée' length (20in/508mm), according to current necklace terminology; it is clear from the photograph of the necklace as worn (Fig. 15.6, 3) that it would have extended slightly below the collarbone, but would not have reached as far as the bust. The degree of flexibility of the necklace would have depended on how tightly the beads had been strung, but even with the fairly tight stringing of the replica, there was still scope for the necklace to curve when laid down.

As for the thread used to string the necklace, there was no unequivocal trace found, although a length of very thin organic fibre in the area of the bead run shown in Figure 15.5, 1 is of the requisite thinness, to judge from the diameter of the narrowest bead perforation (0.7mm). If this fibre is not part of the necklace thread, but is instead a piece of cattle hair associated with the basketry container (which is a distinct possibility), then it is likely, bearing in mind the differential survival of different organic materials in the cist, that the necklace thread was of sinew, which would not have survived. That it had been of some organic substance cannot be doubted, as the use of very thin metal wire would have left some kind of trace, if only as a compositional signature on the beads; no such signature was found during the X-ray fluorescence (XRF) spectroscopic analysis of the clay and shale beads by MD, JD and LT.

The various components of the necklace will now be described according to the raw material used and, for each of these categories, the evidence relating to the manufacture and use-wear of the beads will be presented. These data were gathered by JAS and HQ during visits to the Wiltshire Conservation Centre, following HW's micro-excavation of the beads, and at various stages in their conservation. The beads were examined using a Wild Heerbrugg M8 binocular microscope at magnifications up to ×50. The account presented below also describes the methods used to identify the raw materials and incorporates information about the beads' manufacture gained from the process of replicating them. The following 'Discussion' section considers *comparanda* for each of the elements and for the necklace as a whole, before exploring the broader significance of the necklace.

The tin beads (Figs. 15.1, 15.7)

As indicated above, in addition to the fusiform tin bead, found in Group F (F26: Figs. 15.1, 3 and 15.7, 1–2), there was evidence for the presence among the Group E beads of a second tin bead. The latter showed up most clearly in the X-ray of that group of beads (Fig. 15.1, 2) but it survived only as small silver-grey fragments of tin oxide, having been crushed in antiquity and some of its fragments

having been scattered widely over and around the Group E area. It also survives in the form of tin oxide deposits on many of the shale and clay beads in Group E. Even though its original shape cannot be determined, nevertheless the area with the densest concentration of tin in the X-ray is comparable in its dimensions (*circa* 13 × 7mm) to that of the fusiform tin bead F26, and with the eye of faith it could be argued that this bead had probably also been of fusiform shape.

The fusiform bead, although much better preserved, is nevertheless heavily degraded: the original silvery colour of the tin has been transformed to a dull silvery-grey through oxidation; part of one side and parts of both ends had fallen off and there has been considerable surface loss (probably due to partial dissolution in the cist's watery microenvironment), with only tiny patches of the original shiny surface still surviving (Fig. 15.7, 1–2). As with the other tin bead, its degradation left some tin oxide deposits adhering to some beads nearby. However, enough of the bead survives to show that it had been of fusiform shape, an asymmetric oval in cross-section, with one side less convex than the other; the better-preserved end slopes while the other is ragged. The current length of the bead is 13.8mm, its maximum width approximately 7.8mm and its maximum thickness about 8.7mm. The maximum wall thickness is around 3mm. The width of the thread-hole is hard to gauge but, to judge from an area where the interior of the hole has been exposed (Fig. 15.7, 1, bottom right), it is likely to have measured approximately 1.6 × 1.1mm at its narrowest.

It is clear that the bead had been made by hammer-rolling a sheet of tin back on itself, its ends overlapping. The X-ray (Fig. 15.1, 3) shows very clearly that the 'seam' where the long ends of the tin sheet overlap was not a butt-joint, and was not straight; instead, it has a distinctly convex, sloping edge. Part of this edge had broken away, leaving a hole through the bead (most clearly visible in Fig. 15.7, 1, top right and bottom left). On the other side of the bead the tin sheet had cracked from the process of rolling; this is most clearly evident in Figure 15.7, 1, top left. It is highly likely that, when new, the bead would have been burnished to a high sheen; the replica made by JI (Fig. 15.7, 3) shows how striking it would have appeared when new, with its shiny finish and silver colour.

Due to the current state of the bead it was not possible to detect whether there were any signs of use-wear.

As for the identification of the raw material, macro-scopically, oxidized tin is relatively easy to detect, being a light silver-grey colour and prone to crumbling if oxidized to a sufficient degree. Confirmation that the material had indeed originally been metallic tin was provided by JD's compositional analysis using the portable XRF spectrometer, which revealed that the material matched that of the studs in the armband or bracelet. Several other elements were also detected at trace levels, and these too were present on the tin studs. Whether these had derived from the burial environment or had been an integral part

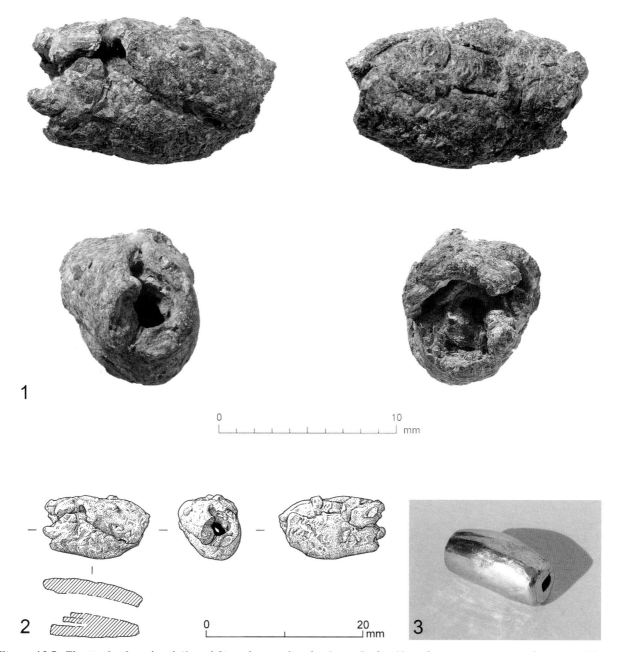

Figure 15.7: The tin fusiform bead (1 and 2) and its replica by Jamie Inglis. Note the curving seam on the original bead. (Drawings: Jane Read. Photographs: 1. Gary Young; 3. Jamie Inglis.)

of the tin's composition remained unclear (Appendix A). No attempt to source the tin was made, since the current state of knowledge about tin exploitation in the south-west peninsula during the Early Bronze Age is insufficient to allow Devon tin sources to be compared with Cornish tin sources. Nevertheless, it would be counter-intuitive to suggest that the source of the tin was anywhere other than from Cornwall or Devon. As such, the material could either have been local – with tin having been exploited on Dartmoor over many centuries back from the recent past – or else it could have travelled up to about 150 km from Cornwall. Tin exploitation around this time is attested at Caerloggas I, St Austell, Cornwall, in the form of tin slag;

part of a Camerton-Snowshill dagger was also found at this site (Miles 1975; Jones and Quinnell 2013).

Creating a replica tin bead

In creating the replica bead, JI started by hammering a piece of metallic tin into a flat sheet around 3mm thick. In order to reproduce the diagonal seam the sheet was cut into a parallelogram shape, rather than a rectangle. The sheet was then bent into a tube by hammering it against the tapering hollow of a swage-block, using a flat-headed wooden mallet. (A shaped block of wood would have sufficed as a swage-block in prehistory.) As the ends of the sheet were hammered into the diminishing-diameter hollow, they slid over each other, producing a sloping edge. During the rolling process, wires of diminishing diameter were used inside the tube to maintain a clear thread-hole and prevent the tube from being flattened. Smoothing the surface to make the seam invisible and tapering the ends of the bead were achieved using a metal planishing hammer, applied gently. The ends were then filed using a stone and the surface burnished using a bronze burnisher, followed by a final polish to a high sheen using jeweller's rouge (iron oxide mixed with fat) on a pad of leather. There is no reason why an Early Bronze Age metalworker could not have used a form of jeweller's rouge and, while leather (in the sense of deliberately tanned, as opposed to cured, hide) would not have been in use when the bead was made, a cured hide could have worked equally well. For the file, a piece of fine-grained sandstone would have sufficed and for the planishing hammer and burnisher a smooth stone could have been used. The slope of the 'seam' proved to be a point of curiosity to JI as a metalworker, particularly as it was more time-consuming to create than a straight seam. After experimentation, however, it was concluded that this was a sophisticated way to produce a seam that would have been invisible when new, since the shearing forces during the hammer-rolling would create a tighter seam than one that could have been achieved using a straight seam. Moreover, this technique would prevent the formation of a straight internal groove into which the necklace thread could have become lodged. Overall, the creation of the bead, from the ingot stage, took 75 minutes, with 15 minutes being taken by the hammering.

The amber beads (Figs. 15.8 and 15.9)

Seven amber beads were found, of various shapes and sizes but none exceeding 10mm in its maximum dimension. Two (E3 and E55) lay within the cluster of beads at the end of the container furthest from its base, while the others were found within the other bead cluster, at the base; the precise location of G1 within the latter could not be determined. The juxtaposition of bead F11 with the fusiform tin bead F26 and the proximity of amber beads F18 and F33 to these has already been noted; it may not be coincidental that these three sub-cylindrical beads are the closest in shape to the fusiform tin bead. The characteristics of the individual beads are as follows:

E55 (Figs. 15.8 and 15.9, 1): small chunky disc bead. Diameter 4mm; perforation diameter 1.5 × 1.4mm; maximum thickness 2.3mm. Orange to reddish, with butterscotch-coloured patches where the amber has become oxidised; despite this surface degradation, it retains some of its original translucency.

The bead is circular in plan and in profile the edge is gently and variably convex; one of the perforated sides is flattish and the other is slightly convex, with a large ancient chip scar running from the perforation to the outer edge.

There is a second, smaller, ancient chip scar on the outer edge. The perforation is central, perpendicular and slightly oval in plan; it is mostly parallel-sided but expands slightly at one end. Its interior is smooth and its outer edges are slightly rounded; it also has tiny specks of black organic material that probably derive from the 'sludge' that had surrounded the contents of the jewellery container (rather than being remains of the necklace thread). The edge and the perforated sides had originally been polished, and patches of this sheen still survive, despite the dulling effect of the oxidation process.

Direct evidence relating to the bead's manufacture is sparse, although the bead had probably been shaped by rubbing a small natural amber pebble against an abrasive surface such as fine sandstone. There is no rilling within the perforation – a feature relating to the rotation of the drill-bit, which is commonly seen in beads that have been perforated with the aid of a bow- or pump-drill – but the shape of the perforation and presence of the large chip scar suggest that the bead had mostly been drilled from one side, with a chip being forced out by the pressure of the drill. The antiquity of both this and the chip scar on the bead edge is clear from the fact that their edges had been smoothed. As for traces of wear, there is no marked thread-wear, although the smoothing of the ends of the perforation (and, to a certain extent, the smoothness of the perforation interior) could be due to thread-wear. Areas of slightly higher sheen around the perforation on each side may be due to bead-on-bead wear, and some of the sheen on the edge of the bead could be due to rotational rubbing against the wearer's skin or a garment, as well as to deliberate polish.

E3 (Figs. 15.8 and 15.9, 2): chunky, very slightly wedge-shaped bead. Length 9.2mm, width 7.7mm, thickness 4.3mm; perforation diameter 2.3mm. Orange to reddish, partly oxidised (particularly on its outer edge) but retaining some of its original translucency.

The bead is oval in plan and asymmetrical and very slightly wedge-shaped in profile, with flat perforated surfaces, one of which is slightly larger than the other, and a variably convex sloping edge. The junction between the sides and the edge varies from sharp to rounded. The perforation is slightly eccentric, perpendicular and mostly parallel-sided, with slightly smoothed ends and traces of the black organic substance as seen in E55, here with the appearance of peaty fibre. It may have been drilled from both ends but mostly from one side, with just a 'starter hole' drilled on the other side to prevent spalling; the existence of the latter is suggested by a partial facet around the end of the perforation on the side that has arbitrarily been labelled 'bottom' in Figure 15.9, 2. There is minor ancient chipping around the hole at both ends, and incipient spalling at one end; this will have been sustained during the drilling process. There are no traces of rilling in the hole.

The bead had been polished all over, including on the flat surfaces that would not have been visible when strung,

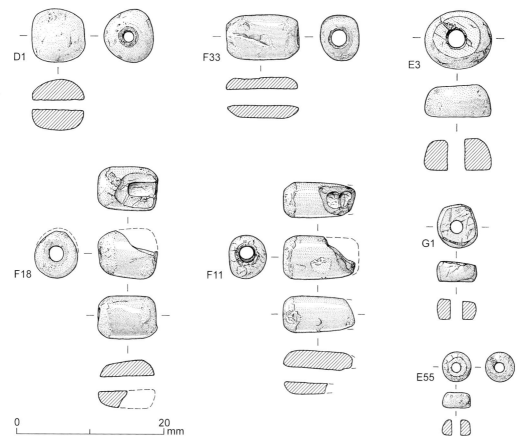

Figure 15.8: The amber beads. (Drawings: Jane Read.)

but post-depositional oxidation has dulled the polish in some areas and has also led to a slight roughening of the outer edge. There are no unequivocal signs of wear: it is unclear whether the absence of rilling in the perforation and the slight smoothing of the edges of the perforation are due to thread wear. Likewise, it is hard to tell whether the polish on the flat surfaces had been enhanced by bead-on-bead wear.

D1 (Figs. 15.8 and 15.9, 3): Plump, almost oblate bead. Length 7.3mm, maximum diameter 6.9mm, perforation diameter 1.4mm. Light reddish–orange, slightly oxidised and less translucent than the other amber beads.

In plan it is a squashed circle and in profile it is bulbous, tapering to flattish, cupped, perforated sides. The junction between the sides and ends is rounded. The perforation is longitudinal, narrow and centrally positioned; it had been drilled from both ends and its ends are slightly funnelled. Broadly-spaced rilling, from the rotation of the drill bit, is visible within the hole at either end.

A flattish area on the convex part of the bead may be part of the original outer surface of the amber piece – probably a pebble – from which the bead had been made, and similarly a small pock-marked area on the convex part of the bead is a natural irregularity which would have been on the pebble's surface. Other, less regular surface

hollows may also have been natural features. The surface had been polished to a fairly high sheen, but this has been partly dulled through post-depositional oxidation. The sheen is highest on the flattish area on one side of the bead (arbitrarily labelled 'top' in Fig. 15.9, 3), and also at the ends, where the perforated surfaces meet the convex side; the latter is likely to be due at least in part to bead-on-bead wear. There are no obvious signs of thread wear. The edges of the perforation are very slightly smoothed but it is unclear whether this had been caused by thread-wear. One tiny spall scar and one shallow scratch on the convex surface represent minor ancient damage.

G1 (Figs. 15.8 and 15.9, 4): Chunky and minimally wedge-shaped disc bead. Diameter 5.5–5.9mm, maximum thickness 2.6mm, perforation diameter 1.6–1.7mm. Light reddish–orange, significantly less oxidised (and thus more translucent) than the other beads.

The bead is sub-circular and slightly faceted in plan and minimally wedge-shaped in profile, with flat perforated sides and a slightly convex edge. The characteristics of the plan shape can be explained in terms of a combination of the original, slightly irregular shape of the parent pebble and faceting caused by grinding to modify that shape into a more circular form. The perforation is central, perpendicular and parallel-sided, although there is a very shallow, crisp bevel at one end that probably relates to the drilling process. No rilling was noted in the perforation. There are shallow, multi-directional grinding striations on both of the flat sides and very faint diagonal grinding striations on the edge, relating to the creation of its slightly convex shape. The bead had been polished to a fairly high sheen all over its exterior. There are no unequivocal signs of wear, although some of the sheen on the flat surfaces and on the outer edge could be due to bead-on-bead wear and bead-on-skin or fabric rubbing respectively (although there is none of the rotational bead-on-bead wear that is sometimes seen on disc beads). There is no obvious thread wear: the ends of the perforation are crisp and the smoothness of the interior of the perforation does not necessarily relate to thread-polish.

F11 (Figs. 15.8 and 15.9, 5): Sub-cylindrical bead, similar in shape to F18 and F33, with a large part of one end missing. Length: 9.7mm; diameter 4.8–5.5mm; perforation diameter 2–2.2mm. Reddish–orange, with only minor oxidation, mostly confined to the bevel at the surviving end; the bead retains much of its original translucency.

In plan, looking down at one perforated end, the bead is a rounded D-shape, with one side considerably less convex than the other. In profile, the bead is asymmetrical, narrowing towards its damaged end where the loss of a large fragment in antiquity left a diagonal scar, and tapering towards gently-pointed perforated ends. The undamaged end is roughly perpendicular to the long axis and, where the body tapers towards this end, the surface is slightly bevelled. The longitudinal perforation is centrally positioned and had been drilled from both ends, although mostly from one end, penetrating nearly the whole length of the bead. There are clear traces of rilling in the perforation, visible where the surface has broken away, and there are also traces of the black organic substance in the interior as noted in some of the other amber beads.

The bead had been polished to a high sheen all over its exterior, although the surviving bevelled end is slightly rougher than the rest of the surface. There are no obvious signs of thread wear, except perhaps for a slight smoothing of the end of the perforation at the surviving end of the bead. It may be that the slight bevelling of the exterior of that end resulted in part from bead-on-bead grinding wear; this might account for the slightly rougher surface at this point and for the fact that this is where the oxidation is most marked. The loss of a large chip at the other end of the bead occurred in antiquity, as is clear from smoothing to part of the edges of the fracture surface. Whether this damage occurred during the bead's manufacture or during its subsequent use cannot be determined.

F18 (Figs. 15.8 and 15.9, 6): Sub-cylindrical bead, similar in shape to F11 and F33; this is the shortest of these three beads. Length 8.2mm; diameter *circa* 4.9mm to *circa* 6mm; perforation diameter 2.2mm. The bead is of the same colour and degree of translucency as F11.

In plan, looking down at one perforated end, the bead is a rounded-triangular shape. In profile the bead is parallel-sided, curving inwards towards slightly flattish ends; faint multi-directional grinding striations from the shaping of the bead are visible on the surface. As with F11, a large chip had been detached from one side of the bead in antiquity, leaving a shiny conchoidal fracture surface. While its edges are fairly sharp, minor, slightly worn chipping at one point confirms that the damage is indeed ancient. The longitudinal perforation is centrally positioned and drilled from both ends. There is faint rilling within the hole and its outer edges are slightly smoothed, with some minor ancient chipping at the intact end. It is unclear whether the smoothing of the perforation ends is due to thread-wear.

The bead had been polished to a high sheen all over its exterior but, as with F11, there is a band of slightly duller, rougher surface at either end, and this is where the oxidation is most marked. It may be that these bands result from bead-on-bead rubbing, leading to surface abrasion.

F33 (Figs. 15.8 and 15.9, 7): Sub-cylindrical bead, similar in shape to F11 and F18. Length 9.6mm; diameter 5.5–6mm; perforation diameter 2.2mm. In colour and translucency the bead matches F11 and F18.

In plan, looking down at one perforated end, the bead is a rounded-D shape. In profile, it has roughly parallel sides, curving in towards the ends; at one end this curvature takes the form of bevelling over part of the circumference. The ends are gently squared off. The longitudinal perforation is centrally positioned and had been drilled from both ends; no rilling was noted in the interior, although it was hard to see far down the perforation. Traces of the black material as noted in some of the other amber beads are present. The ends of the perforation had been slightly smoothed, possibly through thread-wear, and a hollow at one end of the bead may have been caused by thread-pull. There is ancient damage, in the form of a long, diagonal flake scar, on one side.

The bead had been polished to a high sheen, probably all over, but as with F11 and F18, there is a band of dulling and roughening at each end that could well have been caused by bead-on-bead wear. The oxidation is most marked around these bands, and on the diagonal flake scar.

Raw material and techniques of manufacture

Identification of the raw material of the beads as amber was obvious from the colour, texture and warmth of the beads; analysis of one bead by JD using XRF spectrometry was not able to add any further information other than to confirm the organic nature of the material, since XRF is not the most appropriate technique for investigating amber. As for the ultimate origin of the material, this is most likely to be the Baltic Sea region since its distinctive composition has been found in virtually all of the prehistoric amber artefacts that have been analysed in Britain (by infrared spectroscopy: Beck and Shennan 1991) and Ireland (using attenuated

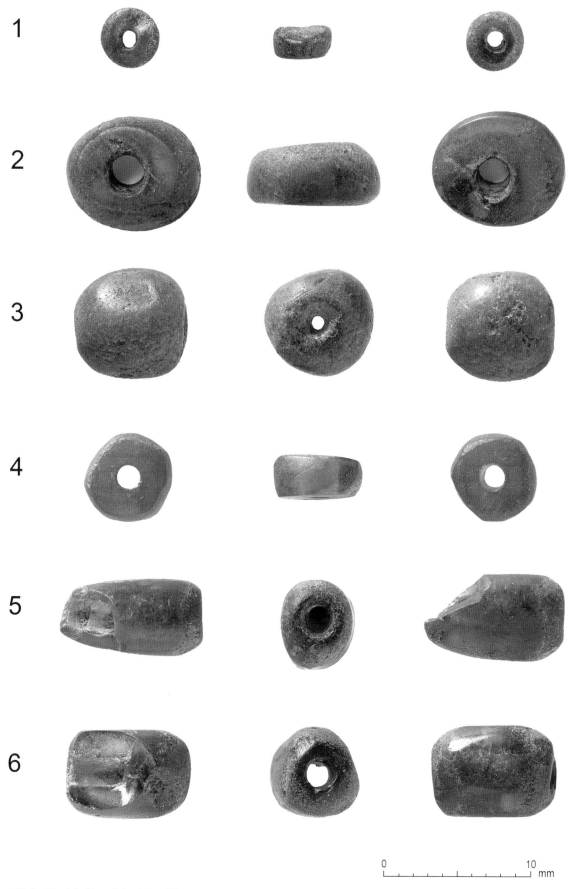

Figure 15.9: 'Top' (left), side/end (middle) and 'bottom' (right) views of the amber beads. 1. E55; 2. E3; 3. D1; 4. G1; 5. F11; 6. F18; 7. F 33. (Photographs: Gary Young.)

total reflection-Fourier transform infrared spectroscopy (ATR-FTIR): Moloney 2013). However, provenancing amber artefacts in these islands is complicated by the fact that the amber that washes up on the east coast of Britain is chemically indistinguishable from Baltic amber, being derived from the same parent deposits; furthermore, as discussed below, the amber-importing activities of elite communities in Wessex may have played a key role in the journey of the amber from its ultimate source to Whitehorse Hill.

Replication work undertaken by KV (Fig. 15.6) demonstrated that the beads could indeed have been made from pebbles of amber, shaped by grinding them against an abrasive such as fine sandstone and perforated using a simple bow- or pump-action drill fitted with a narrow bit made from copper alloy rod, with a diamond-shaped end. Use of such tools would produce the faceting, the striations and the rilling noted in some of the Whitehorse Hill beads. Drilling from both ends is not only a way of accommodating fairly short bits, but also of preventing chipping as the drill approaches the un-perforated end. This part of the manufacturing process would have been undertaken at an early stage in the roughing-out process; subsequent grinding of the perforated surfaces on the disc bead G1 would have removed any of the drilling-related cupping as seen on the other beads. As for polishing, this could have been effected by rubbing the beads against a piece of animal hide or sheepskin, perhaps also using a fine abrasive paste. Overall, the manufacture of the seven replica amber beads took around 14 hours.

The Kimmeridge shale disc beads (Figs. 15.10–15.12)

The 92 disc beads of Kimmeridge shale were distributed through all of the groups of necklace beads; a number (for example, C8: Fig. 15.11, 1) have accretions of tin oxide that had been precipitated from the decay of the two tin beads in the vicinity of the shale beads. With the exception of the large bead F22 which, as noted above, may have served as a fastener for the necklace and which has an external diameter of 9.5mm (Fig. 15.6, 1, left end, and Figs. 15.4 and 15.10; maximum thickness 0.9mm), the beads range between 5.1mm (F70) and 7.7mm (E38) in external diameter and between 0.9mm (D2) and 2.7mm (B6) in thickness, averaging 1.78mm in thickness. All are more or less circular in plan and most have parallel, flat, perforated sides (Fig. 15.11); a few, including B5, are slightly wedge-shaped in profile (Fig. 15.11, 2). The edge is convex, with most beads having a continuously curving, slightly convex edge like that seen in B5; however, some (for example, E19 and E40) have a slightly more angular, bevelled edge, the widest point not always falling at the mid-width of the bead (Figs. 15.11, 3 and 4 and Fig. 15.12). Among these, E40 stands out as being a thick, angular bun-shaped bead, distinctive among the Whitehorse Hill

shale beads but paralleled by F70. Bead C8 (Figs. 15.10 and 15.11, 1) shows another variant, where the edge curves continuously, but more towards one side than towards the other. The junction between the edge and the flat surfaces is consistently fairly crisp. One feature noted on six of the beads that were studied in detail (namely D2, D4, D5, E4, E32 and F70) is faint or very faint 'edge nibble': radial lines extending towards the mid-point of the edge (Fig. 15.13). The significance of this feature is discussed below.

The perforation is perpendicular and central or (as in F22) slightly eccentric and in shape it ranges from circular to ovoid and a rounded D, with the last two shapes indicating that the drill had been repositioned laterally during the perforation process. The perforation diameter ranges from 1.1mm (E17 and E18) to 2.6mm (B5). In most cases, the perforation is hourglass-shaped, with the narrowest point lying either around the mid-thickness of the bead or else closer to one of the flat sides; only a very few parallel-sided perforations were noted, but with these, one or both ends flare from the central part of the hole. The shape of the perforations indicates that the beads had been drilled individually, from both sides. Many, if not most of the beads have chipping to one or (usually) both of the ends of the perforation, caused during the drilling process. Many beads also have shallow chipping or laminar spalling that extends from the outer edge; this, too, will have occurred during the manufacture process and relates to the detachment of the beads from the parent material.

The outer edge of the beads had been polished to a fairly high sheen, while the flat, perforated sides (which would not have been visible when the beads were worn) are matte. As for signs of use-wear, there are no obvious signs of thread-wear: the edges of the perforations are fairly crisp and the absence of rilling in the holes need not be due to wear. Similarly, there are no marked traces of bead-on-bead wear, as is sometimes noted in some disc beads (in the form of concentric scratching on the flat sides, from rotational wear); the only hint of any possible bead-on-bead wear consists of a slight sheen on the high points of each flat surface, and this was consistently present.

Raw material and techniques of manufacture

The colour of the beads ranges from a mottled blackish–brown and dark brown (on the matte flat surfaces) to a darker blackish colour (on the polished edge); very occasional tiny lighter brown inclusion speckles were noted. This colouration, together with the slightly laminar and 'stony' (rather than 'woody') texture of the beads (Fig. 15.14), pointed towards Kimmeridge shale as being the most likely raw material; jet and lignite (including Bovey Tracey lignite) could be ruled out on textural grounds, since the beads lack the 'woody' structure of these materials, while cannel coal could be ruled out on colour and inclusion grounds. The Kimmeridge shale identification was confirmed through comparative compositional analysis by LT using XRF, comparing the beads' composition with

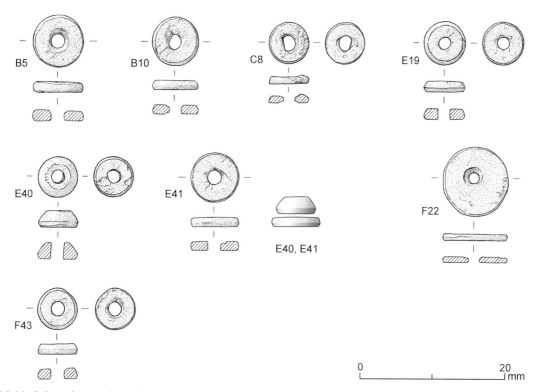

Figure 15.10: Selected examples of Kimmeridge shale beads, including the possible fastener, F22. These convey a sense of the size range of the shale beads, with C8 being almost the smallest and B5 among the largest after F22. Beads E40 and E41 were found adjacent to each other. (Drawings: Jane Read.)

that of Kimmeridge shale, cannel coal and jet; electron microprobe analysis and imaging using a scanning electron microscope, undertaken by MD, also confirmed this identification, as did JD's XRF analysis of one shale bead (Appendix A). The deposits in Kimmeridge Bay lie around 130 km to the east of Whitehorse Hill, as the crow flies.

While several features of the beads offered clues as to their manufacture, the experimental replication of the shale beads by HR-J in the Victorian Jet Works, Whitby, was able to shed further light on the process (Fig. 15.15). It seems most likely that long, pencil-shaped blanks were made by sawing slices (with a flint saw) from a large block of fairly compact yet laminar Kimmeridge shale – with the long axis at right-angles to the natural cleavage planes of the shale – and grinding these into a pencil or narrow cigar shape, first by creating faceted sides then by smoothing the facets. Tapering the ends of that blank could produce not only the dome of the bun-shaped beads seen in E40 and F70 but also the beads where the edge curves outwards but does not curve back. Individual beads would then have been either sawn or cleaved off the blank along the natural cleavage planes, then possibly given a light grinding on the flat surfaces to remove any resultant irregularities. The spalling and chipping that extends inwards from the outer edge of the ancient beads could have been produced by either sawing or cleaving, and the absence of obvious saw marks and of grinding striations suggests that: i) cleavage was the most likely method used to detach beads from the parent 'pencil'; and ii) any post-cleavage grinding had been minimal and did not leave any obvious traces.

The next stage would have been drilling the perforation of each bead; as noted above, this was effected from both sides of the bead, to minimize chipping (although this had been of limited success, given the high incidence of chipping around the perforations). Creating the evenly-curving convex edge shape seen on many of the beads could have been achieved through careful grinding; the 'edge nibble' seen on a few beads was probably a way of facilitating this process (and has also been seen on similarly-shaped disc beads of jet and jet-like materials elsewhere: Sheridan 2015). A final stage of grinding, perhaps involving rolling the edge of the beads against an abrasive surface such as a fine sandstone block, would remove any traces of edge-faceting that might remain, and the beads would have been finished by polishing the edge, probably using an abrasive paste; this could have included shale dust.

The fired-clay beads (Figs. 15.16–5.18)

At least 109 chunky disc beads of fired clay were found, mostly among Groups E and F, with most of the smallest examples being found in Group E. As indicated above, there is some uncertainty as to the precise number that had been present because of the fragmentation of some

Alison Sheridan

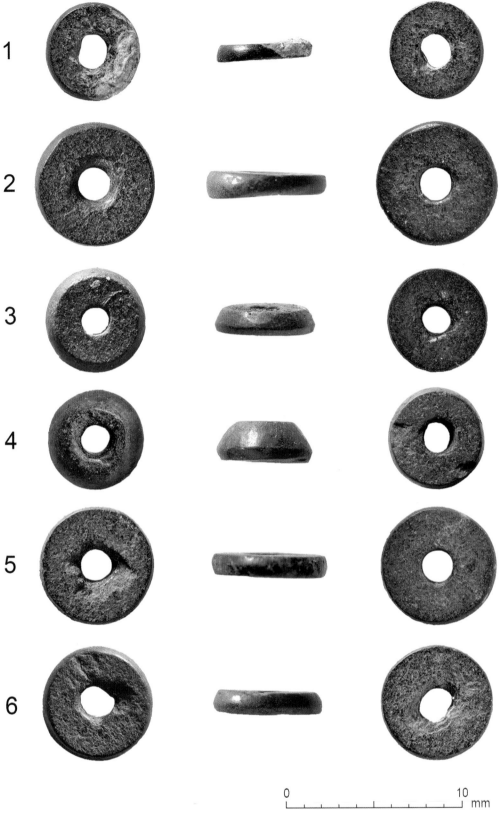

Figure 15.11: The beads shown in Fig. 15.10. Left: 'top' view; centre: side view; right: 'bottom' view. 1. C8, note blob of accreted tin oxide; 2. B5, showing slightly wedge-shaped profile and slight chipping around perforation on 'top' surface; 3.E19, showing asymmetric 'bevelled' profile and slight chipping around perforation on 'bottom' surface; 4. E40, showing truncated, asymmetric bun-shaped profile and chipping from the edge on the 'bottom' surface; 5. E41, showing marked chipping around the perforation on the 'top' surface; 6. B10, showing a slightly bevelled, asymmetric profile and chipping around both ends of the perforation. Continued on Fig. 15.12. (Photographs: Gary Young.)

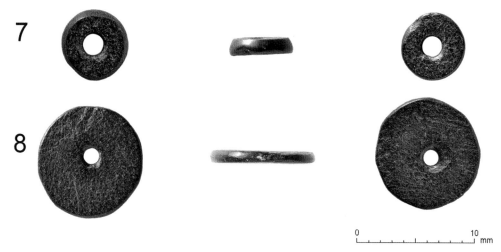

Figure 15.12: (Shale beads continued). 7. F43, showing slightly bevelled, asymmetric profile, minor chipping around the perforation at both ends and edge chipping on the 'bottom' surface; 8. F22, the possible fastener. Note the sheen on the polished edge of each bead. (Photographs: Gary Young.)

Figure 15.13: 'Edge-nibble' – faint transverse striations as seen on G11, probably relating to the creation of a convex edge. Note also the whitish accretions of tin oxide. (Microscope image: Alison Sheridan.)

of the smallest examples into tiny pieces; at any rate, the total will not have been significantly in excess of 109. Their size range (in terms of external diameter) overlaps with that of the Kimmeridge shale beads, with the smallest clay beads – with diameters between 3.3mm (E75) and 4mm (E64) – being smaller than the smallest shale beads, and the largest (D7, at 6.2mm) smaller than the largest shale beads. In thickness, most exceed that of the shale beads, with a range of 2.4mm (D13) to 3.2mm (D3) and an average of 2.63mm. The holes are narrower than those in the shale beads, ranging in diameter from 0.7mm (G13) to 2mm (D7). In plan the beads mostly approximate to a circle, with some resembling a slightly squashed circle. In profile, the edge is fairly flat or else minimally convex, and the surfaces with the thread-hole are mostly slightly convex but in some cases flat and, in a few instances, slightly concave (as in D7: Fig. 15.18, 7). A few beads, including F19 and E45 (Figs. 15.16 and Fig. 15.17, 1 and 5), are irregular in profile and a few are slightly bun-shaped. The junction between the edge and the other surfaces is consistently rounded.

The thread-hole – which is not a drilled perforation, as was the case with the amber and shale beads – is generally perpendicular and roughly central, and is consistently narrow in comparison with the outer diameter of the beads; as noted above, the holes are narrower than those in the shale disc beads, both in absolute terms and in terms of the proportion of hole diameter to maximum diameter. In shape the holes vary from circular to slightly oval or polygonal, or irregular (as with E45, a circle with a 'tail': Fig. 15.17, 1); the ends of the holes are almost invariably curved.

Raw material and techniques of manufacture

The beads had been made by wrapping a tiny 'sausage' of clay around a narrow twig or piece of straw, and then

Figure 15.14: Raw material comparison. 1. Microscope image of G11, showing colour and texture; 2. Block of Kimmeridge shale, showing stony texture of surface cleaved along a lamination plane and polished exterior surface; 3. Samples of Bovey Tracey lignite, showing woody texture. (Photographs: Alison Sheridan.)

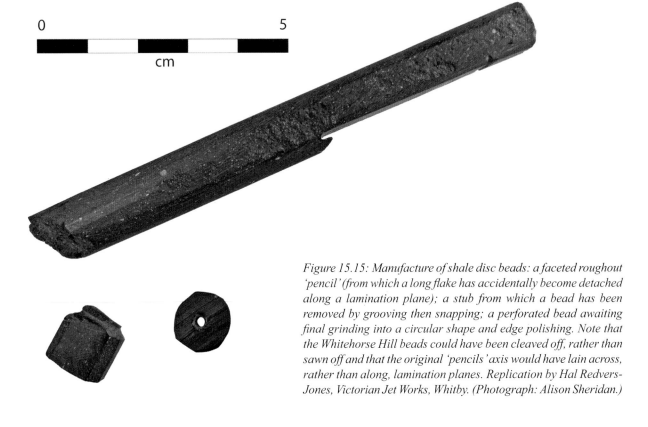

Figure 15.15: Manufacture of shale disc beads: a faceted roughout 'pencil' (from which a long flake has accidentally become detached along a lamination plane); a stub from which a bead has been removed by grooving then snapping; a perforated bead awaiting final grinding into a circular shape and edge polishing. Note that the Whitehorse Hill beads could have been cleaved off, rather than sawn off and that the original 'pencils' axis would have lain across, rather than along, lamination planes. Replication by Hal Redvers-Jones, Victorian Jet Works, Whitby. (Photograph: Alison Sheridan.)

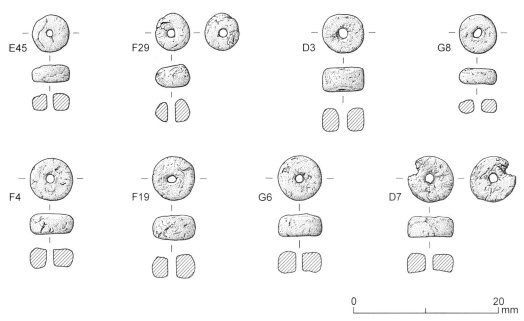

Figure 15.16: A selection of the clay beads. Bead D7 (with E8, not illustrated) is the largest of the clay beads in the necklace, and D3 is the thickest. The smallest clay beads in the necklace are not illustrated here. (Drawings: Jane Read.)

smoothing the seam; vestiges of the seam can be seen in E29 (Fig. 15.17, 2), and the sinuous cracking on one side of E45 (Fig. 15.17, 1) also reflects the process of twisting clay around an organic item. In a few cases, a tiny swirl of upstanding clay is present around the hole, further attesting to this method of manufacture. The hollow 'tail' seen in E45 could well have been caused by the organic support having moved during the shaping of the bead. All these features were reproduced during the experimental replication of the clay beads undertaken by JAS using Fimo modelling clay, and also during the replication using real clay undertaken by Joss Hibbs for the necklace used in the Plymouth Museum display. That the clay had been slightly dry when manipulated is demonstrated in the high incidence of cracks (Fig. 15.17). The absence of 'dragging' in the hole indicates that the narrow organic support – a twig, thorn or piece of straw – had been left in place while the beads were fired; it would have burnt out during that process. (The absence of obvious corrugations within the holes suggests that straw may not have been used, however; such corrugations have been noted by JAS in numerous segmented beads of faience, which were made by wrapping paste around a piece of straw.)

The surfaces of the clay beads are matte and range from smooth to fairly rough. Both organic and inorganic inclusions are present in the clay: a sizeable fragment of weathered stone protrudes through the side of F19, for example (Fig. 15.17, 5), while smaller sub-angular particles of what is most likely to be altered feldspar can be seen in many other beads (for example, G13, Fig. 15.19, 1, and G14, Fig. 15.19, 2). Tiny plant fibres were noted in several beads and one is particularly clear in the scanning electron microscope (SEM) image of G14 made by MD (Fig. 15.19, 3).

One characteristic of the smaller examples is a loss of the interior of the bead, leaving just a very fragile shell or a concave-surfaced bead (Fig. 15.20). It is unclear whether this is due to the post-depositional leaching away of loose-textured clay, to the burning-away of organic-rich clay during the firing process, or to some other factor. In any case, the resulting fragility of the 'shells' is one of the reasons for the difficulty in arriving at a reliable total of the number of small clay beads.

The beads' colour is a rich reddish-brown to dark brown, with an occasional whitish feldspar inclusion. A few beads have accretions of tin oxide on their surface, caused by the decay of the tin beads in the vicinity. A good example is shown on the side of F29 (Fig. 15.17, 3). Others have traces of blackish peat encrusted on their surface; this would have come from the micro-environment within the cist.

While several beads have chips missing (for example, D7, Fig. 15.18) – these appear to represent recent damage, reflecting the fragility of some beads – and others have minor ancient scratches, there is virtually no evidence for either thread or bead-on-bead wear. The smoothness of the interior of the holes could well be due to the use of a smooth twig or thorn, and the splaying of the hole in a few instances will have been a constructional feature, not a sign of thread wear. The only hint of any wear is the frequent presence of a very slight sheen on the high points of the flattish sides of the beads. This could have been caused by bead-on-bead wear.

Raw material identification was carried out through macro- and microscopic examination (including the aforementioned SEM) and through compositional analysis using XRF, with G13 being analysed in Edinburgh by LT and G14 in Cardiff by MD (Appendix A). These confirmed the material as clay, fairly rich in iron. RT's examination

Figure 15.17: Selection of clay beads, as Fig. 15.15 but without G8. 1. E45; 2. F29; 3. D3; 4. F4; 5. F19; 6. G6. Continued on Fig. 15.18. (Photographs: Gary Young.)

Figure 15.18: (Clay beads continued). 7. Clay bead D7. (Photographs: Gary Young.)

 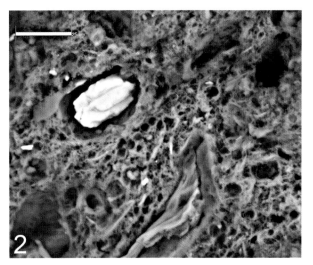

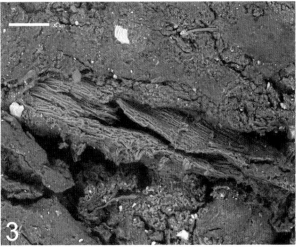

Figure 15.19: Inclusions in the clay beads. 1. Microscope image of surface of clay bead G13, showing whitish mineral inclusion, probably of altered feldspar; 2. Scanning electron microscope (SEM) image showing the same type of inclusion in clay bead G14; 3. SEM image of inclusion of plant material in clay bead G14. (Photographs: 1. Alison Sheridan; 2–3 Mary Davis.)

of A3 and F62 using a binocular microscope at ×20–×40 magnification revealed that the clay had been soft-fired in a reducing atmosphere and contained fine particles of mica, together with sub-angular fragments of off-white mineral, some stained yellow, up to 0.2mm in size (Appendix A). This mineral is suspected to be altered feldspar and if this is the case, it suggests a probable granitic origin for the clay. In other words, it need not have been exotic to Dartmoor. The mineral need not have been added deliberately to the clay, and it is possible that the clay had been levigated before use, to refine it.

Discussion of the necklace

The Whitehorse Hill composite necklace is an example of a type of elite jewellery that was particularly popular in Wiltshire and adjacent counties during the first half, and especially the second quarter, of the second millennium cal

Figure 15.20: Fragments of clay bead E25, showing the hollowness of its interior. (Photograph: Alison Sheridan.)

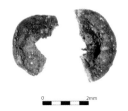

BC, with rare outliers elsewhere in England and in Wales, Ireland and the Netherlands (Woodward *et al.* 2015a; Sheridan *et al.* 2013; Sheridan 2008a; 2012; Haveman and Sheridan 2006). Overall, around 85 Early Bronze Age composite necklaces are known, with around 75% of these coming from Wiltshire, Hampshire and Dorset (Woodward *et al.* 2015a, tables 8.6.1–2 and fig. 12.8, and see also Sheridan *et al.* 2013). The three examples from Devon and Cornwall (other than the Whitehorse Hill necklace) are described below. The key characteristic, as the name suggests, is the use of two or more materials, often including or comprising unusual, exotic and/or rare substances such as jet, amber, fossils, faience and even part of a stalactite in one necklace (from Stockbridge Down, Hampshire: Stone and Hill 1940, 43). The combination of these different materials created multi-colour and multi-textured necklaces.

There is also variety in the shape of the beads within each necklace and, in several cases, a combination of new (or newish) and old components is present, which indicates that beads were not only exchanged between living people but were also passed down the generations, no doubt gaining in ancestral significance as they did so. The probability that the component parts for these necklaces were acquired by their owners over time (rather like charms on a modern charm bracelet), together with the variety in materials, bead shapes and bead ages, means that no two composite necklaces are exactly the same. As discussed elsewhere (for example, Sheridan *et al.* 2013), the ancient beads and those of 'special' substances may well have been believed to have magical powers to protect or to heal – indeed, the shape and colour of the beads may additionally have had a particular symbolic significance – and so the necklaces could well have had an amuletic use, being worn not only as a way of displaying the high status and the identity of the wearer but also as a way of protecting the wearer from harm. The term 'supernatural power dressing' has been coined to describe this high-status use of amuletic jewellery (Sheridan and Shortland 2003). The presence of composite necklaces in funerary contexts implies that they were included not only as a form of conspicuous consumption and identity-marking but also in order to protect the deceased on their journey into the afterlife.

The evolution of these necklaces from Chalcolithic forerunners, such as the example comprising Kimmeridge shale disc beads and a tubular sheet gold bead from a Beaker grave at Chilbolton, Hampshire (Russel 1990), has been discussed elsewhere (for example, Woodward *et al.* 2015a). Found in funerary contexts, mostly with cremated remains but sometimes with unburnt burials, the gender associations of the Early Bronze Age composite necklaces are predominantly, although not exclusively, with females (Sheridan *et al.* 2013; Woodward *et al.* 2015a), and they feature as a major component in Sabine Gerloff's (1975, appendix 7) characterisation of her 'Aldbourne series' of rich female graves in Wessex. This pattern of associations, along with that of the other jewellery found at Whitehorse Hill, reinforces the impression that the occupant of the Whitehorse Hill cist had been female.

Comparanda for the materials and the bead shapes used in the Whitehorse Hill necklace can be cited among other composite necklaces. The use of tin is paralleled in the Early Bronze Age composite necklace found at Exloo in the Netherlands, in the form of segmented and 'chocolate-drop' beads (Haveman and Sheridan 2006), and a further tin segmented bead, now lost, is known from Sutton Veny in Wiltshire (Penhallurick 1986, fig. 24). Other finds of

metallic tin in Early Bronze Age contexts – other than as an alloy or a surface enrichment layer in bronze artefacts, or as tin slag – are, however, extremely rare. They occur as an inlay into a Whitby jet button found at Rameldry Farm, Fife (Sheridan *et al.* 2003), as wire, enclosed within the rim of a sheet gold armlet from Lockington, Leicestershire (Hook and Meeks 2000), and as decorative wire studs inlaid into the pommel of a copper-alloy knife from Bargeroosterveld, Netherlands (Glasbergen 1956; Shell 1979; Needham 2004, 235). Tin was also added to the glaze of faience beads in Britain and Ireland, and while this would have intensified the sheen of the glaze, it was, arguably, primarily an example of conspicuous consumption of a precious material, and may also have been intended to enhance the amuletic capabilities of the faience beads, especially since the transformation of raw cassiterite into metallic tin may have been regarded as a magical process (Sheridan and Shortland 2004). The inclusion of two tin beads in the Whitehorse Hill necklace, and also of the 35 tin studs in the armband, would similarly have constituted not only the conspicuous consumption of this much sought-after material but also a way of maximising the supernatural protection of the cist's occupant. Furthermore, as Dartmoor lies between the tin-producing areas of the south-west region and the rich graves of Wessex – whose wealth in grave goods may be due partly to their occupants' control over the export of tin around Britain and Ireland and into Continental Europe – then the inclusion of tin jewellery at Whitehorse Hill may have signified the basis of the deceased's high status. In other words, control over the movement of tin offered a means for ambitious individuals and groups to gain power and wealth. This movement was probably controlled at many or all stages along the route from producers to consumers. The group to which the deceased individual at Whitehorse Hill belonged may have controlled the flow of tin between the producers and the powerful groups in Wessex.

As for the fusiform shape of the Whitehorse Hill tin bead(s), there are numerous broadly contemporary examples in other materials (principally Kimmeridge shale and jet) from elsewhere in Britain, particularly in Wessex (for example, Upton Lovell G1, Wiltshire: Annable and Simpson 1964, 54 and 108, no. 341). The composite necklaces from North Molton and Upton Pyne in Devon include examples in Kimmeridge shale, while that from Boscregan, Cornwall, includes examples made (unusually) of faience (see below for further details). The bead form originated in the jet and jet-like spacer plate necklaces of the earliest Bronze Age (Sheridan 2008b).

The use of amber beads in the Whitehorse Hill necklace can be paralleled in numerous other Early Bronze Age composite necklaces, most of which have recently been listed by Ann Woodward and colleagues (Woodward *et al.* 2015a, table 8.6.2; also Beck and Shennan 1991; Sheridan 2012, table 2; and Needham *et al.* 2006, 76–77 and fig. 37). As for the beads' shapes, *comparanda* for the chunky disc bead G1 and for the larger bead E3, with their sharp junction between the sides and the edge, are offered by the necklace from Barrow G5J on Net Down, Shrewton, Wiltshire (Beck and Shennan 1991, 169 and fig. 11.12.1). There are numerous other parallels for the use of small amber disc beads (including the form represented by E55); for example, from Chalton, Hampshire (Beck and Shennan 1991, 151 and fig. 11.3.4), and from Solstice Park, Amesbury, Wiltshire, the latter coming from a deposit of cremated bone inside a Trevisker urn, the bone radiocarbon dated to 3240±40 BP (GrA-22371, 1620–1420 cal BC at 95.4%: Sheridan 2012, fig. 28).

Such beads are not only found in composite necklaces: they are also known from an all-amber necklace, associated with a youth (possibly a boy) and radiocarbon dated to 1530–1430 cal BC, found on Boscombe Down, Wiltshire (Barclay 2010). The plump, almost oblate form of D1 is echoed by a bead from a composite necklace from Abingdon, Oxfordshire (Beck and Shennan 1991, 145 and fig. 11.1.1; Garwood and Barclay 2011), while the sub-cylindrical forms of F11, F18 and F33 invite comparison with the slender fusiform beads from the necklaces at Radwell, Bedfordshire (Beck and Shennan 1991, 156–157 and fig. 11.5.3), and Southwick, Hampshire (Beck and Shennan 1991, 170–171 and fig. 11.12.7).

The Whitehorse Hill sub-cylindrical beads are closer to these examples from composite necklaces than they are to the plumper fusiform amber beads that have been found in some amber spacer plate necklaces from Wiltshire and Dorset (for example, Beck and Shennan 1991, 179 and fig. 11.17, and 180 and fig. 11.19.1; *cf* Woodward *et al.* 2015b, table 7.4.4). Indeed, it does not appear that any of the Whitehorse Hill amber beads had started their lives as components in amber spacer plate necklaces, unlike some of the beads in the Exloo necklace (Haveman and Sheridan 2006). However, it is likely that the Whitehorse Hill amber beads had been obtained via contacts with elite groups in Wessex who, as argued elsewhere (Haveman and Sheridan 2006), appear to have obtained supplies of raw amber directly from north-west Jutland, rather than from the coasts of eastern England, and who had it worked up into jewellery of their preferred design by specialist craft workers in Wessex (Beck and Shennan 1991; Clarke *et al.* 1985, chaps 4 and 5, especially p. 215). The *comparanda* mentioned above make it clear that beads of the same, or similar design to those in the Whitehorse Hill necklace were in use in south-central England within the relevant time frame, and Beck and Shennan's distribution map for Early Bronze Age amber objects in Britain shows a clear epicentre in Wiltshire, Hampshire and Dorset (Beck and Shennan 1991, Figs. 6.1, 6.5, 6.6; *cf* Needham *et al.* 2006, fig. 37).

Amber would not only have been sought after as a precious and exotic material. Its symbolic association with the sun (through its colour and its ability to glow with the sun's light) and its electrostatic property would account for its use as an amulet.

As for *comparanda* for the Kimmeridge shale disc beads, the use of Kimmeridge shale is well attested in Early Bronze Age jewellery in southern England, again particularly in Wessex (Woodward *et al.* 2015a; Sheridan 2015), being used not just for disc beads but also for pestle-shaped pendants, for conical V-perforated dress accessories and for non-disc beads of various forms (fusiform, biconical, annular and vertically-ribbed squat oblate). The use of this material in the jet macehead from Clandon, Dorset, as conical studs that were covered with gold foil, should also be noted (Needham and Woodward 2008). Examples of disc beads of this material include those from the composite necklaces found at Southwick, Hampshire (Beck and Shennan 1991, 170), and Upton Pyne, Devon, as discussed below, and also from a bracelet, comprising tiny (2.0–3.18mm diameter) disc beads, found around the right wrist of a skeleton at Roundway, Wiltshire (Sheridan and Davis unpublished).

It may be that some or most of the disc beads that have been described, without analytical confirmation, as being of lignite (for example, Stockbridge Down, Hampshire: Stone and Hill 1940) are actually of Kimmeridge shale, although lignite may indeed have been used in some cases: Gill Bussell's compositional analysis of the disc beads from the composite necklace from Preshute G1a (the 'Manton' barrow), Wiltshire, concluded that they were of '?lignite' (Pollard *et al.* 1981, table 5). The fact that disc beads of Kimmeridge shale have been found in composite necklaces from as early as the third quarter of the third millennium cal BC (at Chilbolton, Hampshire: Russel 1990) to as late as the mid-second millennium (at Solstice Park, Amesbury, Wiltshire; Sheridan 2012) attests to a remarkably long tradition of the use of this material, and for such a specific bead form.

As for where the Whitehorse Hill shale disc beads had originated, as with the amber beads it again seems likely – given the geographical distribution of artefacts made from Kimmeridge shale – that they had been made by a Wessex-based specialist craft worker and obtained through contacts with the Wessex elite. Even though Kimmeridge shale does not have the electrostatic properties of jet (or indeed of amber), nevertheless its superficial resemblance to jet means that it could have been attributed similar supernatural powers and have been sought after for this property as much as for its rarity and aesthetic quality.

The clay beads from Whitehorse Hill do seem to have been made from clay that could have come from Dartmoor, and so they cannot be claimed to be exotic. However, once again there is a pointer towards a link with Wessex insofar as the *comparanda* for the use of fired clay disc beads are to be found there, in a composite necklace from Winterbourne Stoke G64(a), Wiltshire (Annable and Simpson 1964, 61 and 116, no. 481). A few other Early Bronze Age beads of fired clay are known from elsewhere – for example, fusiform and chunky annular beads from Altanagh, County Tyrone (Williams 1986), and, closer to Dartmoor, the fusiform beads from Crig-a-Mennis, Liskey, Cornwall (Christie 1960, 85, fig. 5) – but these do not provide the closeness of fit with the Whitehorse Hill examples as do the Winterbourne Stoke beads. Whether the clay beads at Whitehorse Hill had a particular symbolic significance, or were simply used as a substitute and a space-filler for the more exotic Kimmeridge shale beads, cannot be determined.

Turning specifically to the other composite necklaces that have been found in Devon and Cornwall, and more generally to the incidence of high-status jewellery and other prestigious possessions in these counties, the overall impression is that there were far fewer expressions of wealth here than in contemporary Wessex – an observation that has frequently been made by past commentators (for example, Fox 1948; Fox and Stone 1951) – but that some of the same kinds of precious object were being used in both regions.

Three other composite necklaces are known (Fig. 15.21), from Upton Pyne (barrow 4) and North Molton in Devon (Fig. 21.13–15; Kirwan 1872; Fox and Stone 1951) and from Boscregan in Cornwall (Borlase 1879). Of these, the Upton Pyne example, found in 1868, is the least dissimilar to the Whitehorse Hill necklace. According to Kirwan's account (1872), it comprised around 51 small disc beads of shale, with five larger beads. Of these, three were reportedly of shale, one of which was fusiform to gently biconical in shape and two were annular, with incised decoration on their outer edge; there were also a chunky annular bead, allegedly of 'red clay' and a naturally hollow fossil encrinite that resembles a segmented faience bead. Kirwan's description is a little muddled and his illustration (Kirwan 1872, pl. 1, fig. 2) may be somewhat fanciful as it shows 163 shale disc beads even though only about 51 are mentioned. As currently displayed in the Royal Albert Memorial Museum, Exeter, the necklace comprises 39 small disc beads of shale around 4–5mm in diameter, the fusiform/biconical bead, one of the decorated ring beads, the encrinite bead and the reddish bead. From macroscopic examination (by JAS), it seems likely that the disc beads – like those from Whitehorse Hill – are of Kimmeridge shale, and while the larger, differently shaped, 'shale' beads may also be of this material, they differ in being of a grade that is prone to laminar cracking. The encrinite is correctly identified, but the 'red clay' bead is not of clay and looks as though it could possibly be of oxidized amber; it would certainly repay further study. The latter is approximately 8mm in external diameter and about 4mm thick and, if it is indeed of amber, it invites comparison with the similar-sized bead E3 from Whitehorse Hill (Figs. 15.8 and 15.9, 2).

The Upton Pyne necklace was found among a mass of pyre debris under a round barrow; judging from the shape of the mass, the deposit may have been contained in some kind of wooden 'cist'. An accessory vessel was found close to the beads and at the top of the mass were found a copper-alloy pin and cremated human remains which were claimed to be those of a young adult, possibly a female (Powers 1969; but see also Higgins 2013). The pin had probably secured

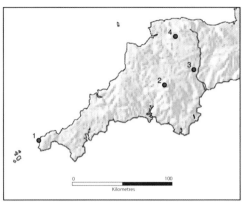

Figure 15.21: Distribution of composite necklaces in south-west England: 1. Boscregan, 2. Whitehorse Hill, 3. Upton Pyne, 4. North Molton. (Map drawn by Stuart Needham based on information provided by Alison Sheridan.)

an organic wrapping or bag for the cremated remains – a fragment of a vertebra was found fused to its shaft – and both the pin and its presumed function invite comparison with the pin found at Whitehorse Hill, as discussed in Chapter 12. Below the cremated remains but above the necklace and accessory vessel was a knife-dagger. A sample of the cremated bone was recently radiocarbon-dated for a research project on daggers and knife-daggers in the south-west peninsula (Jones and Quinnell 2013) and the result of 3220±30 BP (SUERC-39125, 1620–1420 cal BC at 95.4% probability) suggests that this grave post-dates the Whitehorse Hill cist by at least a century.

The composite necklace from North Molton, discovered in 1889, comprises 18 beads, although the chance circumstances of this old find make the total number entirely uncertain (Fox and Stone 1951). Eight of the beads are of faience and of these five are segmented, one is fusiform and two are biconical. Eight are of a dark brown material, variously identified in the past as bituminous shale and as Bovey Tracey lignite; these are fusiform to gently biconical in shape. In addition, there is one plump oblate bead, brownish in parts but mostly greyish, again variously described as being of shale and of lignite (but see below), and one fragment of an oblate bead of amber, with an estimated diameter of approximately 10mm (Fox and Stone 1951). Analysis of the brown beads by LT for National Museums Scotland in Edinburgh in 2006, using XRF and SEM imaging, revealed that the material used for the fusiform to biconical examples is more likely to be shale (and possibly Kimmeridge shale) than lignite, despite Fox and Stone's observation that their specific gravity of 1.39 is comparable to that of Bovey Tracey lignite. The absence of a 'woody' structure under high magnification and similarities with the stony texture and chemical composition of Kimmeridge shale point towards the latter material as being the most likely candidate, although there is scope for further investigation of this matter. As for its specific gravity, there is a reported value of 1.319 for bituminous Kimmeridge shale (Stevenson 1812, 477).

The analysis undertaken in 2006 also included the plump oblate bead (and the faience beads) and revealed that the former may well be of a different material from the fusiform/biconical shale beads. It is of a speckled, fine-grained stone. That it is not lignite is clear from the SEM high-magnification image of its 'stony' surface texture, and the XRF results showed that its composition differs from that of the brown fusiform/biconical beads in having a higher carbon and lower silicon content. Once again, further research may shed more light on its nature and origin.

While the North Molton necklace has fewer obvious points of comparison with the Whitehorse Hill example than the Upton Pyne necklace, nevertheless there is the shared use of amber and the probable shared use of Kimmeridge shale. As noted above, the fusiform/biconical shape of the faience and brown beads also echoes the shape of the best-preserved of the Whitehorse Hill tin beads. The phenomenon of expressing the same design idea (here, the fusiform and biconical shape) in different media is well documented among Early Bronze Age jewellery and has been discussed elsewhere, with regard to faience (Sheridan and Shortland 2004). The North Molton necklace was discovered after a horse trod on what had probably been a cist and the ground gave way. Unfortunately, the associated bones, sherds of pottery and flints did not accompany the necklace into the Royal Albert Memorial Museum and are presumed to be lost.

Like the North Molton necklace, that from Carn Creis III, Boscregan, St Just-in-Penwith, in the extreme west of Cornwall, excavated in 1878 (Borlase 1879), contained several faience beads. Ten of these are segmented and two are of ribbed biconical form, their shape echoing that of the ribbed (and sometimes gold-bound) shale beads of some Wessex series graves (for example, Preshute G1a, the 'Manton' barrow: Annable and Simpson 1964, 47 and 101, no. 196). Tiny disc beads around 4.5mm in diameter, 'of what I take to be Kimmeridge shale' (Borlase 1879, 208), were found wedged into the ends of the biconical beads, to act as stoppers, preventing the ends of the segmented beads from lodging in the ends of the biconical beads. Also present was a naturally-perforated geological freak, 'a heart-shaped stone with flinty excrescence perforated, and probably intended as a charm for the necklace' (Borlase 1879, 209 and pl. iii, F), and part of a broken spherical or oblate bead that had been re-bored with a V-perforation (Borlase 1879, pl. iii, G). The material of the broken bead is stone, not amber (*contra* ApSimon and Greenfield 1972 and *contra* Sheridan 2004–5a), and despite Borlase's claim that this would not have been sufficiently strong to act as the necklace's fastener, nevertheless it remains a distinct possibility that it fulfilled that role. The necklace was found among cremated remains and with a fragment of a flint arrowhead under a cairn, and had apparently not been buried within an urn; the three sherds of thin-walled pottery found with the bones and beads may have come from an

accessory vessel. Other deposits of cremated remains under the cairn had been in Trevisker urns. While this is the least similar of the peninsular composite necklaces to the Whitehorse Hill example, there are points of comparison: the presence of disc beads, possibly of Kimmeridge shale, and the biconical bead form.

Apart from these necklaces, the tally of other 'special' jewellery and other symbols of power and status from Early Bronze Age Devon and Cornwall is relatively small, although far from negligible, with most finds coming from coastal Cornwall, Bodmin Moor, Dartmoor and east Devon.

The earliest expressions of wealth and power within the region in the Early Bronze Age are the two gold lunulae and associated bronze flat axehead from Harlyn Bay, Cornwall (Mattingly *et al.* 2009); the large jet V-perforated button found in a grave with a Beaker and 'knife-dagger' at Fernworthy, on Dartmoor (Shepherd 2009, 357; Jones and Quinnell 2013, 17); and the fancy stone wrist-guard found in another Beaker-associated grave at Cranbrook, Devon (Fiona Roe, pers. comm.). All these artefacts are likely to belong to the period 2200–1950 cal BC; that is, the time when peninsular tin began to be exploited and exported and when, as now appears to be the case from recent lead-isotope analysis of gold artefacts, Cornish gold was also being exploited and exported (Standish *et al.* 2014). At this time, the links with south-west Ireland were particularly strong, as this was where copper was being mined at Ross Island (O'Brien 2015) to be alloyed with tin to make bronze.

After *circa* 2000 cal BC, when the distribution system of peninsular tin appears to have been reorganized and when new sources of copper were being opened in Britain and Ireland (O'Brien 2015), further expressions of wealth and high status appeared in Devon and Cornwall, although with the exceptions of the Rillaton barrow on Bodmin Moor and that on Hameldown, Dartmoor, few of these were in the areas of tin exploitation, suggesting that the people involved in extracting tin were not necessarily the ones who benefited from this valuable resource. It is at this time – during the first half of the second millennium – that connections with wealthy communities to the east, particularly Wessex, are foregrounded in the material culture. Here is not the place for an exhaustive review of the evidence (Chapter 21); suffice it to offer a few observations, focusing mainly on jewellery. (See Chapters 12 and 14 for *comparanda* for the Whitehorse Hill pin and studs.)

The 18 beads made of faience in the North Molton and Boscregan composite necklaces constitute around half of the 37 faience beads, from ten findspots, that are currently known from Devon and Cornwall. The others include a probable necklace of seven segmented faience beads found in ring cairn 2 at Shaugh Moor on Dartmoor (Peek and Warren 1979), along with recent single finds of segmented beads from Willand and Hemerdon in Devon (Naomi Payne, pers. comm.), and from Hendraburnick Down in Cornwall (Jones and Lawson-Jones 2014). As discussed elsewhere (for example, Sheridan and Shortland 2004), the knowhow for making faience seems to have arrived in Britain and Ireland around the twentieth century cal BC, thanks to links with central European communities who were importing peninsular tin. As with other special materials and artefact types, the distributional epicentre for faience beads is Wiltshire and surrounding counties, and more specifically the area around Stonehenge (Sheridan and Shortland 2004, fig. 21.7). It is clear that at least some of the faience beads from the south-west peninsula were made locally, as has been shown for the star-shaped bead from Stannon Down, Cornwall (Sheridan 2004–5b), and seems likely for the Boscregan ribbed biconical beads. Indeed, fusiform and biconical faience beads have a distribution that excludes Wiltshire (Sheridan 2004–5b, fig. 36) and this may be because, as noted above, they are copying a bead form represented there in shale (sometimes embellished with gold). Four bone skeuomorphs of segmented faience beads are known from Farway barrow 31, associated with a date (from cremated human bone) of 3561±34 BP (Wk-20900, 2020–1770 cal BC at 95.4% probability) (Jones and Quinnell 2008).

As for the use of amber in Devon and Cornwall during the first half of the second millennium, there is a handful of finds in addition to those in the Whitehorse Hill, North Molton and (possibly) Upton Pyne composite necklaces. These comprise: i) a pestle-shaped pendant from Halwill, Devon (Miles 1975, 38; Beck and Shennan 1991, 159); ii) a fragment of a V-perforated button from Morwenstow, Cornwall (Miles 1975, 38; Beck and Shennan 1991, 165); iii) a bead, not dissimilar to Whitehorse Hill bead E3 and associated with a date of 3254±31 BP (OxA-13386, 1620–1440 cal BC at 95.4% probability), from Stannon Down (Sheridan 2004–5a); iv) the spectacular amber pommel with gold pins from a Camerton-Snowshill-type dagger from Hameldown on Dartmoor (Jones and Quinnell 2013, with further references); and v) a minimally-modified (but possibly decorated) pebble of amber found with tin slag and part of a Camerton-Snowshill dagger at Caerloggas I, Cornwall (Miles 1975; Jones and Quinnell 2013). These finds show strong stylistic links with elite material culture in Wessex and, as noted above, it is likely that they had been acquired from contacts with the Wessex elite, who were importing raw amber from Denmark and having it worked into artefacts by specialists. The links with Wessex include the Camerton-Snowshill daggers; these, and other daggers and knife-daggers from the south-west, have recently been discussed in detail by Jones and Quinnell (2013).

Shale (presumably Kimmeridge shale) finds other than those in the composite necklaces are very rare in Devon and Cornwall – a pestle-shaped pendant came from Stannon Down, Bodmin Moor (Jones 2004–5, 126–7 and fig. 41) – but, in the case of the two cups from Farway barrows 24 and 32, Devon, they are spectacular (Jones and Quinnell 2008, 33, 38; Needham *et al.* 2006, 101–103, Figs. 53, 54, pl. 13). These cups, along with the corrugated sheet gold cup from Rillaton, Cornwall (Needham *et al.* 2006, 84–87, fig. 41, pls 5–7), have been discussed in detail by Stuart Needham

in his magisterial study of precious cups (Needham *et al.* 2006). Much of their significance lies in what they tell us about social dynamics and the shift of power during the second quarter of the second millennium cal BC; that is, at about the time when the Whitehorse Hill cist was created. While elite groups in inland Wessex continued to flourish, there developed along the Channel coast, on both sides of the sea, a nexus of powerful individuals, interacting in what Needham has termed a 'maritory' (Needham 2009). It was within this Channel maritory that the biconical faience beads that have been found in Brittany and the Netherlands travelled, having probably been made in Cornwall or Devon (Sheridan 2004–5b, fig. 36). There can be no doubt that part of this interaction along and across the Channel featured the movement of peninsular tin from producers to consumers, with those who controlled its flow showing off their wealth and status with ostentatious possessions and funerary monuments.

This, then, was the background within which the Whitehorse Hill necklace (and the other jewellery in the cist) was used. We have seen that the necklace was probably assembled on or near Dartmoor, with some components made locally (that is to say, the clay beads; see above regarding the tin), and with the amber and shale beads probably having been obtained from the east, through links with elite groups in Wessex. Some of the components – notably the sub-cylindrical amber beads F11, F18 and F33 – may have been older than others, to judge from the wear and damage on these beads. As with the pin and the studs, stylistically the necklace shows very close links with the elite material culture of Wessex; and, as argued above, the group of which the cist's occupant was a member may well have derived its wealth through controlling the easterly flow of tin into that region and beyond. The nature of the relationship with the Wessex elite has been much discussed, and older accounts that portrayed it as one of unequal, core-periphery interaction (for example, Fox 1948; Fox and Stone 1951) are being replaced by others that are more nuanced (for example, Needham 2009; Jones and Quinnell 2013) and that emphasise the local character of peninsular practices during the Early Bronze Age (principally Jones 2011). It cannot be denied that the peninsula elite were consciously participating in the 'vocabulary of esteem' that was current in Wessex, putting their own expression on designs that were popular there (for example, through copying fusiform and biconical shale beads in faience). They may have been fewer in number than their counterparts further east, but the wealthy and powerful people of Early Bronze Age Devon and Cornwall seem to have been able to interact as equals, particularly during the second quarter of the millennium.

References

Annable, F. K. & Simpson, D. D. A. 1964. *Guide Catalogue of the Neolithic and Bronze Age Collections in Devizes Museum.* Devizes: Wiltshire Archaeological and Natural History Society.

ApSimon, A. M & Greenfield, E. 1972. The excavation of the Bronze Age and Iron Age settlement at Trevisker round, St Eval, Cornwall. *Proceedings of the Prehistoric Society* 38, 302–381.

Barclay, A. 2010. Excavating the living dead. *British Archaeology*, 36–41.

Beck, C. & Shennan, S. 1991. *Amber in Prehistoric Britain.* Oxford: Oxbow Monograph 8.

Borlase, W. C. 1879. Archaeological discoveries in the parishes of St Just-in-Penwith and Sennen, made during the past year by the President. *Journal of the Royal Institution of Cornwall* 21, 190–212.

Christie, P. 1960. Crig-a-Mennis: a Bronze Age barrow at Liskey, Perranzabuloe, Cornwall. *Proceedings of the Prehistoric Society* 26, 76–97.

Clarke, D. V., Cowie, T. G. & Foxon, A. 1985. *Symbols of Power at the Time of Stonehenge.* Edinburgh: Her Majesty's Stationery Office.

Fox, A. 1948. The Broad Down (Farway) necropolis and the Wessex Culture in Devon. *Proceedings of the Devon Archaeological Exploration Society* 4(1), 1–19.

Fox, A. & Stone, J. F. S. 1951. A necklace from a barrow in North Molton parish, North Devon. *Antiquaries' Journal* 31, 25–31.

Garwood, P. & Barclay, A. 2011. Making the dead. In G. Hey, P. Garwood, M. Robinson, A. Barclay & P. Bradley, *Thames Through Time. The Archaeology of the Gravel Terraces of the Upper and Middle Thames. Volume 1, Part 2: Mesolithic to Early Bronze Age.* Oxford: Oxford Archaeology, 383–432.

Gerloff, S. 1975. *The Early Bronze Age Daggers in Great Britain, and a Reconsideration of the Wessex Culture.* Munich: Prähistorische Bronzefunde VI(2).

Glasbergen, W. 1956. De dolk van Barger Oosterveld. I. Vondstomstandigheden & beschrijving. *Niewe Drentse Volksalmanak* 74, 191–198.

Haveman, E. & Sheridan, J. A. 2006. The necklace from Exloo: new light on an old find. *Palaeohistoria* 47/48 (2005/2006), 100–139.

Higgins, J. 2013. The cremation deposits, 172–175. In A. M. Jones & H. Quinnell, Daggers in the West: Early Bronze Age daggers and knives in the south-west peninsula. *Proceedings of the Prehistoric Society* 79, 165–191.

Hook, D. R. & Meeks, N. D. 2000. The scientific analysis of the gold armlets and the analysis of a fragment from the dagger. In G. Hughes, *The Lockington Gold Hoard: an Early Bronze Age barrow cemetery at Lockington, Leicestershire.* Oxford: Oxbow Books, 27–29.

Jones, A. M. 2004–5. Settlement and ceremony: archaeological investigations at Stannon Down, St Breward, Cornwall. *Cornish Archaeology* 43–44, 1–140.

Jones, A. M. 2011. Without Wessex: the local character of the Early Bronze Age in the south-west peninsula. In S. Pearce (ed.), *Recent Archaeological Work in South-western Britain: papers in honour of Henrietta Quinnell.* Oxford: British Archaeological Report 548, 61–74.

Jones, A. M. & Lawson-Jones, F. 2014. Investigating rock art at Hendraburnick 'quoit', Cornwall. *PAST* 78, 12–13.

Jones, A. M. & Quinnell, H. 2008. The Farway barrow complex in east Devon reassessed. *Proceedings of the Devon Archaeological Society* 66, 27–57.

Jones, A. M. & Quinnell, H. 2013. Daggers in the West: Early Bronze Age daggers and knives in the south-west peninsula. *Proceedings of the Prehistoric Society* 79, 165–191.

Kirwan, R. 1872. Notes on the pre-historic archaeology of East Devon. *Archaeological Journal* 29, 151–165.

Mattingly, J., Marley, J. & Jones, A. M. 2009. Five gold rings? Early Bronze Age gold lunulae from Cornwall. *Journal of the Royal Institution of Cornwall* 2009, 95–114.

Miles, H. 1975. Barrows in the St Austell granite, Cornwall. *Cornish Archaeology* 14, 5–81.

Moloney, L. 2013. Amber in prehistoric Ireland. *Archaeology Ireland* 27(1), 13–15.

Needham, S. P. 2004. Migdale-Marnoch: sunburst of Scottish metallurgy. In I. A. G. Shepherd & G. J. Barclay (eds.), *Scotland in Ancient Europe: the Neolithic and Early Bronze Age of Scotland in their European context.* Edinburgh: Society of Antiquaries of Scotland, 217–245.

Needham, S. P. 2009. Encompassing the sea: 'maritories' and Bronze Age maritime interactions. In P. Clark (ed.), *Bronze Age Connections: Cultural contact in prehistoric Europe.* Oxford: Oxbow Books, 12–37.

Needham, S. P., Parfitt, K. & Varndell, G. (eds.) 2006. *The Ringlemere Cup. Precious Cups and the Beginning of the Channel Bronze Age.* London: British Museum Research Publication 163.

Needham, S. P. & Woodward, A. 2008. The Clandon Barrow finery: a synopsis of success in an Early Bronze Age world. *Proceedings of the Prehistoric Society* 74, 1–52.

O'Brien, W. 2015. *Prehistoric Copper Mining in Europe, 5500–500 BC.* Oxford: Oxford University Press.

Peek, R. A. P. & Warren, S.E. 1979. The faience beads from Shaugh Moor, 26–27. In G. J. Wainwright, A. Fleming & K. Smith, The Shaugh Moor project: first report. *Proceedings of the Prehistoric Society* 45, 1–33.

Penhallurick, R. D. 1986. *Tin in Antiquity.* London: Institute of Metals.

Pollard, A. M., Bussell, G. D. & Baird, D. C. 1981. The analytical investigation of Early Bronze Age jet and jet-like material from the Devizes Museum. *Archaeometry* 23(2), 139–167.

Powers, R. 1969. Report on the cremated bones from a barrow at Stevenstone Farm, Upton Pyne, Devon (No. 7, fig. 1), excavated in 1869, 76. In S. H. M. Pollard & P. M. G. Russell, Excavation of round barrow 248b, Upton Pyne, Exeter. *Proceedings of the Devon Archaeological Exploration Society* 27, 49–76.

Russel, A. D. 1990. Two Beaker burials from Chilbolton, Hampshire. *Proceedings of the Prehistoric Society* 56, 153–172.

Shell, C. 1979. The early exploitation of tin deposits in south west England. In M. Ryan (ed.), *The Origins of Metallurgy in Atlantic Europe: proceedings of the Fifth Atlantic Colloquium.* Dublin: Stationery Office, 251–263.

Shepherd, I. A. G. 2009. The V-bored buttons of Great Britain & Ireland. *Proceedings of the Prehistoric Society* 75, 335–369.

Sheridan, J. A. 2004–5a. Amber bead from site 2, pit [30], 105–106. In A. M. Jones, Settlement and ceremony: archaeological investigations at Stannon Down, St Breward, Cornwall. *Cornish Archaeology* 43–44, 1–141.

Sheridan, J. A. 2004–5b. Star-shaped faience bead SF2 from site 6, context [51], 99–105. In A.M. Jones, Settlement and ceremony: archaeological investigations at Stannon Down, St Breward, Cornwall. *Cornish Archaeology* 43–44, 1–141.

Sheridan, J. A. 2008a. The Bronze Age composite bead necklace. In J. Thomas, *Monument, Memory and Myth: use and re-use of three Bronze Age round barrows at Cossington, Leicestershire.* Leicester: Leicester Archaeology Monograph 14, 80–88.

Sheridan, J. A. 2008b. Towards a fuller, more nuanced narrative of Britain 2500–500 BC. *Bronze Age Review* 1, section 6, online journal, British Museum www.britishmuseum.org/pdf/BAR1_2008_6_Sheridan_c.pdf

Sheridan, J. A. 2012. The ornaments from inside Vessel 11, ring ditch 2 [Earl's Farm Down] 15–18 and Tables 1–3. In J. Valentin, Appendix 13.1. Previous cultural heritage assessment. The excavation of seven ring ditches and other prehistoric features at Earl's Farm Down and New Barn Down, Amesbury, Wiltshire. In Pegasus Group, *Pegasus Group, Regional Distribution Centre Zone D, Solstice Park, Amesbury. Environmental Statement. Volume 2 – Technical Appendix.* Cirencester: Pegasus Group. (Technical Report. Pegasus Planning Group Ltd, Cirencester),. http://repository.nms.ac.uk/view/curators/sheridan=3AJ_A=3A=3A.html

Sheridan, J. A. 2015. Discussion of disc bead and spacer plate necklaces of jet and jet-like materials. In A. Woodward & J. Hunter, *Ritual in Early Bronze Age Grave Goods. An Examination of Ritual and Dress Equipment from Chalcolithic and Early Bronze Age Graves in Britain.* Oxford: Oxbow Books, 341–362.

Sheridan, J. A. and Davis, M. unpublished. The disc bead bracelet from Roundway. Report produced in 2001 for planned publication on excavations at Roundway barrow, Wiltshire, by Sarah Semple.

Sheridan, J. A. & Shortland, A. 2003. Supernatural power dressing. *British Archaeology* 70 (May), 18–23.

Sheridan, J. A. & Shortland A. 2004. '… beads which have given rise to so much dogmatism, controversy and rash speculation': faience in Early Bronze Age Britain and Ireland. In I. A. G. Shepherd & G. J. Barclay (eds.), *Scotland in Ancient Europe. The Neolithic and Early Bronze Age of Scotland in their European Context.* Edinburgh: Society of Antiquaries of Scotland, 263–269.

Sheridan, J. A., Davis, M., Chambers, S., Anheuser, K., Heron, C. & Redvers-Jones, H. 2003. The V-perforated buttons, 89–95. In L. Baker, J. A. Sheridan & T. G. Cowie, 2003. An Early Bronze Age 'dagger grave' from Rameldry Farm, near Kingskettle, Fife. *Proceedings of the Society of Antiquaries of Scotland* 133, 85–123.

Sheridan, J. A., Jay, M., Montgomery, J., Pellegrini, M. & Wilson, J. C. 2013. 'Tara Boy': local hero or international man of mystery? In M. O'Sullivan, C. Scarre & M. Doyle (eds., *Tara – From the Past to the Future*, Dublin: Wordwell, 165–190.

Standish, C. D., Dhuime, B., Hawkesworth, C. J. & Pike, A. W. G. 2014. New insights into the source of Irish Chalcolithic and Early Bronze Age gold through lead isotope analysis. In H. Meller, R. Risch & E. Pernicka (eds.), *Metalle der Macht – Frühes Gold und Silber.* Halle: Landesamt für Denkmalpflege und Archäologie Sachsen-Anhalt, Tagungen des Landesmuseums für Vorgeschichte Halle, Band 11(1), 209–222.

Stevenson, W. 1812. *General View of the Agriculture of the County of Dorset: with observations on the means of its improvement.* London: McMillan.

Stone, J. F. S. & Hill, N. G. 1940. A round barrow on Stockbridge Down, Hampshire. *Antiquaries Journal* 20, 39–51.

Williams, B. B. 1986. Excavations at Altanagh, County Tyrone. *Ulster Journal of Archaeology,* 49, 33–88.

Woodward, A., Hunter, J. & Sheridan, J. A. 2015a. Items of personal adornment IV: composite necklaces: discussion. In A. Woodward & J. Hunter, *Ritual in Early Bronze Age Grave Goods. An Examination of Ritual and Dress Equipment from Chalcolithic and Early Bronze Age Graves in Britain.* Oxford: Oxbow Books, 454–460.

Woodward, A., Hunter, J. & Sheridan, J. A. 2015b. Amber necklaces. In A. Woodward & J. Hunter, *Ritual in Early Bronze Age Grave Goods. An Examination of Ritual and Dress Equipment from Chalcolithic and Early Bronze Age Graves in Britain.* Oxford: Oxbow Books, 363–388.

16. The wooden studs

Alison Sheridan (JAS), Richard Brunning (RB), Vanessa Straker (VS), Gill Campbell (GC), Caroline Cartwright (CC), Stuart King (SK) and Henrietta Quinnell (HQ)

The jewellery found above the human remains in the cist included two pairs of wooden studs, one larger than the other (Figs. 16.1–16.4). All had originally lain at the bottom of the basketry container, with the larger pair (studs 2 and 3) lying side by side; their respective positions are shown in Figure 16.1. The numbering of the studs corresponds to the order in which they were excavated by Helen Williams; the small stud 4 was found after the removal of the others and it lay close to the tin-studded armband or bracelet.

The studs all share the same basic design and all are of the same type of wood; within each pair the sizes are very close (Figs. 16.2–16.4 and Table 16.1). All are neatly circular in plan with low-domed 'inner' and 'outer' surfaces that are of matching or nearly-matching diameters, although a subtle difference in the degree of convexity allows the suggestion that the more convex side had been the outer surface (that is to say, the one facing away from the body, and thereby on public view). Separating these surfaces is a broad and fairly thick 'waist'

which is fairly straight at its mid-point, curving out to a distinct rounded lip around the edge of the convex sides (Figs. 16.2–16.4). The waist on stud 1 has a less smooth curvature than the others.

Tool marks relating to the manufacture of the studs consist of short, parallel incisions running around the waist of stud 2 (Fig. 16.3) and shallow, multi-directional striations on both of the domed surfaces of studs 2, 3 and 4 (Figs. 16.3–16.4). Experimental replication by SK (described below), undertaken in 2013 for the BBC2 *Mystery of the Moor* television programme, demonstrated that the former would have been made by a chisel while the stud roughout was rotating on a lathe, while the latter relate to various stages in the manufacture process, as detailed below. As for the colour of the studs, the same replication work made it clear that the wood would originally have been a creamy-white colour (Fig. 16.11). Immersion in the peaty contents of the cist had stained the studs to a dark brown colour, but the process of freeze-drying lightened them somewhat.

Table 16.1: Summary dimensions of the studs (in mm, rounded to the nearest 0.5mm), together with information on the number of annual growth rings present.

	Larger pair		Smaller pair	
	2	3	1	4
'Outer' side diameter	24 × 23	25 × 25	15.5 × 15	14 × 14
'Inner' side diameter	24 × 23	25 × 25	15 × 14	14 × 14
Min. waist diameter	19	18.5	11	10
Thickness	11	11	9.5	9.5
Min. & max. waist width	4–6	4–6	2.5–5	2.5–5
Waist depth	2.5	3	2	2
Lip width	1.5	1.5	1	1
No. growth rings (approx.)	12	7	11	11

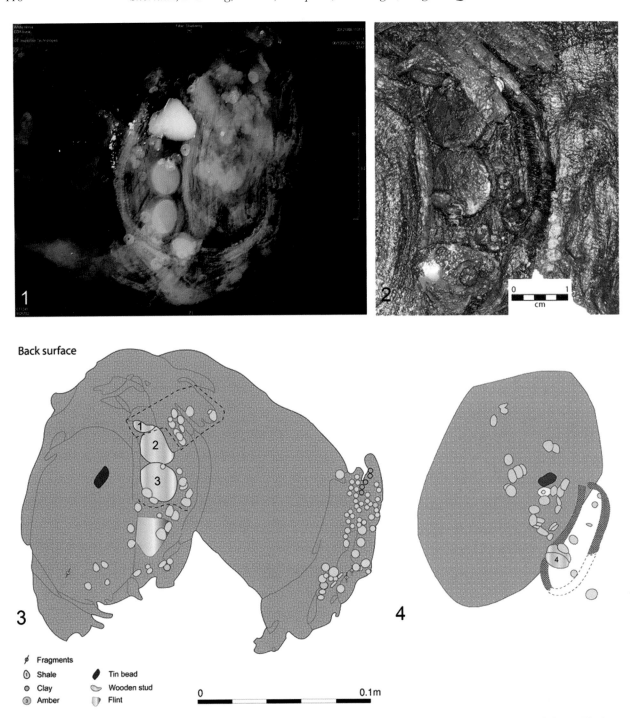

Figure 16.1: The studs in situ. 1. X-ray showing the position of the studs in relation to the lime-bast container's base. The larger pair are close to the flint object (dense white area) and one of the smaller studs (1) can be made out beside large stud 2, on its side. (Image: Mary Davis.); 2. Close-up of the studs; the smaller stud can be seen clearly towards the top. Also visible is the cattle hair whipping that linked the base of the container to its side and, beyond that to the right, the tin-studded armband or bracelet. (Photograph: Helen Williams.) 3. Schematic plans showing (left) studs 1–3 and (right) stud 4, found after the removal of the other studs. Note that the orientation of these plans is at 180° to that of the X-ray and photo. (Image based on information by Helen Williams.)

There were no obvious traces of any use-wear, or of ancient damage. There is minor chipping and localised contraction to the edges of the domed surfaces on stud 2, and slightly more extensive loss of chips from the corresponding areas on stud 3; all of this damage is post-depositional. Tiny detached fragments from stud 3 were used not only to identify the wood species but also to produce the radiocarbon determination of 3709±33 BP (OxA-27915, 2210–1980 cal BC at 95.4% probability; see below and Chapter 20 for discussion).

Figure 16.2: The studs. Note that the numbering corresponds to the order in which the studs were excavated. (Drawings: Jane Read.)

Figure 16.3: Photographs of the larger pair of studs. Stud 2 (left) and Stud 3 (right). The minimally more domed 'outer' surface is at the top. Note the small patch of tin oxide encrustation on the outer surface of Stud 2 (left), and the cutting and grinding striations. (Photographs: Gary Young.)

Figure 16.4: Photographs of the smaller pair of studs. Stud 1 (left) and Stud 4 (right). The minimally more domed 'outer' surface is at the top. Note the grinding striations on the 'outer' surface of both studs and similar striations on the 'inner' surface of Stud 4. (Photographs: Gary Young.)

0   10 mm

S3700CRC 15.0kV 26.1mm x50 BSE3D 40Pa   1.00mm

Figure 16.5: VP-SEM image showing the carefully worked, apparently smoothed surface and curved edge of the wood of one of the small studs, and aspects of a transverse surface in which there seems to be a diffuse-porous arrangement of apparently solitary small vessels and narrow rays (possibly uniseriate).(Image: C.R. Cartwright.)

Raw material identification

Identification of the species of wood used to make the studs was undertaken by CC, GC and VS. All four studs were examined under a low-power dissecting microscope at up to ×50 magnification. Both pairs appeared to be similar to each other, although detailed wood anatomy could not be seen. One of the smaller wooden studs was then studied under a variable pressure scanning electron microscope (VP-SEM) by CC. The VP-SEM examination had to be swift and at a relatively long working distance (approximately 26mm), not least because the stud had to remain moist to avoid deformation or damage under vacuum in the SEM chamber. This examination confirmed that the stud in question was in good condition, despite some already-present small cracks. It rapidly became clear that the VP-SEM examination of the surface was not going to provide sufficient anatomical detail for a secure identification to genus and/or species. However, Figure 16.5, as well as illustrating the carefully worked, apparently

smoothed surface and curved edge of the wood, does show aspects of a transverse surface in which there seems to be a diffuse-porous arrangement of apparently solitary small vessels and narrow rays (possibly uniseriate). While these features alone are insufficient to identify this wood unequivocally as *Euonymus* sp. (spindle), they are among the 30 characteristic criteria for this taxon.

Thin sections of the detached fragments from stud 3 (of the larger pair) were then cut using a razor blade and mounted in Aquamount on standard microscope slides. Transverse sections, tangential longitudinal sections and radial longitudinal sections were obtained from the wood fragments and the resulting slides were examined at up to ×400 magnification on a Leica DM2500 high-power microscope, with photographs taken on a Leica DFC320 camera mounted on the microscope. Reference was made to the identification criteria published in Schweingruber (1982), Gale and Cutler (2000) and Hather (2000), and to modern comparative wood slides held by Historic England, Fort Cumberland, Portsmouth.

The fragments from stud 3 were identified as *Euonymus* sp., and tentatively as *E. cf. europaeus* or common spindle on ecological grounds, as this is the only species native to Britain. However, it should be noted that the different species of *Euonymus* cannot be distinguished on the basis of wood structure.

The main diagnostic anatomical features observed were as follows:

Transverse section: Diffuse porous, mainly solitary vessels <50μm across. Banding of fibres at annual growth ring. Uniseriate rays (Figs. 16.6 and 16.7).
Tangential longitudinal section: Uniseriate, homogenous rays. Spiral thickening in vessels.

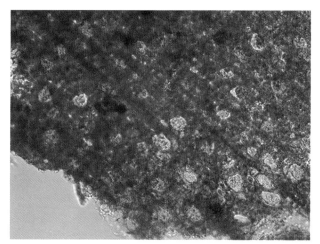

Figure 16.6: Transverse section at ×200 magnification showing diffuse porous pattern of solitary vessels and uniseriate rays.

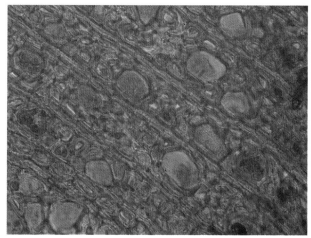

Figure 16.7: Transverse section at ×400 magnification. Scale bar 25 microns.

Figure 16.8: Radial longitudinal section at ×200 magnification showing a simple perforation plate within one of the vessels and spiral thickening.

Figure 16.9: Simple perforation plate, indicated by the arrow, at ×400 magnification.

Figure 16.10: Spiral thickening at ×400 magnification.

Radial longitudinal section: Spiral thickening in vessels; simple perforation plates (Figs. 16.8–16.10).

Additionally, the annual rings as observed in the fragments were not very close together, indicating a relatively fast growth rate. The curvature of the annual rings on both studs was weak, indicating that the studs were manufactured from a large branch or small trunk rather than small diameter roundwood.

Spindle is a small native tree which grows up to 8m in height (Thomas *et al.* 2011, 345). The wood is hard, fine-grained, pale and tough and, as its common name suggests, it was used during the last few centuries for making small objects such as spindles, skewers, pegs, viola bows and virginal keys, with some of these produced by turning (Grigson 1987, 120).

Spindle is currently found mainly on alkaline soils and especially on chalk and limestone, although in mainland Europe it occurs in secondary woodland on acid soils and on moist loam and sandy loam in Belgium. It is quite common as a hedgerow species in southern England, including on the poor soils of the Culm Measures in Devon (Thomas *et al.* 2011, 348). It also currently grows within the National Park (inf. Dartmoor National Park Forestry Officer). In theory, then, it may have grown on Dartmoor during the Early Bronze Age and could therefore have been obtained locally.

Technique of manufacture

The consistency in size of each of the pairs of studs, and the fact that their discs are almost perfectly round (the slight variation being easily accounted for by slightly variable shrinkage rates in different planes following their manufacture), strongly suggested firstly that all four items had been made by the same person or persons, as a set of ornaments, and secondly that they had been turned on a lathe. This is a remarkable finding, as will be explained below, but one that is consistent with the aforementioned

toolmarks. Making a set of replica studs helped to demonstrate what the various stages in the manufacture process are likely to have been, and to show what actions and types of tool will have been involved.

The experimental replication the process of manufacture started by splitting large branches or small trunks of spindlewood in half or in quarters, then trimming their sides to produce a roughly round baton. Further shaping was then done using a simple cord – or strap – operated lathe, wth one person rotating the lathe while the other applied the turning tool (Fig. 16.11, 2). Working in this way speeded up the process, and allowed the turner to work more swiftly and cut more accurately than if both cutting and rotating had been done by one person.

The tool used to cut into the baton must have had a very narrow, slightly curved cutting edge and is most likely to have been made of metal, although the use of a flint tool cannot be ruled out. The process of turning would have involved hollowing out the waist (thereby producing the parallel incisions noted on stud 2), shaping the domes and rounding off their edges (Fig. 16.11, 3). Some of the shallow striations noted on the domes – the few that are concentric with the dome – had probably resulted from this process. Having made the dome shapes the stud could have been twisted off the baton (Fig. 16.11, 5). A knife would then have been used to scrape off any projecting wood from the detachment area (Fig. 16.11, 4) before the domes were ground smooth against an abrasive surface (thereby producing the multi-directional surface striations). To finish off, and to bring out the aesthetic qualities of the wood, the studs may have been oiled; the fact that grinding striations are still visible on the original studs suggests that any polishing that may have taken place had not been sufficient to erase their traces. For further information on the replication process, see http://www.stuartking.co.uk/index.php/articles/woodturning/ (accessed March 2015).

The experimental work also made it clear that lathe-turning would have allowed multiple studs to be made

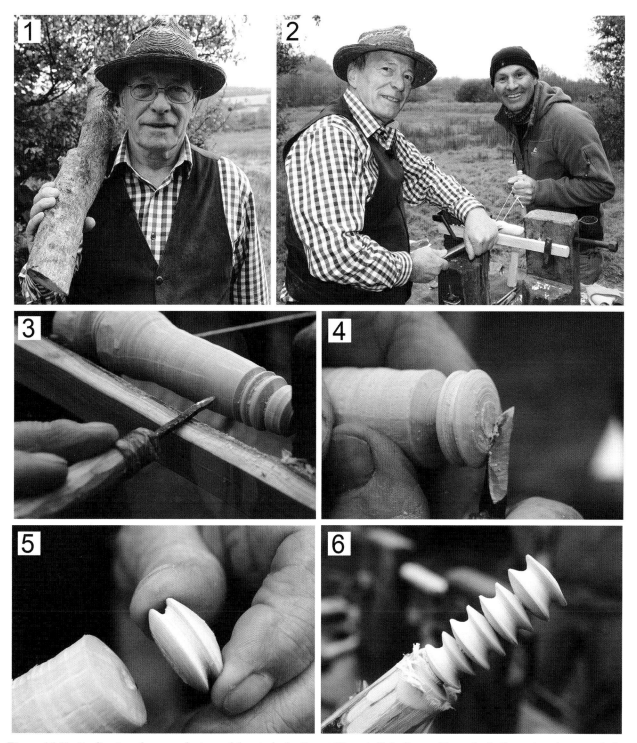

Figure 16.11: Replicating the manufacture of the studs, by Stuart King. 1. Spindlewood branch; 2. Operating the strap-lathe, with presenter Mike Dilger; 3. Presenting the chisel; 4 Trimming the point of attachment; 5. Twisting off a stud; 6. Multiple studs. (Photographs: Dartmoor National Park Authority.)

quickly, in a single episode of turning if desired (Fig. 16.11, 6). It is not known how widespread wooden stud production was during the Early to Middle Bronze Age, however, as the survival of organic artefacts is such a rare phenomenon.

The importance of the discovery that the Whitehorse Hill cist studs had been manufactured by turning cannot be overstated, as this constitutes by far the earliest evidence for wood turning in Britain and Ireland, pre-dating the next evidence by at least half a millennium (Brunning 2007). It seems logical that wood turning may have begun (at least in Britain) with the manufacture of such small items, rather than with the creation of more complex artefacts such as bowls.

Discussion

The Whitehorse Hill studs are unique in having been found as two pairs, in being made from wood and currently constituting the sole evidence for turning in Early Bronze Age Britain and Ireland. They are not, however, unparalleled as an ornament category. Around 60 Early and Middle Bronze Age examples, made from a variety of materials, from 37 findspots (including Whitehorse Hill), are known from Britain and Ireland (Fig. 16.12; Table 16.2). (The slight imprecision in the total is due to uncertainty about the number found in 1723 in Amesbury barrow 44, Wiltshire). Full details of all these objects are presented in Table 16.2 at the end of this chapter; numbers given after findspot names refer to entries in this table. This constitutes the most comprehensive study of this particular type of artefact to have been undertaken to date.

The following basic five-fold classification can be proposed to encompass the variability in form (Fig. 16.13):

Type 1:   Exterior surface concave, interior surface flat (variant 1a) or concave (1b and 1c, with 1c having an elongated waist).

Type 2:   Exterior flat, interior flat (2a) or convex (2b).

Type 3:   Exterior convex (usually conical), interior flat (3a: low-conical; 3b: high-conical) or concave (3c). Variants 3a-c are squat; variant 3d is a slenderer version of 3a, with a conical or domed exterior.

Type 4:   Both surfaces convex. Variant 4a is squat and low-domed; 4b is slender and low-domed; 4c is slender and symmetrical or asymmetrical dumb-bell shaped; 4d is slender and low-conical; and 4e is slender and high-conical (either symmetrical or asymmetrical).

Type 5:   Both surfaces convex, but of different shapes; slender.

The Whitehorse Hill studs belong to Type 4a, a widespread variant that has been found in southern England (at Amesbury, Figheldean and Preshute, Wiltshire, nos. 9–12), northern England (at Stanton Moor, Derbyshire (no. 40), Rishworth Moor, West Yorkshire (no. 47), and Wharram Percy (nos. 51–52) and Fylingdales, North Yorkshire (nos. 55–56)); and in Wales (Brenig 44, Denbighshire (nos. 41–42)).

The materials used to make studs are mostly fired clay (17 examples, including nos. 6, 12 and 36–42) and jet and similar-looking materials, including Kimmeridge shale (36 examples, for example nos. 50–58 of jet and 17–19 and 43 of Kimmeridge shale). One example made from amber is reported to have been found in barrow G44, Amesbury, Wiltshire, in 1723 (no. 9). The only instance of a white or creamy-coloured stud other than the Whitehorse Hill examples comes from Over (barrow 12), Cambridgeshire (no. 20); this was made from limestone marl. It has been suggested (most notably by Richard Bradley in 1977) that certain gold ornaments, such as the plano-conical sheet gold

items from Upton Lovell barrow G2e, Wiltshire (Clarke *et al.* 1985, fig. 4.57), were elaborate versions of studs. This is indeed a possibility, although it arguably requires further investigation, and these items have not been included in Table 16.2.

The geographical distribution of studs is uneven (Fig. 16.12). The highest concentration is in East Anglia and adjacent counties but there are also clusters in Wiltshire and Dorset, in Yorkshire and along the Pennines. Whitehorse Hill is a south-westerly outlier to the southern English distribution, while the examples from Brenig and Cefn Cwmwd in north Wales extend the Pennine cluster westwards. The pair found at Ballinchalla, County Mayo, in the west of Ireland, appear to be a distant outlier and are currently the only unequivocal find from an Irish Early Bronze Age context (Cahill and Sikora 2014, and see note appended to Table 16.2). The heyday of ear-stud use in Ireland occurred several centuries later, during the Late Bronze Age, when spectacular, large, bobbin- and spindle-shaped examples in gold were made (Cahill 1994; 2001).

The overwhelming majority of studs have been found in funerary contexts, associated with both unburnt and cremated human remains. Interestingly, at four findspots in and near East Anglia – Norton Subcourse, Norfolk (nos. 30–31), Langtoft, Lincolnshire (nos. 34–35) and Barleycroft and Over barrow 2, Cambridgeshire (nos. 16–19) – the skeletons were so tightly contracted that it has been suggested that the corpses may well have been bound (Yates *et al.* 2012). Where the sex of the deceased has been reliably identified, in 12 out of the 15 cases (including Whitehorse Hill) it has been identified (with varying degress of certainty) as female. Where more than one individual has been present (as at Ballinchalla, County Mayo (nos. 59–60), this has included a female. The three 'male' identifications – from Winterbourne Steepleton, Dorset (no. 5), Over barrow 12, Cambridgeshire (no. 20), and Langtoft, Lincolnshire (nos. 34–35) – have all been tentative. In two instances studs have been found in domestic contexts (at Bestwall, Dorset (no. 6), and West Row Fen, Cambridgeshire (nos. 22–29)); at the latter site a remarkable total of seven examples made of jet or jet-like material and one example made of fired clay were found. The other find contexts are more ambiguous or poorly-documented, with some being associated with funerary monuments but not with human remains (as at Radwell, Bedfordshire (no. 14), and Thornton-in-Craven, North Yorkshire (no. 50), and others appearing to be stray finds (as with the two found on Rishworth Moor in the West Riding of Yorkshire (nos. 47 and 48), at an unknown distance from each other).

The dating evidence and its reliability for each stud or set or group of studs is reviewed in Table 16.2; see also Chapter 20 for further information on, and discussion of, the Whitehorse Hill dates. With the exception of the date obtained from Whitehorse Hill stud 3 (which calibrates to 2210–1980 cal BC at 95.4% probability), all the radiocarbon dates fall after *circa* 2000 cal BC; indeed,

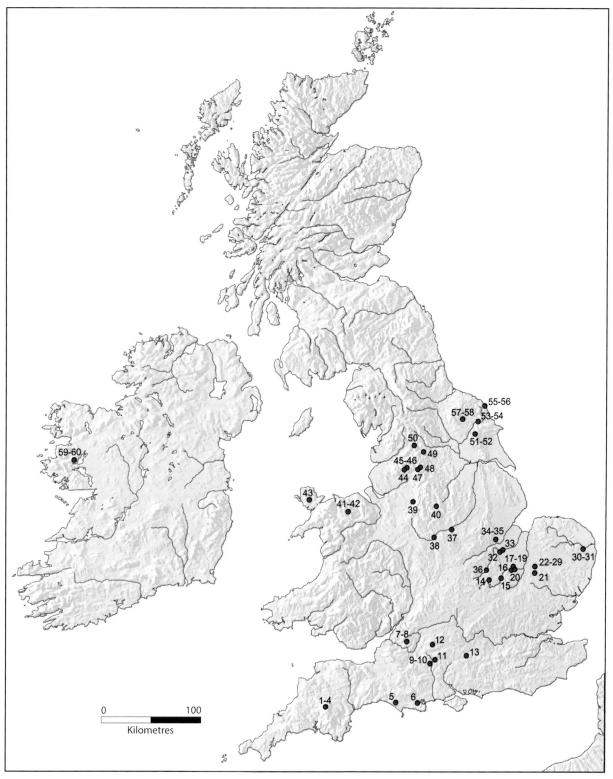

Figure 16.12: Distribution of Early and Middle Bronze Age studs, designed to be worn through the skin. (Map by Stuart Needham based on information provided by Alison Sheridan.)

the fact that all the other Whitehorse Hill dates cluster between *circa* 1900 cal BC and *circa* 1600 cal BC suggests that there is something troublingly anomalous about the studs data which could only be addressed by re-dating the stud. At any rate, there is no sign of heavy wear (or

indeed any wear) to suggest that the studs were ancient when buried. It is pertinent to note that the Type 4a fired clay studs from Brenig 44, Denbighshire (nos. 41–42) are associated with cremated human remains which have produced a date (at 95.4% probability) of 2030–1750

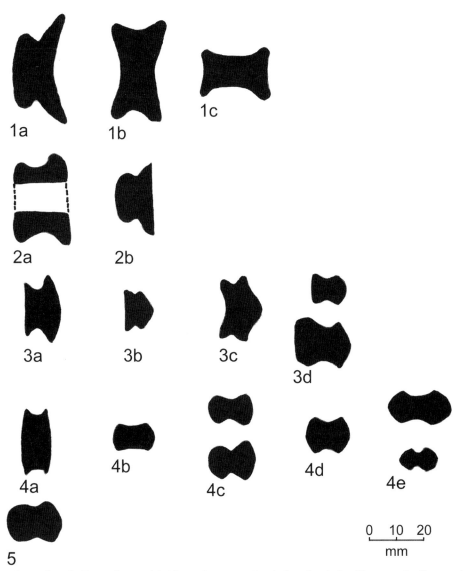

Figure 16.13: Typology of studs. Examples used (with catalogue number in brackets): 1a. Thornton-in-Craven (50); 1b. Bestwall (6); 1c. Ballinchalla (59); 2a. Barton-under-Needwood (38); 2b. Gawsworth (39); 3a. Cefn Cwmwd (43); 3b. Marshfield (7); 3c. Raunds (36); 3d. (top) West Row Fen (22), (bottom) Cowleaze (5); 4a. Whitehorse Hill, stud 2 (1); 4b. St. Neots (15); 4c .(top) Over, barrow 12 (20), (bottom) Langtoft (34); 4d. Norton Subcourse (30); 4e. (top) West Row Fen (27), (bottom) Norton Subcourse (31); 5. Cowdery's Down (13).

cal BC (GrA-22970, 3550±50 BP). That the use of studs persisted over several centuries is indicated by the dates of 1430–1210 cal BC (Beta-299801, 3060±40 BP) for skeleton 2 from Norton Subcourse, Norfolk (nos. 30–31) and of 1490–1300 cal BC (OxA-24535, 3129±30 BP) for the cremated bone associated with the stone stud in barrow 12, Over, Cambridgeshire (no. 20).

As regards the function of these objects, some previous commentators (for example, Cunnington 1907) have described them as dress-fasteners, implying their use as toggles, but this seems unlikely for several reasons. First, although it is theoretically possible to have an unperforated toggle as a dress fastener, it was normal (at least in Bronze Age contexts) for toggles and buttons to be perforated: for examples, see Sheridan 2007, Fig. 14.11, and Shepherd

2009. Second, the position in which some of these items have been found has suggested their use as jewellery, worn through holes in the flesh. There are seven clear instances where a single example, or a pair, has been found close to where the deceased's ear(s) would have been. Six of these findspots are in East Anglia (at Barleycroft (no. 16), Over barrow 2 (nos. 17–19), Chippenham (no. 21), Norton Subcourse (nos. 30–31), Fengate (nos. 32 and 33) and Langtoft (nos. 34–35)); the seventh is in North Yorkshire (at Wharram Percy (nos. 51–52)). Several other pairs have been found, for example, at Brenig 44, Denbighshire (nos. 41–42), here with cremated remains. The 'ear stud' interpretation would account for why one side is often wider than the other, sometimes significantly so (as in the distinctive jet examples with cupped broad surfaces from

Thornton-in-Craven, Crosscliff and Nawton, all North Yorkshire, nos. 50, 53–54 and 57–58 respectively): the narrower, inner surface would facilitate the insertion of the studs into the distended earlobes, while the broader outer surface would create maximum visual impact. These studs would have had to be worn permanently (or at least very regularly) in the earlobes, as otherwise there might have been a danger of the perforations closing up.

At Whitehorse Hill there is a further reason for suspecting that these items were studs worn as jewellery. The fact that they were found inside the container, alongside other items of jewellery, indicates that they had not been attached to a garment when deposited, and suggests instead that they formed part of a set of body ornaments along with the necklace and arm band.

The 'ear stud' interpretation would account for one pair of the Whitehorse Hill studs (arguably the larger pair), but what about the second pair? Several interpretations could be suggested, and again there are potentially informative *comparanda* from elsewhere. At Preshute, Wiltshire (no. 12), a single stud similar in shape to the Whitehorse Hill examples was found in front of the skull of an elderly woman, near the chin. This position suggests its possible use as a labret (a lip stud), worn through the lower lip. A similar explanation could be proposed to account for the third of three studs found close to the head of an adult woman at Over barrow 2, Cambridgeshire (no. 19); this one was found behind the right mandible (to where it could have fallen as the tightly-contracted corpse decomposed), while the other two could have been ear studs. The smaller pair from Whitehorse Hill could therefore have been labrets, perhaps worn at either corner of the lower lip. Alternatively, there is ethnographic evidence for studs of a similar dimension to the Whitehorse Hill examples being worn in the nose (Mary Cahill, pers. comm.), and the use of genital studs is also attested in several parts of the world today, as a casual search of the internet can demonstrate. Alternatively, it has been suggested that the smaller pair of studs may have been the precursors to the larger pair, worn during the process of expanding the holes in the earlobes. It would certainly have been necessary to introduce items of increasing diameter into the perforation in order to achieve the approximately 19mm wide holes (expanding to about 25mm to allow the inner surface to pass through) that were necessary to accommodate the larger pair. Based on present-day experience of stud wearers, the process of enlarging the earlobe to this extent would have taken over two years and would have required the constant wearing of studs. In the current authors' opinion, however, the 'labret' interpretation appears to be the most plausible for the second pair of studs, given that display – of the deceased's status, identity and importance – was clearly a key concern in the choice of objects deposited in the cist, as it probably had been during the life of the young woman in question. If all the jewellery found in the cist had been worn together by that person when alive, it would have created a striking visual impression, with the labrets, ear studs and necklace drawing attention to the head and neck.

It is clear from the discussion of the *comparanda* that studs were part of the vocabulary of bodily display during the Early to Middle Bronze Age in Britain and Ireland (although not apparently on the near Continent at this time, to the authors' knowledge); as noted above, they seem to have been a predominantly female form of jewellery. Although many have been made from fired clay – an unprepossessing-looking material – these objects could well have been indicators of high or otherwise special status, especially since many have been made of jet and jet-like materials and all would have involved an extraordinary investment of effort and time to stretch the skin so that they could be worn. Furthermore, their absolute rarity and their association in Wiltshire with three richly-equipped graves (at Amesbury (nos. 9–10), Figheldean (no. 11) and Preshute (no. 12)) – and possibly others, if one accepts the possible examples in gold – support this suggestion. The Whitehorse Hill studs are of the same type as those found in the three Wessex graves listed above and it may be that, as with the composite necklace, their wearer was emulating or, to put it another way, sharing, the vocabulary of elite fashion in Wessex during the first quarter of the second millennium cal BC.

Acknowledgements

Alison Sheridan wishes to thank the following individuals (in alphabetical order) for providing advice and information relating to the creation of the inventory of studs (Table 16.2): Keith Boughey, Mary Cahill, Chris Evans, John Hargreaves, Frances Healy, Helen Johnson, Deb Klemperer, Susan Lord, Terry Manby, Edward Martin, Sam Walsh, Martin Wills, Ann Woodward and Chris Yeates. She also thanks Stuart Needham for having produced the fine distribution map, Mary Davis for providing superb X-ray images, Helen Williams for her expertise and unfailing helpfulness, Gill Campbell for information about the radiocarbon sample taken from one stud, and Jane Read and Gary Young for their splendid illustrations.

References

Annable, F. K. & Simpson, D. D. A. 1964. *Guide Catalogue of the Neolithic and Bronze Age Collections in Devizes Museum*. Devizes: Wiltshire Archaeological and Archaeological Society.

Barnes, B. 1982. *Man and the Changing Landscape. A Study of Occupation and Palaeo-environment in the Central Pennines*. Liverpool: Merseyside County Council, Merseyside County Museums & University of Liverpool Department of Prehistoric Archaeology.

Barrowclough, D. 2008. *Prehistoric Lancashire*. Stroud: History Press.

Bayliss, A., Hedges, R., Otlet. R., Switsur, R. & Walker, J. 2012. *Radiocarbon dates from samples funded by English Heritage between 1981 and 1988*. Swindon: English Hertage.

Beck, C. W. & Shennan, S. 1991. *Amber in Prehistoric Britain*. Oxford: Oxbow Monograph 8.

Beck, H. C. & Stone, J. F. S. 1935. Faience beads of the British Bronze Age. *Archaeologia* 85, 203–252.

Boughey, K. 2010. *The Harden Moor Ring Cairn: an account of the excavations 1958–60, 1983–4.* Leeds: Yorkshire Archaeological Society.

Boughey, K. 2015. *Life and Death in Prehistoric Craven: Welbury Wilkinson Holgate and the Excavation of the Hare Hill Ring Cairn.* Leeds: Yorkshire Archaeological Society.

Bradley, R. J. 1977. The jet toggle and amber bead. In D. Hall & P. J. Woodward, Radwell excavations, 1974–1975: the Bronze Age ring ditches, 11–12. *Bedfordshire Archaeological Journal* 12, 1–16.

Brindley, A. 2007. *The Dating of Food Vessels and Urns in Ireland.* Galway: National University of Ireland, Department of Archaeology Bronze Age Studies 7.

Brunning, R. 2007. Structural wood in prehistoric England and Wales. Unpublished PhD thesis: University of Exeter.

Burrow, S. 2011. *Shadowland: Wales 3000–1500 BC.* Cardiff & Oxford: National Museum Wales/Oxbow Books.

Cahill, M. 1994. Boxes, beads, bobbins and … notions. *Archaeology Ireland* 8(1), 21–23.

Cahill, M. 2001. Unspooling the mystery. *Archaeology Ireland* 15(3), 8–15.

Cahill, M. & Sikora, M. 2014. More evidence for Bronze Age body-piercing. *Archaeology Ireland* 28(2), 30–31.

Chapman, A., Baker, T., Windell, D. & Woodiwiss, J. 2011. SS 1. Structural evidence: landscape unit reports. In J. Harding & F. M. Healy (eds.), *The Raunds Area Project. A Neolithic and Bronze Age landscape in Northamptonshire. Volume 2. Supplementary studies,* 1–329. Swindon: English Heritage.

Clarke, D. V., Cowie, T. G. & Foxon, A. 1985. *Symbols of Power at the Time of Stonehenge.* Edinburgh: Her Majesty's Stationery Office.

Cunnington, M. E. 1907. Notes on the opening of a bronze age barrow at Manton, near Marlborough. *Wiltshire Archaeological & Natural History Magazine* 35, 1–20.

Elgee, F. 1930. *Early Man in North-eastern Yorkshire.* Gloucester: John Bellows.

Evans, A. J. 1909. [No title]. *Proceedings of the Society of Antiquaries of London* 22, 121–129.

Evans, C. & Appleby, G. 2008. Historiography and fieldwork: Wyman Abbott's Great Fengate ring-ditch (a lost manuscript found). *Proceedings of the Prehistoric Society* 74, 171–192.

Evans, C. & Knight, M. 1998. The Butcher's Rise ring ditches: excavations at Barleycroft Farm, Cambridgeshire. Unpublished Cambridge Archaeological Unit report 283.

Evans, C. & Knight, M. 2000. A Fenland delta: later prehistoric land-use in the lower Ouse reaches. In M. Dawson (ed.), *Prehistoric, Roman, and post-Roman Landscapes of the Great Ouse valley.* York: Council for British Archaeology Research Report 119, 89–106.

Evans, C., Tabor, J. & Vander Linden, M. In press. *Twice-crossed River: prehistoric and palaeoenvironmental investigations at Barleycroft Farm, Over, Cambridgeshire.* The Archaeology of the Lower Ouse valley, Vol. 3. Cambridge: Cambridge Archaeological Unit.

Gale, R. & Cutler, D. 2000. *Plants in Archaeology: identification manual of vegetative plant materials used in Europe and the south Mediterranean to c. 1500.* Kew: Westbury Publishing and Royal Botanic Gardens.

Garrow, D., Meadows, J., Evans, C. & Tabor, J. 2014. Dating the dead: a high-resolution radiocarbon chronology of burial within an Early Bronze Age barrow cemetery at Over, Cambridgeshire. *Proceedings of the Prehistoric Society* 80, 207–236.

Gerloff, S. 1975. *The Early Bronze Age Daggers in Great Britain, and a Reconsideration of the Wessex Culture.* Munich: Prähistorische Bronzefunde VI(2).

Gettins, G. L., Taylor, H. & Grinsell, L. V. 1953. The Marshfield barrows. *Transactions of the Bristol & Gloucestershire Archaeological Society* 72, 23–44.

Grigson, G. 1987. *The Englishman's Flora* (facsimile edition). Frome: Butler and Tanner.

Hall, D. & Woodward, P. 1977. Radwell excavations, 1974–1975: the Bronze Age ring ditches. *Bedfordshire Archaeological Journal* 12, 1–16.

Hather, J. 2000. *The Identification of Northern European Woods: a guide for archaeologists and conservators.* London: University College London.

Hawley, W. 1910. Notes on barrows in south Wiltshire. *Wiltshire Archaeological & Natural History Magazine* 36, 615–628.

Hayes, R. H. 1963. Chapters 1–4: Archaeology: appendix ii–xv. In J. McDonnell (ed.), *A history of Helmsley, Rievaulx and District.* York: Stonegate Press, 335–421.

Hughes, G. 2000. *The Lockington Gold Hoard: an Early Bronze Age barrow cemetery at Lockington, Leicestershire.* Oxford: Oxbow Books.

Hutton, J., 2008. *Excavations at Langtoft, Lincolnshire. The Freeman Land.* Cambridge: Cambridge Archaeological Unit.

Ladle, L. & Woodward, A. 2009. *Excavations at Bestwall Quarry, Wareham 1992–2005.* Dorchester: Dorset Natural History and Archaeological Society Monograph 18.

Leaf, L. S. 1940. Two Bronze Age barrows at Chippenham, Cambridgeshire. *Proceedings of the Cambridge Antiquarian Society* 36, 134–155.

Longworth, I. H. 1984. *Collared Urns of the Bronze Age in Great Britain and Ireland.* Cambridge: Cambridge University Press.

Lynch, F. M. 1993. *Excavations in the Brenig Valley: a Mesolithic and Bronze Age landscape in North Wales.* Cardiff: Cambrian Archaeological Society Monograph 5.

Manby, T. G. 1977. Appendix II, 21–30. In G. Rowley, The excavation of a barrow at Woodhouse End, Gawsworth, near Macclesfield. *Journal of the Chester Archaeological Society* 60, 1–34.

Martin, A. & Allen, C. 2001. Two prehistoric ring ditches and an associated Bronze Age cremation cemetery at Tucklesholme Farm, Barton-under-Needwood, Staffordshire. *Transactions of the Staffordshire Archaeological and Historical Society* 39, 1–15.

Martin, E. & Murphy, P. 1988. West Row Fen, Suffolk: a Bronze Age fen-edge settlement site. *Antiquity* 62, 353–358.

Millett, M. & James, S. 1983. Excavations at Cowdery's Down, Basingstoke, Hampshire, 1978–81. *Archaeological Journal* 140, 151–279.

Mortimer, J. R. 1905. *Forty Years' Researches in the British and Saxon Burial Mounds of East Yorkshire.* London: A. Brown & Sons.

Pollard, A. M., Bussell, G. D. & Baird, D. C. 1981. The analytical investigation of Early Bronze Age jet and jet-like material from the Devizes Museum. *Archaeometry* 23(2), 139–167.

Priestley, J.H. 1936. Local flints, and their prehistoric sequence. *Transactions of the Halifax Antiquarian Society for 1936,* 93–129.

Rowley, G. 1977. The excavation of a barrow at Woodhouse End, Gawsworth, near Macclesfield. *Journal of the Chester Archaeological Society* 60, 1–34.

Schweingruber, F. 1982. *Microscopic Wood Anatomy: structural variability of stems and twigs in recent and subfossil woods from central Europe.* Birmensdorf: Swiss Federal Institute of Forestry Research.

Shepherd, I. A. G. 2009. The V-bored buttons of Great Britain and Ireland. *Proceedings of the Prehistoric Society* 75, 335–369.

Sheppard, T. 1900. *Descriptive Catalogue of the Specimens in the Mortimer Museum of Archaeology and Geology at Driffield.* London: A. Brown & Sons.

Sheridan, J. A. 2007. Dating the Scottish Bronze Age: "There is clearly much that the material can still tell us". In C. Burgess, P. Topping & F. Lynch (eds.), *Beyond Stonehenge: essays on the Bronze Age in honour of Colin Burgess.* Oxford: Oxbow Books, 162–185.

Sheridan, J. A. 2011. Jet studs from Norton Subcourse skeleton 2. Unpublished report for Northamptonshire Archaeology.

Sheridan, J. A. 2012. The shale stud from the Bronze Age cremation cemetery, Cefn Cwmwd. In R. Cuttler, A. Davidson & G. Hughes, *A Corridor Through Time: the archaeology of the A55 Anglesey Road Scheme.* Oxford: Oxbow Books, 149–150.

Smith, M. J. B. 1994. *Excavated Bronze Age Burial Mounds of North-east Yorkshire.* Durham: Architectural & Archaeological Society of Durham & Northumberland Research Report 3.

Stukeley, W. 1740. *Stonehenge, a Temple Restor'd to the British Druids.* London: privately printed.

Thomas, P. A., El-Barghathi, M. & Polwart, A. 2011. Biological flora of the British Isles: *Euonymus europaeus* L. *Journal of Ecology* 99, 345–365.

Tomalin, D. 2011. The character, chronology and cultural implications of the Neolithic and Bronze Age ceramics. In J. Harding & F. M. Healy (eds.), *The Raunds Area Project. A Neolithic and Bronze Age landscape in Northamptonshire. Volume 2. Supplementary studies*, 545–601. Swindon: English Heritage.

Tyson, N. 1995. Whitelow Hill, excavation of a Bronze Age cremation cemetery. *Manchester Archaeological Bulletin* 9, 5–22.

Vine, P. M. 1982. *The Neolithic and Bronze Age Cultures of the Middle and Upper Trent Basin.* Oxford: British Archaeological Report 105.

Walsh, S. 2013. Identity as process: an archaeological and osteological study of Early Bronze Age burials in northern England. Unpublished PhD thesis, University of Central Lancashire: http://clok.uclan.ac.uk/9620/1/Walsh%20 Samantha%20Final%20e-Thesis%20(Master%20Copy)%20 Volume%201.pdf (accessed August 2014).

Woodward, A. 2000. The prehistoric pottery. In G. Hughes, *The Lockington Gold Hoard: an Early Bronze Age barrow cemetery at Lockington, Leicestershire.* Oxford: Oxbow Books, 48–61.

Woodward, A. & Hunter, J. 2015. *Ritual in Early Bronze Age Grave Goods. An Examination of Ritual and Dress Equipment from Beaker Age and Early Bronze Age Graves in Britain.* Oxford: Oxbow Books.

Woodward, P. J. 1991. *The South Dorset Ridgeway. Survey and Excavations 1977–84.* Dorchester: Dorset Natural History and Archaeological Society Monograph 8.

Yates, A., Chapman, A., Inskipp, S. and Sheridan, J. A. 2012. Crouched inhumations from Norton Subcourse Quarry, Norfolk. *PAST* 70, 2–4.

Table 16.2: List of definite and possible examples of Early and Middle Bronze Age studs in Britain and Ireland (compiled by Alison Sheridan).

No	Findspot	No. studs	Stud(s) burnt?	Position of stud(s) in relation to human remains (where present)	Context & associations[1]	Material[2]	Stud type[3]	Dimensions (mm)[4] 'Outer side' diam	'Inner side' diam	Min. waist diam	Th	Principal references	Comments; date[5]; current location of studs
1–4	Whitehorse Hill, Devon	4 (two pairs)	N	Above human remains, in basketry container with other jewellery & a flint	Cist C, aged 15–25, poss. female Garment; bearskin wrapper for cremated remains; basketry container of lime bast; composite necklace; hair & tin armband or bracelet; flint flake; copper-alloy pin; plant material.	Spindle wood	All 4a	2) 24 × 23 3) 25 × 25 1) 15.5 × 15 4) 14 × 14	2) 24 × 23 3) 25 × 25 1) 15 × 14 4) 14 × 14	2) 19 3) 18.5 1) 11 4) 10	2) 11 3) 11 1) 9.5 4) 9.5	This publication	See main text for detailed description & discussion; individual stud numbering as per main text. Measurements rounded to nearest 0.5mm. Stud 3 radiocarbon dated to 3709±33 BP (OxA-27915, 2100–1980 cal BC). This is significantly earlier than other dated material from cist, which has produced dates clustering between c. 1750 cal BC and c. 1650 cal BC. See main text for discussion. Current location: Plymouth Museum.
5	Winterbourne Steepleton (barrow B, cremation 2), Cowleaze, Dorset	1	N	Among cremated remains	Grave pit, possibly secondary to construction of bowl barrow. C, adult, ?male A few small frags calcined animal bone; copper-alloy awl.	Poss. cannel coal	3d	17	13.2	11.7	20.1	Woodward 1991, 60, 67, 102, & figs 34, 55.4; Woodward & Hunter 2015, ID 540	Signs of wear at narrowest part of waist. ID of sex as 'male?' only tentative & might be worth revisiting, since both studs & awls are overwhelmingly associated with females. Charcoal (*Carpinus* and *Quercus* sp.: Bayliss *et al.* 2012, 316) from grave dated to 3120±120 BP (HAR-5620, 1660–1040 cal BC). Date of limited value as it was not obtained from a single-entity sample, including oak charcoal, but it provides a *terminus post quem.* Current location: Dorset County Museum, Dorchester.

No.	Site	Associations / context	Human remains	Burnt	Material	Form						Comments	References
6	Bestwall (pit G87), Dorset	Pit, domestic, next to Late Bronze Age houses '... a significant deposit of Late Bronze Age pottery' (44 sherds) Large quantities of burnt flint & heathstone	No human remains.	N	Fired clay	1b	36	34	28	21		No sign of wear. Stud assumed to be residual from earlier activity, & unrelated to the Late Bronze Age settlement (A. Woodward, pers. comm.). Middle Bronze Age graves with cremated remains are present at Bestwall. Grog & sand present in stud as filler Current location: Dorset County Museum, Dorchester.	Ladle & Woodward 2009, 114, 289–290, & fig 191, 1
7, 8	Marshfield (barrow III), Gloucestershire	On layer of charcoal & burnt earth (suggesting funerary pyre) under approx. centre of kerbed round barrow; primary deposit. C, adult aged 25 to 35-40, poss. female 2 amber beads ('spherical' & 'oval'; both look fusiform on illust.); 1 shale bead, biconical, 'burnt'; copper-alloy awl; part of hedgehog molar (not nec. a grave good).	Found with awl in 'hollow' of kidney-shaped pile of cremated human remains, just below top of 'hollow.'; former presence of organic bag as container for bones suspected.	? (see comment)	Shale*	Both 3b	a) c. 14.6 b) c. 15.2	a) 14.7 b) 15.2	a) 10.2 b) 11.1	a) 12.6 b) 13.8		Excavation report claims that at least 1 stud ('the black example') had been burnt, but no evidence cited to support this, & the fact that amber beads had survived casts doubt on whether 'shale' items had indeed been burnt. Their disintegration need not be due to burning; burning is more likely to have caused complete disappearance of shale items. Current location: originals disintegrated. Replicas: Bristol City Museum.	Gettins et al. 1953; Woodward & Hunter 2015, ID 1168–9 (replicas)
9, 10	Amesbury (barrow G44, Cursus group), Wiltshire	In E mound of twin bell barrow; smaller of the two. C, poss. sub-adult/young adult (judging from engraving). Urn, prob. Vase Urn. Copper-alloy knife dagger and an awl; gold-bound 'earth' (prob. oxidised amber); disc (?pendant); amber spacer plates; Segmented faience beads; fusiform, disc & oblate beads of amber; yellow & black 'glass' beads (will not have been of glass); edge-perforated pendant & other pendants & beads of 'earth' inc. 'many of the button sort ... cover'd with metal'.	Among cremated remains in urn.	N	Amber (+ unspec-ified)	4a, 1b?	a) Prob c. 30 ?b) Prob c. 30	Indet	Indet.	a) and ?b) not much smaller than outer side diam.	Indet.	Found 1723. Unclear from Stukeley's account how many studs had been present. His pl xxxii shows oblique view of what appears to be amber stud, & some way to its left, what seems to be a side view, unlabelled. Unclear if side view of pictured amber stud, or a second stud (as is assumed here); his text refers to 'other [beads] like a pully'. His claim that the remains were those of a girl aged 14 is speculative. There is no sign of any perforation on amber stud even though his text states that the 'beads' 'had holes to run a string thro'. The account is inaccurate in several respects, including claim that artefacts had passed through the pyre. Current location: lost.	Stukeley 1740, 44, table xxxii; Gerloff 1975, 161 (no. 242), pl. 23 E; Beck & Shenman 1991, 147

	Site	No.	Description	Context	N	Material	Type					References	Notes
11	Figheldean (barrow G12, 'Syrencot'), Ablington, Wiltshire	1	Rock-cut, bowl-shaped circular 'cist', primary, under bowl barrow. C, no details. 8 segmented faience beads; 4 jet beads (1 fusiform, 1 plump fusiform, 1 irregular fusiform, 1 chunky annular); kKnife-dagger found immediately above 'cist'.	Found among cremated remains in 'cist'.	N	'jet or shale'*	4a or 3a	c. × 15	No details	No details	No details	Evans 1909; Hawley 1910; Beck & Stone 1935, 239, & fig. 2.8 (knife-dagger) & pl lxiii, fig. 1.2; Gerloff 1975, 168–169 (no. 307) & pl 54B; Woodward & Hunter 2015, ID 420 (but not seen)	Associated beads examined for Woodward & Hunter project; 3 brown-black beads seen then identified as jet. Stud not seen during project visit. Illustrations of top of stud in Beck & Stone 1935 & Gerloff 1975 indicate circular in plan & has v. low peak on outer surface; shape originally described by Evans 1909 as 'precisely resembling a collar stud'. Current location: British Museum 1902.0616.23.
12	Preshute (barrow G1a; Manton barrow), Wiltshire	1	On old land surface under bowl barrow; primary. Traces of wood around head I, tightly contracted, elderly female, lying on left side. Traces & impressions of woven cloth (prob. from funerary garment); 2 accessory vessels, inc. grape cup; 2 knife-daggers (1 with amber pommel) & frags 3 copper-alloy awl. (In group 15–20cm from head); copper-alloy & gold miniature halberd pendant; gold-bound amber pendant; gold-bound biconical shale bead; necklace comprising 150 small disc beads of ?lignite, 5 amber beads & tiny disc bead made from stem joint of fossil encrinite. In group at feet: ribbed ?lignite bead; annular ?steatite bead; chunky annular chalk bead. Mass of small bone frags (presumably unburnt), species not identified.	Beside face, near chin.	N	Fired clay	4a	17.5	18	10.5	12.2	Cunnington 1907; Annable & Simpson 1964, no 201; Gerloff 1975, 161 (no. 241), pls 23,241 & 52C; Woodward & Hunter 2015, ID 1423	'Wilsford series' grave (Wessex 1). Stud interpreted by Cunnington as being dress fastener, but could have been worn as labret (lip stud). Identifications of shale & poss. lignite items as provided by Pollard et al. 1981. Current location: Wiltshire Museum, Devizes (DZSWS 1953.60).

No.	Site		Context	Position		Material						Reference	Notes
13	Cowdery's Down (ring-ditch 3), Basingstoke, Hampshire	1	Grave pit cut into basal fill of ring-ditch. 1 contracted, woman aged 30–40, lying on left side 2 pestle-shaped pendants, 'probably shale'; flint blade.	Under neck, close to pestle-shaped pendants.	N	'Jet'*	5	15	11	c. 9.5	20	Millett & James 1983	Dimensions taken from published drawing. Tool marks & signs of wear noted in published report, & irregularity in shape regarded as sign of un-finished appearance (although if item is indeed of jet, its shape could well have been influenced by shape of parent pebble). Given position (under the neck) & proximity to pestle-shaped pendants, this item can only be regarded as a possible example of a stud. The published interpretation, as a toggle (ie, fastener) for a necklace, could be correct. Stratigraphically earlier than Deverel-Rimbury pottery in same ditch fill. Current location: Hampshire County Museums Service.
14	Radwell (ring-ditch II), Bedfordshire	1	In fill of ring-ditch Small amber disc bead; 1 body sherd shelly pottery; cow femur & sheep tibia from same layer; also charcoal, Prunus sp. (cf blackthorn) & hawthorn.	No human remains present. Found near amber bead.	N	Jet*	4d	13	10	8	17	Hall & Woodward 1977, 11–12, 15	Dimensions taken from published drawing. Excavators suggested that object & amber bead may be redeposited from disturbed central grave. While proximity of sherd suggests that it could have been associated, there is no guarantee that animal bones & charcoal had originally been associated. Charcoal (mostly twiggy fragments) of Prunus and Rosaceae) radiocarbon dated to 3000±90 BP (HAR-1420, 1450–970 cal BC) but charcoal not necessarily contemporary with stud. Current location: The Higgins Art Gallery & Museum, Bedford.

No.	Site	Count	Context	Position	Y/N	Material	Mfr	Dim 1	Dim 2	Dim 3	Wt	Reference	Notes
15	St Neots, Cambridge-shire	1	1. No other details.	No information.	N	?lignite*	4b	11 × 10.8	10.8 × 8.7	9 × 8.2	14.9	Woodward & Hunter 2015, ID 293	Museum catalogue card states: 'Small jet or shale stud found with a skeleton at St Neots. Details of the find are unknown...'. Examined for Woodward & Hunter project. Material unlikely to be jet; is dark grey with black-brown tinge. Pattern of cracking suggests woody structure (as in lignite) but shale cannot be ruled out. Current location: Museum of Archaeology & Anthropology, University of Cambridge (Z.11634).
16	Butcher's Rise, Barleycroft, Cambridge-shire	1	Grave pit; primary grave within monu-ment that developed into ring-ditch I, contracted with ankles & wrists crossed as if bound, adult, indet.sex; lying on right side, head at S end, facing east Oak charcoal.	Next to where ear would have been.	N	Jet	4b	11.75 × 11.2	11.8 × 10.5	8.25–8.35	17.1	Evans & Knight 1998; 2000, 99; Evans *et al.* in press	Oak charcoal dated to 3580±40 BP (OxA-8113, 2040–1770 cal BC); relationship of charcoal to skeleton uncertain, & unclear whether old wood effect exists. However, grave pre-dates deposi-tion of Collared Urn nearby, & subsequent establishment of cemetery featuring Deverel-Rimbury urns, so clearly pre-dates *c.* 1600 cal BC. Current location: c/o excavator.
17–19	Over (barrow 2), Cambridge-shire	3	Round barrow, secondary deposition in barrow mound I, tightly contracted, adult female, lying on left side, head to E.	1 found near forehead, at right eye orbit; 1 behind right mandible; 1 between left scapula & humerus.	N	All Kim. shale	All 4d	a) 14.2 × 12.8 b) 13.9 × 11.7 c) 11.9 × 10.4	a) 13.9 × 12.9 b) 13.25 × 9.9 (dam-aged) c) 11.8 × 9.4	a) 9.5 × 9.2 b) 9.4 × 7.7 c) 8.7 × 7.1	a) 17.3 b) 16.3 c) 14.2	Evans *et al.* in press; Evans, pers. comm.	Key to entries: (a) = SF 022 (896a); (b) = SF 023 (896 b); (c) = SF 024 (896c). Current location: c/o excavator.
20	Over (barrow 12, F1062), Cambridge-shire	1	Round barrow, secondary deposit, in simple pit C, mature adult, ?male.	Among cremated remains.	Y	Stone	4c	11.4 × 11.1	10 × 9.3	6.8 × 6.75	15.4	Garrow *et al.* 2014, 222; Evans *et al.* in press	Stone identified (S. Howard, National Museums Scotland) as limestone marl; could have been obtained reasonably locally. Cremated bone dated to 3129±30 BP (OxA-24535, 1490–1300 cal BC). Current location: c/o excavator.

No.	Site	Qty	Context	Position of stud	Burnt	Material	Type/breakdown	Dim 1	Dim 2	Dim 3	Dim 4	Reference	Notes
21	Chippenham (barrow 5, burial F), Cambridgeshire	1	On base of outer ring-ditch of round barrow I, slightly flexed, lying on right side.	Beneath head.	N	'Shale' *	5	14	13	10	21	Leaf 1940, fig 10, 10	Skeleton too decayed to permit assessment of sex & age. Dimensions taken from published drawing. Contemporary with, or secondary to, primary grave under centre of barrow containing contracted skeleton lying on left side, no visible grave goods. Stratigraphically earlier than graves with cremated remains, with other similar graves at Barrow 5 being associated with Deverel-Rimbury bucket urns. Current location: unknown (not in Museum of Archaeology & Anthropology, University of Cambridge.)
22–29	West Row Fen, Mildenhall, Suffolk	8	Settlement Ceramic type associated with settlement: Collared Urn.	No human remains; not a funerary context.	N	7 × 'jet' * + 1 × fired clay	1 × 3d 1× 4b 3× 4d 2× 4e; clay: 3c	a) 10 b) 12 c) 9 d) 14 e) 12.5 f) 13 g) 13 h) no info	a) 10 b) 12 c) 9 d) 13.5 e) 13.5 f) 12 g) 12.5 h) no info	a) 6.5 b) 10.5 c) 6 d) 9 e) 11.5 f) 8 g) 11 h) no info	a) 12.5 b) 12.5 c) 14 d) 15 e) 18 f) 22.5 g) 22.5 h) no info	Martin & Murphy 1988; Tomalin 2011, 558–559	Dimensions taken from published drawings. Clay example not mentioned in Martin & Murphy 1988 but discussed by Tomalin (2011, 558–559), who studied it & suggested it could have been used to make up a 4th pair with the 7 jet studs. Radiocarbon dates (mostly from mixed-species bulk samples, & submitted in the 1980s) suggest activity in S part of settlement 2020–1740 cal BC, & in N part 1880–1410 cal BC (Bayliss et al. 2012, 202–204). Current location: mostly c/o Suffolk Co. Council; ceramic stud c/o pottery specialist (D Tomalin).
30, 31	Norton Subcourse (skeleton 2), Norfolk	2	Grave pit I, young adult, poss. female, tightly contracted, prob. bound; buried face down Second tightly-contracted, prob. bound skeleton (Sk 1), young adult, prob. male, prob. deposited after Sk 2.	1 found beside position of ear; other under skull.	N	Both jet	1 × 4d 1 × 4e	i) 13.1 ii) 9.1 × 9.6	i) 11.4 × 12.9 ii) 8.3–8.5	i) 9 ii) 5.2 × 5.4	i) 16.3 ii) 13.6	Yates et al. 2012; Sheridan 2011	Sk 2 radiocarbon dated to 3060±40 BP (Beta-299801), 1430–1210 cal BC. Cf date for Sk 1: 3030±40 BP (Beta-299800, 1410–1120 cal BC. Current location: c/o excavator.

No.	Site	No.	Context	Position		Material	Type	Dim. 1	Dim. 2	Dim. 3	Dim. 4	Reference	Comments
32	Fengate, Cambridge-shire	1	In fill of ring-ditch, 'on a "grave" floor which was slightly raised at the head and feet with a hollow for the hips' (Wyman Abbott notebook) I, contracted; no details of age or sex.	Under head, near lower portion of head.	N	'Kim. Shale'*	4c	See comments				Wyman Abbott notes, reproduced in Evans & Appleby 2008, 178	One of c. 28 skeletons (of all ages & both sexes) & c. 80 deposits of cremated remains in fill of ring ditch. Known only from Wyman Abbott's sketch & description; from sketch likely to be comparable in size to Over examples (i.e., c. 14–17mm long). Current location: lost.
33	Fengate, Cambridge-shire	1	In fill of ring-ditch, 'on a "grave" floor which was slightly raised at the head and feet with a hollow for the hips' (Wyman Abbott notebook) I, contracted; no details of age or sex.	Under head, near lower portion of head.	N	'Kim. Shale'*	4b	See comments				Wyman Abbott notes, reproduced in Evans & Appleby 2008, 178	One of c. 28 skeletons (of all ages & both sexes) and c. 80 deposits of cremated remains in fill of ring-ditch. From different skeleton from that found with other stud found at Fengate. Known only from Wyman Abbott's sketch & description; from sketch, likely to be comparable in size to Over examples (i.e., c. 14–17 mm long). Current location: lost.
34, 35	Langtoft, Lincolnshire	2, of which 1 perforated	Grave pit I, tightly contracted, adult aged over 35, ?male, on left side Dog.	On either side of neck, just above shoulders.	N	Both prob. Kim shale	1 × 4c 1 × 4d	a) 13.7 × 12.5 b) 11.7 × 11.2	a) 11.2 × 10 b) 13.4 × 13.4	a) 7.4 × 6.3 b) 11.1 × 10.5	a) 16.8 b) 21	Hutton 2008	Their position is compatible with use as studs, although 1 is perforated (with perforation lying at point where stud would have been concealed within earlobe hole). While this does not rule out use as a stud, an alternative interpretation of perforated example is as a toggle-shaped fastener or pendant. Excavation report refers to 'fine grooves on the indented area suggesting something was wrapped around the middle' although this need *not* indicate wear from cordage, & could instead be a tool-mark. This object could well have been used as a stud. The unperforated item is Type 4c object, & its dimensions are recorded as (a). Current location: c/o excavator.

| 36 | Raunds, West Cotton (on periphery of barrow 6), Northampton-shire | 1 | Grave pit, between outer ditch of barrow 6 & adjacent ditched enclosure; prob. part of secondary activity in area of pre-existing round barrow C, young adult, aged 16–21, ?female Collared Urn, 'stylistically late', buried on its side. | Among cremated remains in Collared Urn; found towards urn's base. | ? | Fired clay | 3c | 22 | c. 20 | c. 17.5 | 15 | Tomalin 2011, 558–559, 598–600 & fig. SS3.84; Chapman et al. 2011, 259–261 | Unclear whether stud burnt or not; described as being of hard reduction-fired grey clay. Comminuted shell present as filler. Some dimensions taken from published drawing. Undated but excavator comments: 'This cremation is likely to lie within phase 7 of the barrow development. Stratigraphically, however, it could have been considerably earlier in date and may have been a cremation within the Ditched Enclosure' (Chapman et al. 2011, 261). 2 Phase 7 pits containing cremated remains nearby radiocarbon dated: grave F3219, from Pomoideae charcoal, to 3610±40 BP (OxA-7866, 2130–1880 cal BC); the other (F3206), from mature Quercus charcoal, to 3347±54 BP (UB-3315, 1760–1500 cal BC; tpq). The stud is arguably more likely to be closer in date to F3219 than F3206. Flint flake & tooth of cow or horse in fill of grave pit not associated with grave: could be residual or intrusive. Current location: c/o Historic England (Fort Cumberland). |

No.	Site		Contents	Human remains	Material	Type					Reference	Notes
37	Lockington (site V, pit 84), Leicestershire	1	Pit. 5 frags from 4 Beakers; 1 sherd 'Bronze Age' pottery; lower part of Late Bronze Age jar; charcoal, charred cereal grains & other charred plant material.	No human remains present.	Fired clay	1b	30	28	26.5	13	Woodward 2000, 56–57; Hughes 2000, 17, 79, table 1	Some dimensions taken from published drawing. Suspected to be disturbed Early Bronze Age grave, with intrusive Late Bronze Age pot; whether Beaker sherds are residual from earlier activity, & whether stud had actually been associated with 'Bronze Age' sherd, is unclear. Grog present as filler in stud; also in Beaker sherds. Charcoal (bulk sample comprising oak, poplar, hawthorn, hazel, blackthorn, field maple, ash & gorse) radiocarbon dated to 3440±80 BP (Beta-83721, 1950–1530 cal BC); it is unknown whether/how this relates to stud's deposition & fact that dated material was not a single-entity sample casts some doubt on its reliability. Current location: c/o Leicestershire County Council Museums Service.
						N						
38	Barton-under-Needwood (pit 824), Staffordshire	1	Grave pit C, indeterminate age & sex Charcoal.	Among cremated remains.	Fired clay	2a	33	28	c. 21	c. 19	Martin & Allen 2001, 10–12	Stud has central vertical perforation 11mm in diam. Grog present as filler in stud. Some dimensions taken from published drawing. Excavators state that stud had probably been through pyre with body. From cemetery of graves containing cremated human remains, inc. pits containing northern English type of Deverel-Rimbury urns. If grave with stud is contemporary, likely to date to mid-second millennium BC. Current location: Birmingham University, awaiting transfer to Potteries Museum & Art Gallery, Stoke on Trent.
						Prob						
39	Woodhouse End (inurned cremation 1), Gawsworth, Cheshire	1	On floor of quarry-ditch for round barrow C, 2 individuals: adult, prob female & immature, indeterminate sex, aged over 6 Collared Urn, Longworth's Secondary Series; Small flint flake; calcined flint implement; charcoal.	Among cremated remains in upright Collared Urn.	Fired clay	2b	c. × 23	c. 15	c. 13	c. 13	Longworth 1984, no 134; Rowley 1977	1 of several 'satellite burials', believed to be secondary to primary putative grave (under centre of barrow) containing long-necked Beaker & flint knife. Publication does not state whether stud had passed through pyre or not. Dimensions taken from published illustration. Current location: Grosvenor Museum, Chester.
						?						

	Site		Context	Stud position	Y/N	Material	Type					Reference	Notes
40	Stanton Moor (mound T13, interment J), Derbyshire	1	Under roughly rectangular mound C, adult female, aged in 20s Small Collared Urn, Longworth's Secondary Series; accessory vessel.	Within accessory vessel inside upright Collared Urn.	Y	Fired clay	4a	24 × 23.2	25.2	16.9	13	Vine 1982, 408, no 999; Longworth 1984, no 320; Woodward & Hunter 2015, ID 1229	Bright orange-red colour, slight surface sheen & softness of fabric all point towards this stud having been on body as it was cremated. Current location: Weston Park, Museums Sheffield (1979:986).
41, 42	Brenig (Llanrhaiadr yn Cinmoerth) (44, pit F20), Denbighshire	2	I, in grave pit associated with ring-cairn, just inside ring C, at least 1 adult & child aged about 5 Collared Urn, Longworth's Secondary Series (= Pot B; decorated); accessory vessel; burnt flint plano-convex knife; second Collared Urn, Longworth's Secondary Series, inverted, containing cremated remains of single individual, prob adult, & some charcoal.	Among cremated remains in inverted Collared Urn; had been pressed into top of mass of cremated remains before urn inverted.	Y	Both fired clay	Both 4a	a) 27.5 b) 30.3–28.2	a) damaged b) c. 30	a) c. 22 b) c. 23	a) 12.3 b) 13.5	Lynch 1993, 129–130; Brindley 2007, 365; Longworth 1984, no 2024, pl. 124; Burrow 2011, 137	Studs reportedly made from 2 different clays. No sign of wear. Waist not quite central in either stud. Cremated bone radiocarbon dated to 3550±50 BP (GrA-22970, 2030–1750 cal BC), replacing old date from charcoal (mixed species, inc. oak, from pit fill) of 3230±70 BP (HAR-503, 1670–1320 cal BC). Some dimensions taken from published illustrations. Current location: National Museum Wales, Cardiff.
43	Cefn Cwmwd (F1009), Anglesey	1	Grave pit, truncated, in unmounded cemetery C, adolescent, indet. sex Collared Urn, Longworth's Secondary Series.	Among cremated remains in inverted Collared Urn.	N	Shale, prob. Kim.	3a	23.9	19.8	14.7 × 14.3	13.4	Sheridan 2012	*Taq* provided by radiocarbon date for oak charcoal from grave pit (F1010) with Collared Urn that cuts F1009: 3587±57 BP (Wk-9289, 2140–1760 cal BC, but possibility of old wood effect). Current location: Oriel Ynys Môn, Anglesey.

| 44 | Whitelow Cairn (cremation E), Ramsbottom, Greater Manchester | 1 | Grave pit, 1 of several secondary graves within ring-cairn C, young adult, prob./poss. female, or adolescent (see comments) Frags bone pin, calcined; calcined flint knife (in frags). | Among cremated remains in pit. | N? | Fired clay | 1b | 30 | 25 | 18 | 13 | Tyson 1995; Barrowclough 2008; Walsh 2013, (vol. 1) 79, 223–235 & fig. 25b, (vol. 2) 101, 303–304; inf. S. Lord, Bury Museum | No obvious heat-damage but pale grey colour raises possibility that it could have passed through pyre Some dimensions taken from published illustration. Not directly dated but see below regarding dating of other deposits in cemetery; judging from these, cremation E prob. dates to *c.* 1800 cal BC. Primary interment had been of cremated remains, under small cairn roughly in centre of area enclosed by ring-cairn. Osteological identification given as 'young adult, possibly female or adolescent' in detailed report (Walsh 2013 vol. 2, 304), but elsewhere as 'young adult female' (e.g., Walsh 2013, vol. 1, 173). Earlier osteological report, by E.L. Patterson, concluded that individual was 'a young, slightly-built adult, probably female' Current location: Bury Museum (BUYGM.T684). |

| 45, 46 | Whitelow Cairn (cremation H), Rams-bottom, Greater Manchester | 2 | Grave pit, 1 of several secondary graves within ring-cairn C, young–middle-aged adult, female Charcoal. | Among cremated remains in pit. | Y | Both fired clay | Both 1b or 2 | a) 20 b) c22 | a) c 20 b) not rec-orded | Not rec-orded | a) 10 b) 50 (incom plete) | Tyson 1995; Barrowclough 2008; Walsh 2013, (vol. 1) 79, 223–235, (vol. 2) 101, 298–299 and fig. 104; inf. S. Lord, Bury Museum, & S. Walsh | From photographs sent to author by S. Lord, it is clear that 2 in-complete studs are present, rather than 1, as stated by previous commentators. Both had clearly been through pyre. Osteological identification given as 'adult, indeterminate sex', in detailed report (Walsh 2013 vol. 2, 299), but elsewhere as 'young to mature adult female' (e.g., Walsh 2013, vol. 1, 173). Oak charcoal from deposit radiocarbon dated, in 1990s, to 3635±20 BP (2115–1935 cal BC; GrN-16616); another sample of oak charcoal dated in 2007/2008 to 3515±35 BP (SUERC-4456, 1940–1740 cal BC). Cannot rule out possibility of old wood effect. Radiocarbon dating of 5 deposits of cremated bone from elsewhere in cemetery in 2012 produced dates ranging between 3599±28 BP (OxA-26844, 2040–1880 cal BC, cremation F) & 3496±28 BP (OxA-26847, 1900–1700 cal BC, cremation G). It is likely that cremations E & H belong within this date bracket, post-dating earliest deposits & probably dating to *c.* 1800 cal BC (Walsh 2013, fig. 104). Note that date for cremation G post-dates associated oak charcoal which previously dated to 3595±20 BP (GrN-16617, 2025–1885 cal BC), indicating an old wood effect. Current location: Bury Museum (BUYGM.T685). |

| 47 | Rishworth Moor, West Yorkshire | 1 | Jet | N | 4a | 21.0 | 18.5 | 15 | 13 | Stray find. See 'Comments'. | No human remains found. | *Transactions of the Halifax Antiquarian Society* 1914, 94–95; Priestley 1936, 128; Manby 1977, 22; Barnes 1982, 116; Barrowclough 2008, 142; inf. C. Yeates, Kirklees Museums & Galleries | 'Found by [H.P.] Kendall in March 1914 on a bare patch of land after the peat had been washed away' (inf. Tolson Museum index card, per C. Yeates). Kendall's account, in the *Trans. Halifax Antiq. Soc.*, says that land had been 'quite undisturbed except for the gradual washing away of the peat'. This account makes no reference to any barrow or cairn, & since Kendall's account went on to mention Mortimer's work on barrows in Yorkshire, had there been any traces of a mound at the stud's findspot, he would have mentioned it. Barrowclough's claim that stud is '[S]aid to have been associated with a barrow' (Barrowclough 2008, 142) is therefore not borne out by available information Current location: Tolson Museum, Huddersfield (on long-term loan from Bankfield Museum, Halifax). |

No.	Site	Qty	Context	Association		Material	Type					Reference	Comments
48	Castle Dean, Rishworth Moor, West Yorkshire	1	Stray find. See 'Comments'.	No human remains found.	N	Fired clay*	1b?	16	16	14	9.5	Barnes 1982, 116; inf. C. Yeates, Kirklees Museums & Galleries	No further details on findspot. Even though stud is similar in size to other Rishworth Moor find, there is insufficient information to be able to say whether they were found close to each other or not The stud is currently attached to a back-board & shape of 1 side cannot be seen; visible side is slightly dished, but unclear whether any of that side had spalled off. If it had, & if surface had been slightly domed, that would make this a type 4a stud. If both sides had been flat, it would be of type 2. Blackish colour seems to represent a deliberate attempt to make this object look like jet. The sub-surface, visible in old chip scars, is much lighter so addition of a surface coating, or some other superficial treatment, is suspected. Material would benefit from re-examination to check whether it is indeed fired clay. Current location: Tolson Museum, Huddersfield (34.61.64, J.H. Priestley collection).
49	Harden Moor, West Yorkshire	1	Grave pit in SW quadrant of ring cairn (pit F127).	Among unurned cremated remains of adult, probably female; some animal bone also present, plus oak charcoal and burnt stone.	Prob.	Fired clay.	3a	28.5	24.5	20.1	13.5	Boughey 2010	Associated oak charcoal radio-carbon-dated to 3530±50 BP (BM-2574), 2020–1690 (recalibrated in 2014 using OxCal 4.2). Other funerary deposits associated with ring-cairn were associated with Collared Urns & accessory vessel, with earliest deposits of cremated remains in centre of ring-cairn dating to 2019–1787 cal BC & latest, in ring-cairn bank, dating to 1745–1634 (Boughey 2010, 20; these dates as cited by Boughey). Part of inner surface missing; condition of clay gives impression that stud had passed through pyre. Current location: last known location was with excavator, Prof. Julian Henderson, University of Nottingham.

No.	Site	Number	Context	Association	Burnt	Material	Form					References	Comments
50	Thornton-in-Craven, Hare Hill (Rectory Allotment, Thornton Moor), N. Yorkshire	1	Isolated find beneath outer circle of a ring-cairn.	Not directly associated with any human remains.	N	Jet	1a	37.3	25.3	18.1	19.2	Boughey 2015, 81–2; inf. K.Boughey, T. Manby & M. Wills (of Craven Museum & Gallery, Skipton)	Outer (cupped) surface highly polished. Criss-cross cracking suggests use of soft jet. Chip missing from edge of outer surface. Current location: Craven Museum & Gallery, Skipton (01075).
51, 52	Wharram Percy (barrow 70), N. Yorkshire	2	Grave pit under round barrow; body surrounded by 'very impervious blue clay' and 'many small, greasy-sided cavities, apparently caused by something that had decayed' (Mortimer 1905, 47) I, aged around 14 yrs, on back with legs flexed to left side; head to SE	Close to the neck and partly under the skull.	N	Both jet	Both 4a	a) 21.7 × 22 b) 21.8 × 21.9	a) 18.4 x18.5 b) 18.5 × 18.7	a) 12.7 b) 13.5	15	Mortimer 1905, 47 and figs 74–5; Woodward & Hunter 2015, ID 200 and 201	David Tomalin (2011, 559); following Mortimer (1905, 402), stated that the skeleton was that of a young female but no grounds are given for this, and it is suspected that it is an assumption. Current location: Hull & East Riding Museum, Hull (335.1942).
53, 54	Crosscliff[e], N.Yorkshire	2	'In a barrow'; no further details.	Assumed to accompany human remains; likely to have been unburnt, by analogy with Wharram Percy & Nawton finds.	N	Both jet	Both 1a	a) 38 b) 35	a) 22.5 b) 29 (incomplete)	a) ≈ 16 b) ≈ 25	a) 19 b) 12.5 (incomplete)	Gettins et al. 1953, 44; Elgee 1930, 111; Manby 1977, 22; inf. T. Manby	'...found by Thomas [Mitchelson] Kendall in a barrow at Crosscliffe, north of Pickering (Yorkshire Museum, 1948)' (Manby 1977, 22). 1 complete, 1 lacking part of its inner surface & edge; complete example has polished outer (cupped) surface & domed inner surface; incomplete example has broader inner surface. Current location: Yorkshire Museum (YORYM 1948.32.1-2; Mitchelson Collection).
55, 56	Near Fylingdales (almost certainly the Peak, nr Robin Hood's Bay), N.Yorkshire	2	From a barrow No details; see 'Comments'.	Assumed to accompany human remains; likely to have been unburnt, by analogy with Wharram Percy and Nawton finds.	N	Both jet	Both 4a	a) 32.5 × 34.5 b) 28.6 × 29.5	a) & b): approx. same as 'outer' surface	a) 21.2 × 23.4 b) 21.5 × 22.6	16.1	Woodward & Hunter 2015, ID 440 & 441	T. Manby (pers. comm.) confirmed this is pair referred to by Mortimer (1905, 47) as having been in Thomas Boynton's collection, & having almost certainly come from diggings into a barrow on the Peak, near Robin Hood's Bay, c. 1870. Boynton bought studs in sale of effects from Peak Hall in 1895, & gifted them to the British Museum. Current location: British Museum (1902.0216.1-2).

No.	Site	N	Context	Human remains	Material	Type	a) / b) dim 1	dim 2	dim 3	dim 4	References	Comments
57, 58	Nawton (Pinderdale Wood, Beadlam), N.Yorkshire	2	Under centre of round barrow; no details as to whether in grave pit or on old land surface I, around 14 years old, 'probably female' (but see 'Comments') Ring or pendant, with asymmetrical perforation; jet 4 complete & one incomplete fusiform beads, jet (& further example discovered later on & mound, along with rough piece of bronze & stone bead or spindle whorl, latter 2 unlikely to be related to grave).	N	Both jet	Both 1a	a) 41.3 × 42.7 b) absent	a) 24.7 × 26.5 b)25.8	a) 21.5 b) 20.6	a) 15.5 b) 6.8+	Hayes 1963, 35, 52, n 14, 345–346; Smith 1994, 21, 110, pl. 23 (NYM 88); Woodward & Hunter 2015, ID 449 & 453	Discrepancy in size between 2 studs due to outer surface of (b) being missing. When new, they would prob. have been roughly same size & shape. Barrow excavated as result of wager between Lord Helmsley & another party; details of context sketchy Sir Arthur Keith stated that individual had been 'probably female' but if age estimate of 14 is correct, it can be very difficult to sex a skeleton. Current location: British Museum (1920.0414.1 and 3).
59, 60	Ballinchalla, County Mayo, Ireland	2	Cist, 3 compartments C, adult female, adult male & adolescent.	Y	Both fired clay	1c & ?	a) c. 15 b) frag	a) c. 13	a) c. 9	a) 26.5	Cahill & Sikora 2014	1 stud is in frags (& may have exploded in pyre). Radiocarbon date (cremated bone): 3442±35 BP (UBA-19254, 1880–1690 cal BC) Current location: National Museum of Ireland, Dublin

[1]Key: C = cremated remains; I = unburnt human remains; [2]Entries marked with asterisk indicate where confirmation of the identification is required, where possible. 'Kim' = Kimmeridge; [3]See Fig. 16.13 for key to stud types; [4]Where two dimensions are given together, this results from the measuring of the diameter at two positions around the circumference, to give a sense of the variability of the diameter; [5]All radiocarbon dates calibrated using OxCal 4.2 and cited at 95.4% probability, rounded out to the nearest decade.

Note: Not included here are the following, some of which are discussed in the main text: i) sheet gold conical objects from Upton Lovell G2e, Wiltshire and the sheet gold 'button covers' from Hengistbury Head, Hampshire, and Barnhill, Broughty Ferry, Angus; ii) 'jet stud' from the Yorkshire Wolds, mentioned by Sheppard (1900, 53); it is unclear whether this had been a stud or a V-perforated button; iii) a large clay object resembling a larger, cruder version of a Type 4a stud from a burnt mound at Cranagh, Co. Wicklow, Ireland (M. Cahill pers. comm.), which is arguably more likely to be a plug for draining a water trough than an item of personal adornment; iv) 'jet ear plug' referred to as associated with a Step 5 Beaker in Lancashire (Barrowclough 2008, fig. 92): no details available concerning the provenance of this claimed example, and it is suspected to be an erroneous entry.

17. The flint

Anna Lawson-Jones

A single flint flake was extracted from inside the basketry container (Chapter 3). It measures 31mm long by 25mm wide by 5mm thick (Fig. 17.1) and was the only flint artefact found during the excavation.

The piece has a banded mid and pale grey ventral face with a paler, partially re-patinated dorsal face. The repatination suggests that the core may have been curated prior to the removal of the flake. The form is suggestive of removal from a larger soft hammered piece, probably a core undergoing reduction soon after the removal of the outer cortical skin, (given the two small dorsal patches of thin white cortex). The flake then saw limited use as a flake tool. The survival of two or three tiny adhering flakelets to the dorsal face reflects a lack of disturbance since deposition following limited use.

The flake is thin with broad rounded corners. Backing retouch can be seen running from the bulb and small platform down the straighter, thickest side of the flake forming a comfortable forefinger hold. The opposing edge is slightly more convex and much thinner, fitting comfortably between the thumb and side of the middle finger. The very slight damage along this edge is the result of abrasion during use. A scrap of leather may have been used to protect the finger and thumb. The modified left- and abraded right-hand sides of the flake reflect how the piece was held and used.

The working edge is located on the left distal side of the flake. Here, focused abrasion can be seen running around a wide notch-like area which extends from the backed edge to half way along the distal end, largely following the most pronounced part of a conchoidal ripple.

This comfortable-to-hold flake tool has seen apparent light use as a broad notched slicing or scraping tool. It is of a simple design, quick to make but highly practical; light in weight and easily modified for a range of uses. Macroscopic analysis suggests that it is most likely to have been used on a soft material, perhaps during the preparation of plant stuffs for food, during bark or leather working, or extracting fibres for basketry work. It would not be suitable for heavy-duty use on hard substances such as wood, bone or horn since these materials would cause significant edge damage, quickly rendering the flake unusable.

Flints represent the most common find from Dartmoor's cists and cairns. Worth (1967, 197) noted that 'flint flakes and implements' have been found in association with Early Bronze Age monuments across Dartmoor, and that some are of a very simple design. Wainwright *et al.* (1979, 29) lists a small number of flint tools associated with the Shaugh Moor cairns on Dartmoor, noting patchy re-patination on some of the pieces and many with evidence for varied use. Further references to Bronze Age sites and flintwork on and around Dartmoor can be found in Butler (1997, 207, 275–277). Previously recorded implements range from finely-worked knives, scrapers and barbed and tanged arrowheads to less strikingly diagnostic worked flints (Butler 1997, 206). The Whitehorse Hill flint would fit well within this picture of variable but utilised flint found associated with Dartmoor cists and barrows.

Significantly, unlike so many of the other flints recovered from Dartmoor, this piece, uniquely, retained much, if not all of its original depositional context, including the basketry container in which it was placed!

Acknowledgements

Thanks to Ryan Smith for photographing the flint.

Figure 17.1: Photograph of the flint. (Photograph: Ryan Smith.)

References

Butler, J. 1997. *Dartmoor Atlas of Antiquities*, Volume 5. Tiverton: Devon Books.

Wainwright, G. J., Fleming, A. & Smith, K. 1979. The Shaugh Moor Project: first report. *Proceedings of the Prehistoric Society* 45, 1–34.

Worth, R. N. 1967. *Worth's Dartmoor*. Newton Abbot: David and Charles.

18. The textile and animal-skin object

Esther Cameron, Susanna Harris and Quita Mould

A textile and animal-skin object lay beneath the animal pelt (Figs. 18.1 and 18.2). The irregularly-shaped remains measured 345 × 260mm but, as no edges could be observed, the object is assumed to be incomplete and the original dimensions are unknown. In burial, the remains had been flattened onto a layer of matted plant material lining the base of the cist. Impressed on the upper face were further traces of plant material and hairs from the animal pelt.

On initial inspection the object appeared to comprise a panel of textile 345 × 65mm with elaborate seams of well-preserved animal skin along its two longer sides and a compacted surface of another organic material extending out beyond them. It was suggested at first that this compacted organic material might be animal skin which had subsequently decayed, leaving little or no trace observable to the naked eye, but it has not been possible to confirm this scientifically (but see 'the surrounding organic remains' below).

Once the upper face had been cleaned and recorded, and samples of the organic materials taken for SEM and dye analysis, the object was turned over. This revealed a layer of decayed plant material, in places up to 8mm thick, which obscured the underside. The material was removed carefully, mindful that further layers of textile and leather could lie within it, but none could be recognised. Inspection of the cleaned surface showed that the object was primarily of a single thickness, albeit with traces of a possible lining in the area of the textile panel (below). No multiple layers were detected which might point to its having been a larger object, deliberately folded or subsequently crushed in the burial.

The three potential components of the object – the textile panel, the animal-skin seams, and the surrounding organic remains – are described in detail below. These sections draw on the findings of SEM analysis conducted separately by Esther Cameron (Cameron *et al.* 2013) and

Caroline Cartwright (Appendix B) and of dye and tannin analysis by Ina Vanden Berghe (Coudray and Vanden Berghe 2013).

The textile panel

The textile component was fragile and heavily encrusted. The thread system running the length of the textile (system 1) was particularly weak and susceptible to disintegration if moved and for this reason there was minimal contact with any part of the textile during analysis. The encrustation was identified under SEM as a variety of plant remains with traces of decayed leather or skin products within it of the same colour as the textile and hence difficult to differentiate from it either by examination with hand lens, optical microscope or SEM (Appendix B). Although the original colour of the textile and animal-skin object has been lost, its elaborate structure suggests that it could originally have been coloured, for example by dyeing.

The central panel was a woven textile. Stitched to either edge were two rows of leather 'beading' and a fringe of outward pointing triangles. The textile component had two layers. The construction of a portion of the textile and animal-skin object in plan and section views is shown schematically in Figures 18.3 and 18.4. The backs of the seams were exposed when the underside of the object was cleaned, which confirmed that it had a front and back. The layer facing upwards in the cist is the 'right' side of the artefact while the layer facing downwards is the 'wrong' side, as the edges of the 'beading' and fringe are visible. These will hereafter be called the upper and lower textile layer.

The preserved area of the upper textile layer measured 350mm long and 65mm wide. Including the leather fringe, the full width of the composite textile and animal-skin band was 105mm. If there were selvedges along the long edge of the textile they were not visible, probably because they were stitched into the animal-skin seam. Due to the

Figure 18.1: The textile and animal-skin object, upper view. (Photograph: M. Wachnik.)

Figure 18.2: Illustration of the textile and animal-skin object, upper view. (Drawing: M. Wachnik.)

absence of selvedges, starting or finishing borders, it was not possible to distinguish warp and weft, so the threads running the length of the textile are denoted system 1 and those across the width system 2. The upper textile layer was woven in repp, which is a variation of plain weave. This means that the textile was woven with a simple under one, over one which alternates each row (plain weave) and the thread count of one system is significantly higher and more tightly packed than the threads of the other system (repp) (Bender Jørgensen 1992, 13). Repp may also be referred to as warp faced or weft faced depending on which thread system dominates the weave (Emery 1966, 76–77, 86–87). Of the upper textile layer, both system 1 and 2 were made of z2S threads, which means they were made of two z-spun threads plied together in an S-direction. (The z and s refer to the direction of spin; s being counter clockwise and z clockwise. The capital letters denote the direction of plying.) Threads of system 1 measured 0.5–0.8mm in diameter and were medium to loosely spun. Threads of

system 2 measured 1–1.2mm in diameter and were loosely spun (65°). In terms of thread count, there is an average of 22 threads per cm in system 1 and 5–6 per cm in system 2.

The lower layer comprised multiple rows of parallel yarn running the length of the band (Fig. 18.5). The threads were 2S, that is, two simple threads plied in an S direction, measuring 0.8mm in diameter. As threads are inclined to tangle if they are not fixed in place, it seems highly likely that they originally belonged to a textile but that only one set of threads remains. Where only one thread system survives it is usually assumed the textile was made of two different raw materials, for example a plant fibre and an animal fibre. In this case, one of these has not survived in the burial environment. In the Whitehorse Hill cist both plant fibres and animal hair were preserved, although the absence of the pelt skin (Chapter 11) demonstrates that not all materials of animal origin were equally preserved. The remaining threads on the lower layer were straight and did not have the crinkly appearance one might expect of a

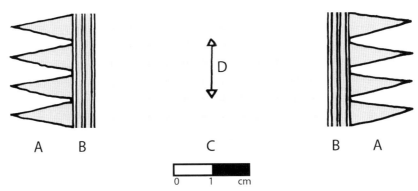

Figure 18.3: Schematic diagram showing the construction of a portion of the textile and animal-skin object, plan view. A = leather fringe of outward pointing triangles, B = two rows of leather 'beading', C = upper layer of textile, D = direction of thread system 1, upper textile layer. (Drawing: S. Harris.)

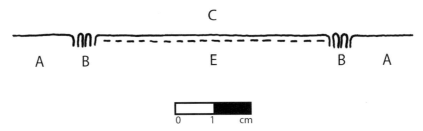

Figure 18.4: Schematic diagram showing the construction elements of the textile and animal-skin object, section view. Annotation as for plan view, E = lower textile layer. (Drawing: S. Harris.)

Figure 18.5: The lower textile layer showing multiple rows of parallel, S-plied yarn running lengthways. (Photograph: Helen Williams, Wiltshire Conservation Centre.)

single set of preserved threads. Therefore, although it seems likely that the lower layer is the remains of a textile, the exact nature of this textile is unclear. Due to the encrusted surface, the threads were only visible for part of the central textile area; therefore the way the lower textile layer was joined to the seam is unclear.

The analysis of threads from the textile component found both to be of vegetable fibre. With the hope of identifying the plant fibre species, the encrusted fibres were cleaned by gently macerating with hydrogen peroxide, distilled water

and glacial acetic acid (Appendix B, below). Following cleaning, the VP-SEM examination carried out by Caroline R. Cartwright concluded that two fibres could be closely matched with nettle (*Urtica dioica*) (Appendix B).

Bronze Age textile manufacture: the wider context

Recent overviews of textile technology in the British Isles have concentrated on the Late Bronze Age and Iron Ages (DeRoche 2012; Wincott Heckett 2012). Hence, the main comprehensive reviews of Early to Middle Bronze Age textiles in Britain remain Henshall (1950) and Bender Jørgensen's chapter on Great Britain and Ireland and the catalogue in her analysis of north European textiles (Bender Jørgensen 1992, 18–19, 197–198). These are supplemented by published and unpublished textile reports (Gabra-Sanders 1994; Crowfoot in Green and Rollo-Smith 1984, 311–312; Harris 2012; Hedges 1974; Jones *et al.* 2011, 89; Walton Rogers 2008).

Fibres: identification and evidence of processing

In Bronze Age Europe the most commonly identified textile fibres are linen from the flax plant (*Linum usitatissimum*) and wool. While it is relatively easy with microscopic examination to distinguish plant (also referred to as vegetable or cellulose) from animal fibre, species identification is more problematic. Although quoted in later literature, early species identifications should be treated cautiously, as for example the 'fine fibre resembling flax' of textiles from Garton Slack, Yorkshire (Mortimer 1905, 234), which seems little more than speculation (Henshall 1950, 142). Although recent fibre identifications for Bronze Age Britain are scarce, both flax and nettle fibres have been identified, albeit sometimes tentatively. Fibres from a plain weave textile from Must Farm, Cambridgeshire, were identified as almost certainly flax, while those from a tapestry weave textile at the same site were identified as possibly flax (Walton Rogers 2008). Fibres on the back of a small, bronze pendant from a vessel containing a cremation at Harlyn Bay, Cornwall (2120–1880 cal BC, SUERC-15536) are identified as 'most likely linen' but could also be from another species (Jones *et al.* 2011, 89).

The identification of nettle fibres is relatively rare on a European scale. A textile from the socket of a spearhead in a hoard found at Pyotdykes, Angus, Scotland (eighth century cal BC), was first identified by Ryder as flax (Henshall 1964, 198) but Hedges later suggested the fibres could be nettle (Hedges 1973, 61–69, 213–214, quoted in Gabra-Sanders 1994, 41). A Late Bronze Age textile (ninth–eighth century cal BC) from Denmark, discovered inside a bronze cauldron at Lusehøj, near Voldtofte in south Funen, was identified as nettle fibre (Mannering *et al.* 2012, 97). More recently, fibres from a plain weave textile from a late Early Bronze Age (1880–1690 cal BC, OxA-24639) cremation in Over Barrow, Cambridgeshire, were identified by Gleba as most probably flax (*Linum* sp.) but with a possibility of being nettle (*Urtica* sp.) (Harris 2012).

It is tempting to see the three possible identifications of nettle in Britain (Whitehorse Hill, Over Barrow, Pyotdykes) as significant, especially the roughly contemporary textile from Over Barrow. However, caution is required. The Pyotdykes find is much later and the Over Barrow fibres are not clearly distinguished from flax. The Whitehorse Hill fibres are the most definitely identified as nettle so far. Although, as Cartwright writes in her SEM report (Appendix B), as only small samples of fibre were taken they may not be representative of the whole textile. The implications are nevertheless intriguing. Nettle fibres are cellulose fibres, which share common properties in that they are absorbent, flammable and resistant to alkalis (Harris 2010; Hencken Elsasser 2010, 58). While ostensibly producing a similar cellulose stem fibre to flax, nettle is typically a foraged plant rather than an agricultural crop, with implications in terms of raw material management and economy.

Threads: identification and evidence of processing

The spin direction and diameter of the yarns used to weave the Whitehorse Hill cist textiles find good comparisons in other British Bronze Age textiles and yarns. Textiles of plant fibre were typically made in 2-ply yarns, in contrast to wool textiles which were spun from simple yarns (Bender Jørgensen 1992, 19). The plied threads of the Whitehorse Hill cist woven textiles fit this pattern. In terms of spin direction, the z-spun and S-plied yarn (z2S) threads from the Whitehorse Hill cist are comparable to the S-plied yarns of Must Farm and Over Barrow, Cambridgeshire (Harris 2012; Walton Rogers 2008). The context in which the Over Barrow textiles belong is dated to the later Early Bronze Age, 1900–1700 cal BC (Evans *et al.* forthcoming; Harris 2015, 73). The textiles from Must Farm were charred in a fire which occurred in the Late Bronze Age 930–790 cal BC (Beta-243230; 2700+40 BP; Knight 2012). Geographically closer, the yarns used to make a plain weave textile from Barrow 5k, Shrewton, Wiltshire, were identified by Crowfoot as loosely S-plied (Green and Rollo-Smith 1984, 311). In terms of thread diameter, the 0.5–0.8mm range of the system 1 yarn can be compared to those from Over Barrow and Must Farm, but is coarser than the finest yarns at either site (Harris 2012; Walton Rogers 2008). The 1–1.2mm thread diameter of the system 2 thread of the Whitehorse Hill cist textile is slightly coarser than might typically be expected but, considering its use as the basis for the repp textile, need not be considered unusual.

For many years it was assumed that in the Bronze Age (and other prehistoric periods) stem fibres such as linen were produced in much the same way as historically, that is by retting, hackling, scutching and combing in preparation for draft spinning (Gleba and Mannering 2012, 9). New studies suggest that in some areas of Europe before the Middle to Late Bronze Age plant fibres were only partially retted and then spliced rather than spun into yarn (Leuzinger and Rast-Eicher 2011), a process documented elsewhere in the ancient world (Granger-Taylor 1998). Due to the state of preservation of the Whitehorse Hill cist textiles no further information can be added to this debate. However, for this reason any statements about fibre processing and thread production should be made warily until further research clarifies these methods.

Weave type and evidence of manufacture

In terms of weave structure, the majority of recorded British Bronze Age textiles are balanced plain weave. This is the case for the small fragments of charred textile found among the cremated bones at Whitehorse Hill cist (Chapter 8). As a repp textile, the upper textile layer from the Whitehorse Hill cist fits into the less common category of textiles. At Must Farm, alongside balanced plain weave textiles, Walton-Rogers (2008) describes several fancy textiles, including a fine repp textile measuring 90 × 15mm. Similar but not directly comparable are occasional examples of balanced plain weaves with repp borders; there are also textiles with decorative effects and one possible example of sprang, a type of netting (Bender Jørgensen 1992, 18–19; Pryor *et al.* 1985; Walton Rogers 2008; Wincott Heckett 2012, 432–436).

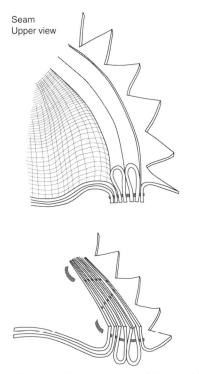

Seam
Upper view

Figure 18.6: Diagram of construction of the 'beaded' seam with fringe, upper and lower views (individual components not to scale). (Drawing: Q. Mould & M. Wachnik.)

Although there are no preserved selvedges or borders to suggest the type of loom used to weave the upper textile layer of the woven band, on the basis of dimension it seems likely that it was woven as a long, narrow strip, with system 1 as the warp threads and system 2 as the weft. If correct this would make it warp-faced, as in this case the warp threads (average of 22 threads per cm) hide most of the wefts (5–6 threads per cm). This alters the visual appearance of the textile, creating a ribbed effect (Chandler 1995, 121). It also changes the physical characteristics of the textile. A repp textile such as the Whitehorse Hill cist upper layer textile lacks the drape of a balanced plain weave; it is sturdier and would be suitable for making a belt or band (Chandler 1995, 119). This dense, sturdy characteristic is further emphasized by the addition of the lower textile layer which acted as a backing, making it stiffer and unlikely to roll up at the long edges.

The animal-skin seams

The construction of the two identical closed seams edging the textile panel was sophisticated, each incorporating two lengths of 'beading' and a decorative fringe, all made of animal skin 1mm in thickness (Fig. 18.6). Each length of 'beading' was folded double, forming a 'U'-shaped profile, with a folded width of 4–5mm and a thickness of 2mm across the fold. Such narrow, folded lengths of material incorporated into a seam are termed 'beading' in leatherworking and 'piping' in dressmaking and upholstery.

The fringe comprised a flat strip with the outer edge carefully cut into a series of small isosceles triangles, each 16–18mm long and a maximum of 7mm wide. The fringe was aligned so that the triangles lay outward, away from the textile panel and on top of the surrounding organic material.

Where the ends of the 'beading' were exposed small round stitch holes could clearly be seen each about 1mm in diameter and spaced approximately 5–6mm apart. Stitch holes were also present in the fringing. All the holes were empty, the stitching medium having decayed during the period since the burial, which suggests it may have been untreated animal sinew. The seams had a sinuous profile and, combined with the nature of the stitch holes in the 'beading', a closed seam sewn with a running stitch is suggested.

Skin: identification, evidence of processing and preservation

The skin of the 'beading' and fringe was robust and flexible; its outer surface smoother than the inner, giving the impression of 'grain' and 'flesh' sides, although no grain pattern was visible. The skin was outwardly hairless, but embedded within it were fragments of fine hair with well-preserved scale pattern which allowed the skin to be identified as calf (*Bos taurus*). There is little indication of how the skin was processed. The lack of a grain pattern, together with its smooth appearance, suggests that it was scraped on both sides but there is no further surviving evidence of the method of treatment used. Investigation of skin clothing from the glacier corpse from the Ötztaler Alps (*circa* 3200 cal BC) suggests that the skins had been processed using a combination of fats and smoke and the indications are that similar methods continued to be used in Western Europe throughout the prehistoric period (Forbes 1966; Ryder 1993; Groenman-van Waateringe 1995; Groenman-van Waateringe *et al.* 1999; Püntener and Moss 2010; Harris 2011; Thomson 2011a, 70–73). Animal skins treated in this way, impregnated with inert fatty materials and slowly dried, are resistant to decay for an extended period as the water-repellent fats coat the individual skin fibres and fill the spaces between them so that the fibres remain too dry for bacterial attack to take place (Thomson 2011b, 4). Although they can withstand repeated wetting they will eventually rot if subjected to prolonged damp conditions, as is the case here. The survival of the seams of the textile and animal-skin object is just one of many examples of human and animal tissues, both treated and untreated, to have been recovered from waterlogged peat environments.

Derivatives of cinnamic and benzoic acids were detected in samples taken from both the textile panel and the animal-skin seam as well as in the matted plant material that lay beneath. It has been suggested that these derived from the animal-skin seams, on the assumption that they had been tanned (Coudray and Vanden Berghe 2013, 7, and tables 3 and 4). As it is unlikely that a skin product of this

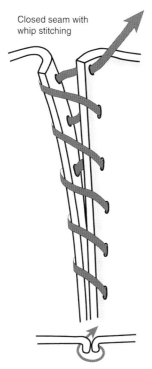

Closed seam with whip stitching

Figure 18.7: Closed seam with oversewn (whip) stitching. (Drawing: Q. Mould & M. Wachnik.)

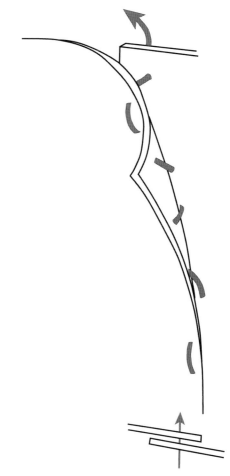

Figure 18.8: Lapped seam with running (tacking) stitching. (Drawing: Q. Mould & M. Wachnik.)

date was vegetable-tanned using polyphenolic vegetable tanning materials, an alternative explanation is required. The survival of the skin may well be due to two factors: a lack of oxygen and the presence of sphagnum moss, the latter being part of the wet heathland flora identified by Cartwright in the matted plant remains (Appendix B, Figs. B20–24). The moss is known to produce a polysaccharide tanning agent – 'sphagnan' – that cross links collagen fibres in skin, preventing decay, and causing it to develop a dark brown colouration similar to that of the skin seams (Painter 1991a; 1991b; 1995). Although the source of the tanning materials found in the textile and animal-skin object has not been scientifically verified it seems probable that they derived from sphagnum moss in the surrounding deposits.

Bronze Age skin working: the wider context

Excavation reports of Bronze Age burials in Britain are littered with descriptions of organic remains, some identified as skin products at the time of their discovery. Judging from the descriptions, such as that for Gristhorpe, Yorkshire, some of these traces appear to have been wrappings or coverings for the dead, while others suggest clothing, particularly a fragment of footwear from Loose Howe, Yorkshire (Melton *et al.* 2010; Elgee and Elgee 1949). Examples of seams and stitching have been observed, as at Cartington, Northumberland, where 'fragments of skin shewing (*sic*) the thong stitching … were found amongst the clay' (Dixon 1913, 82), at King Barrow, Arne, Stoborough, Dorset, where a human skeleton in a log coffin was found

wrapped in several skins neatly stitched together (Dodsley 1767, 70; Grinsell 1959; Needham *et al.* 2006, 103–104), and on knife sheaths from Kirkcaldy and Ashgrove, Fife (Henshall 1968, 195, figs. 40–41f). The type of stitching and the seams employed were not recorded in these early finds, and in most cases their dates are uncertain, so that the details of the seam construction used in the well-dated textile and animal-skin object from the Whitehorse Hill cist are of particular importance.

Evidence of Early Bronze Age skin-working from Danish oak coffin burials, the Hallstatt salt mines, the glacier corpse from the Ötztaler Alps, and Breton tombs such as Trossen-Kergourognon, Côtes d'Armor, indicates that at least two types of seam were in use at that time (Broholm and Hald 1948; Glob 1983; Ryder 1993; Spindler 1994; Prigent 1881). The first and most common type is the simple closed seam with 'oversewn' stitching, also termed 'whip' stitching (Fig. 18.7). The second is an overlapped seam with a running stitch, also called 'tacking' stitch, as seen on the leggings of the glacier corpse (Spindler 1994, 139) (Fig. 18.8). The original whip stitching of these seams is characteristically fine, while more crudely executed stitching has been identified as later repairs (Spindler 1994, 136). In respect of stitches and seams the textile and animal-skin object fits comfortably within this small body of evidence, but for the 'beading' and fringe there are no parallels.

The inclusion of 'beading' in a seam may render it more water tight. Although much later in date, seams with 'beading' are well attested in Roman leatherwork (Winterbottom 2009, 824, fig. 497, and appendix 10, 1387, table 110), including waterproof seams used on tents. The technique is used in animal-skin seams today In some instances it may be considered practical, such as on seal-skin boots (Western Canadian Arctic *mukluks*) made by peoples of the eastern and central Arctic, for example (Oakes and Riewe 1995, 61, fig. 45). In others, contrasting colours are selected for the 'beading' and it appears purely decorative, as seen on the red, single 'beaded' seams used on reindeer-skin bags made by the Sami and the turquoise triple 'beaded' seams used on the dark blue uppers of a Mongolian traditional leather boot (Cambridge Archaeology and Anthropology Museum MAA2003.6 and 1974.12 respectively). In the case of the Whitehorse Hill cist the fringe and the two lengths of 'beading' within the seams were essentially decorative and one might speculate that they were of differing colour to the textile and any animal-skin panels that may have surrounded it. However, no evidence for colouration or pigmentation was observed, nor was any evidence of dyes detected on either the fringe or the seam 'beading', or indeed on the textile (Coudray and Vanden Berghe 2013).

The surrounding organic remains

Organic material, present on the periphery of the textile and animal-skin object beyond the two fringes, extended to approximately 180mm to one side but ended close to the seam on the other. It consisted of an organic substance similar in colour to the textile, fringe and' beading'. The impressions of hair and hair-locks were visible on its surface and hair fibres, similar to those from the pelt, were also present. Below these impressions were plant rootlets and evidence of decayed vegetation which was generally indistinguishable from the layer of matted plant material that lay below the textile and animal-skin object. SEM analysis confirmed that the majority of this was vegetation in various stages of degradation. Vestigial traces of decayed leather or skin products were found intermingled with this wide variety of fragmented plant remains (Appendix B). One sample taken from the area of a seam was identified as a skin product of calf (*Bos taurus*) (Appendix B, Fig. B18). It would appear that within the surrounding organic remains some remnants of an animal-skin product had been preserved. These vestigial traces might be residual: some could have filtered down from the decaying pelt which was positioned immediately above, and the calf skin fragment may well have derived from part of the fringed seam. Alternatively, it is possible that they might represent the highly decayed remains of a separate animal-skin component. Insufficient has survived to be certain of its origins. One might speculate as to whether the textile panel had been part of a larger item made of animal skin that had subsequently decayed. If this had been the case, the seams would have been functional as well as decorative, as they would have served to join the two materials together.

Interpreting the evidence

Small fragments of textiles or dark stains around bodies, interpreted as the remains of textile or leather shrouds, wraps or clothing, have been found in Bronze Age cremation and inhumation burials throughout Britain. In other cases textiles were possibly used to wrap daggers and other items. In barrow 5k, Shrewton, Wiltshire, a dagger was wrapped in moss and textiles (Crowfoot in Green and Rollo-Smith 1984, 311). While there are no comparable composite textile and animal-skin objects in southern England there are textile bands from further afield. An ornate, twill weave horsehair band with elaborate tassels at either end was discovered in Cromaghs, Armoy, Co Antrim, Northern Ireland (Henshall 1950, 132–133, 138, 140, 158; Wincott Heckett 1998; 2012, 432–433); it is dated to the Late Bronze Age, around 800 cal BC, however, and thus rather late for a direct comparison. Of closer date are the narrow repp wool belts which were worn by men and women inhumed in Early Bronze Age barrows in Denmark. For example, there is a striped, tasselled repp belt (30 × 2460mm) worn by a female buried in Grave C, Borum Eshøj, Aarhus Amt (Broholm and Hald 1940, 73–77). In this case the tassel fringe was attached to the band with overstitching. Another tasselled repp belt (25 × 1750mm) was worn by a young woman buried at Egtved, Vejle Amt, dated to 1370 cal BC (Broholm and Hald 1940, 87; Christensen 2006, 221). Typically the Danish belts were woven in plain weave repp, in contrast to the accompanying textile clothing which was woven in balanced plain weave. A similar purpose may be attributed to the textile and animal-skin object in the Whitehorse Hill cist. It is woven in repp rather than plain weave, making it a sturdy rather than draping material; however, at 105mm wide the Whitehorse cist textile and animal-skin object is more than three times as wide as the two comparable textile belts mentioned above. At this width it is still narrow enough to be a belt but other possible uses should be considered: for example, a decorative sash worn on the body, a loincloth (comparable with that associated with the glacier corpse from the Ötztaler Alps), a decorative band attached to another artefact in the cist, or the remains of a component of another item, such as a bag.

The possible biography of the textile and animal-skin object

There are two aspects to consider in terms of understanding the biography of the textile and animal-skin object: its position in the cist and evidence of wear. Placed at the bottom of the cist was a layer of vegetation identified as the leaves and stems of heathland grasses, sedges, heather and moss (Appendix B). Analysis of the matted plant material reveals that the stems were unidirectional, so it appears to have been a bed of plant material carefully laid on the floor of the cist (Chapter 9). Placed on top of this was the textile and animal-skin object, which would have had a striking shape and texture against the 'bedding'. If we consider the orientation of the seam, it was placed with the 'right' side upwards. The cremated remains were then placed on top, wrapped in a pelt with the fur facing outwards. There seems to have been a sense of visual display for the benefit of the mourners: the most visually impressive side of the textile and animal-skin object faced upwards and the pelt encased the cremated bones with the fur on display. Although incompletely preserved, the textile and animal-skin object is without creases, patches or stitched repairs and the leather triangles are cleanly cut. It seems to have been of good quality and in good condition when it went into the cist. The complexity of the seams, compared with the simple oversewn seams used on other surviving examples of Early Bronze Age textile clothing, animal-skin clothing and equipment suggest that the textile and animal-skin object was a prestigious ceremonial item, not intended for 'everyday' use.

Concluding remarks

The only other recorded example of an Early Bronze Age textile and animal-skin object is what has been interpreted as a bag containing flint arrowheads from Tossen-Kergourognon, Prat, Côtes-d'Armor (Prigent 1881). This has not survived. Its traces, which were found inside a wooden box, are described:

> Ces têtes de fleche avaient été primitivement placées dans une double enveloppe de cuir et d'étoffe. J'ai encore en ma possession des fragments de cuir et d'une substance qui me semble être un debris d'étoffe. (Prigent 1881, 20)

The phrase 'inside a double envelope' is ambiguous because it could mean that the arrowheads had been wrapped in a layer of leather and then in a separate layer of textile or basketry and, as there is no mention that the leather and 'cloth' were joined or part of the same item, it would be unwise to suggest it to be closely comparable with the object from Whitehorse Hill cist. The textile and animal-skin object found here is a rare survival, with the complexity of the decorative animal-skin seams apparently unrivalled by discoveries of Bronze Age organic objects to date.

Acknowledgements

Helen Williams is thanked for providing additional photographs and excavation information on the textile and animal-skin object and the woven band with studs; Hero Granger Taylor for discussing the construction technique of the repp textile; Andy Jones for kindly sharing his references; Roy Thomson for his expert opinion on leather-related matters; Clément Nicolas for the Prigent reference, and Magdalena Wachnik for Figures 18.1–2 and 18.6–8.

References

Bender Jørgensen, L. 1992. *North European Textiles until AD 1000*. Aarhus: Aarhus University Press.

Broholm, H. C. & Hald, M. 1940. *Costumes of the Bronze Age in Denmark: contributions to the archaeology and textile history of the Bronze Age*. Copenhagen: NYT Nordisk. Arnold Busck.

Broholm, H. C. & Hald, M. 1948. *Bronze Age Fashion* (trans. J. Andersen*)*. London: Committee of the Exhibition Danish Art Treasures.

Cameron, E., Harris, S. & Mould, Q. 2013. SEM analysis of the textile and animal skin object, and the woven band with tin studs (unpublished report).

Chandler, D. 1995. *Learning to Weave*. Colorado, CO: Interweave Press.

Christensen, K. 2006. Dendrochronology dating of Bronze Age oak coffins from Denmark and Schleswig. *Acta Archaeologica* 77, 163–242.

Coudray, A & Vanden Berghe, I. 2013. *Dartmoor, England: Bronze Age textile and animal skin objects from Whitehorse Hill Cist Project 2011. Organic colorant analyses*. Brussels: Institut Royal du Patrimoine Artistique/ Koninklijk Instituut Voor Het Kunstpatrimonium.

DeRoche, D. 2012. England: the Bronze and Iron Ages. In M. Gleba & U. Mannering (eds.), *Textiles and Textile Production in Europe from Prehistory to AD 400*. Oxford: Oxbow Books, 444–450.

Dixon, D. D. 1913. Cartington oak coffin. *Proceedings of the Antiquaries of Newcastle on Tyne* 3(6), 79–84.

Dodsley, J. 1767. Chronicle, March 12th. *Annual Register 1767*.

Elgee, H. W. & Elgee, F. 1949. An Early Bronze Age burial in a boat-shaped wooden coffin from north-east Yorkshire. *Proceedings of the Prehistoric Society* 15, 87–106.

Emery, I. 1966. *The Primary Structures of Fabrics: an illustrated classification*. Washington DC: Textile Museum.

Evans, C., Tabor, J. & Vander Linen, M. forthcoming. *Twice-crossed River: prehistoric and palaeoenvironmental investigations at Barleycroft Farm/Over, Cambridgeshire*. The Archaeology of the Lower Ouse Valley Volume 3. Oxford: Cambridge Archaeological Unit.

Forbes, R. J. 1966. *Studies in Ancient Technology* Volume 5 (2nd revised edition). Leiden: Brill.

Gabra-Sanders, T. 1994. Textiles and fibres from the Late Bronze Age hoard from St Andrews, Fife, Scotland. In K. Tidow & G. Jaacks (eds.), *Ärchaologische Textilfunde: archaeological textiles*. Neumünster: Textilmuseum Neumünster, 34–42.

Gleba, M. & Mannering, U. 2012. Introduction: textile analysis and technology. In M. Gleba & U. Mannering (eds.), *Textiles and Textile Production in Europe from Prehistory to AD 400*. Oxford: Oxbow Books, 1–24.

Glob, P. V. 1983. *The Mound People*. London: Paladin.

Granger-Taylor, H. 1998. Evidence for linen yarn preparation in Ancient Egypt – the hanks and fibre strips and the balls of prepared rove from Lahun in the Petrie Museum of Egyptian Archaeology, University College London (UC 7421, 7509 and 7510). In S. Quirke (ed.), *Lahun Studies*. Reigate: SIA Publishing, 102–111.

Green, C. & Rollo-Smith, S. 1984. The excavation of eighteen round barrows near Shrewton, Wiltshire. *Proceedings of the Prehistoric Society* 50, 255–319.

Grinsell, L. 1959. *Dorset Barrows*. Dorchester: Dorset Natural History and Archaeological Society.

Groenman-van Waateringe, W. 1995. Pollenanalyse als Indikator für das Gerbeverfahren bei den Tierfellen des Mannes vom Tisenjoch. In K. Spindler, E. Rastbichler-Zissernig, H. Wilfing, D. zur Nedden & H. Nothdurfter (eds.), *Der Mann im Eis: Neue Funde und Ergebnisse*, v. 2. Vienna and New York: Springer, 67–70.

Groenman-van Waateringe, W., Kilian, M. & van Londen, H. 1999. The curing of hides and skins in European prehistory. *Antiquity* 73, 884–890.

Harris, S. 2010. Smooth and cool, or warm and soft; investigating the properties of cloth in prehistory. In E. Andersson Strand, M. Gleba, U. Mannering, C. Munkholt & M. Ringgaard (eds.), *North European Symposium for Archaeological Textiles* X. Oxford: Oxbow Books, 104–112.

Harris, S. 2011. Preparing skins in prehistory, a review of evidence and approaches. In R. Thomson & Q. Mould (eds.), *Leather Tanneries: the archaeological evidence*. London: Archetype, 57–67.

Harris, S. 2012. Report on the textiles from Over Barrow, Cambridgeshire with fibre analysis by Margarita Gleba. Unpublished report submitted Cambridge Archaeological Unit.

Harris, S. 2015. Folded, layered textiles from a Bronze Age pit pyre excavated from Over Barrow 2, Cambridgeshire, England. In K. Grömer & F. Pritchard (eds.), *Aspects of the Design, Production and Use of Textiles and Clothing from the Bronze Age to the Early Modern Era: NESAT* XI. Budapest: Archaeolingua, 73–81.

Hedges, J. W. 1973. Textiles and textile appliances in prehistoric Britain. 1973. Unpublished MA thesis, University of Sheffield.

Hedges, J. 1974. A Late Bronze Age socketed knife and textile from Nydie Mains, Fife. *Proceedings of the Society of Antiquaries of Scotland* 104, 293–295.

Hencken Elsasser, V. 2010. *Textiles: concepts and principles* (3rd edition). New York: Fairchild Books.

Henshall, A. S. 1950. Textiles and weaving appliances in prehistoric Britain. *Proceedings of the Prehistoric Society* 16, 130–162.

Henshall, A. 1964. Appendix 1: Report on the cloth from Pyotdykes, 197–198. In J. M. Coles, H. Coutts & M. Ryder, A Late Bronze Age find from Pyotdykes, Angus, Scotland, with associated gold, cloth, leather and wood remains. *Proceedings of the Prehistoric Society* 30, 186–198.

Henshall, A. 1968. Scottish dagger graves. In J. M. Coles, S. Piggott and D. Simpson (eds.), *Studies in Ancient Europe*. Leicester: Leicester University Press, 173–195.

Jones, A. M., Marley, J., Quinnell, H. & Hartgroves, S. 2011. On the beach: new discoveries at Harlyn Bay, Cornwall. *Proceedings of the Prehistoric Society* 77, 89–109.

Knight, M. 2012. *Must Farm Must Read. Articulating Britain's Lost Prehistoric Landscape*, 11–12 [online at http://www.mustfarm.com/archaeology]

Leuzinger, U. & Rast-Eicher, A. 2011. Flax processing in the Neolithic and Bronze Age pile-dwelling settlements of eastern Switzerland. *Vegetation History and Archaeobotany* 20(6), 535–542.

Mannering, U., Gleba, M., & Bloch Hansen, M. 2012. Denmark. In M. Gleba & U. Mannering (eds.), *Textiles and Textile Production in Europe From Prehistory to AD 400*. Oxford: Oxbow Books, 91–121.

Melton, N., Montgomery, J., Knüsel, C. J., Batt, C., Needham, S. P., Parker Pearson, M., Sheridan, J. A., Heron, C., Horsley, T., Schmidt, A., Evans, A., Carter, E., Edwards, H., Hargreaves, M., Janaway, R., Lynnerup, N., Northover, P., O'Connor, S., Ogden, A., Taylor, T., Wastling, V. & Wilson, A. 2010. Gristhorpe Man: an Early Bronze Age log-coffin burial scientifically dated. *Antiquity* 84, 796–815.

Mortimer, J. R. 1905. *Forty Years' Researches in British and Saxon Burial Mounds of East Yorkshire*. London: Brown and Sons.

Needham, S., Parfitt, K. & Varndell, G. 2006. *The Ringlemere Cup. Precious Cups and the Beginning of the Channel Bronze Age*. London: British Museum.

Oakes, J. & Riewe, R. 1995. *Our Boots: an Inuit women's art*. London: Thames & Hudson

Painter, T. 1991a. Preservation in peat. *Chemistry and Industry* 17 June, 421–424.

Painter, T. 1991b. Lindow Man, Tollund Man and other peat-bog bodies: the preservation and antimicrobial action of spagnan, a reactive glycuronoglycan with tanning and sequestering properties. *Carbohydrate Polymers* 15, 123–142.

Painter, T. 1995. Chemical and microbiological aspects of the preservation process in sphagnum peat. In R. Turner & R. Scaife (eds.), *Bog Bodies: new discoveries and perspectives*. London: British Museum Press, 88–99.

Prigent, abbé 1881. Fouille du grand tumulus de Tossen-Kergourognon en la commune de Prat, Côtes du Nord. *Bulletin et mémoires de la Société d'émulation des Côtes-du-Nord* 19, 15–31.

Pryor, F., French, C. & Taylor, M. 1985. An interim report on excavations at Etton, Maxey, Cambridgeshire, 1982–1984. *Antiquaries Journal* 65(2), 20–311.

Püntener, A. & Moss, S. 2010. Ötzi the Iceman and his leather clothes. *CHIMIA International Journal for Chemistry* 64(5), 315–320.

Ryder, M. 1993. Skin and wool remains from Hallstatt. *Circea* 10, 69–78.

Spindler, K. 1994. *The Man in the Ice* (trans. E. Osers). London: Weidenfeld and Nicolson.

Thomson, R. 2011a. The role of leather science and technology in heritage conservation. Unpublished PhD thesis, University of Northampton

Thomson, R, 2011b. Skin, leather and tanning: some definitions. In R. Thomson and Q. Mould (eds.), *Leather Tanneries the archaeological evidence*. London: Archetype, 3–7.

Walton Rogers, P. 2008. Textiles, including weft-twined work and cordage from Must Farm, near Whittlesey, Cambridgeshire, MUS06. The Anglo-Saxon Laboratory, York for Cambridge Archaeological Unit, unpublished report.

Wincott Heckett, E. 1998. A Late Bronze Age horsehair ornament from Cromaghs, Armoy, in Ireland. In L. Bender Jørgensen & C. Rinalso (eds.), *Textiles in European Archaeology. Proceedings of the 6th NESAT symposium*. Göteborg: Göteborg University, 29–38.

Wincott Heckett, E. 2012. Scotland and Ireland. In M. Gleba & U. Mannering (eds.), *Textiles and Textile Production in Europe from Prehistory to AD 400*. Oxford: Oxbow Books, 428–442.

Winterbottom, S. 2009. The Roman stitched sheet leather. In C. Howard-Davis (ed.), *The Carlisle Millennium Project: excavations in Carlisle, 1998–2001 Volume 2: the finds*. Lancaster Imprints 15. Oxford: Oxbow Books, 817–831.

Section 5:

The cist and the moor: the environmental setting of the site and its wider landscape context

19. The environment of the Whitehorse Hill cist

Ralph M. Fyfe, Jeffrey J. Blackford, Mark Hardiman, Zoë Hazell, Alison MacLeod, Marta Perez and Sarah Littlewood (née Williams)

The preservation of the Whitehorse Hill cist within an area of extant peatland offered a rare opportunity to explore the relationship of the monument to its surrounding contemporary and historic environment, through detailed examination of the peat sequence and the palaeoenvironmental record within it. Dartmoor has been the focus of palaeoenvironmental investigations since the 1960s (for example, Simmons 1964; Smith *et al.* 1981; Caseldine and Hatton 1993; Fyfe *et al.* 2008; Fyfe and Woodbridge 2012); detailed work at Whitehorse Hill can therefore be placed in a broader regional landscape context.

This chapter focuses on several inter-related questions:

1. What were the environmental conditions and land use at the time that the cist was constructed?
2. What is the evidence for environmental change in the wider landscape before, during or after the period of cist construction?
3. Is there any evidence for grazing or burning in the immediate or wider vicinity of the cist?

These questions are addressed by detailed examination, at high temporal resolution, of the record of pollen, non-pollen palynomorphs (NPPs), micro-charcoal, testate amoebae, peat humification, radiocarbon dating and tephrochronology from the peat. Pollen analysis and plant macrosfossils are used as indicators of the character of the local and regional vegetation. NPPs include fungal spores and other fungal remains that may allow inferences about particular environmental conditions (for example, as a consequence of associations with known host plants) or activities such as grazing in the records of obligate dung fungi (Blackford *et al.* forthcoming). Testate amoebae and peat humification are palaeomoisture indicators which can be used to infer past climatic conditions.

Palaeoecological investigations at Whitehorse Hill have been undertaken in two phases of research (Chapter 2). In 2005 a continuous peat sequence immediately adjacent to the cist on its northern side was recovered using overlapping monolith tins (Fig. 19.1) and 5cm thick spits (slices) were also taken. These samples were used both to assess the potential for various analyses and to undertake some detailed palaeoenvironmental reconstruction. In 2011 a second set of monolith tins was taken from the southern side of the cist (Fig. 19.1), again with associated bulk samples. This chapter presents the detailed analyses undertaken on the 2011 samples (WHH11), supplemented by results drawn from the 2005 profile (WHH05) where these add to the understanding of the environment before, during and after cist construction.

Methods

Summary of analyses undertaken

In order to develop datasets suitable to address the key questions concerning the past environment and environmental changes, the methods described here were applied to the 2005 or 2011 profiles, or in some instances both. Palaeoecological methods were also applied at different sampling (and therefore temporal) resolutions. A summary of the methods applied and the resolution of the analyses is provided in Table 19.1. The 2011 profile saw the most detailed analysis, with 72 contiguous 0.5cm slices being analysed for pollen, NPPs and micro-charcoal analysis to develop very high temporal resolution datasets describing vegetation change and suitable for the reconstruction of past land management practices. All depths refer to depth below the ground surface. A glossary of common names of plants used throughout is provided at the end of this chapter (Table 19.4).

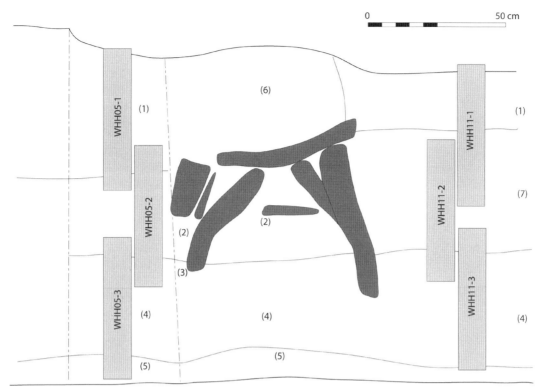

Figure 19.1: The west-facing excavated section, showing the stratigraphic relationships between the cist and the 2005 and 2011 profiles (WHH05 and WHH11 respectively). For explanations of contexts, see Chapter 2.

Table 19.1: summary of the methods applied to the 2005 and 2011 sections.

	2005 section (WHH05)	*2011 section (WHH11)*
Pollen	8cm resolution throughout profile	0.5cm resolution 25–61cm depth
NPPs	4cm resolution throughout profile	0.5cm resolution 25–61cm depth
Testate amoebae	4cm/8cm resolution variously throughout profile	No analysis
Macrofossils	5cm-thick slices throughout profile	No analysis
Humification	4cm resolution throughout profile	No analysis
Tephra	Scanning at 5cm resolution	Full analysis of target tephra horizons
Radiocarbon dating	2 AMS samples on plant macrofossil remains and 4 AMS samples on bulk peat (paired humic/humin samples (Table 20.2)	2 bulk peat samples (Chapter 20)

Pollen, non-pollen palynomorphs (NPPs) and micro-charcoal analysis

Samples for pollen, NPP and micro-charcoal analysis were extracted from the monolith tins in 1cm slices from WHH05 and in 0.5cm slices from WHH11. Microfossils were extracted from the sediment using standard physical and chemical treatments, using potassium hydroxide to disaggregate the samples, hydrochloric acid to remove silicates and acetolysis to dissolve the unwanted organic fraction (Faegri *et al.* 1989; Moore *et al.* 1991). Known numbers of *Lycopodium* (Clubmoss) spores were added to the sub-samples at the earliest stage as an exotic marker to be able to quantify microfossil and charcoal concentrations. The prepared samples were mounted in silicone oil from which pollen, NPPs and micro-charcoal counts were completed. A minimum of 300 total land pollen (TLP) and a minimum of 100 total NPPs (TNPP) were counted from each sample. The counts were converted into proportional data, using TLP for pollen and TNPP for NPPs. Aquatic pollen taxa were included in the pollen count and algae in the NPP count, but these were not included in the TLP or TNPP sums respectively; they are represented in the results as proportions of 'TLP plus aquatics' or 'TNPP plus algae'.

The pollen, NPP and microscopic charcoal content of each sub-sample was recorded using an Olympus binocular microscope at ×400 magnification. Charcoal was counted in two size fractions, based on the length of the long axis (10–50µm and >50µm). Pollen types were identified using the key in Moore *et al.* (1991) and the reference collection at Plymouth University, and use the Bennett

(1994) nomenclature. NPPs were identified using the published illustrations and descriptions of van Geel (1978), Pals *et al.* (1980), Prager *et al.* (2006) and Blackford *et al.* (forthcoming). NPPs were identified taxonomically where possible and where taxa could not be identified they were assigned a type number (van Geel 1978). NPPs are presented grouped by ecological affinities (where these are known or may be inferred from previous research).

Testate amoebae analysis

Preparation for testate amoebae from WHH05 followed the standard procedures of Charman *et al.* (2000). Samples were micro-sieved between 15μm and 300μm and a known quantity of *Lycopodium* spores added as marker grains to enable calculation of testate amoebae concentrations for each sample. Samples were mounted on slides using glycerol and examined under a high-power Leitz Dialux 22 microscope at ×400 magnification. Identifications were made using the key in Charman *et al.* (2000). Where taxonomic identifications were not clear due to poor preservation, individuals were grouped together at genus level (for example, *Heleopera* undiff.). Counting stopped when a total of either 150 tests or 100 *Lycopodium* had been reached.

Plant macrofossil analysis

Macrofossil analysis was undertaken from 10cm³ sub-samples from the 5cm thick slices of peat from WHH05. Samples were sieved through a 125μm mesh using distilled water and examined under a low-power Leica MZ95 light microscope at magnifications up to ×60. Identifications were made using a combination of the modern comparative reference material available at the Environmental Studies Team laboratories, Historic England, Fort Cumberland, and the reference works Beijerinck (1947), Cappers *et al.* (2006) and Ross-Craig (1979). Names are reported as in Stace (1997). Absolute counts of discrete plant components (for example, seeds, leaves, fruits, nutlets) were made and, where appropriate, these were converted to a minimum number of individuals. Abundance of other remains and components (for example, macro-charcoal, mineral, unidentifiable organic matter (UOM)) were estimated using a grouping system (Table 19.2).

For *Sphagnum* identifications, where leaves were

Table 19.2: Plant macrofossil abundance categories.

Category	No.	% abundance
Abundant	5	50–75
Common	4	26–50
Frequent	3	11–25
Occasional	2	5–10
Rare	1	<5

abundant a representative selection was mounted on a slide in Aquatex, and identified. Where fewer than ten leaves were available, all were mounted and identified. Examination was carried out on a high-power Leica DM 2500 light microscope between magnifications of ×100 to ×400. Identifications were made to section level (due to the degraded nature of the remains) using Daniels and Eddy (1985). An overall sample abundance value was also given, reported as *Sphagnum* spp.

Peat humification and loss-on-ignition (LOI)

Moisture content was measured by weighing peat samples from WHH05, and drying them at a moderate temperature (between 50–60°C) to ensure no accidental sample loss via inadvertent burning of organic matter. Samples were reweighed, and moisture content calculated as percentage weight loss. To calculate LOI (that is to say, mineral content), the same samples were combusted at 550°C to burn off all organics and reweighed. Peat humification was measured using the method of Blackford and Chambers (1993). Light transmission through the samples was measured at a wavelength of 550nm on a WPA S106 spectrophotometer at the University of Southampton. Light transmission values are inversely related to the degree of peat humification: higher light transmission suggests reduced peat humification, implying relatively wetter conditions that inhibited peat decay.

Tephra analysis

Sampling for tephra analysis was carried out in three phases. In the first phase monolith WHH11 was scanned for the presence/absence of tephra content by extracting 5cm-long contiguous samples. These were then processed using the following method, modified from Blockley *et al.* (2005). Samples were air dried, combusted for 2 hours at 550°C to remove organics and subsequently carbonates were removed by immersion in 10% HCl. The resulting material was sieved to retain the 15–125μm fraction, and then a two-phase heavy liquid separation procedure was applied to remove remaining organic matter or diatom frustules (at a density 2.0g/cm³) and to extract the fraction which would include tephra and other mineral grains of a similar density (between 2.0–2.5g/cm³). The resulting material was mounted in Canada Balsam and examined optically using an Olympus CX-41 microscope fitted with Vernier stage, cross-polarising filters and ×100, ×200 and ×400 magnification objective lenses. Slides were counted in their entirety to produce quantifiable counts of number of shards per gram of dry sediment.

Where tephra was detected through scanning, phase 2 involved extracting contiguous 1cm-thick samples from across the (already-identified) peaks in shards. Sampling extended 2cm on either side of each peak, in order to ensure that the full shard distribution was encompassed and that the interval of peak shard concentration could be constrained to a single centimetre. These samples were processed using the same method as was applied for phase 1. Depths with peaks in shard content were sub-sampled for geochemical analysis during the third phase. Samples were processed as described above, but were not subjected to drying or incineration as the high temperatures involved may have damaged the structure and altered the chemistry of volcanic glass shards. Shards were mounted on 2.5cm Specifix-40 resin stubs which had been pre-flattened so that they had a maximum vertical grade across the surface of 10–20μm. All ash layers identified in this research were classified as 'cryptotephra' layers and were recovered from samples that contained a significant quantity of other lithic grains in addition to glass shards. To reduce the time spent searching for shards during electron microprobe analysis, glass shards were individually picked out of the extracted material. This was done using a 10 micro-litre gas chromatography syringe fitted with a 100μm (internal diameter) needle attached to a micromanipulator, a process termed 'picking' (Matthews *et al.* in preparation). Stubs were then covered with resin and ground down, using successively finer grades of silicon carbide paper (35μm, 15μm, 8.4μm), until shards became exposed at the surface. Shards were then polished using successively finer grades of diamond suspension (9μm and 3μm) and aluminium oxide powder (0.3μm). This produced a smooth surface suitable for geochemical analysis by Wavelength Dispersive Spectroscopy (WDS).

Analyses of glass shards were carried out at the Tephra Analytical Unit (TAU) at the University of Edinburgh,

using a Cameca SX100 microprobe fitted with five vertical crystal spectrometers and Dynamic Beam tracking software which permits analysis of target areas as small as 3μm. A standard suite of ten major elements was analysed: SiO_2, TiO_2, Al_2O_3, FeO (total), MnO, MgO, CaO, Na_2O, K_2O and P_2O_5. Data were filtered to exclude non-tephra objects (other minerals) and data which returned low 'total' values (below 94.9%). Occasionally, minerals (such as quartz and feldspar) and biological fragments (such as plant phytoliths) optically mimic the appearance of volcanic glass shards. However, chemically these are straightforward to identify and discount.

Data exploration was undertaken using bi-plots and comparison was made with appropriate published data from the literature and database sources such as Tephrabase (www.tephrabase.org). Correlations are based on how well 'unknown' data compare with the collective available information with respect to similarities detected in visual plots. In addition, some stratigraphical control allows the number of potential correlatives to be narrowed down to specific time frames.

Results

Physical characteristics of the peat

Moisture content, LOI and peat humification (light transmission) measurements made on WHH05 are shown on Figure 19.2. At the very base of the profile moisture

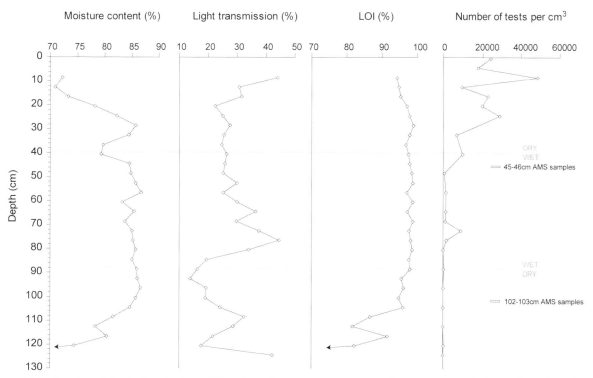

Figure 19.2: Results of physical analysis on WHH05, including moisture content, loss-on-ignition (LOI) and peat humification analysis, and also showing the position of the AMS radiocarbon dates from the profile (Chapter 20). The dry-wet-dry shifts are the palaeomoisture inferences based on the pollen zones derived for the same profile.

content is at a minimum (*c.* 55%), probably due to a combination of more compacted peat and the enhanced mineral content in the basal sample. Upwards to 105cm, moisture content values gradually increase, and then remain relatively constant throughout the middle part of the profile (fluctuating around 85%). This is interrupted by a slight, maintained return to drier values between 35cm and 40cm. Values then decrease upwards to a relatively dry surface peat from approximately 30cm.

Generally, LOI varies little throughout the profile. Values are at a minimum of 40% (in the lowest sample) supporting the evidence of visible mineral grains at this depth. Upwards, from about 105cm, values then fluctuate between 95% and 100%, indicating only a very small mineral component within the peat.

At the very base of the profile, the light transmission value is relatively high, probably due to increased mineral content of the peat. Values drop dramatically at about 120cm, indicating greater humification and suggesting drier conditions, and then increase to a peak at approximately 110cm. Between about 105cm and 85cm, values reach a minimum of about 15%, but then increase upwards to the profile-maximum of approximately 45% at around 80cm, suggesting reduced peat humification resulting from wetter conditions. From here light transmission increases to a constant of approximately 25%, implying relatively dry conditions between 60cm and 20cm. Values then increase (from 20cm to 0cm) to relatively high levels at the surface, indicative of the less decomposed nature of surface peat.

Tephra

Scanning for tephra (Phase 1) was undertaken on both the 2005 and 2011 monolith profiles, and both included distinct sections with significant shard concentrations. High-resolution analysis (Phases 2 and 3) was undertaken on WHH11 (Fig. 19.3), which indicated nine peaks in tephra shard concentrations. Three of these peaks had insufficient shard concentrations for geochemical analysis, therefore analysis was only undertaken on six of the peaks (Table 19.3). The geochemical analysis of the horizons indicates that all layers can be classified as being of Rhyolitic composition, according to the Le Bas *et al.* (1986) scheme, with the most likely source region being Iceland. Figure 19.4 illustrates the variability and similarity of the ash layers' chemical composition.

The six layers for which geochemical data are available are described below. In order to determine the source of the ash layers in the Whitehorse Hill samples, it was necessary to compare the data to that of published and unpublished sources. Within the south-west region, the only published study to which the Whitehorse Hill data could be compared was Matthews (2008), which presented geochemical data from Roman Lode on Exmoor. In the descriptions that follow 'RLO' indicates tephra horizons from Roman Lode, along with their depths in that sequence. Further research on tephras from sites on Exmoor is ongoing (MacLeod, unpublished data).

WHH11 0–4cm: The uppermost layer in WHH11 at 0–4cm (RH0471) has an affinity with RLO 34cm which is considered to represent the BMR-90 tephra layer and has an age of *circa* AD 920 (Hall and Pilcher 2002).

WHH11 9–11cm: The shard counts for this layer included glass which was brown in colour, generally signifying a more Fe (iron)-rich tephra, distinct from the colourless (lower Fe) shards. A distinct and different chemical signature was expected; this was not identified in the chemical data (Table 19.3; Fig. 19.4). Instead, this layer has produced data which is very similar to that of the underlying and largest layer in the sequence, OMH-185, suggesting that there is a degree of re-working of the lower tephra into this interval. This is also evident by the occurrence of a few more OMH-185 data points in the uppermost sample (WHH11 0–4cm). An alternative explanation is that this layer relates to the AD 860 Part A tephra, which is chemically identical to the OMH-185 layer, and has recently been detected on Exmoor (MacLeod, unpublished data). Whilst no brown shards were analysed on this occasion this interval should be a target for future work as it may provide an additional tephra isochron for comparison. At present it is impossible to confidently assign the layer to either eruption.

WHH11 18–19cm: The layer identified in RLO at 52cm appears to have close affinity to that of WHH11 at 18–19cm depth (Fig. 19.5). This layer in both RLO and WHH is characterised by data with two clear populations, one with slightly elevated Ca (calcium) and Fe values. Matthews (2008) identified this as the OMH-185 tephra layer, also known as the Microlite tephra (due to the characteristic mineral inclusions in the glass, also observed at WHH11). This tephra has a modelled age estimate of 2695–2590 cal years BP, 745–640 cal BC (Plunkett *et al.* 2004). The tephra has now been identified in England, Ireland, Germany and Scotland (where it is also known as the BGMT-3 tephra; Langdon and Barber 2001).

WHH11 47–50cm: This layer was analysed as a priority in the hope of obtaining a date close to the assumed position of the cist in the sequence. Due to low shard concentrations (Fig. 19.3) and difficulties in extracting sufficient shards for analysis, this layer was prepared three times. Three analyses were obtained from this layer from single glass shards and these have been compared to published data. This layer classifies as a Rhyolite which has its source in Iceland. It is chemically most similar to both the OMH-185 (Barnsmore) and AD 860 Part A tephra layers. However, as it underlies these layers by a considerable stratigraphic interval and is consistently detected across both overlapping monoliths on multiple occasions, contamination by later tephra is considered unlikely. The tephra most probably dates to 4000–5000 years ago, based upon its stratigraphic position and the age of other tephra layers described here, but does not match the chemical composition of products from the Hekla volcano and thus cannot represent the Hekla 4 eruption

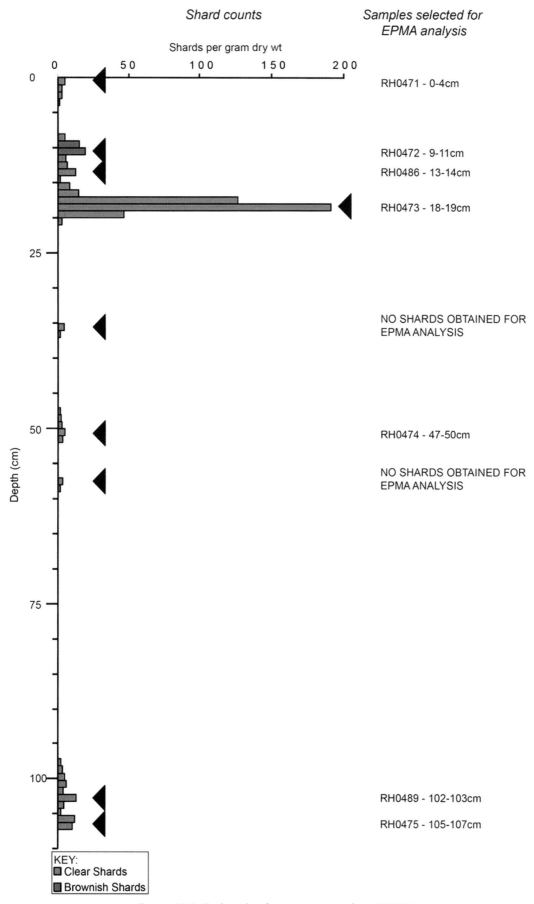

Figure 19.3: Tephra shard concentrations from WHH11.

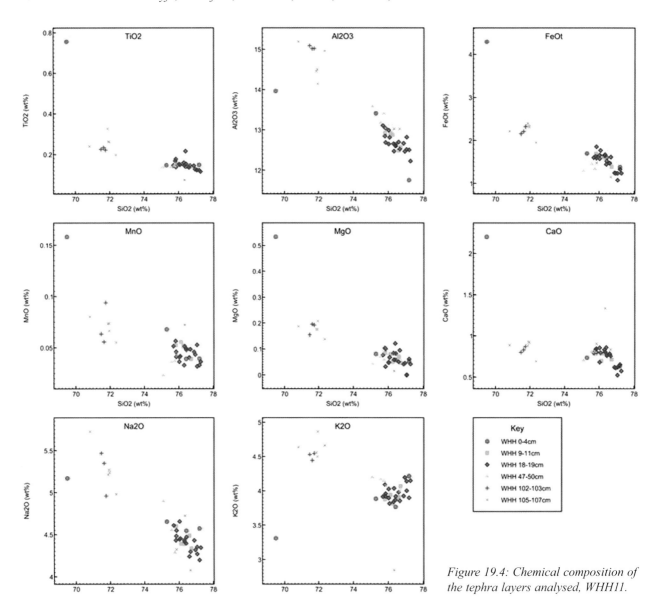

Figure 19.4: Chemical composition of
the tephra layers analysed, WHH11.

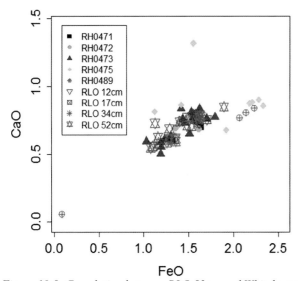

*Figure 19.5: Correlation between RLO 52cm and Whitehorse
Hill 18–19cm (RH0473).*

(Table 19.3; Fig. 19.6). The most likely source volcano,
based on published chemical analyses, is the Snæfellsjökull
volcano in the Snæfellsness peninsula, western Iceland
(Fig. 19.6). An eruption of this volcano, termed Sn-2, has
been reported in Iceland and dated to 4820–4100 cal BP,
2870–2150 cal BC, within the timeframe covered by the
WHH11 sample. However, no glass chemical data exist from
this eruption in order to test this correlation (Johannesson *et
al.* 1981). Comparison between the WHH11 data and other
eruptions of the Snæfellsjökull volcano demonstrates that
this is the most likely source.

WHH11 102–103 and 105–107cm: The lowermost layers
in WHH11 (Fig. 19.7) have produced a chemical signature
which is consistent with both the Lairg A (105–107cm:
6970–6845 cal BP, 5020–4895 cal BC) and Lairg B
(102–103cm: 6625–6550 cal BP, 4675–4600 cal BC) tephra
layers (Chapter 20; Hall and Pilcher 2002). The sample at
105–107cm appears to have a mixed signal of both Lairg A

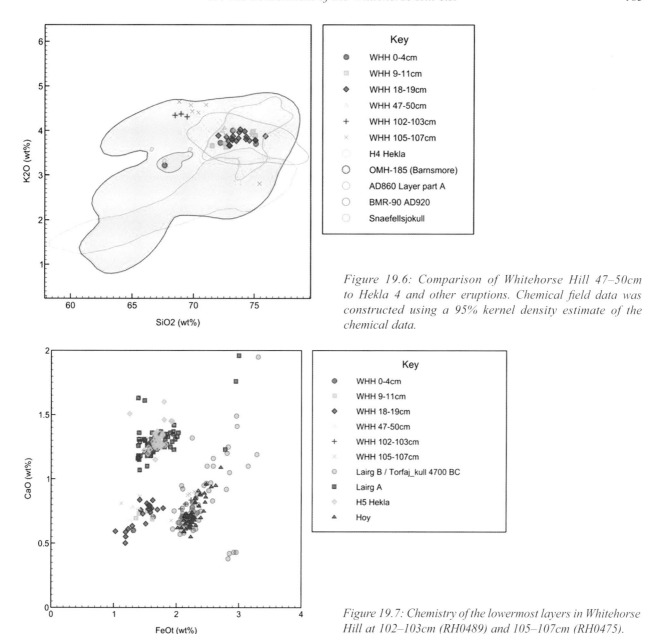

Figure 19.6: Comparison of Whitehorse Hill 47–50cm to Hekla 4 and other eruptions. Chemical field data was constructed using a 95% kernel density estimate of the chemical data.

Figure 19.7: Chemistry of the lowermost layers in Whitehorse Hill at 102–103cm (RH0489) and 105–107cm (RH0475).

and B chemistry. This may represent sampling across the boundary between the two layers which in this instance is difficult to detect using the shard counts alone, given that numbers are so low. This, combined with the fact that they occur so close together in time, has made them difficult to separate. The layer at 102–103cm also has similar chemistry to a layer known as the Hoy tephra (*c.* 6350 cal BP. 4400 cal BC); however, the dating control associated with this layer is poor and it is thought that although they have different names, the Hoy layer may actually represent the same eruption as the Lairg B tephra.

Plant macrofossils

Overall, Ericaceous plant remains are the most commonly occurring plant remains throughout WHH05 (Fig. 19.8).

These are dominated by *Calluna vulgaris* (heather) and *Erica tetralix* (cross-leaved heath), although other *Erica* spp. are also present. The greatest occurrences of *C. vulgaris* remains (dominated by leaves, but variously including stems and seeds) are at 75–95cm and 10–35cm. All three types of remains were found only in the two samples spanning 70–80cm. The dominance of *C. vulgaris* leaves could be due to their charred nature enhancing preservation. *E. tetralix* remains (again, mostly charred) are dominated by leaves and are most common at 70–85cm and 20–25cm. The deepest of these groups coincides with a peak in uncharred *Erica* spp. leaves; these could not be identified further due to their highly degraded nature, but it is likely that they are of *E. tetralix* too. Ericaceous flower heads are also present throughout most of the profile, but with most in the top 35cm of the profile; the dominance

Table 19.3: Geochemical data from tephra sherds analysed, Whitehorse Hill.

	SiO_2	TiO_2	Al_2O_3	FeO	MnO	MgO	CaO	Na_2O	K_2O	P_2O_5	Total
WHH 11 0–4cm	75.12	0.14	12.43	1.58	0.04	0.06	0.77	4.47	3.71	0.01	98.31
	73.22	0.14	11.15	1.31	0.04	0.05	0.60	4.34	4.00	0.02	94.87
	72.21	0.14	12.86	1.63	0.07	0.08	0.71	4.46	3.73	0.02	95.89
	67.66	0.73	13.60	4.18	0.15	0.52	2.15	5.03	3.22	0.11	97.37
WHH 11 9–11cm	71.52	0.15	12.19	1.59	0.05	0.08	0.74	4.33	3.66	0.01	94.32
	72.65	0.14	12.27	1.54	0.05	0.05	0.75	4.18	3.63	0.01	95.27
	74.86	0.14	12.26	1.35	0.04	0.05	0.69	4.23	3.97	0.00	97.59
	72.59	0.13	11.83	1.40	0.05	0.07	0.73	4.25	3.70	0.01	94.76
	75.07	0.15	12.74	1.62	0.05	0.08	0.69	4.33	3.89	0.01	98.62
WHH 11 18–19cm	74.59	0.21	12.31	1.41	0.05	0.12	0.84	4.29	3.78	0.03	97.63
	73.68	0.12	12.26	1.03	0.03	0.00	0.59	4.08	3.83	0.01	95.63
	73.51	0.15	12.12	1.46	0.05	0.08	0.73	4.30	3.77	0.02	96.18
	72.86	0.17	12.53	1.53	0.04	0.03	0.81	4.31	3.77	0.02	96.06
	75.10	0.14	12.27	1.58	0.05	0.09	0.74	4.21	3.78	0.00	97 96
	75.07	0.12	12.16	1.29	0.03	0.06	0.63	4.08	3.79	0.01	97.25
	72.98	0.14	12.29	1.70	0.04	0.07	0.76	4.27	3.66	0.01	95.92
	72.71	0.14	12.42	1.51	0.03	0.05	0.65	4.25	3.85	0.02	95.64
	73.16	0.13	12.24	1.79	0.04	0.10	0.77	4.39	3.82	0.02	96.45
	75.91	0.14	12.51	1.23	0.05	0.04	0.61	4.37	3.88	0.01	98.74
	73.19	0.14	12.67	1.55	0.05	0.07	0.77	4.46	3.79	0.00	96.69
	72.91	0.15	12.09	1.57	0.03	0.08	0.80	4.23	3.67	0.01	95.56
	74.20	0.11	11.74	1.19	0.04	0.04	0.55	4.17	3.98	0.01	96.03
	72.04	0.16	12.21	1.55	0.05	0.10	0.79	4.21	3.89	0.01	95.02
	74.33	0.13	12.32	1.43	0.04	0.05	0.76	4.11	3.86	0.00	97.05
	73.83	0.12	11.96	1.19	0.04	0.04	0.59	4.14	4.03	0.01	95.96
	73.23	0.14	11.97	1.61	0.05	0.06	0.77	4.23	3.87	0.01	95.93
	74.31	0.15	12.36	1.62	0.04	0.05	0.84	4.55	3.81	0.01	97.73
	73.75	0.12	11.98	1.19	0.05	0.00	0.50	4.17	3.96	0.01	95.72
WHH 11 47–50cm	72.36	0.13	12.62	1.39	0.03	0.07	0.77	4.36	3.99	0.02	95.73
	72.54	0.13	13.12	1.25	0.02	0.04	0.68	4.73	4.06	0.01	96.59
	73.36	0.14	12.98	1.30	0.04	0.06	0.78	4.15	4.02	0.01	96.82
WHH 11 102–103cm	69.47	0.23	14.57	2.14	0.05	0.19	0.81	5.19	4.31	0.03	96.99
	68.50	0.22	14.46	2.07	0.06	0.15	0.77	5.24	4.34	0.02	95.83
	68.99	0.21	14.44	2.23	0.09	0.19	0.84	4.77	4.37	0.02	96.15
	64.97	0.01	19.85	0.09	0.02	0.00	0.06	1.09	15.57	0.06	101.70
WHH 11 105–107cm	74.74	0.14	12.70	1.12	0.04	0.06	0.81	3.98	3.90	0.01	97.50
	72.61	0.15	12.49	1.41	0.04	0.10	0.86	4.14	3.90	0.01	95.72
	68.83	0.25	13.53	2.21	0.06	0.20	0.89	5.01	4.65	0.03	95.66
	70.39	0.26	14.20	2.28	0.07	0.17	0.90	5.16	4.40	0.03	97.86
	69.89	0.32	14.05	2.33	0.07	0.17	0.86	5.07	4.43	0.05	97.23
	71.03	0.19	14.69	1.92	0.05	0.14	0.68	4.89	4.58	0.02	98.18
	69.77	0.24	14.97	2.18	0.08	0.18	0.87	5.64	4.57	0.03	98.52
	75.42	0.07	12.86	1.55	0.07	0.01	1.32	4.67	2.81	0.00	98.79

of *C. vulgaris* remains suggests that the flower heads are therefore likely to be of *C. vulgaris*.

Eriophorum vaginatum (hare's-tail cottongrass) sclerenchymatous spindles are found between 95cm and 50cm, with the most abundant sample (of over 100) at 75–80cm. *Sphagnum* spp. leaves are found only in the two samples between 65cm and 75cm. Remains are quite rare and most are highly decomposed. It was, however, possible to identify some to *Sphagnum* section *Acutifolia*, which is generally associated with drier bog conditions.

Occasional other seeds and fruits are also present, but often it was not possible to identify these to species level due to their broken and/or highly degraded nature. They include a *Juncus* sp. seed, cf Poaceae sp. caryopsis, a *Carex* sp. nutlet and an indeterminate seed.

In terms of other sample components, mineral is most abundant at the base of the profile. UOM (unidentified organic material) is present throughout the whole profile, but is consistently high in the top 45cm of the profile. Fungal fruiting bodies and charcoal content are also most abundant towards the surface, coincident with the UOM. Above-ground plant macrofossil remains and humic/humin samples from bulk peat were used to produce AMS radiocarbon dates for two levels within WHH05 (Chapter 20).

Pollen

The analysis of WHH05 at a low sampling resolution provides an overview of the general pattern of pollen deposition around Whitehorse Hill (Fig. 19.9). Three local pollen assemblage zones (lpaz) were distinguished, whose main characteristics are outlined below.

WHH05 lpaz1: 124–88cm, *Calluna vulgaris*. The lowest pollen level is dominated by *Calluna vulgaris* (60–80%). Arboreal taxa comprise 20–40% TLP and include *Quercus* and *Corylus*. *Pinus* is only present in significant amounts in the lowest sample. Micro-charcoal is recorded within the zone.

WHH05 lpaz2: 88–40cm, *Calluna vulgari–Quercus–Corylus–*Cyperaceae. The start of the zone is marked by a decline in *Calluna vulgaris* and increases in arboreal taxa, Cyperaceae and *Pteridium*. Micro-charcoal continues to be recorded throughout the zone. *Calluna vulgaris* returns towards former levels towards the top of the zone.

WHH05 lpaz3: 40–16cm, *Calluna vulgaris*. *Calluna vulgaris* remains dominant in the diagram into the uppermost zone, with levels similar to the basal pollen zone. Arboreal taxa and Cyperaceae decline to low levels. Poaceae increase from trace levels in the preceding zone to around 20% TLP, before declining. The zone is also characterised by elevated levels of micro-charcoal.

Pollen analysis on WHH11 focused on high-resolution analysis before, during and after the period of time that spanned the construction of the cist, and a total of 72 contiguous samples was analysed (Fig. 19.10). Seven distinct local pollen assemblage zones were identified. It should be stressed that the local pollen assemblage zone numbers are not synonymous with the 2005 local pollen assemblage zones, but relate only to WHH11. The main characteristics of the zones are described here. The changes are described upwards through the profile, including within individual local pollen assemblage zones where these are detailed.

WHH11 lpaz1: 60.5–59cm, *Corylus– Quercus–*Cyperaceae. *Corylus* is the most abundant taxon (51% at the bottom of the zone) declining to 40% at the top. *Quercus* is the second most common taxon (23–15%). *Alnus* pollen is also well represented, reaching 12% of the TLP assemblage. Shrub taxa are represented by *Calluna vulgaris,* with an average of 4% of the TLP assemblage. In the herbaceous group Cyperaceae dominate, oscillating between 9% and 12%; Poaceae (6%) and *Ranunculus acris* type (3%) are also consistently present. There are low concentrations of micro-charcoal.

WHH11 lpaz2: 58.5–53.5cm, *Corylus–Quercus–*Poaceae. Tree taxa continue to dominate the assemblage with *Corylus* being the most abundant (average 41%), followed by *Quercus* (average 20%) and *Alnus* (reaching 18%). Other tree taxa are present in low percentages: *Betula* (2%), *Tilia* (1%), *Pinus* (0.5%) and *Salix* (0.5%). *Calluna vulgaris* remains at similar levels to the preceding zone (average 6%). The herb taxa are dominated by Poaceae, reaching 10%. Cyperaceae is also well represented (average 4%), and other herbs include *Plantago lanceolata, Ranunculus acris* type and *Gentiana* type. Micro-charcoal concentration levels remain low.

WHH11 lpaz3: 52.5–50cm, *Corylus–Quercus–*Cyperaceae. The zone is distinguished by an increase in Cyperaceae. *Corylus* remains the most abundant taxon (average of 39%). *Quercus* is the other most common taxon that starts at 13% and reaches values around 22% by the top of the zone. A range of additional tree taxa are constantly present, some at very low levels (*Alnus* ~9%, *Betula* ~3%, *Tilia* and *Ulmus* <1%). *Calluna vulgaris* starts at 11% but it declines through the zone down to 5%. There is a constant presence of various herbs at low values (Poaceae ~3%, *Plantago lanceolata* and *Ranunculus acris* type <1%). Micro-charcoal concentrations rise at the start of the zone.

WHH11 lpaz4: 49.5–38.5cm, Cyperaceae–*Corylus–Quercus*. This zone is characterised by a significant increase in Cyperaceae pollen, averaging 40%, reaching 47% at 42cm but subsequently declining at the top of the zone to 19%. Although Cyperaceae is the most common taxon, tree taxa still represent most of the pollen count. *Corylus* is the second most common taxon (average 30%). *Quercus* is present in lower proportions than in the previous zone but still reaches an average of 20%. Other tree taxa

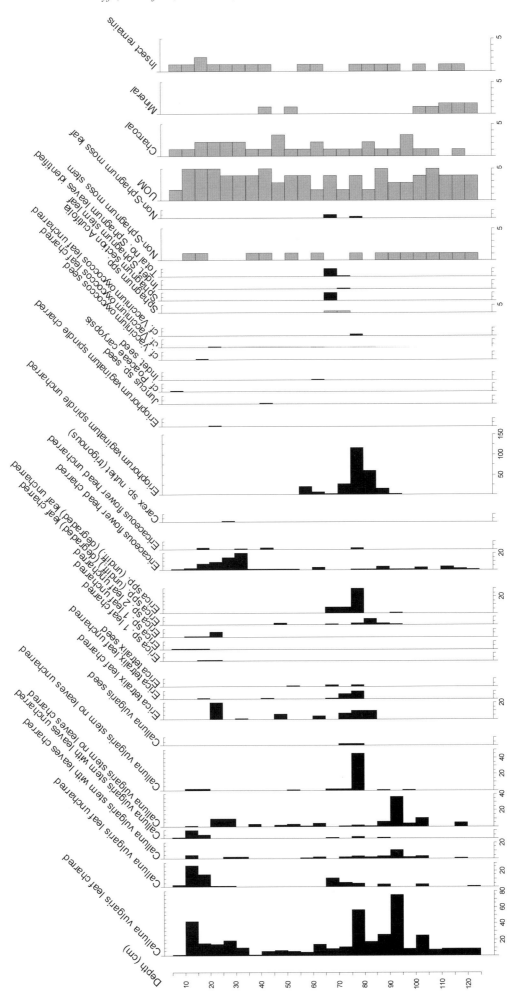

Figure 19.8: Results of plant macrofossil analysis from WHH05. Solid black bars indicate counted remains and light grey bars show the 1–5 abundance scale results. Unless otherwise labelled, the full lengths of the x-axes represent '10'.

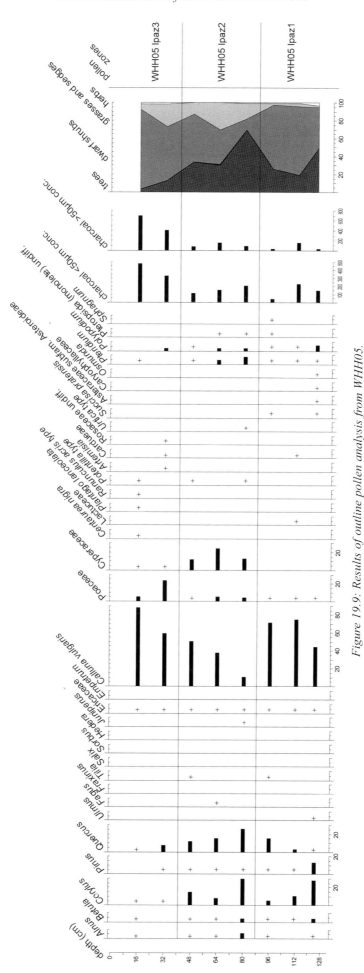

Figure 19.9: Results of outline pollen analysis from WHH05.

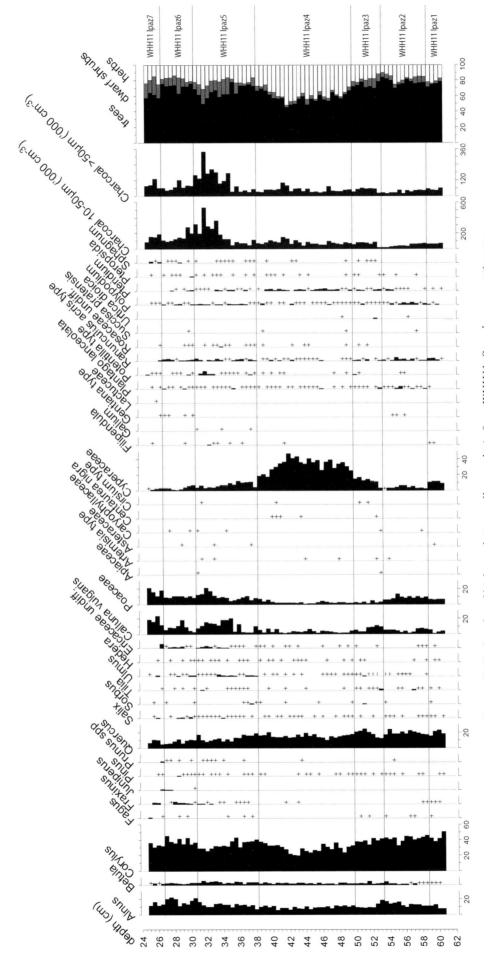

Figure 19.10: Results of high-resolution pollen analysis from WHH11. Samples are contiguous.

Table 19.4: Glossary of the plant types (Latin and common names) as referred to on the pollen and plant macrofossil diagrams.

POLLEN DIAGRAMS (Figures 19.9 and 19.10)

TREES

Alnus	Alder
Betula	Birch
Corylus	Hazel
Fagus	Beech
Fraxinus	Ash
Pinus	Scots pine
Prunus	Wild cherry
Quercus	Oak
Salix	Willow
Sorbus	Mountain ash
Tilia	Lime
Ulmus	Elm

SHRUBS

Hedera	Ivy
Juniperus	Juniper

DWARF SHRUBS

Calluna vulgaris	Common heather, or ling
Ericaceae	Heather family
Empetrum	Crowberry

GRASSES AND SEDGES

Cyperaceae	Sedge family
Poaceae	Grass family

HERBS

Apiaceae	Carrot family
Artemisia	Mugwort
Asteraceae	Sub-family of daisy family, covering daisy-type herbs
Cardueae	Sub-family of daisy family, covering thistle-type herbs
Caryophyllaceae	Pink family
Centaurea nigra	Common knapweed
Cirsium	Genus of daisy family, covering plume thistles
Filipendula	Meadowsweet
Galium type	Bedstraws
Gentiana type	Gentians
Lactuceae	Sub-family of the daisy family, covering dandelion types
Plantago lanceolata	Ribwort plantain
Potentilla type	Cinquefoils
Ranunculus acris type	Buttercups
Rosaceae undiff.	Rose family
Succisa	Devil's-bit scabious
Urtica	Nettles

SPORE PRODUCING PLANTS

Osmunda	Royal fern
Pteridium	Bracken
Polypodium	Polypody fern
Pteropsida	Ferns
Sphagnum	Bog mosses

PLANT MACROFOSSIL DIAGRAM (Figure 19.8)

Calluna vulgaris	Common heather, or Ling
Erica tetralix	Cross-leaved heath
Erica sp.	Heath (or Heather)
Carex sp.	Sedges
Eriophorum vaginatum	Hare's-tail cotton grass
Juncus sp.	Rushes
Vaccinium oxycoccos	Cranberry
Sphagnum	Bog mosses

remain constant through the zone, including *Alnus* and *Betula*. *Calluna vulgaris* is recorded throughout the zone, between 1 and 6%. The herbaceous assemblage (apart from Cyperaceae) remains similar to the previous zone. Additional herbaceous types appear sporadically (*Potentilla* type and Rosaceae). Micro-charcoal concentrations remain similar to the preceding zone.

WHH11 lpaz5: 38–31cm: *Corylus–Calluna vulgaris–Poaceae–Quercus*. The zone is marked by *Corylus* as the dominant taxon, starting at 41% and reducing to 30%, and an increase in *Calluna vulgaris*. Other significant tree taxa include *Quercus* (10–20%), *Alnus* (up to 16%), *Betula* (~4%), and *Fraxinus*, *Pinus*, *Prunus*, *Salix*, *Tilia* and *Ulmus* are recorded at low levels. *Calluna vulgaris* is present at values between 3% and 20% and Poaceae has similar levels (5–20%). Other herbaceous taxa constantly present include *Plantago lanceolata*, *Potentilla* type, *Ranunculus* and Rosaceae. Cyperaceae values decline to around 5%. Micro-charcoal concentrations fall to lower values than in the previous zone.

WHH11 lpaz6: 30.5–27cm: *Corylus–Alnus–Calluna vulgaris*. Zone 6 remains dominated by tree taxa: *Corylus* is still the most abundant taxon (37–41%), *Alnus* pollen increase to 22% and other tree taxa (*Betula*, *Fagus*, *Fraxinus*, *Pinus*, *Salix*, *Tilia* and *Ulmus*) increase slightly while *Quercus* declines to 6%. *Calluna vulgaris* increases from 3% at the bottom of the zone to 8% at the top, with a peak (18%) at 29cm. The herbaceous group is represented by Poaceae (average 10%) and again small but constant percentages of *Plantago lanceolata*, *Potentilla* type, *Ranunculus* and Cyperaceae. The micro-charcoal presence increases steadily along the zone, although this is mainly the charcoal in the smaller size fraction <50 μm.

WHH11 lpaz7: 26.5–25cm: *Corylus–Calluna vulgaris–Poaceae*. The start of zone 7 is marked by an increase in *Calluna vulgaris* and drop in *Alnus*. Overall, tree taxa remain dominant with *Corylus* (average 39%) most abundant. Other tree taxa (other than *Alnus*) remain at levels similar to the preceding zone. *Calluna vulgaris* increases from 9% to 23% at 26cm. Poaceae becomes the dominant herbaceous taxon, increasing from 9% up to 20% at the top of the zone. The other herb taxa present at low levels throughout include *Gentiana* type, *Plantago lanceolata*, *Potentilla* type, *Ranunculus* and Rosaceae. The micro-charcoal percentages reduce considerably in this zone and have the lowest levels of the whole sequence.

Non-pollen palynomorphs (NPPs)

Analysis of WHH05 was undertaken as part of an undergraduate dissertation (Williams 2006); selected recounting and checking of the original material has confirmed the general pattern described from samples spaced 4cm apart through the profile.

Of particular interest in studies linking archaeology, land use and palaeoenvironments are the spore types associated with dung known as coprophilous fungi. The 2005 Whitehorse Hill samples are rich in coprophilous types, with at least some coprophilous spores in every sample. The dominant types are *Sporormiella* (an obligate coprophile) and Types 112 and 261. Also recorded are *Zopfiella* type (Type 501), *Podospora* and *Tripterospora* type, all likely to be indicative of a dung substrate. Various dead-wood decomposers are also abundant, especially *Coniochaeta lignaria* (Type 172) and the ubiquitous *Chaetomium*, a well dispersed fungal spore that is present on grasses naturally, but increases with human presence (van Geel and Aptroot 2006).

The NPP data from 2005 have been used to classify the samples into three broad zones (Fig. 19.11). While each of these could be further subdivided, the two major breaks at 84cm and 54cm show the overall structure in the data set. Some types are common throughout and do not delimit the phase changes (for example *Meliola*, *Tilletia*, Type 90 and *Chaetomium*). The zones are described below.

WHH05 Zone 1 (125–86cm): The earliest phase at Whitehorse Hill is dominated by *Pleospora* and by Type 496 and Type 495, Type 10, the two fire-related species (*Gelasinospora* and *Neurospora*), and *Meliola*. These are mostly indicators of peat-forming, locally-growing plant communities, indicating a dry, grass and Ericoid dominated flora. There is some evidence of grazing animals within the local area.

WHH05 Zone 2 (86–54cm): The second phase shows increases in *Geoglossum* and *Sporormiella*, Type 104, Type 122 and *Coniochaeta xylariispora*. This change includes evidence for wetter conditions, reduced *Calluna vulgaris* cover and increased grazing indicators.

WHH05 Zone 3 (54–0cm): The final phase is dominated by coprophilous taxa, *Pleospora*, Type 10 and *Neurospora* and Type 303. Phase 3 shows a further increase and diversification of grazing indicators, a return of *Calluna vulgaris* and possibly drier peat surface conditions, and a return to a greater fire frequency including on-site burning.

The results from the study of WHH05 indicated that the material was highly suitable for more detailed NPP work, both to understand local mire conditions and to also consider aspects of human management of the local area through the late Neolithic and into the Bronze Age, particularly the presence of grazing animals. WHH11 was therefore used to produce a detailed, high temporal resolution NPP record using the same 72 contiguous 0.5cm thick samples from which the detailed pollen work was undertaken (Fig. 19.12). Eight distinct zones were distinguished within the dataset, which are described here. Again, the zonation is not synonymous with that from the 2005 sequence but is particular to this profile.

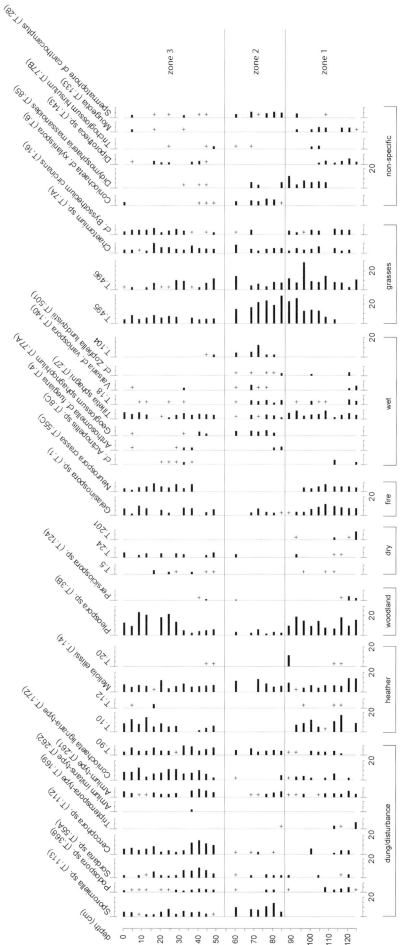

Figure 19.11: Results of non-pollen palynomorph analysis from WHH05.

WHH11 NPP1 Zone 1: 60.5–59cm: *Chlamydospores–Mycelium* **of** *M. ellisii–Thalloconidium* **of** *Sporoschisma.* *Chlamydospores* (Type 12) dominate this zone, oscillating between 74% and 59% of the total spore assemblage. Other spores present include Type 303 (reaching 19% at the top of this zone), *Conidia* (reaching 11%), *Sporormiella* sp. (6%) and Type 91 (3%). The assemblage of this zone is also dominated by Mycelium of *M. ellisii* (21%) and *Thallaconidium* of *Sporoschima* (reaching 16% but disappearing completely at the top of the zone). Type 496 starts to have a high presence at the top of the zone, reaching 17%.

WHH11 NPP1 Zone 2: 58.5–53cm: *Chlamydospores–Type 496–Type 303.* *Chlamydospores* remain dominant in this zone, reaching 67% at 54.5cm, and 58% at the top of this zone. Type 496 spores are abundant in this zone, reaching 39% of the total assemblage at 56cm but diminishing totally at the top of the zone. Type 303 is constantly present, reaching 27% but reducing to 13% at the top of the zone. Other spores present above trace levels include *Conidia* (~5%), *Byssothecium circinans* (increasing to 8%), Type 91 (increasing steadily to reach 21%), *Sordaria* (1%) and *Sporormiella* (~2%). There is a small but constant presence of algal spores in this zone.

WHH11 NPP1 Zone 3: 52.5–38.5cm: *Chlamydospores–Type 303–Conidia.* Zone 3 is dominated by *Chlamydospores*, with an average of 50% of the total assemblage, followed by Type 303, which oscillates between 18% and 40%. The other spore taxa present are *Conidia* (4–20%), *Byssothecium circinans* (3–9%), and *Sporormiella* sp (~3%). Other NPPs appear in bands at localised depths: Type 466 (from 49–46cm), *Sordaria* sp. (from 43.5–42cm) and *Rhytidospora* cf. *tetraspora* (from 45–44cm).

WHH NPP1 Zone 4: 38–36.5cm: *Chlamydospores–Type 496–Conidia.* This zone remains dominated by *Chlamydospores*. The second most abundant spore is Type 496 (average 25%). The other spores that make up the majority of the assemblage in this zone include *Conidia* and Type 303 (both reaching 12% at the top of the zone), *Sporormiella* sp. and *Sordaria* (both ~2%).

WHH NPP1 Zone 5: 36–33.5cm: *Chlamydospores–Type 303–Sordaria* **sp.** This zone remains dominated by *Chlamydospores,* which reach 62% at 35.5cm but diminish to 33% at the top of the zone. Type 303 is again the second most abundant spore (average 20%). *Sordaria* sp. increases from 6% to 20% at the top of the zone, becoming the third most abundant taxon. Other spores which start to increase their percentages include Ascospores (2%), *Gelasinospora* sp. (2%), *Sporormiella* sp. (3%) and Type 206 (2%, but increasing to 8% at the top of the zone). Some algae spores are present, including Zygospores of *Mougeotia* (2%) and *Spirogyra* (average 3%).

WHH NPP1 Zone 6: 33–31cm: *Sordaria* **sp.–Type 206–Chlamydospores.** The most abundant spore taxon in this zone is *Sordaria* sp. (average 55%). The second most abundant is Type 206 (average of 20% but diminishing totally at the top of the zone). *Chlamydospores* have reduced considerably in relation to previous zones, but are still present with significant percentages (9–16%). Type 303 also has a reduced presence but at the top of the zone reaches 14% of the total spore assemblage. Ascospores, *Sporormiella* and Type 406 are also present at low levels.

WHH NPP1 Zone 7: 30.5–27cm: Type 303–Chlamydospores–Sordaria **sp.** In this zone the most abundant spore taxon is Type 303 (between 57% at the bottom of the zone and 63% at the top). *Chlamydospores* are the second most abundant taxa (average 30%). *Sordaria* sp. reduces considerably in comparison with the previous zone, reaching 14% at the bottom of the zone but less than 1% at the top. Other spore taxa present include Ascospores (3%), *Conidia* (2%), *Pleospora* (3%) and *Ustilago* spp (peak of 5% at 28cm). Algae are present at the bottom of the zone – zygospores of *Mougeotia* (average 4%) and *Spirogyra* (average 3%) – but all of them decline and are absent at the top of the zone.

WHH NPP1 Zone 8: 26.5–25cm: Ascospores–Chlamydospores–Type 303. In this zone the Ascospores are the most abundant taxa (average 22%) with *Chlamydospores* the second most abundant (average 20% but with a peak of 40% at 25.5cm). Type 303 increases from 10% at the bottom of the zone to 21% at the top. Other spores present in the zone include *Sordaria* sp. (5%), *Pleospora* (2%), *Glomus* cf *fasciculatum* (10%) and *Urocystis* sp (2%).

Testate amoebae

Testate amoebae were assessed from WHH05 (Hazell 2014). Tests were only present in sufficient concentrations for assemblages to be reliably interpreted in the top 40cm and between 70cm and 80cm depth (Fig. 19.2). Overall, in the top 40cm, taxa are dominated by *Hyalosphenia subflava*, a reliable dry indicator, together with the predominantly dry *Trigonopyxis arcula* type and the cosmopolitan *Cryptodifflugia oviformis*. There are also low occurrences of *Nebela militaris*, another dry indicator. Within the top two near-surface samples (that is to say, above 5cm), the fragile *Corythion dubium* (a predominantly dry indicator) and *Euglypha* spp. (associated with wetter conditions) occur; they are often found in recent, less humified sediments. *Cyclopyxis arcelloides* type (a cosmopolitan taxon) is present in the top 15cm. Between 70cm and 80cm the assemblage is dominated by *Amphitrema flavum*, a wet indicator, with lesser abundances of *Assulina muscorum* and *C. arcelloides* type, both cosmopolitan. This is the only occurrence of *A. flavum* within the interpretable parts of the record.

Due to the highly variable and predominantly low test concentrations throughout the majority of the profile it was not considered appropriate to apply a palaeomoisture

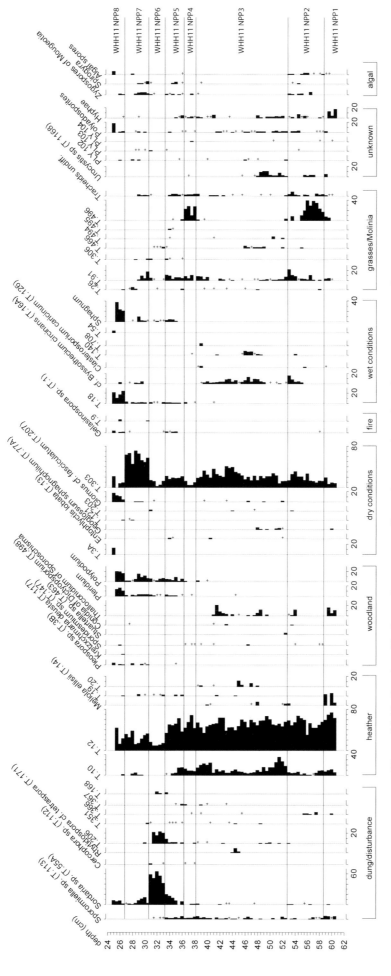

Figure 19.12: Results of high-resolution non-pollen palynomorph analysis from WHH11. Samples are contiguous.

transfer function. The lack of testate amoebae at depth meant that no such work was undertaken from WHH11.

Discussion

The age of the Whitehorse Hill peat sequence and the position of the cist within it

Central to any interpretation of palaeoecological sequences is a secure chronology that allows the results to be placed within their correct time frame. In this particular study, estimating the depth in the peat sequence which correlates with the construction and use of the cist was a key goal, but one that has been frustrated by the difficulties associated with some of the site's radiocarbon dates (in particular, those produced from bulk peat samples from the 2011 peat sequence). As such, a radiocarbon-based chronology for the 2011 peat sequence is not available at this point in time.

The successful recognition and identification of tephra shards within the peat at Whitehorse Hill represents a major advance for palaeoecological research in south-west Britain. Tephra horizons, when present, can provide independent dating horizons for peat sequences and allow precise correlation between sequences. Whitehorse Hill is one of only four sites in the south-west from which tephras have been geochemically linked to their source eruptions, the other three all lying on Exmoor (Roman Lode: Matthews 2008; Ricksy Ball and Spooners: MacLeod, unpublished data). In the case of Whitehorse Hill, the six identified tephra horizons are considered the only secure tie-points for development of an age-depth model. However, due to a lack of published tephra chemical data for comparison, it is difficult to securely determine the precise source eruption of the ash layer which is thought to underlie the archaeology (WHH11 47–50cm). The most likely source eruption is Sn-2, an eruption of the Snæfellsjökul volcano which has an estimated age of 2870–2150 cal BC (Johannesson *et al.* 1981).

Linear interpolation between the key tephra horizons (using age-depth data) has been undertaken to establish the most likely depth in the WHH11 palaeoecological sequence that relates to the construction of the cist. Peat accumulation rates are around 40 years per cm for the profile used for high-resolution analysis: each 0.5cm-thick peat sample thus represents ~20 years. An age estimate for each 0.5cm sample has been produced, resulting in minimum, mid-point and maximum ages for each sample. The relative ages of samples (and thus the duration of events) is secure within this tephra-based approach. However, the absolute age of any particular sample carries an uncertainty of between ±75 and ±400 years, depending on the proximity of the sample to a well-dated tephra horizon. Using the estimated age for the construction of the cist, which retains its own uncertainties (Chapter 20), the age-depth model suggests that the cist 'construction level' lies somewhere between 31cm and 40cm (using the minimum and maximum age ranges of the samples), and 34–35cm depth based only on the midpoint age for each sample.

An alternative method for estimating the depth that most probably correlates to the construction of the cist is to use biostratigraphical principles, comparing pollen assemblages from inside the cist with the pollen assemblages from the peat. This can determine: (a) whether any peat samples provide a reasonable match to the cist samples; and (b) the depths of any samples that do match. This approach relies on a series of assumptions: (i) material deposited within the cist from which pollen is recovered derive from the immediate location; (ii) the pollen within the cist material reflects the local pollen rain in the same way as pollen in the peat (that is, there are no taphonomic differences); and (iii) there is no depositional bias (deliberate selection) of material placed in the cist that would influence the pollen assemblages. In the case of assumption (i), the vegetation matting within the cist has been confirmed as *Molinia caerulea* (purple moor grass) (Chapter 9) which was most probably local in origin to the cist. If the material was taken from near the cist, then this should validate assumption (ii). Surface samples of peat have 'source areas' of pollen of the order of 100–200m (Broström *et al.* 2008): samples close to each other should thus appear very similar. Results of the analysis of pollen from the cist (Chapter 10) indicated a floral tribute had been added, which might challenge assumption (iii). As a result, this particular pollen taxon (*Filipendula,* meadowsweet) was removed from the pollen assemblages before the statistical comparison was made.

Comparison of pollen from the peat and the cist was undertaken by combining all samples together into a single dataset (excluding the counts for *Filipendula*), and calculating a dissimilarity matrix. This is a calculation of the dissimilarity of each sample with every other sample in the dataset. The dissimilarity matrix was then used to undertake an unconstrained cluster analysis, which groups samples on the basis of their dissimilarity score. The results of the analysis confirm that pollen samples from within the cist are all very similar (they are placed within the same broad cluster), and these samples cluster with pollen samples from 31–33cm depth. The cist samples are also similar (although slightly less similar) to the samples from 25–26.5cm depth. The same comparison was undertaken using the NPP assemblages. As the source area of NPPs is much smaller than pollen, there is more potential for differences in NPP assemblages, so the results must be viewed with circumspection. Nevertheless, a good match was found between NPPs from within the cist and from the peat samples at 33–34.5cm depth.

It is reassuring that comparison of the two different approaches to positioning the cist within the peat sequence result in overlap: the depth indicated by biostratigraphy falls within the wider depth range suggested by the tephra-based age-depth model. The development of future dating approaches to the peat (either through collection of material suited to dating, or refinement of tephra horizons) will inevitably result in revision of the age-depth model. For the present, it is assumed that the cist lies somewhere between 31cm and 33cm depth in the peat sequence, until further dating resolves or refines the age of the peat.

The environmental context of the Whitehorse Hill cist

Discussion of the palaeoecological results from the peat profiles allows the cist to be placed within the *longue durée* of landscape character and management around Whitehorse Hill. Analysis of WHH05 focused on a low temporal resolution, longer-term upland history, based on pollen, NPPs and plant macrofossil remains, useful for a 'broad-brush' environmental history. In contrast, WHH11 allows a very detailed picture of local land management, at high temporal resolution, across the later Neolithic and Bronze Age (Figs. 19.10 and 19.12). Unfortunately it is not possible to correlate between the depths in the 2005 and 2011 Whitehorse Hill profiles owing to the paucity of dating, which makes comparison of the two sequences speculative at this time. The Whitehorse Hill material can also be discussed and contextualised alongside other well-dated pollen sequences from northern Dartmoor, particularly those in Fyfe and Woodbridge (2012) on Hangingstone Hill (0.3km north of Whitehorse Hill), Cut Hill (3.2km south-west), Broad Down (4.4km south) and Winneys Down (3.4km south-south-east), and Fyfe *et al.* (2008) on Shovel Down (3.4km east) (Fig. 19.13). While other sequences have been published from the northern moor – for example, Black Ridge Brook (Caseldine and Hatton 1993) – these are largely confined to the Mesolithic or do not have secure chronologies through the Neolithic and into the early Bronze Age (Caseldine 1999).

Some comment is also required about integrating the different strands of evidence, particularly the spatial scale (source area) that each of the different datasets represents. Plant macrofossils are not dispersed far from their source plants and so represent a detailed picture of the plants that were growing at the sampling site in the past. At the other extreme, the pollen record integrates grains from plants that are local (close to or at the sampling site), extra-local (tens to hundreds of metres from the coring site) and the regional pollen rain (Jacobsen and Bradshaw 1981; Sugita 2007), where the 'region' represents Dartmoor and possibly some of the surrounding lowlands. Integration of macrofossil and pollen records is beneficial (Birks and Birks 2000), in particular use of the plant macrofossil data to develop the interpretation of the pollen record. Between these two extremes some NPPs are airborne (for example, *Chaetomium*, *Coniochaeta* and *Kurtzeria*) but most are not (Ingold 1971; Lacey 1996); the airborne ones are not the dominant types in the Whitehorse Hill record. NPPs should therefore be considered local indicators (~10–20 m). Again, combining the NPP and pollen records from the high-resolution profile, particularly when NPPs are associated with particular host plants or conditions, allows a much richer interpretation of past land management and vegetation character.

The longue durée *at Whitehorse Hill*

Long-term moorland development at Whitehorse Hill can be described from the outline pollen diagram from WHH05, combined with the more detailed work from the macrofossils and NPPs in that profile. The pollen analysis suggests three broad phases in the local landscape (Fig. 19.9). The earliest phase was a heather-dominated heath, with hazel woodland in the broad vicinity. This was followed by a wetter phase, indicated by increases in sedge pollen (Cyperaceae) and reductions in heather. The final phase represents a heather and grass-dominated heath, with very little evidence of woodland cover in the wider landscape. This general pattern is borne out by the results of the peat humification, testate amoebae and plant macrofossil analysis. The peat humification results (Fig. 19.2) show consistently enhanced light transmission values in the middle phase, implying wetter conditions. The testate amoebae, although only a partial record, cover the last phase and are dominated by the drier indicator *Hyalosphenia subflava*. Within the plant macrofossil record (Fig. 19.8), above-ground remains of ericaceous material (for example, leaves, stems and seeds of *Calluna vulgaris* and *Erica tetralix*) were recovered throughout the profile, but there is the same distinct middle phase marked by the presence of hare's-tail cotton grass (*Eriophorum vaginatum*) spindles and the only records of *Sphagnum* stems and leaves. The NPPs from 2005 further corroborate the existence of these three phases. They also indicate that, during the transition to the second phase, grasses, and in particular purple moor grass, may have become an important component of the blanket bog vegetation, as Types 495 and 496 in particular have been strongly associated with *Molinia* (van Smeerdijk 1989).

There are strong indications of grazing within the 2005 NPP record, most clearly associated with the shift to wetter, cotton-grass bog vegetation. The obligate dung fungi *Sporormiella* (Type 113) shows a clear 'take-off' at that point. Although there are a range of other fungi associated with dung prior to this point, only *Sporormiella* and *Podospora* are obligate dung fungi. The remaining taxa are also found in rotting vegetation and tend to increase significantly in association with grazing (Blackford *et al*, forthcoming). Taxa such as *Sordaria* sp (Type 55A) prefer a dung substrate, but can live on rotting vegetation. The increased values of these associated taxa thus suggest an increase in grazing in the third broad phase.

Indications of burning within the datasets come from the micro-charcoal curves within the pollen results (Fig. 19.8), the NPP taxa associated with fire (*Gelasinospora* sp. (Type 1) and *Neurospora crassa* (Type 55C): Fig. 19.9), and the macro-charcoal from the plant macrofossil results (Fig. 19.8). The macro-charcoal suggests constant, low-level burning within the vicinity of Whitehorse Hill; however, the NPP taxa *Gelasinospora* sp. and *Neurospora crassa* indicate a strong association with the first and third general phases. These are the periods with most ericaceous

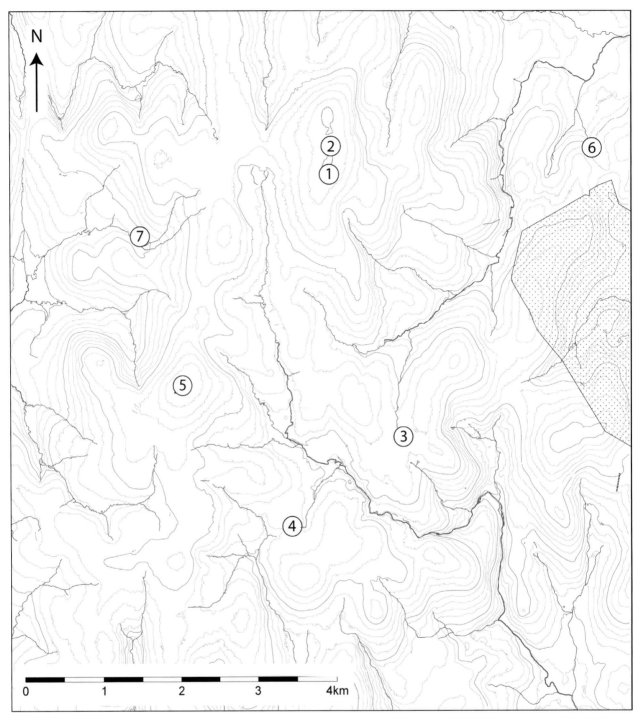

Figure 19.13: Location of Whitehorse Hill and other pollen sites mentioned. 1. Whitehorse Hill, 2. Hangingstone Hill, 3. Winneys Down, 4. Broad Down, 5. Cut Hill, 6. Shovel Down, 7. Black Ridge Brook. The stippled area indicates Fernworthy Forest.

indicators. The final phase also has the highest levels of micro-charcoal. This is, perhaps, not surprising, as wetter mire vegetation (for example, that characterised by *Eriophorum* and *Sphagnum*) is likely to be less flammable than a drier heather-dominant blanket mire community. It is not possible to distinguish anthropogenic burning from natural fires from the data alone, but previous work has strongly argued for human modification of Dartmoor's vegetation through the deliberate use of fire during the

Mesolithic (for example, Caseldine and Hatton 1993), and it seems reasonable to assume that this was also the case in later prehistory.

The Neolithic and Bronze Age environment at Whitehorse Hill

The pollen and NPP work from WHH11 provides a detailed picture of the Neolithic and Bronze Age environs at Whitehorse Hill. The current absence of a secure chronology for WHH11 means that attribution of precise dates for changes in the high-resolution sequence is not possible. The discussion is therefore framed around three broad periods: pre-cist construction, the landscape of the period of cist construction and the post-cist landscape (see previous discussion for the positioning of the cist within the sequence). Beyond this, the discussion uses depths rather than ages, although approximate durations of phases are given where possible, based on the estimates of peat accumulation rates.

The pre-cist landscape

At the start of the high-resolution analysis (61cm) the pollen and NPPs indicate that the peat bog was predominantly heather covered (NPP Type 12 and *Meliola ellisii*), with some sedges (Cyperaceae pollen) locally (NPP zone 1, Pollen zone 1). It is assumed that this sedge pollen is derived in the main from hare's-tail cotton grass (*Eriophorum vaginatum*) on the basis of the plant macrofossil results from WHH05. The high proportions of woodland taxa indicate a predominantly wooded upland away from areas that were peat covered. The woodland would have been dominated by hazel with oak in more sheltered positions and alder on the wetter valley floors. This general pattern of hazel and oak woodland on Dartmoor during the Neolithic is mirrored at the comparable sites reported in Fyfe and Woodbridge (2012), particularly Hangingstone Hill and Cut Hill. There are few radical shifts in the character of this wider 'regional' vegetation character immediately apparent within the entire pollen diagram, but there are hints within the local pollen (sedges, grasses and heathers), indicating changes in the character of the bog vegetation. These subtle changes in the pollen are mirrored by more significant fluctuations in the NPP record.

At around 59cm sedge (Cyperaceae) pollen decreases slightly and grasses (Poaceae) increase. At the same time there is a significant increase in NPP Type 496. This particular NPP is strongly associated with *Molinia* in palaeoecological studies (van Smeerdijk 1989) and these two datasets thus suggest that the local bog vegetation moved into a grass-moor phase. This phase lasted for around 200–250 years and finished with an increase in the fungal spore T91, which is associated in the literature with a transition to fen peat (van Geel 1978). Increases in pollen of sedges and heather, and the occurrences of NPPs Type 91 and Type 10, suggest that for the subsequent ~125 years the vegetation was a mosaic of heather and cotton grasses.

Between 50cm and 40cm depth a distinct sedge-dominated phase is clear, with the dominance of Cyperaceae in the pollen record and NPPs associated with wetter conditions. This phase appears to last for around 500–600 years. Similar Cyperaceae-dominated phases occur in other pollen records from northern Dartmoor, at Hangingstone Hill, for example, between ~3000–1900 cal BC and at Cut Hill between ~3100–2000 cal BC (Fyfe and Woodbridge

2012). Towards the end of this phase at Whitehorse Hill, the increase in NPP Type 10 suggests that *Calluna vulgaris* begins to increase. Between 40cm and 38cm depth the combination of heather (*Calluna vulgaris*) and sedge (Cyperaceae) pollen, alongside NPP Type 10, suggest a mosaic of heather and cotton grasses indicative of a pool-hummock pattern across the bog surface. Between 38cm and 36cm depth there is a distinct increase in NPP Type 496 which, as described above, is associated with *Molinia*. At the same depth grass (Poaceae) pollen increases at the expense of sedge (Cyperaceae) and heather (*Calluna vulgaris*). Based on the age-depth modelling work, this represents the phase immediately preceding the construction of the cist. Throughout this whole pre-cist phase there are only intermittent indications of grazing from the obligate dung fungi (*Sporormiella* sp.) and persistent but low levels of charcoal, suggesting only a low level of fire in the wider landscape.

The landscape of the cist

While the exact depth that relates to the construction of the cist within WHH11 has yet to be established, it is most likely (as discussed above) to lie between 33cm and 31cm depth. Discussion of the contemporary landscape of the cist must, though, recognise events that immediately preceded its construction and also be mindful of the chronological uncertainty. Around the estimated depth of the cist two significant changes are recognised: an increase in burning and a marked increase in taxa associated with grazing.

The indications of increased burning lie between 36cm and 34cm and continue through to around 31–30cm depth. This is primarily reflected in the increase in both size fractions of the micro-charcoal curves (Fig. 19.8), but there is also a slight increase in *Gelasinospora*, an NPP type associated with fire (Boyd 1986). It is not possible to disentangle the causes of the burning recognised in the micro-charcoal, and it remains possible that a shift to warmer and drier climatic conditions towards the end of the third millennium BC, such as that recorded by Amesbury *et al.* (2008) from Tor Royal Bog on Dartmoor, resulted in mire vegetation more prone to burning. Heather is associated with burning in the palaeoecological record (for example, Odgaard 1992; Fyfe *et al.* 2003), and the pollen record suggests increases in heather in the mire vegetation. However, given the clear evidence that societies were marking and using large parts of the upland by the Early Bronze Age, through construction of stone rows, circles and cairns, it seems improbable that responsibility for burning events did not lie with Early Bronze Age communities on Dartmoor.

Indications that grazing became increasingly important on the mire around Whitehorse Hill lie between 35cm and 31cm depth within the NPPs associated with dung. In particular *Sordaria* sp. (Type 55a) increase steadily to 33cm, and between 33cm and 31cm both *Sordaria* sp. and Type 206 dominate the NPP record in a phase lasting around 100–150 years. Although the obligate grazing dung such as *Sporormiella* sp. do not show any particular increase in abundance, both *Sordaria* sp. and Type 206 respond strongly to grazing. According to the rest of the NPP assemblage and the pollen record, the grazing took place on a heather and grass-vegetated bog, with burning continuing in the wider landscape. Once again, there are few indications of localised burning: none of the NPPs associated with fire shows any increase. It is also noteworthy that in spite of the indications that this was the most intense grazing and burning episode in the high-resolution analysis, there is no evidence of wider clearance of the upland: the hazel, oak and alder woodland persisted. It must be assumed that while the high upland was being used for grazing, this was restricted to areas that were already open (that is, the blanket mire communities), and there was no immediate pressure on land or space that resulted in clearance. This continued presence of woodland on the high upland further supports the inferences of Fyfe and Woodbridge (2012), with pronounced clearance of the high upland not apparent until the later Iron Age. This is in contrast to lower areas of Dartmoor, particularly those associated with Bronze Age enclosure, which were predominantly open by the mid-second millennium BC (Smith *et al.* 1981; Fyfe *et al.* 2008).

The post-cist landscape

The final phase of the high-resolution sequence sees a reduction in indicators of both grazing (NPP *Sordaria* sp. and Type 206) and burning (reductions in charcoal curves), although the charcoal concentrations do remain higher than the pre-cist levels. The general indications from the NPPs above 31cm are that the local mire conditions become increasingly dry: Type 303 is associated with drier phases of growth and can become very abundant (Blackford *et al.* forthcoming), as is seen at Whitehorse Hill. The continued dominance of heather (*Calluna vulgaris*) and grasses (Poaceae) in the pollen record confirms a largely heather-grass dominated mire, still surrounded by hazel, oak and alder woodland. From 26cm onwards the pollen and spores suggest wetter local bog conditions but with a different character to the earlier phase at 50–40cm. From 26cm there are the first real indications of bog mosses (*Sphagnum*), both in the pollen and with NPP Type 18 (usually associated with wet shifts in the palaeoecological record and in particular with *Eriophorum vaginatum*).

Conclusions

Two profiles from Whitehorse Hill (WHH05 and WHH11) provide insights into long-term moorland development and detailed changes in the local landscape before, during and after cist construction. There are two broad landscape 'zones' that can be considered from this analysis: first, areas characterised by blanket bog vegetation, and secondly, 'dryland' areas; that is to say, better drained areas and valley

sides and bottoms where blanket bog communities would not have been favoured. The 2005 profile has allowed us to consider the long-term development of the high upland and recognise three broad phases over about the last 5000 years. During the first phase, heather dominated a blanket bog community surrounded by a predominantly hazel and oak woodland. The second phase represents a shift to wetter conditions, with the development of cotton grasses in the blanket bog communities, which remained surrounded by hazel and oak woodland on drier soils. The third phase was a grass and heather dominated moorland, in which woodland had largely disappeared. The timing of these shifts is not clear, but comparison with other sequences from high northern Dartmoor suggests woodland clearance around the Middle to Late Iron Age.

The high-resolution analysis from the 2011 profile spans the Neolithic and Bronze Age, and shows that this broad three-phase upland scheme masks considerable shorter-term variability in the character of the upland, particularly in the bog vegetation, with a series of phases lasting 100–150 years. These changes most probably relate to both changing climatic conditions and the consequences of land use, including both grazing and burning. Chronological difficulties mean that correlation between the peat and the cist remains uncertain, and the best approach relies on biostratigraphical correlation between material deposited within the cist and the detailed pollen record. This relies on the reasonable, but unproven, assumption that vegetative material deposited within the cist is local. On the basis of this correlation, the cist was constructed in a period which was characterised by drier bog conditions and during the most intensive period of grazing and burning recorded in the sequence. Nevertheless, the wider upland landscape, away from the areas characterised by blanket mire vegetation, appears to have retained much of its original woodland cover when the cist was constructed, and there is no evidence for woodland clearance or reductions in woodland cover in the high-resolution analyses. It therefore seems that the communities who constructed the cist at Whitehorse Hill utilised the blanket mire communities for grazing, with some use of fire, but had few discernible impacts on upland woodland above perhaps 400m OD.

References

Amesbury, M., Charman, D., Fyfe, R. M., Langdon, P. G. & West, S. 2008. Bronze Age settlement decline in southwest England: testing the climate change hypothesis. *Journal of Archaeological Science* 35, 87–98.

Beijerinck, W. 1947. *Zadenatlas der Nederlandsche flora.* Wageningen: H Veenman & Zonen.

Bennett, K. D. 1994. *Annotated Catalogue of Pollen and Pteridophyte Spore Types.* Cambridge: University of Cambridge.

Birks, H. H. & Birks, H. J. B. 2000. Future uses of pollen analysis must include plant macrofossils. *Journal of Biogeography* 27, 31–35.

Blackford, J. J. & Chambers, F. M. 1993. Determining the degree of peat decomposition for peat-based palaeoclimatic studies. *International Peat Journal* 5, 7–24.

Blackford, J. J., Innes, J. B. & Clarke, C. forthcoming. *Guide to Quaternary Fungi*. London: Quaternary Research Association Technical Guide.

Blockley, S. P. E., Pyne-O'Donnell, S. D. F., Lowe, J. J., Matthews, I. P., Stone, A., Pollard, A. M., Turney, C. S. M. & Molyneux, E. G. 2005. A new and less destructive laboratory procedure for the physical separation of distal glass tephra shards from sediments. *Quaternary Science Reviews* 24, 1952–1960.

Boyd, W. E. 1986. Vegetation history at Linwood Moss, Renfrewshire, Central Scotland. *Journal of Biogeography* 13, 207–223.

Broström, A., Nielsen, A. B., Gaillard, M.-J., Hjelle, K., Mazier, F., Binney, H., Bunting, M.-J., Fyfe, R. M., Meltsov, V., Poska, A., Räsänen, S., Soepboer, W., Stedingk, H., Suutari, H. & Sugita, S. 2008. Pollen productivity estimates – the key to landscape reconstructions. *Vegetation History and Archaeobotany* 17, 461–478.

Cappers, R., Bekker, R. and Jans, J. 2006. *Digital Seed Atlas of the Netherlands*. Eelde: Barkhuis.

Caseldine, C. J. 1999. Archaeological and environmental change on prehistoric Dartmoor: current understandings and future directions. *Quaternary Proceedings* 7, 575–583.

Caseldine, C. J. & Hatton, J. 1993. The development of high moorland on Dartmoor: fire and the influence of Mesolithic activity on vegetation change. In F. M. Chambers (ed.) *Climate Change and Human Impact on the Landscape*. London: Chapman and Hall.

Charman, D. J., Hendon, D. & Woodland, W. A. 2000. *The Identification of Peatland Testate Amoebae*. Quaternary Research Association Technical Guide 9. London: Quaternary Research Association.

Daniels, R. & Eddy, A. 1985. *Handbook of European Sphagna*. Huntingdon: Institute of Terrestrial Ecology (Natural Environment Research Council).

Faegri, K., Kaland, P. E. & Krzywinski, K. 1989. *Textbook of Pollen Analysis*. New York: Wiley.

Fyfe, R. M., Brown, A. G. & Rippon, S. J. 2003. Mid- to late-Holocene vegetation history of Greater Exmoor, UK: estimating the spatial extent of human-induced vegetation change. *Vegetation History and Archaeobotany* 12, 215–232.

Fyfe, R. M., Brück, J., Johnston, R., Lewis, H., Roland, T. & Wickstead, H. 2008. Historical context and chronology of Bronze Age enclosure on Dartmoor, UK. *Journal of Archaeological Science* 35, 2250–2261.

Fyfe, R. M. & Woodbridge, J. 2012. Differences in time and space in upland vegetation patterning: analysis of pollen data from Dartmoor, UK. *Landscape Ecology* 27, 745–760.

Hall, V. A. & Pilcher, J. R. 2002. Late-Quaternary Icelandic tephras in Ireland and Great Britain: detection, characterization and usefulness. *Holocene* 12, 223–230.

Hazell, Z. 2014. Palaeoenvironmental analysis of an upland peat from Whitehorse Hill, Dartmoor, Devon. Unpublished report, English Heritage.

Ingold, C.T. 1971. *Fungal Spores, their Liberation and Dispersal*. Oxford: Clarendon Press.

Jacobsen, G. L. & Bradshaw, R. H. W. 1981. The selection of sites for palaeovegetation studies. *Quaternary Research* 16, 80–96.

Johannesson, H., Flores, R. M. & Jonsson, J. 1981. A short account of the Holocene tephrachronology of the Snæfellsjökull central volcano, western Iceland (Ljosu oskulogin fra Snæfellsjökli). *Jökull* 31, 23–30.

Lacey, J. 1996. Spore dispersal and its role in ecology and disease: the British contribution to fungal aerobiology. *Mycological Research* 100, 641–660.

Langdon, P. G. & Barber, K. E. 2001. New Holocene tephras and a proxy climate record from a blanket mire in northern Skye, Scotland. *Journal of Quaternary Science* 16, 753–759.

Le Bas, M. J., Le Maitre, R. W., Streckeisen, A. & Zanettin, B. 1986. A chemical classification of volcanic rocks based on the total alkali–silica diagram. *Journal of Petrology* 27, 745–750.

Matthews, I.P. 2008. *The Tephrochronology of Roman Lode, Exmoor, Devon*. London: English Heritage Research Department Report 26.

Moore, P. D., Webb, J. A. & Collinson, M. E. 1991. *Pollen Analysis*. Oxford: Blackwell.

Odgaard, B. V. 1992. The fire history of Danish heathland areas as reflected by pollen and charred particles in lake sediments. *Holocene* 2, 218–226.

Pals, J. P., van Geel, B. & Delfos, A. 1980. Palaeoecological studies in the Klokkeweel Bog near Hoogkarspel (Prov. of Noord-Holland). *Review of Palaeobotany and Palynology* 30, 371–418.

Plunkett, G., Pilcher, J., McCormac, G. & Hall, V. 2004. New dates for first millennium BC tephra isochrones in Ireland. *Holocene* 14, 780–786.

Prager, A., Barthelmes, A., Theuerkauf, M. & Joosten, H. 2006. Non-pollen palynomorphs from modern alder carrs and their potential for interpreting microfossil data from peat. *Review of Palaeobotany and Palynology* 141, 7–31.

Ross-Craig, S. 1979. *Drawings of British Plants, Volume 6: Lobeliaceae to Verbenaceae*. London: Bell and Hyman.

Simmons, I. G. 1964. Pollen diagrams from Dartmoor. *New Phytologist* 63, 165–180.

Smith, K., Coppen, J., Wainwright, G. J. & Beckett, S. 1981. The Shaugh Moor Project: third report – settlement and environmental investigations. *Proceedings of the Prehistoric Society* 47, 205–273.

Stace, C. 1997. *New Flora of the British Isles*. Bath: Bath Press.

Sugita, S. 2007. Theory of quantitative reconstruction of vegetation I: Pollen from large sites reveals regional vegetation. *Holocene* 17, 229–241.

van Geel, B. 1978. A palaeoecological study of Holocene peat bog sections in Germany and the Netherlands, based on the analysis of pollen, spores and macro and microscopic remains of fungi, algae, cormophytes and animals. *Review of Palaeobotany and Palynology* 25, 1–120.

van Geel, B. & Aptroot, A. 2006. Fossil ascomycetes in Quaternary deposits. *Nova Hedwigia* 82, 313–329.

van Smeerdijk, D. G. 1989. A palaeoecological and chemical study of a peat profile from the Assendelver polder (The Netherlands). *Review of Palaeobotany and Palynology* 58, 231–288.

Williams, S. 2006. Environmental change and landscape modification since the early Neolithic, Whitehorse Hill, Dartmoor. Durham University: unpublished undergraduate dissertation.

Section 6:
The radiocarbon dating

20. Interpreting the chronology of the cist

Peter Marshall, Christopher Bronk Ramsey, Nicola Russell, Fiona Brock and Paula Reimer

The wide range of organic material preserved in the cist provided the opportunity for determining a robust chronology for the cremation and its associated grave goods. In addition, the peat mound into which the cist had been placed had the potential to provide an environmental setting and context for the burial.

Radiocarbon dating

Cist

Twelve radiocarbon determinations have been produced on samples of cremated bone, waterlogged wood, plant material and charcoal from the cist (Table 20.1). These were dated between 2012 and 2014 by Accelerator Mass Spectrometry (AMS) at the Scottish Universities Environmental Research Centre in East Kilbride (SUERC), Queen's University, Belfast (UBA), and the Oxford Radiocarbon Accelerator Unit (OxA).

At SUERC the waterlogged wood and plant macro-fossils were pre-treated as described by Stenhouse and Baxter (1983) and the cremated bone followed Lanting *et al.* (2001). The CO_2 obtained from the pre-treated samples was combusted in pre-cleaned sealed quartz tubes (Vandeputte *et al.* 1996) and then converted to graphite (Slota *et al.* 1987). The samples were dated by AMS as described by Freeman *et al.* (2010).

The samples dated at Queen's University Belfast were processed using an acid-alkali-acid pre-treatment as first outlined in de Vries and Barendsen (1952). The pre-treated and dried samples were placed in quartz tubes with a strip of silver ribbon to remove nitrates, chlorides and CuO. The samples were then sealed under vacuum and combusted to CO_2 overnight at 850°C. The CO_2 was converted to graphite on an iron catalyst using the zinc reduction method (Vogel *et al.* 1984). The graphite samples were analysed with an 0.5MeV NEC pelletron compact accelerator, with the $^{14}C/^{12}C$ ratios corrected for fractionation using the on-line measured $^{13}C/^{12}C$ ratio and in accordance with Stuiver and Polach (1977).

Those dated at Oxford were prepared and dated as described by Brock *et al.* (2010), Dee and Bronk Ramsey (2000) and Bronk Ramsey *et al.* (2004).

Three samples failed: at SUERC a fragment of cremated bone (GU-27037) did not produce sufficient CO_2; at Oxford a fragment of pelt (P31392) completely dissolved in the base wash and leather (P31393) from the textile and animal-skin object survived pre-treatment until the bleach step, when it completely dissolved.

Peat monoliths

The eight radiocarbon measurements obtained on samples from the peat monoliths were dated by AMS at SUERC in 2006 and 2012.

The samples dated at SUERC were pre-treated using methods outlined in Stenhouse and Baxter (1983), combusted following Vandeputte *et al.* (1996), graphitised as described by Slota *et al.* (1987) and measured by AMS (Freeman *et al.* 2010; Xu *et al.* 2004). For each of the 'bulk' peat samples both the alkali-soluble ('humic acid') and alkali- and acid-insoluble ('humin') fractions were dated.

Radiocarbon quality assurance

Internal quality assurance procedures and international inter-comparisons (Scott 2003; Scott *et al.* 2010) indicate no laboratory offsets and validate the measurement precision quoted.

The results reported (Tables 20.1 and 20.2) are conventional radiocarbon ages (Stuiver and Polach 1977). The calibrated date ranges have been calculated by the maximum intercept method (Stuiver and Reimer 1986), using the program OxCal v4.2 (Bronk Ramsey 1995; 1998; 2001; 2009) and the IntCal13 data set (Reimer *et al.* 2013). They are quoted in the form recommended by Mook (1986), rounded outwards to 10 years. The probability distributions of the calibrated dates (Fig. 20.1) have been calculated using the probability method (Stuiver and Reimer 1993) and the same data.

The samples

Construction and contents of the cist

The cist was set into a mound of peat and although a cut for the cist was not identified in section it seems improbable that it was a free-standing structure (Chapter 2). It seems conceivable that prior to the construction of the cist the two hazel (*Corylus avellana*) stakes (SF1 and SF2) were pushed into the peat to mark the site. Stakes SF1 (SUERC-40124) and SF2 (OxA-26377 and OxA-27447) were respectively found lying horizontally and vertically outside the cist. The two measurements on SF2 are statistically consistent (T'=0.3; T'(5%)=3.8; v=1) and a weighted mean (WHH11 – SF2; 3447±20 BP) has been taken as providing the best estimate for the age of the stake.

After the cist was constructed, the burial deposit and the accompanying items were placed inside it. The key questions identified were as follows:

- At what point in time was the site marked by the stakes and how does this relate to the finds and burial horizon within the cist?
- What is the date of the cremation and is there evidence for the curation of bone?
- How do the dates of the artefacts relate to the burial deposit and were the artefacts contemporary with one another and with the burial? Were any of the objects heirlooms or were they made for the grave?

The cist was block-lifted and taken for excavation in the laboratory at Chippenham, where it was excavated in spits and by quadrant. This detailed excavation established that the cremation was located beneath a layer of matted plant material and had been placed within an animal pelt. A second layer of matted plant material measuring approximately 325 × 250mm, with fibres running roughly in the same direction, appeared to have been deliberately placed on the granite slab that formed the base of the cist. The two radiocarbon measurements on *Molinia* (purple moor grass) stems from the matting in spit J (see Chapter 9) below the organic artefacts (OxA-30025 and UBA-25301) are statistically consistent (T'=0.2; T'(5%)=3.8; v=1) and could therefore be of the same actual age.

A *Molinia* stem (SUERC-52450) from spit C (see Chapter 9) above the organic artefacts was also dated. As it appears that clumps of purple moor grass were collected for use as matting around the cremation deposit and its associated organic artefacts (Chapters 9 and 21) the dates do not provide a constraint for deposition.

Samples from the following objects recovered from within the block were dated:

- Basketry object (OxA-27543) partially overlying the bear pelt.
- Pelt (OxA-27446) containing the cremation.

Two pairs of wooden studs, one pair smaller than the other, were recovered from within the basketry container during excavation in the laboratory at Chippenham. Fragments of wood had become detached from one of the larger ear studs and these fragments were dated (OxA-27915).

Two fragments of cremated human bone, a fragment of charcoal (*Corylus* sp.) and a charred grass culm base were submitted for dating from the cremation. One fragment of cremated bone failed during pre-treatment. The determinations on the other three samples – calcined bone (OxA-26376), pyre fuel (UBA-25300 and SUERC-52451) – are statistically consistent (T'=6.0; T'(5%)=6.0; v=2; Ward and Wilson 1978) and could therefore be of the same actual age.

The monoliths

The integration of archaeological and palaeoenvironmental chronologies is vital to produce meaningful reconstructions of the environmental context of past human activities (for example, Baillie 1991; Gearey *et al.* 2009; Kintigh *et al.* 2014). Producing robust chronologies for palaeo-environmental sequences, such as pollen diagrams (Chapter 19), presents a specific set of problems. The formation processes of peat, which are the archive for palaeoenvironmental data, may show considerable complexity, including variations in sediment accumulation rates and bioturbation. Although these processes may sometimes be evident in the stratigraphy or biostratigraphy, this is by no means always the case. This has resulted in considerable debate regarding 'best practice' in radiocarbon sub-sampling procedures, in terms of the sediment fractions which might yield the most reliable estimation of the age of the horizon in question (Brock *et al.* 2011; Howard *et al.* 2009; Lowe and Walker 2000; Shore *et al.* 1995; Walker *et al.* 2001).

Environmental sampling of the peat mound into which the cist was set was initially carried out by Historic England (formerly English Heritage) in 2005 (Straker 2006). Two samples were submitted for dating comprising Ericaceous leaves, stems and flower heads, and *Eriophorum vaginatum* (hare's-tail cotton grass) sclerenchymatous spindles from the level of the base of the cist (as it was believed to be in 2005) (see Chapter 2) and the top of the cist.

Given the paucity of identifiable plant macrofossils in the samples assessed from the 2011 monoliths and the lack of radiometric-sized bulk peat samples (Howard *et al.* 2009) due to the on-site sampling programme, the dating of bulk AMS-sized peat samples offered the only potential means of providing a chronology for the sequence adjacent to the cist. Given the inherent difficulties in obtaining accurate

Table 20.1: Whitehorse Hill, cist; radiocarbon dates.

Laboratory Number	Sample Reference	Material and context	Radiocarbon Age (BP)	$\delta^{13}C$ (‰)	Calibrated Date (95% confidence) cal BC	Posterior Density Estimate (95% probability) cal BC
Stakes						
SUERC-40124	WHH11 – SF1	Wood, *Corylus* (hazel) <10 years old (R Brunning). A horizontal stake found on the eastern side of the cist, parallel with and level with the cists' basal stone.	3500±30	−27.8±0.2	1920–1700	1890–1735 (90%) or 1715–1695 (5%)
OxA-26377	WHH11 – SF2	Wood, *Corylus* (hazel) <10 years old (R Brunning). A vertical stake found on the north side of the cist, running up the length of cist stone M.	3437±28	−25.6±0.2	-	
OxA-27447	WHH11 – SF2	As OxA-26377.	3457±27	−25.4±0.2	-	
	WHH11 – SF2	Weighted mean OxA-26377 & OxA-27447 (T'= 0.3; T'(5%)= 3.8; v= 1; Ward and Wilson 1978).	3447±20		1875–1690	1870-1845 (4%) or 1815–1685 (91%)
Cremation						
OxA-26376	WHH11 – cremation (sample A)	Cremated human long bone fragment (S Mays) from spit D, quadrant 3.	3511±29	−21.5±0.2	1930–1740	1895–1740 (93%) or 1710–1695 (2%)
GU-27037	WHH11 – cremation (sample B)	As OxA-26376.	Failed to produce enough CO_2			
SUERC-52451	WHH11 – cremation charcoal (sample A)	Charcoal *Corylus* sp. (hazel) moderate ring curvature, 4 growth rings [20mg] (Z Hazel).	3528±29	−28.0±0.2	1950–1750	1920–1740
UBA-25300	WHH11 – cremation charcoal (sample B)	Charred grass culm base [30mg] (Z Hazel).	3423±34	−27.3±0.22	1880–1630	1860–1845 (1%) or 1810–1800 (1%) or 1780–1635 (93%)

Laboratory Number	Sample Reference	Material and context	Radiocarbon Age (BP)	$\delta^{13}C$ (‰)	Calibrated Date (95% confidence) cal BC	Posterior Density Estimate (95% probability) cal BC
P31393	WHH11 – leather and textile object	Leather (E Cameron) from animal skin and textile object, from spit C (20–30mm).	Failed in pretreatment			
P31392	WHH11 – pelt	Pelt/ (E Cameron) from animal pelt.	Failed in pretreatment			
OxA-27446	WHH11 – pelt	As P31392.	3358±30	−20.9±0.2	1740–1560	1745–1625
OxA-27543	WHH11 – basketry container	Unidentified plant remains from basket.	3405±33	−27.9±0.2	1870–1620	1765–1635
OxA-27915	WHH11 – wooden stud	Euonymus europaeus (spindle) stud (G Campbell).	3709±33	−26.8±0.2	2210–1980	-
Matted plant material						
SUERC-52450	WHH11 – matting – spit C [2–3cm]	Molina (purple moor grass) stem [20mg] (G Campbell).	3433±29	−25.0±0.2	1880–1660	1865–1845 (2%) or 1815–1795 (1%) or 1780–1655 (92%)
OxA-30025	WHH11 – matting – spit J [11–12cm] sample A	Molina (purple moor grass) stem [20mg] (G Campbell).	3357±30	−25.3±0.2	1740–1550	1745–1625
UBA-25301	WHH11 – matting – spit J [11–12cm] sample B	Molina stem [20mg] (G Campbell).	3378±37	-	1760–1560	1750–1630

Table 20.2: Whitehorse Hill, monoliths; radiocarbon dates.

Laboratory Number	Sample Reference	Material	Radiocarbon Age (BP)	$\delta^{13}C$ (‰)	Calibrated date (95% confidence)
SUERC-40113	WHH05 [45–46cm]	Peat: humic acid	3370±30	−28.6±0.2	1750–1540 cal BC
SUERC-40114	WHH05 [45–46cm]	Peat: humin fraction	3410±30	−29.2±0.2	1870–1620 cal BC
SUERC-10198	WHH05 [45–46cm]	Plant macrofossils: *Eriophorum vaginatum* (hare's-tail cotton grass) sclerenchymatous spindles (Z Hazell)	3650±50	−27.0±0.2 (assumed)	2200–1890 cal BC
SUERC-40118	WHH05 [101–102cm]	Peat: humic acid	4280±30	−28.2±0.2	2920–2880 cal BC
SUERC-40119	WHH05 [101–102cm]	Peat: humin fraction	4345±30	−29.0±0.2	3080–2890 cal BC
SUERC-10199	WHH05 [101–102cm]	Plant macrofossils: *Eriophorum vaginatum* (hare's-tail cotton grass) sclerenchymatous (Z Hazell)	4625±50	−27.0±0.2 (assumed)	3630–2140 cal BC
SUERC-40120	WHH11 monolith 3 [1.04–1.05m] bottom	Peat: humic acid	5080±30	−28.1±0.2	3970–3790 cal BC
SUERC-40119	WHH11 monolith 3 [1.04–1.05m] bottom	Peat: humin fraction	5200±30	−28.9±0.2	4050–3960 cal BC
SUERC-40122	WHH11 monolith 1 [24–25cm]	Peat: humic acid	3205±30	−28.6±0.2	1530–1410 cal BC
SUERC-40123	WHH11 monolith 3 [24–25cm]	Peat: humin fraction	3330±30	−28.9	1690–1520 cal BC

results from the dating of bulk AMS-sized peat samples (Bayliss 2008, fig. 9), the following samples were dated:

- From the 2005 monolith sequence, two bulk peat samples (humic and humin fractions) to determine whether consistent results could be obtained with those from 'bulk' plant macrofossils from the same horizons dated in 2005 (SUERC-10198 and SUERC-10199).
- From the 2011 monolith sequence, two bulk peat samples (humic and humin fractions) to determine the consistency of measurements on these fractions.

Results

Construction of the cist

The 12 determinations from the cremation, organic remains buried with the cist, wooden stakes and *Molinia* are not statistically consistent (T'=84.4, T'(5%)=19.7, v=11) and the samples clearly represent material of different ages. This is, however, entirely expected, given the range of materials dated, all of which can be expected to have 'life histories' prior to burial. The wooden stud is clearly older than the majority of material in the cist; as *Eunymus europaeus* (spindle) does not grow to excessive ages a significant age-at-death offset (Bowman 1990) can be discounted as an explanation. In addition the stud had no evidence of any wear (Chapter 16), and is also older than any examples from Britain and Ireland (Table 16.2) and considerably older than any other dated material associated with the cist (Fig. 20.1). We have therefore elected to remove the measurement on wood fragments from stud 3 (OxA-27915) from the analysis below. Further material was

not available for dating to confirm our suspicions about the original measurement. Even excluding the wood stud the remaining measurements from the cist are statistically inconsistent (T'=29.9, T'(5%)=18.3, v=10), reinforcing the interpretation that the materials are not all of the same age.

Simple visual inspection of the calibrated radiocarbon dates does not allow us to assess the date of funerary activity at Whitehorse Hill accurately, since the calibration process does not allow for the fact that the radiocarbon dates in this group are related: they all come from the same site. Bayesian statistical modelling is required to account for this dependence (Buck *et al.* 1992; Bronk Ramsey 2000), which we have undertaken using OxCal v.4.1.2 (Bronk Ramsey 1995; 1998; 2001; 2009). The date ranges from the model defined below are given *in italics* to distinguish them from simple, calibrated radiocarbon dates.

The date for the burial of the cremation and its associated grave goods is most likely that for the latest item deposited in the cist. However, it is actually most likely that the material found within it derives mainly from close to this event, with a few older items being incorporated into it. This can be modelled by an exponential distribution – rising to greatest concentration of samples found from the end of collection, as in the model shown in Figure 20.2. Such a model makes more sense from an archaeological perspective (that is to say, a few items not collected/made for the burial) than assuming that the dated samples represent material derived from a uniform phase of activity (Buck *et al.* 1992) associated with the burial.

The model shown in Figure 20.3 has good overall agreement (A_{model}=107) and provides an estimate for the deposition of the cremation and its associated grave goods in the cist of *1730–1600 cal BC* (*95% probability; cist*

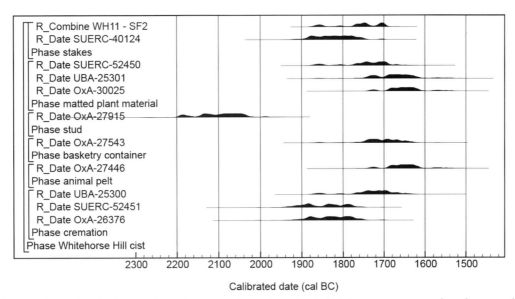

Figure 20.1: Probability distributions of dates from Whitehorse Hill. Each distribution represents the relative probability that an event occurred at a particular time. These distributions are the result of simple radiocarbon calibration (Stuiver and Reimer 1993).

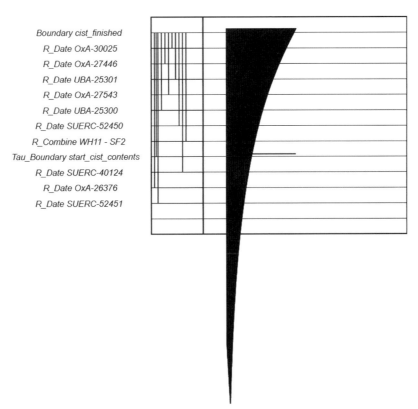

Figure 20.2: Schematic for the model shown in Figure 20.3

finished; Fig. 20.3), probably *1690–1620 cal BC (68% probability)*. It is 87.4% probable that the cremation (*OxA-26376*; Table 20.3) is the oldest item incorporated into the cist, although whether this is just a reflection of a small offset due to an old-wood effect from the fuel (Snoek *et al.* 2014) is impossible to determine. The basketry container and pelt are probably of a similar date (Table 20.3) and

were unlikely to be of any significant age when they were deposited.

The objects used in the construction of the cist (wooden stakes) and incorporated within it represents material with an age span of *60–280 years (95% probability*; Fig. 20.4), probably *125–240 (68% probability)*.

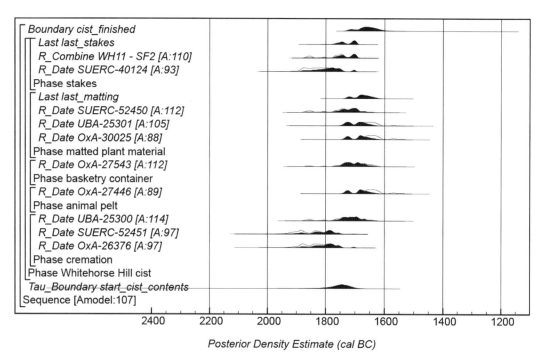

Figure 20.3: Probability distributions of dates from the Whitehorse Hill cist – an exponential distribution has been used for the collection of material associated with the cist. Each distribution represents the relative probability that an event occurs at a particular time. For each radiocarbon date, two distributions have been plotted: one in outline which is the result of simple radiocarbon calibration, and a solid one based on the chronological model used. The other distributions correspond to aspects of the model. For example, the distribution 'cist_finished is the estimate for when the cist was completed. The large square brackets down the left-hand side of the diagram and the OxCal keywords define the overall model exactly.

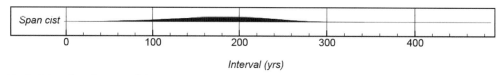

Figure 20.4: Probability distribution of the number of years over which material incorporated into the Whitehorse Hill cist originated. The estimate is derived from the model shown in Figure 20.3.

The monoliths

2005 monoliths

The humic and humin fractions from both samples are statistically consistent and the weighted mean of these samples therefore provides the best estimate for their ages; WHH05 (45–46cm); 3390±22 BP (T'=0.9, T'(5%)=3.8, v=1; Ward and Wilson 1978) and WHH05 (101–102cm); 4313±22 BP (T'=2.3, T'(5%)=3.8, v=1).

But at both depths, the weighted mean of the humic and humin fractions of these samples is significantly younger than the bulk plant macrofossils (Fig. 20.5) 3390±22 BP (WHH05: 45–46cm) and 3650±50 BP (SUERC-10198); (T'=23.2, T'(5%)=6.0, v=2); 4313±22 BP (WHH05: 101–102cm and 4625±50 BP (SUERC-10199); (T'=33.5, T'(5%)=6.0, v=2).

Although the humin (acid and alkali-insoluble) fraction is thought to be most representative of the original plant material (Shore *et al.* 1995), it is clearly much younger than the bulk plant macrofossils dated from these horizons (Fig. 20.6), and we are unable to say with any confidence which, if any, measurement provides a reliable estimate of the age of the deposits.

2011 monoliths

The humic and humin fractions from the two samples dated from the 2011 monoliths are not statistically consistent; WHH11 (24–25cm) (T'=8.7, T'(5%)=3.8, v=1) and WHH11 (1.04–1.05cm) (T'=8.0, T'(5%)=3.8, v=1). In both cases the humic acid fraction is younger than the humin fraction (Fig. 20.7). This is in agreement with much previously published work (for example, Brock *et al.* 2011; Bayliss *et al.* 2008), and suggests the downward movement of humic acids (Shore *et al.* 1995). However, given that from the 2005 core we know the humin date is not statistically consistent with the plant macrofossils, we are unable to say with any confidence which measurement provides a reliable age estimate for the formation of the deposits.

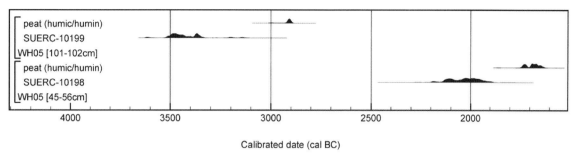

Figure 20.5: Probability distribution of radiocarbon dates from the Whitehorse Hill 2005 monolith.

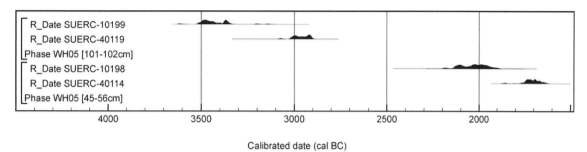

Figure 20.6: Probability distribution of radiocarbon dates on the humin fraction (SUERC-40114 and SUERC-40119), and bulk plant macrofossils (SUERC-10198–9) from the Whitehorse Hill 2005 monolith.

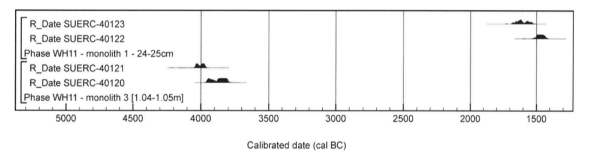

Figure 20.7: Probability distribution of radiocarbon dates on humic (SUERC-40120 and SUERC-40122), and humin (SUERC-40121 and SUERC-40123) fractions from the Whitehorse Hill 2011 monolith.

Table 20.3 Percentage probabilities of the relative order of artefacts and materials incorporated into the Whitehorse Hill cist. The cells show the probability of the distribution in the left-hand column being earlier than the distribution in the top row. For example, the probability that the calcined bone (OxA-26376) is earlier than the animal pelt (OxA-27446) is 98.9%.

	OxA-26376	OxA-27446	OxA-27543	last_matting	last_stakes
OxA-26376		98.9%	96.6%	99.5%	91.9%
OxA-27446	1.1%		31.2%	65.5%	13.3%
OxA-27543	3.4%	68.9%		81.7%	26.9%
last matting	0.5%	34.5%	18.3%		5.7%
last_stakes	8.1%	86.7%	73.1%	94.3%	

Tephra

Further independent scientific dating evidence with which to evaluate the radiocarbon results from the 2011 monoliths exists at Whitehorse Hill from tephra dating (Chapter 19).

Estimates for the Lairg A, Lairg B and OMH-185 tephra horizons identified in the 2011 monoliths were derived from age-depth modelling the individual radiocarbon dated sequences from Sluggan Bog (Pilcher *et al.* 1996) and Glen West (Plunkett *et al.* 2004).

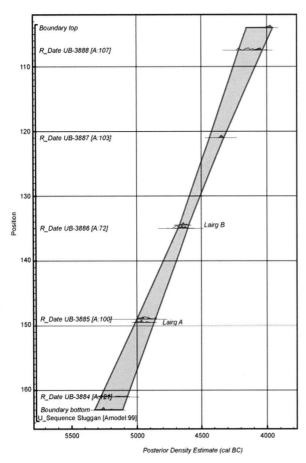

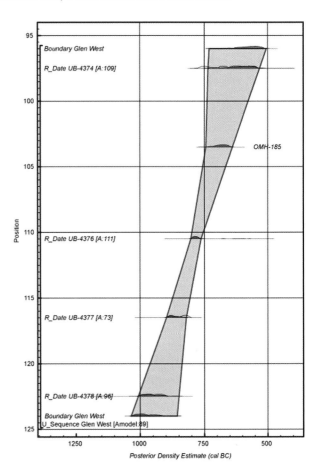

Figure 20.8: Bayesian age-depth model of the chronology of the sediment sequence at Sluggan Bog (U_Sequence model; Bronk Ramsey 2008) and estimates for the dates of the Lairg A and B tephra's. The coloured band shows the estimated date of the sediment at the corresponding depth, at 95% probability. For radiocarbon dates, the lighter distribution is the result of simple calibration and the darker distribution is the posterior density estimate provided by the model/

Figure 20.9: Bayesian age-depth model of the chronology of the sediment sequence at Glen West (U_Sequence model; Bronk Ramsey 2008) and estimates for the date of the OMH-185 tephra. The format is identical to Figure RC6.

Revised age estimate for the OMH-185 tephra

A uniform-aged depth model (U-Sequence, Bronk Ramsey 2008; Fig. 20.9) shows good overall agreement (A_{model}=89) between the radiocarbon dates (Plunkett *et al.* 2004) and stratigraphy. The model provides an estimate for the date of the OMH-185 tephra of *745–640 cal BC (94% probability; OMH-185; Fig. 20.9).*

Revised age estimates for the Lairg A and Lairg B tephras

A uniform aged depth model (U-Sequence, Bronk Ramsey 2008; Fig. 20.8), in which the accumulation rate is unknown but assumed to be constant (Christen *et al.* 1995), shows good overall agreement (A_{model}=99) between the radiocarbon dates (Pilcher *et al.* 1996) and stratigraphy. The model provides estimates for the date of the Lairg A tephra of *5020–4895 cal BC (94% probability; Lairg A; Fig. 20.8)* and Lairg B of *4675–4600 cal BC (95% probability; Lairg B; Fig. 20.8).* The estimate for the Lairg B event is in agreement with that obtained from the annual laminated record of Lake Belau, Germany (Dörfler *et al.* 2012), of *4980–4760 cal BC (95% probability)* and that suggests the age-depth model (Fig. 20.8) is robust and accurate.

Tephra and radiocarbon results

Figure 20.10 shows the radiocarbon results from the 2011 monoliths and estimates for the dates of three tephras (Chapter 19) derived above. The results suggest that the radiocarbon measurements from near the base of the profile (104–105 cm) are too young by as much as 800 years. Explaining such a large offset in both the humic and humin fractions is difficult, although downward movement of water-soluble organic materials would lead to the age of the humic fraction being too young and downward penetration of rootlets could result in the humin sediment fraction also being too young. Given that the radiocarbon measurements were from AMS-size bulk samples this remains a possibility.

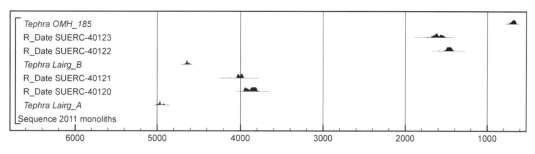

Calibrated date (cal BC)/*Posterior Density Estimate (cal BC)*

Figure 20.10: Probability distribution of radiocarbon dates on peat: humic (SUERC-40120 and SUERC-40122) and humin (SUERC-40121 and SUERC-40123) fractions from the Whitehorse Hill 2011 monolith, and estimates for the dates of the Lairg A, Lairg B, and OMH-185 tephras derived from the models shown in Figures RC6 and RC7.

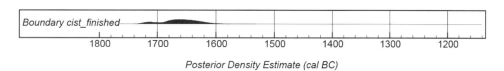

Posterior Density Estimate (cal BC)

Figure 20.11: Probability distribution for the completion of the Whitehorse Hill cist. The distribution is derived from the model shown in Figure 20.3.

Conversely, the radiocarbon determinations from near the top of the monoliths (24–25 cm) may be too old!

Discussion

The independent dating evidence provided by the tephra analysis, although one might argue for a degree of circularity in that the age of the tehpras is derived from radiocarbon dating, clearly demonstrates the difficulties in providing reliable chronologies for peat sequences when AMS-size samples are used. The sole reliance on material from both sets of monolith tins for providing samples for radiocarbon dating was with hindsight unsound when the section (Fig. 19.1) could have been sampled to provide radiometric sized [>200g] samples from 1cm slices (*cf* Howard *et al.* 2009).

Given the fact that a robust chronology for the peat sequence could not be provided the environmental work (Chapter 19) on the sequences from the monoliths has no independent dating framework beyond the broad parameters provided by the tephrachronology.

The chronology

Given we have no reason *a priori* to expect all the dated samples from the cist and its construction to be of the same actual age (cf Hamilton and Kenney 2015), such a model as that shown in Figure 20.3 will inherently produce a less precise but more robust estimate for the archaeological date of interest (the burial event) than other methods (for example, simply combining all the measurements). The estimated date for the completion of the cists and incorporation of the material into it is

1730–1600 cal BC (*95% probability*; *cist_finished;* Fig. 20.3), probably *1690–1620 cal BC* (*68% probability*). It is very probable that the cremation, and at the very least the calcined bone, was older than the other artefacts buried with it (see Chapter 21 for further discussion of this point). It is also probable that the calcined bone was older than the stakes (91.9% probability) initially used to delineate the position of the cist.

References

Baillie, M. G. L. 1991. Suck in and smear: two related chronological problems for the 90s. *Journal of Theoretical Archaeology* 2, 12–16.

Bayliss, A, 2008. Introduction: Scientific dating and the Aggregates Levy Sustainability Fund 2004–7. In A. Bayliss, G. Cook, C. Bronk Ramsey, J. van der Plicht, & G. McCormac, *Radiocarbon Dates From Samples Funded by English Heritage Under the Aggregates Levy Sustainability Fund 2004–7.* Swindon: English Heritage, vii–xvii.

Bowman, S, 1990. *Radiocarbon Dating.* London, British Museum.

Brock, F., Higham, T., Ditchfield, P. & Bronk Ramsey, C. 2010. Current pretreatment methods for AMS radiocarbon dating at the Oxford Radiocarbon Accelerator Unit (ORAU). *Radiocarbon* 52, 103–112.

Brock, F., Lee, S., Housley, R. & Bronk Ramsey, C. 2011. Variation in the radiocarbon age of different fractions of peat: a case study from Ahrenshöft, northern Germany. *Quaternary Geochronology* 6, 505–555.

Bronk Ramsey, C. 1995. Radiocarbon calibration and analysis of stratigraphy. *Radiocarbon* 36, 425–430.

Bronk Ramsey, C. 1998. Probability and dating. *Radiocarbon* 40, 461–474.

Bronk Ramsey, C. 2000. Comment on 'The use of Bayesian

statistics for 14C dates of chronologically ordered samples: a critical analysis'. *Radiocarbon* 42, 199–202.

Bronk Ramsey, C. 2001. Development of the radiocarbon calibration program. *Radiocarbon* 43, 355–363.

Bronk Ramsey, C. 2008. Deposition models for chronological records. *Quaternary Science Review* 27, 42–60.

Bronk Ramsey, C. 2009. Bayesian analysis of radiocarbon dates, *Radiocarbon* 51, 337–360.

Bronk Ramsey, C., Higham, T. & Leach, P. 2004. Towards high precision AMS: progress and limitations, *Radiocarbon* 46, 17–24.

Buck, C. E., Litton, C. D. & Smith, A. F. M. 1992. Calibration of radiocarbon results pertaining to related archaeological events. *Journal of Archaeological Science* 19, 497–512.

Christen, J. A., Clymo, R. S. & Litton, C. D. 1995. A Bayesian approach to the use of 14C dates in the estimation of the age of peat, *Radiocarbon* 37, 431–442.

Dee, M. W. & Bronk Ramsey, C. 2000. Refinement of graphite target production at Oxford Radiocarbon Accelerator Unit, *Nuclear Instruments and Methods in Physics Research, Section B* 172, 449–453.

Dörfler, W., Feeser, I., van den Bogaard, C., Dreibrodt, S., Erlenkeuser, H., Kleinmann, A., Merkt, J. & Wiethold, J. 2012. A high-quality annually laminated sequence from Lake Belau, northern Germany: revised chronology and its implications for palynological and tephrochronological studies. *Holocene* 22, 1413–1426.

Freeman, S. P. H. T., Cook, G. T., Dougans, A. B., Naysmith, P., Wicken, K. M. & Xu, S. 2010. Improved SSAMS performance, *Nuclear Instruments and Methods in Physics Research, Section B* 268, 715–717.

Gearey, B. G., Marshall, P. & Hamilton, D. 2009. Correlating archaeological and palaeoenvironmental records using a Bayesian approach: a case study from Sutton Common, South Yorkshire, England, *Journal of Archaeological Science* 36, 1477–1487.

Hamilton, W. D. & Kenney, J. 2015. Multiple Bayesian modelling approaches to a suite of radiocarbon dates from ovens excavated at Ysgol yr Hendre, Caernarfon, North Wales. *Quaternary Geochronology* 25, 72–82.

Howard, A. J., Gearey, B. R., Hill, T., Fletcher, W. & Marshall, P. 2009. Fluvial sediments, correlations and palaeoenvironmental reconstruction: the development of robust radiocarbon chronologies. *Journal of Archaeological Science* 36, 2680–2688.

Kintigh, K. W., Altschul, J. H., Beaudry, M. C., Drennan, R. D., Kinzig, A. P., Kohler, T. A., Limp, W. F., Maschner, H. D. G., Michener, W. K., Pauketat, T. R., Peregrine, P., Sabloff, J. A., Wilkinson, T. J., Wright, H. T. & Zeder, M. A. 2014. Grand challenges for archaeology. *American Antiquity* 79, 5–24.

Lanting, J. N., Aerts-Bijma, A. T. & van der Plicht, J. 2001. Dating of cremated bone. *Radiocarbon* 43, 249–254.

Lowe, J. J. & Walker, M. J. C. 2000. Radiocarbon dating the last glacial-interglacial transition (14C ka BP) in terrestrial and marine records: the need for new quality assurance protocols. *Radiocarbon* 42, 53–68.

Mook, W. G. 1986. Business meeting: recommendations/ resolutions adopted by the Twelfth International Radiocarbon Conference. *Radiocarbon* 28, 799.

Pilcher, R. A., Hall, V. A. & McCormac, F. G. 1996. An outline tephrochronology for the Holocene of the north of Ireland. *Journal of Quaternary Science* 11, 485–494.

Plunkett, G. M., Pilcher, J. R., McCormac, F. G. & Hall, V. A.

2004. New dates for first millennium BC tephra isochrones in Ireland. *Holocene* 14, 780–786.

Reimer, P. J., Bard, E., Bayliss, A., Beck, J.W., Blackwell, P., Bronk Ramsey, C., Buck, C. E., Cheng, H., Edwards, R. L., Friedrich, M., Grootes, P. M., Guilderson, T. P., Haflidason, H., Hajdas, I., Hatté, C., Heaton, T. J., Hoffmann, D. L., Hogg, A. G., Hughen, K. A., Kaiser, K. F., Kromer, B., Manning, S. W., Niu, M., Reimer, R. W., Richards, D. A., Scott, E. M., Southon, J. R., Staff, R. A., Turney, C. S. M. & van der Plicht, J. 2013. IntCal13 and Marine13 radiocarbon age calibration curves 0–50,000 years cal BP. *Radiocarbon* 55, 1869–1887.

Scott, E. M. 2003. The third international radiocarbon intercomparison (TIRI) and the fourth international radiocarbon intercomparison (FIRI) 1990–2002: results, analyses, and conclusions. *Radiocarbon* 45, 135–408.

Scott, E. M., Cook, G. & Naysmith, P. 2010. The fifth international radiocarbon intercomparison (VIRI): an assessment of laboratory performance in stage 3. *Radiocarbon* 53, 859–865.

Shore, J. S., Bartley, D. D. & Harkness, D. D. 1995. Problems encountered with the ^{14}C dating of peat. *Quaternary Science Review* 14, 373–383.

Slota, P. J., Jr., Jull, A. J. T., Linick, T. W. & Toolin, L. J. 1987. Preparation of small samples for ^{14}C accelerator targets by catalytic reduction of CO. *Radiocarbon* 29, 303–306.

Snoeck, C., Brock, F. & Schulting, R. 2014. Carbon exchange between bone apatite and fuels during cremation: impact on radiocarbon dates. *Radiocarbon* 56, 591–602.

Stenhouse, M. J. & Baxter, M. S. 1983. ^{14}C dating reproducibility: evidence from routine dating of archaeological samples. *Proceedings of the First International Symposium, ^{14}C and Archaeology, Groningen, 1981, PACT* 8, 147–164.

Straker, V. 2006. Dartmoor 2005: palaeoenvironmental sampling from Cut Hill and Whitehorse Hill. Unpublished report, English Heritage.

Stuiver, M. & Polach, H. A. 1977. Reporting of ^{14}C data. *Radiocarbon* 19, 355–363.

Stuiver, M. & Reimer, P. J. 1986. A computer program for radiocarbon age calculation. *Radiocarbon* 28, 1022–1030.

Stuiver, M. & Reimer, P. J. 1993. Extended ^{14}C data base and revised CALIB 3.0 ^{14}C age calibration program. *Radiocarbon* 35, 215–230.

Vandeputte, K., Moens, L. & Dams, R. 1996. Improved sealed-tube combustion of organic samples to CO_2 for stable isotope analysis, radiocarbon dating and percent carbon determinations. *Analytical Letters* 29 (15), 2761–2773.

Vogel, J. S., Southon, J. R., Nelson, D. E. & Brown, T. A. 1984. Performance of catalytically condensed carbon for use in accelerator mass-spectrometry, *Nuclear Instruments and Methods in Physics Research*, Section B 233, 289–293.

de Vries, H. & Barendsen, G. W. 1952. A new technique for the measurement of age by radiocarbon. *Physica* 18, 652.

Walker, M. J. C., Bryant, C., Coope, G. R., Harkness, D. D., Lowe, J. J. & Scott, E. M. 2001. Towards a radiocarbon chronology of the Late-Glacial: sample selection strategies. *Radiocarbon* 43, 1007–1021.

Ward, G. K. & Wilson, S. R. 1978. Procedures for comparing and combining radiocarbon age determinations: a critique. *Archaeometry* 20, 19–31.

Xu, S., Anderson, R., Bryant, C., Cook, G. T., Dougans, A., Freeman, S., Naysmith, P., Schnabel, C. & Scott, E.M. 2004. Capabilities of the new SUERC 5MV AMS facility for 14C dating. *Radiocarbon* 46, 59–64.

Section 7:
Discussion, interpretation and conclusions

21. The results from the project

Andy M. Jones

There are approximately 187 recorded cists on Dartmoor (Butler 1997, 173) (Fig. 21.1) but this is almost certainly an underestimate: others are very likely to exist under unexcavated cairns and barrows and, in the light of the results from the Whitehorse Hill cist, it is very probable that other sites await discovery beneath the peat.

As a class of monument, cists are the most frequently excavated type on the moor and, from the last quarter of the nineteenth century until the first quarter of the twentieth, they were the subject of intensive investigation, with annual reports on the results of fieldwork appearing in the *Transactions of the Devonshire Association*. By the time that a hiatus in the campaign of cist digging occurred, some 44 sites had been investigated (Butler 1997, 173).

The last documented investigation of a cist was in 1949 (Dixon 1953), when two flints were found within Harford 1. This site contained rather more in the way of artefacts than most. Indeed, aside from a few notable exceptions (see Table 21.1), the contents of most of Dartmoor's cists proved to be unexceptional. In part the paucity of artefacts recovered was due to the techniques available at the time, although the prevalent acidic soil conditions were not favourable to survival for organic finds and, as will be argued below, certain types of non-organic artefact, including post-Beaker ceramics, seem to have been excluded from being incorporated within them. Despite these limitations, hints of the former presence of organic finds were made at a very small number of sites, and some patterns such as cist orientation and the deposition of charcoal and of flint were identified early on. It should be noted that the publication record was for its time impressive and, as discussed in Chapter 2, the results of earlier work on the moor inevitably shaped expectations for the Whitehorse Hill excavations.

It is noticeable how infrequent excavations of ceremonial monuments of both rescue and research type have been in the 70 years since the last cist excavation, with the exception of the Shaugh Moor cairn complex and the stone rows at Cholwichtown and Cut Hill (Wainwright *et al.* 1979; Eogan and Simmons 1964; Fyfe and Greeves 2010). Instead, most of the investigations that have taken place since the 1970s have focused upon Middle Bronze Age settlements and field systems (for example, Fleming 1988; Wainwright and Smith 1980; Gerrard 2000; Brück *et al.* 2003; Marchand and Hughes 2012).

In part this switch in focus has been due to increasing levels of monument protection and the decline in research-led investigation in England into non-threatened sites. However, it is also the case that research into roundhouse settlements and field systems was perceived as likely to reveal bigger dividends in terms of answering questions about occupation, settlement economy and land-use, than investigation of another 'empty' stone chest.

However, the Whitehorse Hill cist has revealed that, given the right conditions for preservation, these assumptions are incorrect. The assemblage of so many organic objects is exceptional and without parallel in a British context, where, in general, there have been few new discoveries since Henshall (1950) compiled her corpus of organic materials from the Bronze Age. With the exception of the outstanding range of artefacts associated with the Gristhorpe log coffin burial (Melton *et al.* 2013), the nearest comparable surviving finds, in terms of quality, are those from bogs and waterlogged barrows outside mainland Britain. Examples include the basketry recovered from Irish bogs (Raftery 1970) and, in Europe, the clothing from Danish bogs and log coffin burials (Hald 1980). Indeed, it is the Danish log coffin burials, such as that from Borum Eshøj, which provide the nearest comparanda in terms of the range of organic materials, including hide, wood, leather and bark containers (Glob 1983, 40–2); however, these are a few centuries younger than the finds from Whitehorse Hill (Randsborg and Christensen 2006).

Although Early Bronze Age organic remains, including hide and wood, have occasionally been recorded in northern Britain (for example, Mortimer 1905; Dixon 1913; Noble and Brophy 2011; Melton *et al.* 2013), organic objects from burial sites in southern Britain remain extremely scarce (Table 21.2). Their existence has been inferred from the positions of non-organic items such as copper-alloy pins (Burgess 1980, 180–192), or traces have survived as mineralised impressions on metalwork, have appeared as dark stains or are documented from antiquarian excavations (for example, Ashbee 1978; Green and Rollo-Smith 1984; French 1994; Annable and Simpson 1964, 45–46; Dixon 1913).

A small number of organic finds or impressions from them have been recorded in the south-west region (here taken to be Devon and Cornwall). On Dartmoor, coils of 'hair' were reported within the cist at Manaton 9 (Soussons Plantation south) (Burnard 1903, 142; Butler 1997, 277) and at Lydford 50 'hair' was also said to have been found (Grinsell 1978). Beyond Dartmoor, organic finds include a 'chaplet' or 'wreath' of 'oak and birch leaves' recorded from beneath a cremation at the Huntshaw barrow in north Devon (Doe 1875). Across the Tamar in Cornwall fabrics and woven objects have only survived as mineralised fragments or impressions (Table 21.2).

The Whitehorse Hill cist also produced non-organic artefacts, including the largest number of amber and shale beads to be found in the south-west peninsula, and the surrounding mound was also rich in environmental material. Given the scarcity of such artefacts and data from Dartmoor and indeed nationally, the opportunity has been taken to discuss them in their wider context.

The following sections consider the results from the excavation under a number of key themes. First the Beaker-period origins for the cist tradition on Dartmoor – pre-dating the construction of the Whitehorse Hill cist – will be discussed and their influence on subsequent Early Bronze Age cists assessed.

The next theme is the Early Bronze Age cist tradition itself. Within this section the choice of location and the methods used in cist construction will be considered and compared with other sites on Dartmoor and more widely in the south west. Where appropriate, parallels with other sites beyond this region are also drawn.

The third section reviews the artefactual assemblage from the cist. This includes both non-organic and organic objects as well as other materials deliberately deposited, including charcoal and the cremation itself. Discussion in this section is not just concerned with comparanda but is also focused on the materiality of the objects; that is to say, what they were made from, their colour and texture, where they came from and the symbolism that they may have held. Consideration is also given to what was not included within the cist.

The fourth section addresses how the contents of the

cist were drawn together, the time frame for the cist and how the contents may have been choreographed to create a particular image or reading.

The fifth section looks at the after-life of Whitehorse Hill and the mound in which the cist was found. Discussion centres on the influence that the site may have exerted in the landscape after the Early Bronze Age.

The synthesis concludes with a final overview of the project and the implications for further work on Dartmoor.

Origins of the cist tradition on Dartmoor: Beaker beginnings

Despite being a commonly found site type on Dartmoor (usually as an element of cairn construction), direct dating for cists is extremely limited. As can be seen in Table 21.1, none of the other cists on Dartmoor have associated radiocarbon dates and very few have produced closely diagnostic finds.

Cists are widely distributed across the British Isles and as a site type they have a very long pedigree, with the earliest being associated with Early and Middle Neolithic burials in Britain and beyond (Benson and Whittle 2007, 81; Kinnes 1979; Gibson 2007; Scarre 2011, 105). However, evidence from across Britain and Ireland places the majority of cists in the Beaker-using and Early Bronze Age periods (for example, Savory 1972; Carlin and Brück 2012; Jones 2005). In a local context, with the possible exception of the cist at Meacombe, which, on the basis of its remarkably large capstone (weighing over 2 tons), has been suggested as being of Neolithic date (Grinsell 1978; Butler 1997, 155), none of the Dartmoor cists or indeed those of the south-west region generally can be demonstrated to pre-date the last quarter of the third millennium cal BC (Jones 2012).

In common with the south-west peninsula as a whole (Jones 2011a), the earliest securely dated cists on Dartmoor are those which are associated with Beaker ceramics; these are likely to date from the latter part of the third millennium to the early second millennium cal BC. Currently, the only scientifically dated example from a Beaker-associated cist in the south west is that from beside the Try menhir in west Cornwall (Jones and Quinnell 2006a), and this is a very late example dating to 1880–1600 cal BC (GrA-30170; 3410+50 BP).

The pottery from several cist sites on Dartmoor is too poorly recorded to assign a type. However, five or six sites (Table 21.1) with Beaker pottery have been found there (Quinnell 2003). Three cists contained objects which are of the same period. Three barbed and tanged arrowheads were found at Shaugh Prior 8 (Worth 1967, 199), Cornwood 3 produced a stone 'sponge finger' (Smith and Simpson 1966) and a stone bracer was recovered from Lydford Archeton 39 (Burnard 1901; Woodward and Hunter 2011, 167).

It seems likely that these sites are a localized development from the Beaker-associated burials which are recorded across Britain from the middle of the third millennium cal BC (Bradley 2007, 150; Gibson 2013). In the lowlands,

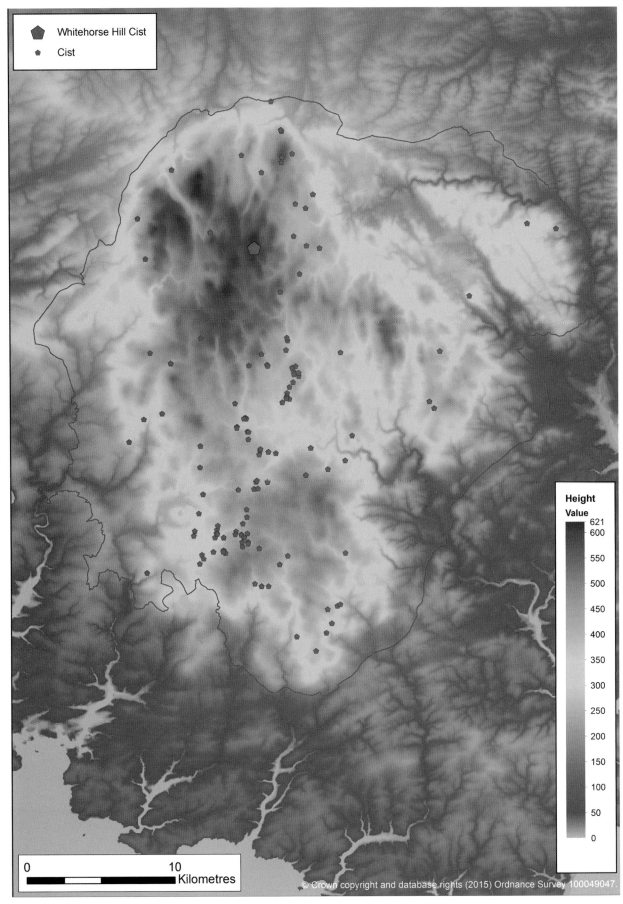

Figure 21.1: The distribution of cists within the boundary of Dartmoor National Park.

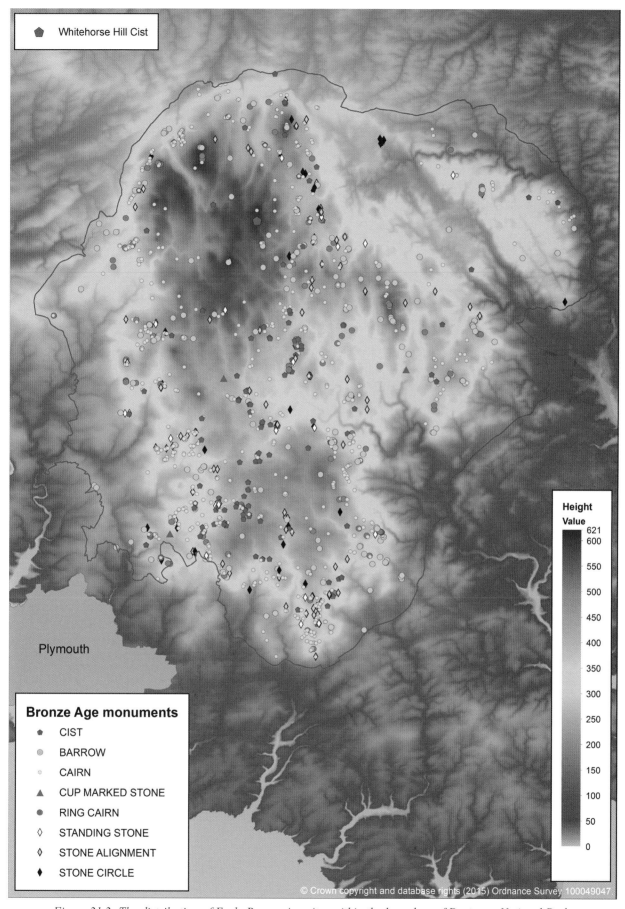

Whitehorse Hill Cist

Bronze Age monuments
- CIST
- BARROW
- CAIRN
- ▲ CUP MARKED STONE
- ● RING CAIRN
- ◇ STANDING STONE
- ◊ STONE ALIGNMENT
- ◆ STONE CIRCLE

Plymouth

Height
Value
621
600
550
500
450
400
350
300
250
200
150
100
50
0

© Crown copyright and database rights (2015) Ordnance Survey 100049047

Figure 21.2: The distribution of Early Bronze Age sites within the boundary of Dartmoor National Park.

Table 21.1: Excavated Dartmoor cists, cairns and barrows.

Site name	Grinsell no.	Radiocarbon date	Cist/cairn/barrow	Artefactual associations	Reference
Dartmoor Chagford, (Thornworthy)	3	–	2 cists beneath a cairn.	Cairn contained 2 cists. Larger cist contained flint knife & flake. Smaller contained sherds from a Beaker.	Grinsell 1978; Quinnell 2003.
Chagford (Chagford Common)	4	–	Cairn covering a central cist.	Complete Beaker found in corner of small cist which had been packed with clay. Unlikely to have held a burial.	Burnard 1897; Grinsell 1978; Quinnell 2003.
Chagford (Chagford Common)	10		9 small cairns investigated. 4 covered pits.	All cairns produced charcoal. 4 covered pits, 1 produced burnt human bones.	Baring-Gould 1901.
Cornwood	3	–	Cairn covering 'some kind of cist'.	Cist was found to contain stone 'sponge finger' & sherds from a Beaker, now lost.	Bate 1872; Grinsell 1978.
Cornwood	5	–	Circle of stones surrounding a pit at end of stone row.	The pit was excavated but no finds were recovered.	Eogan & Simmons 1964.
Harford	1	–	Cairn covering a cist.	The cist was found to contain two flints.	Dixon 1953; Grinsell 1978.
Headon, 684, Sparkwell	–	SUERC-47201: 3849±39 BP, 2470–2150 cal BC. Unidentified tuber dated.	Pit-circle possibly within ring cairn.	The pits formed a ring which was possibly inside a removed ring cairn. Oak charcoal was recovered.	Quinnell and Dyer 2013.
Headon, 750A and 750B, Sparkwell	–	Wk 20136: 3429±35 BP, 1880–1630 cal BC. *Quercus* sp. dated. SUERC-47207: 3469±39, 1900–1680 cal BC. Unidentified rhyzomes dated. SUERC-47208: 3415±39, 1880–1620 cal BC. *Corylus avellana* nutshell and charcoal dates.	2 conjoining turf-built barrows were found to cover pits.	Cut features below turf covering of barrows contained charcoal but no other finds.	Quinnell & Dyer 2013.
Headon, 751, Sparkwell		SUERC-47205: 3554±39, 2020–1760 cal BC. *Quercus* sp. dated.	Pits had been cut into a 'barrow-like' knoll which may have once been covered by a mound.	Cut features within area of natural rise contained charcoal but no other finds were recovered.	Dyer & Quinnell 2013.
Holne Moor, Holne	4	–	Cairn covering a central pit.	Pit contained burnt bones & charcoal.	Burnard 1905.
Lydford	1	–	Cairn covering a cist.	Cist contained burnt human bone.	Grinsell 1978.
Lydford	15 b and 15 c	–	2 small cairns.	2 cairns excavated. 1 covered pit with charcoal.	Burnard 1902; Grinsell 1978.
Lydford	16	–	Cairn covering a pit.	Cairn covered pit containing charcoal.	Baring-Gould 1898.
Lydford	16a	–	Cairn covering a pit.	Cairn covered pit containing charcoal.	Baring-Gould 1898.
Lydford	17	–	Cist without cairn.	Cist contained a flint flake.	Grinsell 1978.

Lydford	17c	–	Cairn covering a pit.	Cremation in pit associated with 2 burnt flints.	Grinsell 1978.
Lydford	22	–	Cairn.	Flint recovered from cairn.	Grinsell 1978.
Lydford	23	–	Cist covered by a cairn.	Cist contained cremated bone & charcoal in pit cut into floor.	Baring-Gould 1898.
Lydford (Fernworthy)	24	–	A cist covered by a cairn.	Cist contained a Beaker with sherds from another. Copper-alloy knife-dagger, jet button & flint scraper also found. No trace of body & cist appeared to have been full of stones.	Baring-Gould 1898; Grinsell 1978; Quinnell 2003.
Lydford	28	–	Cairn covering pit.	Pit beneath cairn held cremation deposit & worked flint.	Burnard 1896b; Grinsell 1978.
Lydford	30	–	Cairn covering a pit.	Cairn covered pit & pottery. Part of a Collared Urn found over stone slab which covered a pit containing charcoal.	Burnard 1901; Grinsell 1978.
Lydford (Archeton Newtake)	39	–	Cairn covering a cist.	Below centre of cist was pit which contained flint flake, stone bracer & charcoal.	Burnard 1901; Grinsell 1978; Woodward & Hunter 2011, 167.
Lydford	40	–	Large cist in a cairn.	Cist contained burnt bones, flint scraper & possible arrowhead.	Worth 1902; Grinsell 1978.
Lydford	41	–	Cairn covering cist	Flint scraper found in cist.	Grinsell 1978.
Lydford	42	–	Cairn covering one or possibly two cists.	'Faint indications bone ashes' recorded in pit covered by stone slab.	Grinsell 1978.
Lydford	43	–	Cairn covering a pit.	Charcoal recovered from pit.	Grinsell 1978.
Lydford	44	–	Cairn covering a central depression.	Charcoal & burnt bones recovered from 'central depression' below cairn.	Grinsell 1978.
Lydford	46	–	Cist.	Coarse pot sherd said to have been found in cist in 1832.	Grinsell 1978.
Lydford	50c	–	Cist.	Human hair said to have been recovered from cist in 1827.	Grinsell 1978.
Lydford (Lakehead Hill)	52	–	Cist.	Sherds from 2 vessels found within cist. Form of larger vessel unknown but smaller may have been a Beaker. 3 fine flint scrapers also recorded but no trace of burial.	Worth 1967, 198; Grinsell 1978; Quinnell 2003.
Lydford	57	–	Small cairn covering a pit.	Pit beneath cairn contained charcoal.	Grinsell 1978; Baring-Gould 1901.
Lydford	67a	–	Cist.	Cist contained sherds of pottery, a flint & quartz stones. Charcoal recorded but no burial.	Grinsell 1978; Burnard 1914.
Manaton	5	–	Barrow covering a cist.	Charcoal & a flint found in the cist.	Baring-Gould 1903; Grinsell 1978.
Manaton	6	–	Barrow covering a pit.	Cremated bone & charcoal found in central pit under barrow. More burnt bone & charcoal found within & below paved area adjacent to pit. Two frags copper-alloy found on floor of barrow & flint arrowhead found in barrow mound.	Baring-Gould 1903; Grinsell 1978.
Manaton	9	–	Cairn covering a cist.	2 coils 'human hair' found in pit below N end of cist.	Burnard 1903.

Manaton (Hameldown Single barrow)	11	–	Barrow covering cairn.	Beneath barrow was deposit of cremated human bone, charcoal & flint flake.	Bate 1872; Grinsell 1978.
Manaton, (Hameldown Two barrows)	12	–	Barrow covering cairn.	Copper-alloy dagger with amber & gold-studded pommel recovered from underneath barrow, below paving in S part of site. Dagger associated with deposit of cremated bone.	Bate 1872; Jones and Quinnell 2013.
Moretonhampstead	5a	–	Cairn.	Cairn recorded as containing frags of 'earthen ware vessels' & burnt wood.	Grinsell 1978.
Moretonhampstead	6	–	Cairn? Covering a cist.	?dagger 'spearhead' of copper-alloy, with 2 'pegs or screws' found in cist with blue & white 'glass' beads, stone amulet & cremated bones & ashes.	Grinsell 1978.
Peter Tavy (White Hill)	6a	–	3 cairns, 2 covering pits & a third over a possible cist.	Charcoal recovered from both pits & within the cist.	Grinsell 1978.
Peter Tavy	17	–	Cairn.	Cairn covered charcoal & ash.	Grinsell 1978.
Peter Tavy	18	–	Cairn.	Small cairn contained charcoal & a flint scraper.	Grinsell 1978.
Peter Tavy	22	–	Cairn	2 flints found within cairn.	Baring-Gould 1899; Grinsell 1978
Peter Tavy	24	–	Cairn.	Elongated perforated stone found under cairn.	Baring-Gould 1899; Grinsell 1978.
Peter Tavy	27	–	Cairn covering cist.	Cist did not contain any artefacts.	Baring-Gould 1899; Grinsell 1978.
Peter Tavy (Langstone Moor)	39	–	Cairn covering a cist.	Small cist 0.5m long × 0.3m wide. Charcoal & a little 'bone' ash recovered from paved base of cist.	Baring-Gould 1898; Grinsell 1978.
Peter Tavy (Langstone Moor)	40	–	Cairn covering a central pit.	Pit did not contain any artefacts.	Baring-Gould 1898; Grinsell 1978.
Peter Tavy (Langstone Moor)	40a	–	Cairn covering a central pit.	Pit had been filled with soil.	Baring-Gould 1898; Grinsell 1978.
Peter Tavy (Langstone Moor)	41	–	Cairn covering a central pit.	Pit below cairn did not contain any artefacts.	Grinsell 1978.
Peter Tavy (Langstone Moor)	41a	–	Cairn covering a central pit.	Pit beneath cairn had been filled with soil.	Grinsell 1978.
Shaugh Moor, Ring cairn 1, Shaugh Prior		HAR-2216: 3520±70 BP, 2040–1680 cal BC. Bulk charcoal dated.	Ring cairn.	Ring cairn built around natural boulder. Several cut features including charcoal-filled pit. Plano convex flint knife of Early Bronze Age date recovered from on top of old land surface. 2 sandstone whetstones found in turf layer over site.	Wainwright *et al.* 1979.
Shaugh Moor Cairn 126, Shaugh Prior	–	HAR-2221: 3350±70BP, 1880–1460 cal BC. Bulk charcoal dated. HAR-2285: 3400±90 BP, 1940–1490 cal BC. Bulk charcoal dated.	Simple cairn.	Charcoal-filled pit found on SW side of cairn.	Wainwright *et al.* 1979.

Shaugh Moor, Ring cairn 2, Shaugh Prior	–	HAR-2220: 3430±90 BP, 1960–1500 cal BC. Bulk charcoal dated. HAR-2214: 3240±90 BP, 1740–1300 cal BC.	Ring cairn.	7 segmented faience beads recovered from small near-central pit within ring cairn. Pit also contained charcoal & a pot base.	Wainwright *et al.* 1979.
Shaugh Moor, Cairn 4, Shaugh Prior			Robbed-out cairn badly disturbed.	Sandstone whetstone found in peat over cairn.	Wainwright *et al.* 1979.
Shaugh Moor, Cairn 70, Shaugh Prior	–	HAR-2219: 3430±80 BP, 2030–1610 cal BC. Bulk charcoal dated.	Simple cairn.	Charcoal-filled pit found within cairn.	Wainwright *et al.* 1979.
Shaugh Moor, Cairn 71, Shaugh Prior	–	HAR-2213: 3430±80 BP, 1950–1520 cal BC. Bulk charcoal dated.	Cairn.	Charcoal & sherds of pottery recovered from small depression under cairn.	Wainwright *et al.* 1979.
Shaugh Prior (Great Gnat's Head)	1a	–	Cairn covering a pavement.	Cairn covered a paved area, without any finds.	Worth 1901; Grinsell 1978.
Shaugh Prior (Calveslake)	3	–	Cairn enclosing a cist.	3 flint flakes, a tanged arrowhead & a quartz crystal recovered from cist.	Worth 1967, 199; Grinsell 1978.
Shaugh Prior (Deadman's Bottom)	5	–	Cairn covering a pavement.	Heat-reddened floor in paved area revealed, but no artefacts recovered.	Worth 1900; Grinsell 1978.
Shaugh Prior (Deadman's Bottom)	7	–	Cairn covering a cist.	Cist did not contain any finds.	Worth 1900; Grinsell 1978.
Shaugh Prior (Deadman's Bottom)	8	–	Cairn enclosing a cist.	Sherds from a Beaker recovered from cist together with 3 barbed-and-tanged arrowheads.	Worth 1967, 199; Grinsell 1978; Quinnell 2003.
Shaugh Prior (Hentor Warren)	7	–	Cairn covering a cist.	Cist did not contain any finds.	Worth 1901; Grinsell 1978.
Shaugh Prior	47a	–	Barrow covering a platform.	Small barrow was found to cover 'hearth' or platform of granite & a flint pebble.	Worth 1896; Grinsell 1978.
Sheepstor	21	–	Cairn covering a pit.	Pit beneath cairn contained charcoal mixed with earth.	Grinsell 1978
Sheepstor	22	–	Cairn covering a cist.	Cist devoid of any finds.	Worth 1901; Grinsell 1978
Sheepstor	24	–	Cairn covering a cist.	Cist contained a little charcoal.	Grinsell 1978.
Sheepstor	25a	–	Cairn covering pit.	Pit beneath cairn contained only charcoal but 3 flints, including a scraper, found in cairn material.	Grinsell 1978.
South Tawton	5b	–	Cairn.	Small cairn did not contain any finds.	Grinsell 1978.
Sparkwell	8a	–	Barrow?	Barrow said to have cover-ed large flint scraper & 3 flint flakes.	Grinsell 1978.
Throwleigh	2	–	Cairn covering cist.	Circular pit in bottom of cist contained charcoal.	Baring-Gould 1903; Grinsell 1978.

Walkhampton	5	–	Cairn covering a cist.	Cist beneath cairn contained flint scraper, flint flake & polishing stone.	Baring-Gould 1895.
Walkhampton (Raddick Hill)	14a	–	Cairn covering a cist.	Copper-alloy artefact found inside cist. Object type unknown, although it was suggested by Grinsell to be a possible knife-dagger blade.	Burnard 1899; Grinsell 1978.
Walkhampton (Raddick Hill)	17	–	Cairn covering a cist.	Charcoal recovered from cist.	Burnard 1899; Grinsell 1978
Widecombe-in-the-Moor	18	–	Cairn.	'Old jar' or 2 recorded as being found in cist.	Grinsell 1978.
Whitehorse Hill, Lydford	–	(see Chapter 20)	Cist located in peat mound.	This volume.	This volume.

timber-lined graves are sometimes found (for example, Ashbee 1978; Fitzpatrick 2011; Booth *et al.* 2011, 140), whereas, by contrast, stone-lined cists occur in the uplands, including examples in northern England and Scotland (for example, Baker *et al.* 2003; Manby 1969; Smith 1994). In the south west both Dartmoor and West Penwith have concentrations of Beaker-associated cists (Jones and Quinnell 2006a; Jones, forthcoming). Both areas are also associated with sources of tin and copper and it is tempting to see this distribution as being in some way related to the increased mobility and journeying in search of metalliferous deposits which have been suggested for the later third millennium cal BC (Fitzpatrick 2013). However, unlike the situation in south-west Ireland (O'Brien 2004), to date none of the Beaker pottery assemblages on Dartmoor or in the south-west region as a whole can be closely associated with evidence for metal extraction or working (Jones *et al.* 2012).

It is also evident that, from the outset, activity associated with Beaker cists on Dartmoor diverged from that found elsewhere and seems to have developed according to local understandings of 'Beaker'-associated tradition and burial practices (below).

Only one of the Dartmoor cists with Beaker pottery, Lydford 24, also contained objects: a copper-alloy knife-dagger and a jet button (Baring-Gould 1898; Gerloff 1975, 165). These belong with the classic range of artefacts associated with Beaker burials. None of the Beaker cists on Dartmoor contain human remains and, although the moors' acidic soils are likely to have destroyed all traces of unburnt human remains, at least one, Chagford 4 (Burnard 1897), is very small and unlikely to have been large enough to have held an inhumation. Instead it is likely to have been used as a repository to hold the Beaker (Quinnell 2003; Jones 2013) and this may also have been the case at other Beaker-associated cists across the Moor. Indeed, from this period, throughout the south west, cists and stone-lined pits appear to have been constructed as containers for curated objects or heirlooms, as well as for burials (Jones 2013). Given the increasing evidence for the manipulation and movement of human remains in the Beaker-using period and Early Bronze Age generally (for example, Parker

Pearson *et al.* 2004; Fitzpatrick 2011, 201–2; Bailey *et al.* 2013), it is also possible that bone, together with artefacts, could have been taken in and out of cists. It may therefore be a mistake to see them as 'final' resting places for human remains. This point will be returned to. The treatment of artefacts also varied in character, with complete Beaker vessels at some sites but just sherds deposited at others (Quinnell 2003). Taken together, it seems probable that the single inhumation burial associated with Beakers which is found to the east in Wessex was a rarity across the region.

Nonetheless, it does seem very likely that the Beaker-associated sites on Dartmoor directly contributed to the subsequent cist building tradition of the second millennium cal BC. In addition to the obvious shared characteristics in construction methods, continuity of tradition can be seen in their alignment, predominantly north-west–south-east (Worth 1967; and see below), and in the incomplete or fragmentary nature of the pottery placed within them (Quinnell 2003).

However, it is of interest that, by contrast with the rest of the south-west peninsula, Beaker pottery represents the first and, with very few exceptions, the last diagnostic pottery style to be placed within a cist in Dartmoor. This meant that subsequently throughout the Early Bronze Age pottery formed a fairly minor part of the repertoire of objects for inclusion within cists and barrows.

The Whitehorse Hill cist and its context: Early Bronze Age cists and cairns on Dartmoor

Although there are few other radiocarbon dates and only a comparatively small number of closely diagnostic finds from excavated cists and cairns on Dartmoor, the majority of dated cairns and barrows in the south west belong to the period between 2000 cal BC and 1500 cal BC (Jones 2011a; 2012; Garwood 2007b). The radiocarbon dating from the Whitehorse Hill cist is wholly consistent with this pattern (above). It is therefore very probable that, although some may fall earlier or later than this period, most cairns and cists on Dartmoor will also date to the

Figure 21.3: The cairn in the centre of the southern stone row at Merrivale, looking west. (Photograph: Henrietta Quinnell.)

first half of the second millennium cal BC. This section will therefore consider the results from the Whitehorse Hill cist in the light of information from other excavated Early Bronze Age sites on the moor and, where appropriate, elsewhere in Britain.

As with Whitehorse Hill, most Dartmoor cists are found singly, although a small number of paired examples are known, as at Chagford 3 and possibly Lydford 42 (Grinsell 1978). However, there appears to be little evidence for the multiple cist tradition which is found in northern and western Britain and in Ireland (Savory 1972; Watkins 1982; Butler 1997, 176).

Given the relatively small numbers of cremations found within the 12% of excavated cists and cairns across the Moor (Butler 1997, 205: see Table 21.1 and below) there does not appear to have been the same level of emphasis on the burial of cremated human remains (token, whole or multiple), as is found in other uplands of the south-west peninsula (Christie 1988; Bonnington 2011). However, there may be other reasons why cremated human remains have not been found, and this will be discussed below.

Key points for discussion in the following section include the factors which may have influenced the siting of the Whitehorse Hill cist, the construction of the cist in relation to other sites on the moor, the processes involved in the formation of its contents, and the evidence for a distinctive tradition of cist building on Dartmoor.

Location

The relative isolation of the Whitehorse Hill cist from other sites, in an elevated, remote part of the Moor, could be considered a little unusual. Many Dartmoor cists are found in close proximity to other forms of monument, being within or under Early Bronze Age cairns, situated at the end of stone rows or located close to larger ceremonial monument complexes, as at Merrivale or Shovel Down (for example, Butler 1991; 162–8; 1994, 23–32; Carnes 2014, 14–16) (Figs. 21.2 and 21.3). Summit cairns (Fig. 21.4), such as those on Hameldown Down or Three Barrows (Ugborough 1), are set in similar elevated positions but these tend to be visible in the wider landscape (Butler 1997, 166) and are of rather a different scale to the Whitehorse Hill cist.

The setting for the burial

The landscape situation of the Whitehorse Hill cist is therefore of interest. It is located in an elevated position, on a watershed, overlooking the heads of several streams and the interfluves between them in an area which was in places boggy. Despite having views out into the distant landscape, the site is, however, unlikely to have been visible from the surrounding lower-lying ground. In common with other barrows in the south west, it may have been the views out into the surrounding landscape which were significant

Figure 21.4: Photograph of Broad Barrow, Hameldown, from the south. (Photograph: Henrietta Quinnell.)

(Lewis 2007; Jones 2011b). As described in Chapter 19, the environmental sequence suggests that the cist was set in a treeless hilltop location that was becoming a grassy peatland, increasingly used for grazing as coarse pasture. Trees are likely to have been found on the slopes of the hill, so we might envisage the site as located in a large clearing in what was otherwise a predominantly wooded landscape.

Although the hill is now peat covered, the place-name Whitehorse Hill is suggested to have derived from the white granite which is said to have been exposed in 'large flat masses almost like a pavement' (Chudleigh 1892, 15). Of course, the name is comparatively recent and it is not certain whether or how much, if any, granite was exposed in the Bronze Age.

The site would have been then, however, as it is today, on an elevated, flat area. The ridge, of which Whitehorse Hill forms the southern end, may have been considered as a liminal place, a platform raised above and set apart from the surrounding landscape, a place which could be seen only from a distance. Given the association between ritual deposition of artefacts and human remains at watery and peaty places across Britain and Ireland during the Bronze Age (Bradley 1990; Becker 2013; Schulting and Bradley 2013), the boggy character of the area around the Whitehorse Hill cist may have given it added significance. This juxtaposition of high and wet, together with the extensive views to the east and west, may have meant that it was considered to be a special place, ideally suited for the siting of the cist and for the burial of human remains.

Mounds and swellings

Although there is no evidence for a ceremonial complex on the hill, it may be significant that the Whitehorse Hill cist occupies a similar topographical position to the Hangingstone Hill cairn, located 700m away at the northern end of the ridge; another cairn has recently been found on the slopes of Hangingstone Hill (J. Marchand, pers comm.). Taken together, and with the possibility that further cists could survive buried in the peat (or have already been removed by peat cutting), these sites might suggest that the hill had become associated with burial and funerary activity.

The preference for mounds, or more commonly cairns, as places for cists also raises the question as to whether the Whitehorse Hill cist was located in a natural hummock in the peat which resembled a 'barrow mound'. As described in Chapter 1, in the modern landscape the peat 'mound' in which the cist is set now stands proud and is a visually distinctive feature. Peat had already been growing for a considerable period of time prior to the construction of the cist, probably since the Mesolithic period if the tephra horizon from the base of the section is taken into account (Chapter 19). However, it is clear that the present extent of the 'mound' and its current visual prominence are the result of nineteenth-century peat cutting (Chapter 2).

It is, therefore, given changes to the landscape, uncertain as to how far the site stood out above the surrounding peat in the Early Bronze Age. It is possible that there was a small natural mound or 'swelling' (cf Ingold 2010), which could have made it a distinctive, or at least a sufficiently dry place to build a cist. If it was a slight mound it would have been visible from some distance. Indeed, the distinction between natural and cultural mounds is likely to be more of a concern to archaeologists than to people in prehistory, and a place that conformed to a circular archetype favoured for burial may have been of more importance (for example, Bradley 2012).

It is certainly the case that in other parts of Britain natural 'barrow-like' mounds could become the focus for burial and ritual activity in the Early Bronze Age. On the

Figure 21.5: Shaugh Moor ring cairns 1and 2. Note outcropping rock within the nearest ring cairn. (Photograph: Henrietta Quinnell.)

Surrey heaths, for example, it has proved very difficult to distinguish between natural sandy mounds and round barrows, which occur in relatively close proximity to one another. Supposedly natural mounds at Thursley Common and at the Kings Ridge at Frensham, for example, were in fact barrows (Graham *et al.* 2004; 2008). By contrast, other natural mounds resembling barrows became the foci for human activity. The King Henry VIII mound in Richmond Park, for example, may have been entirely natural, although 'ashes' were placed within it. At Barrow Green, near Oxted, a large natural mound was heightened by the addition of earth on top (Grinsell 1934; Whimster 1931, 69).

Comparable practices have also been identified in East Anglia and the English Midlands. At Longham, in Norfolk, one complete and two partial Beakers were recovered from a 'barrow' which was revealed to be a natural periglacial mound 3m in diameter and 0.8m high (Wymer and Healy 1996). In the Midlands, too, Bronze Age cremation burials were sometimes placed into natural mounds; at Anc's Hill in Staffordshire, for example, a double Food Vessel, associated with human remains (Chitty 1929), was inserted into a natural 'barrow'.

Dave Mullin (2001) has argued that such instances occurred because people deliberately 'forgot' the past, in order to manipulate and give new meanings to places in the landscape. While this argument has merit, it is also the case that when natural places were encountered, they would have been understood in terms framed by the spirituality which permeated the minds and actions of people in prehistory

(Insoll 2004, 150). Therefore, a distinction between things 'cultural' and things 'natural' is probably meaningless in a prehistoric context (for example, see Bradley 2000; Cummings 2002). When encountered, features resembling barrow mounds may well have been thought of as ancestral places of burial or the works of supernatural beings. The act of 'manipulation' may have been the appropriation of a perceived ancient place for burial or other activities.

This process of using natural features is also apparent on Dartmoor and in other parts of the south west (Jones 2013). On Headon Down, a ring of Early Bronze Age pits were cut into a natural rise (Dyer and Quinnell 2013). Unlike Whitehorse Hill, the site was not associated with any burials but it is possible that activity occurred at this location because the rise had a barrow-like appearance.

In addition to 'barrow-shaped' swellings it is also evident that other natural landscape formations proved attractive to cairn builders. Several cairns and cists on Dartmoor, such as the excavated group on Shaugh Moor (Wainwright *et al.* 1979) or the kerbed cairn with central cist on Royal Hill (Lydford 90) (Figs. 21.5 and 21.6), can be seen to incorporate natural rock outcrops within them. Although not 'barrow like', these outcrops may also have been perceived as 'ancestral' or supernatural works (Bradley 1998; Tilley 2010) and their incorporation represented the drawing of distinctive topographical features into the cultural realm. Returning to Whitehorse Hill, it is noticeable that beyond the area of peat cuttings, natural hummocks occur in the blanket peat. Had there

Figure 21.6: A kerbed cairn incorporating outcropping stones at Royal Hill, Dartmoor. (Photograph: Henrietta Quinnell.)

been a rise in the peat where the Whitehorse Hill cist was located, it is possible that it too may have been perceived to have been an 'ancient' work, and as such was a ready-made and highly suitable receptacle for the cist.

Distancing the dead

Although the locations of contemporary Early Bronze Age settlements on Dartmoor are unknown, it is probable that the choice of Whitehorse Hill as the site of the cist would have involved carrying the cremated remains high above and away from the more sheltered and lower-lying areas which were probably the long-term focus of occupation at this time, as well as above the areas where the larger-scale ceremonial monument complexes or 'sanctuaries' comprising stone rows, stone circles and a diverse range of cairns were located. Major complexes are found, for example at Merrivale, Shovel Down, Drizzlecombe and Fernworthy (Fox 1964, 61–64; Quinnell 1994a) (Fig. 21.7), and they are likely to have been used by large aggregations made up of several communities or extended family groupings. The emphasis on funerary activity at Whitehorse Hill also contrasts with the broadly contemporary ceremonial activity which has been found in association with other forms of Early Bronze Age monument, for example, the ring cairns at Shaugh Moor, where no human remains were deposited (Wainwright *et al.* 1979). Again, the Shaugh Moor cairn group is located somewhat closer to areas which would have been more suited for occupation, and it may have been used for smaller communal gatherings by family-sized groups (Jones 2012).

The approximately 1000 Early Bronze Age cists and cairns on Dartmoor (Fig. 21.8) are likely to have been constructed over a span of several centuries, from *circa* 2200 cal BC with the Beaker-associated cists down to around 1500 cal BC (below). This means that the number of sites constructed per year was probably not great. As has been found elsewhere, even assuming that all burial sites were used for multiple burial deposits, it is clear that only a small proportion of people were afforded formal burial (for example, Fowler 2013, 6). The majority of people who inhabited Dartmoor cannot have been formally buried within a cist or beneath a cairn. Those who were formally buried may have been drawn from leading families, but they may also have been feared individuals or people who had undertaken certain roles in society or died in inauspicious circumstances. For example, among the Nuer of south Sudan, people killed by lightning were buried differently from those who died by other means (Evans-Pritchard 1956, 54–56). Given that only a selected number of people were treated in this way, it is likely that the location of the Whitehorse Hill cist is unlikely to have been a chance affair and its siting is likely to have been deliberated over.

Anthropological study also makes us aware that attitudes to death and to the disposal of human remains are rarely neutral and can involve complex reactions (Evans-Pritchard 1956, 144–76; Metcalf and Huntington 1993; Gibson 1995; Waterson 1997, 199–228). Where people who are selected for burial finally end up often matters not just to their immediate kin but also to the wider community, who may want to pay respect to the deceased and, perhaps as importantly, be seen by others to be acting 'correctly'.

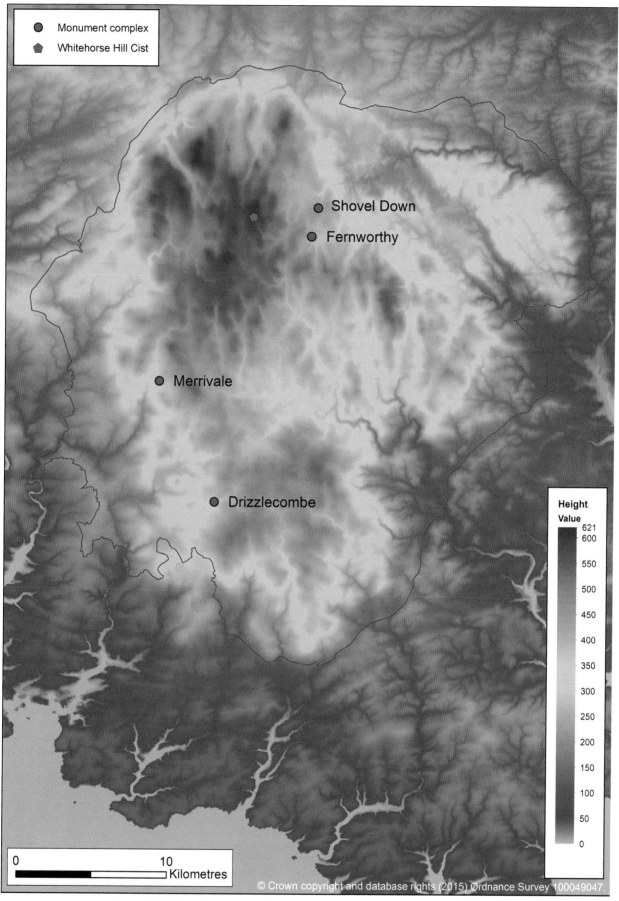

Figure 21.7: The distribution of major Early Bronze Age monument complexes.

Andy M. Jones

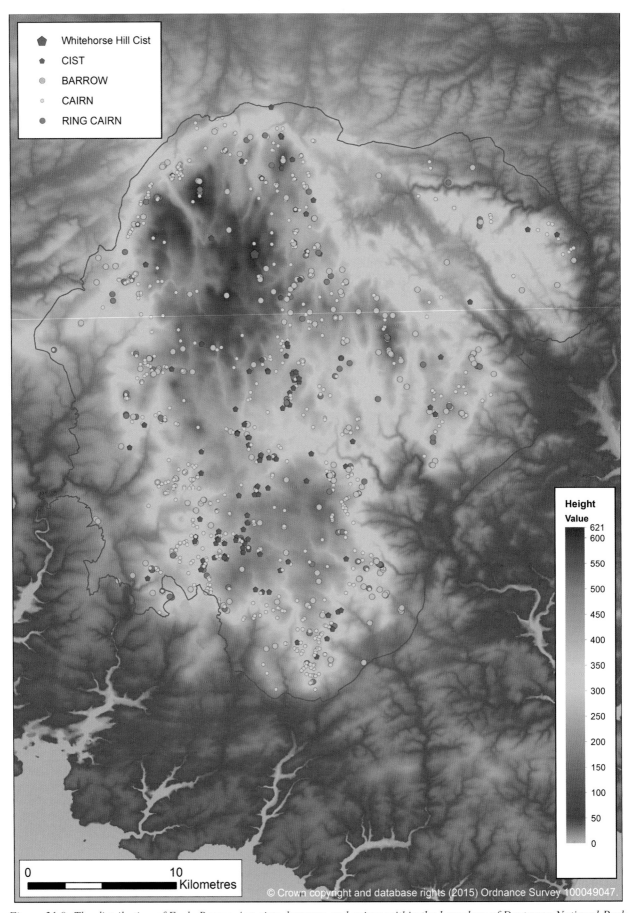

Figure 21.8: The distribution of Early Bronze Age cists, barrows and cairns within the boundary of Dartmoor National Park.

Human remains, as will be discussed below, can sometimes hold significance as a symbolic or powerful material and as such may become a valued resource for use in other places and contexts (below).

By contrast, the fear of the consequences from supernatural revenge by the deceased is also well-documented both in the anthropological and historical record, and a desire to place the dead well beyond the inhabited spaces of the living is a frequent concern for communities (Weiner 1987; Parker Pearson 1999; Watkins 2013, Chapter 2).

Presencing the dead

Use of a site such as Whitehorse Hill for funerary purposes may have implicitly or explicitly included the establishment of a claim to tenure through the installation of the remains of a 'community member' in a monument. Several archaeological studies have stressed how the physicality of the mounds within Early Bronze Age round barrow cemeteries may, as well as setting apart the dead and removing them from the domain of the living, have acted as territorial markers dividing up tracts of land; the human remains inside the mounds may have been used in funerary rituals that were linked to the creation of lineages and used to lay claim to particular tracts of the landscape (Fleming 1971; Garwood 1991; Barrett 1994, 123–129).

It has been argued of some places away from the south-west peninsula that barrow construction could have been linked with settlement or agricultural expansion. For example, in Denmark it has been argued that the upsurge in barrow building coincided with the extension of grazing (Holst *et al.* 2013) and in central and southern England it has been suggested that after 2000 cal BC areas were laid claim to through the construction of new barrow complexes (Field 1998; Garwood 2007a, 152–154). Later still, towards the end of Early Bronze Age, small barrows were constructed on what had been marginal land, close to settlement areas (Bradley and Fraser 2010). In a landscape without physical boundaries, rights of tenure may have been established and maintained through ties to the land which were made manifest through acts of deposition at particular sites, including cists.

Therefore, in addition to distancing the dead for supernatural or cosmological reasons, the choice of site for the Whitehorse Hill cist could have arisen as a consequence of changing patterns of land use. Given that the Early Bronze Age communities who occupied Dartmoor, especially those using the higher moors, are likely to have been pastoralists, burials could have occurred along routes and on tracts of land which had become important for grazing, places where the community had formed a growing attachment as a result of seasonal movement. The 'presencing' of human remains and the deposition of high-status or supernaturally charged artefacts (below) may therefore have allowed for the establishment, legitimisation and manipulation of land rights, with regard to who had use of the hill both for burial and for other purposes.

Constructing the cist

Once the site of the cist had been selected, the materials needed for its construction would have been gathered together and the sequence for its furnishing agreed.

Nearly all of the recorded cists on Dartmoor are of simple 'stone chest' appearance, formed by long side stones and shorter ends (Worth 1967, 173) (Fig. 21.9). Although a small number of sites, such as Ugborough 16 (Worth 1967, 170; Grinsell 1978; Butler 1997, 168–177) may have originally been free-standing, the majority of identified cists are set within or covered by cairn material. The Whitehorse Hill cist shares many features in common with such sites; however, its setting within a peat mound differs from other cists. The setting, has however, enabled the construction sequence to be examined in greater detail.

Marking the site

After the site had been chosen but prior to actual construction of the cist, its location was marked by two hazel stakes, and it is possible that all four corners of the cist were originally marked in this way. Chronological modelling (Chapter 20) provides estimates for the dates of the stakes of *1890–1735 cal BC* (*90% probability; SUERC-40124*; Fig. 20.3) or *1715–1695 cal BC* (*5% probability*) and *1870–1845 cal BC* (*4% probability; WH11 – SF2*; Fig 20.3) or *1815–1685 cal BC* (*91% probability*), probably *1765–1735 cal BC* (*33% probability*) or *1720–1690 cal BC* (*35% probability*). Small posts and stakeholes are known from a large number of barrows in southern Britain, although in most cases it is not possible to tie their use down to the marking of the site prior to burial. For example, on Bodmin Moor posts were found near to Colliford site CRIVA (Griffith 1984) and at Caerloggas III on the St Austell granite (Miles 1975) two branches were sealed beneath the mound. The formal marking of the place of burial itself with posts and stakes has only occasionally been identified at other Early Bronze Age sites. An early example of this type of practice was identified at the grave of the Amesbury Archer, which had a stake-hole in the bottom of it (Fitzpatrick 2011, 71). However, it is more common for other types of pre-burial structure (for example, post-rings) to be found beneath burial mounds. At Deeping St Nicholas in Lincolnshire, for example, a posthole structure that pre-dated barrow construction may have been used to enclose the body of a child prior to burial (French 1994, 24).

It is very possible that the marking out of the site for the cist would have involved some kind of ritual, and the use of the hazel wands to mark the site is likely to have been symbolic and the choice of wood a deliberate one. It may be relevant to note that hazel was considered to have supernatural properties and was important in early Welsh and Irish folklore traditions, for example, as rods for divining (MacKillop 1998, 235). Although we cannot draw a direct parallel from such early historic sources, they do highlight the possibility that the wood used for the stakes may have had such associations.

Evidence for marking sites with stakes has not been identified at any of the other excavated Dartmoor cists. However, given that most were opened by antiquarians who were searching for artefacts and that wood is unlikely to have survived at most other sites, it is unsurprising that evidence for marking out sites has gone unrecorded. Another form of possible ritual associated with the initiation of cist sites has, however, been observed at a number of sites. This takes the form of small pits cut into the base of the cist, as at Lydford 23 and Manaton 9 (Baring-Gould 1898; Burnard 1903). It seems quite likely that these pits were associated with some form of foundation rite. In most cases no artefacts have been found, although charcoal has often been recovered (below and Table 21.1). The frequent occurrence of charred wood within pits in cairns across the south west indicates that it was probably considered to contain symbolic properties (below).

Cutting, lining and capping

After the site had been marked as the place for the cist, the next stage of the construction process would have involved the cutting out of an area to hold the structure of the cist. This would have been fairly hard work, given the consistency of the peat and the dense concentration of the root mat which had to be penetrated. Once the cut was made, the bottom and sides were lined with pieces of granite.

The stones used in the cist's construction were quite carefully selected, and it is to be expected that there was intimate landscape knowledge of where the most suitable pieces could be obtained (Hawkes 1959, 110). The source of the stones is likely to have been fairly local, as they are all of granite. However, given that the hilltop was already covered by a blanket of peat by the Early Bronze Age, it is possible that they were carried some distance to the cist site. The sides of a watercourse or perhaps a well-trodden trackway on the hill slope may have exposed pieces of granite within the natural 'growan' subsoil.

A flat slab was selected for the base stone and tapering 'tooth'-shaped stones were chosen for the sides, and the latter were driven tapering end down into the peat around the edge of the cut. Smaller stones were used to fill gaps. The use of a base stone is unusual as nearly all other excavated cists have a subsoil floor. Notable exceptions are Peter Tavy 39, which had a paved floor, and Sheepstor 22, which was constructed directly on the outcropping granite (Baring-Gould 1898; Grinsell 1978). The base stone may have been used at Whitehorse Hill because of the wet conditions within the peat mound, and / or the desire to have a flat surface upon which to place the contents of the cist.

Finally, a very distinctive piece of granite was selected and brought to the site to be used as the capstone. After the contents of the cist had been carefully and ceremonially deposited it would have been placed on top of the side stones. The placing of the capstone would in itself have been a highly dramatic and symbolic act, 'completing' the monument. It seems likely from the soil micromorphological work (Chapter 5) that the capstone was left exposed, and this means that the site would have been visible in the landscape for some time after the cist was constructed. Outsized stones are a feature of several cists across the British Isles and can be seen to be part of the ostentation which is a feature of many Early Bronze Age burial sites (Parker Pearson *et al.* 2013). Distinctive capstones are also a feature of other cists on the moor, and when not covered by cairn material this may have given them a distinct, individual character (Fig. 21.10). This would have been recognized by the communities who inhabited the area, thereby contributing to the biographies of the sites. The stones themselves may also have been considered to be symbolically charged pieces of place (for example, Leary *et al.* 2013, 209–210), which could have sanctified the cist.

Building on tradition

Given its peat-mound setting, the cist inevitably deviated in construction techniques from the majority of known cists on Dartmoor, a substantial proportion of which are located within or beneath cairns (for example, Butler 1994, fig. 50.2.1). Most Dartmoor cists are regular in plan and constructed from large pieces of granite, which form rectangular or, less frequently, square (for example, Sheepstor 2) structures. The Whitehorse Hill cist may have been sub-rectangular when first constructed, but its unstable peat setting probably caused it to become more irregular over time (Chapter 2). Despite some differences, it is clear that the Whitehorse Hill cist was following a well-established tradition. With external dimensions of 0.78m long by 0.68m wide and 0.3m high, it falls within the established size range of cists on Dartmoor, albeit towards the smaller end.

Furthermore, the discovery during the excavations that the long axis of the cist was aligned broadly north-west–south-east, means that its orientation conforms with around 95% of all the other recorded cists on Dartmoor (Butler 1997, 176). This figure is remarkably high, especially so when it is considered that less than 60 km to the west on Bodmin Moor there is no such uniformity in cist alignment (Trahair 1978; Johnson and Rose 1994, 40) (Fig. 21.11). Such patterning strongly points to a well-defined tradition of building to which the Whitehorse Hill cist belongs (Jones 2012).

Finally, it may be significant, given the 'organic' nature of the surrounding environment, that a cist, rather than an unlined grave, was constructed within the peat at all. After all, non-cisted burials in pits and within graves beneath earthen barrow mounds were typical of Early Bronze Age burial practices elsewhere in Britain and across those parts of Devon which lay beyond Dartmoor (Radford and Rogers 1947; Pollard and Russell 1969; Jones and Quinnell 2008). This again points to a desire to adhere to a locally traditional way of doing things – the creation of a defined stone-lined receptacle, crowned by a visually distinctive

Figure 21.9: A large cist at Drizzlecombe, Dartmoor, showing its box-shaped construction and displaced capstone. (Photograph: Adrian Oakes, Dartmoor National Park Authority.)

Figure 21.10: A cist at Merrivale, Dartmoor, with a distinctive and outsized capstone. (Photograph: Adrian Oakes, Dartmoor National Park Authority.)

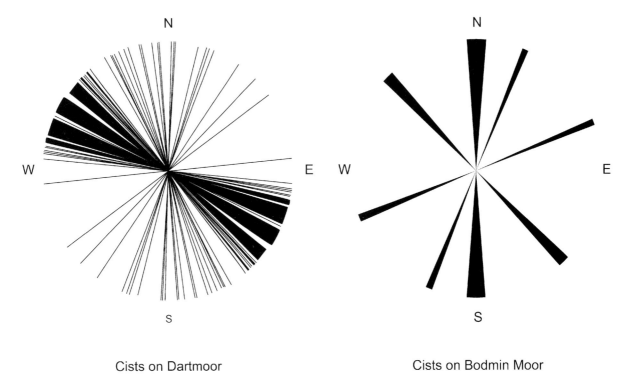

Cists on Dartmoor   Cists on Bodmin Moor

Figure 21.11: The orientation of cists on Dartmoor (left) and Bodmin Moor (right). (After Butler 1997 and Trahair 1978.)

and perhaps symbolically significant capstone – which went beyond the simple expedience of disposing of a corpse.

Having considered how the cist was constructed we will now turn to its contents.

The contents: artefacts from the cist

The Whitehorse Hill cist has significantly altered our knowledge of the variety of artefacts which were placed in the region's cists. Earlier investigations had largely revealed sites that appeared to be devoid of contents or only contained charcoal or an occasional flint (Butler 1997, appendix 3 and Table 21.1 this volume). The variety of finds from the Whitehorse Hill cist has increased the range of artefacts known to have been made in the British Early Bronze Age and has shed invaluable light on the techniques used to make them. At the same time, the role of the 'craftsman' is also receiving greater attention as it is becoming recognised that the actual production of artefacts can be bound up with cosmological ideals and symbolism. As Mary Helms (2009) has argued, the act of producing artefacts was in antiquity often linked with 'replication of the original creativity of the deities' and craft persons were frequently seen as being guided by the divine. In light of the range of materials included within the Whitehorse Hill cist and the very high levels of craftsmanship expressed in the artefacts discussed in the preceding chapters, attention here will be given to the potential social and symbolic elements of the assemblage.

This section therefore considers each class of artefact in terms of the material from which it was made (tin, wood,

amber and others), and discusses parallels for them in their local and regional context. The condition and sourcing of the objects is considered, in terms of how far the object might have travelled in order to be included within the cist. Anthropological and archaeological studies have revealed that artefacts can have complex histories and some objects can become 'known' and gain in prestige over time and distance from their source (for example, Helms 1988; Woodward 2002; Woodward and Hunter 2015).

Archaeological research increasingly shows that many materials are likely to have been associated with particular places (Bradley 2000; Brittain 2004) and were potentially thought of as containing supernatural properties; in some cases they may even have been considered to be animate substances in their own right (Vitebsky 1995, 12–14; Ingold 2000, 96–98; Tilley 2004; Jones *et al.* 2011, 34). Likewise, objects derived from animals or plants may have been considered to be totemic or to hold the properties of the animal from which they were derived (Vitebsky 2005, 259–264; Reynolds 2012).

The materiality of the objects is therefore discussed in terms of the socially constructed qualities with which they might have been perceived to be imbued because of their colour, derivation (place, or species of animal or plant), texture, or unusual characteristics such as electrostatic properties (Sheridan and Shortland 2004; Hurcombe 2014, 10; Harris 2014a).

Ceramics: an absence of evidence

Before moving onto the objects which were included in

the cist it is, however, worth considering briefly what was not there. The absence of ceramics from within the Whitehorse Hill cist is consistent with the wider pattern across the moor. As discussed above, one of the most intriguing and striking aspects of Dartmoor's cists and barrows is the near absence of ceramic vessels from the post Beaker-using period. Indeed, when Beakers are taken out of the equation, only *circa* 5% of the excavated barrows on Dartmoor have been found to contain ceramics. This paucity stands in contrast with excavated sites in lowland Devon, where a variety of ceramic vessels have been found (Pollard and Russell 1969; Watts and Quinnell 2001; Jones and Quinnell 2008), and especially with Cornwall, where ceramics have been found in well over half of excavated barrows (Quinnell 1988) and were widely used to contain cremations as well as for other non-burial related purposes (for example, Jones 2005; 2012).

In particular, Trevisker Ware, very commonly found to the west in Cornwall and occasionally in Devon on a range of Early Bronze Age sites, beginning *circa* 2000 cal BC (Jones 2011a; Quinnell 2012), appears to be absent from cists and cairns on Dartmoor. However, Trevisker Ware pottery is known from Middle Bronze Age settlements on Dartmoor (Wainwright and Smith 1980; Marchand and Hughes 2011). There may, therefore, have been a deliberate cultural decision to exclude it from the burial contexts of the earlier second millennium cal BC.

Alternatively, the lack of Trevisker Ware may reflect the general paucity of this form from Devon in general (Quinnell 2012). However, it is interesting that other forms of ceramic such as Food Vessels, Collared Urns and accessory vessels, which are recovered from barrows elsewhere in Devon, as, for example, at Farway (Hutchinson 1880; Jones and Quinnell 2008), are also absent or rare on Dartmoor. For example, only one Collared Urn has been recovered, from Hurstone Ridge, Lydford 30 (Burnard 1901). In general, where ceramics do occur, as at Shaugh Moor 71 or Lydford 67a (Wainwright *et al.* 1979; Burnard 1914), they are fragmented and plain, and therefore cannot be placed within a known ceramic tradition. Again this must represent a cultural choice as communities on the moor will have interacted with lowland communities who did deposit ceramics and vessels would have been easily produced.

Early Bronze Age life-ways on Dartmoor may have meant that ceramics were not widely used (Quinnell 1994a). Pastoralist herders grazing their animals on the moor could have preferred lighter and less bulky containers to pots (below). Even in the nineteenth century shepherds on the Sussex Downs would carry their possessions in baskets known as frails (for example, Wills *et al.* 1989, 77). At Whitehorse Hill, the use of the pelt to wrap the cremation deposit and of the basketry container to hold the beads, the wooden studs and the flint flake demonstrates that non-ceramic containers and animal hide wraps were used to carry objects, and the survival of chance finds from waterlogged and peatland sites elsewhere in western and northern Europe makes it certain that such containers were

much more commonly used than is apparent from what has survived in the wider archaeological record (Keller 1866, 325; Raftery 1970; Randsborg and Christensen 2006; Sheridan *et al.* 2013; Hurcombe 2014, chap. 2). The apparent non-use of pottery may have originated from a lack of need or from a preference by transhumant pastoralists for not carrying heavy and potentially fragile pots, giving rise to a 'moorland pastoralist identity' or tradition of not depositing ceramics with burials.

Metalwork: tin and copper alloy

The Whitehorse Hill cist contained a small number of metallic items of jewellery. The copper-alloy pin was found in the folds of the pelt which was wrapped around the cremation, and the tin bead and probably the braided armband or bracelet with tin studs were in a basketry container beside the pelt (Chapters 12, 14 and 15). A second fragmented tin bead is also likely to have been present in the container. The reasons for its fragmentation are unclear. It may have been due to the conditions within the cist or to an act of destruction. As with ceramics, Early Bronze Age metalwork is exceedingly rare on Dartmoor (Table 21.1) and often of uncertain form, as at Moretonhampstead 6 (Grinsell 1978).

Copper-alloy pin

There are no recorded examples of copper-alloy pins or awls from Dartmoor (Chapter 12) and in Devon as a whole only one burial at Upton Pyne is associated with a pin (Kirwan 1872; Jones and Quinnell 2013). To the west, in Cornwall, the nearest comparanda are finds of awls or pins which are associated with funerary sites at Harlyn Bay, Treligga and Indian Queens (Pearce 1983, 100; Christie 1985; Knight *et al.* 2015, 31; Nowakowski and Johns 2015). Some awls may have been used like pins or even have been pins which have been misinterpreted. Nicholas Thomas (2005, 222) has suggested that awls without handles may have had their handles removed as a form of 'ritual killing' but an alternative explanation might be that awls without handles functioned as pins to hold bags containing cremations together.

Both pins and awls are rather more frequent to the east in Wessex, where a number of have been found in barrows (for example, Annable and Simpson 1964; Ashbee 1986; Thomas 2005; Woodward and Hunter 2015, 175–181). In some instances pins and awls have been associated with bags containing cremated remains, as at Snail Down in Wiltshire (Thomas 2005, 111) and Upton Pyne barrow 4 (Kirwan 1872). The copper-alloy pin from Whitehorse Hill was found in the folds of the pelt and may been used to hold it in place, although alternatively it could have been placed on top to symbolically mark the closure of the deposit.

Pins are, of course, decorative items and, as discussed in Chapter 12, the Whitehorse Hill pin is an example of a rare and precious item which is likely to have denoted the status

Figure 21.12: The tin bead and studs in the replicated jewellery. This reveals just how shiny they would have been when new. (Photograph: Dartmoor National Park Authority.)

of the wearer and their social identity. Traditionally copper-alloy pins and especially awls appear to be associated with female burials (for example, Thomas 2005, 222), and Janet Spector (1991) has, through anthropological analogy, made the point that in the nineteenth-century Dakota Culture of Minnesota awls were an important indicator of the status and social standing of women. However, pins are also found with male burials (Annable and Simpson 1964, 26) and it was not possible to determine the gender of the Whitehorse Hill burial (Chapter 6), although the association with beads may support the hypothesis of the burial being that of a female.

Tin: beads and studs

All three of the artefacts made of metal, or incorporating items of tin, from the Whitehorse Hill cist, are small. They are likely to have been personal objects of high value which probably denoted the social identity of their wearer(s) and of the deceased individual.

It is notable that both the bead and studs are of unalloyed tin, rather than copper-alloy. In the light of the local availability of the resource it is, of course, very probable that the bead(s) and studs were made of tin from the south west. However, it is not possible to be more specific as unlike the tin sources in west Cornwall (Haustein *et al.* 2010), those on Dartmoor are not adequately characterized to establish this (Chapter 15).

Securely dated Early Bronze Age smelting in the south-west peninsula is limited to tin slag recovered from a barrow at Caerloggas, Cornwall, (Miles 1975), but there is evidence that cassiterite pebbles, from which tin could be extracted, were being collected from streams. For example, excavations at Tremough, Cornwall, (Jones *et al.* 2015, 172), led to the discovery of a cassiterite pebble in a lightly-built structure which has been dated to the earlier Bronze Age. Very recently a collection of over 100 cassiterite pebbles has been found in a pit associated with Trevisker pottery at Tregurra valley, Truro. This site is not currently dated but the ceramic association means that it is likely to be of Early to Middle Bronze Age date (Taylor 2015). Given that many people in the south west are likely to have engaged in mobile pastoralism, it is possible that pebbles to be used for smelting were collected during the seasonal round.

The reconstructions of the jewellery from the Whitehorse Hill cist demonstrate that, by contrast with the current appearance of the artefacts, when new the studs were the visually dominant element of the braided band, and the tin bead (or beads) is likely to have been the centre point of the necklace. In both reconstructed items it is the shininess of the tin which is so remarkable and this would have been true of the original pieces when they were newly made (Fig. 21.12). However, despite tin being a locally available material, no other pure tin artefacts dating to the Early Bronze Age have been recorded on Dartmoor and they are exceptionally rare elsewhere in Britain as a whole.

In fact, the tin studs in the braided band are without immediate parallel, although one other tin bead, a segmented example (now lost) from a barrow in Sutton Veny in Wiltshire (Annable and Simpson 1964, 60), is known from Britain. Further afield, in Ireland, a tin-plated silver earring was recovered from a pit grave at Rosnaree in Meath (Waddell 1990, 21) and in the Netherlands a composite necklace which included both tin and amber beads was found at Exloo (Haveman and Sheridan 2005/2006).

Some copper-alloy objects may, however, have been tin-enriched in order to obtain a shiny surface. In Cornwall, at Harlyn Bay, a copper-alloy pendant found with a multiple cremation deposit was found to have had a tin-enriched surface, possibly to give it a silvery reflective face (Jones *et al.* 2011).

Beads of other metals are extremely rare. A silver bead was reported from a barrow in Dorset (Bradley 1997, 28; Needham 2000, fig. 18). In Scotland a necklace including four lead beads was found inside a cist (Hunter and Davis 1994). When polished, both the silver and lead beads would have gleamed like those found at Whitehorse Hill.

In light of the extensive anthropological and historical evidence for ritualized practices associated with the production of metal objects (Eliade 1988, 472–474; Helms 1993, 59–60), metalworking is likely to have been seen as a magical process in the Early Bronze Age, and the hard, reflective substances may well have been believed to have held supernatural qualities. Tin is very likely to have been viewed as being a magical material, transformed from the living rock into a different substance, first liquid and hot and then hard and cool, and the silvery light reflected by it could have been seen as containing or emitting supernatural properties (Keates 2002; Barber 2003, 165).

With such potential associations, tin is likely to have denoted the social identity of its wearer and potentially their wealth. The near absence of pure tin artefacts and the scarcity of copper-alloy items from cairns and barrows across Dartmoor might therefore be considered unusual, considering the availability of sources.

Indeed, until now, the only significant Early Bronze Age metalwork find from Dartmoor is the copper-alloy Camerton-Snowshill type dagger from the Hameldown barrow (Manaton 11) (Bate 1872; Jones and Quinnell 2013). Although this artefact is likely to have expressed a rather different kind of identity from the decorative objects within the cist, it too was a particularly fine piece, with a unique amber pommel studded with gold pins (Fig. 21.21). In terms of workmanship, this dagger stands apart from the other examples found in the south west and arguably it may have been the pommel and the goldwork which made it a special object which was appropriate for deposition.

The marked scarcity of metalwork from cairns and cists on Dartmoor contrasts with the evidence from surrounding areas of the south west, where copper-alloy finds such as daggers, although infrequent, are not uncommon (Quinnell 1988; Pearce 1983; and see fig. 1 in Jones and Quinnell 2013). The rarity of metalwork again perhaps represents a cultural choice, given that deposits of tin and copper are found both on Dartmoor and in the wider region. It is, however, conceivable that to moorland communities their value as materials lay outside the realm of burial. Instead they were exchanged with distant groups in return for desirable items which were more highly valued by upland dwellers. These may have included livestock, which could have enhanced the social standing of pastoralists (Evans-Pritchard 1969, chap. 1; Harding and Healy 2007,

258–260), or other forms of 'exotica' such as finely worked textiles, the bear pelt, amber beads from Wessex or items with perceived symbolic or magical properties (Needham 2000; Helms 1988; Woodward and Hunter 2015).

Beads: shale, clay and amber

The cist contained a composite necklace which, in addition to the tin bead(s), included others of amber, shale and clay (Chapter 15).

The regional comparanda

As discussed in Chapter 15, composite necklaces are well-documented in Wessex but beads are only known from a few sites on Dartmoor and even then only in small numbers (Chapter 15; Table 21.1).

Beyond Dartmoor, composite necklaces are uncommon in Devon and only one, from Boscregan (Borlase 1879), is known from Cornwall. The composite necklaces from the south west have been fully described in Chapter 15. Discussion here is therefore limited to discussion of points of similarity with the Whitehorse Hill cist.

The composite necklaces known from Devon are all associated with cremation burials which are distinct from most of the other finds of beads in the region, which are mostly found in small quantities and not necessarily with burial deposits. The necklace from North Molton was found with a cremation and 'potsherds and flints' in a hole made by a ploughman in 1889 (Fox and Stone 1951). A second composite necklace was recovered from a 'cist-like' structure within Upton Pyne barrow 4 (Kirwan 1872, 153), one of the 15 or so barrows within a group (Fox 1969; Pollard and Russell 1969). The necklace was associated with a cremation and was also accompanied by a number of other artefacts, including an accessory vessel, a copper-alloy pin and a dagger.

The North Molton burial is lost and the gender of the deceased is unknown, but the presence of beads supports the suggestion that it, and the burials from Whitehorse Hill and Upton Pyne, were of females (see Sheridan and Shortland 2004; Sheridan 2008, 84). The North Molton necklace is not very similar in form to that from Whitehorse Hill but, as noted in Chapter 15, the amber and the possible Kimmeridge shale beads suggest a shared desire to have necklaces made from certain materials from specific sources (Fig. 21.13).

The Upton Pyne necklace has a number of other associations which parallel those of the Whitehorse Hill cist. Both cremations have been identified as those of young people (Chapter 6; Fox 1969) and were deposited in wrappings held together with copper-alloy pins. Both necklaces have similarities in their colour schemes, with both combining beads which are predominately dark in colour with a smaller number of larger, lighter-coloured ones (Figs. 21.14–21.16). Colour symbolism was undoubtedly important to prehistoric communities, both for

Figure 21.13: The beads of faience (top), amber (middle) and possibly shale (bottom) forming the North Molton composite necklace. (Photograph: National Museums of Scotland.)

Figure 21.14: The North Molton composite necklace as restrung. (Photograph: Royal Albert Memorial Museum, Exeter.)

Figure 21.15: The Upton Pyne composite necklace as restrung (Photograph: Royal Albert Memorial Museum, Exeter.)

monuments and artefacts (Jones and MacGregor 2002) and the use of a range of colours and of the contrast between dark and light is consistent with that from other Bronze Age grave assemblages (Woodward 2000, 111).

As argued in Chapter 15, the necklaces from Whitehorse Hill, Upton Pyne and North Molton show an awareness of Wessex fashions and testify to contacts with that region. It is interesting, however, how they stand apart from other bead find-spots in the region. Even the composite necklace from Boscregan was found with a multiple cremation deposit and not that of an individual (Borlase 1879; Jones forthcoming).

Individual beads and finds of small numbers are occasionally discovered in the south west, although their contexts vary considerably and many are not found with burial deposits. On Dartmoor seven segmented faience beads were found in a pit within Shaugh Moor ring cairn 2; these were not associated with a burial but were instead found with a deposit of charcoal and a pot base. By contrast, 'blue and white' beads said to have come from inside a cist at Moretonhampstead 6 (Grinsell 1978) appear from their description also to have been of faience and were found with burnt bone.

Small numbers of beads have been recovered from other sites in Devon (Grinsell 1970; 1978; 1983). At Halwill 1 a single amber bead or pendant was found in a barrow with a small quantity of burnt bone identified as being from an animal (Burnard 1896a; Beck and Shennan 1991, 159). At Farway 31 segmented bone beads imitating faience beads were recorded in direct association with a cremation (Kirwan 1870; Jones and Quinnell 2008).

In Cornwall many beads have also been found as single

Figure 21.16: The replica of the composite necklace from Whitehorse Hill. (Photograph: Plymouth Museum.)

items. At Stannon Down, Bodmin Moor, a pit beside cairn 2 produced an amber bead and at a ring cairn (site 6) a faience bead was found inside the structure (Jones 2004–5). In neither instance was the bead associated with a buried individual. Clay beads from a barrow at Crig-a-Mennis, Perranzabuloe, were found in a Trevisker vessel with flints, a quartz pebble, charcoal and a tiny amount of burnt bone (Christie 1960).

The small numbers of beads which are typically found could indicate restricted access to prestige items. However, it has been suggested that necklaces may have been broken up on the death of an individual and shared out between community members (Woodward *et al.* 2005). It also the case that the marking of individuality in the south west may have been exceptional and differed from that in other regions; the possible reasons for this are discussed below.

Materials from afar

Another of the striking things about the Whitehorse Hill necklace is that, aside from the locally sourced clay (and possibly the tin), the beads of which it is composed must have travelled over considerable distances. The Kimmeridge shale beads came from the Dorset coast, which lies more than 130km to the east. The amber used in the beads originated in the Baltic, but the beads are likely to have been obtained through exchange with communities in Wessex (Chapter 15), over 180km to the east, where they had probably been fashioned.

Obtaining these items is likely to have involved a complex social exchange network. The beads could have been obtained through adjacent communities who acted as intermediaries, or have involved a journey which may have included several days' walk each way, across unfamiliar landscapes, potentially through the territories of communities who may have been more or less friendly. Anthropological study has long revealed that exchange frequently leads to the creation of cycles of reciprocity and social debt, which extend beyond mere monetary value (for example, Weiner 1987, 139–154); it is very likely that the acquisition of beads and other items was bound up in complex exchange networks which went beyond simple trade. However, the undertaking of potentially dangerous, long-distance journeys in search of exotica and items which possessed perceived magical power, such as amber or shale beads, may have enhanced the status and renown of those who undertook such travels (Needham 2000). In fact there is now good evidence for the circulation of items which included precious cups, beads and metalwork over large areas and across the sea in the period after 2000 cal BC (Needham *et al.* 2006; Needham 2009). Such items are likely to have become known, and to have possessed biographies of ownership.

Once obtained, the objects would have conferred prestige on their wearers but it is also probable, as Sheridan and Shortland (2004) suggest, that the seemingly 'magical', electrostatic properties of both the amber and the shale would have been apparent; amber has in the past also been associated with curative properties (Pliny the Elder 2004, 370; Woodward 2000, 109). Like the tin with its silvery reflection, the shine from the amber and the shale may well have been associated with supernatural powers.

Both substances also have other properties which are likely to have made them the subject of stories and desire. The small creatures that can sometimes be found imprisoned within amber and the shale cliffs which could burst into flame at Kimmeridge are likely to have been a source of wonder and myth.

Flint

A single flint flake tool was recovered from inside the basketry container (Chapter 17). Flints are commonly found in association with cists and barrows across the south west (Worth 1906; Dudley 1964; Pollard and Russell 1969; Christie 1988), although in many cases a direct association with a burial is not proven, and in some cases the flint may have been residual and associated with earlier occupation. For example, at the Watch Hill barrow on the St Austell granite many flints came from the turf stack which formed the mound (Jones and Quinnell 2006b). Others are likely to have been deposited as part of funerary-related activities, such as feasting around the barrow, as, for example, at Constantine Island on the north Cornwall coast (Jones 2009–10).

In light of this, it is of interest that, given the general

overall paucity of finds, flint tools represent the most commonly found artefact from Dartmoor cists (Worth 1967, 197; Butler 1997, appx 3). Flints are included within cists from the Beaker-using period onwards and, aside from the arrowheads noted above from Shaugh Prior 8, these are typically recorded as being flakes or scrapers (Worth 1967, fig. 70): a flint from Fernworthy (Lydford 24) can now be identified as a knife related to plano-convex examples (H. Quinnell, pers. comm.). Finds of flints from post-Beaker cists include those from Lydford 17, 40, 41 and 52, Manaton 11, Peter Tavy 18, Shaugh Prior 3, Sheepstor 25a, Sparkwell 8a and Walkhampton 5 (Grinsell 1978; Table 21.1). This suggests that on Dartmoor flint tools were preferentially selected for inclusion in cists and with burial-related activity, perhaps to a greater extent than elsewhere in the south west. As with site orientation, the inclusion of flints within Dartmoor cists could represent a regional practice.

The flint flake from the Whitehorse Hill cist therefore fits a wider pattern of artefactual association found across Dartmoor. Although it could be dismissed as an apparently simple flake tool, there may have been a particular reason for its placement within the basketry container: it could, for example, have been included to signify the intended social identity or the 'personhood' (Fowler 2004) of the interred individual and it may therefore be a mistake to view it as a merely 'mundane object' (Lemonnier 2012). The form of the flint would have carried cultural resonances in terms of the tasks it had been used for, including the preparation of vegetable substances or meat, or for bark or leather working (Chapter 17), or given its find context for personal grooming, such as cutting hair; the wear along its edges would have displayed a history of use. Taken together, these could have given the flint its own 'biography', derived from associations with the person who had used it or with particular activities (Spector 1991; Gosden and Marshall 1999). It is also possible that it was knapped from an old curated core, which had its own biography (Chapter 17). In this way, the inclusion of the flint within the basketry container may have referenced the gender or the perceived identity of the deceased just as much as the beads or any of the other artefacts did.

The organic finds

The organic artefacts form the most exceptional aspect of the site, as they are made from materials which do not normally survive in the archaeological record. Their survival has shed light on the ways that organic materials were worked during the Early Bronze Age; for example, the turning of wood, the combining of plant fibres and animal skins and the use of lime bast (Chapters 8, 11, 13, 14, 16 and 18).

Given the lack of comparanda any one of these artefacts would by itself have been a notable occurrence, but as a group they represent an unparalleled assemblage. However, it is important to remember that objects made of organic materials, as opposed to metals or stone, would have formed the majority of material culture in the Bronze Age (Hurcombe 2014, chap. 1). Wood, basketry, hides and textiles for clothing were part of the everyday world but are materials which normally only survive in wetland contexts and are missing from most excavated sites (Coles and Coles 1986, 184). Seen in these terms, the assemblage from the Whitehorse Hill cist represents only a small proportion of the range of organic objects likely to have been in use during the Bronze Age, but does provide an indicator of what may be missing from other supposedly 'empty' cists on Dartmoor and beyond.

The selected artefacts are remarkable for their craftsmanship and as individual items represent hours of work in their preparation. Likewise, the skill involved in their production and the associations which they may have carried would have rendered them as significant to the communities who used them as the non-organic items discussed above.

The remainder of this section focuses upon the materials from which the organic objects were made, their sources and the properties which they might have been considered to possess.

The matted plant layers

The first and last items to be placed within the cist were layers of 'matted' plant material. Because of its poor level of preservation, the upper layer could not be identified. The lower layer was comprised of purple moor grass (*Molinia caerulea*) (Chapter 9). This grass still grows locally on Dartmoor today, and it is very probable that the grass deposited was gathered in the late summer to early autumn from the area adjacent to the cist. This seasonality is also suggested by the presence of pollen from meadowsweet found within the cist, which would also have been present in the summer (Chapter 10).

Although there did not seem to be any structure to the plant layer, the stems of the grasses were unidirectional and appear to have been laid flat along the base of the cist. The lining of cists, coffins and graves with plant material has been recorded at a number of sites across Britain (Table 21.2). For example, at Ashgrove Farm in Fife plants had been used to line the base of the cist (Henshall 1963–64). Leaves were found in association with the cremation at Huntshaw 2 in Devon (Doe 1875) and at Loose Howe and Gristhorpe plant materials were found inside log coffins (Elgee and Elgee 1949; Sheridan *et al.* 2013). It is therefore likely that this was a widespread practice during the Early Bronze Age and that graves and cists were routinely lined with plants or branches as part of funerary rituals. This practice may be seen as an aesthetically pleasing action. It is also possible that the offering of living greenery into the cist or grave was heavy with symbolism, referencing, for example, beliefs involving birth, death and rebirth.

Meadowsweet pollen has been identified in several cists in the British Isles, including sites in Scotland and Wales (Dickson 1978; Murphy and Murphy 2013). It has usually been interpreted in two ways. The first is that it is

Table 21.2: Organic artefacts (hides, basketry, matting and textiles) identified from British Bronze Age barrows.

Site name & county	Grinsell no.	Radiocarbon date	Organic remains & associated artefacts	Reference
England				
Berkshire				
Lambourn	–	-	Barrow contained inhumation burial associated with accessory vessel, & copper-alloy awl & dagger. Traces of plain-weave textile found as impression on dagger.	Smith 1921
Cambridgeshire				
Barnack	–	HAR-1158: 3800±200 BP, 2880–1690 cal BC	3 of the inhumation burials (6, 7 & 40) beneath barrow covered by dark stains, interpreted as shrouds.	Donaldson 1977
Over, Barrow 2	–	OxA-024639: 3477±30 BP, 1880–1690 cal BC	Plain weave textiles found preserved in charred clumps within cremation pit pyre beneath barrow. Cremated bone, bone needle/ pin & 2 small sherds of Collared Urn also recovered. Textiles may have been placed in piles as offerings beside body or used as means of binding it.	Harris 2015
Cornwall				
Carthamartha Woods	–	-	Cist beneath cairn contained small piece of bone 'thought to be the top joint of a finger'. At bottom of cist was 'dark discolouration', which may have been decayed fabric or caused by 'infiltration of water'.	Walford & Quinnell 1997
Carvinack	–	-	Small cairn beneath barrow covered cremation. Clay beneath cremation produced impressions of textile bag.	Dudley 1964.
Pit 32093, Harlyn Bay	–	SUERC-15536: 3610±35 BP, 2120–1880 cal BC	Pit contained cremation inside Trevisker vessel. Copper-alloy pendant from inside pot covered in mineralized fibres from cloth bag or clothing.	Jones *et al.* 2011
Isles of Scilly				
Knackyboy, St Martins	–	OxA-26474: 3837±38 BP, 2470–2140 cal BC; OxA-26363: 3319±29 BP, 1690–1510 cal BC; OxA-26364: 3365±28 BP, 1740–1610 cal BC; OxA-26365: 3157±29 BP, 1500–1320 cal BC; OxA-26366: 3145±29 BP, 1500–1310 cal BC; OxA-26368: 3215±28 BP, 1600–1420 cal BC; OxA-26369: 3066±28 BP, 1420–1230 cal BC; OxA-26370: 3276±29 BP, 1630–1490 cal BC; OxA-26371: 3146±29 BP, 1500–1310 cal BC; and OxA-26372: 3386±29 BP, 1750–1610 cal BC	Excavation of Scillonian entrance grave revealed chamber containing ceramic vessels, faience beads & cremation burials. Impressions of matting found on bases of 2 vessels.	O'Neil 1952; Sawyer 2015, 87–89
Devon				
Huntshaw	1	–	Barrow covered cist with cremation with possible traces of cloth wrapped around it.	Doe 1875; Grinsell 1970
Huntshaw	2	SUERC-38738: 3600±30 BP, 2040–1880 cal BC; and SUERC-38739: 3535±30 BP, 1950–1760 cal BC	Barrow covered cremation associated with copper-alloy dagger. Traces of sheath & handle survived, along with leaves, forming layer, suggested by excavator to have formed a 'chaplet' or wreath.	Doe 1875; Grinsell 1970; Jones & Quinnell 2013

Site name & county	Grinsell no.	Radiocarbon date	Organic remains & associated artefacts	Reference
Manaton	9	–	Cist found to contain 2 coils of 'human hair' within pit under paving at N end of cist.	Burnard 1903, 142; Grinsell 1978; Butler 1997 207–208
Lydford	50c	–	Cist investigated in 1827 said to have contained human hair.	Grinsell 1978; Butler 1997, 207
Upton Pyne 4	2	SUERC-39125: 3220±30 BP, 1600–1420 cal BC	Low barrow covered cremation which may have been in bag fastened by copper-alloy pin, which found on top of cremation. Copper-alloy dagger, incense cup & composite necklace also recovered.	Kirwan 1872; Fox 1969; Grinsell 1983; Jones & Quinnell 2013
Whitehorse Hill Cist	–	This volume (Chapter 20)	Cist contained cremation wrapped in bear pelt, which may have been held together by copper-alloy pin. Cist also held basketry container inside which were beads of amber, shale, clay & tin, 2 pairs wooden studs & a flint. In addition there was a braided bracelet or armband with tin studs, a textile & animal-skin object & layers of matted plant material.	This volume
Derbyshire Shuttlestone	–	–	Barrow covered central cairn below which was inhumation burial covered by skin of dark red colour with 'hairy surface'. Burial accompanied by copper-alloy dagger & axe. Traces of 'leather' on 1 side of axe.	Bateman 1861, 34–35
Dorset King Barrow, Arne, Stoborough	19	–	Beneath bowl barrow was skeleton in log coffin stitched together. Wood or shale cup found at head end & gold 'lace' accompanied burial.	Grinsell 1959; Needham *et al.* 2006, 103–104
Bincombe	13	–	Bell barrow contained inhumation with Beaker. Position of body suggested it had been wrapped in cloth held together with copper-alloy pin.	Grinsell 1982
Dewlish	8	–	Bowl barrow covered cremation with dagger still with leather sheath evident.	Grinsell 1959
Edmonsham	2	BM-708: 3069±45 BP, 1440–1210 cal BC; & BM-709: 3477±52 BP, 1940–1660 cal BC	Barrow covered cremation burial associated with copper-alloy Camerton-Snowshill dagger with traces of leather sheath adhering.	Proudfoot 1963; Grinsell 1982
Long Crichel	18	–	Bowl barrow covered inhumation. Position of body suggested it had been wrapped.	Piggott & Piggott 1944, 68–69; Grinsell 1959
Weymouth	8	–	Barrow covered 2 inhumation burials & a cremation. 3 copper-alloy daggers recovered, 2 had traces of their wooden sheaths. Impressions of plain-weave textile found on copper-alloy axe. 2 gold pommel mountings also found.	Henshall 1950; Grinsell 1959
Winterborne St Martin	44	–	Secondary cremation under bowl barrow wrapped in 'woven pouch' made from some kind of grasses.	Grinsell 1959; St George Gray & Prideaux 1905
Winterborne Steepleton	19c	–	Pond barrow enclosed large no. pits, some containing cremations. Cremation G said to have been buried in wooden keg or basket, 1 or 2 twigs survived.	Grinsell 1959; 1982; Atkinson *et al.* 1951
Hampshire Weaver's Down	44	–	Log coffin under barrow recorded. 'Hair', probably animal, identified but no bone found inside coffin.	Grinsell 1938

Site name & county	Grinsell no.	Radiocarbon date	Organic remains & associated artefacts	Reference
Kent				
Ringwould	Ringwould with Kingsdown 1	–	Burnt material 'resembling linen' found in accessory vessel inside Collared Urn containing cremation beneath Ringwould barrow.	Woodruff 1874
Lincolnshire				
Deeping St Nicholas, Grave 483	–	GU-5358: 3540±60 BP, 2040–1690 cal BC	Child burial in log coffin under barrow mound contained black stain at head, may have been remains of shroud.	French 1994, 25–34
Deeping St Nicholas, Grave 46	–	GU-5342: 3440±60 BP, 1910–1610 cal BC	Female inhumation cut into primary barrow mound associated with black stain thought to be shroud.	French 1994, 25–34
Deeping St Nicholas, Grave 47	–	GU-5344: 3350±70 BP, 1880–1460	Male inhumation cut into primary barrow mound associated with black stain thought to be either mat or shroud.	French 1994, 25–34
West Ashby, Grave F48	–	–	Log coffin cut into barrow mound. Traces of hide cover or cloth found.	Field 1985
West Ashby, Grave F66	–	–	Second log coffin cut into barrow mound. Interior coffin fill suggested former presence of organic material such as cloth, hide or small branches. Food Vessel recovered from grave.	Field 1985
Staffordshire				
Throwley	–	–	Barrow covered cremation which appeared to have been deposited into pit inside basket. Copper-alloy pin, accessory vessel & a flint also found.	Bateman 1861, 130
Norfolk				
Weasenham Lyngs	–	BM-877: 3339±56 BP, 1750–1490 cal BC	Multiple cremation deposit found under mound with sherds from Collared Urn & charred frags of charred cloth with 'tabby' weave.	Lawson 1986, 73
Northumberland				
Cartington	–	GU-1648: 3790±65 BP, 2470–2020 cal BC	Beneath cairn within barrow was Beaker-associated burial in log coffin. Bracken fronds present in coffin. Fragments of a stitched animal skin thought to be from kid or calf. May represent clothing or wrapping.	Dixon 1913; Melton *et al.* 2013
Ford, Doddington	–	–	Burial in cist found within sandy knoll. Inhumation clothed in 'leathern dress', parts of which still showed stitching. Food Vessel & flint knife were found with burial.	Greenwell 1877, 411; Kinnes & Longworth 1985, 101
Wiltshire				
Amesbury	51	BM-287: 3738±55 BP 2300–1970 cal BC	Bell barrow covered Beaker burials within timber structure. Considerable quantity of 'something which appeared to be decayed leather' was over 1 burial. Interpreted by Ashbee as folded hide or leather object.	Ashbee 1978
Amesbury	58	–	Bell barrow covered cremation, upon which was small knife-dagger, wrapped in cloth with substance, possibly moss.	Ashbee 1960, 82
Amesbury	85	–	Burial under bell barrow had been laid on moss, traces of which preserved by corrosion products from accompanying copper-alloy dagger.	Moore & Rowlands 1972, 44

Site name & county	Grinsell no.	Radiocarbon date	Organic remains & associated artefacts	Reference
Bishop's Canning	81	HAR-2998: 3540±70 BP 2120–1680 cal BC & NPL-139, 3745±135 BP, 2570–1770 cal BC	Hemp Knoll barrow. Low barrow mound covered Beaker inhumation burial in coffin. Beside coffin were head & hooves from an ox. Character suggested that hide had been deposited.	Robertson-Mackay 1980
Collingbourne Ducis	4	–	Beneath double bell barrow was crema-tion in wooden coffin containing acces-sory vessel, copper-alloy dagger in scabbard & copper-alloy ring-headed pin. Dagger bore textile impression & traces of wooden sheath visible on blade. Mineralised remnants of horn hilt also survived.	Grinsell 1957; Thomas 2005, 223–225
Durrington	11	–	Bowl barrow covered cremation in Collared Urn. Traces of cloth wrapping survived where they had been replaced by carbonate of lime.	Grinsell 1957
Durrington	43b	–	Bowl barrow covered Urn inverted over cremation wrapped in cloth.	Grinsell 1957
Durrington	48	–	Bowl barrow covered cremation wrapped in cloth.	Grinsell 1957
Milston	23	–	Bowl barrow covered cist. Cremation had been wrapped in cloth, traces of which survived in floor of the barrow.	Grinsell 1957
Ogbourne St Andrew	11	–	Bowl barrow covered cremation wrapped in cloth.	Grinsell 1957
Preshute ('Manton Barrow')	1a	–	Inhumation burial beneath bowl barrow had been wrapped in cloth, impressions of which visible in clay soil. Accom-panied by 2 accessory vessels, flat copper-alloy dagger, copper-alloy 'blade' with amber pommel, shale bead with gold bands, 3 copper-alloy awls & composite necklace comprised of 150 shale beads, 5 amber & a fossil.	Cunnington 1907; Grinsell 1957
Shrewton	5j	–	Inhumation burial of elderly female cut into mound of barrow. She had been buried with composite necklace which included 2 wooden beads.	Green & Rollo-Smith 1984
Shrewton	5k	–	A low mound covered several inhumations, including a central burial with a Beaker and a copper-alloy dagger. The dagger appears to have been wrapped in moss, which in turn was covered by a woven fabric.	Grinsell 1957; Green & Rollo-Smith 1984
West Overton	6b	–	Bowl barrow covered central Beaker inhumation burial. Burial covered by thin layer interpreted as remains of cloak or hide. Analyses of deposit suggested it was made from animal material.	Smith & Simpson 1966
Wilsford, Bush Barrow	5	–	Primary inhumation below barrow accompanied by large number of artefacts, including lozenge-shaped gold sheet, copper-alloy objects, bone mounts, gold belt hook, smaller gold lozenge-shaped sheet, polished mace-head, copper-alloy rivets, 1000s of minute gold pins, 2 copper-alloy daggers & a copper-alloy axe. Fragments of wood associated with small dagger which also bore traces of wood & 'leather' sheath. Traces of wooden sheath also found adhering to	Hoare 1812; Annable and Simpson 1964.

Site name & county	Grinsell no.	Radiocarbon date	Organic remains & associated artefacts	Reference
			large dagger, & remains of wooden hilt survived. Copper-alloy axe bore traces of cloth on 1 side.	
Winterborne Stoke	47	–	Disc barrow with central cremation. Burial accompanied by copper-alloy dagger said to have traces of leather sheath. Analysis of surviving material revealed mineralised textile fragments, perhaps associated with rush matting.	Gingell 1988
Winterborne Stoke	62	–	Bowl barrow covered cremation wrapped in cloth inside large urn.	Grinsell 1957
Winterborne Stoke	63	–	Bowl barrow covered cremation wrapped in cloth.	Grinsell 1957
Yorkshire Blanch 241	–	–	Barrow covered pit with inverted urn containing cremation & bone pin. Black deposit around urn seemed to represent traces of basketry.	Mortimer 1905, 327–328
Garton Slack 82	–	–	Grave I beneath barrow was found to contain inhumation with 'string' & small pieces of textile.	Mortimer 1905, 234
Gristhorpe	–	OxA-17454: 3669±30 BP, 2140–1940 cal BC; OxA-19219: 3743±32 BP, 2280–2030 cal BC; OxA-16844: 3671±32, BP, 2150–1940 cal BC; OxA-16812: 3375±31 BP, 1750–1610 cal BC; HAR-4424: 3590±100 BP, 2210–1680 cal BC	Log coffin under barrow contained inhumation accompanied by copper-alloy dagger & flints. Found to contain cattle hide, bone pin & paws or pelts of fox & pine marten. Also an 'organic ornament', bark & wood container, wooden fastener & plant matter.	Melton *et al.* 2013
Kelleythorpe, C38	–	–	Inhumation in cist associated with Beaker, amber necklace, copper-alloy dagger & upper part of 'hawks head and beak'. Body lay upon mass of 'linen cloth'.	Mortimer 1905, 275
Loose Howe	–	–	Log coffin found below barrow. Coffin lined with rushes, reeds or straw with pillow of grass or straw at head. Inhumation could have been clothed or wrapped in linen cloth. Fragment of foot wrapping an ankle bone & small piece of shoe with 2 lace holes also survived. Copper-alloy dagger also accompanied burial.	Elgee & Elgee 1949; Melton *et al.* 2013
Rylstone	–	–	Burial beneath barrow found in log coffin. Inhumation wrapped in wool cloth.	Greenwell 1877, 376, Kinnes & Longworth 1985, 97
Towthorpe 139	–	–	Inhumation burial found in log coffin in pit beneath large barrow. Burial associated with copper-alloy dagger in sheath, stone macehead with haft of ash, & plano-convex flint knife. Under & over dagger was large quantity of dark matter, resembling decayed & compressed leaves.	Mortimer 1905, 3–6
Scotland Ashgrove Farm, Methil, Fife	–	–	Beaker-associated burial found in cist accompanied by dagger with horn & cattle-hair sheath. Floor of cist covered by black deposit formed by plant remains, 'consisting of leaf fragments, bark, twigs, and plant tissue. For the most part, it was too decayed for	Henshall 1963-64.

Site name & county	Grinsell no.	Radiocarbon date	Organic remains & associated artefacts	Reference
			identification, with the exception of one or more fragments of birch, cross-leaved heath, rush, moss and fairly abundant sphagnum moss'. A '1 foot' long 'stick', probably a rhizome, also found lying across the body.	
Barns Farm, Dalgety, Fife	–	SRR-528: 3796±80 BP, 2480–1980 cal BC (2 further determinations gave Neolithic dates & are not reproduced here.)	Barrow mound found to cover 6 cists, 3 graves & several pits, which included cremations & inhumations. Associated finds included a Beaker & Food Vessels, battle-axe, shale necklace, jet beads & pendants, various flint tools, copper or copper-alloy knife & copper-alloy awl. Head of inhumation within cist 1 rested upon piece of hide. Copper alloy knife from grave 3 had probably been wrapped in hide & there may also have been wooden sheath but analysis could not confirm this. Based on shape of soil stain, coffin used for burial in grave 2 may have been a reused coracle, made from animal skin.	Watkins 1982
Bishopmill, Elgin, Morayshire	–	–	Cist containing copper-alloy dagger also contained portions of skin identified as coming from an 'ox'.	Davidson 1866–68; McAdam 1982
Blackhills, Tyrie	–	–	Cist containing inhumation was covered by a hide, identified at time as an ox hide. Burial was accompanied by a Food Vessel.	Callander 1908–09
Broomend, near the Inverurie Paper-Mills, Aberdeenshire	–	OxA-13214: 3720±35 BP, 2210–2020 cal BC	Cist containing 2 male inhumation burials were covered by probable ox hide. Burials accompanied by 2 Beakers, flint flake, flint knife & bone belt ring.	Chalmers 1866–68; Sheridan 2004
Broomend, near the Inverurie Paper-Mills, Aberdeenshire	–	–	Second cist containing skeletons of an adult & a child covered by hide or cloth. Burial accompanied by horn ladle & Beaker. Second smaller ceramic vessel also found.	Davidson 1866–68
Cabrach, Aberdeenshire	–	–	Cist containing inhumation burial accompanied by ceramic vessel & flints. In addition to finds 'a darkish fibrous-looking substance like dry moss was found beside and under the remains of the body. What it had been, whether hair, wool, or vegetable matter, could not be discovered'.	Christie 1862–64
Graignish, Argyllshire	–	–	Cist containing Food Vessel & stone axe associated with inhumation uncovered. Hair, identified as 'bovine' also present.	McAdam 1982
Cuninghar, Tillicoultry	–	–	Cist contained remains of inhumation. Matted substance found at spot where head rested, & appeared to be of 2 materials, a 'lighter coloured, composed of the matting of roots' & a 'darker coloured' belonging to an animal, possibly stoat. The burial accompanied by Food Vessel.	Robertson 1894–95; Ryder 1963–64
Dalrigh, Argyll and Bute	–	OxA-6813: 3555±60 BP, 2120–1700 cal BC	Log coffin found under mound. Fragments sewn birch bark found inside coffin. These may have been part of coffin cover or wrapping for body.	Mapleton 1879; Melton et al. 2013

Site name & county	Grinsell no.	Radiocarbon date	Organic remains & associated artefacts	Reference
Forteviot, Perth and Kinross	–	SUERC-26112: 3675±30 BP, 2150–1950 cal BC; SUERC-29196, 3690±30 BP, 2200–1970 cal BC SUERC-29200: 3705±30 BP, 2200–1980 cal BC; SUERC-29198: 3590±30 BP, 2030–1880 cal BC; SUERC-29199: 3740±35 BP, 2280–2030 cal BC	Cist burial covered by cairn inserted into henge monument. Burial accompanied by copper-alloy dagger & organic remains including wood, flower buds, animal hide & bier or mat of birch bark.	Noble & Brophy 2011
Keas Cottage, Spinningdale, Dornoch, Firth, Sunderland	–	SUERC-41427: 3635±30 BP 2130–1910 cal BC SUERC-41428: 3700±30 BP 2200–1980 cal BC	Cist within substantial pit contained remains of crouched inhumation of middle-aged female with signs of spinal joint disease. Tripartite Food Vessel urn placed to west of skull & some wool or sheepskin recovered from under skeleton.	Arabaolaza 2013
Langwell Farm, Strath Oykel, Sutherland	–	SUERC-24680 & SUERC-33918 Weighted mean 3653± 25 BP (T'=2.3, T'(5%)=3.8, v=1; Ward and Wilson 1978); 2140–1940 cal BC	Cist found to hold the flexed body of woman wrapped in brown cow or bull hide, with woven materials & hazel stick.	Lelong 2012
Lunanhead, Angus	–	–	Gravel knoll contained inhumation inside cist. Burial associated with layer of matted material & jet necklace.	McAdam 1982
Masterton, Fife	–	–	Burial in cist accompanied by dagger with traces of horn handle, 2 copper-alloy armlets, small copper-alloy blade & necklace of jet beads. Floor of cist covered by an animal/cattle hide.	Henshall 1962–63
Parkhill, Aberdeenshire	–	–	Mound covered Beaker-associated inhumation inside cist. Burial covered by layer of matted hair.	McAdam 1982
Seafield West, Inverness	–	GrA-27037 & GrA-27039 Weighted mean 3603± 29 BP (T'=1.8, T'(5%)=3.8, v=1; Ward and Wilson 1978); 2040–1880 cal BC	Log coffin burial (probably crouched inhumation) found beneath cairn inside ring-ditch. Associated with copper-alloy dagger with wood & animal/cattle skin sheath.	Cressey & Sheridan 2003; Sheridan 2004
Wales Dysgwylfa Fawr, Cardiganshire	–	HAR-2677: 3300±80 BP, 1760–1410 cal BC	Secondary cremation burial found in log coffin within barrow. Pieces of fur lay over cremation. Food Vessel & a flint found with burial.	Forde 1939; Savory 1980, 80

a residue from an intoxicating drink akin to mead (Dickson 1978), which may have been consumed during ritualised drinking as part of the funeral (cf Sherratt 1991; Clarke *et al.* 1985, 201–203): this interpretation has normally been put forward in relation to pollen found in ceramic vessels. At Whitehorse Hill, however, the pollen was from inside the cist, and its survival suggests that any libation must have been a large one. The alternative hypothesis is that the meadowsweet pollen is derived from floral tributes placed in the grave (Hughes and Murphy 2013; Tipping 1994; 1997). Given the evidence for the placing of other plant material in the cist at Whitehorse Hill, this seems

to be the more likely explanation for its inclusion. The widespread discovery of meadowsweet pollen in Early Bronze Age graves does, however, suggest that the plant, with its distinctive white flowers and sweet smell, was widely used in burial-associated rituals and, much like flowers in modern western European funerals, is likely to have carried symbolic associations (for example, Barley 1995, 154–155).

The pelt

The pelt represents another rare survival. Although several

hides or pelts have been identified in association with Early Bronze Age burials, it is rare that the species of the animal has been confirmed using modern methods. The evidence for hides and pelts generally only survives in the form of 'dark stains' within grave cuts, as at West Overton 6b in Wiltshire (Smith and Simpson 1966; Table 21.2), indicating the former presence of hides or textiles.

The presence of hides has also been inferred from the presence of animal bones; for example, the head and hooves of an ox found within the Hemp Knoll barrow in Wiltshire led to the suggestion that a cattle hide had been buried with the individual (Robertson-Mackay 1980).

Other instances are old finds which no longer survive and where the animal species cannot be verified, as, for example, the stitched garment said to have been of deer skins, from the King Barrow, Arne, Stoborough, Dorset (Grinsell 1959). Many identifications of surviving hairs are old (Table 21.2) and they may therefore be open to question. However, the recent study of the Gristhorpe log coffin burial (Sheridan *et al.* 2013), has identified a cattle hide.

The identification of the Whitehorse Hill pelt was therefore a great surprise. Analysis of the fur (Appendix C) revealed that it was from an animal of the bear genus. Given that the find came from temperate Europe it is likely to have been from a brown rather than a polar bear (Curry-Lindahl 1972). On the mainland of the south-west peninsula there are no immediate comparanda for the bear pelt from the Whitehorse Hill cist; a single bear claw found within a post-Roman midden on Tean, in the Isles of Scilly, is not thought to have come from a locally resident animal (Thomas 1960). Bears are, however, thought to have survived in parts of northern Britain into at least the Romano-British period (Hammon 2010) and a review of animal remains of the Neolithic and Bronze Age in southern England has identified four Late Neolithic sites which contained bear bones (Serjeantson 2011, 45). In southern England a high-status Late Iron Age burial from Welwyn Garden City, Hertfordshire, had been wrapped in a bear pelt before the body was cremated (Stead 1967). As at Whitehorse Hill, however, it is uncertain whether this was an imported pelt or derived from a local animal.

Animals are often considered by contemporary non-western societies to possess an agency of their own and they therefore become totemic. Products from them such as pelts, claws and teeth can be used to invoke the materiality of the animal from which they came (for example, Hurcombe 2014, 115).

There is widespread evidence that bears had a special significance for prehistoric societies. The fact that the bear can walk on two legs like a human and 'disappears' in winter is likely to have made it a focus for myths and symbolic belief; they may have been seen as mediators between the human and the animal world (Aldhouse-Green and Aldhouse-Green 2005, 72–73; Zeiler 2006). This symbolism is well-documented by both historical and anthropological studies across Europe and Asia. Eliade (1967, 201–210) recounts the complex rituals associated with the sacrifice and consumption of bears by the Ainu of Japan. In northern Europe comparable rituals appear to have been undertaken to appease the spirit of the bear before it could be skinned and eaten. In the Finnish epic poem the *Kalevala,* for example, the hunted bear is treated with absolute respect (Lönnrot, 2008 598–613) and the Saami people of this region would carefully bury the bones of bears after skinning the animal and consuming the meat, in the belief that the bears would be resurrected (Aldhouse-Green and Aldhouse-Green 2005, 42). By contrast, despite valuing the medicinal powers of its body parts, the Eveny of Siberia consider bears to be too human-like under their fur and generally avoid killing them (Vitebsky 2005, 264).

Pelts from skinned animals are often deemed to hold special powers. In Norse mythology the donning of wolf skins led Sigmund to become a wolf (Byock 1999, 44) and Viking berserkers would wear either wolf or bear pelts to obtain the power held within them (Williams 2001). Indeed, there is still some belief amongst modern non-western societies that bear pelts contain magical power. For example, there is a belief among the Eveny that the shaking of a bear pelt can cause rain (Vitebsky 2005, 101).

The bear which produced the Whitehorse Hill pelt may also have held symbolic meaning and its skin would almost certainly have been regarded as a high-status item. As was described in Chapter 11, it was taken from the rear quarters of the animal, the highest quality part of the animal pelt, and also the warmest and most comfortable to wear. As such, the pelt could have conferred status upon its wearer and have been a prestigious item in the way that the jewellery was. The wrapping of the cremated bones in the pelt would therefore have hidden and contained them. At the same time it could have empowered the remains by enveloping them in a layer which would have conveyed meanings associated with the animal that it was derived from, including status and magical symbolism (Douny and Harris 2014).

The ear studs or labrets

The two pairs of ear studs or labrets from the cist were made from turned spindle wood (Chapter 16). They represent the earliest evidence for wood turning in Britain (Brunning *et al.* 2013, 174) and are also the only wooden studs to survive from the Early Bronze Age in Britain. The larger studs are thought to have been worn in the ears and the smaller pair elsewhere on the body, perhaps through the lips or cheeks. Piercing is well-documented in the anthropological record, with many groups across Africa and the Americas choosing to wear ear studs and labrets (for example, Giddings 1967, 118; Reynolds 1968, 196; Jenness 1977, 143; Fisher 1984, 12, 136, 288–289). We might therefore expect piercings of one form or another, as well as tattooing, to have been a common form of bodily decoration in prehistory (for example, Spindler 1993, 167–173).

As demonstrated in Chapter 16, non-wooden examples of ear studs or labrets survive across Britain, with the

Figure 21.17: Late Bronze Age gold ear spools from Ballinesker, Co. Wexford. (Photograph: National Museum of Ireland.)

Figure 21.18: The replica spindle wood ear studs. This image reveals how pale in colour they were when new. (Photograph: Dartmoor National Park Authority.)

nearest instance to Whitehorse Hill being that from Cowleaze Barrow B, in Dorset, where an example in shale was found (Woodward 1991, 102). Further away, several gold objects from Ireland dating to the later Bronze Age have recently been reinterpreted as ear spools (Cahill 2001) (Fig. 21.17). These are likely to have been high-status items and their circular shape may have had symbolic importance (Leahy 2008). The symbolism associated with the circle was widespread during the Bronze Age in Western Europe, in terms of the architecture of monuments and decoration on objects (Bradley 2012, chap. 3). The gold colour of the Irish examples could have made reference to the sun and it may be significant that when freshly made the studs from the Whitehorse Hill cist would also have been a warm, yellowish colour which may similarly have carried a solar symbolism (Fig. 21.18).

The Whitehorse Hill studs are, however, made from a rather less exotic material than those from either Ireland or Cowleaze. The spindle tree still grows on the fringes of Dartmoor and it is very likely that the wood used for the studs was derived from local sources. In later periods

spindle wood was used because of its suitability for turning a variety of intricate objects. The wood for the studs could have been selected because there was already a body of knowledge about turning and which woods were most suitable for producing fine objects. The craftsmanship employed in producing them is likely to have made them valued pieces.

The fact that there were two set of studs within the Whitehorse Hill cist may be significant. They may have been worn on two parts of the body (Chapter 16), with the larger pair being worn as ear studs and the smaller pair elsewhere on the body; for example, in the lips or cheeks; there are plenty of ethnographic examples of studs or labrets being worn in a variety of places on the body. Alternatively, they may represent two stages of ear piercing, with the smaller ones representing a first set and the second an adult set, although the shape of the smaller pair perhaps makes this less likely (Chapter 16). Either way, changes to appearance, in attire or hairstyles, for example, are often used to denote the end of childhood and are well-documented in the anthropological record (for example, Richards 1956, 102). As such, the studs could have signified a stage in the interred individuals' life, such as the change from child to adult, as well as their status.

The radiocarbon determination from a piece from one of the studs, 3709±33 BP, 2200–1980 cal BC (OxA-27915), is rather earlier than any of the other dates from the cist, including that of the cremation. This date is also earlier than the majority of other dated studs from other sites (Chapter 16). It might, if accepted, imply that the studs had been handed down as heirlooms between generations and, as such they may have held particular significance for the person who wore them. If heirlooms, they could also have represented a link to past generations and the cycle from youth to maturity.

The basketry container

The basketry container from the Whitehorse Hill cist is an exceptionally rare artefact. A review of British prehistoric wooden artefacts carried out in the late 1970s revealed that very few items of basketry have survived from prehistory, by comparison with other forms of worked wood (Coles *et al.* 1978). Although further objects have been recovered through more recent excavations of wetland sites, the number of earlier Bronze Age basketry objects in Britain and Ireland remains small. The surviving prehistoric examples cover a wide time-span, with Mesolithic fish traps and other baskets from Clowanstown, Co Meath, and North Wall, Dublin (Fitzgerald 2007), to bags from Aghintemple, County Longford (Raftery 1970), dating to the Neolithic and eel traps from Must Farm, Cambridgeshire, to the later Bronze Age (Symonds 2012). Most evidence for basketry takes the form of impressions in pottery. On the Isles of Scilly, impressions of matting have been identified on the bases of Early Bronze Age pottery found with the Knackyboy entrance grave (O'Neil 1952, pl. xiv) and frequently on Bronze Age ceramics from Scillonian settlements, especially at Nornour (Butcher 1978, fig. 36). However, as discussed above, despite the limited surviving evidence, basketry must have been a very commonly used medium for containers.

The Whitehorse Hill basketry container was made from three sections of bundle-coiled and sewn lime bast, sewn together with cattle hair to form an elongated container which would probably have resembled a lidded pot (Chapter 13). Although found in the Alpine region of Europe (for example, Harris 2010) and from Danish sites (Hald 1980, 128), lime bast has been much less frequently identified as a medium for prehistoric artefacts in Britain, where other materials such as hazel, alder and birch were employed for more robust baskets, and grasses, sedges and rushes for finer items (Henshall 1950; Brunning *et al.* 2013).

In part, the paucity of comparable lime bast artefacts is due to preservation conditions in Britain (Coles *et al.* 1978), but it may also be due to the fact that working with lime bast must have been a seasonal occupation and may have

therefore been less common than other forms of basketry, such as those using hazel or sedge, which could be quickly produced all year round. This is because bast fibres come from inside the bark of the tree. Production would have involved removing the bark with the bast fibres attached in the spring. The outer and inner bark was then removed and this was followed by the process of 'retting', soaking the stripped bast layers in water for several weeks until they separated. If not retted the pectin from the material oozes out in a mass (Hurcombe 2014, 30). The bast fibres then had to be rinsed and dried, at which point they could be used (Reichert 2007; Higgitt *et al.* 2011).

Despite involving a seasonal and lengthy process of manufacture, lime provided fibres which would have been durable and they have also been found to have useful properties in terms of the low absorption of water (Harris 2010). This would have meant that it was an ideal medium for containers, as the contents would have remained dry. As discussed above, in the absence of pottery, a light, durable and water-resistant material (Lord and Wood 1999) would have been very valuable to pastoralists moving their animals across upland areas such as Dartmoor, where the weather can be unpredictable and any reduction in the weight of things to be carried would have been appreciated.

The lime trees used for the basketry container cannot be closely sourced. Although towards the northern edge of their tolerance, and less common than in central lowland England where non acidic soils are found (Rackham 1986, 68–70), evidence for lime trees has been found in prehistoric contexts across south-west England and Wales (Taylor 1980; Orme and Coles 1983; Fyfe *et al.* 2003), which are more often characterized as being covered by oak and hazel woodlands. The pollen record for Dartmoor has produced little evidence for lime trees, although they are likely to have been present on the gravels in the deeper river valleys which fringe the moor (R. Fyfe, pers. comm.). This means that the lime bast container from the Whitehorse Hill cist could have been manufactured from relatively local trees. It is also possible that the container came from further afield and was an item which had been obtained through exchange, perhaps with communities to the east in the Exe Valley (Fyfe *et al.* 2003) or further away on the chalk, where lime was a dominant species in the wildwood and where its working was perhaps more common.

The cattle hair used to attach the sections of basketry together may have been chosen to create a decorative effect, as the hair around the top created a band comprising a pattern of light and dark segments. These are particularly evident in the reconstructed basketry container (Fig. 21.19). Indeed, the function of this patterning could be argued to have made the container distinctive, in the same way that decoration on pottery may have done. As discussed below, the cattle hair may also have carried symbolic resonances, especially if manufactured locally with hairs from particular animals.

The manufacture of the basketry container was certainly a fine example of craftsmanship, and for this reason, as

Figure 21.19: The replica basketry container (minus the lid). Note the decorative effect formed by the cattle hair. The original basketry container is in the background (Photograph: Plymouth Museum).

well as its water-resistant properties, it is likely to have been a valued item. Given the lack of evidence for ceramic vessels, it is likely that basketry was commonly used by communities on Dartmoor. As such, it may also have been a type of object which was closely linked to the social identity of moorland communities.

Braided armband or bracelet: cattle hair

The tin studs within the braided band have been discussed above, and here the discussion is focused on the materiality of the organic element. As has been described in Chapter 16, the bracelet or armband was made from cattle hairs and their braiding together involved considerable skill.

It is important to remember that the fibres which formed the body of the band may not have been randomly chosen and were possibly of as much significance as the tin element. Although there are no direct comparanda in the Early British Bronze Age, woven bands made from horse hair have been found in association with a Late Bronze hoard from Co Antrim in Ireland (Herity and Eogan 1989, 199). Animal hair may very well have carried its own symbolism, perhaps related to its colour or the animal it came from. Horses, for example, in both the Iron Age and early historic periods were symbols of status associated with the supernatural and religion (Wincott Heckett 1998; Green 1986, 91–94; Williams 2001; Poole 2013).

A close relationship between cattle and people would be unsurprising: anthropological study has revealed that cattle are frequently valued animals, especially for pastoralists who often form close bonds with their animals (Evans Prichard 1969; Turton 1980; Insoll *et al.* 2015), and it is likely that this was no less true in prehistoric Britain. Ray and Thomas (2003), for example, have suggested that there were no such things as 'mere' animals and that cattle and people were bound up in complex social relationships. Julian Thomas (2014, 408–410) has pointed out that cattle

were not just a material resource but that the herds were a repository of a collective history of exchange, feasts and alliances. Individual animals would have displayed their origins via their hair colour and build and are likely to have been displayed at gatherings.

Thomas's argument is based on evidence from Neolithic contexts but is probably also applicable for the Early Bronze Age. Cattle bones are known from barrows, as, for example, at Raunds, where a large-scale slaughter of animals is likely to have taken place (Harding and Healy 2007, 258–260). As noted above, cattle hides have also been identified at a number of burial sites (Table 21.2), again suggesting a close relationship between bovines and people.

If, as seems probable, the communities on Dartmoor were largely pastoralist herders then it is likely that cattle would have held a particular symbolic importance for them. The cattle hair from Whitehorse Hill may have come from a known animal from the herd and have been associated with a particular biography. It may have imbued the band, and thereby the wearer, with the spirit of the animal it was derived from and / or reinforced the link between people and animals.

The textile and animal-skin object

The textile and animal-skin object is comprised of two layers of nettle textile, edged with calf-skin beading fringed with triangles (Chapter 18). The animal skin was attached to the nettle textile by stitching of an exceptional standard. As with the lime bast, the preparation of nettle fibres would have required considerable labour, involving retting or manual stripping of the fibres using a stone tool, before they could be used to create a textile (Hurcombe 2014, 57).

The item is incomplete and it may have been part of a larger garment partly made from other materials which have not survived the conditions within the cist. The lack of certainty regarding the overall size of the item and the possibility that it may have been part of something larger makes identification difficult. This is made harder by the fact that the object from the Whitehorse Hill cist is almost without comparanda in a British context. Early Bronze Age textiles are relatively well-documented in Britain, but most survive as scraps or impressions (below).

Worked animal skins (as opposed to hides, above) are far less common and actual clothes from the British Bronze Age rarely survive. Where garments have been preserved they have most commonly been found in association with log coffin burials (Table 21.2). At King Barrow, Arne, in Dorset, a skeleton in a log coffin was found in 'deer skins stitched together' (Grinsell 1959). In Northumberland fragments of a skin, possibly of calf or kid, were found inside a log coffin at Cartington (Dixon 1913), and at Ford in Northumberland the inhumation within a log coffin was said to have been clothed in a 'leathern dress' with the stitching still visible (Greenwell 1877, 411). At Loose Howe, Yorkshire, an inhumation within a log coffin was recorded as being clothed or wrapped in a linen cloth (Elgee and Elgee 1949).

Earlier Bronze Age clothing, although of slightly later date, is much better documented in southern Scandinavia, where several Danish log coffin burials have produced finely made textile garments, as, for example, those from Borum Eshøj, Muldhhøj and Storehøj (Glob 1983; Randsborg and Christensen 2006). A range of textile clothes are known from these burials, including wraps, skirts, shirts and caps (Randsborg 2011; Harris 2012; 2014b). A similar range of clothing would probably have been found in Britain, and we could anticipate that it too would have been regarded as finery, although its deposition in the grave may have carried more meaning than simply status.

The calf skin used for the fringing and the beading may have carried its own symbolism: as discussed above, cattle would have been valued animals and, just as the hair chosen to make the braided band and to sew the basketry together may have involved a selection process, and have incorporated materials redolent with perceived symbolic properties, so the calf skin may also have carried particular meanings. Although no evidence for dyes could be detected (Chapter 18), the object may well have had a deliberately contrasting colour scheme, consisting of a lighter-coloured nettle textile central section fringed by dark animal-skin triangles. The contrasting of dark and light elements is found with both the necklace and the basketry container described above. All these objects may have been made in a world with a much more muted range of everyday colours than we are used to today (Hurcombe 2014, 121), but were intended to be as visually striking as possible (Fig. 21.20).

The materials used in the production of the textile and animal-skin object were therefore likely to have been highly valued in their own right and the distinguished quality of the sewing which joined the two materials together also suggests a prestigious item.

The question remains as to what the textile and animal-skin object from the Whitehorse Hill cist was. It may have

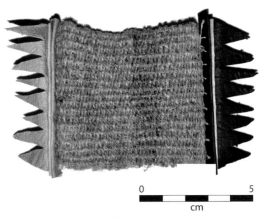

Figure 21.20: A section of the replica textile and animal-skin object. (Photograph: Plymouth Museum.)

been part of, or attached to, a larger garment, or it may have been a belt or a broad band or sash. Comparable, although narrower belts have been found in Denmark, as at Borum Eshøj, and these are likely to have signified the group affinity (age or gender) or status of their wearers. In Denmark, female graves are associated with the broadest and finest examples (Randsborg 2011, 35). The Whitehorse Hill cist item had not been repaired and was in very good condition. Like all the other items in the cist, it was a finely-crafted object which is likely to have taken hours to make. It had also been laid in the cist face up (Chapter 18), so that the workmanship and the symbolism of the object would have been readily evident to the onlooker when it was placed into the cist. This implies that it was not an everyday item and may have been worn as a ceremonial garment, a symbol which would have the denoted the social identity of the wearer and of the community who placed it there.

Textile fragments

By contrast with the unique textile and animal-skin object, the fragments of textile from the cist represent one of the more commonly found organic remains which are recovered from barrows (Table 21.2). In common with most other Early Bronze Age textiles, the identifiable fragments from the Whitehorse Hill cist were of a plain weave, although the material from which they were made could not be established (Chapter 8; Henshall 1950).

Most Early Bronze Age textiles do not survive as objects but instead are preserved as mineralised fragments on copper-alloy objects or as impressions in softer materials, or their former existence is inferred from other evidence. Mineralised fragments form the most commonly encountered evidence. In the south-west, at Harlyn Bay pit 32093, in Cornwall, for example, mineralized textile fragments had been preserved where they had come into contact with a copper-alloy pendant (Jones *et al.* 2011). Similarly, several copper-alloy objects found in Wessex barrows have revealed traces of textiles (Henshall 1950; Grinsell 1957; Table 21.2).

In addition to mineralised fragments, good evidence for textiles has survived where they have been preserved as impressions, as at Carvinack, Cornwall, where the imprint of a woven object was found in the clay beneath a barrow mound (Dudley 1964). More unusually, at the Manton barrow (Preshute G1a), in Wiltshire, impressions of a cloth associated with an inhumation burial were preserved in calcium carbonate (Grinsell 1957).

Rather more commonly, the presence of textiles has been inferred from the positions of other objects, such as the arrangement of human remains. For example, at Bincombe 13 in Dorset the positioning of the body suggested that it had been wrapped in a cloth which was held together by a copper-alloy pin (Grinsell 1982). Only very exceptionally have small amounts of actual textile been found preserved (Table 21.2). In Yorkshire, for example, small fragments of textile were found in association with an inhumation burial in grave 1 at Garton Slack 82 (Mortimer 1905, 234).

The textile fragments from the Whitehorse Hill cist had been burnt and were found in association with the cremated bone. As such, with the exception of a possible burnt wooden object (Chapter 7), it was the only artefactual material to have been burned with the body on the funeral pyre. Given the temperature that the pyre would have burned at, the fragments must have been part of a much larger piece of textile, most of which would have been consumed by the flames. Evidence for the burning of textiles as part of cremation rites has occasionally been found elsewhere, as at Weasenham Lyngs, Norfolk (Lawson 1986, 73). However, in most cases where textiles have been identified with Early Bronze Age cremations, as for example at Huntshaw 1, in Devon, (Doe 1875) or Durrington 11, Wiltshire (Grinsell 1957), they do not appear to have been burned. This implies that in the majority of instances, the burnt bone was collected from the pyre site and then wrapped in a cloth after the cremation had taken place. It might also imply that in most cases, the textile only needed to be large enough to hold the fragments of bone in a bundle. By contrast, at Whitehorse Hill it seems probable that the body had been wrapped in a large shroud or garment which was burned with the body.

As discussed above, evidence from elsewhere in Europe suggests that textiles were highly-valued items (Randsborg 2011, 116–118; Harris 2012). As such, the burning of a substantial piece of textile would have involved the destruction of a very valuable item. The ability to make such a sacrifice may have denoted the status of the deceased or of the family who consigned the textile to the flames. Given that the cremation may have been attended by a number of people, this could be seen as an extravagant act which would have added to the public spectacle of the rite of cremation.

Wood preserved as charcoal

The Whitehorse Hill cist contained a quantity of charcoal which was mostly derived from oak, although a smaller amount of hazel was also included (Chapter 7). The environmental evidence (Chapter 19) suggests that the oak is unlikely to have grown near to the cist and would therefore have been introduced to the site with the cremated bone. It could be argued that this was coincidental and represents the accidental incorporation of pyre material during the collection of the cremated bone. However, to dismiss it in this way would lose sight of the fact that the deposition of charcoal played a significant role in a wide range of ceremonial monuments across the south west (Tilley 1996; Jones 2005; Jones and Quinnell 2008) and particularly in relation to Bronze Age monuments on Dartmoor.

Indeed, charcoal is the mostly widely documented material to have been recorded from Dartmoor's cists and cairns, especially within pits (Johnston 2005; Table 21.1). Again, while it could be argued for some cases that it had been accidentally introduced, there are others where this was patently not the case. At Throwleigh 2, for example, a deposit of charcoal was recovered from a pit cut into the base of a cist (Burnard 1902). Comparable pits have been recorded in Dartmoor's cairns, as, for example, at Shaugh Moor, where four of the five sites within the cairn group were found to contain small pits packed with charcoal (Wainwright *et al.* 1979). A similar pattern has been found at Headon Down, where two turf barrows were found only to cover charcoal-rich pits (Dyer and Quinnell 2013). With this in mind, it is probable that the inclusion of charcoal within the Whitehorse Hill cist was deliberate.

The selection of oak is also likely to have been deliberate as it would have made a good choice of wood for use on the pyre; it was commonly selected as pyre material and is also recovered from ceremonial monuments across the south west and beyond (Jones 2005; Pollard 1967; 1971; Finn 2012, 81).

Oak charcoal is frequently found in association with upland ceremonial monument complexes (Tilley 2010; Jones 2004–5) and this is of interest because oak trees are unlikely to have grown on the high moors during the Bronze Age. This is undoubtedly true for Whitehorse Hill, which is exposed and was already a place where peat was developing (Chapter 19). This implies that oak was selected from a range of available trees found in more sheltered locales and taken for use in pyres and fires before being deliberately buried as charcoal in cists and cairns. As Zoë Hazell comments in Chapter 7, the wood used in the Whitehorse Hill cist pyre was not freshly cut but had either been in a stockpile or had been collected as dead windfall material. Given the amount of wood required to cremate a body it is likely that it had been stored for a while prior to use in the cremation.

This need not be surprising. Anthropologists have found that all over the world, rituals marking human life cycles make use of trees, which through their longevity, growth and natural cycles, can become loaded with symbolism (Rival 1998; Brennand and Taylor 2003). Trees themselves can be conceived as being 'alive', or containing spirits, or as having metaphorical analogies with the human body (Bonnemere 1998) and the cycle of growth and death (Parker Pearson *et al.* 2013). For these reasons, certain species of tree frequently become important to particular communities for use in ritual and burial-related activities (for example, Busia 1954; Hackett 1996, 40; Giambelli 1998).

The symbolic importance of particular trees to prehistoric communities of later periods is well-documented in Europe. Iron Age communities in Britain and Gaul were reported by classical sources as identifying deities with trees and sacred groves were associated with temples and places of worship; the oak tree was often seen as acting as an *axis mundi* in cosmological schemes (Green 1986, 22; Aldhouse-Green 2000; Helms 2009). Oak was also used in Early Bronze Age funerary contexts in another way, in the form of log coffins, and it has been suggested that there may have been a symbolic link between the deceased person and the wood of the coffin (Parker Pearson *et al.* 2013).

With these examples in mind, it therefore seems very probable that oak was consciously chosen for use in ceremonial monuments across Dartmoor and elsewhere across the south west, reduced to charcoal by burning and incorporated into the fabric of cists and cairns. Oak was perhaps therefore burnt with the body in order to help convey the human spirit to a different cosmological level; perhaps the perceived symbolic spirit or essence of the burnt tree was, like the cremated bone, captured and placed into the appropriate context.

The presence of so much oak charcoal might also have implications for the location of the pyre. It is possible that the wood was carried to a pyre site on Whitehorse Hill; however, this would have involved hauling a large amount of heavy wood to the summit of the hill. This is possible, but perhaps it is more likely that the cremation took place on lower ground, nearer to a place where oak woodland was found.

The cremation

Given that the deceased cannot control what happens to their mortal remains, either in terms of their treatment or the choice of the place where they are finally laid to rest, we can consider those remains as having been a resource to be manipulated or displayed in much the same way that the other deposits in the cist were. In short, as Parker Pearson (1982) made clear in his study of post-medieval burial practices in Cambridge, the dead do not bury themselves and their interment is tied up in a web of social and symbolic practices and strategies.

The cremation deposit was poorly preserved (Chapter 6) and this may in part reflect localised conditions within the cist and the peat mound, as cremated bone normally survives well in the acidic soils (Kalsbeek and Richter 2006) which predominate across the south-west peninsula (Jones and Quinnell 2008). In fact, most of the recorded Early Bronze Age burials in the region are cremations. However, the cremation from the cist was underweight

and, as will be discussed below, the poor condition of the cremation may have been due to its treatment and storage prior to burial.

Cremations are known from other cists and cairns on Dartmoor, as at Lydford 23 and Manaton 12 (Baring-Gould 1898; Bate 1872; Table 21.1), and no inhumation burials have been recorded. Of course, this may largely be a consequence of preservation conditions, which are unfavourable for the survival of unburnt bone. Recent study has, however, made it apparent that there is widespread evidence for differing treatment of human remains across the south west (Jones 2011a) and, as noted above in relation to Chagford 4, there are also cists which are both too small to have held articulated inhumation burials and which are lacking in any cremated human remains. This might imply that some cists never contained human remains or that in certain circumstances remains may have been partly or totally removed for use elsewhere (below).

The gender of the Whitehorse Hill burial could not be established through osteological analysis. It was possible to determine that it was a person probably aged between 15 and 25, however, and the artefactual associations suggest that the deceased is likely to have been female. Although no further data are available for Dartmoor, young people have been recorded at other funerary sites across the south west, including the recently analysed burial from Harlyn Bay (Jones *et al.* 2011), and, as elsewhere, it is evident that the deaths of some children were dealt with in the same way as those of adults who were afforded a burial (Fowler 2013, 244). Female cremations are also well represented in the burial record in the wider south-west region, including those from an excavated site at Elburton, near Plymouth (Watts and Quinnell 2001). In short, on current knowledge, age and gender do not seem to have been a factor in determining whether a person was cremated, although it is possible that the treatment of human bone and the artefacts selected to accompany them may have been influenced by these factors.

One reason why the burial could not be sexed was that it was of a low weight for the age of the person. With a weight of 708g the cremation was less than half of what might be expected from an Early Bronze Age burial of an adult (McKinley 1997; 2000). This might simply imply that people had been less than effective in collecting the burnt bone from the pyre site or were unconcerned about completeness. However, although the burial is rather lighter than those found in Wessex, it is fairly typical of the south west as a whole, where complete single cremations appear to be a rarity. By contrast, multiple, partial and token deposits are increasingly being identified (Jones 2012) and the range of burial practices found during the Early Bronze Age parallels those found in other regions outside Wessex (Gamble and Fowler 2013).

Unfortunately, with the exception of the Whitehorse Hill cremation, none of the human remains from Dartmoor has been the subject of modern osteological analysis. Nonetheless, there are hints that this pattern of partial or token deposition of cremated bone is found at other cists across the moor. For example, at Lydford 42 'faint indications of bone ashes' were recovered from a stone-covered pit beneath a cairn, and at Peter Tavy 39 'a little bone ash' was recovered from the paving at the base of the cist (Grinsell 1978; Baring-Gould 1898). The small amounts of bone which are said to have come from these sites suggest that in many cases less than complete remains of cremated bodies were being placed into cists on Dartmoor. Beyond the moor incomplete burials have been recorded from barrows in east Devon, as at Farway, and the Upton Pyne 248b barrow produced only fragments of bone (Jones and Quinnell 2008; Pollard and Russell 1969). To the west, in Cornwall, token and partial burials are known from a number of sites, including Treligga barrows 1 and 2 on the north Cornish coast, Davidstow sites III, XIX, and XXV on Bodmin Moor, and Chysauster in Penwith, where five cremations averaged just 150g (Christie 1985; 1988; Smith 1996).

When considered in relation to these sites, the Whitehorse Hill cremation can be clearly seen to fit a wider pattern of activity found across the south west, which frequently involved only part of the remains of a person or persons being formally interred within cairns, barrows or cists. In some cases where the burial deposit is extremely small, it is possible that, in common with other materials such as quartz or charcoal, the human bone itself may have become a symbolic or magical substance (Brück 2004a; Rebay-Salisbury 2010; Booth *et al.* 2011, 134; Jones 2012) which had become divorced from any notion of individual identity. However, in the case of the Whitehorse Hill cremation, enough material had been gathered together to form a coherent deposit, and had not been intermixed with other materials, such as quartz.

It is also possible that cremated bone from the cist had been curated for some time before it was buried, although the radiocarbon dating from the Whitehorse Hill cist cannot prove this (Chapter 20). Delays between cremation and burial have been suggested elsewhere. For example, the recent radiocarbon dating of cremated bone from Barrow 1 at Cossington, Leicestershire, strongly indicates that one of the cremations had been curated for some time before burial within the barrow (Thomas 2013). Recent work on Early Bronze Age burials from Orkney has revealed that not only are cremations incomplete in terms of skeletal remains but that they are consistently earlier than the charcoal they are found with, implying that human remains had been burnt as part of secondary rites long after death had occurred (Richards and Wright 2014, 46) or that parts of 'old' cremations had been curated and were being deposited with 'new' charcoal.

As discussed above, it is likely that the Whitehorse Hill body had not been burnt on the site but had been cremated in a valley below and the cremated bone subsequently brought to the cist. As a result, there may have been a time lag between cremation and burial. Consequently, it is possible that there was a delay between the act of cremation and that of deposition while an appropriate site for the burial was chosen and the cist constructed, or because social custom dictated that there should be a deliberate gap between the act of cremation and that of burial. Stages between death, funerary rites and final place of burial are, of course, well-documented in the anthropological record (Hertz 2009; Metcalf and Huntington 1993, 116), and these are often associated with an underlying desire by the community to be seen to control the disruption caused by the process of death and also to remove the pollution thought to have arisen from it (for example, Bloch and Parry 1982; Douglas 1992, 176–179). During such a period, pieces of bone could, of course, have become lost or have deliberately been removed from the Whitehorse Hill cremation.

However, if human bone was considered important in its own right, then perhaps portions of it were circulated to mourners or other members of the community (Woodward 1993; Brück 2004b; 2006; 2009). In historical times human remains in the form of saint's bones were kept as relics and pieces of hair from a deceased person retained as objects of mourning (Hutton 2013, 335; Llewellyn 1996, 95–96). Pieces from the cremation could therefore have been deposited elsewhere in other contexts. Indeed, study of Bronze Age monuments in the south west has revealed that small amounts of cremated bone ended up in a variety of contexts, including ceremonial monuments and in other places such as pits (Jones 2005; Jones and Quinnell 2014, 132). Elsewhere, cremated bone has even been found to be incorporated within the fabric of pottery (Curtis *et al.* 2010).

Again, activity associated with the breaking down and circulating of human remains has been widely documented by anthropological studies; for example, the Yąnomamö of the Amazon are known to have ground up cremated bone for use in drinks that were consumed at funerary rituals (Chagnon 1997, 115). By contrast, some North American Indian societies kept bones and other human remains in what are termed 'soul bundles' or 'death bundles' (Hall 1997, 24–31). These could be made of either cloth or hide and, as well as the human remains, could contain other personal items, such as awls. They were respected and could be passed on as heirlooms, and after appropriate ceremonies to release the soul, they could in some societies be reburied (Hall 1997, 29). Although it is not possible to make direct analogies for the treatment of human remains between societies which are separated to such a degree in time and space, these ethnographic instances offer some insight into the potential range of practices involving the circulation of human remains.

Despite the difficulty with drawing direct anthropological analogy, the circulation of human remains might account for why some sites have produced very tiny amounts of bone, as, for example, the Honiton 3 ring cairn and Farway 21 in east Devon, or Treligga barrow 2 on the north Cornish coast (Christie 1985; Pollard 1971; Jones and Quinnell 2008). It may also explain why the Whitehorse Hill cist cremation was underweight and potentially 'older' than some of the other artefacts within the cist.

Summary: what do the contents of the cist tell us?

The evidence from the Whitehorse Hill cist makes it clear that a potentially large range of organic finds must be missing from other excavated sites across the moor and beyond. The artefactual assemblage can be viewed as a collection of high-status objects, and collectively they certainly constitute the 'richest' known Early Bronze Age burial from Dartmoor. The organic survival means that it is one of most important assemblages from the whole of south-west Britain. All of the items were finely made, demonstrating high levels of craftsmanship and/or made from rare materials, with several items, notably the amber and the shale beads, clearly originating far beyond the moor. As has been demonstrated elsewhere (Needham 2009; Needham *et al.* 2006), long-distance journeys and exchanges were undertaken by at least some individuals and it has been argued that this would have led to certain people accruing status, which in turn becomes evident in the burial record (for example, Fitzpatrick 2011). The contents of the cist make it evident that the people who moved across Dartmoor with their animals did not exist in isolation from more distant communities.

Once on Dartmoor, however, it is likely that the objects were understood and deployed according to local tradition and custom: the importance of regional variation and preferences has been acknowledged in the preceding discussion. For example, it is evident that for much of the Early Bronze Age certain categories of find, including ceramics and metalwork, were largely excluded from the burial repertoire. The artefacts from the cist may have empowered the wearer but their materiality and the way that they were worn may also have 'identified' the wearer as a member of a pastoralist community. This is likely to have extended to the composition of the burial deposit itself, which, it has been argued, falls within the wider pattern of burial practices found across the south-west peninsula.

It has also been argued that the materials from which the artefacts were made were themselves important, some because they were rare or difficult to work, others, perhaps, because they were of a particular colour or reflectivity. Many of the items may have been significant because they carried connotations or the essences of the things they were made from, or because they denoted particular places or other things (for example, animals and plants) which were significant to people in the Bronze Age. Some artefacts were newly made whereas others may already have had biographies. In some cases the properties of the materials themselves may well have been believed to possess powers that were associated with the supernatural. Possessing or wearing these objects may quite literally have 'empowered' those individuals who had access to them.

Choreographing the burial

Background

This section of the chapter considers the assemblage within the cist in terms of how the burial and artefactual material came together and how it was intended to be viewed.

In recent years, it has been recognised that far from being neutral places of interment, where riches were deposited beside a body simply to display wealth, prehistoric graves were complex spaces containing objects with diverse temporalities which were designed to be read. It has also become increasingly evident that graves could be revisited and were not necessarily sacrosanct spaces that could not be reopened.

Several studies have focused on the placing of signifying artefacts around the graveside, but there has been a tendency to assume that objects were directly associated with the deceased person (for example, Thomas 1991). Some commentators have considered the 'biography' of artefacts which are found within Early Bronze Age graves, and have pointed out that these could have different life histories from one another, with some being curated heirlooms (Woodward 2002; Healy and Harding 2004; Woodward *et al.* 2005). Even within the same grave, some objects could be newly made whereas others were old and worn (Woodward and Hunter 2015, chap. 10), and the combining of artefacts with different biographies is likely to be significant. Laurent Oliver (1999), in a seminal paper on central European Iron Age 'princely' graves, has focused on the need to consider the temporalities of the artefacts which are found within 'high-status' graves, and has argued that they arose from a variety of interactions across time and space, which include the life-cycle of objects from creation to deposition and their relationship with the dead person extending from the erection of the burial monument and its later use or reuse.

A second, related strand of enquiry has been to consider the role of the deceased's kin and community over selecting what was, or conversely was not, included within the grave and how the open grave may have been read by onlookers. Julian Thomas (1991) and John Barrett (1994, 126–127) have suggested that Early Bronze Age grave-associated objects were selected and arranged by the living to create a particular set of potentially fictionalised meanings which could be 'read' by mourners at the graveside. Joanna Brück (2004a) has argued that grave-goods could have represented the relationships between the deceased and the people who were organising the burial. Likewise, Chris Fowler (2004, 75) has suggested that artefacts and human remains were used by the community to create and express particular ideas about identity or 'personhood' which may have been different from the actual lived reality of the individual. In other words, once the body had ceased to belong to the individual, it lost its autonomy and became controlled by the community. As such it could be used to focus social relations at a particular place (Fowler 2013, 100).

It is also true to say that the cist as a structural form lends itself to detailed interpretation *par excellence*. The shape and well-defined, bounded character of the cist meant that it was an ideal device to 'frame' events and to cut them off and contain them. But, as will be discussed, it was also a structure which could be revisited.

With these themes in mind the remainder of this section considers the time period over which the assemblage from the cist was brought together and the biographies of the objects. The status and personhood of the individual, and the structuring / 'wrapping' of the contents, are contemplated. Lastly, the continuing accessibility of the cist to community members will also be discussed.

Assembling the cist's contents

Time and tempo

Over the last few decades several writers have highlighted the importance of the biographies of objects (Appadurai 1986). Gosden and Marshall (1999), for example, in relation to Fijian sperm whale teeth necklaces, have highlighted that items can gain in prestige because of the patina which they have developed through being exchanged and touched by individuals. The study of artefacts from Early Bronze Age burials elsewhere in Britain has revealed that older objects could be buried in much later contexts. For example, at Pendleton in Lancashire, Beaker-period goldwork has recently been found with a much later Early Bronze Age Collared Urn and a cremation burial (Barrowclough 2014). On Dartmoor, inspection of the pommel from the Hameldown barrow (Manaton 11) revealed repairs, which, suggested that it was not new at the time of burial; the same is true of the Rillaton cup from Cornwall, which was judged to be well-worn (Needham *et al.* 2006; Needham and Sheridan 2014).

As discussed above, some of the artefacts from the Whitehorse Hill cist were newly made and had immediate connotations. Others may have been part of the life histories of numerous individuals and as such carried many associations; these may have been included because they evoked connections with other places or the past (cf Edmonds 2012). The coming together of the artefacts within the cist represents a moment in time when the life histories of the artefacts were drawn together to form an assemblage. Of course, their biographies have continued from the time that they were excavated, analysed, interpreted and displayed (Fowler 2013, chap. 2).

The focus of this section is, however, to consider the artefactual assemblage up to the point that it became sealed within the cist and prior to when it was reopened in 2011. It is also worth noting that with the exception of a fragment from a possible wooden artefact and a textile shroud, none of the artefacts had been placed in the funeral pyre. So none need have been directly associated with the time or act of burning the body.

Two strands of evidence from the cist can potentially assist with building up a picture of the processes by which things came together as an assemblage. The first is radiocarbon dating; the second derives from the results of the analyses of the artefacts themselves, in terms of the wear and condition that they display and the order in which they were found inside the cist.

Chronological modelling (Chapter 20) provides estimates for the dates of material incorporated into the cist spanning a period *60–280 years* (*95% probability*; Fig. 20.4), probably *125–240 years* (*68% probability*), from *1845–1685* (*95% probability*; *start_cist_contents*; Fig 20.3) probably *1780–1719 cal BC* (*68% probability*) to *1730–1600 cal BC* (*95% probability*; *cist_finished*; Fig 20.3), probably *1690–1620 cal BC* (*68% probability*). The material from the cist clearly represents material of different ages (T'=29.9, T'(5%)=18.3, ν=10). The cremated bone (*OxA-26376*) is earlier than the pelt (*OxA-27446*) and basket (*OxA-27915*); 95.5% probable. It is therefore very probable that the cremation was not buried immediately, this might explain the low mass of cremated bone that was recovered (Chapter 6).

Assuming that the cremation had not been buried immediately and considering the condition of the artefacts themselves, we can perhaps begin to construct a model for the relationships between the items.

Again, there are contrasts between artefacts. For example, within the composite necklace, several of the amber beads were worn and had probably been restrung, but the clay and shale beads were by contrast fresh and may have been specifically acquired or made for incorporation within it. The necklace was therefore a hybrid of old and new, as well as of the local and the distant. As such it may have been a possession which belonged to the deceased individual, or, could have been assembled to accompany the deceased, made up from a combination of 'heirloom' items and newly acquired or made items.

The pelt appears to have been in good condition and is unlikely to have been very old at the time that the cremation was put into the cist. This was certainly also the case for the basketry container and the textile and animal-skin object, both of which appeared to be in very good condition. Likewise, the flint had only been lightly used and is unlikely to have been curated for any significant period of time. Given that these artefacts were very new they may not have been directly connected with the deceased individual, and therefore could represent objects which were selected by the community as items which were appropriate for inclusion.

Lastly, the matted plant material represents the shortest temporal cycle which could be identified. The identification of purple moor-grass and meadowsweet pollen suggests that the plant materials were collected locally in the late summer. This is perhaps congruent with the cycle of upland moorland use by the pastoralists who assembled the burial.

In summary, rather than interpreting the contents of the cist as the product of one moment in time, it is also possible to see them as a combination of intersecting temporal cycles which involved things with different biographies being drawn together to form the deposit. That is to say, the assemblage included things which might have pre-dated the deceased person, the cremated remains themselves and things which could have been contemporary with them, objects which post-dated the act of cremation, and finally the plant remains which belonged to the season when the contents of the cist were assembled.

By considering the contrasting timeframes of the components of the assemblage it can be argued that the contents represent an 'orchestrated' collection of objects. The way that these may have been intended to be 'read' is considered in the next part of this section.

The context of the cist: status and display

In the first part of this chapter much of the emphasis was placed on the craftsmanship, rarity and value or status of the artefacts, the latter qualities both in terms of their inherent symbolism and their ability to potentially denote the social standing of the deceased and, by association, that of the community. This section considers how the artefacts came to be assembled within the cist and the ways they and the burial deposit itself could be read or interpreted.

Given the large number of finely made artefacts, a straightforward interpretation of the burial deposit would be that we are looking at the high-status burial of a 15–25 year old, probably female individual from a well-connected family or community. Indeed, this is largely the interpretation given up to this point. The non-organic finds are broadly comparable to other Early Bronze Age cremation burials and barrow-associated assemblages found across the British Isles (for example, Harding and Healy 2007; Barclay and Halpin 1999, 163; Thomas 2008; Needham 2012) and western Europe (Harding 2000, chap. 3; Rebay-Salisbury 2010) throughout the later third to mid-second millennium cal BC. It is of interest that the Whitehorse Hill cist, which is likely to be that of a younger woman, dates to the period when ostentatious female cremation burials become more evident in the archaeological record (Brück 2009; Sheridan 2012).

Indeed, in light of the clear contacts which existed across Europe in the second millennium, and the extended connections which have been demonstrated by some of the artefacts, it would be fanciful not to perceive the Whitehorse Hill burial within the context of a wider Bronze Age world (for example, Kristiansen and Larsson 2005; Needham 2009; Needham *et al.* 2006). It is, therefore, at one level entirely correct to see the Whitehorse Hill cist burial as a rich interment related to (and within) a wider tradition of high-status burials, including those found in Wessex in which wealth was frequently displayed.

Nonetheless, it is also important to remember that there was a good deal of regional diversity in the burial record across north-west Europe during the second millennium cal BC (Wilkin and Vander Linden 2015), and that attitudes and reactions to death are complex and culturally specific (for example, Seale 1998, 144). High-

status objects in burial contexts can be a relative and not always a straightforward indicator of the actual wealth of the deceased individual in the wider world. For example, relatively recently documented burials of members of the Romany community include examples of gold and silver jewellery and money being deposited into the grave (Vesey-Fitzgerald 1973, 85–88), whereas, by contrast, other contemporary affluent communities strongly avoid such actions in commemorating the dead. It is therefore necessary to consider how 'high-status' the Whitehorse Hill burial was in relation to other burials in the south west and, in particular, to those on Dartmoor. That is to say, how it sits within its local and regional context.

As we have seen from the discussion of the artefacts above, and as Table 21.1 demonstrates, the Whitehorse Hill burial is, in a Dartmoor context, exceptional. Despite there being over 100 recorded excavations, most Dartmoor cists and cairns appear to have been, beyond the occasional flint flake, 'empty'. This is, however, very likely to be an erroneous picture because of the complete decay of organic remains at other sites and, of course, in the case of the largely antiquarian excavations, the possibility of previous disturbance which was not recognised or recorded. Nonetheless, a straightforward comparison between the non-organic components of the Whitehorse Hill assemblage (pin, composite necklace and flint) and other burials, the only site to approach it in terms of non-organic exotica is the Hameldown Barrow (Manaton 11), with its very fine and broadly contemporary Camerton-Snowshill dagger with an amber and gold-studded pommel (Fig. 21.21). Given the lack of other comparably 'rich' burials on Dartmoor, if we are to interpret the Hameldown and Whitehorse Hill interments as elite burials on the basis of their non-organic components, they would have been the product of a very narrow or short-lived hierarchy.

Moving beyond Dartmoor, richer burials are occasionally found in Devon in the period after *circa* 2000 cal BC and more commonly after *circa* 1750 cal BC. Examples include those at North Molton, Upton Pyne and Farway (Pollard and Russell 1969; Kirwan 1872; Jones 2011a). The cremation at Upton Pyne barrow 4, for example, was associated with an accessory vessel, a copper-alloy dagger and a copper-alloy pin (Kirwan 1872; Jones and Quinnell 2013) (Figs. 21.22 and 21.23) and has recently been dated to the end of the Early Bronze Age, 3220±30 BP, 1600–1420 cal BC at 92.6% (SUERC-39125) (Jones and Quinnell 2013), which is later than the Whitehorse Hill cist.

However, closer inspection of the record for these exceptional sites reveals that many of the 'exotic' artefacts, such as the shale cup from Farway 32 (Fig. 21.24) or the Camerton-Snowshill dagger from Huntshaw 2, were not placed in direct association with the burial but were separated from it (Jones and Quinnell 2008; 2013). As such they differ from most of the richer Wessex burials and cannot necessary be directly associated with the deceased person. In other words, 'exotic' items such as these may have signified the status of the community and / or the

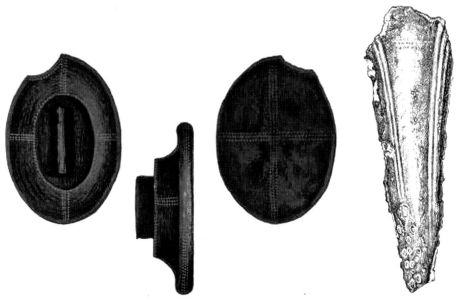

Figure 21.21: The Hameldown Camerton-Snowshill dagger with the amber and gold pommel. (After Bate 1872.)

Figure 21.22: The accessory vessel from Upton Pyne. (Photograph: Royal Albert Memorial Museum, Exeter.)

symbolism of the buried artefact more strongly than the importance of the buried individual.

The same pattern is also true for Cornwall: barrow-associated artefacts become more numerous after 2000 cal BC but few 'rich' artefactual assemblages are directly linked with the remains of individuals. The Rillaton barrow on Bodmin Moor (Smirke 1867; Jones 2012) provides a rare example of an individual who was associated with high-status 'grave goods', including the gold cup, a Camerton-Snowshill dagger, beads and pottery. Elsewhere, however, the link is less direct. At Harlyn Bay, for example, inhumation burials were not accompanied by artefacts, as opposed to mixed, multiple cremation deposits which were (Jones *et al.* 2011; Jones and Mikulski in prep.). This pattern could be seen as marking a community of ancestors and denying, rather than acknowledging, individuality.

In summary, the Whitehorse Hill cist burial was assembled at a time when high-status burials are found

Figure 21.23: The copper-alloy knife-dagger from Upton Pyne. (Photograph: Royal Albert Memorial Museum, Exeter.)

Figure 21.24: The artefacts from Farway barrow 32. (After Hutchinson 1880.)

across Britain and Europe and many of the objects found within the cist reflect the tastes of the period. It also occurred at a time when barrow-associated artefacts were becoming more prevalent in the south-west region, although frequently not in direct association with a buried individual. By contrast with the overwhelming majority of excavated cists on Dartmoor and wider region, the Whitehorse Hill cist burial represents the placing of high-status objects with an individual. The following section will consider whether this reflected the social standing of the interred individual or that of the wider community.

Constructing personhood

Returning to the Whitehorse Hill cist itself, we can envisage a scenario where, following the construction of the cist, on arrival at the site, the items were placed into the cist on a layer of plant material, in view of the participants, and the cremation, wrapped inside the pelt was put at one end. The objects could have been displayed in the cist, where their quality and associations may have been admired by onlookers. The artefacts were then covered by a second matted plant layer and the peaty layer (8), although the latter could have entered at a much later date in time (below). Finally the capstone was lowered. Arguably the

prestige of those who had arranged the burial would have been enhanced and the place remembered as the resting place of a high-ranking individual.

This basic sequence is likely to be correct but, given that a period of time could have elapsed between the death of the individual and their burial, the family and community members had a period of time to gather and assemble the finely-made, precious things which reflected the position both of the deceased person and of those who contributed items to the cist.

If there was a significant span of time between the death of the interred individual and the act of burial, it is worth considering how far it was the actual identity of the deceased which was being commemorated. In other words, was this person remembered as a specific individual? Or was the 'personhood' created by the act of burial an idealised creation, which said more about family or community status, identity and beliefs, than straightforward remembrance of a deceased individual. The name of the individual may still have been remembered but their actual life history and deeds may have been forgotten, embellished or mythologized.

Similarly, if the accompanying objects had been amassed over a lengthy period of time, there is a question of how 'rich' the burying community was in reality: had people been gathering and storing materials until sufficient things were available, or could be spared? It is possible that a delay between death and the burial had occurred, during which complex funerary rituals of separation, transformation and reincorporation took place (Van Gennep 1960, 146–165) and appropriate items could be acquired for deposition. Alternatively, it is possible that the time was right for some things, including the cremation and its pelt wrapping, to pass out of circulation in daily life and into the cist. Viewed in this way, the artefacts could be seen as being as much about the conveying of a contrived image associated with the deceased, rather than as direct markers of individual status. The assembled artefacts could have been intended to signify an elite female persona, but it is also possible that some other identity was indicated, relating, for example, to some form of specialist knowledge or particular skills and abilities of the deceased, or to the social or kin group with which they were associated (Fowler 2013, 88).

'Wrapping' the cist

It is worth briefly considering the 'cremation bundle' as a component of the overall assemblage. The interment within the cist obviously involved funerary activity and human remains, but it is possible that it had become a valued magical bundle of bones which belonged to the community. Bundles of cremated material could have become significant supernaturally charged items, with their own 'personalities'. As noted above, token amounts of cremated bone are frequently recorded in barrows across the south-west, and these often end up in 'ritual', rather than straightforward burial-related contexts. The cremation could have ended up in the cist because it was a propitious time for the bundle to be deposited, and the other artefacts could also have reached the point in their 'biographies' where it was appropriate for them to be taken out of circulation.

Some light can perhaps be shed on this by considering the order in which things were placed in the cist and how they were arranged, in the way that a structured deposit within a pit might be analysed (for example, Richards and Thomas 1984; Brittain 2004). At the base of the cist was the matted plant layer, and directly upon this the textile and animal-skin object was laid out. This was placed face up, so that the workmanship and symbolism of the object was visible. However, it would not have been visible for long as it was directly overlain by the next object, which was the pelt with the cremation inside it. This would have entirely hidden the textile and animal-skin object from view. The pelt effectively wrapped and concealed the cremation and the copper-alloy pin, which may itself have represented a symbolic closure of the 'bundle'; the pelt would have been more than adequate to enclose the deposit of bones, and it would have become lost amongst the hair of the pelt.

The final item to go in was the basketry container. This partly rested on the pelt and the cremation. It held the beads, the studs, the flint and almost certainly the braided tin-studded band. Although they could have been circulated beforehand, all of these collected items would, because they were inside the container, have *de facto* been invisible to mourners once the basketry container was inside the cist. This meant that much of the contents of the cist were layered and enclosed within wrappings which concealed their contents and potentially transformed or added meanings to them, including those of persona or status (Harris 2014b). It may have been the case, as Harding and Healy (2007, 243) have pointed out, that most of the artefacts in Early Bronze Age burials were wrapped or otherwise hidden and not put on display.

In other words, if we think about the assemblage within the cist as a deliberately structured deposit, it becomes evident that not all things were on display at the same time, and they in no way 'framed' the cremated remains to create a holistic, immediately 'readable' persona. Instead, there was a collection of diverse things, mostly contained in wrappings, which had been packaged as discrete bundles.

Consequently, as a group, they could not be 'read' by onlookers unless those individuals were directly involved with bringing the objects together, with viewing or inspecting items during the infilling of the cist, or by subsequently taking them out and unwrapping them. This latter possibility is considered in the following section.

Community chest

The possibility that the contents of the cist were accessible raises intriguing questions as to whether all the items arrived at one time as a group or whether they were placed and re-placed on more than one occasion. Some or all

of them may have been considered not to be in a final resting place but only 'temporarily resting'; they may have been circulated in the past and could be circulated in the future. As a parallel, Stuart Needham (2001), for example, has argued that Bronze Age metalwork could have been retrieved from hoards for ritual uses, and in Ireland sacred objects such as lunulae may have been taken out of bogs for use in ceremonies (Becker 2008). Again, the opening of ancient graves is well-documented in early medieval literature, sometimes for grave robbing but also to obtain items. In the *Laxdaela* saga, for example, a sword known as *Skofnung* was retrieved from a burial mound (Magnusson and Palsson 1969, 239).

Likewise, there is also anthropological evidence for the opening of cists. For example, the Konyak Nagas of northern India would separate the head from their dead chief's body and bury it in a stone cist, with the eyes facing towards the village path. A year later they would reopen the cist and turn the skull around so that it looked away from the path (Fürer-Haimendorf 1969, 92).

There is in fact a growing body of evidence for both the reuse of monuments and for the movement of human remains during the Early Bronze Age. It is apparent that graves were frequently revisited and accessed and what we see in the archaeological record may often represent only the last time a site was visited. At Raunds in Northamptonshire, for example, several barrows showed evidence for later burials being cut into earlier graves whereas in other cases graves appear to have been opened without further burials being made within them (Harding and Healy 2007, 228).

The frequent presence of disarticulated bone within Early Bronze Age funerary deposits may also indicate that human remains were either being taken away or added to existing burials (Petersen 1972; Harding and Healy 2007, 229–230). For example, at Barnack in Cambridgeshire, an adult inhumation was found in a grave which had probably been disturbed by the insertion of the disarticulated remains of an infant (Donaldson 1977). Cremations and inhumations are also found together in graves in the north of Britain; Petersen (1972) suggested that in that area monuments may have been intended from the outset to hold subsequent burials.

Most identified evidence for post-burial revisiting of graves has been associated with inhumations, but there is also evidence for cremations being moved. At ring-ditch site C at Roxton, Bedfordshire, excavation revealed that an original adult cremation deposit associated with Collared Urn sherds had been exhumed and redeposited into another context (Taylor and Woodward 1985).

Unmounded cists are more accessible than cists and other graves below barrows, the positions of which can become lost. This is especially true of sites such as the Whitehorse Hill cist where distinctive capstones are likely to have been left exposed and not covered by a cairn or mound. In fact, investigation of several cist sites has revealed evidence for them being re-opened after the original deposition. At Barns Farm, Dalgety, in Fife, for example, cist 1 was found to contain a cremation and an inhumation which may have been added subsequently (Watkins 1982). In north-east England, at Dour Hill, Northumberland, a cist with a massive capstone was opened and more remains were probably inserted at least once after the original burial was deposited (Fowler 2013, 165). Likewise, at Hasting Hill, Tyne and Wear, one of the cists beneath a cairn was found to contain the remains of three individuals (Gamble and Fowler 2013); these included bones from a young child which appear to be weathered, implying that they had not been buried immediately. The number of interred individuals makes it likely that there was sequential use of the cist or deliberate co-mingling of skeletal material deposited within it (Gamble and Fowler 2013). Revisiting a cist also seems to have occurred at Gains Law ring cairn, Northumberland, where a sherd missing from a Food Vessel accompanying a cremation in one cist was found in a second (Fowler 2013, 239).

This widespread activity suggests that during the Early Bronze Age, human bones could be stored, moved, reburied, and recovered, possibly for circulation in other contexts. As Fowler (2013, 245) states, such activity might have involved rituals when objects and bones were added to or removed from cists. If, as has been argued elsewhere (Jones 2013), cists in the south west can be seen as part of a continuum of features which acted as receptacles for curated items and heirlooms, then burials may also have been viewed as a form of 'community property'. The removal of artefacts and cremated bone from cists on Dartmoor could partly explain why so many were found 'empty'.

Returning to the Whitehorse Hill cist, the evidence for the movement or circulation of items is far from unequivocal. However, there are a few indications which suggest that there might have been some interest in the site after the burial deposit had formed. Starting with the cist itself, it has already been suggested that the capstone was left as a visible marker and this would have rendered it accessible for people to lift up and examine its contents. Indeed, the capstone's shape and size could have made the site a distinctive place in the landscape. Disturbance to the peat which eventually formed over the capstone might also suggest that it had been at least uncovered at a later point in time. It is also possible that the peaty layer (8) could have entered the cist at this time, although soil layers have been recorded in other Dartmoor cists (Baring-Gould 1898; Burnard 1897; 1899; Quinnell 2003).

There are slight hints from the contents of the cist that some disturbance may have occurred. During the excavation in the laboratory some detached triangular calfskin pieces from the textile and animal-skin object were recovered from the level of the basketry container (Chapter 3) and textile fragments were found in layer (8). Given that the animal skin and textile object was the first item to be placed inside the cist and was below the pelt, any detached pieces might have resulted from items being taken in and out of the cist. Likewise, the sideways collapse of the basketry container and the destruction of a tin bead could relate to post-burial disturbance, although this is speculative and the bead may have fallen apart due to conditions inside the cist. It is also possible that some cremated bone could have been taken away from the cist for circulation after it had been deposited, depleting the deposit until it amounted only to the surviving partial burial.

Finally, there are hints that there had been things in the cist which were no longer present when it was excavated. Initial analysis of the hairs from the pelt indicated the presence of keratins from other animal-derived materials which were not present within the cist (Enrico Cappellini pers. comm.). Of course, this may be entirely due to differential preservation, and some materials, as with the skin on the inner side of the pelt, may simply have dissolved. However, it is also possible that the traces of animal-derived materials represent items which are no longer there because they were removed in prehistory.

Rather than being an 'open and shut case', therefore, the Whitehorse Hill cist may have functioned as a 'community chest' where items were curated, taken out and admired and in some cases added or taken away.

Summary: how did the cist come together?

By considering the infilling of the cist in detail, it has been suggested that the contents of the cist represent the gathering together of items with different biographies, the old and the new as well as the local and the distant. Some items possibly belonged to the deceased whereas others may not have been directly associated with the interred individual because they either pre-dated or post-dated the cremation.

The idea that the contents were intended to be 'read' was considered and the notion discussed that a particular image or personhood was being created. It was concluded that the cist was infilled in such a way that it would not have been easily 'read' by onlookers other than at the time of its formation. It was accepted that a 'persona' could have been created through the artefactual associations – for example, that of a 'high-status' younger woman – but it is possible that this was an identity which was mythologized and divorced from the reality of the lived life.

Finally, the concept that the burial and all the other objects within the cist were conceived of as belonging to the community and not to the deceased person was discussed, as was the growing body of evidence for the revisiting of graves and the manipulation of human remains. This evidence suggests that the place of burial in the Early Bronze Age was not necessarily seen as the final resting places for bodies or artefacts. While the evidence from Whitehorse Hill does not lead to any certain conclusion on this matter, one question which does emerge is whether the emptiness of other cists on Dartmoor is solely a reflection of the complete lack of organic survival elsewhere or of objects being moved in and out of them?

After the cist: a place for Middle Bronze Age grazing?

Recent archaeological research has demonstrated that although some sites appear to have faded from memory in the period after their use, many other monuments were 'remembered' and often had 'lives' which extended beyond the intentions of their builders. Some sites may have been reclaimed and manipulated by subsequent generations, to assist, for example, with establishing 'ancient' rights of tenure or ownership of place (Bradley 2002, 112–124), or with maintaining the ties of individuals with particular places. The modification, reuse and referencing of older prehistoric burial monuments is well-documented in the south-west peninsula and across Britain and western Europe (Jones and Quinnell 2006b; Harding and Healy 2007, 222; Hoan and Loney 2013; Artelius 2013; Amkreutz 2013).

Interestingly, the referencing of older sites does not seem to have occurred only at large monuments but also at much more ephemeral sites (Chadwick and Gibson 2013), which suggests that certain places may have been embedded into the social memory of individuals and groups, whereas others apparently became forgotten. Indeed, those sites which remained in contact with routine human activity, visible, for example, during the course of routine patterns of animal movement and grazing, often became places which remained in the consciousness of later generations (Hoan and Loney 2013). Likewise, anthropological study of pastoralist communities has demonstrated that quite ephemeral remains of ancient sites can frequently become associated with myths and stories and sometimes require respect or particular offerings as they are passed by to avert ill effects from spirits (Humphrey 1997, 150; Vitebsky 2005; 322–325).

In south-west Britain there is a growing body of evidence for a continuing interest in earlier monuments. This sometimes takes the form of diagnostic Middle Bronze Age artefacts found on earlier sites, as, for example, at the Lovehayne barrow in Devon, where copper-alloy palstaves were recovered (Pearce 1983, 438; Jones and Quinnell 2008). At Stannon Down, Bodmin Moor, radiocarbon dating revealed the reuse of a cairn in the Middle Bronze Age and at Constantine Island on the north Cornish coast an inhumation burial was inserted into an earlier mound (Jones 2006; 2009–10). The evidence for Middle Bronze Age reuse of monuments is less apparent on Dartmoor, although copper-alloy palstaves have recently been recovered during excavations of cairns at Hemerdon, implying that the sites became of interest to later communities (AC Archaeology 2013). Richard Bradley (2002, 72–81) has observed the relationship between Middle Bronze Age field walls and earlier cairns on Dartmoor and pointed out that boundaries often run up to or incorporate cairns and other monuments but rarely destroy or rob them.

As noted above, the paucity of contents within many Dartmoor cists might point to objects or cremations having been removed for use by later communities. However, in terms of radiocarbon and artefactual information the Whitehorse Hill cist is securely dated to the centuries before 1500 cal BC, with no evidence for subsequent disturbance. The next securely dated horizon is formed by a layer of tephra (OMH-185) in the peat above the cist which has an Early Iron Age modelled age estimate of 2705–2630 cal years BP, 755–680 cal BC (see Chapter 19). Prior to this, there is evidence for non-pollen palynomorphs or fungal spores which had grown on animal dung around the time that the cist was constructed, continuing, albeit at lower levels, after the cist had been built.

The presence of these non-pollen palynomorphs is very interesting, for two reasons. The first is that before the level of the construction of the cist, for which chronological modelling (Chapter 20) provides an estimate of *1730–1600 cal BC* (*95% probability*; *cist_finished*), probably *1690–1620 cal BC* (*68% probability*), there is very little evidence in the environmental model for animal grazing around the mound (Chapter 19). This picture appears to change around the time of the construction of the cist, when a heather-grassland environment became more widespread and there are increased indications of the presence of animals. In the light of the discussion above regarding land tenure, it is unfortunate that the lack of close chronological resolution of the mound beyond the cist means that we cannot tell exactly how long after the construction of the cist this grazing activity continued, although it is very possible that its location would have been known to the Middle Bronze Age pastoralist communities whose animals grazed the high moors. What we can say is that animal grazing around the cist is likely to have continued during the period for which there is widespread evidence for settlement and large-scale enclosure on lower-lying portions of Dartmoor (Fleming 1988, 103–107; Balaam *et al.* 1982; Smith *et al.* 1981; Fyfe *et al.* 2008; Quinnell 1994b) (Fig. 21.25). Evidence from animal footprints found during excavations at Shaugh Moor suggests that sheep, cattle and horses were present in settlements on the moor during the middle centuries of the second millennium cal BC (Balaam *et al.* 1982).

The second point of interest lies in the fact that although the non-pollen palynomorph sequence cannot currently be closely dated, it may suggest that grazing extended into the later Bronze Age. This is noteworthy because it has been argued (for example, Burgess 1980, 350) that due to climatic deterioration the Late Bronze Age witnessed a hiatus in occupation of upland areas which resulted in the moors being largely abandoned until the medieval period. More recent work, however, has cast doubt on this assumption (Tipping 2002). On other upland areas across the south west there is growing evidence for continuing use (Jones 2004–5; Jones and Quinnell 2011). On Dartmoor, Late Bronze Age or Iron Age ceramics have long been known within roundhouses at Foales Arrishes (Radford 1952) and Kestor (Fox 1954), with Early Iron Age pottery found more recently in a roundhouse at Teigncombe

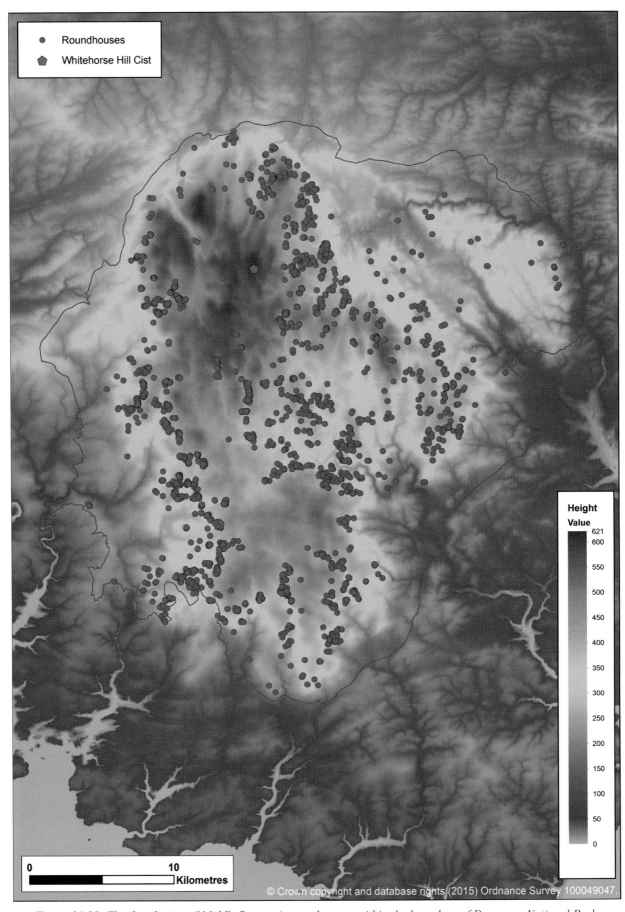

Figure 21.25: The distribution of Middle Bronze Age settlements within the boundary of Dartmoor National Park.

Figure 21.26: The Middle Bronze settlement on Shaugh Moor, which was reused in the later Bronze Age and Iron Age. (Photograph: Henrietta Quinnell.)

(Gerrard 2000). Radiocarbon dating of Shaugh Moor house 19 and structure 804 demonstrated occupation of later Bronze Age and Early Iron Age date and there are artefacts from the site which are broadly Middle Iron Age (Wainwright and Smith 1980) (Fig. 21.26). Harold Fox (2012, chaps 4 and 5) has also made a substantial case for seasonal transhumance to the higher parts of Dartmoor in the early medieval period.

The non-pollen palynomorphs from Whitehorse Hill are therefore significant because they add further to the picture of animal grazing in the period during and following the construction of the cist, and because they reveal that Bronze Age communities made use of even the highest parts of the moor. In light of this, it is wrong to consider any part of Dartmoor as an empty, non-cultural space.

The hilltop location of the Whitehorse Hill cist made it a potential factor in the social strategies of subsequent groups using the summit of the hill. Pastoralists in the Middle Bronze Age are likely to have been very aware of the existence of even quite ephemeral traces of the cist. Although the identity of the individual buried within may have been long lost the cist may have continued to feature in the stories of those who grazed their animals on the hill.

Conclusions: a remarkable discovery and the excitement of the ordinary

The excavations at Whitehorse Hill have radically transformed our knowledge of material culture in Early Bronze Age Britain. A remarkable sample of the 'missing majority' was recovered, those perishable items which archaeologists know must have existed but which are usually overlooked in accounts because they do not survive. The artefacts will undoubtedly provide a resource for further analysis and interpretation.

The interpretation offered here has been that the objects within the cist are likely to have carried symbolic associations and to have denoted the social identity of the deceased – albeit, perhaps, in a way which was decided upon by their family or community – and that they were deployed in the context of local traditions of practice.

The results of this work are significant for considering other apparently 'empty' cists on Dartmoor. Highly-prized garments made from textiles or animal pelts and other objects made of organic materials comparable with those from White Horse Hill have not survived at other excavated sites on, or indeed beyond, the moor. Perceptions of the relative importance of areas based on where 'rich' grave assemblages have been found has largely been biased towards places where non-organic 'bling' was deposited, such as Wessex. In other words, we need to maintain a note of caution when we discuss regional distributions of 'rich' graves and status: what we are really highlighting may simply be those areas where 'rich' objects survive, as well as those where communities chose to leave 'rich' things for us to find.

Despite the major advances in knowledge, which have arisen from the project, inevitably questions and issues remain. For example, did the tin used in the bead(s) and studs come from local production on Dartmoor? Was the bearskin from a local animal? Conditions inside the cist meant that some things, such as textiles, survived better than, for example, animal skin, and this raises the question of whether other items were also originally present. It is not possible to be certain whether the cist was opened in prehistory, so do the contents reflect the time that the burial was made or the last time it was looked at? A broad chronology for the peat could only be derived from the tephra layers given the inconsistent and potentially inaccurate radiocarbon measurements obtained from different peat fractions. Further work on the identification of the tephra layers could potentially refine the chronology for the development of the mound and provide a framework for interpreting the environmental proxies.

Further questions are, of course, inevitable and we should be excited about the Whitehorse Hill cist. Its discovery, together with other recent work on Dartmoor at Cut Hill and Headon Down, has demonstrated the huge potential for new sites of national importance to survive. We must expect many more to survive, especially beneath the peat in areas which have been thought of as empty wilderness.

Acknowledgements

I would like to thank Graeme Kirkham, Henrietta Quinnell and Ralph Fyfe for their comments on this chapter. I would also like to thank Tom Cadbury, Mary Cahill, Jane Marchand and Fiona Pitt for supplying and giving me permission to reproduce their photographs.

References

AC Archaeology 2013. AC Archaeology in Devon: Hemerdon. *Devon Archaeological Society Newsletter* 116, 6–7.

Aldhouse-Green, M. 2000. *Seeing the Wood for the Trees – the Symbolism of Trees and Wood in Ancient Gaul and Britain.* Aberystwyth: University of Wales.

Aldhouse-Green, M. & Aldhouse-Green, S. 2005. *The Quest for the Shaman.* London: Thames and Hudson.

Amkreutz, L. W. S. W. 2013. Memorious monuments. Place persistency, mortuary practice and memory in the Lower Rhine Area wetlands (5500–2500 cal BC). In D. R. Fontijn, K. Wentink, A. J. Louwen & S. van der Vaart (eds.), *Beyond Barrows. Current Research on the Structuration and Perception of the Prehistoric Landscape Through Monuments.* Leiden: Sidestone Press, 43–80.

Annable, F. & Simpson, D. 1964. *Guide Catalogue of the Neolithic and Bronze Age Collections in Devizes Museum.* Devizes: Wiltshire Archaeological and Natural History Society.

Appadurai, A. 1986. *The Social Life of Things: commodities in cultural perspective.* Cambridge: Cambridge University Press.

Arabaolaza, I. 2013. *Spinning the Yyarn: a cist at Keas Cottage, Spinningdale.* Glasgow: Guard Archaeology, Archaeology Reports Online ARO5 [online at http://www. archaeologyreportsonline.com/PDF/ARO5_Keas_Cottage. pdf]

Artelius, T. 2013. Inventions of memory and meaning. Examples of Late Iron Age reuse of Bronze Age monuments in south-western Sweden. In D. R. Fontijn, K. Wentink, A. J. Louwen & S. van der Vaart (eds.), *Beyond Barrows. Current Research on the Structuration and Perception of the Prehistoric Landscape Through Monuments.* Leiden: Sidestone Press, 21–40.

Ashbee, P. 1960. *The Bronze Age Round Barrow in Britain.* London: Phoenix House.

Ashbee, P. 1978. Amesbury barrow 51: excavations, 1960. *Wiltshire Archaeological and Natural History Magazine* 70/71, 1–60.

Ashbee, P. 1986. The excavation of Milton Lilbourne barrows 1–5. *Wiltshire Archaeological and Natural History Magazine* 80, 23–96.

Atkinson, R. J. C., Brailsford, J. W. & Wakefield, H. G. 1951: A pond barrow at Winterbourne Steepleton, Dorset. *Archaeological Journal* 58, 1–24.

Bailey, L., Green, M., & Smith, M. J. 2013. Keeping the family together, Canada Farm's Bronze Age burials. *Current Archaeology* 279, 20–26.

Balaam, N. D., Smith, K. & Wainwright, G. 1982. The Shaugh Moor project: fourth report – environment, context and conclusion. *Proceedings of the Prehistoric Society* 48, 203–279.

Baker, L., Sheridan, A. & Cowie, T. 2003. An Early Bronze Age dagger grave from Rameldry Farm, near Kingskettle, Fife. *Proceedings of the Society of Antiquaries of Scotland* 133, 85–123.

Barber, M. 2003. *Bronze and the Bronze Age: Metalworking and Society in Britain c. 2500–800 BC.* Stroud: Tempus

Barclay, A. & Halpin, C. 1999. *Excavations at the Barrow Hills, Radley, Oxfordshire.* Oxford: Oxford Archaeological Unit.

Baring-Gould 1895, S. Second report of the Dartmoor exploration committee. *Transactions of the Devonshire Association* 27, 81–92.

Baring-Gould, S. 1898. Seventeenth report of the barrow committee. *Transactions of the Devonshire Association* 30, 77–79.

Baring-Gould, S. 1899. Sixth report of the Dartmoor exploration committee. *Transactions of the Devonshire Association* 31, 146–155.

Baring-Gould, S. 1901. Seventh report of the Dartmoor exploration committee. *Transactions of the Devonshire Association* 33, 129–138.

Baring-Gould, S. 1903. Ninth report of the Dartmoor exploration committee. *Transactions of the Devonshire Association* 35, 143–145.

Barley, N. 1995. *Dancing on the Grave: encounters with death.* London: John Murray.

Barrett, J. C. 1994. *Fragments from Antiquity: an archaeology of social life in Britain, 2900–1200 BC*, Oxford: Blackwell.

Barrowclough, D. 2014. Golden biographies: The production, curation, fragmentation and deposition of the Armoricantype rolled-gold bead-like ornaments found at Pendleton, Lancashire, *Archaeological Journal* 172, 30–60.

Bate, C. S. 1872. Researches into some ancient tumuli on Dartmoor. *Report of the Transactions of the Devonshire Association* 5, 549–558.

Bateman, T. 1861. *Ten Years' Diggings in Celtic and Anglo Saxon Grave Hills, in the Counties of Derby, Stafford, and York*. London: J Russell Smith.

Beck, C. & Shennan, S. 1991. *Amber in Prehistoric Britain*. Oxford: Oxbow Books.

Becker, K. 2008. Left but not lost. *Archaeology Ireland* 22, 12–15.

Becker, K. 2013. Transforming identities – new approaches to Bronze Age deposition in Ireland. *Proceedings of the Prehistoric Society* 79, 225–265.

Benson, D. & Whittle, A. 2007. *Building Memories: the Neolithic Cotswold long barrow at Ascott-under-Wychwood, Oxfordshire*. Oxford: Oxbow Books.

Bloch, M. & Parry, J. 1982. Introduction: death and the regeneration of life. In M. Bloch & J. Parry (eds.), *Death and the Regeneration of Life*. Cambridge: Cambridge University Press, 1–44.

Bonnemere, P. 1998. Trees and people: some vital links. Tree products and other agents in the life cycle of the Ankave-Anga of Papua New Guinnea. In L. Rival (ed.), *The Social Lives of Trees: anthropological perspectives on tree symbolism*. Oxford: Berg, 113–132.

Bonnington, P. 2011. Earlier Bronze Age cemetery mounds and the multiple cremation rite in western Britain. In S. Pearce (ed.), *Recent Archaeological Work in South-western Britain: papers in honour of Henrietta Quinnell*. Oxford: British Archaeological Report 548, 75–93.

Booth, P., Champion, T., Foreman, S., Garwood, P., Glass, H., Munby, J. & Reynolds, A. 2011. *On Track. The Archaeology of High Speed 1 Section 1 in Kent*. Oxford: Oxford/Wessex Archaeology.

Borlase, W. C. 1879. Archaeological discoveries made in the parishes of St. Just in Penwith and Sennen. *Journal of the Royal Institution of Cornwall* 6, 190–213.

Bradley, R. 1990. *The Passage of Arms: an archaeological analysis of prehistoric hoards and votive deposits*. Cambridge: Cambridge University Press.

Bradley, R. 1997. *Rock Art and the Prehistory of Atlantic Europe*. London: Routledge.

Bradley, R. 1998. Ruined buildings, ruined stones: enclosures, tombs and natural places in the Neolithic of south-west England. *World Archaeology* 30, 13–22.

Bradley, R. 2000. *An Archaeology of Natural Places*. London: Routledge.

Bradley, R. 2002. *The Past in Prehistoric Societies*. London: Routledge.

Bradley, R. 2007. *The Prehistory of Britain and Ireland*. Cambridge: Cambridge University Press.

Bradley, R. 2012. *The Idea of Order: the circular archetype in prehistoric Europe*. Oxford: Oxford University Press.

Bradley, R. & Fraser, E. 2010. Bronze Age barrows on the heathlands of southern England; construction, forms and interpretation. *Oxford Journal of Archaeology* 29, 15–34.

Brennand, M. & Taylor M. 2003. The survey and excavation of a timber circle at Holme-next-the-Sea, Norfolk, 1998–9. *Proceedings of the Prehistoric Society* 69, 1–84.

Brittain, M. 2004. Layers of life and death: aspects of monumentality in the Early Bronze Age of Wales. In V.

Cummings & C. Fowler (eds.), *The Neolithic of the Irish Sea*. Oxford: Oxbow Books, 224–232.

Brück, J. 2004a. Material metaphors: the relational construction of identity in Early Bronze Age burials in Ireland and Britain. *Journal of Social Archaeology* 4, 307–333.

Brück, J. 2004b. Early Bronze Age burial practices in Scotland and beyond: differences and similarities. In I. A. G. Shepherd and G. J. Barclay (eds.), *Scotland in Ancient Europe*. Edinburgh: Society of Antiquaries of Scotland, 179–188.

Brück, J. 2006. Death, exchange and reproduction in the British Bronze Age. *Journal of European Archaeology* 9, 73–101.

Brück, J. 2009. Women, death, and social change in the British Bronze Age. *Norwegian Archaeological Review* 42, 1–23.

Brück, J., Johnston, R. & Wickstead, H. 2003. Excavations of Bronze Age field systems on Shovel Down, Dartmoor, 2003. *Past* 45, 10–12.

Brunning, R., Last, J., Anderson-Whymark, H., Campbell, G., Sheridan, A., Dungworth, D., Davies, G. & Middleton, A. 2013. Technology and domestic objects. In M. Canti, G. Campbell & S. Greaney (eds.), *Stonehenge, Wiltshire. Stonehenge World Heritage Site Synthesis: prehistoric landscape, environment and economy*. Portsmouth: English Heritage, 159–204.

Burgess, C. 1980. *The Age of Stonehenge*. London: Dent.

Burnard, R. 1896a. Exploration of a barrow in the parish of Halwill. *Transactions of the Devonshire Association* 28, 86–89.

Burnard, R. 1896b. Fifteenth report of the barrow committee. *Transactions of the Devonshire Association* 28, 84–86.

Burnard, R. 1897. Sixteenth report of the barrow committee. *Transactions of the Devonshire Association* 29, 66–71.

Burnard, R. 1899. Eighteenth report of the barrow committee. *Transactions of the Devonshire Association* 31, 94–100.

Burnard, R. 1901. Seventh report of the Dartmoor exploration committee. *Transactions of the Devonshire Association* 33, 129–138.

Burnard, R. 1902. Eighth report of the Dartmoor exploration committee. *Transactions of the Devonshire Association* 34, 160–165.

Burnard, R. 1903. Twenty-second report of the barrow committee. *Transactions of the Devonshire Association* 35, 141–142.

Burnard, R. 1905. Twenty-fourth report of the barrow committee. *Transactions of the Devonshire Association* 37, 87–95.

Burnard, R. 1914. Thirty-third report of the barrow committee. *Transactions of the Devonshire Association* 46, 93–94.

Busia, K. A. 1954. The Ashanti of the Gold Coast. In D. Forde (ed.), *African Worlds: studies in the cosmological ideas and social values of African peoples*. Oxford: Oxford University Press, 190–210.

Butcher, S. 1978. Excavations at Nornour, Isles of Scilly, 1969–73: the pre-Roman settlement. *Cornish Archaeology* 17, 29–112.

Butler, J. 1991. *Dartmoor Atlas of Antiquities*. Volume 2: the north. Tiverton: Devon Books.

Butler, J. 1994. *Dartmoor Atlas of Antiquities*. Volume 3: the south-west. Tiverton: Devon Books.

Butler, J. 1997. *Dartmoor Atlas of Antiquities*. Volume 5: the second millennium B.C.. Tiverton: Devon Books.

Byock, J. (trans). 1999. *The Saga of the Volsungs*. London: Harmondsworth.

Cahill, M. 2001. Unspooling the mystery. *Archaeology Ireland* 57, 9–15.

Callander, G. J. 1908–9. Notice of the discovery in Aberdeenshire of five cists, each containing a drinking-cup urn. *Proceedings of the Society of Antiquaries of Scotland* 43, 76–92.

Carlin, N. & Brück, J. 2012. Searching for the Chalcolithic: continuity and change in the Irish Final Neolithic/Early Bronze Age. In M. J. Allen, J. Gardiner, & A. Sheridan (eds.), *Is there a British Chalcolithic? People, Place and Polity in the Late 3rd millennium*. Oxford: Oxbow Books/Prehistoric Society, 281–297.

Carnes, A. 2014. *The evolution of Neolithic and Bronze Age landscapes: from Danubian longhouses to the stone rows of Dartmoor and northern Scotland*. Oxford: Archaeopress.

Chadwick, A. & Gibson, C. 2013. 'Do you remember the first time?' A preamble through memory, myth and place. In A. Chadwick & C. Gibson (eds.), *Memory, Myth, Place and Long-term Landscape Inhabitation*. Oxford: Oxbow Books, 1–31.

Chagnon, N. A. 1997. *Yąnomamö*. Fort Worth: Harcourt Brace.

Chalmers, J. H. 1866–68. Notice of the discovery of a stone kist at Broomend, near Inverurie, Aberdeenshire. *Proceedings of the Society of Antiquaries of Scotland* 7, 110–114.

Chitty, L. 1929. Twin Food Vessels preserved at Aqualate Hall, Staffordshire. *Antiquaries Journal* 9, 137–140.

Christie, J. 1862–64. Account of the opening of an ancient cist in the parish of Cabrach, Aberdeenshire. *Proceedings of the Society of Antiquaries of Scotland* 5, 362–364.

Christie, P. 1960. Crig-a-mennis: a Bronze Age barrow at Liskey, Perranzabuloe, Cornwall. *Proceedings of the Prehistoric Society* 26, 76–97.

Christie, P. 1985. Barrows on the north Cornish coast: wartime excavations by C. K. Croft Andrew 1939–1944. *Cornish Archaeology* 24, 23–122.

Christie, P. 1988. A barrow cemetery on Davidstow Moor, Cornwall: wartime excavations by C. K. Croft Andrew. *Cornish Archaeology* 27, 27–169.

Chudleigh, J. 1892. *Devonshire Antiquities*. London: H. R. Allenson.

Clarke, D. V., Cowie, T. G. & Foxon, A. 1985. *Symbols of Power at the Time of Stonehenge*. Edinburgh: National Museum of Antiquities of Scotland.

Coles, B. & Coles, J. 1986. *Sweet Track to Glastonbury: the Somerset Levels in prehistory*. London: Thames and Hudson.

Coles, J., Heal, S. V. E. & Orme, B. 1978. The use and character of wood in prehistoric Britain and Ireland. *Proceedings of the Prehistoric Society* 44, 1–46.

Cressey, M. & Sheridan, A. 2003. The excavation of a Bronze Age cemetery at Seafield West, near Inverness, Highland. *Proceedings of the Society of Antiquaries of Scotland* 133, 47–84.

Cummings, V. 2002. All cultural things: actual and conceptual monuments in the Neolithic of western Britain. In C. Scarre (ed.), *Monuments and Landscape in Atlantic Europe*. London: Routledge, 107–121.

Cunnington, M. E. 1907. Notes on the opening of a bronze age barrow at Manton, near Marlborough. *Wiltshire Archaeological & Natural History Magazine* 35, 1–20.

Curry-Lindahl, K. 1972. The brown bear (*Ursus arctos*) in Europe: decline, present distribution, biology and ecology. In S. Herrero (ed.), *Bears, Their Biology and Management. IUCN New Series* 23, 74–80.

Curtis, N., Popovic, L., Wilkin, N. & Wright, M. 2010. The moon, the bonfire and the Beaker? Analysing white inlay from Beaker pottery in Aberdeenshire. *Past* 65, 1–3.

Davidson, C. B. 1866–68. Notice of further stone cists found at Broomend, near the Inverurie Papermills. *Proceedings of the Society of Antiquaries of Scotland* 7, 115–118.

Dickson, J. H. 1978. Bronze Age mead. *Antiquity* 205, 108–113.

Dixon, C. E. B. 1953. Seventy-first report on barrows. *Transactions of the Devonshire Association* 85, 176–177.

Dixon, D. D. 1913. Cartington oak coffin. *Proceedings of the Antiquaries of Newcastle on Tyne* 3, 6, 79–84.

Doe, G. 1875. The examination of two barrows near Torrington. *Report of the Transactions of the Devonshire Association* 8, 102–105.

Donaldson, P. 1977. The excavation of a multiple round barrow at Barnack, Cambridgeshire, 1974–76. *Antiquaries Journal* 57, 197–232.

Douglas, M. 1992. *Purity and Danger: an analysis of the concepts of pollution and taboo*. London: Routledge.

Douny, L. & Harris, S. 2014. Wrapping and unwrapping, concepts and approaches. In S. Harris & A. J. Veldmiejer (eds.), *Wrapping and Unwrapping Material Culture: archaeological and anthropological perspectives*. Walnut Creek CA: Left Coast Press, 15–40.

Dudley, D. 1964. The excavation of the Carvinnack barrow, Tregavethan, near Truro, Cornwall. *Journal of the Royal Institution Cornwall* 4, 414–451.

Dyer, M. & Quinnell, H. 2013. Excavation of a group of Early Bronze Age monuments on Headon Down, Sparkwell. *Proceedings of the Devon Archaeological Society* 71, 55–80.

Edmonds, M. 2012. Biographies and afterlives. In A. Jones, J. Pollard, M. Allen & J. Gardiner (eds.), *Image, Memory and Monumentality: archaeological engagements with the material world*. Oxford: Oxbow Books/Prehistoric Society, 146–162.

Elgee, H. W. & Elgee, F. 1949. An Early Bronze Age burial in a boat-shaped wooden coffin from north-east Yorkshire. *Proceedings of the Prehistoric Society* 15, 87–106.

Eliade, M. 1967. *From Primitive to Zen*. London: Collins.

Eliade, M. 1988. *Shamanism, Archaic Techniques of Ecstasy*. London: Arkana.

Eogan, G. & Simmons, I. G. 1964. The excavation of a stone alignment and circle at Cholwichtown, Devonshire. *Proceedings of the Prehistoric Society* 30, 25–34.

Evans-Pritchard, E. E. 1956. *Nuer Religion*. Oxford: Oxford University Press.

Evans-Pritchard, E. E. 1969. *The Nuer: a description of the modes and livelihood and political institutions of a Nilotic people*. Oxford: Oxford University Press.

Field, D. 1998. Round barrows and the harmonious landscape: placing Early Bronze Age burial monuments in south-east England. *Oxford Journal of Archaeology* 17, 309–326.

Field, N. 1985. A multi-phased barrow and possible henge monument at West Ashby, Lincolnshire. *Proceedings of the Prehistoric Society* 51, 103–136.

Finn, N. 2012. *Bronze Age Ceremonial Enclosures and Cremation Cemetery at Eye Kettleby, Leicestershire: the development of a prehistoric* landscape. Leicester: University of Leicester.

Fisher, A. 1984. *Africa Adorned*. New York: Harry N. Abrams.

Fitzgerald, M. 2007. Catch of the day at Clowanstown, Co Meath, *Archaeology Ireland* 21, 4, 12–15.

Fitzpatrick, A. 2011. *The Amesbury Archer and the Boscombe Bowmen: Bell Beaker burials at Boscombe Down, Amesbury, Wiltshire*. Salisbury: Wessex Archaeology.

Fitzpatrick, A. 2013. The arrival of the Beaker set in Britain and

Ireland. In J. T. Koch & B. Cunliffe (eds.), *Celtic from the West 2: rethinking the Bronze Age and the arrival of Indo-European in Atlantic Europe*. Celtic Studies Publications 16. Oxford: Oxbow Books, 41–70.

Fleming, A. 1971. Territorial patterns in Bronze Age Wessex. *Proceedings of the Prehistoric Society* 37, 138–166.

Fleming, A. 1988. *The Dartmoor Reaves: investigating prehistoric land divisions*. London: Batsford.

Forde, D. 1939. Dysgwylfa Fawr barrow, Cardiganshire: a Food-Vessel and dug-out trunk cremation burial. *Antiquaries Journal* 19, 90–92.

Fowler, C. 2004. *The Archaeology of Personhood: an anthropological approach*. London: Routledge.

Fowler, C. 2013. *The Emergent Past. A Relational Realist Archaeology of Early Bronze Age Mortuary Practices*. Oxford: Oxford University Press.

Fox, A. 1954. Excavations at Kestor. *Transactions of the Devonshire Association* 86, 21–62.

Fox, A. 1964. *South West England*. London: Thames and Hudson.

Fox, A. 1969. Appendix: the Upton Pyne cemetery. *Proceedings of the Devon Archaeology Society* 27, 75–78.

Fox, A. & Stone, J. F. S. 1951. A necklace from a barrow in North Molton parish, North Devon. *Antiquaries Journal* 31, 25–31.

Fox, H. 2012. *Dartmoor's Alluring Uplands: Transhumance and Pastoral Management in the Middle Ages*. Exeter: University of Exeter Press.

French, C. 1994. *Excavation of the Deeping St Nicholas Barrow Complex, South Lincolnshire*. Heckington: Lincolnshire Archaeology & Heritage.

Fürer-Haimendorf, C. 1969. *The Konyak Nagas; an Indian frontier tribe*. London: Holt Rinehart and Winston.

Fyfe, R. M., Brown, A. G. & Coles, B. J. 2003. Mesolithic to Bronze Age change and human activity in the Exe Valley, Devon, UK. *Proceedings of the Prehistoric Society* 69, 161–181.

Fyfe, R. M., Brück, J., Johnston, R., Lewis, H., Roland, T. & Wickstead, H. 2008. Historical context and chronology of Bronze Age enclosure on Dartmoor, UK. *Journal of Archaeological Science* 35, 2250–2261.

Fyfe, R. M. & Greeves, T. 2010. The date and context of a stone row: Cut Hill, Dartmoor, south-west England. *Antiquity* 323, 55–70.

Gamble, M. & Fowler, C. 2013. A re-assessment of human skeletal remains in Tyne and Wear Museums: results and implications for interpreting Early Bronze Age burials from northeast England and beyond. *Archaeologia Aeliana* **42**, 47–80.

Garwood, P. 1991. Ritual tradition and the reconstitution of society. In P. Garwood, D. Jennings, R. Skeates & J. Toms (eds.), *Sacred and Profane: proceedings of a conference on archaeology, ritual and religion, Oxford, 1989*. Oxford: Oxford University Committee for Archaeology, 10–32.

Garwood, P. 2007a. Late Neolithic and Early Bronze Age funerary monuments and burial traditions in the West Midlands. In P. Garwood (ed.), *The Undiscovered Country: the earlier prehistory of the West Midlands*. Oxford: Oxbow Books, 134–165.

Garwood, P. 2007b. Before the hills stood order: chronology, time and history in the interpretation of Early Bronze age round barrows. In J. Last (ed.), *Beyond the Grave: new perspectives on barrows*. Oxford: Oxbow Books, 30–52.

Gerloff, S. 1975. *The Early Bronze Age daggers in Great Britain*. Munich: Prähistoric Bronzefunde VI(2).

Gerrard, S. 2000. *Dartmoor Bracken and Archaeology Project Interim Report for the 2000 Season*. Privately published.

Giambelli, R. A. 1998. The coconut, the body and the human being. Metaphors of life and growth in Nusa Penida, Bali. In L. Rival (ed.) *The Social Lives of Trees: anthropological perspectives on tree symbolism*. Oxford: Berg, 133–158.

Gibson, A. 2007. A Beaker veneer. In M. Larsson & M. Parker Pearson (eds.), *From Stonehenge to the Baltic: living with cultural diversity in the third millennium BC*. Oxford, British Archaeological Report S1692, 47–64.

Gibson, C. 2013. Beakers into bronze: tracing connections between Western Iberia and the British Isles 2800–800 BC. In J. T. Koch & B. Cunliffe (eds.), *Celtic from the West 2: rethinking the Bronze Age and the arrival of Indo-European in Atlantic Europe*. Celtic Studies Publications 16. Oxford: Oxbow Books, 71–100.

Gibson, T. 1995. Having your house and eating it: houses and siblings in Ara, South Sulawesi. In J. Carsten & S. Hugh-Jones (eds.), *About the House: Levi-Strauss and beyond*. Cambridge: Cambridge University Press, 129–148.

Giddings, J. L. 1967. *Ancient Men of the Arctic*. New York: Borzoi Books.

Gingell, G. 1988. Twelve Wiltshire round barrows. Excavations in 1959, and 1961 by F. de M. and H. L. Vatcher. *Wiltshire Archaeological and Natural History Magazine* 82, 19–76.

Glob, P. V. 1983. *The Mound People*. London: Paladin.

Gosden, C. & Marshall, Y. 1999. The cultural biography of objects. *World Archaeology* 31, 169–178.

Graham, D., Graham, A. & Wiltshire, P. 2004. Investigation of a Bronze Age mound on Thursley Common. *Surrey Archaeological Collections* 91, 151–166.

Graham, D., Graham, A., Farr, L. & Branch, N. 2008. A probable Bronze Age mound on the King's Ridge, Frensham Common. *Surrey Archaeological Collections* 94, 181–189.

Gray, H. St George. & Prideaux, C. S. 1905. Barrow digging at Martinstown, near Dorchester 1903. *Proceedings of the Dorset Natural History and Archaeological Society* 26, 6–39.

Green, C. & Rollo-Smith, S. 1984. The excavation of eighteen round barrows near Shrewton, Wiltshire. *Proceedings of the Prehistoric Society* 50, 255–319.

Green, M. 1986. *The Gods of the Celts*. Stroud: Bramley Books.

Greenwell, W. 1877. *British Barrows: a record of the examination of sepulchral mounds in various parts of England*. Oxford: Clarendon Press.

Griffith, F. M. 1984. Archaeological investigations at Colliford Reservoir, Bodmin Moor 1977–78. *Cornish Archaeology* 23, 47–140.

Grinsell, L. V. 1934. An analysis and list of Surrey barrows. *Surrey Archaeological Collections* 42, 26–60.

Grinsell, L. V. 1938. Hampshire barrows. *Proceedings of the Hampshire Field Club and Archaeological Society* 14, 9–40.

Grinsell, L. V. 1957. Archaeological gazetteer. In B. Pugh (ed.), *Victoria County History of Wiltshire*, vol. I. London: Oxford University Press, 21–279.

Grinsell, L. V. 1959. *Dorset Barrows*. Dorchester: Dorset Natural History and Archaeological Society.

Grinsell, L. V. 1970. The barrows of north Devon. *Proceedings of the Devon Archaeological Society* 6, 340–355.

Grinsell, L. V. 1978. Dartmoor barrows. *Proceedings of the Devon Archaeological Society* 36, 85–180.

Grinsell, L. V. 1982. *Dorset Barrows Supplement*. Dorchester: Dorset Natural History and Archaeological Society.

Grinsell, L. V. 1983. The barrows of south and east Devon. *Proceedings of the Devon Archaeological Society* 41, 5–46.

Hackett, R. I. J. 1996. *Art and Religion in Africa*. Oxford: Oxford University Press.

Hald, M. 1980. *Ancient Danish Textiles from Bogs and Burials: a comparative study of costume and Iron Age textiles*. Copenhagen: National Museum of Denmark.

Hall, D. 1997. *An Archaeology of the Soul: North American Indian belief and ritual*. London: Longmans, Green and Co.

Hammon, A. 2010. The brown bear. In T. O'Connor & N. Sykes (eds.), *Extinctions and Invasions: a social history of British fauna*. Oxford: Oxbow Books, 95–103.

Harding, A. 2000. *European Societies in the Bronze Age*. Cambridge: Cambridge University Press.

Harding, J. & Healy, F. 2007. *The Raunds Project: a Neolithic and Bronze Age landscape in Northamptonshire*. London: English Heritage.

Harris, S. 2010. Smooth and cool, or warm and soft; investigating the properties of cloth in prehistory. In E. Andersson Strand, M. Gleba, U. Mannering, C. Munkholt & M. Ringgaard (eds.), *North European Symposium for Archaeological Textiles X*, vol. 5. Oxford: Oxbow Books, 104–112.

Harris, S. 2012. From the parochial to the universal: comparing cloth cultures in the Bronze Age. *Journal of European Archaeology* 15, 61–97.

Harris, S. 2014a. Introduction. Leather in archaeology: between material properties, materiality and technical choice. In S. Harris & A. J. Veldmiejer (eds.), *Why Leather? The Material and Cultural Dimensions of Leather*. Leiden: Sidestone Press, 9–22.

Harris, S. 2014b. Wrapping the dead: the Bronze Age mound burials of southern Scandinavia through a wrapping analysis. In S. Harris & L. Douny (eds.), *Wrapping and Unwrapping Material Culture: archaeological and anthropological perspectives*. Walnut Creek CA: Left Coast Press, 115–134.

Harris, S. 2015. Folded, layered textiles from a Bronze Age pit pyre excavated from Over Barrow 2, Cambridgeshire, England. In K. Grömer & F. Pritchard (eds.), *Aspects of the Design, Production and Use of Textiles and Clothing from the Bronze Age to the Early Modern Era. NESAT* XII. Budapest: Archaeolingua, 73–81.

Haustein, M., Gillis, C. & Pernicka, E. 2010. Tin isotopy – a new method for solving old questions. *Archaeometry* 52, 816–832.

Haveman, E. & Sheridan, A. 2006. The Exloo necklace: new light on an old find. *Palaeohistoria* 47/48, 101–139.

Hawkes, J. 1959. *A Land*. London: Harmondsworth.

Healy, F. & Harding, J. 2004. Reading a burial: the legacy of Overton Hill. In A. Gibson & A. Sheridan (eds.), *From Sickles to Circles: Britain and Ireland at the time of Stonehenge*. Stroud: Tempus, 176–193.

Helms, M. 1988. *Ulysses' Sail: an ethnographic odyssey of power, knowledge and geographical distance*. Princeton: Princeton University Press.

Helms, M. 1993. *Craft and the Kingly Ideal; art, trade and power*. Austin TX: University of Texas.

Helms, M. 2009. The master(y) of hard materials: thoughts on technology, materiality and ideology occasioned by the Dover boat. In P. Clark (ed.), *Bronze Age Connections: cultural contact in prehistoric Europe*. Oxford: Oxbow Books, 149–158.

Henshall, A. 1950. Textiles and weaving appliances in prehistoric Britain. *Proceedings of the Prehistoric Society* 26, 130–162.

Henshall, A. 1962–63. A Bronze Age cist burial at Masterton, Fife. *Proceedings of the Society of Antiquaries of Scotland* 96, 145–154.

Henshall, A. 1963–64. A dagger-grave and other cist burials at Ashgrove, Methilhill, Fife. *Proceedings of the Society of Antiquaries of Scotland* 97, 166–179.

Herity, M. & Eogan, G. 1989. *Ireland in Prehistory*. London: Routledge.

Hertz, R. 2009. *Death and the Right Hand*. London: Routledge.

Higgitt, C., Harris, S., Cartwright, C. R. & Cruickshank, P. 2011. Assessing the potential of historic archaeological collections: a pilot study of the British Museum's Swiss lake dwelling textiles. *British Museum Technical Research Bulletin* 5, 81–94.

Hoan, A. & Loney, H. L. 2013. Landesque capital and the development of the British uplands in later prehistory: investigating the accretion of cairns, cairnfields, memories and myths in ancient agricultural landscapes. In A. Chadwick & C. Gibson (eds.), *Memory, Myth, Place and Long-term Landscape Inhabitation*. Oxford: Oxbow Books, 124–145.

Hoare, R. C. 1812. *The Ancient History of South Wiltshire*. London: William Miller.

Holst, M. K., Rasmussen, M., Kristiansen, K. & Beck, J-H. 2013. Bronze Age 'Herostrats': ritual, political and domestic economies in Early Bronze Age Denmark. *Proceedings of the Prehistoric Society* 79, 265–296.

Hughes, G. & Murphy, K. 2013. Fan Foel round barrow, Mynydd Du, South Wales: archaeological excavation and palaeoenvironmental analysis, 2002–4. *Archaeologia Cambrensis* 162, 67–105.

Humphrey, C. 1997. Chiefly and shamanist landscapes in Mongolia. In E. Hirsch & M. O'Hanlon (eds.), *The Anthropology of Landscape*. Oxford: Oxford University Press, 135–162.

Hunter, F. & Davis, M. 1994. Early Bronze Age lead – a unique necklace from southeast Scotland. *Antiquity* 261, 824–830.

Hurcombe, L. 2014. *Perishable Material Culture in Prehistory: investigating the missing majority*. London: Routledge.

Hutchinson, P. O. 1880. Report on barrows near Sidmouth. *Report of the Transactions of the Devonshire Association* 12, 122–151.

Hutton, R. 2013. *Pagan Britain*. London: Yale University Press.

Ingold, T. 2000. *The Perception of the Environment: essays in livelihood, dwelling and skill*. London: Routledge.

Ingold, T. 2010. The round mound is not a monument. In J. Leary, T. Darvill & D. Field (eds.), *Round Mounds and Monumentality in the British Neolithic and Beyond*. Oxford: Oxbow Books, 253–260.

Insoll, T. 2004. *Archaeology, Ritual, Religion*. London: Routledge.

Insoll, T., Clack, T. & Olirege, R. 2015. Mursi ox modification in the Lower Omo Valley and the interpretation of cattle-rock art in Ethiopia. *Antiquity* 343, 91–105.

Jenness, D. 1977. *The Indians of Canada*. Toronto: University of Toronto Press (1st pub 1932).

Johnson, N. & Rose, P. 1994. *Bodmin Moor: an archaeological survey*, vol. 1. London: English Heritage.

Johnston, R. 2005. Pattern without a plan: rethinking the Bronze Age coaxial field systems on Dartmoor, south-west England. *Oxford Journal of Archaeology* 24, 1–21.

Jones, A., Freedman, D., O'Connor, B., Lamdin-Whymark, H., Tipping, R. & Watson, A. 2011. *An Animate Landscape: rock art and the prehistory of Kilmartin, Argyll, Scotland*. Oxford: Windgather Press.

Jones, A. & MacGregor, G. (eds.), 2002. *Colouring the Past*. Oxford: Berg.

Jones, A. M. 2004–5. Settlement and ceremony: archaeological investigations at Stannon Down, St Breward, Cornwall. *Cornish Archaeology* 43–44, 1–141.

Jones, A. M. 2005. *Cornish Bronze Age Ceremonial Landscapes,* c. *2500–1500 BC*. Oxford: British Archaeological Report 394.

Jones, A. M. 2006. Monuments and memories set in stone: a Cornish Bronze Age complex in its landscape on Stannon Down. *Proceedings of the Prehistoric Society* 72, 341–365.

Jones, A.M. 2009–10. Excavation of a Bronze Age barrow on Constantine Island, St Merryn, Cornwall. *Cornish Archaeology* 48–49, 67–98.

Jones, A. M. 2011a. Without Wessex: the local character of the Early Bronze Age in the south west. In S. Pearce (ed.), *Recent Archaeological Work in South-western Britain: papers in honour of Henrietta Quinnell*. Oxford: British Archaeological Report 548, 61–74.

Jones, A. M. 2011b. The Botrea barrow group: regional identity in Early Bronze Age Cornwall. In A. M. Jones and G. Kirkham (eds.), *Beyond the Core: regionality in British prehistory*. Oxford: Oxbow Books, 75–86.

Jones, A. M. 2012. Going west: ceremony, barrows and cairns in the south west peninsula. In W. Britnell and R. J. Silvester (eds.), *Reflections on the Past, Essays in Honour of Frances Lynch*. Welshpool: Cambrian Archaeological Association, 172–194.

Jones, A. M. 2013. Memory, myth, place and landscape inhabitation: a perspective from the south-west peninsula. In A. Chadwick & C. Gibson (eds.), *Memory, Myth, Place and Long-term Landscape Inhabitation*. Oxford: Oxbow Books, 55–75.

Jones, A. M. forthcoming. Early landscape and ceremony. In P. Herring, N. Johnson, A. M Jones, J. A. Nowakowski & A. Sharpe. *Archaeology and Landscape at the Land's End, Cornwall. The West Penwith Surveys 1980–2010.* Truro: Cornwall Council.

Jones, A. M., Gossip, J. & Quinnell, H. 2015. *Settlement and Metalworking in the Middle Bronze Age and Beyond: new evidence from Tremough, Cornwall*. Leiden: Sidestone Press.

Jones, A. M., Marley, J., Quinnell, H. & Hartgroves, S. 2011. On the beach: new discoveries at Harlyn Bay. *Proceedings of the Prehistoric Society* 77, 89–110.

Jones, A.M. & Mikulski, R. in preparation. After the storm: an Early Bronze Age cist burial at Harlyn Bay, Cornwall, 2014.

Jones, A. M. & Quinnell, H. 2006a. Cornish Beakers: new discoveries and perspectives. *Cornish Archaeology* 45, 31–70.

Jones, A. M. & Quinnell, H. 2006b. Redating the Watch Hill barrow. *Archaeological Journal* 163, 42–66.

Jones, A. M. & Quinnell, H. 2008. The Farway barrow complex in East Devon reassessed. *Proceedings of the Devon Archaeological Society* 66, 27–58.

Jones, A. M. & Quinnell, H. 2011. Bosiliack: a later prehistoric settlement in Penwith, Cornwall. *Archaeological Journal* 168, 96–132.

Jones, A. M. & Quinnell, H. 2013. Daggers in the west: Early Bronze Age daggers and knives in the south west peninsula. *Proceedings of the Prehistoric Society* 79, 165–191.

Jones, A. M. & Quinnell. H. 2014. *Lines of Archaeological Investigation Along the North Cornish Coast*. Oxford: British Archaeological Report 594.

Jones, A. M., Taylor, S. R. & Sturgess, J. 2012. A Beaker-associated structure and other discoveries along the Sennen to Porthcurno SWW pipeline. *Cornish Archaeology* 51, 1–69.

Kalsbeek, N. & Richter, J. 2006. Preservation of burned bones: an investigation of the effects of temperature and pH on hardness. *Studies in Conservation* 51, 123–138.

Keates, S. 2002. The flashing blade: colour and luminosity in north Italian Copper Age society. In A. Jones, & G. MacGregor (eds.). *Colouring the Past*. Oxford: Berg, 109–126.

Keller, F. 1866. *The Lake Dwellings of Switzerland and Other Parts of Europe*. London: Longmans, Green and Co.

Kinnes, I. 1979. *Round Barrows and Ring-ditches in the British Neolithic*. London: British Museum.

Kinnes, I. & Longworth, I. 1985. *Catalogue of the Excavated Prehistoric and Romano-British Material in the Greenwell Collection*. London: British Museum Press.

Kirwan, R. 1870. Notes on the prehistoric archaeology of east Devon, part iii. *Report of the Transactions of the Devonshire Association* 4, 295–304.

Kirwan, R. 1872. Notes on the prehistoric archaeology of east Devon. *Archaeological Journal* 29, 34–44.

Knight, M. G, Ormrod, T. & Pearce, S. 2015. *The Bronze Age Metalwork of South Western Britain: a corpus of material found between 1983 and 2014*. Oxford: British Archaeological Reports 610.

Kristiansen, K. & Larsson, T.B. 2005. *The Rise of Bronze Age Society: travels, transmissions and transformations*. Cambridge: Cambridge University Press.

Lawson, A. 1986. *Barrow Excavations in Norfolk 1950–82*. East Anglian Archaeology 7. Dereham: Norfolk Archaeological Unit.

Leahy, D. 2008. Piercing the Neolithic. *Archaeology Ireland* 57, 32–33.

Leary, J., Field, D. & Campbell, G. (eds.). 2013. *Silbury Hill: the largest prehistoric mound in Europe*. Swindon: English Heritage.

Lelong, O. 2012. Langwell Farm, Strath Oykel. *PAST* 72, 12–14.

Lemonnier, P. 2012. *Mundane Objects: materiality and non-verbal communication*. Walnut Creek CA: Left Coast Press.

Lewis, J. 2007. The creation of round barrows on the Mendip Hills, Somerset. In J. Last (ed.), *Beyond the Grave: new perspectives on barrows*. Oxford: Oxbow books, 72–82.

Llewellyn, N. 1991. *The Art of Death*. London: Reaktion Books.

Lönnrot, E. (Bosley, K. trans), 2008. *The Kalevala*. Oxford: Oxford University Press.

Lord, J. & Wood, J. 1999. Making a spear and the Iceman's outfit. *British Archaeology* 49, 8–11.

McAdam, E. 1982. Comparative background: the cemetery, 120–129. In T. Watkins, The excavation of an Early Bronze Age cemetery at Barns Farm, Dalgety, Fife. *Proceedings of the Society of Antiquaries of Scotland* 112, 48–141.

MacKillop, J. 1998. *Dictionary of Celtic Mythology*. Oxford: Oxford University Press.

McKinley, J. 1997. Bronze Age 'barrows' and funerary rites and rituals of cremation. *Proceedings of the Prehistoric Society* 63, 129–145.

McKinley, J. 2000. The analysis of cremated bone. In M. Cox & S. Mays (eds.), *Human Osteology in Archaeology and Forensic Science*. London: Greenwich Medical Media, 403–421.

Magnusson, M. & Palsson H. (trans). 1969. *Laxdaela Saga*. Harmondsworth: Penguin.

Manby, T. 1969. Rudston barrow LII: Beaker cremation associations. *Yorkshire Archaeological Journal* 42, 254–258.

Mapleton, R. J. 1879. Notice of the discovery of an old canoe in a peat-bog at Oban. *Proceedings of the Society of Antiquaries of Scotland* 13, 336–338.

Marchand, J. & Hughes, S. 2012. Bronze Age Bellever: settling Dartmoor in the 2nd millennium BC. *Current Archaeology* 266, 36–41.

Melton, N., Montgomery, J. & Knüsel, C. J. (eds.) 2013. *Gristhorpe Man: a life and death in the Bronze Age*. Oxford: Oxbow Books.

Metcalf, P. & Huntington, R. 1993. *Celebrations of Death: the anthropology of mortuary ritual*. Cambridge: Cambridge University Press.

Miles, H. 1975. Barrows on the St Austell granite. *Cornish Archaeology* 14, 5–81.

Moore, C. N. & Rowlands, M. 1972. *Bronze Age Metalwork in Salisbury Museum*. Salisbury: Salisbury and South Wiltshire Museum.

Mortimer, J. R. 1905. *Forty Years' Researches in British and Saxon Burial Mounds of East Yorkshire*. London: Brown and Sons.

Mullin, D. 2001. Remembering, forgetting and the invention of tradition; burial and natural places in the English Early Bronze Age. *Antiquity* 289, 533–588.

Murphy, K. & Murphy, F. 2013. The excavation of two round barrows at Pant y Butler, Llangoedmor, Ceredigion, 2009–10. *Archaeologia Cambrensis* 162, 19–32.

Needham, S. 2000. Power pulses across a cultural divide: cosmologically driven acquisition between Armorica and Wessex. *Proceedings of the Prehistoric Society* 66, 151–208.

Needham, S. 2001. When expediency broaches ritual intention: the flow of metal between systemic and buried remains. *Journal of the Royal Anthropological Institute* 7, 275–298.

Needham, S. 2009. Encompassing the sea: 'maritories' and Bronze Age interactions. In P. Clark (ed.), *Bronze Age Connections: cultural contact in prehistoric Europe*. Oxford: Oxbow Books, 12–37.

Needham, S. 2012. Putting capes into context: Mold at the heart of a domain. In W. Britnell & R. J. Silvester (eds.), *Reflections on the Past, Essays in Honour of Frances Lynch*. Welshpool: Cambrian Archaeological Association, 210–236.

Needham, S., Parfitt, K. & Varndell, G. 2006. *The Ringlemere Cup: precious cups and the beginning of the Channel Bronze Age*. London: British Museum.

Needham, S. P. & Sheridan, J. A. 2014. Chalcolithic and Early Bronze Age goldwork from Britain: new finds and new perspectives. In H. Meller, E. Pernicka and R. Risch (eds.), *Metals of Power: early gold and silver. Proceedings of the 6th Archaeological Congress of Central Germany*. Halle: Landesmuseum für Vorgeschichte Halle, Tagungen des Landesmuseums Band 11, 903–941.

Noble, G. & Brophy, K. 2011. Ritual and remembrance at a prehistoric ceremonial complex in central Scotland. *Antiquity* 329, 787–804.

Nowakowski, J. A. & Johns, C. 2015. *Bypassing Indian Queens. Archaeological excavations 1992–1994. Investigating prehistoric and Romano-British settlement and landscapes in Cornwall*. Truro: Cornwall Archaeological Unit, Cornwall Council & Highways Agency.

O'Brien, W. 2004. *Ross Island: mining, metal and society in early Ireland*. Galway: University of Galway Press.

Oliver, L. 1999. The Hochdorf 'princely' grave and the nature of archaeological funerary assemblages. In T. Murray (ed.), *Time and Archaeology*. London: Routledge, 109–138.

O'Neil, B. H. St J. 1952. The excavation of Knackyboy cairn, St Martins, Isles of Scilly, 1948. *Antiquaries Journal* 32, 221–234.

Orme, B. & Coles, J. 1983. Prehistoric woodworking from the Somerset Levels 1: timber. In J. Coles (ed.), *Somerset Levels Papers 9*. Exeter: University of Exeter, 19–44.

Parker Pearson, M. 1982. Mortuary practices, society and ideology: an ethno-archaeological study. In I. Hodder (ed.), *Symbolic and Structural Archaeology*. Cambridge: Cambridge University Press, 89–98.

Parker Pearson, M. 1999. Fearing and celebrating the dead. In J. Downes & T. Pollard (eds.), *The Loved Body's Corruption: archaeological contributions to the study of human mortality*. Glasgow: Cruithne Press, 9–18.

Parker Pearson, M., Sharples, N. & Symonds, J. 2004. *South Uist: archaeology and history of a Hebridean island*. Stroud: Tempus.

Parker Pearson, M., Sheridan, A. & Needham, S. 2013. Bronze Age tree-trunk coffins in Britain. In N. Melton, J. Montgomery & C. J. Knüsel (eds.), *Gristhorpe Man: a life and death in the Bronze Age*. Oxford: Oxbow Books, 29–67.

Pearce, S. 1983. *The Bronze Age Metalwork of South Western Britain*. Oxford: British Archaeological Report 120.

Petersen, F. 1972. Traditions of multiple burial in later Neolithic and Early Bronze Age Britain. *Archaeological Journal* 129, 22–55.

Piggott, S. & Piggott, C. 1944. Excavation of barrows on Crichel and Launceston Downs, Dorset. *Archaeologia* 90, 47–80.

Pliny the Elder, (trans Healy, R.) 2004. *Natural History: a selection*. London: Harmondsworth.

Pollard, S. 1967. Seven prehistoric sites near Honiton, Devon. Part I. A Beaker flint ring and three cairns. *Proceedings of the Devon Archaeological Society* 25, 19–39.

Pollard, S. 1971 Seven prehistoric sites near Honiton, Devon. Part II Three flint rings. *Proceedings of the Devon Archaeological Society* 29, 162–180.

Pollard, S. & Russell, P. 1969. Excavation of round barrow 248b, Upton Pyne. *Proceedings of the Devon Archaeological Society* 27, 49–74.

Poole, K. 2013. Horses for courses? Religious change and dietary shifts in Anglo-Saxon England. *Oxford Journal of Archaeology* 32, 319–334.

Proudfoot, E. 1963. Report on the excavation of a bell barrow in the parish of *Edmondsham*, Dorset, England. *Proceedings of the Prehistoric Society* 29, 395–425.

Quinnell, H. 1988. The local character of the Devon Bronze Age and its interpretation in the 1980s. *Proceedings of the Devon Archaeological Society* 46, 1–12.

Quinnell, H. 1994a. New perspectives on upland monuments – Dartmoor in earlier prehistory. *Proceedings of the Devon Archaeological Society* 52, 49–62.

Quinnell, H. 1994b. Becoming marginal? Dartmoor in later prehistory. *Proceedings of the Devon Archaeological Society* 52, 75–84.

Quinnell, H. 2003. Devon Beakers: new finds, new thoughts. *Proceedings of the Devon Archaeological Society* 61, 1–20.

Quinnell, H. 2012. Trevisker pottery: some recent studies. In W. Britnell, & R. J Silvester (eds.), *Reflections on the Past: essays in honour of Frances Lynch*. Welshpool: Cambrian Archaeological Association, 146–171.

Rackham, O. 1986. *The History of the Countryside*. London: Dent

Radford, C. A. R. 1952. Prehistoric settlements on Dartmoor and the Cornish moors. *Proceedings of the Prehistoric Society* 18, 55–84.

Radford, C. A. R. & Rogers, E. H. 1947. The excavation of

two barrows at East Putford. *Proceedings of the Devon Archaeological Exploration Society* 3.4, 156–163.

Raftery, J. 1970. Prehistoric coiled basketry bags. *Journal of the Royal Society of Antiquaries of Ireland* 100, 167–168.

Randsborg, K. 2011. *Bronze Age Textiles: men, women and wealth*. London: Bristol Classical Press.

Randsborg, K. & Christensen, K. 2006. Bronze Age oak-coffins. *Acta Archaeologia* 77, 49–74.

Ray, K. & Thomas, J. S. 2003. In the kinship of cows: the social centrality of cattle in the earlier Neolithic of southern Britain. In M. Parker Pearson (ed.), *Food, Culture and Identity in the Neolithic and Early Bronze Age*. Oxford: British Archaeological Report S1117, 37–44.

Rebay-Salisbury, K. 2010. Cremations: fragmented bodies in the Bronze and Iron Ages. In K. Rebay-Salisbury, M. L. S. Sorensen & J. Hughes (eds.), *Body Parts and Bodies Whole: changing relations and meanings*. Oxford: Oxbow Books, 64–71.

Reichert, A. 2007. *Bast, Rushes, Stinging Nettles. Textile Materials from the Stone Age. Archaeological Reconstructions by Anne Reichert*. Dithmarschen: Museum für Archäologie und Ökologie Dithmarschen.

Reynolds, B. 1968. *Kariba Studies; the material culture of the peoples of the Gwembe valley*. Manchester: Manchester University Press.

Reynolds, F. 2012. Totemism and food taboos in the Early Neolithic: a feast of roe deer at the Coneybury 'Anomaly', Wiltshire, southern Britain. In H. Anderson-Whymark & J. Thomas (eds.), *Regional Perspectives on Neolithic Pit Deposition*. Oxford: Oxbow Books, 171–186.

Richards, A. 1956. *Chisingu: a girl's initiation ceremony among the Bemba of Zambia*. London: Faber and Faber.

Richards, C. & Thomas, J. 1984. Ritual activity and structured deposition in later Neolithic Wessex. In R. Bradley & J. Gardiner (eds.), *Neolithic Studies: a review of some current research*. Oxford: British Archaeological Reports 133, 189–218.

Richards, C. & Wright, J. 2014. Monuments in the making: the stone circles of western Scotland. In C. Richards (ed.), *Building the Great Stone Circles of the North*. Oxford: Windgather Press, 31–61.

Rival, L. 1998. Trees, from symbols of life and regeneration to political artefacts. In L. Rival (ed.), *The Social Lives of trees: anthropological perspectives on tree symbolism*. Oxford: Berg, 1–38.

Robertson, R. 1894–95. Notice of the discovery of a stone cist and urns at the Cuninghar, Tillicoultry; with notes on the contents and the sculptured covering stone of the cist; and on the microscopical examination of the fibrous or hairy substance found in the cist. *Proceedings of the Society of Antiquaries of Scotland* 29, 190–197.

Robertson-Mackay, M. E. 1980. A 'head and hoofs' burial beneath a round barrow, with other Neolithic and Bronze Age sites, on Hemp Knoll, near Avebury, Wiltshire. *Proceedings of the Prehistoric Society* 46, 123–176.

Ryder, M. L. 1963–64. Report on the hair and skin remains from Ashgrove, Methilhill, Fife, and other Bronze Age sites. In A. Henshall, A dagger-grave and other cist burials at Ashgrove, Methilhill, Fife. *Proceedings of the Society of Antiquaries of Scotland* 97, 174–176.

Savory, H. N. 1972. Copper Age cists and cist-cairns in Wales: with special reference to Newton, Swansea, and other 'multiple-cist cairns'. In F. Lynch, & C. Burgess (eds.), *Prehistoric Man in Wales and the West: essays in honour of Lily F Chitty*. Bath: Adams and Dart, 117–140.

Savory, H. N. 1980. *Guide Catalogue of the Bronze Age Collections*. Cardiff: National Museum of Wales.

Sawyer, K. 2015. *Isles of the Dead? The Setting and Function of the Bronze Age Chambered Cairns and Cists of the Isles of Scilly*. Oxford: Archaeopress Archaeology.

Scarre, C. 2011. *Landscapes of Neolithic Brittany*. Oxford: Oxford University Press.

Schulting, R. & Bradley, R. 2013. 'Of human remains and weapons in the neighbourhood of London': new AMS ^{14}C dates on Thames 'river skulls' and their European context. *Archaeological Journal* 170, 30–77.

Seale, C. 1998. *Constructing Death: the sociology of dying and bereavement*. Cambridge: Cambridge University Press.

Serjeantson, D. 2011. *Review of Animal Remains from the Neolithic and Early Bronze Age of Southern Britain (4000 BC–1500 BC)*. Portsmouth: English Heritage.

Sheridan, A. 2004. The National Museums of Scotland radiocarbon dating programmes: results obtained 2003/4. *Discovery and Excavation in Scotland* 5, 174–176.

Sheridan, A. 2008. Bronze Age composite bead necklace. In J. Thomas, *Monument, Memory and Myth: use and Reuse of Three Bronze Age Round Barrows at Cossington, Leicestershire*. Leicester: Leicester University Archaeology Monograph 14, 80–88.

Sheridan, A. 2012. Contextualising Kilmartin: building a narrative for developments in western Scotland and beyond, from the Early Neolithic to the Late Bronze Age. In A. Jones, J. Pollard, M. Allen & J. Gardiner (eds.), *Image, Memory and Monumentality: archaeological engagements with the material world*. Oxford: Oxbow Books/Prehistoric Society, 163–183.

Sheridan, A., Needham, S. O'Connor, S., Melton, N, Janaway, R, Cameron, E. & Evans, A. 2013. The Gristhorpe coffin and its contents. In N. Melton, J. Montgomery & C. J. Knüsel (eds.), *Gristhorpe Man: a life and death in the Bronze Age*. Oxford: Oxbow Books, 148–165.

Sheridan, A. & Shortland, A. 2004. '… beads which have given rise to so much dogmatism, controversy and rash speculation': faience in Early Bronze Age Britain and Ireland. In I. A. G. Shepherd & G. J. Barclay (eds.), *Scotland in Ancient Europe*. Edinburgh: Society of Antiquaries of Scotland, 263–282.

Sherratt, S. 1991. Sacred and profane substances: the ritual use of narcotics in later Neolithic Europe. In P. Garwood, D. Jennings, R. Skeates & J. Toms (eds.), *Sacred and Profane: proceedings of a conference on archaeology, ritual and religion, Oxford, 1989*. Oxford: Oxford University Committee for Archaeology, 33–42.

Smirke, E. 1867. Some account of the discovery of a gold cup in a barrow in Cornwall. *Archaeological Journal* 24, 189–195.

Smith, G. 1996. Archaeology and environment of a Bronze Age cairn and prehistoric and Romano-British field system at Chysauster, Gulval, near Penzance, Cornwall. *Proceedings of the Prehistoric Society* 62, 167–220.

Smith, I. F. and Simpson, D. 1966. Excavation of a round barrow on Overton Hill, north Wiltshire. *Proceedings of the Prehistoric Society* 32, 122–155.

Smith, K., Coppen, J., Wainwright, G. & Beckett, S. 1981. The Shaugh Moor project: third report – settlement and environmental conditions. *Proceedings of the Prehistoric Society* 47, 205–274.

Smith, M. 1994. *Excavated Bronze Age burial mounds of north-east Yorkshire*. Durham: Architectural and Archaeological Society of Durham and Northumberland.

Smith, R. 1921. The Seven Barrows at Lambourn. *Archaeological Journal* 78, 47–54.

Spector, J. 1991. What this awl means: towards a feminist archaeology. In J. Gero & M. Conkey (eds.), *Engendering Archaeology: women and archaeology*. London: Blackwell, 388–405.

Spindler, K. 1993. *The Man in the Ice*. London: Weidenfeld and Nicolson.

Stead, I. M. 1967. A La Tène III burial at Welwyn Garden City. *Archaeologia* 101, 1–62.

Symonds, M. 2012. Waterworld: Must Farm's Bronze Age boats. *Current Archaeology* 263, 12–19.

Taylor, A. F. & Woodward, P. J. 1985. A Bronze Age barrow cemetery and associated settlement at Roxton, Bedfordshire. *Archaeological Journal* 142, 73–149.

Taylor, J. A. 1980. Environmental changes in Wales during the Holocene. In J. A. Taylor (ed.), *Culture and Environment in Prehistoric Wales: selected essays*. Oxford: British Archaeological Report 76, 101–130.

Taylor, S. R. 2015. *Truro Eastern District Centre, Cornwall: archaeological watching brief archive report*. Truro: Cornwall Archaeological Unit.

Thomas, A. C. 1960. Excavations on Tean, Isles of Scilly, 1956, and problems of the Scillonian submergence. Unpublished report, University of Edinburgh.

Thomas, J. 2008. *Monument, Memory and Myth: use and re-use of three Bronze Age round barrows at Cossington, Leicestershire*. Leicester: Leicester University Press.

Thomas, J. 2013. Mounds, memories and myths: ancient monuments and place in the Leicestershire landscape. In A Chadwick & C. Gibson (eds.), *Memory, Myth, Place and Long-term Landscape Inhabitation*. Oxford: Oxbow Books, 76–98.

Thomas, J. S. 1991. Reading the body: Beaker funerary practice in Britain. In P. Garwood, D. Jennings, R. Skeates & J. Toms (eds.), *Sacred and Profane: proceedings of a conference on archaeology, ritual and religion, Oxford, 1989*. Oxford: Oxford University Committee for Archaeology, 33–42.

Thomas, J. S. 2014. *The Birth of Neolithic Britain: an interpretative account*. Oxford: Oxford University Press.

Thomas, N. 2005. *Snail Down, Wiltshire. The Bronze Age Barrow Cemetery and Related Earthworks in the Parishes of Collingbourne Ducis and Collingbourne Kingston; excavations 1953, 1955 and 1957*. Devizes: Wiltshire Archaeological and Natural History Society/English Heritage.

Tilley, C. 1996. The powers of rocks: topography and monument construction on Bodmin Moor. *World Archaeology* 28, 161–176.

Tilley, C. 2004. *The Materiality of Stone: explorations in landscape phenomenology*. Walnut Creek CA: Left Coast Press.

Tilley, C. 2010. Rocks as resources: landscapes and power. In C. Tilley (ed.), *Interpreting Landscapes: geologies, topographies, identities*. Walnut Creek CA: Left Coast Press, 353–426.

Tipping, R. 1994. Ritual floral tributes in the Scottish Bronze Age – palynological evidence. *Journal of Archaeological Science* 21, 133–139.

Tipping, R. 1997. The soil and pollen stratigraphy beneath the cairn. In R. Mercer and M. S. Midgley, The Early Bronze age cairn at Sketewan, Balnaguard, Perth and Kinross.

Proceedings of the Society of Antiquaries of Scotland 127, 281–338.

Tipping, R. 2002. Climatic variability and 'marginal' settlement in upland British landscapes: a re-evaluation. *Landscapes* 3, 10–28.

Trahair, J. 1978. A survey of the cairns on Bodmin Moor. *Cornish Archaeology* 17, 3–24.

Turton, D. 1980. There's no such beast: cattle and colour naming among the Mursi. *Man* 15, 320–338.

Van Gennep, A. 1960. *The Rites of Passage*. Chicago IL: University of Chicago Press.

Vesey-Fitzgerald, B. 1973. *Gypsies of Britain*. Newton Abbott: David and Charles.

Vitebsky, P. 1995. *The Shaman: voyages of the soul, trance, ecstasy and healing from Siberia to the Amazon*. Chicago: University of Chicago Press.

Vitebsky, P. 2005. *Reindeer People: living with animals and spirits in Siberia*. Chicago IL: University of Chicago Press.

Waddell, J. 1990. *The Bronze Age Burials of Ireland*. Galway: Galway University Press.

Wainwright, G. J., Fleming, A. & Smith, K. 1979. The Shaugh Moor Project: first report. *Proceedings of the Prehistoric Society* 45, 1–34.

Wainwright, G. J. & Smith, K. 1980. The Shaugh Moor project: second report – the enclosure. *Proceedings of the Prehistoric Society* 46, 65–122.

Walford, G. F. & Quinnell, N. 1997. C K Croft Andrew's Excavations in Tavistock Woodlands in 1937 and 1938. *Cornish Archaeology* 36, 77–94.

Waterson, R. 1997. *The Living House: an anthropology of architecture in south-east Asia*. London: Thames and Hudson.

Watkins, C. 2013. *The Undiscovered Country: journeys among the dead*. London: Vintage.

Watkins, T. 1982. The excavation of an Early Bronze Age cemetery at Barns Farm, Dalgety, Fife. *Proceedings of the Society of Antiquaries of Scotland* 112, 48–141.

Watts, M. & Quinnell, H. 2001. A Bronze Age cemetery at Elburton, Plymouth *Proceedings of the Devon Archaeological Society* 59, 11–44.

Weiner, A. B. 1987. *The Trobrianders of Papua New Guinea*. Belmont: Wadsworth/Thomson.

Whimster, D. C. 1931. *The Archaeology of Surrey*. London: Methuen.

Wilkin, N. & Vander Linden, M. 2015. What was and what would never be: changing patterns of interaction and archaeological visibility across north-west Europe from 2500 to 1500 cal BC. In H. Anderson-Whymark, D. Garrow & F. Sturt (eds.), *Continental Connections: exploring cross-Channel relationships from the Mesolithic to the Iron Age*. Oxford: Oxbow Books, 99–121.

Wills, B., Pailthorpe, R. & Payne, S. 1989. *The Downland Shepherd*. Sutton: Stroud.

Williams, H. 2001. An ideology of transformation: cremation rites and animal sacrifice in early Anglo-Saxon England. In N. Price (ed.), *The Archaeology of Shamanism*. London: Routledge, 3–16.

Wincott Heckett, E. 1998. A horsehair woven band from County Antrim, Ireland: clues to the past from a later Bronze Age masterwork. In Textile Society of America, *Creating Textiles: makers, methods, markets*. Earleville MD: Textile Society of America, Textile Society of America Symposium Proceedings 173, 150–157.

Woodruff, C. H. 1874. On Celtic tumuli in east Kent. *Archaeologia Cantiana* 9, 16–31.

Woodward, A. 1993. The cult of relics in prehistoric Britain. In M. Carver (ed.), *In Search of Cult: archaeological investigations in honour of Philip Rahtz*. Woodbridge: Boydell Press, 1–8.

Woodward, A, 2000. *British Barrows: a matter of life and death*. Stroud: Tempus.

Woodward, A. 2002. Beads and Beakers: heirlooms and relics in the British Early Bronze Age. *Antiquity* 294, 1040–1047.

Woodward, A. & Hunter, J. 2011. *An Examination of Prehistoric Stone Bracers from Britain*. Oxford: Oxbow Books.

Woodward, A. & Hunter, J. 2015. *Ritual in Early Bronze Age Grave Goods. An Examination of Ritual and Dress Equipment from Chalcolithic and Early Bronze Age Graves in Britain*. Oxford: Oxbow Books.

Woodward, A., Hunter, J., Ixer, R., Maltby, M., Potts, P., Webb, P., Watson, J. & Jones, M. 2005. Ritual in some Early Bronze Age grave goods. *Archaeological Journal* 163, 31–64.

Woodward, P. J. 1991. *The South Dorset Ridgeway: survey and excavations*. Dorchester: Dorset Natural History and Archaeological Society Monograph.

Worth, R. H. 1900. Nineteenth report of the barrow committee. *Transactions of the Devonshire Association* 32, 46–54.

Worth, R. H. 1901. Twentieth report of the barrow committee. *Transactions of the Devonshire Association* 33, 117–122.

Worth, R. H. 1902. Twenty-first report of the barrow committee. *Transactions of the Devonshire Association* 33, 104–146.

Worth, R. H. 1906. Twenty-fifth report of the barrow committee. *Report of the Transactions of the Devonshire Association* 38, 57–66.

Worth, R. H. 1967. (G. M. Spooner and F. S. Russell eds)*Worth's Dartmoor, compiled from the published works of the late R Hansford Worth,*. Newton Abbot: David and Charles.

Worth, R. N. 1896. Fifteenth report of the barrow committee. *Transactions of the Devonshire Association* 28, 84–89.

Wymer, J. J. & Healy, F. 1996. Neolithic and Bronze Age activity and settlement at Longham and Beestone with Bittering. In J. J. Wymer (ed.), *Barrow Excavations in Norfolk, 1984–88*, East Anglian Archaeology 77. Dereham: Norfolk Museums Service, 28–53.

Zeiler, J. T. 2006. The bear, the wolf, the otter and the weasel: carnivorous mammals in the Dutch Neolithic. In D. Serjeantson and D. Field (eds.), *Animals in the Neolithic of Britain and Europe*. Oxford: Oxbow Books, 24–31.

Appendix A: Chemical analysis of beads from the Whitehorse Hill cist

Joanna Dunster

Seven beads and a woven band of organic material decorated with studs of an unknown metal were analysed to determine the elemental composition. The analysis was performed prior to cleaning and conservation in order to assist in designing the most appropriate strategy for a rare find of great antiquity. The portable XRF was chosen as a non-destructive surface technique with low limits of detection for a range of diagnostic elements. The metal studs on the band were found to be mostly made of Sn, one bead was consistent with amber, one was found to be of an organic material and therefore composed of elements too light for detection by the pXRF, and three were found to be consistent with shale (Chapters 14 and 15).

Method of analysis

A portable X-ray Fluorescence Spectrometer (Niton XL3Dt) was used for the analysis of the objects. The methodology followed Dungworth and Girbal (2011), under the condition Mining Mode to access the greatest range of elements, and using a He flush in order to allow the detection of light elements (in the range of Mg – P).

The beads were analysed following excavation and prior to cleaning and conservation. As a result, the data obtained may be subject to some or all of the following limiting factors.

- The surface of the artefacts was wet. This layer of water attenuates the X-rays as they pass through, but not evenly, as the lighter X-rays have lower energy and are more drastically affected. This can prevent the detection of lighter elements and bias the results towards heavier elements.
- The surface of the artefacts was contaminated by mud. This not only attenuates the X-rays, it also introduces other elements into the path of the detector which cannot readily be distinguished from the composition of the bead, potentially resulting in a misleading composition.
- The surface of the artefacts was obscured. The material may contain variations such as paint or inlay which may have a different chemical composition. There may also be areas of corrosion or damage where the surface material differs. Without a full view of the surface it is impossible to be confident that the area sampled is the most representative of the total composition.
- The areas sampled were curved. This means that the reflection of X-rays was not uniform across the surfaces and many may have been deflected away from the detector entirely, resulting in a misleading composition.
- The area sampled was smaller than the detector. This means that X-rays were able to escape and the analysed total is not equal to 100%.

The artefacts were individually subjected to one reading totalling one minute, which consists of 15 seconds at four different accelerating voltages and with different secondary targets (Ag, Mo and Fe). The relative heights of the peaks in each spectra were used to determine the presence and relative abundance of elements.

Results

Braided band with tin studs

The main target for analysis in this case was any one of the round studs attached to the band, which had been identified as metal following excavation. The studs appeared to be of a similar size and shape, but it was impossible to comment on their visual similarity until cleaning had been

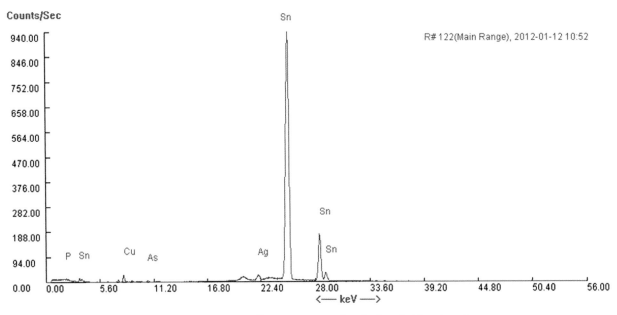

Figure A.1: Main Range spectrum for the braided band stud.

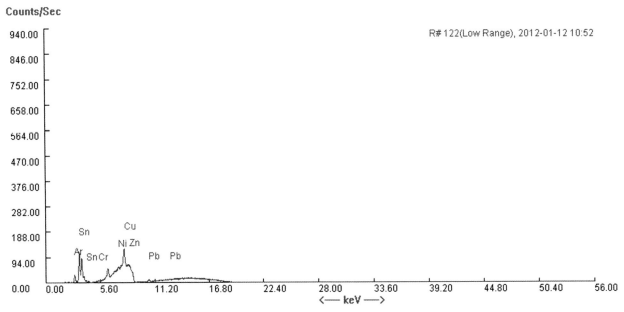

Figure A.2: Low Range spectrum for the braided band stud.

carried out. The area analysed showed a strong Sn peak under the Main and High-energy conditions (Fig. A.1) and low levels of Cu, Zn, Pb and Cr under the Low- and Light-energy conditions (Fig. A.2). These results support the interpretation that the metal from which the studs were constructed was Sn. However, it cannot be concluded whether the trace metals can be attributed to impurities in the tin or were components of the burial environment which were either adhering to the band or had been absorbed by the organic woven material.

Additionally, a terminal of the the band was analysed, as it appeared to contain some solid material. The levels of the elements detected were so low that no diagnostic composition could be assigned, and it was concluded that the principal components were too light for detection using this method, suggesting that the material was organic.

Large wooden stud

This object was selected for analysis because it is significantly different in size and shape, and it was therefore thought to be of a different composition. It is a squat cylinder shape with no obvious perforation, although this and the colour could not be conclusively stated until

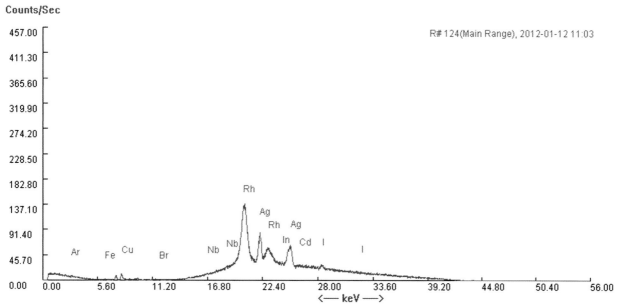

Figure A.3: Main Range spectrum for the large wooden stud.

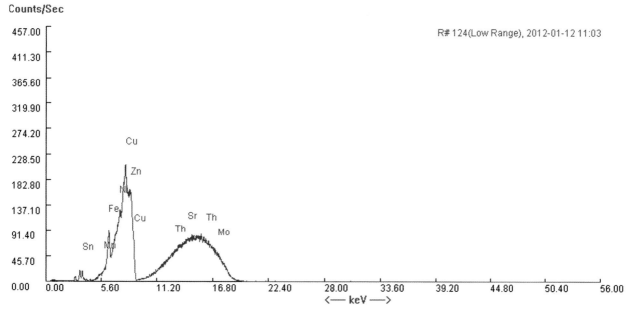

Figure A.4: Low Range spectrum for the large wooden stud.

after cleaning. Under all energy conditions, there were no clear or significantly high peaks. This is evident in the relatively high level of background noise present in the spectra (Figs. A.3 and A.4). It was concluded that the principal components are elements too light for detection, suggesting that the material is organic.

Tin bead

This object was selected for analysis because it was significantly different from the other beads in size and shape, and its surface was covered in a grey-brown granular

substance consistent with a metal corrosion product. The original shape was most probably tubular and a perforation was evident at one end. Under the Main and High-energy conditions, it showed a large, clear Sn peak (Fig. A.5), while the Low and Light-energy conditions resulted in a range of trace metals (Fig. A.6). These were compared with those in the studs attached to the woven band (above) and were found to be present at similar levels. The analysed surface of this bead is therefore consistent with tin, although, as noted above, it cannot be conclusively stated whether the source of the trace metals is the tin itself or the burial environment.

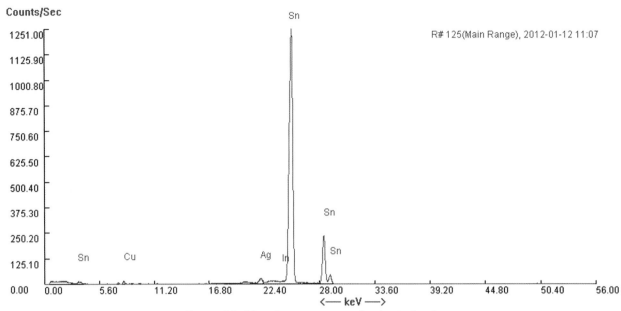

Figure A.5: Main Range spectrum for the tin bead.

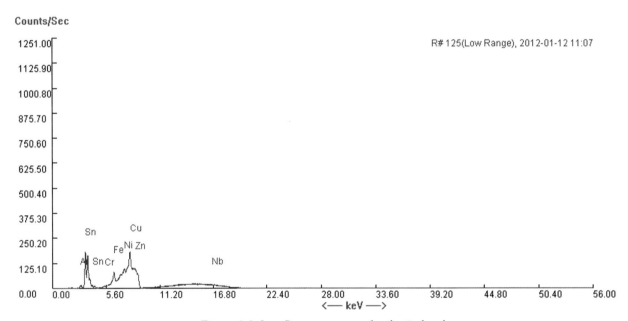

Figure A.6: Low Range spectrum for the tin bead.

Amber bead

This bead was selected for analysis because its size and shape were significantly different from those of the other beads in the assemblage. It is relatively large and tubular in shape with a perforation from end to end. In areas where there is less soil adhering, it is obviously transparent with an orange–yellow colour consistent with amber. Under all energy conditions, there are no clear or relatively high peaks (Figs. A.7 and A.8) and a high level of background noise, meaning that the composition is most probably dominated by light elements which cannot be detected in this case.

This result is consistent with the organic composition of amber (Beck *et al.* 1965).

Small round bead 1 (shale)

This bead was selected for analysis because it appeared to be representative of many of the beads in the assemblage in terms of size and shape. It is relatively small and round with flattened ends and a wide perforation throughout. The colour could not be commented on prior to cleaning, although it was thought to be similar to another excavated example

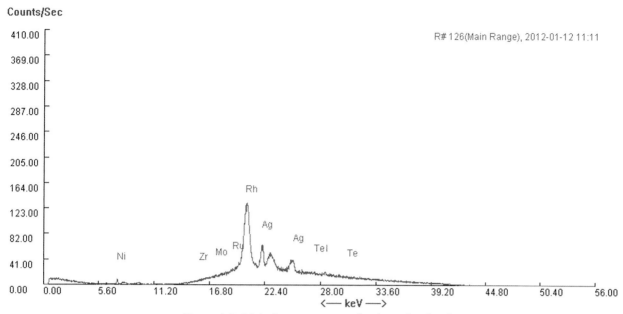

Figure A.7: Main Range spectrum for the amber bead.

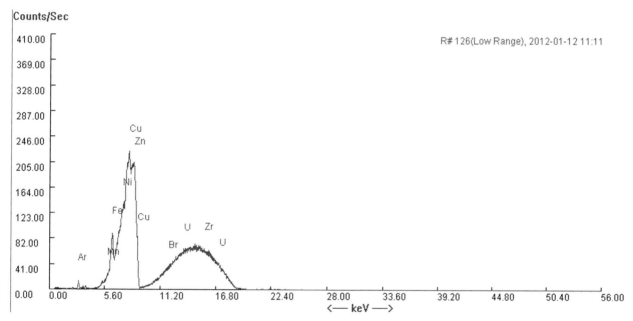

Figure A.8: Low Range spectrum for the amber bead.

which is grey and consistent with shale (below). Under all four energy conditions, there were no clear, relatively high peaks, and a high level of background noise (Figs. A.9 and A.10). This means that the composition is likely to be principally light elements which cannot be detected in this case, and is consistent with an organic material.

Small round bead 2 (shale)

This bead was selected for analysis because it also appeared to be representative of many of the beads in the assemblage

in terms of shape and size. However, it was still hoped to prove a similarity with the allegedly shale bead which was among the first discovered at the site (Chapter 2). The bead is relatively small and round in shape with flattened ends and a wide perforation throughout. Under the Main and Low-energy conditions (Figs. A.11 and A.12 respectively) a strong Fe peak can be seen. There are trace levels of other metals which may originate from the bead material, or from the burial environment. Under the Light-energy condition (Fig. A.13) a moderate Si peak can be seen, which supports the interpretation of shale.

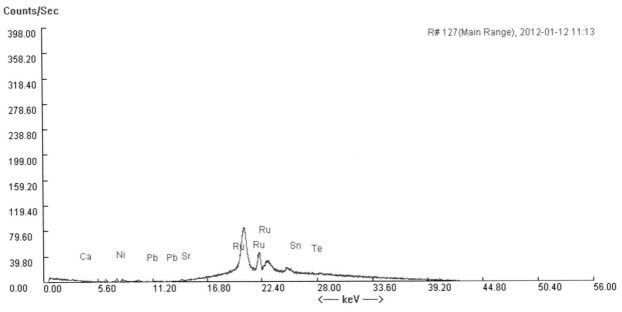

Figure A.9: Main Range spectrum for the small round bead 1.

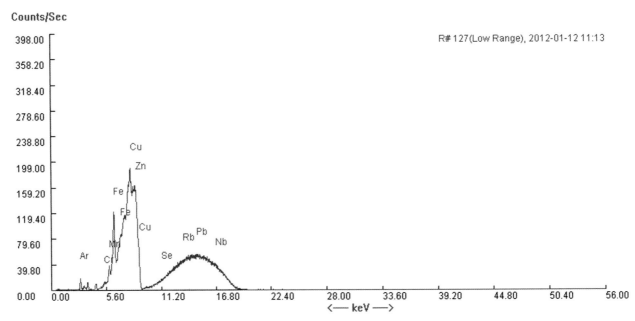

Figure A.10: Low Range spectrum for the small round bead 1.

The spectra compare well with those obtained from analysis of the bead which was among the first to be excavated and which was originally interpreted as shale (Figs. A.14–A.16).

It can be concluded from this comparison that the composition of both beads is very similar, and that they are probably made from the same material, although what the material is cannot be determined by the pXRF.

Very small round bead (shale)

This bead was selected for analysis because, although similar to the small round beads, it is significantly smaller. Under the Main and Low-energy conditions (Figs. A.17 and A.18 respectively), it shows a strong Fe peak with trace metals which compare well with the small round shale beads discussed above. The presence of a moderate

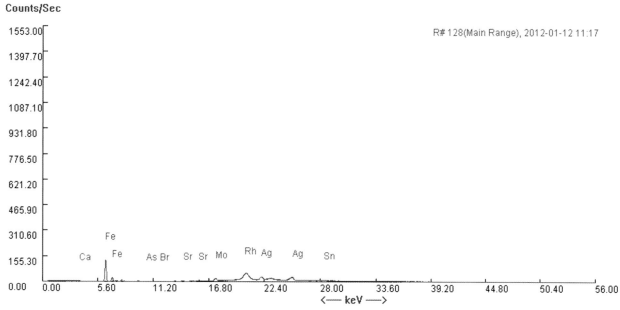

Figure A.11: Main Range spectrum for the small round shale bead.

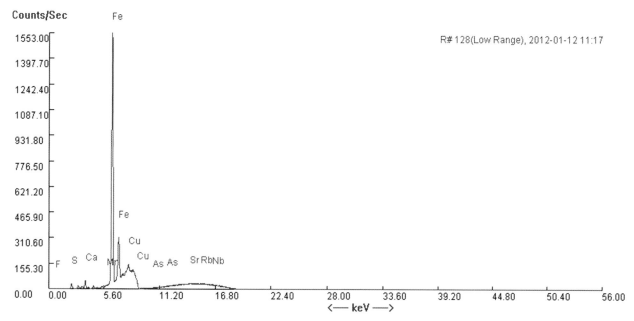

Figure A.12: Low Range spectrum for the small round shale bead.

Si peak under the Light-energy condition supports this identification (Fig. A.19).

It can be concluded from this comparison that the very small round bead shares a similar elemental composition with the small round beads, and that they are probably made from the same material. Again, it is not possible to confirm what that material is using the pXRF.

References

Beck, C., Wilbur, E., Meret, S., Kossove, D. & Kermani, K. 1965. The infrared spectra of amber and the identification of Baltic amber. *Archaeometry* 8, 96–109.

Dungworth, D & Girbal, B. 2011. *Walmer Castle, Deal, Kent. Analysis of Window Glass*. Research Department Report 2/2011. Portsmouth: English Heritage.

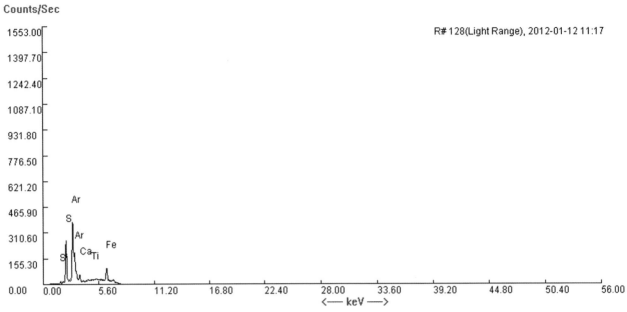

Figure A.13: Light Range spectrum for the small round shale bead.

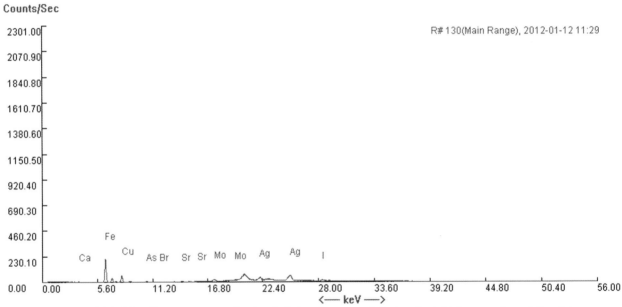

Figure A.14: Main Range spectrum for the shale bead recovered during the initial excavation of the cist.

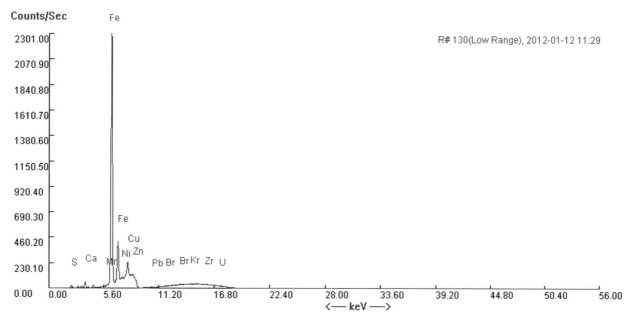

Figure A.15: Low Range spectrum for the shale bead recovered during the initial excavation of the cist.

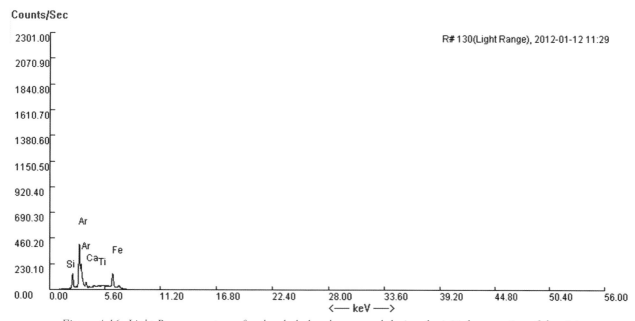

Figure A.16: Light Range spectrum for the shale bead recovered during the initial excavation of the cist.

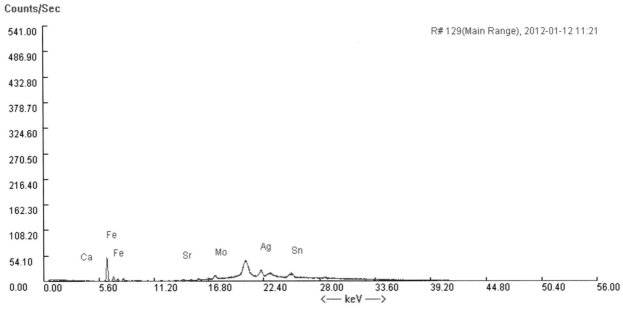

Figure A.17: Main Range spectrum for the very small round bead.

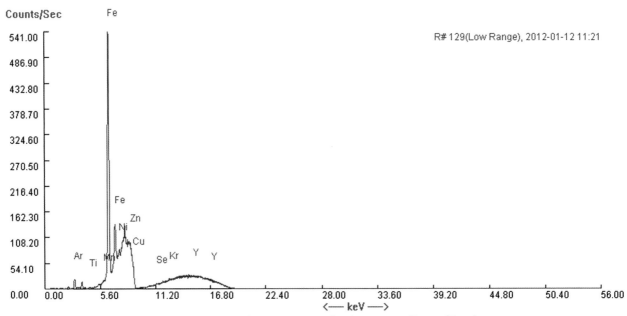

Figure A.18: Low Range spectrum for the very small round bead.

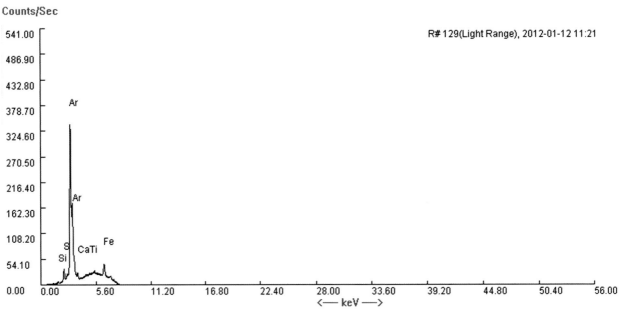

Figure A.19: Light Range spectrum for the very small round bead.

Appendix B: Report on the scanning electron microscope (SEM) examination of the basketry container and other organic artefacts from Whitehorse Hill cist

Caroline Cartwright

The excavation of the cist on Whitehorse Hill revealed unusual conditions of preservation of damp organic material within the acid peat environment. The organic objects included a basketry object containing beads and wooden studs, an animal pelt enclosing cremated human bone, a textile and animal skin object beneath the pelt and a braided band with tin studs. Two layers of matted plant material were present, one above and the second below the burial.

The organic material studied

Following the submission of an initial assessment report on the organic artefacts and associated plant remains (Cartwright 2012), which contained 21 variable pressure scanning electron microscope (VP-SEM) images of samples examined, a further stage of analysis was undertaken on organic remains from the cist. The artefacts included the basketry container (Chapter 3), a textile and animal-skin object and a braided band with tin studs. A subsequent request was made for the VP-SEM examination of one small (intact) wooden ear stud from the basketry container, with a view to possibly identifying the wood used (Chapter 16).

Method of examination

Examination of samples from the organic artefacts and the matted plant layers was undertaken in a VP-SEM (Hitachi S-3700N) using the backscatter electron (BSE) detector, mostly at 15kV (but sometimes at 12kV or 20kV), with a working distance of about 14mm. As the fibrous material of the samples was in a fragile condition, the SEM chamber was only partially evacuated (40 Pa). The 3D mode (rather than Compositional) was selected to maximize the opportunity to reveal diagnostic features on the fibres and other plant cells, as well as the animal hairs and leather/skin products. Uncoated samples were placed on adhesive carbon discs mounted onto aluminium stubs; no other sample preparation was required. Principles, procedures and identification criteria from publications (for example, Higgitt *et al.* 2011 and references therein; Cartwright and King 2012), as well as reference collection specimens and reference SEM images compiled by the author, were used for comparison with the Whitehorse Hill samples.

As all of the samples had been kept moist, use of the environmental secondary electron detector (ESED) on the VP-SEM was required for some samples (such as the textile and animal-skin object). Mindful of the possible need to control the water evaporation from these moist samples, the use of a Deben Coolstage was mooted, particularly for the examination of the wooden ear-stud. However, that was not possible due to the limited amount of time that the object was available for VP-SEM examination.

Discussion was held on the subject of the possible deployment of raking light (oblique) photography for characterisation of weave structures of possible textiles or remnant textile impressions. Ultimately this was not implemented as it would have necessitated the transfer to London of the organic objects during the time when they were still undergoing conservation. Furthermore, the existing corpus of imagery combined with input from the team of textile specialists involved was deemed (by the

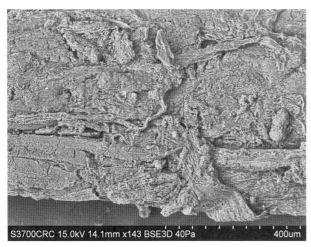

Figure B.1: VP-SEM image showing the constituents of a sample from the basketry container. (Image: C.R. Cartwright.)

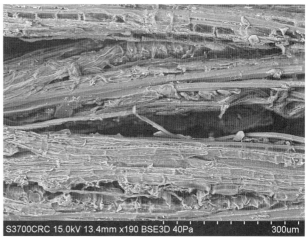

Figure B.3: VP-SEM image showing lime/linden (Tilia sp.) bast fibres from a circular disc (basketry container) sample. (Image: C.R. Cartwright.)

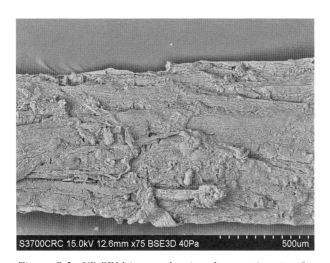

Figure B.2: VP-SEM image showing the constituents of a sample from one of the circular discs of the basketry container. (Image: C.R. Cartwright.)

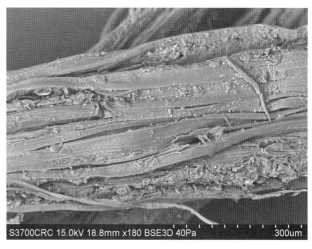

Figure B.4: VP-SEM image showing lime bast fibres from a circular disc (basketry container) sample. (Image: C.R. Cartwright.)

team members involved) to provide sufficient information at the current point in time.

Results

The basketry container

Initial sampling of the bag was problematic inasmuch as some of the materials used for the construction of the artefact (Fig. B.1) appeared in their wet condition to be very similar to those in the matted plant layers; distinguishing the different elements was not straightforward. A further complication was introduced by what appeared to be degraded remnants of leather/hide or skin products overlying or interweaving amongst the plant fibres. However, subsequent sampling after conservation had advanced was more productive. Samples taken from

the circular discs (Fig. B.2), the 'tube' and the stitching were examined using the VP-SEM (above) and compared with modern experimental archaeological and historical reference specimens of plant fibres.

Figures B.3 and B.4 show that the circular discs are made up of lime/linden (*Tilia* sp.) bast fibres. The woven 'tube' also consists of lime bast fibres (Figs. B.5 and B.6). Lime bast fibres were also used for the ties or stitching which hold together the coils of lime bast (Fig. B.7 and B.8).

Other organic items

Braided band with tin studs

The braided band with tin studs comprises braided fibres, initially thought to be of horse hair or plant material. Owing

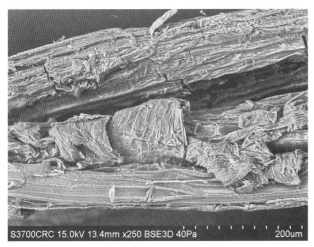

Figure B.5: VP-SEM image showing lime bast fibres from a woven 'tube' (basketry container) sample. (Image: C.R. Cartwright.)

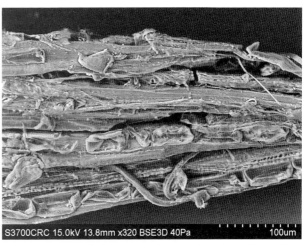

Figure B.8: VP-SEM image showing lime bast fibres from a basketry container tie/stitching sample. (Image: C.R. Cartwright.)

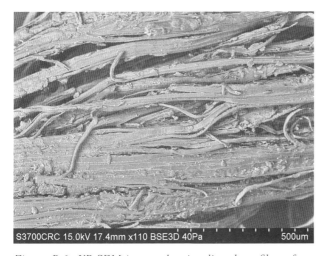

Figure B.6: VP-SEM image showing lime bast fibres from a woven 'tube' (basketry container) sample. (Image: C.R. Cartwright.)

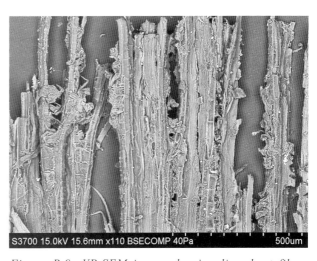

Figure B.9: VP-SEM image showing lime bast fibres experimentally stripped from the bark by S. Harris. (Image: C.R. Cartwright.)

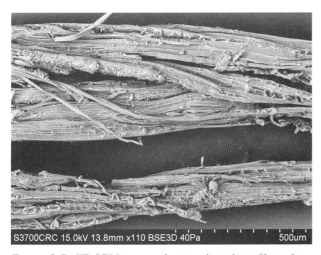

Figure B.7: VP-SEM image showing lime bast fibres from a basketry container tie/stitching sample. (Image: C.R. Cartwright.)

to the extreme rarity of the object and the complex, intricate nature of its fabrication, only two tiny samples of fibres/hairs were taken for identification; these may not represent all the fibres and/or hairs present. Figure B.10 shows the larger fibre, ostensibly an animal guard hair rather than a plant fibre, despite the absence of clear scale patterning. It was debated whether some features could be vestigial (or ghost) remnants of cuticular scales (Chapter 14). Within the author's corpus of comparative SEM images of guard hairs from many animal taxa (including horse), some guard hair specimens do appear remarkably smooth. This can arise in archaeological or historical fibres where wear, usage, damage, ageing, burial and other such factors may have impacted on the surface scale features (Cartwright and King 2012). Either way, identification to a specific animal was not possible on the basis of this sample. However, subsequent analysis (Appendix C) revealed that the band was of bovine hair.

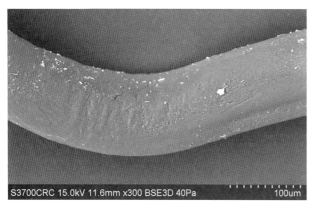

Figure B.10: VP-SEM image showing an animal guard hair from the braided band with tin studs. (Image: C.R. Cartwright.)

Figure B.11: VP-SEM image showing a fine animal underfur hair from the braided band with tin studs. (Image: C.R. Cartwright.)

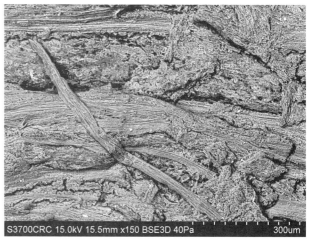

Figure B.12: VP-SEM image showing the different constituents of the plant fibre textile and animal-skin artefact. (Image: C.R. Cartwright.)

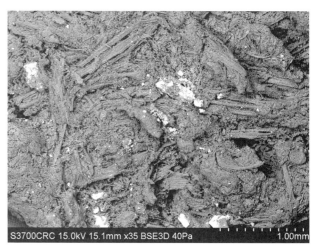

Figure B.13: VP-SEM image showing the different constituents of the plant fibre textile and animal-skin artefact. (Image: C.R. Cartwright.)

Figure B.11 shows the second sample taken from the braided band. It shows a very fine underfur animal hair which cannot (in my opinion) be identified to taxon on the basis of this single hair, despite the fact that cuticular scales survive. It is also questionable whether it might, in fact, be a stray hair from the pelt.

Textile and animal-skin artefact

The piece described as of textile and animal skin consists of several types of organic materials in a variety of orientations and preservation. Selected samples were examined using the VP-SEM as described above. Figures B.12–B.15 provide a representative illustration of this material. Figures B.12 and B.13 illustrate, again, the problem of distinguishing between plant remains present naturally in the peat envelope containing the cist burial, the matted plant layers and any plant remains deliberately selected or modified to create artefacts. Figures B.14–B.17 appear to show vestigial traces of decayed leather or skin products intermingled with a wide variety of fragmented

plant remains. Figure B.18 shows a sample that had a close match with reference specimens for calf (*Bos taurus*) leather/hide.

Small samples of the textile yarns were examined by Esther Cameron, Susanna Harris and Quita Mould (Chapter 18) in order to establish details of the weave (as well as analysing the leather). Mindful of the difficulty (alluded to above) of differentiating the textile fibres from other associated plant remains, prior to the VP-SEM examination a gentle maceration (using hydrogen peroxide, distilled water and glacial acetic acid) of the plant fibres was undertaken in order to obtain a better understanding of the range of plant fibres present. In this way, it was hoped that the textile fibres themselves could be pin-pointed. This proved successful; inasmuch as two fibres could be identified as being a very close match with *Urtica dioica*, nettle (Fig. B.19). However, some caution is urged with

Figure B.14: VP-SEM image showing the different constituents of the plant fibre textile and animal-skin artefact. (Image: C.R. Cartwright.)

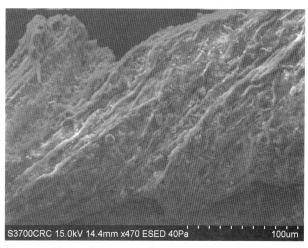

Figure B.17: VP-SEM image showing the different constituents of the plant fibre textile and animal-skin artefact. (Image: C.R. Cartwright.)

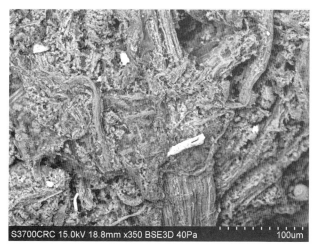

Figure B.15: VP-SEM image showing the different constituents of the plant fibre textile and animal-skin artefact. (Image: C.R. Cartwright.)

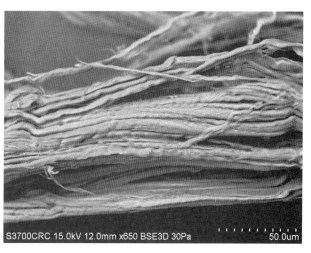

Figure B.18: VP-SEM image showing a sample from the textile and animal-skin artefact that had a close match with reference specimens for calf (Bos taurus) leather/hide. (Image: C.R. Cartwright.)

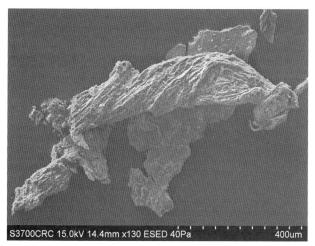

Figure B.16: VP-SEM image showing the different constituents of the plant fibre textile and animal-skin artefact.(Image: C.R. Cartwright.)

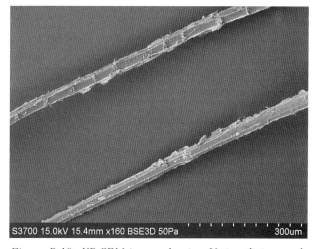

Figure B.19: VP-SEM image showing Urtica dioica nettle fibres present in the textile part of the textile and animal-skin artefact. (Image: C.R. Cartwright.)

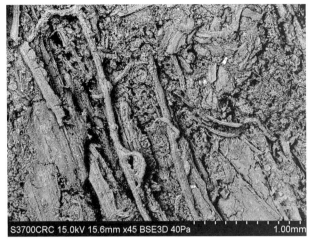

Figure B.20: VP-SEM image showing the diverse plant macros in samples from the matted material. (Image: C.R. Cartwright.)

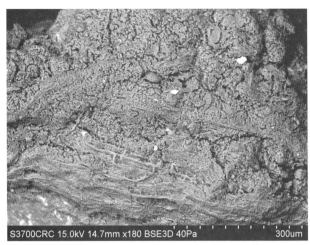

Figure B.22: VP-SEM image showing the diverse plant macros in samples from the matted material. (Image: C.R. Cartwright.)

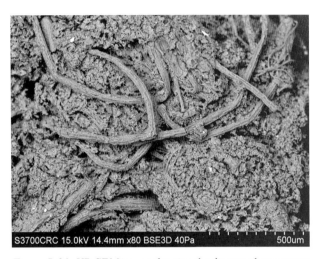

Figure B.21: VP-SEM image showing the diverse plant macros in samples from the matted material. (Image: C.R. Cartwright.)

Figure B.23: VP-SEM image showing the diverse plant macros in samples from the matted material. (Image: C.R. Cartwright.)

regard to interpretation; as with all such samples these represent a selected part of the whole, and should not necessarily be construed as meaning that nettle is being the principal or indeed only plant fibre comprising the textile element of this artefact.

Matted plant material

The matted plant material consists of a number of plant remains in a complex state of orientation, fragmentation and preservation (Figs. B.20–B.24). Despite careful sampling, it was difficult to differentiate between the plant remains present in the peat, those in the matted layers and any plant remains deliberately selected or modified for artefacts. Samples from the matted remains have also been analysed by Julie Jones (Chapter 9), who kindly shared her results with me during the process; this has proved very helpful

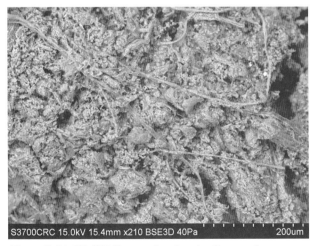

Figure B.24: VP-SEM image showing the diverse plant macros in samples from the matted material. (Image: C.R. Cartwright.)

in corroborating the results of my VP-SEM examination of plant macros in these layers.

As Figures B.20–B.24 show, much of the material consisted of monocot leaf and plant stem fragments with culm nodes – probably grasses – often uni-directionally orientated (J. Jones, Chapter 9). Flatter and more fragmented monocot stems were frequently randomly dispersed amongst the more aligned stem fragments. *Sphagnum* sp. (Sphagnaceae) leaves were also present. *Eriophorum vaginatum* (Cyperaceae) and ericaceous plant macro-remains were found within or adjacent to the matted material, including *Erica tetralix* and *Calluna vulgaris*. The identification of the presence of *Molinia caerulea* (purple moor grass) by Julie Jones has shed light on some of the more elusive Poaceae examples viewed in the VP-SEM.

Acknowledgements

I would like to thank Helen Williams, Senior Conservator, Wiltshire Council, for facilitating several sampling visits to the conservation laboratory at the Wiltshire and Swindon History Centre in Chippenham, and for providing information and data. Grateful thanks are due to Julie Jones, Gill Campbell and Esther Cameron who generously shared their results with me during their analyses.

References

Cartwright, C. R. 2012. Whitehorse Hill Cist: Assessment report on organic artefacts examined. Unpublished assessment report submitted to English Heritage.

Cartwright, C. R. & King, J. C. H. 2012. Identifications of hairs and fibres in Great Lakes objects from the eighteenth and nineteenth centuries using variable pressure scanning electron microscopy. *British Museum Technical Research Bulletin* 6, 69–81.

Higgitt, C., Harris, S., Cartwright, C. R. & Cruickshank, P. 2011. Assessing the potential of historic archaeological collections: a pilot study of the British Museum's Swiss lake dwelling textiles. *British Museum Technical Research Bulletin* 5, 81–94.

Appendix C: Report on the proteomic analysis of hairs from the basketry container, the braided band and the pelt from the Whitehorse Hill cist

Caroline Solazzo

The excavation of the Whitehorse Hill cist revealed a number of organic objects containing animal hair components. These included a pelt, a braided band with tin studs and a basketry container. This section reports on the results of proteomic analysis undertaken to identify which animals had produced the hairs.

Experimental procedure

The hair samples were solubilised in 8 M urea/50 mM Tris/40 mM DTT (dithiothreitol) at pH 8.8 by overnight shaking.

Whitehorse Hill	mg	Buffer ml
Braided band	0.6	100
Basketry container	1.5	100
Pelt	2.6	200

Alkylation of the samples was done on 100μL of supernatant with 2.8mg IAA (iodoacetic acid), 4h in the dark. Samples diluted to 400μL with 300μL of 50 mM Ambic pH 8.0 Overnight digestion of 100μL with 1μg of trypsin at 37°C.

The samples were dried after digestion and resolubilised in 10μL of 0.1% TFA (trifluoroacetic acid). The samples were desalted and concentrated using C18 zip-tip (elution 50%/50% Acetonitrile/0.1% TFA), then dried and resolubilised in 10μL of 0.1% TFA. One μL of analyte was deposited on the Maldi plate and mixed with 1μL of alpha-cyano-4-hydroxycinnamic acid matrix, then left to dry.

The plate was loaded in an Ultraflex™ III mass spectrometer (Bruker Daltonics GmbH, Germany), and analyses were carried out in positive reflector mode using an Nd: YAG laser operating at 337nm. Spectra were acquired using flexControl 3.0 (Bruker Daltonics GmbH, Germany) on a mass range of 800–4000 Da with an accumulation of 500 shots on the standards and 1000 shots on the samples. The calibration standard (Bruker Daltonics) was prepared according to the manufacturer's instructions for instrument calibration and consisted of angiotensin I, ACTH clip(1–17), ACTH clip(18–39) and ACTH clip(7–38) peptides.

Reference database

The mass spectra obtained on the archaeological samples were compared to a series of reference spectra obtained from common species in archaeology and common wool-producing animals (including sheep, goat, cow, rabbit, dog, horse and camel). The main diagnostic peptides usually recognisable in common species are given in Table C.1 for a few species (for further information and data see Solazzo et al. 2013).

Table C.1: Diagnostic peptides usually recognisable in common species. In red unique bovine peptides; in orange other characteristic bovidae peptides.

m/z	Peptide sequence	Domestic sheep	Domestic goat	Cow	Deer	Reindeer	Camel	Dog	Horse
952.50	LQFFQNR	+	+		+				
968.49	LQFYQNR	+	+	+	+	+	+		+
1041.49	WQFYQNR							+	+
1169.55	WQFYQNQR	+	+	+			+	+	+
1051.48	DVEEWFAR						+		
1109.53	DVEEWYIR	+	+	+		+			
1625.85	LNVEVDAAPTVDLNR	+	+	+	+	+	+	+	+
1896.86	DVEEWFTTQTEELNR								+
1834.98	TVNALEVELQAQHNLR	+	+	+	+	+	+		
1848.99	TVNALEIELQAQHNLR							+	+
2063.03	SDLEANSEALIQEIDFLR	+	+	+		+			
2072.02	LEAAVTQAEQQGEAALTDAR							+	
2075.06	SDLEANVEALIQEIDFLR			+					
2191.12	KSDLEANSEALIQEIDFLR	+		+		+			
2203.16	KSDLEANVEALIQEIDFLR			+					
2563.34	YSSQLSQVQGLITNVESQLAEIR								+
2577.30	YSCQLAQVQGLIGNVESQLAEIR			+	+	+			
2583.35	YGSQLSQVQGLITNVEHQLAEIR						+		
2593.27	YGSQLAQMQCLIGNVEAQLAEIR							+	
2665.35	YSCQLSQVQSLIVNVESQLAEIR	+							
2680.32	YSCQLNQVQSLISNVESQLAEIR	+	+						
2692.36	YSCQLNQVQSLIVNVESQLAEIR		+						
2712.30	YSSQLNQVQCMITNVESQLAEIR							+	

Results on hair from the basketry container and the braided band

The peak at *m/z* 1835 is characteristic of bovidae (for instance sheep, goat, cow, muskox), cervidae (deer, reindeer, caribou, elk, moose), and camelidae (camel, llama) and therefore excludes all other species belonging to canidae, felidae, equidae families, etc. The peaks at *m/z* 2075 and 2203 are unique to **bovine** (cow, yak); they are both present in the basketry container and the braided band (see zooms on peaks below).

The shifts in *m/z* visible in the archaeological samples come from the deamidation of asparagine (N) and glutamine (Q), a very common modification in ancient materials, that adds +1 for each amino acid modified (there are 4 Q/N in *m/z* 1835, 2 Q/N in *m/z* 2075 and 2203). Deamidation happens at different rates for each amino acid, resulting in the modification of the isotopic envelope.

Note that African antelopes and giraffe also have the *m/z* 2075/2203 peak but lack the *m/z* 2577 peak, which is present in the archaeological samples, albeit as a minor peak with also heavy deamidation (5 Q/N).

Mass spectra of the braided band

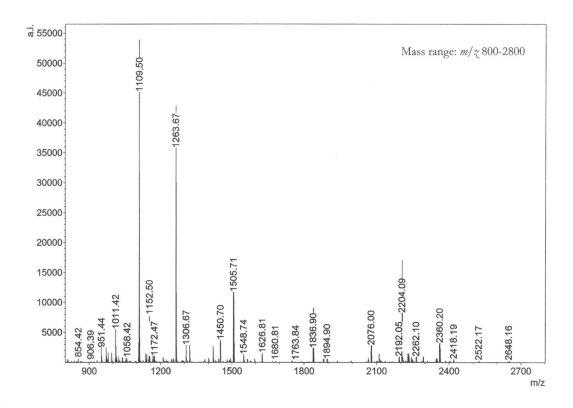

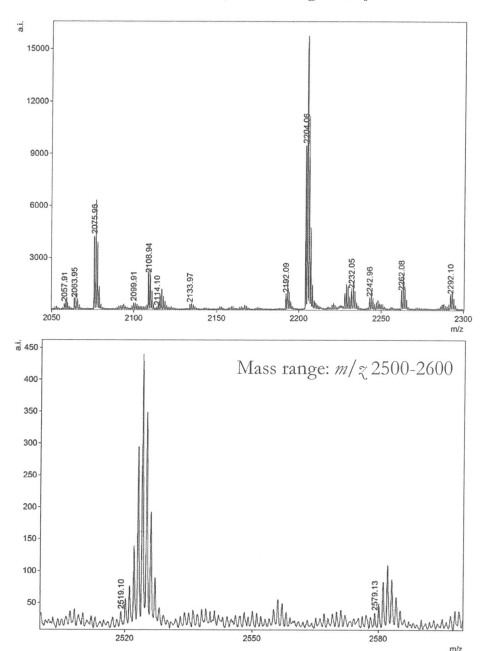

Zooms on the braided band (blue), compared to cattle (orange): *m/z* 1835, *m/z* 2075, *m/z* 2203, *m/z* 2577 (different scaling)

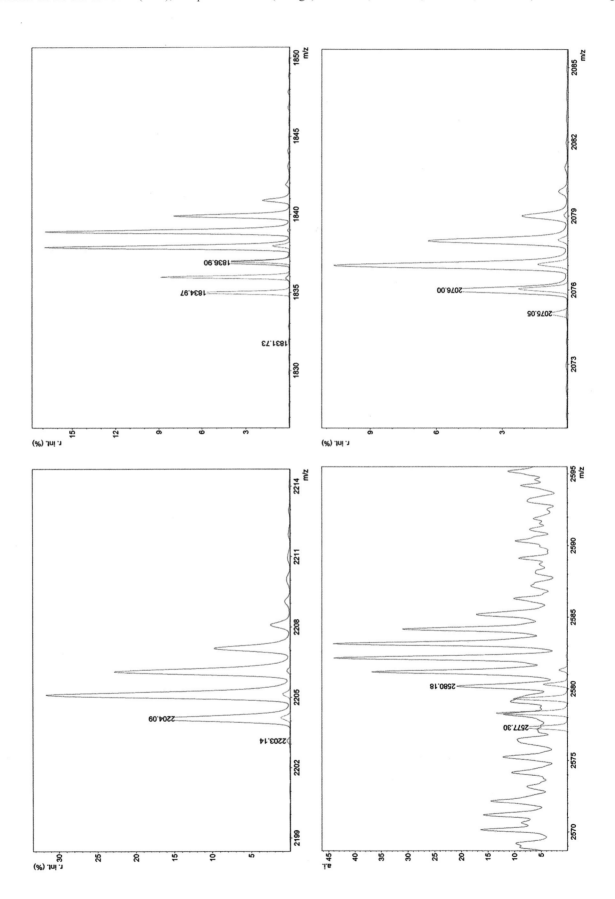

Mass spectra of the basketry container

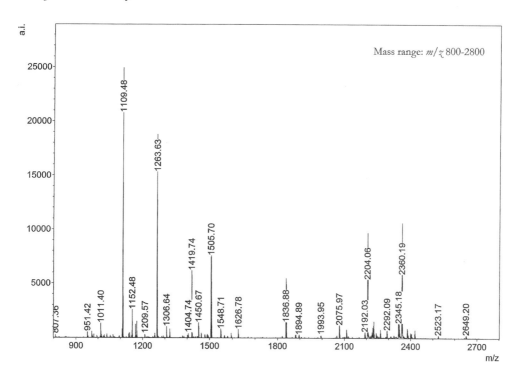

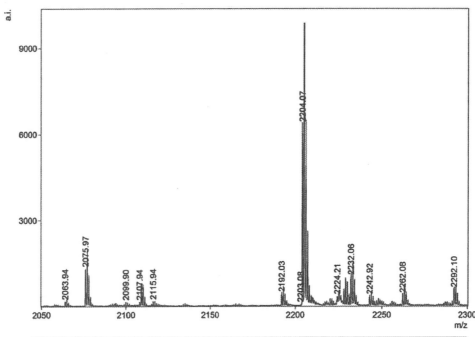

Mass range: *m/z* 2050-2300

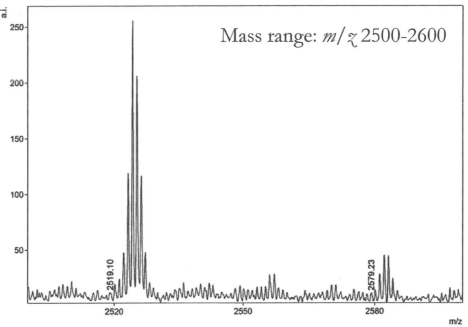

Mass range: *m/z* 2500-2600

Zooms on the basketry container (green), compared to cattle (orange): *m/z* 1835, *m/z* 2075, *m/z* 2203, *m/z* 2577 (different scaling)

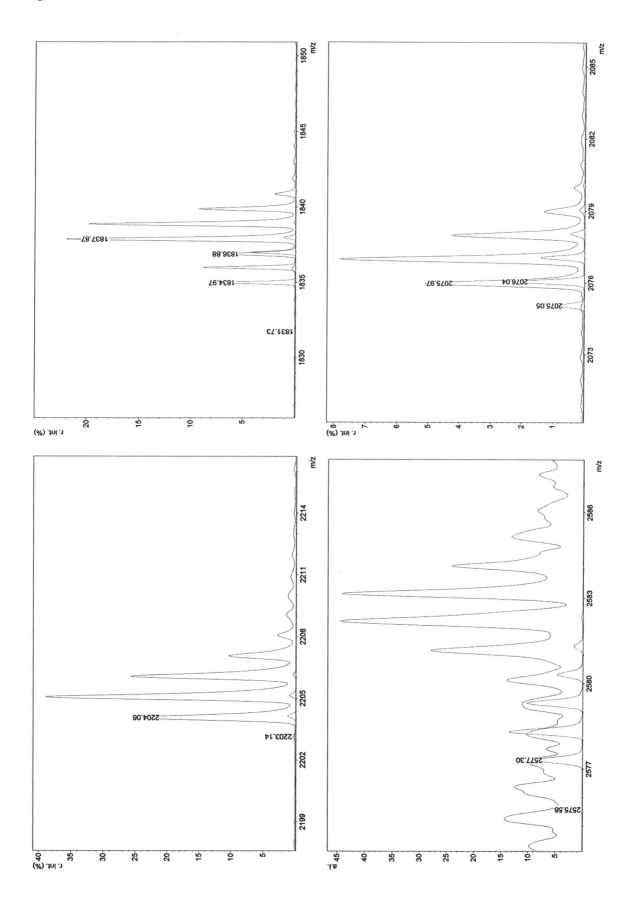

Results on the pelt

The absence in the pelt of the peak at *m/z* 1835 as well as the *m/z* 1109 (which is also characteristic of bovidae and cervidae) exclude the identification of the pelt as sheep or a relative species, as well as a cervidae. The pelt had instead the peaks at *m/z* 1848 and *m/z* 1041. Both peaks are found in dog and a horse, and 1848 is found in rabbit. However, unique peptides for horse and dog at *m/z* 2563 and 2593 (Table C.1) were absent. A major peak belonging to dog at *m/z* 2072 was also absent.

A new series of reference species was therefore analysed for further comparison, based on a large range of fur mammals, including new canidae (wolf, fox, coyote), felidae (puma, lynx, bobcat), mustelidae (marten, mink, etc), and a few more species, including black bear. The experimental data for reference materials are given at the end of this report. Note that all species were obtained from the American continent, so there could be some differences with their European equivalents.

Table C.2 summarises the main diagnostic peaks identified in the pelt and in the new reference species. The pelt has a peak at *m/z* 2088 and not 2072, excluding all canidae. The peak is present in the mustelidae, skunk, muskrat and beaver, but these species, except for sea otter and badger, don't have the peak at *m/z* 2114. Finally badger lacks the peak at *m/z* 2036 and sea otter the peak at *m/z* 1419.

Conclusion: only the black bear has a perfect match with the pelt, and the data best fit the *Ursus* genus.

Fur species	Family	Sub-order	mg	Buffer ml
Arctic hare	Leporidae	Lagomorpha	3.11	200
Badger	Mustelidae	Caniformia	5.00	200
Beaver	Castoridae	Rodentia	2.08	200
Black bear	Ursidae	Caniformia	5.00	200
Bobcat	Felidae	Feliformia	3.13	200
Coyote	Canidae	Caniformia	5.00	200
Lynx	Felidae	Feliformia	2.09	200
Marten	Mustelidae	Caniformia	3.52	200
Mink	Mustelidae	Caniformia	3.75	200
Muskrat	Cricetidae	Rodentia	2.01	200
Opossum	Didelphidae		5.00	200
Puma	Felidae	Feliformia	2.90	200
Raccoon	Procyionidae	Caniformia	2.43	200
Red fox	Canidae	Caniformia	3.85	200
Sea otter	Mustelidae	Caniformia	1.69	200
Alaskan seal	Phocidae	Caniformia	5.00	200
Skunk	Mephitidae	Caniformia	5.04	200
Weasel	Mustelidae	Caniformia	0.85	200
Wolf	Canidae	Caniformia	4.90	200
Wolverine	Mustelidae	Caniformia	4.75	200

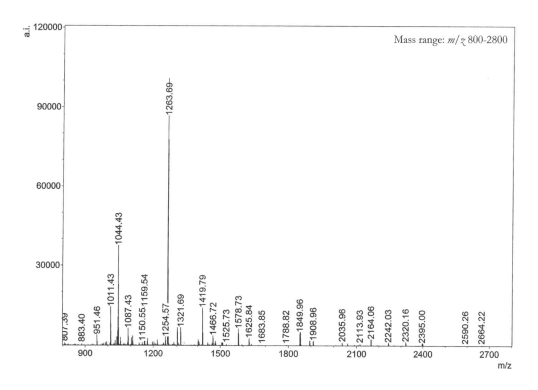

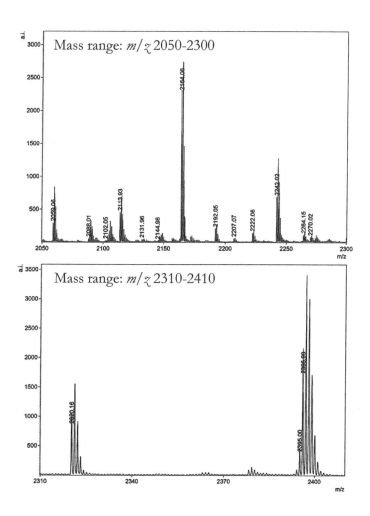

Orange: pelt and blue: bear

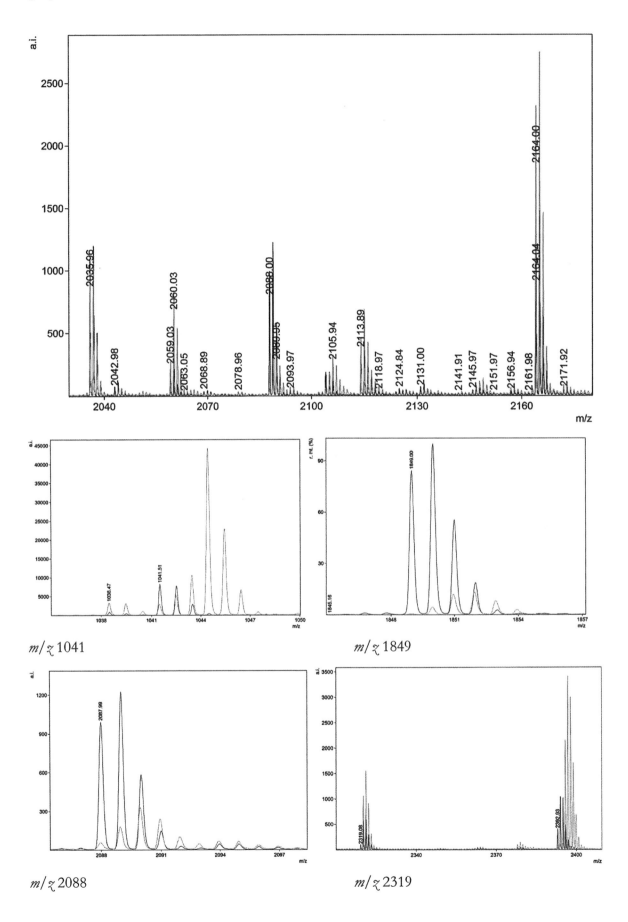

m/z 1041   *m/z* 1849

m/z 2088   *m/z* 2319

Mass spectra of black bear: in red, peptides identified from newly sequenced *Ursus maritimus* keratin proteins (made available in Pubmed August 2014); in blue, peptides identified from *Ailuropoda melanoleuca* (panda) keratin sequences.

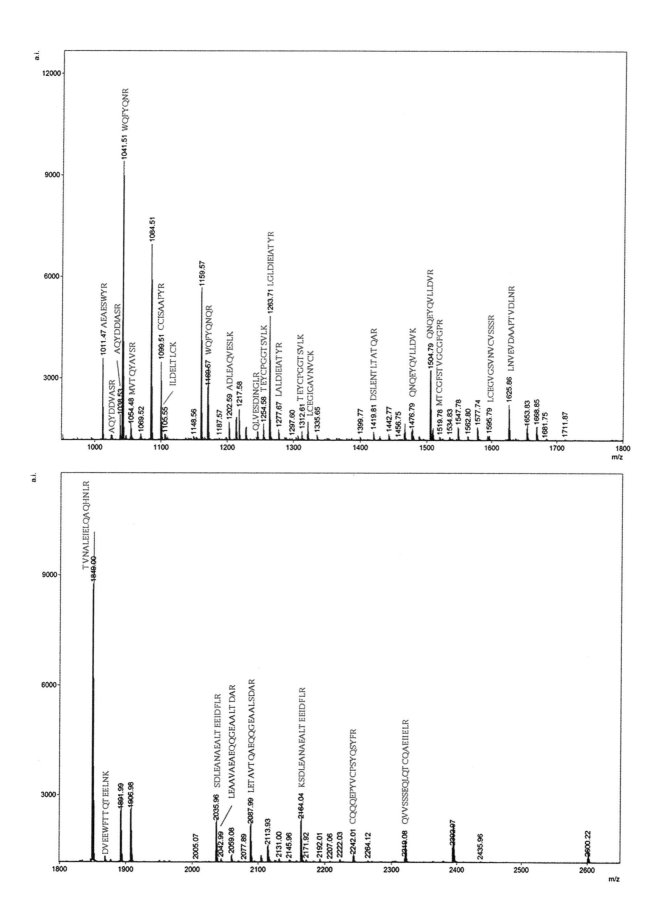

Reference materials

As for archaeological samples, the hair samples were solubilised in 8 M urea/50 mM Tris/40 mM DTT (dithiothreitol) at pH 8.8 by overnight shaking.

Table C.2: Summary of the main diagnostic peaks identified in the pelt and in the new reference species.

m/z	pelt	Black bear	Red fox	Dog	Coyote	Wolf	Sea otter	Badger	Marten	Mink	Wolverine	Weasel	Skunk	Raccoon	Alaskan seal	Opossum	Muskrat	Beaver	Bobcat	Lynx	Puma
1041	+	+	+	+	+	+	+	+	+	+	+	+	+	+	−	+	+	+	+	+	+
1419	+	+	−	−	+	+	−	+	+	+	+	+	+	−	−	−	+	+	−	+	−
1849	+	+	+	+	+	+	+	+	+	+	+	+	+	+	+	+	+	+	+	+	+
2036	+	+	+	+	+	+	+	−	+	+	+	+	−	+	−	−	−	−	−	−	−
2059	+	+	+	+	+	−	+	+	+	+	+	−	−	−	−	−	−	−	−	+	+
2072	−	−	+	+	+	+	−	−	−	−	−	−	−	−	−	−	−	+	−	−	−
2088	+	+	−	−	−	−	+	+	+	+	+	+	+	−	−	−	+	+	−	−	−
2114	+	+	+	?	+	+	+	+	−	−	−	−	−	+	+	−	−	−	+	+	+
2164	+	+	+	+	+	+	+	+	+	+	+	+	−	+	−	−	−	−	−	−	−
2319	+	+	−	−	−	−	−	−	−	−	−	−	+	−	−	−	+	+	−	−	−
2393	+	+	+	−	+	+	+	+	−	+	+	−	−	+	−	−	−	−	+	+	+

Alkylation of the samples was done on 100µL of supernatant with 2.8 mg IAA (iodoacetic acid), 4h in the dark. Samples diluted to 400µL with 300µL of 50 mM Ambic pH 8.0. Overnight digestion of 100µL with 1µg of trypsin at 37°C.

The samples were dried after digestion and resolubilised in 10µL of 0.1% TFA (trifluoroacetic acid). The samples were desalted and concentrated using C18 zip-tip (elution 50%/50% Acetonitrile/0.1% TFA), then dried and resolubilised in 10µL of 0.1% TFA. One µL of analyte was deposited on the Maldi plate and mixed with 1µL of alpha-cyano-4-hydroxycinnamic acid matrix, then let to dry.

The plate was loaded in an Ultraflex™ III mass spectrometer (Bruker Daltonics GmbH, Germany), and analyses were carried out in positive reflector mode using an Nd: YAG laser operating at 337nm. Spectra were acquired using flexControl 3.0 (Bruker Daltonics GmbH, Germany) on a mass range of 800–4000 Da with an accumulation of 500 shots on the standards and 1000 shots on the samples. The calibration standard (Bruker Daltonics) was prepared according to the manufacturer's instructions for instrument calibration and consisted of angiotensin I, ACTH clip(1–17), ACTH clip(18–39) and ACTH clip(7–38) peptides.

Acknowledgements

The analysis of the samples was possible thanks to Prof. Matthew Collins, University of York, who kindly offered access to BioArCh's facilities and to the Proteomics Bioscience Technology facility. Dr Ursula Arndt is particularly thanked for her help with the project.

Reference

Solazzo, C., Wadsley, M., Dyer, J. M., Clerens, S., Collins, M. J. & Plowman, J. 2013. Characterisation of novel α-keratin peptide markers for species identification in keratinous tissues using mass spectrometry. *Rapid Communications in Mass Spectrometry* 27, 2685–2698.

Index

Numbers in *italic* denote pages with figures, numbers in **bold** denote pages with tables.

Italic text is used for Latin terms.

Place names are in Devon, unless indicated otherwise.